Regulating Internet Gaming

Challenges and Opportunities

Anthony Cabot and Ngai Pindell, editors

UNLV Gaming Press

UNLV Gaming Press
4505 Maryland Parkway, Box 457010
Las Vegas, Nevada 89154-7010

Regulating Internet Gaming:
Challenges and Opportunities

Library of Congress call number GV1302.5.R43 2013

Paperback edition ISBN 978-1-939546-04-3

Cover design by 15-North, Inc.
Layout by David G. Schwartz

Set in Minion Pro.

Anthony:
To my Mom and Dad for teaching me the value of hard work

Ngai:
To my family: Sara, Colin, and Theo

Contents

Contents

Editors' Note

On February 21, 2013, Governor Brian Sandoval signed Assembly Bill 114 legalizing online gaming in Nevada. Although the state has long been a leader in gaming regulation in the United States and abroad, this was a significant legislative step and highlights Nevada's recent entry into *online* gaming regulation. Until recently, a handful of jurisdictions outside of the United States licensed online gaming operators and provided Internet gaming products to customers throughout the world, including customers in the United States. As a result, the initial development of Internet gaming has been shaped by both the brick and mortar casino industry in the United States, and by operators and regulators in many countries.

Although legal online gaming is new to the United States, it has a longer history abroad. At the same time, several states, most notably Nevada and New Jersey, have decades of experience with brick and mortar gaming and have developed sophisticated regulatory regimes. This book builds on the experiences of both American and international regulatory systems to describe current approaches and suggest best practices for the development of Internet gaming regulation and infrastructure globally.

The book was inspired by a conference held at the UNLV Boyd School of Law in spring 2012 that brought together national and international experts to discuss the future of Internet gaming regulation. Their contributions are collected here in eleven chapters outlining best practices in Internet gaming law, regulation, and policy.

In Chapter One, Tony Cabot begins by discussing how governments can best create an Internet gaming licensing structure, including suggestions for how to identify and weigh relevant public policy and economics goals. In Chapter Two, Peter Kulick adds detail to the licensing scheme by examining accounting, auditing, and recordkeeping practices, applying lessons and experiences from casino brick and mortar experiences to an online regime. In Chapter Three, Sanford Millar focuses on the taxation of regulated Internet gaming using examples and approaches from around the world to illustrate emerging trends and to offer recommendations for best practices. In Chapter Four, Richard Williamson describes the necessary controls gaming operators and regulators should employ to monitor data and assets. In Chapter Five, Nick Nocton focuses on best practices of protecting customer funds in a global, online gaming regime. In Chapter Six, Stuart Hoegner continues the discussion of finances by focusing on money laundering and prevention practices.

Chapter Seven begins a shift in focus from finance and regulation to other policies important to online gaming. In Chapter Seven, Lawrence Walters describes current advertising rules for online gaming and offers suggestions for best practices. In Chapter Eight, Frank Catania, Sr., Gary Ehrlich, and Antonia Cowan describe the special challenges that Internet gaming will face in maintaining socially responsible gaming practices. In Chapter Nine, Alan Littler continues the focus on customer protection by discussing how regulation can best address the fraud and cheating challenges posed by global online gaming. In Chapter Ten, J. Blair Richardson analyzes online age verification tools and regulations that prevent minors from gambling. Finally, in Chapter Eleven, Marketa Trimble discusses geolocation and the potential for an international convention to facilitate the enforcement of regulations and policy among countries with differing gaming law and policy objectives.

An effort of this size and scope would not be possible without the work of many contributors. UNLV Boyd School of Law students Jason Aldridge, Kenton Eichacker, Michael Gianelloni, Christopher Humes, Morgan Petrelli, Marisa Rodriguez, and Adam Tully edited the individual chapters and worked with the authors. David Schwartz, Professor and Director of the UNLV Center for Gaming Research, led the publication effort and was the architect of the new UNLV Gaming Press. Finally, thank you to UNLV Provost John White, Karl Rutledge and the gaming attorneys at Lewis and Roca in Las Vegas, UNLV Lied Library Dean Patricia Iannuzzi, all of the contributors to the May 2012 Internet Gaming Regulation Symposium, and the faculty and staff at the UNLV Boyd School of Law for their support of the Symposium and for the development of the UNLV Gaming Press.

Anthony Cabot and Ngai Pindell, editors
March 2013

1

Licensing

Anthony Cabot

INTRODUCTION

This chapter recommends a model approach for government licensure of the Internet gaming industry. Unlike some other areas of regulation, no best licensing practices exist. Each government must consider what is the best licensing structure to employ in light of its unique circumstances, such as its public policy, regulatory funding and resources, industry resources, and market size. All of these factors can influence the regulatory structure in general and licensing in particular.

A model approach, as opposed to best practices, provides a framework for what the government should consider in crafting and implementing a licensing system that best reflects the government's goals and resources. The starting point for such an approach is an understanding of the government's interest in licensing parties involved in the industry. This requires the government to identify public policies and policy goals by determining its position toward Internet gambling, what goals it hopes to achieve related to such gambling, and how regulation in general and licensing in particular can help achieve these goals. This inquiry is covered in section 1. Section 2 covers the economics of licensing. Governments need to understand the costs of imposing licensing and the non-licensing alternatives for achieving policy goals. Once the government determines the goals of licensing and considers the attendant costs, it must put into place a structure that considers who the government needs to license, the level of scrutiny for such licensing, and the standards and criteria for evaluating license requests. The government/licensor must understand the range of parties interested in Internet gaming, the responsibilities of those parties, and how each could impact the government's policy goals before it can decide who needs to be licensed. Section 3 addresses these issues.

Licensing and Public Policy

Licensing is a tool to achieve specific public policy goals by excluding persons from an industry, occupation or profession before their actions can compromise public policy. Licensing is not unique to Internet gaming. Governments often impose licensing requirements on various professions to protect the public. For example, lawyers, doctors, contractors and even beauticians have to go through some level of licensing scrutiny before they can offer their services.[1] Licensing is most valuable as a tool to shield the public from abuse where the person being licensed holds a special position of trust, the public is in a vulnerable position, regulatory violations are difficult to detect, and enforcement is of limited utility. For example, a gaming site operator could easily victimize the public by using rigged games. One scandal that plagued the online poker industry allegedly involved associates of a former poker site owner. Those associates accessed an internal system which allowed them to view other player's hands at the poker table.[2] This method of cheating gave the cheaters a significant advantage and resulted in players losing millions of dollars.[3] Since these types of occurrences may be difficult to police through enforcement, licensing provides governments with a tool to achieve policy goals, such as maintaining the fairness of the games by preventing dishonest persons from operating licensed gaming sites.

Considering the risks and vulnerabilities associated with Internet gaming, licensing is a prophylactic exercise. Some cases may exist where the applicant has such a sordid history or poor reputation that his or her mere association with the industry is inconsistent with policy goals. But, this is rare and most often regulators attempt to use licensing to exclude unfit persons before they enter the gaming industry, as well as to inform those qualified persons of the standards expected of them. In this light, licensing is a means to predict the behavior of the license applicant with the objective that only those qualified entities and individuals, i.e. those who do not pose a threat to the public, withstand licensing scrutiny.

The foundation of gaming licensing is a determination of the government's public policy toward gambling generally and Internet gaming specifically. From this public policy, governments can craft policy goals that it hopes to accomplish through regulation. Suppose that the only policy goals are to assure that the games offered on regulated sites are fair and honest. The suitability review of applicants for an operator's license may not be limited to dishonesty; it may also require that applicants have sufficient competency to detect and prevent schemes by employees or third

---

[1] *In re* Application of Cason, 294 S.E.2d 520, 523 (Ga. 1982) (*citing* Penobscot Bar v. Kimball, 64 Me. 140, 146 (Me. 1875)).

[2] Mike Brunker, *Poker site cheating plot a high-stakes whodunit*, MSNBC.com, (Sept. 18, 2008), http://www.msnbc.msn.com/id/26563848/ns/us_news-crime_and_courts/t/poker-site-cheating-plot-high-stakes-whodunit/

[3] *Id.*

parties designed to cheat players. In this context, licensing would seek to protect the public by requiring licensing of persons with responsibilities that if not performed competently and honestly could compromise the honesty or fairness of the games. This, as an example, could include site owners, software architects and programmers, data and server centers and other persons with access to sensitive areas of the Internet gaming systems. It could include reviews of the applicant's honesty, experience, competency, or technology infrastructure. If the goals are expanded to assuring that player funds are protected, the scope of the licensing review may include the financial strength of the operator. Suppose further that a government expands its policy goals to assure that the gaming markets are competitive to allow licensees to compete in world markets or to assure the lowest costs to players. In this case, the government needs to balance the cost and impact of licensing on competitive market conditions.

Absent an understanding of what the government wants to accomplish through regulation and licensing, regulators have no context for the various licensing requirements. This can result in widely inconsistent actions by regulators who substitute their own beliefs or assumptions, or those of their perceived constituency, as to the goals and methods of regulation. This can create conflicts in approach to licensing between agencies, regulators, and even staff.

Once a government formulates a public policy toward Internet gambling, it must set and implement policy goals based on that public policy. Implementation usually involves both adopting and enforcing laws designed to achieve policy goals. These laws can restrict, mediate or promote the activities of, or by, private parties.[4] Regulation is a common method of implementation. This is the process by which government achieves policy goals by restricting the choices of private parties.[5]

In the context of gambling, public policy most often focuses on either player protection or government protection, or a hybrid of these policies.

Player Protection Policies and Goals

Public policy that focuses on player protection has among its primary goals to assure that the games are fair and honest and that player transactions (deposits, payments, and transfers) and account balances are secure.

Honesty refers to whether the site operator offers games whose chance elements are random. The concept of random is elusive and its precise meaning has long been debated among experts in the fields of probability, statistics and the philosophical sciences. A standard dictionary might define random in a general sense as "having no specific pattern or objective; haphazard," or "made, done, or happening without conscious decision." These same dictionaries also might provide a meaning in a more

[4] BARRY M. MITNICK, THE POLITICAL ECONOMY OF REGULATION 8, 9 (1980).
[5] Id. at 20.

specific statistical sense such as "a phenomenon that does not produce the same outcome or consequences every time it occurs under identical circumstances," or "an event having a relative frequency of occurrence that approaches a stable limit as the number of observations of the event increases to infinity," or even "governed by or involving equal chances for each item." All of these definitions are lacking in some way for purposes of establishing necessary criteria for randomness in games of chance. Randomness in the context of gaming is the observed unpredictability and absence of pattern in a set of elements or events that have definite probabilities of occurrence. For example, a slot machine is honest if the outcome of each play is not predetermined or influenced beyond the established house advantage (or player's skill) in the gaming operator's or another player's favor.

A second aspect of honesty is whether forces outside of the established rules of the game influence the outcome. Take, as an example, community poker. The method of shuffling/distributing cards has to meet prescribed standards of randomness. But, beyond this, the game must be free of collusion between players and have controls to prevent players from gaining an advantage by having access to hole cards or unexposed cards in the deck. Like much of Internet gambling, detection of collusion is not a problem that can be solved exclusively by technology. HUDS (heads up displays) can provide operators with monitoring, but interpretation of that information, like casino surveillance, is an art requiring training, competency and integrity.

Fairness deals with whether the operators are offering games that give the players a reasonable opportunity of winning. This is a form of price setting because game odds determine the cost that players have to pay to play house banked casino games and rake requirements determine the cost of playing community pooled poker. In a perfect economy, market forces would determine pricing because the players would have access to all the information necessary to determine the costs of playing and could chose the best price among multiple competitors. In house banked casino games, the cost of playing is reflected in the house advantage. In community games, it is the house commission such as the amount of the rake in poker. Most gaming markets are not perfect and regulators may attempt to ensure fairness by either requiring disclosure of game odds or setting the maximum price a casino can charge players for the gambling experience. Ensuring a competitive market through full disclosure of odds information and price setting on house commissions can accomplish policy goals related to fairness, though the competitive market is more efficient at setting a fair price than regulators.

Fairness in the online poker industry may also extend to other prohibitions. As an example, governments may prevent the use of certain software programs (often called "bots") used by some participants in non-house banked games. Bots use probability driven algorithms to create a statistical advantage over most human players. Other examples of fairness concerns related to online poker may include allowing player collusion or allowing a player to have more than one seat at a poker table.

Player protection goals also extend to industry regulations that minimize undesirable social consequences. These social consequences can apply to the general population or focus on a specific sub-population that is considered worthy of special protection. One broader concept is the notion that gaming operators should not exploit the public by encouraging them to gamble, should not exploit players by encouraging them to gamble beyond their means, and should not convince players to wager more than they otherwise would without encouragement. Governments may adopt laws that prevent gaming operators from advertising, offering incentives to gamble or conducting other activities that stimulate demand for more gambling.

While broad prohibitions on advertising or incentives are rare in the Internet gaming industry, other measures directed at the general population are more common. These efforts to minimize undesirable social consequences could include a general prohibition against the use of credit, operator or player set daily loss limits, maximum or player set playing times, display of time at play, or requirements that sites or advertisements contain language regarding the dangers of problem gambling or access to problem gambling help lines.

Some player protection goals, such as excluding underage players, may relate to specific subgroups. One group that is often given special consideration is problem players. A solution for problem players could be mandatory exclusion of problem players who are voluntarily or otherwise entered onto a list.

Player protection also can focus on protecting the player from other potential harms, most notably protection from risks to player data and privacy that are derived from playing on the gaming site.

Finally, player protection also can focus assuring that the site operators timely pay winnings and protect and return player funds on deposit with the site.

From a licensing perspective, unsuitable persons under the player protection goals could include those who would (a) cheat the players, (b) fail to take measures to prevent others, including employees or players, from cheating or taking advantage of others through the use of bots, by collusion or otherwise, (c) provide or permit games that are unfair, (d) fail to timely pay winnings or protect player funds, (e) evade regulations that discourage the stimulation of gaming demand or fail to implement such measures, or (f) violate or fail to take measures to protect the public generally or vulnerable classes of persons, specifically including problem gamblers.

Government Protection Goals

Governments may have a more selfish reason to prevent the involvement of persons who could, indirectly or directly, jeopardize the government's economic stake in the Internet gaming industry. While the player protection goals support regulation for the player, a government protection framework sets goals and provides regulation to protect the interests of the government. By way of analogy, banks tend to place restrictions on businesses they lend to: if the bank lends a few hundred dollars to a borrower, a simple promissory note might be a few pages long; however, if a bank lends a hundred million dollars, the loan documents may be hundreds of pages long. In both cases, the bank wants to see the businesses succeed, but it puts more restrictions on the second borrower because the bank's interest is greater.

Government protection goals often predominate where the government places a heavy reliance on the industry to meet tax expectations. Persons who can do direct harm to government interests include those who skim funds without paying taxes or are so incompetent that the government will lose tax revenues through employee or player theft or poor management. Governments may also have an economic interest in the regulated industry's impact on job creation and economic development. Government protection goals would also shield the industry from threats to its existence, thereby protecting the government's revenue stream and any other economic benefits created by the industry. The gaming industry faces eradication if the public, or public officials, perceives it as too problematic for any number of reasons, including that it is too intrusive, not subject to proper regulation, or is infiltrated by persons who are dishonest, associated with organized crime, have dubious reputations or otherwise taint the industry For example, in the United States, if a state government permits Internet gaming, its regulations must assure that persons physically located in other states which prohibit Internet gaming cannot access and play on the licensed sites. Failure to do so could result in a federal prohibition of all Internet gaming to protect the interests of the states that prohibit online gambling or because of the negative publicity associated with criminal proceedings against licensed online operators that failed to respect jurisdictional prohibitions. In addition to the federal threat, state voters or legislators can change the laws permitting Internet gaming. Gaming is different from most other industries because it is often perceived as a vice. Its very existence may be tenuous, as public perception of the benefits and burdens may change and influence the legality of the activity.

Besides the threat of legislative intervention, players collectively have the economic ability to impact the government's tax and economic interests by not playing on licensed sites. For example, assuring the honesty of the games is important because the public must perceive that gambling is honest before it will play. If one operator cheats, the public may believe or fear that the entire industry is dishonest. Additionally, the gaming industry can suffer credibility problems if the media exposes a site owner or operator as having criminal ties, regardless of whether the owner or operator otherwise complies with all regulations and acts ethically.

A third policy for governmental involvement is to assure that the gaming industry does not interfere with other government goals. For example, the government's best interests dictate that the online gaming industry not become a conduit for money laundering. Malta specifically looks to whether the applicant has followed practices to prevent money laundering and other suspicious activities before issuing Internet gaming licenses.[6]

Finally, government protection also is promoted if the jurisdiction does not suffer reputational damage and resulting loss of business if a site operator fails to timely pay winnings and protect and return player funds on deposit with the site.

From a licensing perspective, unsuitable persons under a government protection framework could include those who would (a) cheat the players, (b) fail to take measures to prevent others including employees or players from cheating, (c) provide or permit games that are unfair, (d) fail to pay winnings or protect player funds, (e) evade the payment of taxes, (f) associate with persons whose reputations can harm the industry, or (g) violate, or fail to take measures to prevent violations, of laws designed to protect the industry or the government's other interests.

Hybrid Systems

Most frequently, governments do not strictly follow either the government protection or player protection goals, but instead blend aspects of both goal sets. For example, a jurisdiction could view the financial reward from gambling to be generally greater than the potential harm. These hybrid systems may try to reap the revenues from gambling, but minimize the harms, particularly to its citizens, by using regulation to limit those aspects of the industry that do the most harm. If done properly, the government can assess the cost of the regulation (as reflected by the cost of implementation and loss of revenues) and compare that value to the cost of not regulating the matter at issue (costs to the government, the public or the players).

Because government and the player protection goals often overlap and most jurisdictions are hybrid systems, the basic structures of many gaming license regimes are often quite similar. However, sophisticated jurisdictions demonstrate nuanced differences in all aspects of regulation including licensing.

---

[6] Malta Remote Gaming Regulations, § 8(2)(g) (2004) (amended 2011), *available at* http://www.lga.org.mt/lga/content.aspx?id=87374

LICENSING AND ECONOMICS

Licensing would be fairly simple if jurisdictions could design licensing systems without concern for the cost to the government, those regulated and the market being regulated. This is not realistic because an overly burdensome licensing scheme can, in different ways, impact the government's goals, the financial viability of regulated industry and those who the regulations are intended to protect. Much of this is attributable to how regulation, including licensing, can impact market economics.

The theory of market economics specifies a number of basic conditions needed for a market to set prices efficiently. The greater the deviation from these conditions, the less efficient the market system becomes. A basic condition of efficient pricing is that markets must be competitive. Of all factors necessary to support a free market model, a key is the absence of barriers to entry.[7] Barriers to entry are factors that discourage entry into an industry by potential competitors and, thus, allow established firms to earn super-normal profits. Government restraints, including licensing requirements, are barriers to entry that can prevent the casino industry from forming a competitive market.

The online gambling industry does not have many natural barriers to entry. For example, online gaming is not necessarily a capital intensive venture. Likewise, gambling is fairly fungible, with the exception of the few proprietary games. Similar dismissals of the other types of barriers to entry can be made with one major exception - government intervention including licensing.

Licensing, as a government restraint, will have economic costs. As an example, if licensing costs or requirements are too high, licensed gaming companies or vendors will gain protection from competition. The resulting monopoly and oligopoly markets create higher cost to the consumer, less innovation, lower service levels, and lower output. In the gaming industry, lower output means higher net profits on lower gross revenues. If a government bases tax rates on gross revenues, it will suffer a lower overall tax return.

---

[7] These barriers can take on a number of different forms. Barriers to entry include:
A. Extreme or significant capital requirements resulting from scale effects.
B. The existence of patents or copyrights.
C. Scarcity of or control over a necessary resource.
D. Excessive skill or knowledge requirements.
E. Social, cultural, or religious taboos.
F. Absolute cost advantages, *i.e.* advantages possessed by established firms who are able to sustain a lower average total cost than new entrants irrespective of size of output.
G. Large initial capital requirements.
H. Product differentiation, either natural or artificial, such as advertising.
I. Retaliation or pre-emptive actions.
J. Vertical integration, *i.e.* requiring entry at two or more levels.
K. Governmental restraints.

Governments must strike the proper licensing balance, consistent with their policy goals. Entry barriers can hinder other government goals. Silicon Valley in Northern California, a world center for high tech companies, would not likely exist if start-up companies with great ideas and little capital had licensing barriers. If a government has a goal to attract new technology companies and resulting employment through the legalization of Internet gambling, licensing barriers can prevent start up or thinly capitalized companies from entering the market.

Notwithstanding the above, licensing often has an important role to play in the gaming context. Indeed, the proper balance between licensing and barriers to entry is crucial. If licensing is too lenient, the industry may suffer if a scandal develops that harms the industry's reputation or results in legislation to prohibiting legal gambling.

Likewise, player protection goals may seek to insure that the players get the fairest price when they play with a licensed online site. If licensing results in oligopoly or monopoly pricing, this results in games that are less fair to the players. Consistent with government protection goals, the proper balance between licensing and barriers to entry is crucial.

A market can become a monopoly, oligopoly or competitive market through explicit licensing restraints, *e.g.* state law may dictate there only be a very limited number of site operators or system providers. As an example, the Nevada regulations only allow existing Nevada casino licensees to become licensed Internet gambling operators. There are certain other requirements, depending on the location of the establishment within the state, that existing licensees to have either a resort-hotel, a certain number of rooms or seats or have held a license for at least five years. Likewise, California has proposed legislation that would restrict licenses for site operators to certain tribes, card rooms and race tracks as well as limit the number of licensed systems providers that could service these site operators. If the federal government passes legislation, it will likely restrict operators' licenses to casinos, Indian tribes, racetracks and card rooms. Each of these decisions could impact competitive markets by allowing those fortunate enough to qualify for a license to reap greater than competitive returns. Any categorical restriction on who may obtain a license will create some level of entry barrier.

Barriers need not be explicit. They can result from cost, risk, time, opportunity costs or reputation. Even when the law does not dictate the number of site operators, it may influence whether a given market becomes a monopoly, oligopoly or competitive market. A government requiring a substantial investment to qualify for a license is an example. California legislation creates a vignette by requiring non-refundable deposits against the operator's tax liabilities in the amount of $30 million. Any minimum investment requirement will create some level of entry barrier. Even if California allowed an unlimited number of licenses, the $30 million deposit would constitute a significant barrier to entry. Such legislation may make investment attractive for the first entrant who can make monopoly profits and, perhaps, even a few other entrants. At some point, however, potential competitors will not be willing to enter the market because the potential profits do not justify the capital costs.

Besides cost, the licensing system employed by a state will influence the number of competitors. In a perfect, competitive system, competitors will enter the market if the existing entrants are making extraordinary profits. How quickly or easily they can enter the market is greatly influenced by licensing. Existing competitors will have an advantage if the licensing process creates a significant barrier. Licensing can create barriers to entry in five major ways.

First, it can add uncertainty and risk to the decision on whether to enter a market, especially when regulators regularly deny licenses to applicants. All things being equal, a company will devote its resources to a market where it can more likely obtain a license.

Second, the length of time that a licensing investigation takes may create a barrier. Companies that want to enter a market do so based on the current market economics. If licensing takes a substantial amount of time, the company must forecast the economics for when it might obtain its license. This adds risk to the decision to enter the market. Moreover, the time and effort required in the licensing process are an opportunity cost; as such, effort could instead be directed to creating markets or expanding existing markets. For example, in Malta, the Lotteries and Gaming Authority (LGA), which regulates gaming in Malta, takes about two to three months to investigate an applicant and issue a license. This expeditious handling of license applications allows the prospective licensees to plan deployment and marketing strategies. Such planning is very difficult when licensing might take a year or more.

The third barrier is the cost of licensing. A potential entrant will consider the cost of licensing when deciding if its money will generate a higher return in this market as opposed to another.

Fourth is the burden that the licensing places on the applicant's resources. This includes the efforts of officers, directors, and staff needed to complete applications and successfully navigate the licensing process.

Finally, the licensing process may cause social stigma and embarrassment to a potential entrant. This may discourage some companies, especially diversified companies, where embarrassing disclosures in the licensing process could negatively impact its brand and other businesses.

These barriers can be particularly problematic as they relate to providers of goods or services. As an example, one emerging casino jurisdiction mirrored the regulations of a larger casino jurisdiction that required licensure for companies that manufactured chips and tokens. The cost of licensing under the regulations of the larger casino jurisdiction exceeded the value of any contract to supply chip to the emerging casino district. Had a company stepped forward and obtained a license, it could have effectively charged rates so high that the casino would have forfeited a substantial portion of its table game profits just to purchase chips needed to offer the games. In the interactive gaming world, this can occur with service or software providers like site security or payment processors. The issue, posed as a question, is "will the largest and potentially the best providers of a service or software invest in the effort, time and cost of licensing for Internet gaming when other markets exist for its product without such barriers?"

Where reasonably efficient, proactive standards and enforcement can achieve public goals, they are generally preferred to licensing for two reasons. First, enforcement can provide a more certain and measureable result. Licensing attempts to predict behavior where standards and enforcement control behavior. Protecting player funds is an example. The licensing process tries to predict whether a future licensee is likely to divert player funds for other purposes. Conversely, a proactive standard might require licensees to physically segregate player funds under the control of a trusted third party thereby allowing the regulator to control the funds. Additionally, reasonable standards and enforcement may not create the same level of barrier to entry as licensing.

This does not mean that barriers to entry are not justified in many instances. For example, requiring that applicants have minimum reserves to assure the protection of players' deposits is a barrier to entry which may prevent less financially endowed companies from entering the market. However a reserves minimum is a barrier that may be justified in jurisdictions that have a strong player protection sentiment.

Governments need to understand the costs of imposing entry barriers to assess their cost versus the benefits that they hope to achieve through implementation of those barriers. Simply put, the most efficient regulation is one that accomplishes key policy goals with the least impact on a free market economy.

LICENSING FUNDAMENTALS

Differences between licensing systems are based on five major factors: breadth, depth, level of review, criteria, and standards of the licensing process.

Breadth means the extent to which a government requires persons or entities associated with the gaming industry to obtain a license. For example, does a company that provides payment processing solutions for Internet gaming sites have to obtain a license?

Depth of licensing means the extent to which a government requires persons within a licensable entity to undergo an individual investigation. This could require that certain officers, directors, shareholders and employees associated with an entity applying for a gaming license file individual disclosures and undergo a background investigation.

Level of review refers to the intensity of the investigative process. A low-level review might include simple criminal background checks. A high-level review may entail the regulatory agency train special agents to conduct a complete and independent review of the applicant, including both background and finances.

Criteria are those matters that the government considers in granting licenses. These can include moral character, honesty, connections to criminal elements, financial ability and business experience.

Standards refer to how rigidly the regulators will apply the criteria. For example, under the same set of facts, an applicant may obtain a license in one jurisdiction, but not another because one jurisdiction requires a higher standard of conduct than the other. As such, the minimum attributes of qualified applicants varies based on the standards used.

Breadth of Licensing

The Internet gaming ecosphere has many participants. Besides the owner and operator of the Internet gaming site, others—such as suppliers, service and providers—may serve integral roles in the creation and operation of an Internet gaming site.

The first major subset includes those with an economic interest in the success of the site, such as owners or investors, those who receive a percentage of profits and some creditors.

A second major subset is comprised of game software suppliers. These could include: the manufacturers of game content or systems including sports betting and exchange systems, casino games, poker software, bingo software and system software. These suppliers provide software for game play that may be exhibited in browser software, mobile or other applications. These vendors may or may not provide the back end software otherwise known as the system software. An operator may own this software, or license the game play layer.

A third major subset contains contracted non-gaming service and software providers. This is divided into two categories: software providers and service providers. Non-gaming service providers include payment processors, fraud prevention, customer service, domain name acquisition and management, affiliate management, bonus and loyalty management, network and chat management, hosting services, age and location verification, site optimization, and others. Non-gaming software providers include those whose products integrate into back-end gaming platforms to perform such functions as account management, affiliate and agent software, customer service tools, customer relationship management (CRM) tools, fraud and security tools, registration platforms, integrated cashier, centralized reporting tools, bonus and loyalty tools, network management tools and site optimization tools.

A fourth subset is network specific services including data and server centers and site security.

A fifth subset includes affiliates, marketing partners and other marketing resources.

Those Having a Direct Economic Interest in the Success of the Business

Owners

Owners hold the rights to conduct the online business. Owners may either operate the gaming site or hire a service provider to run the gaming site on their behalf. While owners who are not operators do not have direct contact with the software or with customers, they may have considerable influence over the website and typically share in gaming profits. Land-based casino jurisdictions generally require that casino owners be licensed.

Requiring owners to be licensed certainly advances player protection policies and goals. The owner has direct influence over the honesty and fairness of the gaming operations as well as control over player funds. These are key considerations for best regulatory practices in licensing. The owner also has the financial responsibility and ability to implement all the necessary systems and procedures to assure that players are protected from third party cheating, privacy violations and data theft. Owners also have primary responsibility for implementing compliance systems and programs designed to address problem gambling and other regulatory requirements.

Owner licensing is also consistent with government protection goals and policies. A government must consider not only the potential influence that an owner has over an operation, but also public perception of unsuitable owners (assuming the public knows who owns the domain name or any part of the online business). Indeed, the owner is typically the most visible person to the public.

Therefore, under both government protection or player protection goals, owners should be given highest licensing priority.

Persons Entitled to Profits

Persons entitled to profits are parties that bargain for their goods or services to be paid for by a percentage of the other party's profits. In an online gaming environment, such profits will mainly be a percentage of revenues derived from player losses or rake. This is a sensitive area for gaming regulators because ownership interest can be easily disguised as a vendor's participatory interest in the gaming operation. The potential for abuse has led to some states, like Nevada, and some Internet gaming regulations to require anyone sharing in a percentage of gaming revenues to be licensed. For example, Antigua requires suppliers to be licensed if they receive a percentage of gaming revenues.[8] This rule has the advantage of certainty and ease of application.

Still, the majority of profit participation agreements in the Internet gaming space are likely to be legitimate and consistent with existing Internet

---

[8] Ant. & Barb. Internet Gaming and Interactive Wagering Regulations, pt. IV, §§ 87 (2007), *available at* http://www.antiguagaming.gov.ag/files/Antigua_and_Barbuda_Gaming_Regulations-Final.pdf

marketing practices. A good example of parties that might be entitled to share revenue are websites that drive traffic to the gaming site. Such affiliate marketing is widely used in the online retail space where companies that sell books, electronics, and clothing provide a percentage of each sale to the operator of the site that referred the customer to the seller. Other potential revenue sharers may include those who provide security software services, equipment, financing, or management.

Capturing revenue sharing affiliates in the licensing net disturbs the natural economy of Internet commerce. The effects can be twofold. First, sites and suppliers may alter their economic relationships by using formulas that are less reflective of the actual value of their services. For example, the value of a player referred by an affiliate is best measured by the player's losses. If licensing barriers obstruct this method of measuring and sharing value, a different and probably less efficient formula for compensation will have to be derived between the operators and affiliates. Second, fewer affiliates or suppliers may be attracted to the market, which may impact competitive pricing.

Governments that tend toward government protection goals are sensitive that allowing persons of unsavory reputation to share in revenues can damage the industry's reputation. For this reason, government protection goals and policies would counsel greater attention to the suitability of any parties sharing in profits.

Jurisdictions that tend toward the player protection goals are more concerned with the ability of profit sharers to influence operations based on their relationship to the gaming operator. As detailed in the section on level of review, regulators may decide to tier this group into smaller sub-groups for purposes of licensing review. One distinction could be based on the total revenue paid to a person. For example, are substantial regulatory concerns invoked if a poker teaching site is paid a nominal, monthly fee of a few thousand dollars based on a revenue share for recommending and referring players to a licensed poker site? Having different levels of licensing (or none at all) based on cumulative annual payments to vendors and suppliers is common in the gaming industry.

Another possible distinction is based on the nature of the entitlement. For example, a person that licenses a game patent and receives a percentage of the net revenues of that game may not have to undergo licensing, but a private person that finances the Internet gaming site and receives 20 percent of net profits may have to obtain a license. The reason is that a person who receives a small percentage of the revenue of one game is unlikely to have any significant influence over the site's operation. Exempting such parties from licensing would allow for the creation and promotion of new game content that is based on the game's real value to the gaming site.

In addition, relaxed standards may exist for persons sharing in overall revenues based on the nature of the transaction. An example of this may be where a finance company shares in revenues, and that type of sharing is typical of financing in broader contexts.

Elements of an Internet Gaming Site

Game Content

Sports Betting/ Exchange	Casino (RNG)	Poker (RNG)	Bingo (RNG)	Pari-Mutuel

Backend Platform Software- System Backbone (API System)

Cashier	Fraud	Site Security	Account Management	Centralized Reporting Tools
Bonus And Loyalty	Registration Platform	Site Optimization	Customer Service	Affiliate/ Agent

Services (Requiring Integration Into Backend)

Payment Processors	Fraud Prevention	Age And Identification Verification	Location Verification
Affiliate Management	Network And Chat Management	Registration Services	Tax Allocation/Management Services
Security Services	CRM/Bulk Mail	Site Optimization	Customer Service/Call Centers

Hosting Services - Load Balancing

Site Services (Not Requiring Integration)

Domain Name Acquisition/ Management	Marketing Campaign Management	Audit/ Accounting	Banking	Legal

Financial

Lenders	Creditors	Revenue Sharing

As such, both government and player protection goals would prescribe policies for licensing at least some parties who share in the profits of Internet gaming sites. Still, there are notable circumstances where jurisdictions may consider a lower level (or no) licensing, including site affiliates who receive a small percentage of revenue for directing players to gaming websites, game patent holders who receive a portion of revenues that their games generate, and contexts, like financing, where revenue sharing is generally practiced.

C. Lenders/Creditors

Lenders/Creditors are common parties to most business agreements. Examples in an online gaming context could include lenders of money, suppliers of certain software, and vendors who sell equipment like servers or computers on credit. While licensing of every lender/creditor would ensure that people can neither hide ownership interests in online gaming operations nor exert undue control over operations, such regulation could be very costly to implement and regulate.

Four considerations surround the degree of regulatory scrutiny accorded creditors. First, creditors that lend money or provide financing expect a return on their money commensurate with the costs and risks involved in the transaction. Second, the initial cost of capital may decrease if the lender has the opportunity to share in revenues. Third, as the amount lent or financed increases, so does the creditor's vested interest in the success of, and potential influence over, the business. Fourth, unsuitable persons may use the cover of lender or creditor not as a method to lend moneys to a gaming operation at market interest rates but as a guise to participate in revenues from the gaming operations without obtaining necessary licensing. Regulation must balance the first and second considerations against the latter two.

Full licensing helps assure that loans are not used to hide ownership in gaming operations and that a party having potential influence over a gaming site is suitable. Requiring full licensing of all creditors, however, raises costs and creates barriers that will deter many legitimate lenders. This policy may result in higher interest costs to gaming operators since competition between lenders will be diminished and lenders will pass on investigation costs to borrowers. Likewise, vendors of equipment and goods may not be willing to provide goods on credit if it requires them to bear the expense of licensing. Such a regime would place the gaming operators in the position of having to either have cash available for purchases or seek loans from a limited number of approved lenders at interest rates potentially higher than the broader market.

Short of full licensing for all creditors, regulators can exempt certain creditors from licensing scrutiny. One possible exemption focuses on the difference between commercial and noncommercial creditors. There are four major types of commercial creditors: (1) banks or savings and loan associations regulated by the government, (2) national insurance companies, (3) government-regulated pension or retirement funds, and (4) foreign-regulated banking institutions. Exempting commercial creditors from licensing is based on the idea that other government agencies regulate these lenders. These institutions would not likely violate controls prohibiting their involvement in gaming operations because it could jeopardize their other licenses. Moreover, because they are in the business of lending money, they spread their risk over many loans. Therefore, these institutions are less likely to feel compelled to influence gaming operations to protect their investment. Finally, the initial structuring of a loan with a commercial creditor is unlikely to be a scam under which the lender is actually an equity participant.

A second possible exemption is based on the extent and context of credit provided. This exemption recognizes that many transactions by noncommercial creditors are done in the ordinary course of business. This may include suppliers that ship their product, bill the gaming operator and expect payment within a certain time. Requiring the operator to prepay all suppliers or pay on delivery would burden gaming operators. Therefore, a standard can be set that exempts creditors from obtaining licensing when the credit extended is below a certain dollar threshold. For example, only creditors owed more than a certain amount may have to register with the regulators, and those over a higher amount must obtain a license.

A third possible exemption may be for transactions that are not secured by gaming assets, such as gaming receipts and gaming stock. This would recognize that lenders with certain security interests pose the greatest regulatory concern. These creditors have a substantial remedy against the gaming operator for failure to pay its debt. As such, a secured creditor of a financially distressed gaming operator can exercise much greater control over gaming operations than an unsecured creditor. This can also be addressed by requiring registration of secured interests, and giving them greater scrutiny than unsecured transactions. Another option is to require approval of secured transactions, but not necessarily a licensing investigation of the creditor. A third option is to require prior approval for the secured creditor to foreclose on a security interest in gaming equipment, gaming receipts, or stock.

Instead of granting broad exemptions, regulators may require the gaming operator to report all credit transactions. After reviewing the reports, the regulators would then have the discretion to require the creditor to file an application and undergo licensing. This allows the regulators to maintain control over the transaction with only minimal interference in financial markets. The mere possibility of having to obtain a license might result in some lenders refusing to serve the gaming industry, but will not be as significant an obstacle as mandatory licenses. Moreover, regulators can allay many concerns of potential lenders by judiciously exercising their discretion only when serious concerns arise.

Governments may be best served by taking a balanced approach to licensing lenders and other creditors. While full licensing would prevent hidden ownership interests and protect operators from the undue influence of unsuitable persons, such a licensing regime could result in higher costs for obtaining credit and a dearth in competition among creditors. There are several types of creditors which could be exempted from licensing requirements without undercutting governmental policy goals. Additionally, some jurisdictions may find that an *ad hoc* review of credit transactions is sufficient to insulate the Internet gaming industry from unsuitable or hidden interests

2. Key Game Suppliers

A. Operators - Hosted Service Providers

A white label product or service is a product or service produced by one company (the producer) that other companies (the marketers) rebrand (or "skin") to make it appear as if they made it. Companies that provide white label services are Hosted Service Providers (called an xSP). These "turnkey" solutions are in essence a combination of Internet functions including gaming and non-gaming applications (Software as a Service), infrastructure, customer service, player hosts, web design and maintenance, regulatory oversight, security, monitoring, storage, and hosting email. Typically, the casino customer can brand the site through providing the art and audio for the site and are responsible for marketing the site. xSPs can provide different degrees of customization or permit the customer to assume responsibility for some aspects of the site. xSPs benefit from economies of scale and operate on a business to business model, delivering the same software and services to several casino customers, who may not have the economic incentive or expertise to operate their own Internet gaming service. Smaller casinos can also take advantage of the liquidity that a larger network can provide to its customers. When offering community based games, like poker, this assures the player has a variety of available games, limits, and, when offering house banked games, a wider array of games.

Hosted service providers should be given the highest priority in licensing breadth because of their importance in controlling the systems that assure the honesty and fairness of games, protection of player funds, and the other goals of both the players and government protection goals. While the profile of the hosted service provider may not, in many circumstances, be as visible as the actual owners, scandals or issues at such a level can harm players and significantly taint the industry.

B. Gaming Software Provider and Manufacturers of Internet Gaming Systems

Just as manufacturers of slot machines and other gaming devices are crucial in the operational ability of traditional casinos, manufacturers of gaming software are essential for an online gaming operation. Because such suppliers develop the machinery or code, suppliers can produce flaws in the machine or imbed bad code which can compromise the honesty or fairness of the games. As such, online gaming operators and the government regulators need to depend not only on the integrity of the software maker, but also on the technical ability of the software maker to prevent future breaches of security and performance. Therefore, many governments specifically require software providers to obtain licenses. For example, in Alderney, an "associate" needs to be licensed.[9] While "associate" might seem like it means "a business partner," the definition of an associate includes a software contractor that designs the code.[10] Alderney's laws, in particular, have a wide breadth as they relate to what the jurisdiction perceives as a critical player protection function. In contrast, Antigua only requires key personnel to be licensed, which do not include suppliers such as software contractors.[11] In fact, suppliers need to be licensed only if they receive a percentage of gaming revenues.[12]

The extent to which a jurisdiction requires software providers to be licensed may depend on several factors. For example, the complexity of game software may go beyond the capacity of many regulatory agencies to understand or test. A sophisticated gaming laboratory is expensive; indeed, it can be more than the entire regulatory budget in many places. Jurisdictions without a testing laboratory may use private testing companies to fill the void. Either in-house or private testing may satisfy regulators that the design and operation quality of the gaming sites, and its myriad of functions, meet government standards. Even with a state-of-the-art laboratory, some aspects of Internet gaming sites are so complex that unscrupulous persons can still exploit them without detection. Regulators must therefore rely on the manufacturer's integrity to assure that the gaming sites and the games thereon are fair and honest.

Licensing becomes more important to the extent that regulators do not have the money, expertise, or technical resources to assure that the games are fair and honest through testing and enforcement.

The manufacturer of the system platform may be different from the manufacturer of the game content. The issue in such case is whether to require licensure of both manufacturers. A jurisdiction may decide to only license the system platform manufacturer. This relies on the system platform manufacturer to have a contractual relationship with the game content providers and to exercise all necessary due diligence to assure that the game content software meets all regulatory requirements. The regulators are, therefore, relying on the honest and competency of system platform manufacturer along with an independent review of the software by an independent laboratory.

---

[9] Alderney, The Alderney eGambling Ordinance § 17 (2009)

[10] *Id.* at § 30, "business associate."

[11] Ant. & Barb., *supra* note 8 at pt. II, § 10 (persons requiring licenses); pt. I, "Key person(s) (defining key person); pt. IV, §§ 87-8 (suppliers and licensing).

[12] *Id.* at pt. IV, §§ 87, 88.

Another issue is the history of the software. Other non-licensed developers may have touched the code in the past. Software is a living, breathing entity and code is rarely derived from the ground up. Moreover, with software increasingly being coded by team members or third party contractors in various remote locations, governments cannot guarantee the code has only been handled by licensed resources. Therefore, governments need to rely more heavily on the accountability of licensed operators, systems architects, and potentially the test labs to be accountable for the integrity of the integrated code in its current and future configurations.

A subset of game software is the random number generator, which is the core of many game systems. This is the software algorithm that generates a sequence of numbers or symbols that lack any pattern, or appear to a testable degree to mimic a random event. Malta and other legislations typically certify a number of RNG producers and require licensees to use only a certified random number generator.

Non-Gaming Related Services And Software

Application Service Providers.

An application service provider (ASP) is an Internet based business service. The ASP typically provides software application, operates and maintains the servers, and offers the Internet service through web browsers, mobile devices, or otherwise. Even a gaming company that intends to own and operate its own Internet gaming site contracts certain services to third-party ASPs for services such as payment processing, geo-location, age and identification verification, or customer relations management. The reason for such integration with third-party services can be that the Internet site lacks expertise in a particular service area or it is much less expensive to contract for the service than to provide it directly. Some risk, however, exists in integrating some services including the loss of control of corporate data and potential security risks.

The extent to which ASPs should fall within the breadth of licensing should depend on the type of service being provided.

An Application Programming Interface (API) Provider

In this context, the API is the supplier of a complete interface for multiple software components to communicate with each other. In Nevada, these platform providers are tasked with greater responsibility than merely a component provider to an operator. They are tasked with assuring that all gaming components on the system meet regulatory requirements. In this context, the regulators require them to obtain a license. Without delegating this additional authority, the API provider could be no differently than another software provider whose software does not determine win or lose.

In jurisdictions with higher levels of technical resources and competency, licensing may be less important than those jurisdictions where the honesty and competency of the manufacturer is more critical.

Payment Processors

Internet gaming sites can process payments directly with their bank, called the merchant bank. In this case, the site will apply for and obtain a merchant account. This allows the site to accept credit/debit cards, and other forms of card payment based on the card not present (CNP) transaction principles. A payment processor typically is a third-party company appointed by a merchant to handle credit card transactions for merchant-acquiring banks. Most payment processors act as "middleman" where the player pays the processor, which in turn pays the site less a processing fee. Besides securely transferring the money between the various bank accounts, the payment processor can provide other services including anti-fraud and anti-money laundering measures, as discussed below.

Advantages to using a payment processor can include increased security, fraud prevention, and lower system infrastructure costs (such as purchasing or developing a payment gateway). A large payment processor may allow the gaming site operator to utilize credit card merchant facilities with multiple premier banking institutions with preapproved mainstream payment mechanisms such as PayPal, Visa or MasterCard.[13]

Payment processors are largely unrelated to the major policy goals of both player and government protection. For example, a payment processor has no opportunity to cheat the player or impact the honesty or fairness of the games offered on the site. Payment processors may, however, handle player payments and receipts. In this process, some payment processors may have custody of player funds. The policy goal of assuring that these funds are adequately protected is consistent with both player and government protection goals. This can be achieved in several ways short of requiring licensing of the payment processors. The first way is to require the site owner to have reserves in place even for funds in temporary possession of the payment processor. If this is done, even if the payment processor absconded with the funds, the players would be protected. A second method would be to require the payment processor to bond or otherwise insure the moneys in their possession. A third method is to regulate the accounts that the payment processor is using to assure that they are properly restricted. This can include procedures and approvals for segregation of players' funds outside of operators' control. Two or more trusted third parties, which could include the payment processor, regulated financial institutions, and regulated escrow agents or insured

---

[13] The use of ewallet structure versus aggregate accounting structure present different software bookkeeping and controls. Ewallets, as an example, tie to a user's social security number. Nevertheless, fraud and anti-money laundering controls are typically written into the software system layer.

certified accountants, could share control of the segregated funds. In any of these cases, enforcement mechanisms may assure better policy results than interfering with market competition through licensing.

Besides the security of players' funds, the government may have legitimate concerns as to whether the payment processor can adequately protect player data. This may be addressed through technical standards or by reference to third party data protection standards. For example, major credit card companies adopted PCI (Payment Card Industry) compliance standards for financial institutions and merchants that secure customers' personal data when using a credit card. As a matter of practice, Malta requires that all payment processors be PCI compliant.

Payment gateways are different from payment processors in that a payment gateway merely facilitates the transfer of information between the Internet gaming site and the player's bank (called the issuing bank). A key function of a payment gateway is encryption. A payment gateway uses encoding technology to encrypt and decrypt all the transferred information, including credit card numbers and other account information. The payment gateway processor validates the provided card account details and authorizes the payment amount. It is probably more significant to note what the payment gateway does not do. It is the card issuer that transfers the funds directly from the player's card balance to the acquiring bank. The acquiring bank then transfers the funds into the Internet gambling site's own merchant account. Payment gateways should have low priority because they have no direct effect on any policy goals regardless of whether the focus is on government or player protection.

Payment processors and payment gateways are a useful, and in many cases essential, tool for online gaming sites to securely and efficiently transfer funds. Because these systems are uniquely removed from many of the government and player protection goals discussed in this chapter, licensing them is not an especially pressing matter. In fact, enforcement mechanisms and other non-licensing, regulatory requirements are likely sufficient to ensure that governments and players are adequately protected from the risks associated with payment processors and payment gateways.

Fraud Prevention

Fraud prevention consists of fraud screening techniques designed to maximize the efficiency of the payment verification process. It is often conducted by the payment processor as a part of the services that they provide to online sites. These techniques can involve address verification (comparing the address information provided by the player against the billing address information that the issuer has on record for the account), card verification methods (to ensure that the person submitting the transaction is in possession of the actual card), comparison of data in positive and negative files (Office of Foreign Assets Control list lookups or 'black-list' lookups),[14] and conducting

---

[14] According to the official US Treasury website, the Office of Foreign Assets Control

risk analysis based on IP address, country of origin, and velocity pattern analysis.[15] In most cases, the provider that offers fraud prevention services does not decide whether to accept or reject a transaction; rather if the fraud criteria set by the operator and administered by the service provider indicates an exception, the transaction is referred to the operator for resolution. In such cases, the servicer provider is further removed from responsibility for decisions that could impact revenues and hence, less important to achievement of policy goals; therefore the benefits of licensure are greatly reduced.

Site Security

Site security is a very broad concept and can entail many aspects including network management, site redundancy, firewalls, intrusion detection, intrusion prevention, hacking prevention, social engineering, anti-virus, anti-Trojan, anti-worm, physical security, a secure uncrackable RNG, and disaster recovery. Certain forms of hacking, such as Denial of Service attacks[16], that cannot cripple a brick-and-mortar casino, would prevent the gaming operation from operating and can cause serious damage to an Internet-based gaming operation. This can be of special concern for jurisdictions that focus on government protection goals as it can impact tax revenues and the public perception of the sufficiency of the regulations. Moreover, from a player protection prospective, compromised site security could allow hackers to steal personal player data or impact the fairness or honesty of the games. Thus, site security is an important aspect of regulatory oversight. It may, however, be more appropriately the subject of technical standards and regulatory enforcement as opposed to licensing.

Site security is important to all Internet commerce from small businesses to multi-billion dollar banking institutions. The methods that each uses to protect their sites can be, and often are, state of the art solutions. Isolating who can provide services to the gaming sites based on licensing will likely prevent the gaming sites from always using state of the art security services

---

"publishes a list of individuals and companies owned or controlled by, or acting for or on behalf of, targeted countries. It also lists individuals, groups, and entities, such as terrorists and narcotics traffickers designated under programs that are not country-specific. Collectively, such individuals and companies are called "Specially Designated Nationals" or "SDNs." Their assets are blocked and U.S. persons are generally prohibited from dealing with them." http://www.treasury.gov/resource-center/sanctions/SDN-List/Pages/default.aspx

[15] Velocity pattern analysis is a method of determining the potential of fraud in an online transaction based on the number of uses of a data element such as the use of a credit card in a predefined period such as 24 hours. A sudden increase in the number of transactions can signal the greater likelihood of a fraudulent transaction. http://www.merchantaccount.at/processing101/antifraud/velocity-pattern-analysis/

[16] "A Denial of Service attack (DoS) is any intended attempt to prevent legitimate users from reaching a specific network resource." George Loukas and Gulay Oke, *Protection against Denial of Service Attacks: A Survey*, THE COMPUTER JOURNAL, Volume 53, Issue 7, page 1, Oxford Journals, http://staffweb.cms.gre.ac.uk/~lg47/publications/LoukasOke-DoSSurveyComputerJournal.pdf.

and software needed to ensure the security of the site from hackers and other external threats.

Age, Identity, and Location Verification Systems and Services

Age and Identification verification refers to systems or services used by Internet gaming sites to confirm that the users attempting to access their website are who they claim to be and are of the age required by law to participate in gaming. This service involves the documenting, tracking, and logging of identification and age verification. Age and identification verification providers also interface with age and identification databases provided by 4th parties, including other governments.

Location verification refers to systems or services sites designed to confirm that the users are physically located in a jurisdiction where they are permitted to play and where the site is permitted to accept players. This service involves documenting tracking and logging of location verification.

Both age and location verification systems are widely available and used in a variety of existing online businesses. For example, both age and location verification are important for Internet sales of alcohol and tobacco products as well as age-restricted materials. Allowing Internet gaming sites to use existing technologies without placing substantial licensing barriers on providers assures that the most technically advanced technology is available to the operator. This is particularly important for compliance with the laws of other jurisdictions. The need to license age and location verification services is further diminished where regulators set reasonable standards for age or location verification systems or services. Reasonable regulatory standards would include privacy protections and the parameters for how the operator should determine who meets relevant age and location requirements at both the automated systems level and when exceptional circumstances require non-automated verification.

Bonus and Loyalty Management

Bonus and loyalty management software and services allow the Internet site to measure customer feedback and allocate resources including bonuses based on the customer loyalty. These systems include customer loyalty metrics that measure and aggregate a customer's loyalty, track ongoing customer feedback, and provide methods for utilizing that information, including player bonuses based on the data and feedback collected. To the extent that third party service providers can access player data or can interface with game systems, regulatory oversight may be useful. To the extent that these concerns can be addressed through technological standards, the need to invoke licensing or registration may be diminished. Where third parties do not have access to either game systems or player data, responsibility for bonus and loyalty management systems can legitimately lie exclusively with the licensed operator.

Internet Hosting Services

An Internet hosting service allows individuals and organizations to make their website accessible to players. Web hosts are companies that provide space on a server for use by clients, as well as Internet connectivity, typically in a data center. Web hosts can also provide data center space and connectivity to the Internet for other servers located in their data center, called co-location. In this scenario, the user owns the server; the hosting company provides physical space that the server takes up and takes care of the server. The co-location provider may contribute little to no support directly for their client's machine, furnishing only an environmental control system, uninterruptable power supplies, battery backups and diesel generators, Internet access, and secured storage facilities for the server.

Hosting service plays two important roles of concern to regulators: security of the site servers and uninterrupted service. Private certification of a data center is made based on the level of capability of the data center, with the highest tier (4) being the most redundant capacity components and multiple distribution paths serving the site's computer equipment and, thus, least likely to have interrupted service. Security of the data centers can also vary from insecure to meeting the highest standards for critical government and banking servers. As governments are more likely to want licensees to use the most secure and robust data centers, as opposed to self-housing their servers, they may want to regulate the use of third party co-location data centers through technical standards and enforcement rather than by licensing.

Independent Marketing Agents, Affiliates and Other Referral Websites, Agents, and Virtual Hosts.

Search engines, e-mail, website syndication, and marketing affiliates have long played an important role in driving customers to Internet gaming sites. Some sites have more than 70 percent of their revenue coming from affiliates.

Affiliates of an Internet gaming operator are entities that are paid to bring customers into the gaming operation's web portal. Usually, affiliates are websites that have business arrangements with the gaming operation in which the affiliates agree to connect their users to the gaming website. For example, a gaming news website that directs its members to the casino would be considered an affiliate. In return, the affiliates are compensated for their referral by either a fixed fee per referral or a percentage of the expected gaming revenue derived from each referral. In the realm of Internet gaming, affiliate websites perform the roles that junket representatives[17] and hosts perform in traditional casinos. Affiliates do not know or have access to the revenues that a gaming operation generates. In fact, the only time that

---

[17] A junket representative is a commissioned contractor that bring patrons to the casino. ANTHONY N. CABOT, CASINO GAMING: POLICY, ECONOMICS, AND REGULATION 254 (2001).

affiliates have a connection with the gaming operations of a website is when affiliates are paid a percent of actual gaming revenues.

Advertisers are external entities that work with the marketing department within the gaming operation to promote the gaming site. The very purpose of the advertiser is to stimulate demand for gambling on the licensed site. An example of such an entity is a company that posts advertisements, known as banner ads, on various web pages. These ads are posted for the gaming operation in return for a fee per view or a fee per click. The largest groups of online advertisers include search engines and social media websites. Rather than affiliates who might be paid an estimated or actual percent of gaming revenues, advertisers in the online world are generally paid per click. Several common methods exist to compensate marketing affiliates including revenue sharing or pay per sale (PPS), cost per action (CPA), and cost per click (CPC) or cost per mille (CPM). As the name suggests, cost-per-click advertising means that the advertisers put the gaming operation's advertisements on many websites to gain potential clients, and the gaming operation pays the advertiser once a prospective gaming customer clicks on the advertisement and is directed to the gaming operation's website. Advertisers are fairly isolated from gaming revenues and the gaming operations. CPA arrangements typically pay the affiliate (a) a flat fee for each registered player, (b) a flat fee for each registered player who makes a deposit, (c) a percentage of the gross revenue of a player, or a combination of (a) plus (c) or (b) plus (c).

Regardless of whether a jurisdiction's policies focus on government or player protection, the use of affiliates poses certain concerns.[18] Unlike casino employees, affiliates act independently of the gaming site. This creates less accountability to corporate codes of ethics and internal controls. Affiliates can serve as "barkers" whose sole goal is to drive traffic to the gaming sites. This can be done through the use of false or misleading advertisements or offers. For example, a site may pose as an independent consumer review provider, while actually giving falsely positive reports and ratings to only those sites that pay them bounties. Moreover, the affiliates can operate beyond the jurisdiction of the regulators.

Site operators must adopt corporate policies if they want to control affiliate behaviors. Regulators can shift the responsibility to maintain regulatory controls over the affiliates to the site operators through mandatory policies and practices that can be reviewed and measured by regulators if desired. Moreover, technologies exist to help control affiliates. Governments can implement "crawler" software, that can collect data on the marketing activities of the affiliates of their licensees. If violations of advertising standards are detected, then the regulators can force the termination of the affiliate relationship or take other corrective action. While potentially effective, this method is reactive as opposed to proactive.

---

[18] Under the most conservative player protection goals, the use of affiliates to promote gaming activities could be prohibited as it stimulates demand.

Internal marketing employees pose fewer problems than affiliates because they are subject to corporate codes of ethics and internal controls.

Operation and People Services

Other services such as customer service, domain name acquisition and management, affiliate management, network and chat management, and site optimization are not critical to the core policy goals related to either player or government protection. Regulators may want to understand the interface of these systems with more critical system functions or the extent of access to customer data. Only where technical requirements cannot adequately protect critical systems should consideration be given to requiring registration or licensure of these types of providers.

Non-Gaming Software Providers

Among others, gaming site operators may use products that integrate into back-end gaming platforms to perform such functions as account management, affiliate and agent software, customer relationship management tools, fraud and security tools, registration platforms, integrated cashier, centralized reporting tools, bonus and loyalty tools, network management tools and site optimization tools.

Recommendation

As detailed above, the necessary breadth of licensing is highly contextual. Apart from owners and hosted service providers, which should be given the highest licensure priority, the need for licensing depends greatly on the extent to which a party can influence a variety of factors like the honesty and fairness of games, the public's perception of the online gaming industry, a party's ability to affect gaming operations, the economic and innovative costs of licensing requirements, and whether licensee oversight, technical requirements, and regulatory enforcement sufficiently protect against risks related to malfeasance or incompetence. More simply, the breadth of licensing will vary based on a jurisdiction's particularized policy concerns and its ability to adequately address those policy concerns through methods other than licensing.

Depth of Licensing

When a government requires a license to engage in gaming-related activities, the entity that must apply for and obtain a license often is not an individual. For example, the owners of most Nevada casinos are publicly traded corporations. Depth of licensing refers to which persons associated with the applicant-entity must file an application and obtain a license.

Regardless of the type of approval sought, it is first necessary to determine which parties associated with the applicant need to be licensed. Jurisdictions around the world have varying requirements as to who within or associated with an applicant needs to be licensed. Decisions on who must be licensed are based mostly on the relationship between the party required to be licensed and the applicant-gaming operation. For example, in the Isle of Man, for the business' gaming license to come into force, a designated official of the company must first be approved by the Commissioners.[19] Thus, determining the depth of who needs to be licensed requires an analysis of the involvement of parties in the management and operations of the online gaming operation. Many jurisdictions require significant depth in terms of who needs to be licensed.

Most owners, operators, suppliers, and vendors for Internet gaming sites will be some form of business entity, usually a corporation. A corporation is an artificial person or legal entity that the government authorizes to conduct business. The principal benefits of a corporation are the limited liability of equity owners (known as shareholders), transferability of interest, and continuity of existence.

Structures for corporations differ between countries, but usually involve officers, directors, shareholders, and employees. Shareholders are persons or entities that hold equity, as represented by shares, in a company. Shares entitle the holders to control the corporation through voting for the board of directors. In the discretion of the board of directors, shareholders are entitled to earnings through current or accumulated dividends and to pro-rata distribution of assets upon liquidation.[20] Shareholders typically elect directors who manage the corporation through corporate officers. Officers are corporate agents, and have management responsibilities that the board of directors delegates to them.

Depth of licensing for corporations concerns which directors, shareholders, officers and employees must undergo licensing scrutiny. Similar considerations are needed for other business formations, such as general and limited partnerships, trusts, joint ventures, limited liability companies, and joint stock associations.

Officers/Key Employees

Gaming executives are responsible for overseeing gaming operations. One gaming executive that is particularly critical to gaming operations and the well being of the Internet gaming company is the Chief Executive Officer (CEO). The CEO manages all online gaming operations, ensures efficiency of the website, and establishes internal policies and rules. Sometimes, an online gaming portal may divide the CEO's responsibility into two: the CEO would have the role of managing the business aspects of the gaming operation, and an employee with specialized technical skills, known as the Chief Technology Officer (CTO), would manage the site itself. Among the CTO's responsibilities are to ensure that the site is

---

[19] Isle of Man, Online Gambling Regulation Act § 10 (2001), *available at* http://www.gov.im/lib/docs/gambling/Regulations/onlinegamblingregulationact2001.pdf
[20] HARRY HENN AND JOHN ALEXANDER, CORPORATIONS (HORNBOOK SERIES) 396 (1983).

always accessible, that it is secure, that it can sustain anticipated traffic, and that the software and hardware implemented meet regulatory and internal standards. Other important technical persons include the chief architect and chief systems administrator. System administrators play a significant role in site security. They can govern everything from safety of the operating system to new software versions. The Chief Financial Officer (CFO) is typically responsible for managing the financial risks of the corporation, budgeting and financial planning, record-keeping, financial reporting, and data analysis.

Since executives have access to nearly all of the gaming operation's financial information and have the ability to manipulate the data, they are the group most likely to receive regulatory attention and intensive licensing review. Regulations can designate these individuals in different ways. For example, the Kahnawake, a Mohawk Territory in Canada, designate the titles of key officers that must be licensed including the CEO, CFO, COO, CTO and Office Manager.[21] In Malta, regulators require licensed directors to be Maltese residents.[22] Other jurisdictions designate who needs a license based on function as opposed to title. For example, the United Kingdom requires that key personnel be licensed, but defines key personnel based on function rather than title.[23] Those functions include anyone responsible for the overall strategy of gaming operations, financial planning, control, budgeting, marketing, commercial development, regulatory compliance, IT provision, and gaming related security.[24] Still others use compensation to determine who needs a license by either setting a compensation amount that triggers licensure or simply requiring a fixed number of the most highly compensated executives to file an application.

Regardless of whether they are defined by job title, function, or compensation, corporate agents performing essential functions are likely to be subject to some degree of licensing in most jurisdictions.

Other Employees

Hardware and Software Technicians

Software engineers are some of the most numerous employees of an online gaming operation. Led by a chief software engineer, the role of software engineers is to write computer code that will impact every aspect of the website. The most common types of code that the engineers focus on are code directing the randomness/probability of casino games,

---

[21] Kahnawake, Regulations Concerning Internet Gaming, §§ 60-62 (1999) (amended 2011), *available at* http://www.gamingcommission.ca/docs/RegulationsConcerningInter-activeGaming.pdf

[22] Malta, *supra* note 6 at § 2 "key official," 15, 18.

[23] Gt. Brit. Gambling Act, Pt. 5, §§ 67, 80 (2005), *available at* http://www.legislation.gov.uk/ukpga/2005/19/contents

[24] *Id.* at § 80.

code to direct the movement of money between accounts, and reporting functions. Although the group, also known as computer programmers, might seem as if it has the ability to markedly impact gaming operations, software engineers are not heavily involved while the gaming operation is functional. The programmers' role of writing code is undertaken offline and is verified by multiple parties, internal and external, before the software is implemented in a live setting.

Governments need to understand their own resources and the limitations of testing strategies even when performed by independent testing facilities. While controls over the software can be implemented to ensure that the computer code is fully functional and that no avenues exist for the programmers to insert malicious code that would change probabilities or transfer funds to incorrect accounts, these things cannot be accomplished with absolute guarantees. The degree of assurance is dependent on many factors including the stringency of the standards, the quality of the manufacturers' internal testing and controls, the competence and capability of the testing agency, and the degree and sophistication of the government's industry-wide oversight. Once the software is implemented into the operations, except for follow up releases and bug fixes, software engineers are not involved; the technical operations personnel take over the role of managing the software.

Although an online gaming operation does not have a physical location, the website runs off certain hardware. This hardware is comprised of servers and hosting computers, which are managed by information technology employees with expertise in the field. This group is perhaps farthest removed from gaming operations because hardware employees typically do nothing more than monitor the physical components used to run the website, and not the software upon which the website operates.

Technical Support and Operations Personnel

In the ecommerce world, technical support staff is often broken into levels. Level 3 personnel would be highly trained technical system administrators and support engineers. Key individuals in this group are discussed above. Level 2 personnel would have some technical knowledge but much less than Level 3. Level 1 personnel are not very tech savvy but interface with the customers. Most important for the purposes of regulatory licensing is not the personnel level but the functionality and access assumed by each level of technical support staff. For example, technical operations personnel are a subgroup of technical support that is unique to Internet gaming. This group is responsible for ensuring that the website is operational and that it is secure. A major role of technical operations personnel is to monitor the website and ensure that it is safe for players, that there is no cheating, and that the integrity of the gaming operation is not compromised. To meet the responsibilities of this function, technical operations personnel are given very broad access and have the ability to move funds into or out of client accounts, to monitor and change game outcomes, to contact clients regarding their accounts, and to access the funds of the gaming operation to settle monetary disputes. Due to the ability of this group to access and change sensitive information, it should have exposure to stringent licensing requirements.

Therefore, the level of system access a particular job function requires should dictate which technical support personnel need to be licensed and not the job's level of technical knowledge.

Customer Support

Customer support employees, in any business, are meant to interact with customers and resolve any issues the customers face. In Internet gaming, some common customer service roles include providing information about the website to potential clients, knowing the games offered, and settling client disputes with the gaming operator. In the long-run, effective customer support can help the website achieve a reputation for being user-friendly, which will certainly help the business. To perform effectively, customer service employees need access to information that might be sensitive.

To solve some of the more sensitive customer issues, such as those involving funds, customer support may need to access private information, like information regarding customer funds and bank accounts. Furthermore, to settle disputes, customer support may be able to move a limited amount of funds either to or from player accounts. Much of this may depend on whether payment processing is outsourced and whether sensitive data is available only to the payment processor. Although this group has access to sensitive customer information, the regulatory need for strict licensing of the group is not high because the actions of customer support can be traced and, if necessary, reversed. Additionally, much of the information that is available to customer support is on a read only basis, which means that customer service employees can view, but not change, the information. Nevertheless, depending on the functionality and access accorded to customer support, governments may consider some limited form of licensing for customer support such as employee registration or work cards.

Fraud and Surveillance

The fraud and surveillance department of an online gaming operation seeks to prevent players from cheating both the gaming operation and other players. The department, led by the director of surveillance, monitors games and their outcomes in order to determine the probability that players are using software to cheat the gaming operation. By looking at the risk/returns of many games, the fraud department can also detect players who are banning together and bilking other players out of money. Another key function of the fraud and surveillance department is to prevent fraudulent forms of payment. As identity theft and credit card fraud rise, the burden on the department to verify payments rises so that the gaming operation and other players can be awarded their winnings.

Along with the functions of a traditional casino, such as monitoring games to prevent collusion among players, the online frontier imposes many additional duties on the fraud and surveillance department. For example, the department monitors the website for collusion, chip dumping, and robotic programs. The fraud and surveillance department also ensures that the users of the site are real persons.

The main tool that the department has to enforce its anti-cheating and -fraud measures is exclusion. Just as traditional casinos can remove players from the property, the fraud and surveillance department of an online gaming operation can exclude a player from participating in the website's operations.

Generally the department has read-only access. Thus, while the director of surveillance has access to information that would make him critical in gaming operations, the access is not one that can be used to manipulate gaming data. As such, the need for licensing in the fraud and surveillance department is not particularly compelling.

Marketing Employees

The marketing department of a gaming operation is responsible for the creation and implementation of a marketing strategy to drive traffic to and promote the gaming operation. In the context of Internet gaming, a marketing director leads the marketing department and works with affiliates and advertisers to seek more customers. Some key roles of the marketing director include developing promotions, installing rewards programs, and ensuring that the gaming operation's image is not undermined in the media. The marketing director is also responsible for ensuring that all marketing strategies and all interactions with affiliates, advertisers, and potential customers comply with all relevant gaming statutes and regulations.

In Internet gaming, marketing employees are responsible for some unique tasks. For example, the marketing department of an online business has to monitor online activity targeting the gaming operation. Search engine optimization, social media marketing, and banner advertisements on websites are some of the common functions that an online gaming operation's marketing department performs. All such roles, while not directly related to the gaming operations, indirectly influence the revenues of the gaming operation.

Internal marketing employees pose fewer problems than affiliates because they are subject to corporate codes of ethics and internal controls. Because they are employees, gaming site operators have greater interest and control over their actions. Because licensee oversight is likely sufficient to ensure marketing employees do not contravene a government's Internet gaming regulations and policies, licensing is largely unnecessary.

Finance and Accounting

The finance department of a gaming operation, led by the Chief Financial Officer (CFO), makes financing decisions such as issuing debt, ensuring compliance with regulations, and monitoring projects to generate positive cash flows for the gaming operation. The accounting department is led by the gaming operation controller. It is the duty of the controller to reconcile accounting transactions, enforce internal controls, approve the general ledger, and work with the internal audit department to monitor money flows. Together, the finance and accounting departments maintain the gaming operation's financial records, prepare licenses and tax forms, and balance the gaming operation's books.

Although the two departments seem to have access to much of the gaming operation's financial records and bank accounts, the access is very limited. The employees of the two departments can view the financial information, but generally cannot alter the data. Furthermore, internal policies are in place to prevent the employees from transferring any of the gaming operation's funds into other accounts. Thus, the departments are not deeply associated with actual gaming activities. Because their duties are primarily post-gaming (i.e. journaling entries, reporting results, etc...) licensure is not especially pressing.

Internal Audit

The role of the internal audit department is to analyze and verify the gaming operation's transactions to ensure that they meet established regulatory and internal guidelines. Internal auditors, led by the director, also determine if the various gaming departments are following accounting rules, custodial policies, and control procedures. While internal auditors are focused on the workings of gaming departments, audit clerks audit revenue generating areas. Audit clerks verify the accuracy of revenue and expenditure figures, correct discrepancies, audit online balances, and prepare reports about daily operations. The internal audit department seeks to verify information post-event and so is not directly involved in actual gaming operations. As with the financing and accounting departments described above, the audit department's post-gaming role greatly mitigates the need for licensing.

Non-Gaming Employees

A website needs to hire employees for non-gaming purposes. For example, a website could have employees that manage its servers and decide which types of games to offer players. Such roles are isolated from the actual game play and therefore need not be licensed.

Notable exceptions are computer information service employees. As gaming operations become more computer-based, the staff dedicated to the maintenance of these systems increases. A gaming operation can have many different sensitive computer systems, including player tracking systems, slot tracking systems, debit card systems, marker issuance and collection systems, bingo and keno systems, accounting systems, and sports and horse race totalizators.[25] Such employees may have greater opportunity to manipulate game outcomes or player/operator accounts.

Except for certain computer service employees, non-gaming operation employees generally are of the lowest regulatory priority. Effective implementation of internal control systems should adequately protect gaming operator assets from potential theft by non-gaming employees. Regulators, however, may wish to make computer service employees, particularly those with access to software, a higher regulatory priority.

Directors

Directors have a duty to the corporation to use their best judgment in deciding and executing corporate policy. Their duties include (1) selecting officers and setting officer salary and compensation, (2) making major policy decisions, and (3) deciding major financial matters, including dividends and financing. Directors often are described as inside or outside directors. An "inside" director is a board member who is an employee, officer, or significant shareholder in the company. An "outside" director is not an employee, significant shareholder, or otherwise charged with operational responsibilities; an "outside" director is considered independent of management. Outside directors can be selected because of their general business or specific industry knowledge or experience. As a result, outside directors are often viewed as having objective, informed opinions regarding the company's decisions, health, and operations and bring diverse experience to the company's decision-making processes.

Governments often only require inside directors to obtain licenses. In Nevada, as an example, only inside directors of public and certain private companies have to file licensing applications.[26] They include the chairman of the board, those holding greater than five percent of any class of voting securities, those serving on the executive committee or any comparable committee with authority over the casino activities, those who are also gaming employees, and those who regulators determine supervise gaming activities.[27] This is a reasoned approach because outside directors are independent of the company and have less opportunity to impact daily management or operations most subject to regulatory sensitivities.

---

[25] A totalizer is a computer used in pari-mutuel horse race wagering to register and divide the total of all wagers made after the race track has subtracted its commission among all the persons having placed a wager on a winning horse or combination of horses. *See* Princeton's Wordnet.

[26] Nev., Regulations of the Nevada Gaming Commission and State Gaming Control Board, §§ 5A.030 (licensing regime for Internet gaming mirrors traditional licensure), 15.585.7-5 (corporate licensure requires that any person described in 16.410-15 have a license), 16.410-15 (licensing officers, employees, and directors) (1959) (current as of March 27, 2012), *available at* http://gaming.nv.gov/modules/showdocument.aspx?documentid=2957

[27] *Id.*

Moreover, as outside directors are most often paid based on fixed criteria such as a monthly or meeting fee, they are less subject to financial or other pressures that could lead to compromising regulatory integrity. Finally, a goal of selecting outside directors is to have the most qualified persons to serve in that position. The pool of eligible outside directors would likely be significantly smaller if licensing were a prerequisite.

Shareholders

All forms of business entities that a license applicant may use include the concept of equity ownership. In corporations, the most common form of business entity is equity held by shareholders. A corporation can be either public or private. A publicly-traded company is a corporation whose stock is traded on a public market. An attractive feature of being a publicly-traded corporation is the ability to raise capital through a public offering. Most often, a public offering occurs when the company sells either stock or debt instruments to the public through brokers. Public company stock is attractive to investors because it usually provides liquidity. If a person buys the stock, he can usually sell it in the public market by simply contacting his broker.

Benefits aside, allowing publicly traded corporations to own and operate gaming operations poses regulatory issues. As a practical matter, a publicly-traded corporation cannot be licensed if all its shareholders must be licensed. A public company can have thousands of shares traded daily. Therefore, if a jurisdiction wants to encourage publicly-traded corporations to invest in its gaming industry, it must allow licensing without each shareholder having to obtain a license.

Waiving licensing requirements for some shareholders, however, may allow unsuitable persons to buy shares and have an ownership interest in the gaming companies. This may not pose substantial problems if the person owns a few shares out of millions, but can create regulatory issues if the person owns a significant percentage of the stock. Public perception problems may occur where the media exposes that a notorious criminal has major holdings in a publicly-traded gaming company. Moreover, regulatory problems may occur where the person's holdings allow him to exert influence or control over the corporation.

Jurisdictions that want publicly traded corporations must balance these regulatory concerns with market realities. They can do this by setting thresholds at which shareholders in publicly traded corporations must apply for and obtain a gaming license. In the United States, these levels are commonly set at 5 percent, 10 percent, or 15 percent.[28] As an example, a license application may ask the applicant to name and provide a curriculum vitae of every shareholder that holds more than 5 percent of the company. These levels are often tied to government reporting or filing requirements for when a shareholder acquires a beneficial interest greater than a certain

---

[28] CABOT, *supra* note 17, at 275.

amount. Some places, such as Nevada and New Jersey, allow institutional investors to hold over 10 percent.[29] Institutional investors are entities such as banks, insurance companies, registered investment companies, advisors, and employee benefit or pension funds. Falling within this category are mutual fund companies that often control and invest billions of dollars for their clients. In Nevada, the regulators set a maximum limit that an institutional investor may hold without obtaining a license.[30] In both Nevada and New Jersey, the institutional investor must show it is holding the stock for investment purposes only.[31]

Some jurisdictions do not distinguish between private and public companies and set levels for shareholder licensing based solely on percentage of ownership. For example, Kahnawake requires the suitability of each individual who owns more than 10 percent of outstanding shares,[32] while Antigua sets the bar at 5 percent.[33] The historical experience of some jurisdictions has provided little reason to distinguish between public and private companies. These jurisdictions licensed gaming before the advent of public gaming companies. They made general exceptions to the requirement that all shareholders be licensed to allow public companies to enter the industry. This limited relaxation of regulatory oversight was deemed an acceptable tradeoff for the benefits brought by public company investment. The requirements were not relaxed for private companies. Even Nevada, however, has since relaxed requirements that all shareholders of private companies must obtain a license.

Therefore, typically the need for licensing shareholders is linked to the extent of that shareholder's investment. It is important to note that the nature of institutional investors may allow them to avoid licensure where individuals may not. Another important regulatory consideration is whether a company is public or private, since requiring all public shareholders to carry a license is a practical impossibility.

Levels of Review

Levels of review in regulatory systems consist of "tiered" licensing. Tiered licensing involves categorizing groups of individuals or entities that are associated with the gaming industry into two or more tiers. Each tier is then subject to a different level of licensing scrutiny. For example, regulators may decide to extend the breadth of licensing to both owners

---

[29] Nev., *supra* note 26, at § 16.430(1) (for public companies) and at § 15.430(1) (for private companies); N.J. STAT. ANN. § 5:12-85.1(g) (West 1977) (current as of Feb. 1, 2011)

[30] Nev., *supra* note 26, at § 16.430(1) (for public companies) and at § 15.430(1) (for private companies).

[31] *Id.* at § 16.430(1, 3) (for public companies) and at § 15.430(2) (for private companies); N.J. STAT. ANN. § 5:12-85.1(g) (West 1977) (current as of Feb. 1, 2011)

[32] Kahnawake, *supra* note 21, at §§ 24(b)(iv) (traditional gaming context), 30(d) (Internet gaming context).

[33] Ant. & Barb., *supra* note 8, at pt. II, §§ 10(b), 16, 17.

and gaming employees. The level of review, however, might be different. Owners may have to undergo a thorough investigation that requires the regulators to spend months reviewing all aspects of the owner's life, while the review of the gaming employees is merely a check of their police records. These checks take on several forms depending on the jurisdiction. In Malta, the licensing authorities review personal background information, financial information, participation in legal activities, criminal records, and even interests of the applicant to determine whether the owner can be licensed.[34] Key personnel face similarly stringent requirements and a check of their police records. In the United Kingdom, the licensing authorities analyze personal details, civil litigation history, prior gaming industry and general business history, competencies, references, and prior bankruptcies to determine the ability of key personnel to be licensed.[35] Similarly, Panamanian authorities consider criminal records, suitable references, and general national employment regulations to determine levels of review.[36] From an economic perspective, these tiers can be seen as different sized barriers; high scrutiny is a substantial barrier to entry and low scrutiny is a low barrier to entry.

The most expensive and intrusive investigation is a full licensing investigation. It is a comprehensive independent review of the applicant's financial history and personal background. Full investigations are expensive because the government investigators review primary source materials. For example, rather than relying on an acquittal as a determination of innocence, government investigators may reinvestigate the incident. They will seek to learn if other evidence, perhaps that was not admissible in the criminal proceeding, might suggest guilt. In a financial context, investigators may not rely on tax returns, but instead analyze cash-flow by reviewing actual deposits and withdrawals to figure out both net worth and source of funds. These investigations are expensive and time consuming.

Partial investigation involves reviewing only limited areas on each application. Instead of a field background investigation, the regulators may conduct only a computer review of federal, state, and local police data banks. If the review does not reveal any arrests, convictions, or investigations of the applicant, the regulators may issue a license. Partial investigations provide less protection to the government. A partial investigation usually consists of a criminal history check, reviewing responses from the applicant's references, and sometimes a personal interview.[37] Partial investigations have two disadvantages. They may not provide enough information or personal contact with the applicant to provide a basis for accurate prediction of future

---

[34] Malta, *supra* note 6, at § 5(2)(i-vi)

[35] Gt. Brit., *supra* note 23, at §§ 128 (personal licenses are reviewed under the provisions for operational licenses), 69-70.

[36] Pan., Resolution No. 065 Panama, Art. 11(d) (2002), *available at* http://www.mef.gob.pa/Documentos-JCJ/REGLA%20Ingles.pdf

[37] Deborah L. Rhode, *Moral Character as a Professional Credential*, 94 YALE L .J. 491, 512 (1985).

conduct. Moreover, a cursory investigation with insufficient information verification often yields questionable information.[38] Nevertheless, a partial investigation provides some benefits. Most notably, it may inhibit persons with extensive criminal histories from obtaining employment in the online gaming business. Additionally, regulators may obtain useful derogatory information about applicants from third parties that may lead to denial of the application despite the absence of a negative criminal record.

Limited licenses are commonly issued to gaming employees. In such a case, the extent of the partial investigation can be tiered, with key employees being subjected to higher review than lower-level employees. Similarly, the licenses issued can place very specific restrictions on the applicant's employment activities or employment category. For example, New Jersey issues different licenses to key gaming employees, regular gaming employees, and non-gaming employees.[39] To differentiate types of licenses, jurisdictions may use different terminology, such as a work "permit" or "card" for the licensing of gaming and non-gaming employees.

Nevada constructed a formal tiering structure for Internet gaming service providers by identifying three classes and conducting a different level of investigation for each class.[40] Class 1 service providers are those who (a) manage, administer, or control wagers that are initiated, received, or made on an interactive gaming system; (b) manage, administer, or control the games with which wagers that are initiated, received, or made on an interactive gaming system are associated; (c) maintain or operate the software or hardware of an interactive gaming system; (d) receive payments based on earnings or profits from a game, or (e) any other applicant for a service provider license who the regulators believe should have a Class 1 license.[41] Applicants for Class 1 licenses have to undergo the most stringent investigations. Class 2 services providers are any other service provider that the regulators deem as having a critical role with the gaming site's operation.[42] These service providers have to undergo a more cursory review. Any person who is a service provider other than a Class 1 or Class 2 is a Class 3 service provider.[43] A Class 3 license is a probationary license more akin to a registration, and is limited to those who act as a marketing affiliate for an operator of interactive gaming.[44] Here, a "marketing affiliate" is a type of interactive gaming service provider who shares customer databases with operators, or companies that intend to license their brands to operators.

To determine a level of review, placing service providers and employees

---

[38] *Id.*

[39] *See generally* Nicholas Casiello, Jr., *New Jersey, in* INTERNATIONAL CASINO LAW, SECOND EDITION (Cabot, *et al.*, eds., 2d ed., 1993).

[40] Nev., *supra* note 26, at § 5.240(3)

[41] *Id.* at §§ 5.240(2)(d), 5.240(3)(a), 5A.020(4)

[42] *Id.* at § 5.240(3)(b)

[43] *Id.* at § 5.240(3)(c)

[44] *Id.* at § 5.240(3)

in different tiers is of foremost importance. This requires consideration of three factors. First is the relationship between the group under consideration and public policy goals. For example, if the principal governmental policy is to assure the honesty of the game, the most obvious persons who need to obtain licenses are the game operators and the software suppliers or programmers. If governmental policy attempts to prevent gaming profits from going to criminals who may use them to fund criminal operations, then the licensing breadth must extend to persons sharing in profits from the games. Another example includes a government's goal to ensure that criminals have absolutely no involvement in the industry. This may mandate that suppliers of non-gaming goods and services undergo regulatory scrutiny.

Another consideration is capability and budget. Placing all groups into a mandatory licensing tier with full investigations will require a government to commit a substantial number of trained personnel to conduct the investigations or rely on third party investigations whose quality is difficult to maintain. Therefore, governments often place groups into tiers based on regulatory priority. Usually, the top priorities are owners and operators, followed by persons sharing in profits, distributors, manufacturers, and key employees. The government then assigns different levels of licensing scrutiny to each tier taking into account the budget and capacity of its investigative division.

A third consideration is the economic impact of requiring licenses for certain groups. As discussed earlier in this chapter, requiring licensure may discourage persons from applying because they are unwilling to devote the time, pay the cost, or suffer the embarrassment of the licensing process.

In sum, tiered licensing is a commonly used method for prioritizing regulatory investigation. The different tiers typically apply varying degrees of scrutiny determined by three factors: (1) the relationship between the applicant-group and public policy goals, (2) the investigative capability and budget of the regulatory body, and (3) the economic impact of licensing scrutiny.

Criteria

Gaming regulators can consider many different criteria in assessing an application for a gaming license. Criteria can be of a fixed or discretionary nature. Fixed criteria are quantifiable ones that an applicant either meets or does not. Fixed criteria can include whether person has not been convicted of a felony (South Dakota)[45] or ensuring that a person has not been convicted of any crime involving gambling, prostitution, or sale of alcohol to a minor (Mississippi).[46]

Discretionary criteria are minimum qualifications that are not subject to

---

[45] S.D. CODIFIED LAWS § 42-7B-33(3) (1989) (current as of 2012).
[46] MISS. CODE. ANN. § 75-76-67(3) (West 1990) (current as of 2011).

quantification, but are based on the discretion of the gaming regulators. For example Great Britain requires that the person is likely to act consistently with the licensing objectives.[47] The most common discretionary criteria involve good character, associations, management capabilities, and financial abilities.

Good Character

Statutes and regulations often require regulators to consider "good moral character" as a factor in screening applicants for professional and other vocational licenses involving a high degree of public trust. In Alderney, as an example, gaming commissioners will examine the applicant's character.[48] Besides privileged licenses such as gaming, it is often a criterion in considering whether to grant a professional license, such as accounting, law, or medicine. Despite its common use, the term has limited practical utility because it is difficult to define and apply. The major problem with using "good moral character" as a criterion is the inherent subjectivity involved when judging another's character.[49]

Deciding a person's qualification to hold a gaming license based on character functions as a total grant of discretion to the regulators. "Good" character, as opposed to "bad" character, lacks useful definition. What is good or bad is ultimately based on the individual perceptions of the person making the judgment. What is "good" or "bad" to a Baptist minister or a Bronx numbers operator will differ greatly. The former might find any applicant for a gaming license to be of "bad" character because of his choice of profession. In this context, the concepts of good and bad vary based on the political, social, religious, and psychological orientation of the regulator.

Judicial attempts to define the phrase and give concrete standards to the term "good character" are infrequent and unhelpful. One leading case that attempts to define the term is *Konigsberg v. State Bar of California*.[50] In that case, the State Bar denied an applicant admission because of "questionable moral character" based on the applicant having made certain political statements.[51] The Court, discussing the definition of "good moral character" stated that:

The term, by itself, is unusually ambiguous. It can be defined in an almost unlimited number of ways for any definition will necessarily reflect the attitudes, experiences, and prejudices of the definer. Such a vague qualification, which is easily adapted to fit personal views and predilections, can be a dangerous instrument for arbitrary and discriminatory denial. ...[52]

Other courts have struggled with the same ambiguities. The Arizona

---

[47] Gt. Brit., *supra* note 23 at § 70(2)(b).
[48] Alderney, *supra* note 9 at § 5(2)(a).
[49] Rhode, *supra* note 37 at 529.
[50] Konigsberg v. State Bar of Cal., 353 U.S. 252 (1957).
[51] *Id.* at 258-59.
[52] *Id.* at 262-63.

Supreme Court, ten years after *Konigsberg*, conceded that "the concept of good moral character escapes definition in the abstract," and held that each case must be judged on its own merits in an *ad hoc* determination.[53] Thus, the conclusion that the individual has good moral character and, therefore, is fit, is a subjective opinion only reached by comparing the individual to one's personal concept of what is moral or immoral.

Other courts' attempts to define "good moral character" usually resulted in defining the vague, highly subjective phrase with more vague and highly subjective phrases. For example, the North Carolina Supreme Court defined "good moral character" as:

[S]omething more than an absence of bad character. ... It means that he must have conducted himself as a man of upright character ordinarily would, should, or does. Such character expresses itself not in negatives, nor in following the line of least resistance, but quite often in the will to do the unpleasant thing if it is right, and the resolve not to do the pleasant thing if it is wrong.[54]

The Arizona Court adopted, as a means of determining bad moral character, a test that inquires "whether that behavior truly portrays an inherent and fixed quality of character of an unsavory, dishonest, debased, and corrupt nature."[55]

The overall standard in this area was stated by the United States Supreme Court.[56] In that case, an applicant for admission to the Bar was rejected for questionable moral character because of his membership in the Communist Party.[57] The Court reversed, stating that:

[A] state can require high standards of qualification, such as good moral character or proficiency in its law, before it admits an applicant to the Bar, but any qualification *must have a rational connection* with the applicant's fitness or capacity to practice law.[58]

The Court found that membership in the Communist Party alone was not rationally related to one's ability to practice law, and ordered the applicant to be admitted.[59] Applying this in a context other than the practice of law, any "good moral character" requirement would have to be rationally connected to the qualities and abilities needed to engage in that particular occupation.

A second approach that courts take in attempting to interpret "good character" is to engage in judicial interpretation of the licensing goals. For example, the United States Supreme Court, interpreting California decisions on bar admissions stated that the practical definition of "good moral character" tended to be stated in terms of an absence of proven acts

---

[53] Application of Klahr, 433 P.2d 977, 979 (Ariz. 1967).

[54] In re Farmer, 131 S.E. 661, 663 (N.C. 1926).

[55] *Klahr*, 433 P.2d at 979 (*citing* In re Monaghan, 126 Vt. 53, 60, 222 A.2d 665, 671 (Vt. 1966)).

[56] Schware v. Bd. of Bar Exam. of State of N.M., 353 U.S. 232 (1957).

[57] *Id.* at 238.

[58] *Id.* at 239 (emphasis added).

[59] *Id.* at 246-47.

that raise substantial doubts about the applicant's honesty, fairness, and respect for the rights of others and for the laws of the state and nation.[60] Here, the courts determine relevancy by deciding what are good attributes for licensing in the profession being considered, and holding that good character equates to those attributes. This definition has been adopted by several other states.[61] While this is a reasonable approach by courts that are faced with standard-less criteria, from a policy perspective, establishing more concrete criteria in the first instance is preferable.

Another problem with using "good character" as a criterion is attempting to define an individual as good or bad. The concept of character necessitates a review of all the person's traits. Character, by definition, is "the pattern of behavior or personality found in an individual."[62]

As one commentator noted:

One problem of sorting people into two categories -- those of good moral character and those who are not -- is that most people range across the dividing line. Many, if not most, people are usually of good moral character, but not always; are frequently honest, but once in a while untrustworthy; are often loyal, but sometimes unfaithful; will be generally competent, but occasionally careless; and so on. They range along a continuum, usually acting above minimum standards, but at times falling below.[63]

Defining "good" behavior based on a single event in a person's life may, or may not, be justified depending on the nature of the event. If the person sold confidential government information to enemies of this country, that lone event would probably meet most people's criteria of "bad" character. But, what about other single events? Take, for example, an applicant who had been arrested for a single instance of child abuse, agreed to counseling, and had the charges dismissed. A regulator who had been abused as a child might view this single instance as disqualifying while another might not.

Another problem with "good character" as a criterion is that regulators and investigators usually give little credence to "good" acts, but instead concentrate on trying to prove bad character. Thus, a person has "good moral character" if there are no demonstrable instances where the individual showed "bad moral character." A definitional difficulty arises because reasonable people can differ about what conduct would raise substantial doubts about one's moral character.[64] Defining a positive ("good moral character") through the absence of a negative ("bad moral character") is unhelpful unless there are standards provided to determine when the negative exists.

---

[60] *Konigsberg,* supra note 50, at 263.

[61] *See, e.g.,* In re Florida Bd. of Bar Examiners, 373 So. 2d 890 (Fla. 1979); Reese v. Bd. of Com'rs of Alabama State Bar, 379 So. 2d 564 (Ala. 1980); BLACK'S LAW DICTIONARY 693 (6th ed. 1990).

[62] WEBSTER'S NEW WORLD DICTIONARY 125 (Second Concise Edition (1976)).

[63] Banks McDowell, *The Usefulness of "Good Moral Character,"* 33 WASHBURN L .J 323, 323 (1992) .

[64] Rhode, *supra* note 37, at 530..

Generally, conduct evidencing "bad moral character" (in a Bar admissions context) is "[c]onduct evidencing dishonesty, disrespect for law, disregard for financial obligations, or psychological instability."[65] Conduct that is most damaging to one's character is conduct evidencing "moral turpitude," another standard open to varying interpretations.[66] Moral turpitude is an act or behavior which gravely violates moral sentiment or accepted moral standards of the community.[67] It is present in some criminal offenses, but not all.[68] Thus "moral turpitude" is similar in definition to "good moral character" and carries the same definitional inadequacies. According to one commentator, "[f]or purposes of Bar discipline, the 'moral turpitude' criteria does nothing to refine the inquiry, but merely removes it one step from its announced concern-- fitness for legal practice."[69]

While "good moral character" is a common criterion for licensure, it is an inherently vague bench-mark which, in reality, tends to function as a total grant of discretion to regulators. While courts have tried to narrow the definition of "good moral character," they have been largely unsuccessful. Furthermore, courts are not the ideal venue for establishing a more concrete definition because it is preferable to have a workable standard from the first instance.

Integrity, Honesty, and Truthfulness

Integrity, honesty, and truthfulness are three concepts that licensing statutes use as criteria to assess an applicant's suitability for a license. For example, in the Isle of Man, the commissioners will grant a license only if the company is under the control of person(s) of integrity.[70] Under Kahnawake law, besides character, the commission reviews the applicant's honesty and integrity by taking into consideration the following: personal, professional, and business associations, history of criminal convictions, history of civil litigation, credit history, bankruptcies, and personal and professional references.[71]

While related, these concepts of integrity, honesty, and truthfulness have different meanings. Truthfulness means simply to tell the truth. Truthfulness is only one component of honesty. One can be truthful, but dishonest. It is dishonest to use true facts and not disclose other facts in order to create a false impression.[72] For example, a person who was arrested by state police can truthfully state that he was never arrested by

---

[65] *Id.* at 532.
[66] *Id.* at 551.
[67] BLACK'S LAW DICTIONARY 1009 (6th ed. 1990).
[68] *Id.*
[69] Rhode, *supra* note 37, at 552.
[70] Isle of Man, *supra* note 19, at § 4(2)(a).
[71] Kahnawake, *supra* note 21, at § 24(a)
[72] Wiggins v. Texas, 778 S.W.2d 877, 889 (Tex. App. 1989).

city police. If, however, he responded to a question about his criminal record by stating he had never been arrested by the city police, it would be dishonest.

Similarly, honesty is only one component of integrity. "The word 'integrity'… means soundness of moral principal and character, as shown by one's dealing with others in the making and performance of contracts. . ."[73] A person can be honest, but lack integrity if, for example, he knowingly takes advantage of people in his business dealings.

Integrity is a complex concept that involves commitments to prioritized, personal moral principles. These principals can include honesty, family, friendship, religion, honor, country, or fairness. Persons prioritize these commitments such that it is acceptable to violate some commitments in order to honor others. For example, most people believe that it is acceptable to lie if necessary to protect another from harm or injustice.

Integrity means to upholding these commitments for the right reasons in the face of temptation or challenge.[74] For regulators to attempt to test a person's integrity, they would have to understand the person's personal priorities, and then decide whether the person is consistently true to these commitments and their priority. This is an impossible task in a neutral setting, but becomes even more problematic because the regulators' sense of personal priorities might be different from the applicant's.

Integrity might be inconsistent with regulatory policy due to the priority of the applicant's commitments. For example, suppose the applicant values personal friendship highly. Unfortunately, he has been friends since childhood with a person who is of a notorious reputation. The regulators demand that licensees not associate with such persons; however, the applicant's personal integrity places his personal commitment to friendship above the dictates of regulation. The applicant, to maintain his integrity, would continue to maintain his friendship. This may make him unsuitable to hold a gaming license. Therefore, regulators must be adept at defining which commitments are most important to good regulation and to testing the person's behavior against those commitments.

Commitments that are important to meeting regulatory objectives differ between regulatory goals. Fairness and respect are more important to protecting the player than the government. Both government and player protection goals place importance on honesty. Government protection goals place greater emphasis on complying with law.

As a licensing criterion, "honesty" is generally preferable to truthfulness or integrity. Regulators want applicants and licensees to not only tell the truth, but to convey accurate impressions by full disclosure. Therefore, "honesty" as a criterion is preferable to truthfulness. While conceptually

---

[73] In re Bauquier's Estate, 88 Cal. 302, 307, 26 P. 178 aff'd, 88 Cal. 302, 26 P. 532 (Cal. 1891).

[74] Lynne McFall, *Integrity*, Ethics 5, 9 (October 1987).

"integrity" appears preferable to "honesty," it suffers because of its difficulty in application. Attempting to decide a person's personal priorities and testing his behavior against those priorities is difficult, if not impossible.

With that being said, how useful is "honesty" as a criterion? Shakespeare wrote, in Hamlet, "Ay sir, to be honest, as this world goes, is to be one man picked out of ten thousand."[75] Thomas Fuller conveyed a similar thought when he wrote, "He that resolves to deal with none but honest men must leave off dealing."[76] The sentiments that both men convey is that no matter how committed to honesty a person may be, few, if any, people can claim to be completely honest in all their dealings.

When applying the "honesty" criterion, regulators must apply a materiality standard. An applicant is unlikely to be denied a license if he told his son that he could not take him fishing because he had to work, when, in fact, he was going to a football game. Two general rules emerge. First, that the honesty criterion generally is reviewed in a business, as opposed to a personal, context. This is justified because the purpose of licensing is to predict the behavior of the applicant as a gaming licensee. Therefore, his behavior in other business relationships is more germane to the inquiry than his personal relationships.

Second, honesty in business conduct becomes more relevant with the importance of the transaction. For example, it may be of minor materiality that an applicant, in order to cut short a telephone conversation, lied by telling the salesman that he recently bought the product being offered. The materiality increases dramatically if the applicant misrepresents the value of inventory to convince a lender to loan money to his business.

The criteria of integrity, honesty, and truthfulness all suffer from some degree of difficulty in application. Honesty, however, is an important policy goal in both the player and government protection contexts. Moreover, it is the easiest of the three for regulators to measure and judge in a meaningful way, provided the inquiry is limited to material, business-related behaviors.

Competency/Management Abilities

Operating a gaming site takes special knowledge and skills. Regulators may have concerns that otherwise honest persons might frustrate governmental goals if the operators lack the capacity to properly manage their gaming operations. For example, poor managers may not recognize when dishonest software programmers install gaff in computer programs to cheat players or steal from the site. This may frustrate a primary governmental goal by failing to ensure that games are honest. Similarly, professional cheaters and dishonest employees can more easily steal from gaming operations with poor management. This may frustrate

---

[75] WILLIAM SHAKESPEARE, HAMLET act 2, sc.2.
[76] THOMAS FULLER, GNOMOLOGIA 93 (1st ed. 1732), *available at* http://books.google. com/books?id=3y8JAAAAQAAJ&pg=PP1#v=onepage&q&f=false

governmental goals of collecting taxes on all revenues derived from gaming operations. Therefore, some jurisdictions, like Kahnawake, require applicants to have the appropriate services, skills, and technical knowledge to provide online services.[77]

Testing for adequate management skills varies depending on the complexity of the applicant's organization and the gaming operation. The former addresses the nature of the applicant. If it is a large diverse public company, regulators generally do not expect the chairperson of the board of directors to have operational experience. Instead, the emphasis is on the management structure established for the gaming operations. Regulators often require applicants to provide organizational charts designating the persons in each position, their responsibilities, and lines of authority. These are then tested against standards of depth, *i.e.*, is there enough management coverage? Are all key management areas covered? Are responsibilities properly segregated? Does the person have adequate knowledge and experience?

The second variable is the complexity of the gaming operation. If the gaming operation is small and has only on-line electronic gaming devices that are subcontracted to a licensed hosted service provider, the requisite level of management skill is minimal and can be acquired.

In addition to management competency, regulators should investigate and consider technical competence as Internet gambling presents new challenges. While traditional gaming has become more technologically complex, Internet gambling is unique in that governments are certifying information technology which creates an internet-enabled channel in a regulated and secure environment. A gaming commission may need a devoted software architect to decide if an operator is technically competent to manage and operate an Internet gaming site, if their architecture is sound, and whether their hardware and software are well written. Relying purely on post-licensing system certification may not be sufficient if the operator has purchased or licensed the software from a third party and has no practical or technological resources to operate the site. This could be equivalent to allowing a child to drive a Porsche without a driver's license.

Incompetence can be just as destructive to a jurisdiction's policy goals as malfeasance. For this reason, regulators should scrutinize managerial competency proportionate to the complexity of the organization and gaming operation. Additionally, regulators may benefit from a dedicated software architect who can test the technical competency of applicants and their systems.

Financial Abilities

A government may have varying degrees of concern with the financial ability of an applicant to succeed. In a monopoly- or small oligopoly-

---

[77] Kahnawake, *supra* note 21, at § 24(b)(iii).

economy, the government may have a strong interest in assuring that the prospective gaming operator is properly financed. For example, the Isle of Man requires the applicant to have adequate financial means available to conduct online gaming.[78] Similarly, Alderney's gaming commissioners review the applicant's current financial position and background. Malta is more focused on the applicant's ability to maintain the minimum required reserve.[79]

In a competitive economy, the government may have fewer concerns about a new gaming operation's economic viability because there are already adequate assurances in place to protect player's funds and/or government tax revenues. Market forces in a competitive economy often are the best judge of what is viable. If this is done by the government, the market may lose a potential competitor that could succeed by introducing innovations or creating new markets. However, there may be some legitimate concerns for regulators. For example, will the operator go to some unsuitable source to get money if times get tough or will it try to create profits by cheating players? These concerns can be addressed by careful monitoring of the operator and requiring submission of periodic reports.

A closure may not hurt a competitive economy. Instead, it often helps the economy. Suppose a market can only support five gaming sites when there are six. The most marginal site has some market share. If the sixth sites closes, this market share would go to the other five sites. With the sixth site open, the other five sites are less healthy because they earn less. They are also less attractive to lenders and investors. When the sixth site closes, the other sites quickly absorb their capacity and become healthier. Usually the site that fails is the one that is the least competitive because it is under financed, has an inferior product, or is overpriced.

Therefore, while the financial ability of an applicant is of some concern to regulators, it may not be necessary to make financial ability a licensing criterion. Market forces and regulatory oversight may provide sufficient protection without creating artificial barriers to entry.

Compliance With Law

An applicant's compliance with all laws applicable to its business is material to the granting of a gaming license. One function of the licensing process is to predict whether, if granted a license, the applicant will comply with all gaming laws and regulations. Strict compliance with these laws and regulations is essential to achieving the policy goals underlying them. Nothing is more predictive of future compliance with business laws and regulations than a review of past compliance in the same context. Indeed, Maltese regulators look to whether the applicant has been tainted by any illegal practices.[80]

---

[78] Isle of Man, *supra* note 19, at § 4(2)(d).
[79] Malta, *supra* note 6, at § 8(2)(d).
[80] *Id.* at § 8(2)(f).

Like application of the "honesty" criterion, some instances of noncompliance may be less material than others. Less material noncompliance might include matters that do not involve dishonesty, are civil violations, involve negligence, occurred may years ago, were isolated incidences, were corrected before criminal action occurred, were self reported, or were minor compared to size of business. More material incidents of noncompliance include matters involving dishonesty, criminal violation (particularly felonies), illegal gambling, intentional or reckless acts, recent acts, repetitive acts, and acts where the applicant denied or attempted to hide violations.

Jurisdictions like the United Sates that are late-comers in the Internet gaming industry will be faced with a difficult decision as to whether Internet operators that have directly or indirectly (through their licensee) accepted U.S. players are ineligible for a license. No precedent exists as to whether this is or is not a disqualifying factor to obtain a license. Some jurisdictions' laws and regulations do not have rigid criteria for determining suitability. For example, in some jurisdictions, a felony conviction or an offense involving gambling may be a disqualifying factor and pose an insurmountable hurdle for convicted applicants. Other jurisdictions follow more flexible standards. There, regulators will have to make a qualitative decision based on a totality of factors as to whether the person or company is suitable. Compliance with the law is an important aspect of that review. Compliance is much more than whether the company has violated or not violated the law, but whether it has institutional controls for assuring compliance with all laws. This is not only compliance with United States and state laws, but also with foreign laws. This ultimately might evolve into an inquiry about compliance with the laws of foreign countries, and specifically whether the company has made efforts to review and comply with the laws of all the jurisdictions where they accept wagers.

There has been much discussion about whether October 16, 2006, the date when the Unlawful Internet Gaming Enforcement Act ("UIGEA") went into effect, should be a determining date. The thought goes that after that date, site operators knew that accepting U.S. play was unlawful. The recent California legislation proposes a December 31, 2006, date, indicating that there should be some flexibility to extend past the October 16th date.[81] In reality, setting a specific date is too simplistic. For example, even if we assume that UIGEA was the first federal statute that clearly prohibited accepting U.S. play on poker or games of chance, the UIGEA date may be less relevant to those companies that accepted sports wagers. In 2001, Jay Cohen's conviction for accepting U.S. play on sports wagering was upheld.[82] A question arises, therefore, as to whether 2002 is a better date for those that accepted sports wagers. In addition,

---

[81] S.B. 1463, 2012 Reg. Sess. Art. 4, § 19990.23(f)(8) (Cal. 2012) *available at* http://www.leginfo.ca.gov/pub/11-12/bill/sen/sb_1451-1500/sb_1463_bill_20120224_introduced.pdf
[82] *See* United States v. Cohen, 260 F.3d 68, 78 (2d Cir. 2001).

these foreign operators may have additional issues with state laws such as Nevada Revised Statute 465.092 that prohibits a person who is not licensed in Nevada from accepting or receiving a wager over the Internet from a person located in Nevada. This law has been in place since 1997. Moreover, inquiry is not likely to be limited to gaming laws. Focus may shift to compliance with U.S. and state tax reporting and payment.

Prior material violation of laws is a useful licensing criterion because past compliance is a strong indicator of future compliance. Compliance with law inquiries typically include an applicant's compliance with the law of all jurisdiction in which it accepts wagers. An unsettled question in this area is how U.S. regulators should handle applications from Internet gaming operators who accepted wagers from U.S. players when doing so was a violation of U.S. law.

Manner Of Doing Business

Different people have different manners of doing business. While some are reconciliatory, and successfully resolve most disputes without the need for litigation, others are more adversarial and regularly litigate disputes. The adversarial type may create disputes to delay payment and seek favorable settlement by threatening or bringing a lawsuit. In dealing with regulators, the reconciliatory type is cooperative, and agrees on appropriate behavior. The adversarial type challenges the authority of the regulators and ties up regulatory resources in court challenges.

Reconciliatory types make better gaming licensees. They are more willing to conform their behavior to the expectations of the regulators. By not challenging the regulatory authority through litigation, regulatory costs are reduced. On the other hand, adversarial types may provide an important check on regulators. If no licensee challenges regulatory actions that exceed the regulator's authority or that are inconsistent with legislative policy, public policy goals might be frustrated without the knowledge of either the legislature or the chief executive. In addition, citizens in most societies have the right to seek judicial redress of grievances. Prejudicing an applicant for exercising legal rights would appear unjust.

In any circumstance, where an applicant abuses the legal system, regulators may justifiably consider this in assessing suitability for a license.

Criminal History and Prior Convictions

Several jurisdictions that regulate online gaming, including Malta, Kahnawake United Kingdom, and Panama, investigate the applicants' criminal history, background, or records.[83] Given that regulators must necessarily focus on past actions to determine moral character, especially past criminal actions, what type of history should disqualify someone

---

[83] Malta, *supra* note 6, at § 5(2); Kahnawake, *supra* note 21, at § 24(a) (investigating convictions only); Gt. Brit., *supra* note 23, at § 71; Pan., *supra* note 36, at Art. 11(d).

from obtaining a license? A jurisdiction may take two approaches. First, the jurisdiction may use a fixed criterion system which holds that anyone convicted of a felony, a crime involving gambling, or a crime involving "moral turpitude" is ineligible for a gaming license. A second approach would be to allow the introduction of a criminal conviction as evidence of the person's unsuitability, but still consider other evidence to decide overall suitability. Under this view, a criminal conviction creates a presumption of unsuitability and shifts the burden on the applicant to rebut that presumption by showing rehabilitation.[84] In the case of *In re Application of Cason*, the Georgia Supreme Court stated that this rebuttal must be by clear and convincing evidence.[85] The Court went on to state that for Bar fitness purposes, the applicant must reestablish his or her reputation by showing a return to a "useful and constructive place in society."[86] This cannot be evidenced by merely paying a fine or serving time, but must be evidenced by affirmative action, such as community service, occupation, or religion.[87] This "test" allows licensing committees considerable leeway in determining eligibility based upon their own subjective attitudes. Still, it does little to establish that a person who has committed crimes in the past will not commit them again in the future.

Under the discretionary approach, no definitive tests are available to decide whether a person with a history of criminal activities can earn a gaming license. In some instances, convicted criminals may receive gaming licenses. Similarly, the gaming authorities may deny licenses to persons never convicted of a crime, but who failed to show a lack of involvement in criminal activities. Gaming regulators may consider several facts in assessing whether to deny an application based on prior criminal activities. These include:

- The nature of the crime; criminal activities involving moral turpitude, such as thievery or embezzlement, are very significant;
- Mitigating or extenuating circumstances;
- Proximity in time of the criminal activity;
- Age at time of the criminal activity;
- A pattern or high frequency of criminal activity; and
- The applicant's honesty and forthrightness in revealing the past criminal activity to gaming investigators.

Some past crimes committed by an applicant may have no relation to their ability in some particular occupations. For example, a person convicted of child molestation 15 years ago is probably unfit to be licensed to operate a child care center, but it does not follow that the same person is

---

[84] Maureen M. Carr, *The Effect of Prior Criminal Conduct on the Admission to Practice Law: The Move to More Flexible Admission Standards*, 8 GEO. J. LEGAL ETHICS, 367, 383 (1995).
[85] *In re* Cason, 294 S.E.2d at 522.
[86] *Id.*
[87] *Id.*

not "morally" suitable to operate a gaming operation. There is no rational connection between the two, and the fact that the person was convicted of child molestation in the past provides a poor basis for predicting that the person is morally incapable of operating a fair gaming operation.

Predicting the morality of future behavior using an applicant's criminal history may be an imperfect assessment, but it is perhaps some of the strongest predictive evidence available to regulators. A fixed criteria approach is an easy standard to implement, but may not be a strong predictive tool, especially when the applicant's criminal history and license obligations do not correlate. A nuanced discretionary approach can address some of the shortcomings of the fixed criteria test by looking to the circumstances surrounding an applicant's criminal history and the applicant's subsequent conduct.

Associations With Unsuitable Persons

If gaming licensees have friends with notorious backgrounds, the public may believe that the unsuitable persons have an interest in, or influence over, the gaming operations. A person's willingness to associate with disreputable people may also call into question his own character.

The problem with the concept of association is definitional. One court noted "the word 'associate' is not of uniform meaning but is, rather, vague in its connotation."[88] For example, do incidental contacts with known criminals constitute association? What about involuntary contacts? What if the applicant had no knowledge of the other person's unsuitability?

Some courts define association as more than incidental contact with unsuitable persons. In interpreting a regulation prohibiting police officers from "associating" with criminals, one court held that the term means more than "incidental contacts" between police officers and known criminals.[89] The issue in another case was whether a parolee violated his parole by "associating" with undesirable persons.[90] There the court defined association as "to join often, in a close relationship as a partner, fellow worker, colleague, friend, companion, or ally."[91]

While difficult to define, the concept of unsuitable "associations," should focus on the following:

- Nature and intensity of the relationship. Facts considered include: (1) type of relationship; *i.e.*, business or friendship; (2) knowledge of the second person's unsuitability; (3) whether the relationship was voluntary; (4) frequency or involvement of the relationship; and (5) the applicant's attitude after becoming aware of the concern by gaming authorities with the relationship;

---

[88] Weir v. United States, 92 F.2d 634, 638 (7th Cir. 1937), *cert. denied*, 302 U.S. 761, 58 S. Ct. 368, 82 L. Ed. 590 (1937).

[89] Sponick v. City of Detroit Police Dept., 49 Mich. App. 162, 211 N.W.2d 674 (1973).

[90] State v. Morales, 137 Ariz. 67, 668 P.2d 910 (Ariz. Ct. App. 1983).

[91] *Id.* at 68.

- The influence or control over the applicant by the other person;
- The nature of the concern about the second person and how that concern poses a threat to the public interest; and
- The number of questionable relationships.

An inquiry based on these factors is more likely to avoid the injustices of a simple "guilt by association" approach while preserving regulators' ability to exclude persons who are truly unsuitable due to their associations.

Conduct During the Investigation

Statutes or regulations generally require applicants to make full and true disclosure of all information requested by the regulatory agents during the investigation.[92]

The applicant's conduct during the investigation may become relevant to his suitability for many reasons. If the applicant attempts to hide or mischaracterize a past transgression, the regulators may question the applicant's current credibility. If the applicant is not cooperative, the regulators may question whether the applicant will adopt such an attitude when it comes to compliance with the controls. If the applicant keeps disorganized and incomplete financial and personal records, the regulators may question the applicant's ability to account properly for taxes.

Standards of Proof

In licensing matters, the burden of proof is usually on the applicant. This is logical because the applicant has the most direct access to the information regulators may use to decide his suitability. If the applicant cannot produce this evidence, then it probably does not exist. Similarly, the burden of persuading the regulators of the applicant's suitability should be on the applicant.

A party that has the burden of proof must, at a minimum, present evidence to support the requested decision. For example, if an applicant has the burden of proving his suitability, then the applicant must provide at least enough evidence to allow the regulators to decide whether the applicant is suitable. In matters such as licensing, the burden of proof may also insinuate the burden to persuade the regulators of the applicant's suitability.

The agency decides factual matters by weighing the evidence and making a decision. But, not all decisions are made by stacking evidence on different sides of the scale and choosing the side with the most substantial evidence. Decision-makers have different ways to "weigh" evidence. Perhaps the most commonly recognized standards are "beyond a reasonable doubt," and "a preponderance of evidence." The former emanates from the standard used in criminal trials; the amount of evidence supporting a particular decision

---

[92] *See, e.g.*, Nev. Rev. Stat. §463.339.

should be sufficiently substantial so as to eliminate any reasonable doubt that a contrary conclusion could be reached.

The common standard for a civil trial is a preponderance of the evidence. This is the "scale of justice" test. It requires the decision-maker to look at the evidence and decide which of different conclusions is more likely to be true. Suppose, for example, a dispute arises over whether the player placed a wager on a roulette table before or after the dealer called for no further bets. The decision-maker may hear contradictory testimony from many persons, including the player and the dealer. The decision-maker must then decide which was more likely to have occurred. Having a conclusion, the decision-maker would then apply the relevant law.

Another standard is "clear and convincing evidence." This standard calls for the party with the burden of proof to provide "clear and convincing evidence" to support the requested decision. This standard is higher than a preponderance of the evidence, but less than beyond a reasonable doubt.

An even higher burden than "beyond a reasonable doubt" would be to prove a matter "beyond any doubt." If an applicant for a gaming license must prove his suitability "beyond any doubt," he has a substantial burden. If the investigation revealed any evidence that raised any doubt as to his suitability, then the agency should deny the application. For example, suppose the applicant was convicted of shoplifting while a college student, but had no other criminal transgressions. This instance alone might create doubt as to his suitability, but may not rise to the level of reasonable doubt.

The highest burden is when the applicant must prove no evidence exists that he is unsuitable to hold a license. This is an unrealistic standard because virtually every person has some incidences in the course of a lifetime that would provide negative evidence. In most cases, however, they are minor and should not disqualify the person from holding a license.

Given discretion to either grant or deny a license, regulators must assess the evidence in a given application against some standard. This can be pre-defined or left to the intuition of the regulators. For example, the regulators may be given a statutory directive to deny an application if the regulators have any reason to believe that the person does not qualify. This standard would result in fewer licenses being approved compared to a standard that would require the regulators to grant a license based on a preponderance of the evidence. For example, suppose a person was convicted twenty years ago of theft, and a licensing criterion is honesty. Obviously, theft involves dishonesty. Therefore, the theft is evidence of the person's lack of honesty. If regulators are compelled to deny a license when any evidence exists to suggest that the applicant does not qualify, the person would be denied a license. Suppose, further, that the person has led an exemplary life since that conviction for taking the cement sleeping bear mascot from a motel's lawn as a college prank. Under the preponderance standard, he would probably obtain a license.

Standards of proof can vary depending on the state's public policy. Under both the player and government protection goals, the government has a strong interest in assuring that unsuitable persons are not involved in the gaming industry. In these circumstances, the standard of proof should exceed that of a preponderance of the evidence. The level to which this standard rises depends on the intensity of government's policy. If the government insists on and enforces a "clear and convincing" standard, it will have a high efficiency rate, *i.e.* it will likely succeed in keeping out nearly all criminal elements. It also will create a moderate barrier to entry. As the government increases the level of the standard of proof, the less likely it is that criminal elements will infiltrate the gaming industry, but the barriers to entry will also increase.

2

Accounting, Audits, and Recordkeeping

Peter J. Kulick*

INTRODUCTION

Developing an effective Internet gaming regulatory regime should begin with an understanding of the underlying purposes for regulations and the Internet gaming business model. Several underlying reasons exist for the various regulations that govern the operation of the gaming industry. The regulation of the gaming industry in the United States historically targeted curtailing participation of organized crime in the gaming industry. Regulations initially developed to assure that unlicensed individuals did not share in the profits of a licensed gaming operation and that the government received the proper tax revenue.[1] Moreover, rules were implemented to protect players by ensuring that games were fair and not rigged to allow the owners to always win.[2]

As the gaming industry has evolved into a major economic force,[3] regulations relating to accounting, audit, and recordkeeping play an important role in maintaining the integrity of operations and ensuring a healthy, viable gaming industry. Accounting, audit, and recordkeeping rules are largely now contained in minimum internal control standards ("MICS").[4]

---

* Mr. Kulick acknowledges the generous contributions of his colleagues, preeminent gaming lawyers, Robert W. Stocker II and Michael D. Lipton, Q.C.

[1] See ANTHONY N. CABOT, CASINO GAMBLING: POLICY, ECONOMICS, AND REGULATION 395 (1996).

[2] See id.

[3] See AMERICAN GAMING ASSOCIATION, State of the State: The AGA Survey of Casino Entertainment (2011) for comprehensive information concerning the economic impact of the commercial gaming industry in the United States.

[4] See, e.g., NEV. REV. STAT. § 463.157; NEV. REG. 6.090; ALCOHOL AND GAMING COMMISSION OF ONTARIO, CANADA: DRAFT iGAMING REGISTRAR'S STANDARDS 8.1 (hereinafter "AGCO Standards"); BRITISH COLUMBIA, CANADA TGS5, TECHNICAL GAMING STANDARDS FOR INTERNET GAMING SYS. (IGS) (2009) (hereinafter "BC IGS Standards"); MALTA REMOTE GAMING REGULATIONS: Compliance Audit Questionnaire (2004).

Internal controls derive from accounting and audit concepts.[5] The particular internal control standards ("ICS"), which embody any required MICS of a regulating jurisdiction, define the procedures for operating a casino game. They include the procedures and methods for determining income/loss generated from gambling activity. In the brick-and-mortar casino industry,[6] ICS have a significant impact concerning how casino staff responsibilities are assigned, the recording of revenue, and how the games are conducted. ICS likewise provide procedures for assigning responsibilities, recording revenue and how games are offered within the Internet gaming industry.[7]

The lessons learned from the regulation of the brick-and-mortar casino industry can serve as a logical resource to develop best practices in the regulation of Internet gaming.[8] The rationale for examining the regulatory approach used in the brick-and-mortar industry is simple: both brick-and-mortar casinos and Internet gaming operators have a common attribute. That is, the ultimate activity that is subject to regulatory oversight is gambling. The prospective universe of gambling games offered online and on a casino floor is identical.[9]

While Internet gaming and land-based gaming share a common underlying activity, the practical means of conducting gaming and

---

[5] *See, e.g.,* Martin Lipton, et al., Audit Committee Guide & Best Practices, *ALI-ABA Course of Study Materials: Eleventh Annual Corporate Governance Institute,* 19 (2004).

[6] The terms "brick-and-mortar" and "land-based" are used interchangeably throughout this Chapter to refer to physical casinos that offer in-person gaming.

[7] *See, e.g.,* Alderney Gambling Control Commission, Technical Standards and Guidelines for Internal Control Sys. and Internet Gambling Sys. (2010) (*hereinafter* "Alderney ICS"). AGCO Standards, *supra* note 4, 3.38 (providing that software development roles must be segregated).

[8] *See* Ian Abovitz, *Why the United States Should Rethink its Legal Approach to Internet Gaming: A Comparative Analysis of Regulatory Models that have Been Successfully Implemented in Foreign Jurisdictions,* 22 Temp. Int'l & Comp. L.J. 437, 451 (2008). Abovitz suggests that "[a]n effective scheme for internet gambling should be similar to that of traditional gambling and should be based on a balance between government's right to tax and supervise and its duty to protect the industry's actors." *Id.* As explored in depth below, many of the principles of brick-and-mortar gaming regulation are adaptable to the regulation of Internet gaming. In some respect, developing Internet gaming regulations in major emerging jurisdictions -- notable the United States -- offers an opportunity to improve upon regulatory approaches advanced in other Internet gaming jurisdictions and regulatory practices which have traditionally been employed in the brick-and-mortar industry.

[9] For example, whether on a casino floor or through the virtues of the Internet, the universe of games which can be offered run the gambit of table games -- baccarat, blackjack, craps, poker, roulette and the numerous permeations of these table games -- and "slot-machines." In the modern gaming industry, the use of the "slot-machine" nomenclature is an archaism of the early gambling devices where gamblers deposited coins into devices which were operated by electro-magnetic spinning- reels with randomly produced characters. A modern slot-machine has evolved into a highly sophisticated computerized device, capable of offering extensive games and functions.

the business model differ. The economic model, cost structure, means of operating games and the roles of suppliers differ in the Internet gaming industry from that of the land-based gaming industry. Accordingly, effective Internet gaming laws and regulations must be sensitive to these differences and embrace regulatory approaches that adhere to the realities of the Internet gaming industry.

Developing best regulatory practices for accounting, audit, and recordkeeping requirements of regulated Internet gaming are influenced by several factors. At the macro-level, policy goals and the regulatory philosophies/attitudes can, and will, affect the scope of accounting, audit, and recordkeeping rules. To that end, this Chapter first explores the policy goals sought to be achieved by implementing accounting, audit, and recordkeeping rules for regulated Internet gaming.

Regulatory tools that have been used are introduced in summary fashion. Next, the Chapter embarks on a discussion of the theory and history of casino accounting, auditing, and recordkeeping requirements. The discussion is presented in the context of subscribing to the notion that an appreciation of the history and theories of casino accounting, audit and recordkeeping can assist in developing efficient and effective Internet gaming regulatory practices. This Chapter then presents a more detailed discussion of mechanisms used in the field of gaming accounting, audit, and recordkeeping regulations. Finally, we end our journey by enumerating aspirational best practices for the regulation of accounting, audit, and recordkeeping functions within the field of regulated Internet gaming.

The Internet Gaming Business Model; Identifying Policy Goals and Regulatory Tools Used to Implement Policy Goals

The regulation and operation of a regulated business conceptually is similar to a three-tiered pyramid. At the apex of the pyramid is the public policy developed by policymakers. Typically the policymakers are legislative bodies and the policies are adopted in the form of laws. In the middle tier lie implementing rules adopted by regulatory agencies. The regulations add flesh to the policies through interpretative guidance with respect to actions, which should, or should not, be undertaken by the regulated business in the conduct of its affairs.[10] Administrative agencies are charged

---

[10] An entire body of law has developed in the United States dedicated to administrative law. *See, e.g.*, Ronald M. Levin, *The Administrative Law Legacy of Kenneth Culp Davis*, 42 San Diego L. Rev. 315 (2005) (discussing the development of United States administrative law practice). Issues commonly encountered in the field of administrative law include the binding nature of a rule to the level of deference afforded the rules promulgated by the administrative agency. *See, e.g.*, Matthew C. Stephenson, *Mixed*

with the task of interpreting and enforcing the policies embraced in the laws and enforcing regulations promulgated under the governing law. At the base of the pyramid are actual operating systems adopted by the regulated business that are intended to comply with the legal requirements.

Besides the policy goals embraced in authorizing laws, understanding the business model is essential to develop efficient and effective regulations. A failure to appreciate the business model can inadvertently lead to the implementation of non-sensical or impractical rules. An extreme example is illustrative. One can envision the well-intentioned regulator advocating for a rule that requires an agency staff person to be physically present any time cash from poker rakes is physically counted by an Internet gaming operator. With an understanding of the business model, our well-intentioned regulator would quickly recognize that the Internet gaming operator collects its "cash" through electronic fund transfers.[11]

The discussion below first provides an overview of the typical Internet gaming business model. Second, policy goals applicable to accounting, audit, and recordkeeping requirements for the regulated Internet gaming industry are identified. Finally, a summary overview of regulatory mechanisms implemented to achieve the policy goals is set forth.

Overview of the Internet Gaming Business Model

A simple rule of thumb to understand any business operation is to "follow the money." To develop robust regulations, policymakers and regulators should first gain an understanding of the flow of money in the conduct of Internet gaming and the Internet gaming business model. While the business of Internet gaming shares a common activity with its brick-and-mortar brethren, it has a different business operational model. Capital needs, operating costs, the role of suppliers, and staff needs can all substantially differ from the brick-and-mortar gaming industry.

The flow of money in the operation of an Internet gaming operation differs from brick-and-mortar casinos. Typically, a player will use a credit or debit

Signals: Reconsidering the Political Economy of Judicial Deference to Administrative Agencies, 56 ADMIN. L. REV. 657, 658-660. Not infrequently, persons subject to regulations will challenge the validity of a rule, often asserting that the rule exceeds the authority granted to the administrative body under an enabling law. *See, e.g. id.* A comprehensive discussion of the basic tenets of administrative law is well-beyond the scope of this Chapter. Suffice to say, regulators must be cognizant of the legal limitations on the scope of rules adopted in the course of developing Internet gaming regulations. *See id.*

[11] At best, a regulation has been adopted that will never be used because an Internet gaming operator will not have a physical count. At worst, a regulation has been introduced that is difficult to interpret, potentially confusing and impractical. That is, would an agency interpret the rule to mean that an agency staff person must be physically present when an operator reviews computer data and reconciles bank statements? The example is extreme and likely not to occur in the real world. The example is intended to be shocking to illustrate the importance of understanding business models and how tasks are capable of being carried out in the real world.

Figure 1. i-Gaming Business Flow of Money

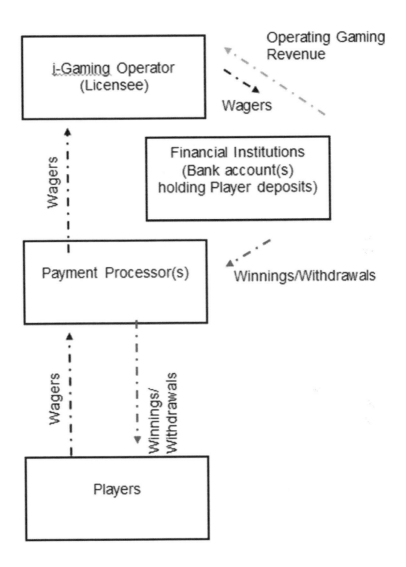

card to transfer money to an account held in the name of the Internet gaming operator.[12] The credit or debit card transfer will be effectuated by a money processor, which may or may not be directly affiliated with the Internet gaming operator. The funds will be held on account for the player with the Internet gaming operators. The funds held on deposit in a financial institution may be deposited in a segregated account or commingled with funds of other players or even other funds of the Internet gaming operators. Figure 1 graphically illustrates the flow of funds.

Like any other business, including land-based gaming operators, there is no one-size fits all organizational structure. The three categories of providers operating within the Internet gaming sphere are business-to-business ("B2B"); business-to-consumer ("B2C"); and business-to-government ("B2G"). Internet gaming operations normally encompass eight distinct spheres of activities. These activities consist of: (1) the game software; (2) the gaming license granted by a licensing jurisdiction; (3) payment processing; (4) liquidity management; (5) site hosting; (6) customer service; (7) marketing; and (8) back-end support. Figure 2 depicts the 8 spheres of Internet gaming business activities.

What can differ among Internet gaming businesses are which activities the operator will directly undertake and which functions will be provided by third-parties.

A business, which obtains an Internet gaming license, operates as a B2C business. The B2C interfaces directly with consumers/players. The licensee may enter into agreements with B2B providers to perform certain functions in the operation of an Internet gaming website. Two basic business models have developed in the Internet gaming industry for the operation of Internet gaming websites. The activities, which the licensee assumes, will depend upon the business model adopted. The business model, which an Internet gaming licensee adopts, will depend on a variety of business factors, such as in-house IT capabilities and payment processing expertise.

The first model used in the Internet gaming industry is known as the "white label" or "skin" model. In the skin model, the licensee is purely a B2C business. The Internet gaming licensee will obtain a gaming license from a jurisdiction and then enter into licensing arrangements with one or more B2B providers to supply game software, payment processing, website hosting, liquidity management, and other services. The game software provider will necessarily be required to obtain a gaming license as a software provider.

The second business model is a B2C model or a software license model. In a B2C model the Internet gaming licensee will hold a gaming license, as well as own underlying game software. The gaming licensee also may enter into agreements with B2B providers to perform certain other spheres of services. For example, in the software license model, the gaming licensee may engage third party affiliates to provide marketing services.

---

[12] Players may use other methods to fund a player account, such as sending in a live-check, use of electronic funds transfers, wire transfers, automated clearinghouse transfers, debit cards, or other means of electronic payments.

Figure 2. i-Gaming Business Model—Spheres of Activities

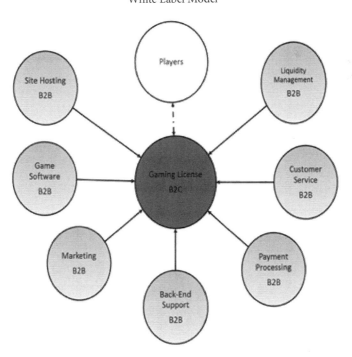

White Label Model

B2C/Software Model

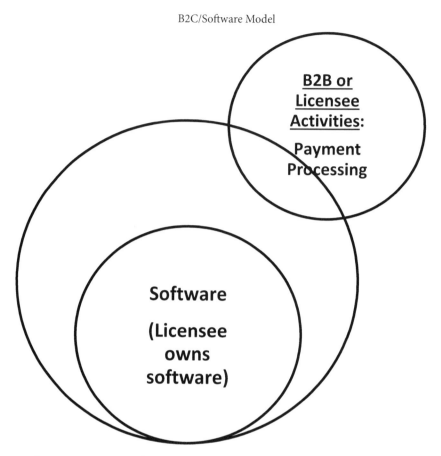

In summary, armed with an understanding of the Internet gaming business model, policymakers and regulators can develop a robust regulatory model, which can support the development of the Internet gaming industry without threatening economic viability.

Identifying Policy Goals for Internet Gaming Accounting, Audit, and Recordkeeping Requirements

Accounting, audit, and recordkeeping rules at their root have the policy prerogative of protecting the flow of funds. For government revenue purposes, however, they also ensure only licensed persons share in profits.[13] Well-designed regulations focus on the purpose for imposing financial-related regulatory burdens. Poorly designed regulatory practices ultimately end up requiring processes to be undertaken, or materials to be provided, which are at best tangentially related to the underlying policy and at worst trumpeting bureaucratic form over substance.

---

[13] *See* Cabot, *supra* note 1, at 395.

With a starting point that accounting, audit, and recordkeeping rules are intended to assure the legitimate flow of funds from gaming operations, other policy goals may also come to light.[14] To expound upon the ultimate goal of protecting the flow of funds, rules governing gaming accounting, audit, and recordkeeping can be classified into four categories: (1) ensuring the government receives the proper tax revenue; (2) preventing unlicensed persons from sharing in the profits of the gaming operations; (3) protecting against fraud; and (4) protecting the integrity of the games. Further examination of these four policy goals is appropriate to gain a better understanding of the underlying concerns.

Ensuring the government receives the proper tax revenue

Regulations governing accounting, audit, and recordkeeping, both for the Internet gaming and land-based gaming industry, at the core are directed at ensuring the government actually receives the appropriate tax revenue.[15] In the United States, tax laws are based on self-assessment—or voluntary compliance—whereby taxpayers determine their own tax liability and are responsible for timely paying the tax liability.[16] A hallmark of self-assessment systems is a requirement that taxpayers not only must file reports (the reporting obligation), but also maintain adequate records to substantiate the positions taken on such reports (the records obligation).[17] Thus, requiring gaming licensees to maintain records is not unique to gaming laws. Accordingly, promulgating gaming regulations that embrace a policy goal to ensure that the proper amount of tax is reported and paid has a longstanding tradition.

The unique aspect of the gaming industry compared to other business sectors is the nature of how revenue is generated. Gaming conducted in brick-and-mortar casinos occurs at a fast pace with several transactions

---

[14] *See* Cabot, *supra* note 1, at 395. Accounting and audit regulations have traditionally been directed at ensuring the government receives its proper share of tax revenue and prohibiting unlicensed individuals from sharing in profits.

[15] *See id. See also* Michael A. Santaniellio, *Casino Gambling: the Elements of Effective Control*, 6 SETON HALL LEGIS. J. 23, 25 (1982) (noting that "[t]he reported gross profit or loss of the casino, with its accompanying tax consequences, is dependent upon the continued integrity" of the control mechanisms to ensure that cash and casino chips reach the counting process.).

[16] *See, e.g.,* I.R.C. §§ 6001 and 6011. While the characterization of the United States tax system as voluntary may suggest that taxes are paid only out of altruistic motivation, the legal requirement imposed by United States tax laws is not at all altruistic. Rather, the qualitative "voluntary" aspect of the United States tax system means that taxpayers determine tax liability as opposed to the government computing tax liability.

[17] *See, e.g.,* I.R.C. § 6001; U.S. TREAS. REG. § 1.6001-1. United States Treasury Regulations generally obligate "any person required to file a return of information with respect to income, shall keep such permanent books of account or records, including inventories, as are sufficient to establish the amount of gross income, deduction, credits, or other matters required to be shown by such person in return of such tax or information." U.S. TREAS. REG. § 1.6001-1(a).

occurring either simultaneously or in rapid-fire succession. As a result, recording most individual gaming transactions is impractical.[18] To address the realities of gaming transactions in brick-and-mortar casinos, aggregate accounting methods and special rules have developed to ensure procedures are in place to properly record the results of each transaction, along with the corresponding revenue and tax liability.[19]

Like the regulation of brick-and-mortar gaming operations, Internet gaming laws share the common goal of ensuring the proper tax is paid by licensees. The means by which revenue is received from the conduct of Internet gaming differs from traditional brick-and-mortar operations. By virtue of having electronic transactions, Internet gaming affords the opportunity to depart from aggregate accounting. From a practical standpoint, this distinction will lead to very different regulatory content with respect to developing best practices to ensure that revenue is properly recorded in an effort to determine the proper tax liability.

PROTECTING AGAINST UNLICENSED INDIVIDUALS SHARING IN PROFITS

The protection of the public integrity of the gaming industry has long been an underlying public policy of the regulation of the industry.[20] Measures to prevent unsavory or unsuitable persons from having a direct or indirect involvement in the gaming business further the public integrity of the gaming industry.[21] Accounting, audit, and recordkeeping rules help fulfill this policy goal by offering the opportunity to trace revenue and the distribution of revenue to ensure that money is not being skimmed from gaming operations.

Protecting against fraud

The emergence of Internet commerce presents new threats for fraudulent activity.[22] Internet-based fraudulent activities range from

---

[18] *See* Santaniellio, *supra* note 15, at 25 (noting that "[t]he reported gross profit or loss of the casino, with its accompanying tax consequences, is dependent upon the continued integrity" of the control mechanisms to ensure that cash and casino chips reach the counting process.). In the context of the brick-and-mortar casino, numerous opportunities for inaccuracies—both intentional and unintentional—exist which can occur in the process of collecting and recording profits. *See id.* As an example, inadequate controls that allow a dealer to pocket chips can result in underreporting of revenue and the corresponding tax.

[19] *See id.* at 24. "Due to the impracticality of recording each gaming transaction, a [brick-and-mortar] casino must rely on aggregate amounts of cash, checks, and gaming chips to determine its gross profits or loss." *Id.* For further discussion of the control procedures used in brick-and-mortar casinos to ensure income and loss are properly reported, *see generally* Santaniellio, *supra* note 15.

[20] *See* Robert W. Stocker II & Peter J. Kulick, *Gambling with Bankruptcy: Navigating a Casino Through Chapter 11 Bankruptcy Proceedings*, 57 DRAKE L. REV. 361, 369 (2009).

[21] *Id.*

[22] *See generally* Edward M. Roche, *Internet and Computer Related Crime: Economic and Other Harms to Organizational Entities*, 76 MISS. L.J. 639 (2006) (discussing the costs of

money-laundering and terrorist financing activities, payment fraud, to identity theft.[23] Online fraud often centers on electronic identity theft and payment fraud.[24] The very nature of Internet gaming as an activity conducted through the Internet, which can involve significant and frequent monetary transactions, exposes the Internet gaming industry to threats of criminal activity through electronic means.[25] Accordingly, advancing the integrity of Internet gaming includes having protocols that assure the public that Internet gaming sites have safeguards to reasonably protect against unwittingly becoming mechanisms for online fraudulent activities.

Protecting the integrity of the games

The ICS developed to satisfy accounting, audit, and recordkeeping requirements can further be used to detect irregularities in the conduct of games. For example, surveillance controls can detect uncommon or unusual moves in the play of a game, which, in turn, may indicate that the integrity of the game has been compromised.[26] Therefore, accounting, audit, and recordkeeping requirements also can be used to further the policy goal of protecting the integrity of the online games. As an example, software may be used to detect unusual betting patterns or wagers.

Summary

Four basic policy goals have been identified above. Jurisdictions may have additional policy goals, which can be advanced through accounting, audit, and recordkeeping requirements.[27] A variety of factors, such as cul-

---

Internet crime).

[23] See Sonya Crites, *Best Practices in Addressing Online Cash Management Security,* 23 COM. LENDING REV. 21, 23-24 (2008). Crites notes that many organizations lack "appropriate controls needed to adequately protect a company's financial assets" from electronic fraud involving identity theft and payment fraud. *Id.*

[24] *Id.* at 23.

[25] Beyond offering gambling games through the internet, Internet gaming is intertwined with online banking and cash management systems. Wager amounts are transferred by payment processors to the operators and from the operators to players. Consequently, Internet gaming regulations will necessarily touch on practices designed to ensure the integrity of the payment processing systems.

[26] See Santaniello, *supra* note 15, at 34.

[27] As an example, a particular jurisdiction may decide to implement a stringent problem-gambling policy that allows for self-exclusion for a specified period of time. Consequently, to further the self-exclusion policy, a jurisdiction may require Internet gaming operators to maintain records that identify players who have opted to self-exclude. The scope of recordkeeping may further identify such information as the date of self-exclusion and the length of the self-exclusion period.

Legal requirements can operate to assist in achieving secondary policy goals. Theoretically, it could be argued that accounting, audit, and recordkeeping should be limited simply to protecting the flow of money. While a theoretically pure regulatory approach has many positives, adopting public policy is not always as simple as what common sense would

tural or political proclivities, can influence public policy.

The policy goals of a particular Internet gaming jurisdiction will impact the content of accounting, audit, and recordkeeping requirements. In the purest sense, the accounting, audit, and recordkeeping functions should be designed with the initial goal of protecting the legitimate flow of funds. Ultimately, the Internet gaming regulations must be reflective of the policy goals embraced in the enabling laws. A careful balance must be maintained with respect to the scope of the regulatory requirements. If Internet gaming regulations unduly burden operators with unnecessary requirements, or requirements that are impractical, the viability of the Internet gaming industry can be undermined.

Overview of Regulatory Tools to Achieve Accounting, Audit, and Recordkeeping Requirements

Regulations can serve as one of the means to effectuate general policy goals embodied in an enabling law. Regulations can interpret the laws and offer guidance with respect to fulfilling the statutory, or code based, requirements. The land-based gaming regulatory field has used several different regulatory tools to carry-out these financial policy goals. The regulatory tools that have historically been used to further accounting, audits, recordkeeping policy goals can be adapted for use in the regulation of Internet gaming.

Regulatory mechanisms, which can be implemented, to effectuate the oversight of Internet gaming accounting and audit controls include:

(1) *Active governmental participation in the accounting process;*[28]
(2) *Government conducted audits;*[29]
(3) *Independent audits;*[30]
(4) *Development of minimum internal control standards (or MICS);*[31]
(5) *Imposition of financial and operational recordkeeping requirements;*[32] and
(6) *Reporting requirements.*[33]

---

dictate. The point being, regulations governing accounting, audit, and recordkeeping can be adapted to assist with achieving secondary policy goals beyond protecting the legitimate flow of funds.

[28] *See* Cabot, *supra* note 1, at 396-97. Governmental involvement in the accounting process raises both an efficiency and practical question with respect to the appropriate level of governmental intrusiveness during the accounting process. For example, regulations could mandate the presence of onsite regulatory personnel to supervise accounting functions. The reliance on active governmental participation in the accounting process, consequently, can raise efficiency and economic feasibility concerns. *Id.*

[29] *Id.* at 396.

[30] *Id.*

[31] *Id.*

[32] *Id.* As discussed further below, recordkeeping requirements present the question concerning the appropriate scope of records an operator must maintain. Scope consists of the type, content, and period records must be maintained.

[33] *Id.* From a financial perspective, the primary reporting obligation is ordinarily a requirement to periodically file tax returns. Reporting requirements also can have

Ultimately, several factors will influence the particular tools implemented to further accounting, audit, and recordkeeping goals.

HISTORY AND THEORIES OF CASINO ACCOUNTING, AUDITING, AND RECORDKEEPING

Distinctive approaches to accounting, auditing, and recordkeeping requirements have developed in the land-based casino gaming industry. Procedures used in the land-based gaming industry can be beneficial for developing best practices in the regulation of Internet gaming. Understanding the theory for imposing regulatory requirements is beneficial in two respects. First, it reveals why certain requirements have been incorporated into rules. That is, what is the harm the rule seeks to protect against or what information is sought to achieve the policy goals. Second, understanding the theory allows for the development of rules that can be adopted for the unique business differences within the Internet gaming industry.

The notion of accounting invokes the method by which a business records its receipts and expenditures. Accounting methods answer questions such as what items are considered expenses and income, as well as the timing when expenses and income are recognized.

At the most fundamental level, an audit is a compliance check to assess the fairness of financial statements to ensure that financial results are accurately reflected in all material respects.[34] The meaning of an "audit" has expanded in the regulatory field to include so-called "certification" audits. A certification audit involves an auditor certifying that a business has complied with other requirements, including non-financial regulatory requirements.[35]

Recordkeeping involves the exercise of identifying the type and scope of information businesses maintain, the medium for maintaining the information, and the length of time that the information must be maintained (usually a minimum of 5-7 years).

Casino Accounting

Accounting is an exercise of recording transactions to determine financial results. The accounting process relies upon *control* mechanisms to ensure that transactions are properly recorded.

---

significant overlap with other regulatory requirements. For instance, Internet gaming regulations could impose reporting requirements to further anti-money laundering protections, suitability and licensing requirements, integrity/fairness of the games, player protections/problem gambling, and age and location verification.

[34] *See* David F. Birke, *Comment: The Toothless Watchdog: Corporate Fraud and the Independent Audit - How Can the Public's Confidence Be Restored?*, 58 U. MIAMI L. REV. 891, 896 (2003).

[35] *See* Amy Shapiro, *Who Pays the Auditor Calls the Tune?: Auditing Regulation and Clients' Incentives*, 35 SETON HALL L. REV. 1029, 1036 (2004).

A Background Primer on Casino Accounting

Standard accounting practice entails identifying revenue and expenses to arrive at the business' profit/loss.[36] Supporting data must be examined to determine the results of each transaction. For most businesses, accounting consists of a review of receipts and other records to trace the inflow of money (i.e., income) and the outflow of money (i.e., expenditures). The process of accounting requires use of internal controls to provide assurances that transactions are accurately and properly recorded.[37]

The method of accounting is an often overlooked, but critical aspect of accounting. In the United States, the non-accountant, and even perhaps the accountant, will defer to the use of "generally accepted accounting principles" ("GAAP") without a full appreciation of what GAAP really means.[38] GAAP may be an easily identifiable standard; however, it is also a complex system that allows for multiple approaches to account for transactions.[39] Accordingly, simply dictating the use of GAAP does not necessarily provide an assurance that the accounting records will provide the information regulators are seeking.

Standard accounting practices have not historically been used in the brick-and-mortar gaming industry.[40] "Casinos are unique because millions of dollars continually change hands among thousands of people on the casino floor without a complete transactional record being made of how much money is exchanged, how many people are involved, or who those individuals are."[41] To record every transaction would mean that the

---

[36] *See, e.g.,* Cabot, *supra* note 1, at 396.

[37] *See* Lipton, *supra* note 5, at 19. The use of internal control standards in the casino industry—often simply referred to using the acronym of ICS or MICS—has evolved into special meaning vis-à-vis regulatory-mandated operations within the gaming industry. The minimum internal control standards, or MICS, are regulatory standards that establish exactly what the name means—the minimum procedures which a licensee must employ for the ultimate purpose of recording each gaming transaction. The internal control standards, or ICS, are those control procedures actually adopted by a licensee to record gaming transactions. As discussed further below, MICS and ICS will provide more detail and cover significantly more subject matters than simply recording an individual gaming transaction.

MICS and ICS are analogous to a staircase. That is, the MICS and ICS require the licensee to undertake several steps in the process which will arrive at an accurate record of the gaming transaction. While ICS have derived special meaning within the gaming industry, the notion of internal control policies (alternatively referred to as internal control procedures) is a much broader accounting concept. Internal control policies set forth procedures businesses implement to ensure transactions are accurately reported. Businesses universally rely on internal control policies. In the public company context, internal control policies are an important element in the accounting and audit process, as well as assuring compliance with the Sarbanes Oxley Act of 2002, 15 USC 7201 et seq, ("SARBOX"). *See id.*

[38] *See* Shapiro, *supra* note 35, at 1051-52.

[39] *Id.*

[40] *See* Cabot, *supra* note 1, at 396.

[41] Santaniello, *supra* note 15, at 23.

gambling activity necessarily would come to a standstill.[42] As a result, standard accounting practices have proved to be impractical in the brick-and-mortar gaming industry.[43] Consequently, a unique system of accounting and internal control procedures is necessary for the land-based casino industry. This unique accounting method is known as aggregate accounting.

At a very basic level, the aggregate accounting method used in land-based casinos is simple to explain. Revenue results are measured over a specified period of time. Win or loss is measured by comparing the beginning chip inventory, the amount of cash or credit received and the remaining chip inventory at the end of the specified period.[44] The real difficulty lies with having proper, effective internal controls.[45] In a brick-and-mortar casino, chips must be delivered to tables ("fills"), money is constantly being deposited at tables and in electronic gaming devices ("drops"), and "drops" collected.[46] Lack of control procedures at each step of this process can cause inaccuracies.[47]

Use of Internal Controls

To ensure accurate accounting, businesses rely upon internal control policies.[48] Internal control policies are a fundamental aspect of financial accounting.[49] The policies and procedures within the purview of internal controls include policies that: (1) address the maintenance of records in reasonable detail to accurately reflect transactions and dispositions of company assets; (2) provide reasonable assurances that the transactions are recorded in a manner that allows financial statements to be prepared in accordance with the accounting system; (3) ensure that receipts and expenditures are made only in accordance with the authorization of management and directors; and (4) provide reasonable assurances to either prevent or allow for timely detection of unauthorized transactions involving company assets that could have a material effect on financial statements.[50]

---

[42] *Id.*

[43] *Id.* at 24.

[44] *Id.*

[45] *See* Richard A. Meyer, *Accounting for the Winnings - Auditing Gambling Casinos*, 12 Conn. L. Rev. 809, 811 (1979).

[46] *Id.* at 811-812.

[47] *See* Santaniello, *supra* note 15, at 23. The significance of using internal controls when aggregate accounting is used can be illustrated by a simple example. At the outset, aggregate accounting measures beginning and ending values over a period of time. If a dealer pockets chips during the measurement period, absent controls, aggregate accounting will not necessarily detect the theft. Therefore, the use of internal controls becomes important to prevent irregularities and ensure an accurate measure of income/loss.

[48] *See generally* Lipton, *supra* note 5, at 19. Internal control procedures are alternatively often referred to as internal control policies. *See id.*

[49] *Id.*

[50] *Id.*

Based on the nature of operations in a brick-and-mortar casino, "special procedures to ensure that [the casinos'] financial records properly reflect the actual results of gaming transaction" must be used.[51] Similar to any other business, the purpose of internal controls in the gaming industry is "to act as checks on the handling of financial operations."[52] The benefits derived from the use of ICS in land-based gaming have been described as "assist[ing] both the state and federal governments in their efforts to control gambling operations, protect the betting public, and collect taxes and fees from the casinos."[53]

The types of internal control procedures adopted in the gaming industry focus on documentation controls, physical/access controls, and personnel controls.[54] Casino internal control policies include provisions to provide for the "separation of functions, and extradepartmental [sic] reviews of transactions."[55]

Summary

Common considerations exist between Internet gaming and land-based gaming related to accounting procedures and the types of internal controls, which may be used. Operators in both the context of internet-based and in-person gambling share the common desire to ensure that the win/loss from the operation of a game is properly recorded. While the goal is similar, the nature of how games are conducted differs substantially. As a result, while traditional casino accounting and internal controls have some application in Internet gaming operations, the accounting and internal controls must be adapted to reflect the reality of how Internet gaming is conducted. The means by which Internet gaming is conducted affords an opportunity to receive more detailed records because each gaming transaction can be readily recorded during the course of play without bringing play to a standstill.

Casino Audits

Audits serve several important functions. Audits are beneficial for internal business purposes to serve as a check on the activities of the busi-

---

[51] Meyer, *supra* note 45, at 812.

[52] *Id.*

[53] *Id.* at 813.

[54] *See* Cabot, *supra* note 1, at 399-401.

[55] *Id.* at 812. In-person gaming occurring on the casino floor is a fast-paced environment, which can literally include dozens of separate gaming transactions in the course of each incidence of play. For example, depending on the number of seats at a blackjack table (typically 5 to 7 seats), a single game of blackjack could consist of over a dozen isolated wagers, not to mention players exchanging cash for chips or "coloring-up" chips to greater dollar denominations, all taking place within the course of a matter of minutes. As a result, the internal control procedures which developed in the land-based gaming environment have been designed to "guarantee that cash, checks, and gaming chips will be properly handled during the gaming day and that they will reach the counting process." Santaniello, *supra* note 15, at 25.

ness.[56] Financial markets also depend on audits to assess the worth and creditworthiness of companies. Audits further serve as a method of assuring regulatory compliance through certifications.

The United States Supreme Court has characterized the role of the auditor as that of the "public watchdog."[57] While the auditing vocation may not necessarily embrace the role of being the "public watchdog," the public relies on auditors to provide an independent assessment of the fairness of financial statements.[58] "Audits" have expanded beyond simply serving as a tool to assess the fairness of financial statements.[59] The concept of an audit is "now used in a variety of contexts to refer to new or more intense account-giving and verification requests."[60] This is especially the case for publicly traded companies, where audits are required to comply with SARBOX.

Without an appreciation of the reason for requiring audits and the role of the auditor, the potential value of an audit can quickly disappear. Regulations and the regulators enforcing the regulations should gain an appreciation of: (1) the role of the auditor; (2) the purpose of the audit; and (3) content that should be included in an audit.

The Role of an Auditor

The traditional role of the auditor is to serve as a detective for the owner of a company.[61] "The standard task of what is now called internal auditing is to inform owners of the activities of their agents and employees."[62] Over the past century, auditors have taken on a secondary role of certifying information for third-party disclosure.[63] In the certifying function, an auditor is a gatekeeper for the third-party user.[64] In connection with publicly traded companies, the role of the auditor has been effectively expanded by SARBOX.

Purpose of the Audit

The objective of an audit will depend on whether the auditor is acting in the role of a detective or certifier. In the "detective" function, the purpose of an audit of the financial statements of a business is to express an opinion with respect to the fairness of the presentation of financial statement in disclosing, in a material respect, the financial position and results of the

---

[56] See Birke, *supra* note 34, at 894-95.

[57] See *United States v. Arthur Young & Co.*, 465 U.S. 805, 818 (1984).

[58] See Birke, *supra* note 34, at 894-95.

[59] See Sasha Courville, et al, *Auditing in Regulatory Perspective*, 25 Law & Pol'y 179 (2003).

[60] *Id.*

[61] See Shapiro, *supra* note 35, at 1034 (2004). Shapiro provides a detailed overview of the traditional role of the auditor.

[62] *Id.*

[63] *Id.* at 1036.

[64] *Id.*

business.[65] In the certification function, an audit is examining whether financial records satisfy an accounting or other standard.[66] Thus, "the audit is seen as a particularly important tool of regulation, accountability, and governance."[67]

Audit Content

The content of the audit will turn on the purpose of the audit and the accounting system used by the business subject to the audit. At the base level, an audit will include notes explaining significant financial transactions and the accounting of those transactions. A certification audit, such as would be expected in the regulated gaming industry, may also include a summary of the licensee's ICS and a certification with respect to whether the ICS satisfy regulatory requirements.[68]

Audits within the Gaming Industry

For the gaming industry, the function of the auditor is typically twofold. First, the auditor—as with any other audit engagement—is responsible for expressing an opinion with regard to whether the income or loss of the gaming business is properly reported.[69] Second, state gaming laws typically impose additional certifications.[70] For instance, the gaming laws and regulations in several jurisdictions ordinarily require an auditor to provide an assessment of the internal control procedures of the casino licensee.[71]

---

[65] *Id.* at 896 (quoting AICPA PROFESSIONAL STANDARDS: Statements on Auditing Standards No. 1, AU § 110.01 (American Inst. of Certified Pub. Accountants 2001)).

[66] *Id.* at 1037. "Accounting standards are vital to certification auditing because the third party information user needs some way to evaluate the information received." *See id* at 1050. Too often, policymakers, attorneys and regulators will simply express the relevant accounting standard as ensuring that financial records are prepared in accordance with GAAP -- that is, "generally accepted accounting standards" -- published by the professional society of accountants. *Id.* at 1051 n.90 (citations omitted). The problem with GAAP is that it "is not only complex, but provides numerous ways to account for even common items such as inventory and depreciation as well as exotic ones such as derivatives." *Id.* at 1052. Accordingly, without understanding the accounting system, a certification audit may prove to be of little value.

[67] Courville, *supra* note 59, at 179.

[68] *See, e.g.*, MICH. COMP. LAWS ANN. § 432.214 (requiring quarterly audits of the financial conditions of casino licensees); MICH. ADMIN. CODE (2000) R 432.11201 to 432.11209; NEV. REV. STAT. § 463.157; *see also* Meyer, *supra* note 45, at 817.

[69] *See* Meyer, *supra* note 45, at 810 ("[audits] are essential parts of the proper reporting of income or loss by gambling casinos."). Beyond ensuring that income or loss is reported, the tasks of the auditor also include studying and evaluating the casino's ICS. The evaluation of ICS can be tied to the process of ensuring that the audit is performed in adherence with professional standards. In the United States, auditors typically conduct audits in accordance with Generally Accepted Auditing Standards ("GAAS").

[70] *See id.* at 817.

[71] *See, e.g.*, BC IGS Standards, *supra* note 4, 1.3.1, 2.26, 4.2.8, and 4.4.2; MICH. COMP. LAWS ANN. § 432.214 (requiring quarterly audits of the financial conditions of casino licensees); MICH. ADMIN. CODE (2000) R 432.11201 to 432.11209; NEV. REV. STAT. § 463.157; and

This requirement is also found in laws specifically applicable to Internet gaming.[72]

The function of the audit, therefore, plays an important role of not only ensuring that gaming revenue is properly recorded, but also for determining compliance with the underlying gaming laws and regulations. The internal controls operate as the backbone of gaming businesses by establishing procedures for, among other matters, recording gaming transactions, document control and access control. Casino accounting procedures and the audit requirements are intertwined within the regulatory body governing the financial aspects of casino operations.

Recordkeeping Requirements

Recordkeeping is simply the obligation of operators to document certain transactions, retain the documents and disclose information. Records are the evidence used to support the results of the transactions of the operator and demonstrate compliance with regulatory requirements. The prospective scope of records can be expansive, ranging from records relating to financial results to records, which demonstrate compliance with gaming laws and rules. In the regulation of Internet gaming, as discussed below, recordkeeping will cover the substance of matters such as recording of wagering transactions, player and location verification, and the conduct of games.

REGULATORY TOOLS

Government regulation of the gaming industry represents government intervention into an economic market. Government intervention can affect economic efficiency and lead to market failures.[73] The economic costs of compliance must carefully be considered when designing regulatory models. In particular, efforts should be undertaken to ensure that regulations do not adversely affect market efficiency. In addition, the cost-benefits of the regulations should be carefully measured.[74]

AGCO Standards, *supra* note 4, at 8.1; *see also* Meyer, *supra* note 45, at 817.

[72] *See* BC IGS Standards, *supra* note 4, at 4.1.1; MALTA REMOTE GAMING REGULATIONS: *Compliance Audit Questionnaire* (2004); AGCO Standards, *supra* note 4, at 8.2; and NEV. REG. § 6.090(9).

[73] *See* TEVFIK F. NAS, COST-BENEFIT ANALYSIS: THEORY AND APPLICATIONS 11 (1996). Economic efficiency is the goal for allocating goods in a market. *See, e.g.,* STEVEN E. RHOADS, THE ECONOMIST'S VIEW OF THE WORLD: GOVERNMENT, MARKETS, & PUBLIC POLICY 63 (1994). *Pareto* optimality dictates that markets reach a state of efficiency "where no one person can be made better off without simultaneously making at least one person worse off." Nas, *supra* note 73, at 11. Government intervention can threaten the ability of a market to achieve *Pareto* optimality and impose welfare costs (or dead-weight losses) on markets. *See* Rhoads, *supra* note 73, at 64.

[74] *See* AUSTRALIA PRODUCTIVITY COMMISSION: GAMBLING, REPORT NO. 50 (2010), at

Various mechanisms can be implemented to effectuate accounting and audit policy goals within the Internet gaming regulatory field. Accepted policy analysis principles allow for the assessment of the economic costs of regulatory requirements.[75] Cost-benefit analysis is particularly useful to ascertain the market costs of regulations and the impact on market efficiency.[76] Cost-benefit analysis involves identifying both the costs and benefits of a prospective regulation.[77] Quantifying the costs and benefits can often be a difficult and complicated task. Besides examining cost-benefits, feasibility of technological requirements of a regulation must be contemplated to avoid imposing standards, which are not technologically capable of being achieved.[78]

Accounting and audit regulations are ordinarily intricately intertwined with internal control procedures. Internal control procedures, whether cast in the form of required minimum internal control systems or merely the procedures adopted by Internet gaming operators, can serve as a practical regulatory model. In the land-based gaming industry, the use of required MICS has been adopted in many jurisdictions as an effective approach to identify accounting, audit, and recordkeeping procedures.[79] Similarly, MICS also have found use in the regulation of Internet gaming to identify required accounting, audit, and recordkeeping procedures.[80] The use of MICS, therefore, can serve as the main tenet of accounting, audit, and recordkeeping regulations.

Ultimately in designing an effective regulatory model, regulatory bodies should strive to keep policy goals front and center. Losing sight of the forest for the trees is far too easy. Therefore, by constantly asking whether a regulatory requirement furthers an underlying policy goal is a good practice when developing best regulatory practices.

17.24, Canberra, Australia (*hereinafter* "Australian Gambling Study").

[75] *Id.*

[76] *See* Nas, *supra* note 73, at 11.

[77] *Id.* The actual application of cost/benefit analysis is simple in theory. Consider the following illustration. Suppose that a regulation is implemented requiring the jurisdiction to implement online monitoring of all interactive games, with the costs of the system being directly passed to the regulated Internet gaming operators. If the costs to operators are $200 per year, while operations can only be expected to generate $100 per year, little incentive exists to actually engage in commercial activity. In the example, the costs of the regulation destroyed any potential economic benefit.

[78] *See* EUGENE MARTIN CHRISTIANSEN, CENTRAL SYSTEMS FOR MACHINE GAMING: A GOOD POLICY? (2003). The Christiansen Study outlines a classic example of regulatory requirements creating inefficient redundancies.

[79] *See, e.g.,* NEV. REV. STAT. § 463.157; MICH. ADMIN. CODE R. 432.1901 to 432.1907 (Michigan gaming rules regarding ICS); *see also* Meyer, *supra* note 45, at 815.

[80] *See, e.g.,* BC IGS Standards, *supra* note 4; MALTA REMOTE GAMING REGULATIONS: *Compliance Audit Questionnaire* (2004).

Examining Accounting and Audit Regulatory Tools: the Practicality of Direct Government Involvement, Government Audits, Independent Audits, and other Tools

As previously identified, gaming regulations have generally resorted to the use of six basic categories of requirements to effectuate accounting, audit, and recordkeeping requirements. These six tools—government participation, governmental audits, independent audits, mandatory minimum internal control procedures, recordkeeping, and reporting—in isolation can have individual merit. These regulatory tools also can have considerable overlap among one another. Thus, often a mix of the six regulatory categories proves to be an efficient and effective regulatory approach.

Government Participation

Government involvement in accounting and audit functions can take the form of direct governmental participation in gaming operations.[81] A method of government participation in the Internet gaming regulatory field could entail the use of central monitoring of the conduct of games and monetary transactions.

Louisiana experimented with direct participation by means of a central monitoring system for electronic gaming devices ("EGD").[82] The lessons of the Louisiana experiment have application to the regulation of Internet gaming. Specifically, the purpose of the Louisiana central monitoring system was to provide state gaming regulators with the ability to remotely monitor EGDs and related monetary transactions. Eugene Martin Christiansen conducted a study to assess the feasibility of the Louisiana experiment.[83]

Louisiana has authorized both commercial gaming and video lottery terminals ("VLT"). Commercial gaming is conducted at land-based and riverboat casinos. VLT machines were authorized to be located at establishments selling alcohol, truck stops, racetracks and off-track betting facilities. The Louisiana central monitoring system was intended to be a "State-operated central *monitoring and control* system providing regulators with control over individual slot-machines, including the ability to shut down malfunctioning machines, in addition to audit and financial monitoring for individual machines and for slot gaming as a whole in real time."[84]

The Christiansen Study concluded that the Louisiana's direct participation through use of a central monitoring system of EGD ultimately "is

---

[81] Cabot, *supra* note 1, at 396. Cabot explains government participation can involve direct supervision of the count process and transactions involving money, credit or cash equivalents. *See id.*

[82] *See* Christiansen, *supra* note 78, at 5-7.

[83] *Id.*

[84] *Id.* at 7.

a weak *monitoring* system … and essentially duplicates the financial audit controls provided to licensed operators by casino computer monitoring systems designed for this purpose."[85] Christiansen's study emphasizes several salient points: (1) operators and state regulators share a common interest in accurate machine reporting and the integrity of each gaming device; (2) technological challenges add costs and compromise the strength of a regulatory system; and (3) redundancy may produce no additional benefits.[86]

What does the Louisiana experiment mean for the development of Internet gaming regulatory practices? At the threshold, the Louisiana approach introduces a potential method for monitoring compliance with Internet gaming accounting, audit, and recordkeeping requirements. Specifically, the Louisiana system highlights a method for government regulators to directly monitor electronic games which could similarly be used in the regulation of Internet gaming. The Christiansen Study, however, calls into question whether any added benefits can be derived from direct government participation. The Christiansen Study found that any benefits were minimal and merely duplicative of existing accounting and audit reports produced by the EGDs for the licensees.[87] Moreover, the Louisiana central monitoring system was expensive to develop and maintain.[88] As a result, the Christensen Study reveals that the costs of government participation through monitoring games and monetary transactions are significant and outweigh the benefits. Essentially, the Louisiana system created an unnecessary redundancy when there was no evidence that current accounting and audit regulations were ineffective. Therefore, the Christiansen Study suggests that direct government participation through central monitoring is not only inefficient, but of little regulatory benefit.

Government Audits

The term "government audit" typically evokes the tax audit by government revenue officials designed to ensure the proper payment of taxes. Audits, however, can address a variety of subjects with respect to regulatory oversight, accountability, and corporate governance.[89] Accordingly, a threshold matter for a governmental audit requirement necessitates answering the question of what are regulators seeking to accomplish as a result of a government audit.[90]

---

[85] *Id.* (emphasis present).
[86] *Id.* at 5-8.
[87] *Id.*
[88] *Id.*
[89] *See* Courville, *supra* note 59, at 179.
[90] In the brick-and-mortar gaming industry, government audits have been justified as an enforcement mechanism to ensure compliance with required minimum internal control procedures, tracking the flow of money to ensure unlicensed individuals do not economically share in revenues, properly reporting revenue and paying all fees and taxes. Cabot, *supra* note 1, at 397-98.

As a compliance check and deterrent tool, government audits can be effective.[91] The *ability*—as opposed to a *mandate*—to conduct governmental audits may serve as a useful regulatory purpose.[92] To the extent that regulations require independent audits, requiring periodic government audits will likely be an unnecessary duplication of the independent audit.[93] Therefore, the flexibility to conduct discretionary and random audits can be a practical regulatory tool. Requiring the government to periodically audit all Internet gaming operators, however, may not add sufficient benefits compared to the resulting costs imposed on licensees.

Independent Audits

Independent audits are an efficient method to ensure compliance with accounting, audit, and recordkeeping requirements for Internet gaming businesses.[94]

ICS and MICS: Internal Controls Procedures and the Role of Mandatory Minimum Internal Controls

As discussed above, internal control procedures are not simply a creation of gaming regulations.[95] Internal control procedures are paramount for ensuring accurate accounting of the operations of any business. The internal controls identify the procedures to carry out transactions and record

---

[91] Cabot, *supra* note 1, at 398.

[92] *Id.* Certainly on the tax-side, the ability of the government to conduct audits is an important mechanism to ensure that revenue is being properly reported and the proper amount of tax is paid on the revenue. This is particularly the case for North American jurisdictions which depend upon voluntary compliance. The tax systems are voluntary in the sense that taxpayer compliance is voluntary.

[93] The independent audit is designed to be an independent, unbiased check of the fairness of financial statements and certification of compliance with regulatory requirements. *See* Mark Allan Warden, Note, *Securities Regulation: Private Auditor Independence for Non-Audit Services - An Evolving Standard*, 55 Okla. L. Rev. 513 (2002). In other words, an independent audit is not the situation where a gaming licensee presents its most optimistic and favorable explanation of the results of its operations. *See id.* That is, the independence of the audit is intended for third parties to be able to rely upon the fairness, in all material respects, of the matters subject to the audit. *See* Birke, *supra* note 34, at 896. Accordingly, requiring annual government audits would likely not add any greater value than an independent audit. In contrast, the ability to conduct discretionary and random audits to verify information or, to conduct further investigations if red flags are raised, can be a useful regulatory tool. *See* Cabot, *supra* note 1, at 397-98. Discretionary and random audits can serve as an incentive to ensure compliance. *See id.* That is, the threat of the government audit can serve to strike a sufficient amount of fear in the licensee to ensure the licensee will use best efforts to remain in material compliance with regulatory requirements. Similarly, the discretionary audit can be helpful for regulators to conduct further investigation when suspected problems, be it with respect to the integrity of games or financial viability, arise.

[94] For Internet gaming operators, which are part of a publicly-held company, independent audits will likely be required under SARBOX. Lipton, *supra* note 5, at 19.

[95] Albeit, the ICS receive considerable attention within the gaming industry with respect to daily operational procedures.

the results of the transactions.[96] Not only do "[internal control procedures] prevent improprieties and promote the integrity of the transactions and the records of results," they also provide detailed procedures for the conduct of Internet gaming operations.[97]

Jurisdictions have promulgated regulations that set forth required MICS.[98] MICS generally serve the purpose within gaming regulations to "safeguard casino assets, ensure the reliability of financial records, and guarantee that all transactions are authorized by casino management."[99] Internal control procedures within the gaming industry cover three categories, consisting of documentation controls, access/physical controls, and personnel controls.[100]

Documentation controls center on the types of records an Internet gaming operator must maintain in connection with preparing financial statements and demonstrating compliance with gaming laws and rules. Documentation controls within Internet gaming regulatory models often bridge not only technology related recordkeeping obligations, but also records that relate to player accounts. Internet gaming regulatory standards further typically include comprehensive documentation and recordkeeping requirements relating to the underlying gaming software.[101] The documentation requirements often consist of maintaining records that detail all technology related changes, and software and hardware updates.[102] Examples of player account document controls include requirements to maintain records relating to deposits to and withdrawals from player accounts, summary reports of player account balances, gaming play reports, and revenue reports of Internet gaming operators.[103]

Access/physical controls are procedures, which identify the personnel that may have access to company records and assets.[104] As an example,

---

[96] *See* Alderney ICS, *supra* note 7.

[97] Meyer, *supra* note 45, at 812; *see also* Alderney ICS, *supra* note 7.

[98] *See* Nev. Rev. Stat. § 463.157; *see also* Meyer, *supra* note 45, at 815-16.

[99] Meyer, *supra* note 45, at 815.

[100] *See* Cabot, *supra* note 1, at 399-401; Meyer, *supra* note 45, at 815.

[101] *See, e.g.,* AGCO Standards, *supra* note 4, at 3.55 to 3.59.

[102] *See, e.g.,* BC IGS Standards, *supra* note 4, at 2.3.1.

[103] *See* Nev. Gaming Control Board: *Minimum Internal Control Standards: Interactive Gaming* (2012) 130 to 143 (hereinafter "Nevada Interactive Gaming MICS"); AGCO Standards, *supra* note 4, at 2.10.

[104] *Id.* at 11 ("[r]emote access to the interactive gaming system components (production services, operating system, network infrastructure, application, database and other components) should be limited to authorized IT department personnel employed by the operator of the interactive gaming system."). Other Internet gaming regulatory models require the implementation of access controls. *See* Malta Remote Gaming Regulations: *Compliance Audit Questionnaire* (2004) 9.1 to 9.2. For example, the Ontario, Canada Draft iGaming Registrar's Standards impose access controls which limit access to player account and player information to operator personnel when such information is appropriate to carry out the personnel's job responsibilities. *See* AGCO Standards, *supra* note 4, at 7.4. Furthermore, access must be appropriately authorized by the operator. *See id.*

access controls may provide that only certain IT personnel can be allowed access to gaming software.[105] Similarly, many Internet gaming jurisdictions impose access controls that restrict access to player accounts and related player information.[106] Access controls also can be in the form of maintaining records, which identify each instance of access by operator personnel and establish security procedures for operator personnel to access software.[107]

Personnel controls are procedures, which establish an organizational structure for the approval of transactions.[108] Typically, personnel controls rely on the division of duties and responsibilities.[109] Personnel control also can include the use of checks and balances to ensure that no single department or person within the Internet gaming operator organization has unfettered control.[110]

The scope of required MICS for Internet gaming operators have ordinarily included a requirement for independent audits, preparation of detailed reports concerning player account deposits/withdrawals, and detailed reports concerning the conduct of games.[111] The content of accounting control systems typically includes both general accounting procedures, as well as establishing audit and recordkeeping procedures. The detail with respect to the types of controls and records that must be maintained that are set forth in Internet gaming regulatory models differs by jurisdiction. The following presents an overview of the content of accounting, audit, and recordkeeping rules adopted by different Internet gaming jurisdictions.

An Overview of Documentation, Access and Personnel Controls Used in Internet gaming MICS: Alderney ICS

The Alderney ICS present an overview of the general content of Internet gaming MICS. The Alderney ICS are illustrative of the fact that the same categories of controls -- documentation, access/physical, and personnel

---

In the context of land-based gaming, access/physical controls have included the use of physical safeguards such as surveillance cameras and restricting the personnel that have access to slot-machine drops or other gaming equipment. *See* Cabot, *supra* note 1, at 399. For further discussion of access/physical controls used in the land-based gaming industry, *see generally* Cabot, *supra* note 1, at 399-400.

[105] *See* Nevada Interactive Gaming MICS, *supra* note 103, at 11.

[106] *See* BC IGS Standards, *supra* note 4, at 3.1.7(a); AGCO Standards, *supra* note 4, at 7.4.

[107] *See* Nevada Interactive Gaming MICS, *supra* note 103, at 12.

[108] *See, e.g.*, Alderney ICS, *supra* note 7, at 4 (providing that a licensee's ICS should include administrative controls detailing organizational structure and decision-making processes).

[109] *See* Santaniello, *supra* note 15, at 32 (discussing division of responsibilities in the context of land-based gaming operations).

[110] *Id.*

[111] *See, e.g.*, Alderney ICS, *supra* note 7, at 24-30; AGCO Standards, *supra* note 4, at 2.1 (all financial transactions must be completely and accurately logged); MALTA REMOTE GAMING REGULATIONS: *Compliance Audit Questionnaire* (2004) 2.4 (operators must adequately record financial transactions); and Nevada Interactive Gaming MICS, *supra* note 103, at 144.

-- are adaptable for application in the regulation of Internet gaming. The Alderney ICS accounting control procedures require licensees to identify:

- Internal accounting controls that consist of identifying procedures for documenting transactions, maintaining accounting records, providing controls over the safeguarding of physical and financial assets, controlling the expenditures of funds, and reconciling customer accounts and profits and losses;
- List of all accounts used in the operation of the licensee's operations;
- Internal reporting procedures;
- External reporting procedures include the submission of various reports to gaming regulators, such as monthly reports concerning operations and quarterly financial reports;
- Reports evidencing that licensees meet prescribed capital ratios;
- Procedures for the preparation and approval of annual budgets and forecasts;
- Identification of the licensee's external auditor and timing for preparation of external audit;
- Description of accounting software used by the licensee, including such information as procedures for backing-up accounting software data and the secure storage of accounting data;
- Access controls for the computerized accounting systems;
- Record retention policy;
- Bank accounting information; and
- Information pertaining to how customer funds are held, such as identifying whether customer funds are held in segregated or comingled accounts.

Similarly, the Nevada Interactive Gaming MICS require operators to have independent audits,[112] reconcile certain payment reports,[113] and periodically prepare and review various gaming related data.[114]

Audit Requirements: Use of Certification Audits

Similar to land-based gaming, Internet gaming regulatory models have embraced mandating the use of independent audits. The Ontario, Canada Draft iGaming Registrar's Standards require the engagement of a reputable independent auditor.[115] Under the standards, the auditor is required to perform a compliance audit to verify operators have appropriate system and manual controls that comply with the underlying regulations.[116]

The Nevada Interactive Gaming regulations adopt a comparable approach. Nevada requires an independent auditor be engaged to prepare a

---

[112] Nevada Interactive Gaming MICS, *supra* note 103, at 144.
[113] *Id.* at 145, 147, 148, 151, and 154.
[114] *Id.* at 146.
[115] See AGCO Standards, *supra* note 4, at 8.1.
[116] See *id.* See also NEV. REG. 6.090.

written report of the licensee's compliance with the MICS.[117]

Regulatory models also have adopted standards, which afford wide discretion to regulators with respect to audit subjects. As an example, the British Columbia, Canada standards authorize regulators to request audits of specific areas of operation to ensure compliance with Internet gaming regulations.[118] The discretionary standard can be useful to assess the health of a licensee when other red flags may arise. Nonetheless, policymakers and regulators must proceed with caution when embedding discretionary standards within a regulatory model. The reason being is that discretionary standards can cause uncertainty with respect to what actions licensees must undertake to satisfy regulatory requirements and unnecessarily increase compliance costs.

When audits discover deficiencies with regard to compliance with ICS, most regulatory regimes obligate licensees address the deficiencies.[119] The Nevada Interactive Gaming regulations, for instance, require the licensee to submit a statement with the independent auditor's report addressing each instance of noncompliance.[120] Imposing a timeframe for disclosing an independent report, as well as the response to compliance deficiencies is beneficial to afford early detection of operators potentially experiencing greater difficulties. Thus, Nevada requires that a licensee's statement addressing items' noncompliance must be submitted within 150 days following the end of the licensee's fiscal year.[121]

Self-Assessment of ICS

Consistent with the approach of requiring audit certifications of compliance with MICS, gaming regulatory models often impose an obligation on licensees to assess the effectiveness of MICS.[122] Self-assessment can be a useful tool for operators to measure operations and identify weaknesses in operational aspects, such as online security protocols, as well as business practices.

The Ontario, Canada Draft iGaming Registrar's Standards address the timing of when self-assessment should occur. The standards provide that testing the effectiveness of MICS is not simply a snapshot on a periodic annual date.[123] Rather, ensuring effectiveness of internal controls is an

---

[117] NEV. REG. 6.090.

[118] See BC IGS Standards, *supra* note 4, at 1.3.1, 2.2.6, 4.2.8, and 4.4.2; AGCO Standards, *supra* note 4, at 8.1.

[119] See AGCO Standards, *supra* note 4, at 8.2; NEV. REG. 6.090(9).

[120] See NEV. REG. 6.090(9).

[121] Id.

[122] See BC IGS Standards, *supra* note 4, at 4.1.1; MALTA REMOTE GAMING REGULATIONS: *Compliance Audit Questionnaire* (2004) Rule 20; NEV. REG. 6.090(9); and AGCO Standards, *supra* note 4, at 8.2.

[123] See AGCO Standards, *supra* note 4, at 8.2.

on-going regulatory requirement.[124] Hence, the Ontario, Canada standards provide that the frequency of measuring effectiveness is based on the risk exposure of the operator.

Recordkeeping: Player Account Records

Internet gaming regulatory systems typically require operators maintain accurate records of all financial transactions.[125] A general obligation to maintain accurate records of financial transactions would likely equate to the maintenance of records relating to player accounts, including account deposits, credits and withdrawals.

The Nevada Interactive Gaming regulations specifically enumerate detailed content, which operators must maintain with respect to player accounts. This information includes records of account deposits and withdrawals, the amount of money wagered during each table session, money won during each table session, promotional or bonus credits wagered during each table session, manual adjustments to the player account, and any other information required by regulators.[126]

Recordkeeping: System Reports

The very nature of the data driven aspects of an Internet business activity allows for flexibility in the development of the content to be included in operational reports of licensees. The Nevada Interactive Gaming regulations identify a comprehensive list of system reports that licensees are obligated to disclose to regulators.[127] The scope of reports includes logs of user access, identifying closed or inactive player accounts, daily players' funds transactions, monthly revenue reports, system configuration settings, and game session reports.[128] British Columbia, Canada and Ontario, Canada Internet gaming standards have embraced a more flexible approach by requiring that operating systems have the capability to provide custom and on-demand reports to regulators.[129] Finally, regulatory models also typically include comprehensive guidance with respect to the methods, which must be used to maintain records.[130]

---

[124] *Id.*
[125] *See* BC IGS Standards, *supra* note 4, at 3.1.10; AGCO Standards, *supra* note 4, at 2.10; and MALTA REMOTE GAMING REGULATIONS: *Compliance Audit Questionnaire* (2004) 2.4.
[126] NEV. REG. 14.
[127] *Id.*
[128] *Id.*
[129] *See* BC IGS Standards, *supra* note 4, at 4.3; AGCO Standards, *supra* note 4, at 7.11.
[130] *See* BG IGS Standards, *supra* note 4, at 4.3; MALTA REMOTE GAMING REGULATIONS: *Compliance Audit Questionnaire* (2004), Rule 20 and Audit Questionnaire 1.1; and AGCO Standards, *supra* note 4, at 8.5. The regulations typically obligate licensees to maintain records in an organized and systematic fashion.

Summary

In summary, the tenet of internal control principles developed for the brick-and-mortar gaming industry can be adapted to the regulation of Internet gaming. Documentation controls have application in the field of Internet gaming regulation similar to the brick-and-mortar industry. Documentation controls can be specifically customized with regard to the maintenance of records concerning software and gaming activity.[131] Access/physical controls will also have application in the regulation of Internet gaming operators by, for example, establishing procedures with respect to the access to player account information and access to software by the IT personnel of the software licensee or operator.[132] Finally, personnel controls also can play an important role with regard to identifying organizational structures and describing decision-making processes.

DEVELOPING BEST PRACTICES FOR INTERNET GAMING ACCOUNTING, AUDIT, AND RECORDKEEPING REGULATIONS

Several guiding principles from mature Internet gaming jurisdictions and from brick-and-mortar gaming regulations can be elicited with respect to developing best practices for Internet gaming accounting, audit, and recordkeeping regulations. Lessons learned from Internet gaming jurisdictions across the globe, such as Alderney, Canada, Malta, Nevada and the United Kingdom, can serve as a good resource for the development of best practices. Internet gaming accounting, audit, and recordkeeping regulatory requirements are not necessarily an opportunity to recreate the regulatory wheel, but rather offer an opportunity to improve upon existing regulatory practices to develop a robust Internet gaming regulatory model.

To develop effective and efficient regulations, regulators must first understand the business model of Internet gaming. This means that Internet gaming regulators should understand both the business organizational models, such as the skin or B2C model, and the flow of money in the operation of an Internet gaming site. As the background section illustrates, the business model for Internet gaming differs from traditional land-based gaming and introduces the potential for new types of suppliers. Understanding the Internet gaming business model and the flow of funds can permit the development of robust Internet gaming regulations, which are carefully balanced to not pervasively impinge upon the efficient operation of economic markets.

An initial guiding principle for the development of robust Internet gaming regulatory practices centers on a full comprehension of the policy

---

[131] *See* AGCO Standards, *supra* note 4, at 7.4 (Internet gaming operating systems must be capable of providing unfettered custom and on-demand reports).
[132] Access controls also can be imposed which obligate licensees to develop personnel user access protocols. *See* Nevada Interactive Gaming MICS, *supra* note 103, at 12.

goals of a particular jurisdiction. Comprehending the policy goals allows for the implementation of regulations, which seek to further the governing policy goals.

The basic rational for imposing accounting, audit, and recordkeeping regulations is to protect the legitimate flow of funds. Specifically, ensuring that (1) the government receives the lawfully correct tax revenue, (2) non-licensed persons do not impermissibly share in profits of Internet gaming operations, and (3) player funds deposited with Internet gaming operators are adequately protected.

In the process of promulgating rules, administrative agencies must consider the costs of compliance. Imposing regulatory burdens that are too costly to meet will effectively cause market failures. To that end, cost-benefit analysis should be employed to assess the costs and benefits of regulations.

The following are suggested guiding principles for developing best practices for Internet gaming accounting, audit, and recordkeeping regulations:

(1) Understand the business model of an Internet gaming operator and the flow of funds.

(2) Requesting information on the corporate structure can be a good regulatory practice.[133] Disclosure of the corporate structure not only reveals which individuals are potential qualifiers that are subject to a finding of suitability, but also can reveal relationships with vendors, what functions the Internet gaming licensee will undertake, how decisions are made, and the individuals responsible for making decisions. A review of corporate structure also can disclose that proper control procedures are in place to ensure that all transactions are properly approved and recorded. In other words, regulators can quickly gain confidence in the ICS adopted by the Internet gaming operators.

(3) Understand the accounting system used by the Internet gaming operator. The accounting system will reveal how items are recorded as revenue, when expenses are recognized and other important financial information. For example, if regulations require GAAP, regulators should know precisely what the implications of GAAP accounting means for the presentation of financial statements and the certifications, which may be provided by independent auditors.

(4) Use independent audits. Independent audits are a cost-effective and efficient means for not only obtaining an independent, unbiased opinion of the financial results of the Internet gaming operator, but also certifications

---

[133] The collapse of Full Tilt Poker is illustrative of the benefits of timely information. The independent report prepared by Peter Dean (the "Dean Report"), the former chairman of the British Gambling Commission, at the behest of the Alderney Gaming Control Commission offers some insight with respect to the impact of regulatory reporting. The Dean Report is available online at http://www.gamblingcontrol.org/userfiles/file/FTP%20Report%2026%20March%202012.pdf.

with respect to regulatory compliance. The independent audit is more efficient and less costly to the markets, as compared to requiring annual governmental audits. Allowing for discretionary and random audits can, however, serve as a useful incentive to encourage Internet gaming licensees to use best efforts to materially comply with the Internet gaming laws and regulations.

(5) Identify the purpose(s) for independent audits. The purpose of the independent audit will guide the scope of the audit and what auditors should certify.

(6) Internet gaming licensees are in a unique position to electronically record transactions and present detailed reports with respect to player accounts, the results of games, and the ability to reconcile accounts. Regulations should require licensees to maintain such records. Regulatory models have adopted different levels of detail with respect to the type of reports, which must be maintained. Nevada has comprehensively enumerated numerous reports that operators are obligated to maintain. In contrast, British Columbia, Canada has embraced an approach giving regulators greater flexibility to seek custom reports. The flexible approach must be used with caution because too much flexibility can result in uncertainty with respect to what is required of licensees, with the requirements susceptible to frequent changes. Nevertheless, some flexibility can be beneficial to the extent that the flexibility allows regulators to adapt regulatory requirements to the realities of actual operations. Furthermore, best practices would also dictate that licensees should strive to maintain all records in an organized and systematic fashion.

(7) Developing MICS is a good idea—within reason. The Alderney MICS and Nevada Interactive Gaming MICS are examples of minimum required internal control procedures. A balance must be maintained to allow flexibility to Internet gaming operators regarding the internal control processes and procedures that are implemented.

An inherent criticism of the gaming regulatory MICS leveled by auditors has been a failure to identify the overall objective of the MICS.[134] "Routine adherence to mechanical procedures without considering the overall objectives of a casino audit may prevent an auditor from detecting a well-designed fraud."[135] Hence, in designing MICS, a fundamental question must be raised with respect to the objectives and goals the MICS are intended to achieve. Are the MICS intended to ensure the integrity of the Internet gaming games, insure appropriate player and site identification, help identify and prevent problem gambling behaviors, incorporate anti-money laundering protections, or to ensure revenue is properly recorded or all of the above?

The Alderney ICS, British Columbia, Canada IGS Standards, Nevada Interactive Gaming MICS and Ontario, Canada Standards all provide models for the development of best practices for Internet gaming account-

---

[134] *See* Meyer, *supra* note 45, at 816.
[135] *Id.*

ing, audit, and recordkeeping regulations. The Alderney ICS offer a coherent statement of objectives.[136] The Alderney ICS identify four objectives for internal controls: administrative control with respect to the organizational structure and decision-making process of the licensee; accounting controls to ensure transactions are executed in accordance with management authorization and transactions are properly recorded to prepare financial statements; controls are in place over the operation of customer accounts and the calculation of gaming activities; and safeguards in place in relation to physical and electronic security of the licensee's systems.

Finally, a few regulatory approaches are not best practices. Most notably, as the Christiansen Study illustrates, direct government participation in monitoring activities will likely cost far in excess of any benefits received. Moreover, the accounting and audit information that can be obtained through a central monitoring system duplicates the information that the Internet gaming operators can already obtain.

---

[136] *See* Alderney ICS, *supra* note 7, at 4-5.

3

Taxation of Regulated Internet Gambling

Sanford I. Millar*

Introduction

This Article surveys global licensing and taxation models applied to Internet gambling. Part II provides a categorical overview of Internet gambling licensing and taxation models, and summarize each model's apparent advantages and disadvantages. Part III surveys a broad sample of regulated online gambling licensing models, describing how particular models are implemented within each jurisdiction, and then comment on the strengths and shortcomings of each approach. Part IV then provides an overview of the current regulatory environment and emerging trends in the United States among jurisdictions considering legalization of Internet gambling. Part V concludes with recommendations, as well as a summary of the survey from Part III.

Internet Gambling Licensing and Taxation Models

Internet gambling licensing and models generally can be described within the following categories: (1) monopoly models, such as lotteries operated by state, provincial, or national governments; (2) free market models, which have licensing fees with nominal up-front or ongoing costs and where there is no pre-set limit on the number of licenses that can be issued; (3) limited free market models where the total number of licenses granted is determined in advance by legislation or regulation; (4) hybrid models involving combinations of the above, usually with splits among game types and/or local jurisdiction. Within these licensing models are taxation models. The taxation models are in the form of an ongoing licensing fee, which can be based upon (a) Gross Gaming Revenue ("GGR"); or (b) Gross deposits or "Net" deposits, or turnover, each of which are discussed below.

Monopoly Models

Monopoly models exist where state, regional (or provincial) or national governments operate online interactive gambling sites either directly or through a government sponsored entity ("GSE"). While a few exceptions exist, monopoly model jurisdictions generally prohibit competitive sites, including offshore gambling[1] sites.[2] Monopoly models are used to regulate a wide variety of Internet gambling activities, from lotteries and fixed-odds games,[3] to pari-mutuel betting[4] and bookmaking,[5] as well as peer-to-peer ("P2P") and other traditional casino games.[6]

The primary regulatory advantage of a monopoly model is the amount of control it places in the hands of the relevant governing body. The governing body in these jurisdictions is either an operator itself (directly or through a government agency or GSE), or the governing body licenses a single operator. Because the governing jurisdiction is the sole licensed operator, it faces little or no lawful competition. It may face competition, however, from unlicensed sites and from sites operating under an extraterritorial license.

As in any jurisdiction outlawing online gambling in general, monopoly models may encourage unlicensed competition, both from domestic and extraterritorial sites. That is, customers may seek gaming services from unlicensed operators either from within the jurisdiction or—perhaps more likely—from offshore operators located in jurisdictions that do not prohibit such operators from providing services extraterritorially, or even *only* grant extraterritorial licenses.[7] Similarly, the revenue that might be enjoyed

---

[1] "Offshore gambling" as used throughout this chapter is gaming activity by a customer geographically located within a particular jurisdiction through an operator based outside of that jurisdiction.

[2] For example, the Austrian government enforces its monopoly over games of chance with respect to offshore operators, but does not criminalize offshore gambling by Austrian residents. *See* Federal Ministry of Finance, Regulation of Games of Chance, http://english.bmf.gv.at/Tax/RegulationofGamesofChance/_start.htm (last visited Mar. 5, 2012).

[3] *See id.* (describing Österreichische Lotterien's license for offering electronic lotteries via the Internet).

[4] For example, the Hong Kong Jockey Club is the only entity licensed to offer online betting services to Hong Kong residents. United States General Accounting Office, Internet Gambling: An Overview of the Issues (Dec. 2002), http://www.gao.gov/new.items/d0389.pdf.

[5] *See, e.g.,* GamingZion, Turkey, http://gamingzion.com/turkey (last visited Mar. 5, 2012) (describing the Turkish government's ownership of the only legal Internet gambling operator there, IDDAA, which provides sports betting only).

[6] The Netherlands is proposing to offer online bingo, poker, casino games, and sports betting through a government-owned operator. *Dutch Government Paves the Way for Legalized Online Gambling*, Casino People, May 21, 2011, http://www.casinopeople.com/news/dutch-government-paves-the-way-for-legalized-online-gambling.html.

[7] For example, Alderney, Malta, and Kahnawake grant extraterritorial licenses permitting operators to solicit customers from only outside of their jurisdictions, and such licensees generally are not licensed in each jurisdiction in which such operators accept customers. *See infra* Part III.

from multiple operators competing to attract customers could also be sacrificed. Monopoly model revenue could be further constrained if the monopoly has a limited product offering. Thus, under a monopoly regulatory model, a certain amount of operator revenue may be lost to competitive operators who have extraterritorial licenses. Furthermore, the regulatory control which is absolute as applied to the licensed operator does not offer consumer protection from competitive offshore operators.

Free Market Models

Jurisdictions intending to attract the maximum number of Internet gambling site operators (including those that offer extraterritorial licenses only) typically adopt free market regulatory models focused on the provision of licenses for fees. The specific structure of such licensing differs by jurisdiction, but most involve an application fee, initial license fee, subsequent renewal fees and on-going taxation, all of which might differ within the jurisdiction depending on the type and size of the operation. In free market jurisdictions, the number of licenses granted are unlimited and the types of games permitted are not constrained.

As the practical antithesis to a monopoly model, the free market models benefit from the number of operators they license, and how attractive the jurisdiction is to operators. In the competitive global marketplace of Internet gambling, operators may move to jurisdictions with favorable regulatory and taxation environments. The attraction to the jurisdiction of licensing more Internet gambling businesses is the revenue generated both directly from licensing, and indirectly through ancillary businesses based in the jurisdiction (such as financial institutions, technology providers, and hosting services). The lower the license fees and the operating costs to the site operator, the more operators are attracted to the jurisdiction.

Finally, perhaps the greatest advantage from a regulatory perspective is that regulators can structure the licenses so that they receive flat fees up front (for each period of licensure). For example, the licensing body might require an advance deposit that it would credit against license fees in the ensuing years of operation. This is a "use it or lose it" approach, designed to minimize the revenue risk to the licensing body.[8]

Limited Free Market Models

Limited free market models attempt to address some of the disadvantages of the unlimited free market models by capping the number of licenses granted, offering a few licenses with higher probity standards or more stringent license applications, imposing stricter regulatory control

---

[8] *See, e.g.,* The Internet Gambling Consumer Protection and Public-Private Partnership Act of 2012, S.B. 1463, 2011-2012 Sess. (Cal. 2012) (proposing such a deposit in the amount of $30 million).

over licensees, or by implementing any combination of these restrictions and limiting the services to within the jurisdiction.

Operating in a limited free market jurisdiction, however, can still be affected by competition from offshore operators who have extraterritorial licenses. Until the issuance of extraterritorial licenses is approached on a cooperative international basis, the recourse of each jurisdiction can be problematic.

Licensing Fee Models Based Upon Gross Gaming Revenue Tax

Under a Gross Gaming Revenue ("GGR") tax model, operators pay a percentage of their revenues, calculated on the basis of the amount wagered by all of their customers minus the winnings returned to the players. This is often subject to additional deductions for certain expenses such as software licensing and development costs, chargebacks on credit cards, and other overhead, but deductions can be capped at a certain percentage of GGR.[9] As illustrated in Parts III and IV, the GGR tax model is a method often used by some jurisdictions that license Internet gambling and also may be hosts for land-based casinos. GGR tax rates on Internet gambling generally range from 2-5 percent in the Caribbean to 15-30 percent in the European Union.[10] They are typically consistent across various types of gaming within a jurisdiction, but sometimes vary, with different games sometimes being subject to differing license fees.[11]

The most commonly cited advantage of a GGR model (as opposed to a turnover, deposit model or net deposit model) is that operators enjoy lower business risk as they are only taxed on their gaming profits, not on player bets or deposits. Jurisdictions often use the GGR model for Internet Gambling when the jurisdiction is already taxing land-based casinos using the GGR model.

While a GGR tax lowers the business risk operators face in Internet gambling in comparison to a deposit model, the primary disadvantage of a GGR model, however, is that taxes are collected in arrears—at the end of the year or customer life cycle—so regulators do not receive tax revenue in as timely or predictable a fashion. Furthermore, the interim period between an Internet gaming operator's initial gaming revenue (amount wagered) and payout of winnings is potentially indefinite because customers establish revolving accounts with these operators. This becomes an issue of special significance where operators are free to offer promotional credits, a common practice in the Internet gambling industry.

Therefore the GGR amount has to be calculated periodically, rendering the taxes more complex and somewhat variable even between periods of

---

[9] In Antigua and Barbuda, for example, deductions for software licensing and development are capped at 40 percent of net win (GGR). SloGold, Antigua and Barbuda Gambling License, http://www.slogold.net/antigua_gambling_license_get_gambling_licence_on_antigua.html (last visited Mar. 5, 2012).

[10] *See infra* Part III.

[11] *See infra* Part III.

similar gaming activity. The alternative—waiting for a customer to close out his or her account before calculating GGR—would mean that taxes are never collected when accounts are left open, even while operators enjoy the benefits of the intervening float (for example, the ability to invest the money deposited in player accounts). Finally, the higher complexity of a GGR model in the context of Internet gaming—especially across multiple jurisdictions—increases transactional costs in general, and adds the risks of arrears tax collection (for example, operator insolvency) to the governing body's risk burden.

Licensing Fee Models with Deposit or a Turnover Tax

The chief alternative to a licensing model with GGR taxation is to base a tax on the funds the player deposits with an operator. Licensed operators must pay a tax calculated by applying a stipulated percentage to the amounts deposited by players. The rate used under such a model is usually much lower than the GGR rate in a particular market—from less than 1 percent in free-market-oriented jurisdictions such as Malta and Belize to 5 to 7.5 percent in other European nations.[12]

A deposit tax model is more efficient to apply to online gambling than a GGR for the reasons outlined herein—the primary distinction being that it is collected in advance as opposed to collection "in arrears," which reduces the revenue risk to the licensing jurisdictions. Furthermore, the deposit tax is game neutral, unlike the calculation of tax on GGR for an operator offering a variety of game types, thus simplifying the tax calculation, and remission processed, particularly in cases where the deposit tax is implemented across multiple jurisdictions. Finally, a deposit tax provides a mechanism for strengthening enforcement of gambling laws against unlicensed operators, whereby players might themselves incur liability for the deposit tax (plus penalties) if playing with unlicensed or otherwise "illegal" operators.

Some critics of the deposit tax model claim that such a regime deters the establishment of regulated gambling.[13] These claims are overly simplistic, however, as an operator's preference among jurisdictions is a function of the tax models, rates, and methods of collection—where the overall tax liability (primarily determined by rate) is the predominant factor. A deposit tax is more straightforward to calculate and enforce, reducing transactional costs and uncertainty in general. And the increased operator-side business risks involved with a deposit tax (mainly that funds might be

---

[12] *Infra* Part III(E).

[13] *See, e.g.*, Remote Gambling Association, Turnover Tax Proposals Will Prevent the Successful Development of an Online Gambling Industry in Spain (Jan. 12, 2011), http://www.rga.eu/data/files/Pressrelease/final_spain_con_pr_jan_2011final. pdf (urging the Spanish government to adopt a tax regime based on gross profits); KPMG, Taxation of Online Gambling: The Case for a Tax Regime Based on Gross Profits (2010) (on file with author) (arguing for the continued use of a GGR model in the United Kingdom, rather than reverting to the previously used turnover model).

deposited without being used for gaming, while still being taxed) can be mitigated by allowing operators to charge fees for early withdrawals, or by granting operators tax credits for customer account withdrawals.

Thus, the primary disadvantage of levying a deposit tax is that most established operators are accustomed to paying a GGR tax, which they perceive as less risky to themselves than being taxed on total gaming volume. Also, while unlikely in the real world, competitors or other malicious persons could "deposit" funds in an account and immediately withdraw the funds without activity, with the goal of causing economic injury to the operator. Even if operators could impose fees on customers for early customer account liquidation, that possibility alone may have the effect of deterring potential legitimate customers from using those operators' sites.

Operators and their associations lobby heavily to implement GGR tax models in countries proposing new online gambling legislation or already levying a turnover tax.[14] But as discussed, a licensed operator could receive a full credit on the deposit tax for those funds withdrawn from player accounts at the end of each payment period. Such a method might thus be more accurately described as a "net deposit tax" model, and would mitigate the business risks and potential risks of unused or malicious deposits.

Hybrid Models

A few economically large jurisdictions such as Australia, Italy, and Spain use hybrids of the models described above.[15] Typically such hybrids involve structuring the licensure and taxation schemes by game type, where certain games may be permitted under a monopoly model, others taxed on a GGR basis, others on deposit basis, and still others on a low-cost, license-only free market model. Different types of games flourish or suffer under different models. The primary advantage of creating a mixed approach to the regulation and taxation of online gambling is that it allows the regulator to mitigate these problems. For example, when the United Kingdom shifted from a turnover tax to a GGR tax to slow the movement of bookmakers to offshore locations, which was threatening gambling duty revenue as a whole, but the imposition of a gross profits tax caused reduced revenue in bingo and pools gambling.[16]

Thus, a jurisdiction can use carefully crafted hybrid models to maximize tax revenue according to the market dynamics of individual games, types of operators, or locality. It can then maximize the advantages of each model incorporated into the hybrid. Of course, the higher transactional cost involved with a more complex hybrid model is the most obvious

---

[14] *See id.* In countries already using a GGR model, such lobbying tends to emphasize maintaining the existing model while, of course, lowering the tax rate.

[15] *See infra* Part III.

[16] HM Customs and Excise, Gambling Duties: Report by the Comptroller and Auditor General 2 (Jan. 14, 2005), *available at* http://www.nao.org.uk/publications/0405/gambling_duties.aspx.

disadvantage. Furthermore, another detriment of adopting a highly complex hybrid model (especially one that may not adapt to changing market conditions flexibly enough) is that the jurisdiction's gaming industry as a whole may end up either more overburdened or under-taxed, cutting into overall potential license revenue.

Finally, the risks and disadvantages of each model also are potentially present in any hybrid system incorporating such a model. For example, a hybrid model incorporating a GGR tax will still require the regulator to collect at least some taxes in arrears, doing little to mitigate the problems outlined above in Section D. Ultimately, a model's structure should be crafted to balance these factors as the various market forces in a particular jurisdiction require.

APPLICATION OF REGULATORY AND TAXATION MODELS BY JURISDICTION

This Part of the Article provides a survey of certain jurisdictions' regulation and taxation of legalized Internet gambling, organized using the categorical approach described above. Monopoly models are used in Austria, Canada, Hong Kong, Hungary, Macau, the Netherlands, New Zealand, Sweden, and Turkey. Free market jurisdictions include Alderney, Costa Rica, the Isle of Man, Kahnawà:ke, and Panama. Belgium provides an illustration of a limited free market model jurisdiction with an emphasis on very limited licensure opportunities.

The surveyed jurisdictions using a GGR model include Antigua and Barbuda, Curaçao, the Dominican Republic, Estonia, Greece, the Philippines, and the United Kingdom. Belize, Cyprus, France, Malta, and Poland use turnover tax models. Finally, Australia (including Tasmania), Denmark, Gibraltar, Italy, Spain and Vanuatu round out the sampling as hybrid model jurisdictions.

Monopoly Models

Austria

Regulated online gambling in Austria comprises all games of chance, including via telecommunications services such as the Internet and telephone.17 The Ministry of Finance operates a state monopoly, Österreichische Lotterien, which is the only major licensed provider of online gaming services within Austrian territory, and is not permitted to provide extraterritorial services.[18]

---

[17] Federal Ministry of Finance, Regulation of Games of Chance, http://english.bmf.gv.at/Tax/RegulationofGamesofChance/_start.htm (last visited Mar. 6, 2012).

[18] Viaden Gaming, Austria Online Gambling License, http://www.viaden.com/products/austria_license.html (last visited Mar. 6, 2012).

A few exceptions from the state monopoly exist for low stakes betting and games of skill, but operators falling into the exceptions are regulated by the Federal States of Austria and their regional laws and can only accept Austrian players.[19] Interestingly, the supply of online gaming services by offshore operators is prohibited (as subject to the state monopoly). Offshore operators can not advertise or operate within Austria, but Austrian citizens are not subject to penalty for gambling on foreign sites and the government does not block or otherwise blacklist foreign online gambling sites.[20]

Canada

A few provinces in Canada have set up state-run online gambling sites, with others considering following suit. The British Columbia Lottery Corporation ("BCLC") is the sole licensee in British Columbia to offer lotteries and other fixed odds games, casino gaming, and sports betting online.[21] For the fiscal year 2010-11, BCLC distributed C$1.104 billion to the provincial government.[22] Quebec provides similar offerings through Loto-Québec Corporation, generating C$3.675 billion in gross revenue, of which C$1.247 billion was paid directly to the provincial government.[23]

Likewise, Ontario is establishing an online casino offering a comprehensive assortment of games.[24] A private company will operate the casino under strict regulation by the provincial government. As of this writing, the Ontario Lottery & Gaming Corporation is considering bids and will assess which operator is the most well-suited to deal with everything from design to financial transfers and all other aspects related to both lottery and online casino products.[25] Ontario regulators anticipate provincial revenue of about C$100 million per year within five years, to add to the roughly C$2 billion it receives through land-based casinos, lotteries, and bingos.[26]

---

[19] Federal Ministry of Finance, *supra* note 17.
[20] GamingZion, Online Gambling Sites in Austria, http://gamingzion.com/Austria (last visited Mar. 6, 2012).
[21] British Columbia Lottery Corporation, http://www.bclc.com (last visited Mar. 6, 2012); British Columbia Lottery Corporation, BCLC Online, http://www.playnow.com (last visited Mar. 6, 2012).
[22] British Columbia Lottery Corporation, Benefiting BC, http://www.bclc.com/cm/benefitingbc/home.htm (last visited Mar. 6, 2012).
[23] Loto-Québec, Social Responsibility, http://lotoquebec.com/corporatif/nav/en/social-responsibility (last visited Mar. 6, 2012). *See also* Loto-Québec, Espacejeux, https://www.espacejeux.com (last visited Mar. 6, 2012).
[24] Casino People, A Look at Online Gambling in Ontario, Canada, Dec. 18, 2011, http://www.casinopeople.com/news/a-look-at-online-gambling-in-ontario-canada.html.
[25] *Ontario Should Have Online Gambling by Mid 2012*, Off Shore Gaming Association, Dec. 17, 2011, http://www.osga.com/artman/publish/article_9865.shtml.
[26] *Ontario to Gamble on Lotteries, Online Gaming*, CTV News (Feb. 6, 2012), http://toronto.ctv.ca/servlet/an/local/CTVNews/20120206/olg-online-tickets-120206/20120206/?hub=TorontoNewHome&cid=top.

Hong Kong

Only pari-mutuel betting and the government lottery are permitted in the Hong Kong Special Administrative Region of the People's Republic of China.[27] The Hong Kong Jockey Club is the only operator licensed to provide online gaming services to Hong Kong residents, and the betting duty paid by the Jockey Club accounts for about 10 percent of government revenues.[28]

Besides live racetracks in Hong Kong, covered events include foreign horse racing and soccer. All other gambling is illegal in Hong Kong, and both operators and customers face stiff criminal penalties if convicted.[29]

Hungary

Hungary's state-owned Szerencsejáték has exclusive rights to provide lottery, sports betting, and prize draw ticket games—all of which are available online.[30] All other forms of Internet gambling are treated somewhat similarly to online gambling under the Unlawful Internet Gambling Enforcement Act ("UIGEA")[31] in the United States—that is, Hungary prohibits financial institutions from conducting transactions with offshore providers for the purpose of online gambling, but Hungarians do not face personal penalties for gambling online through offshore providers.[32]

Macau

Despite (or perhaps because of) its robust land-based gaming industry (with revenues over $33 billion in 2011[33]), Macau does not license online casino gambling.[34] But Macau permits pari-mutuel horse betting online through the only licensed online operator, the Macau Jockey Club, which pays a 35 percent tax on gross revenue. However, horse racing as a whole only accounts for slightly more than 0.5 percent of Macau's total gaming revenue.[35]

---

[27] UNITED STATES GENERAL ACCOUNTING OFFICE REPORT TO CONGRESSIONAL REQUESTERS, INTERNET GAMBLING: AN OVERVIEW OF THE ISSUES 47-48 (Dec. 2002), http://www.gao.gov/new.items/d0389.pdf (hereinafter "GAO Report").

[28] *Id.*

[29] *Id.*

[30] GamingZion, Online Gambling Sites in Hungary, http://gamingzion.com/hungary (last visited Mar. 6, 2012).

[31] Unlawful Internet Gambling Enforcement Act of 2006, Pub. L. No. 109-347, § 801, 120 STAT. 1952 (codified at 31 U.S.C. §§ 5361-67 (2006)). UIGEA prohibits the acceptance of any financial instrument in connection with unlawful Internet gambling, and it puts a burden on financial institutions to identify and block restricted transactions according to regulations implemented by the Federal Reserve System. *Id.* §§ 5363-64.

[32] GamingZion, Online Gambling Sites in Hungary, *supra* note 30.

[33] Except where otherwise indicated, "$" denotes amounts in U.S. Dollars.

[34] University of Nevada Las Vegas Center for Gaming Research, Macau Gaming Summary, http://gaming.unlv.edu/abstract/macau.html (last visited Mar. 6, 2012).

[35] *Id.*

The Netherlands

The Netherlands is proposing to legalize online gambling fairly liberally, but operates online casinos, bingo, poker, and sports books under a government monopoly.[36] Its attitude towards offshore operators is quite negative, as illustrated by its implementation in 2008 of a blacklist of foreign internet sites with which Dutch banks are forbidden from doing business. This restriction is being challenged, with the European Union pressuring the Netherlands to move away from its state-operated monopoly.[37]

New Zealand

The Totalizator Agency Board ("TAB") and New Zealand Lotteries Commission are the only entities allowed to offer online gambling in New Zealand.[38] For the fiscal year 2010-11, the Lotteries Commission's online sales channel, MyLotto, generated about 5 percent of its NZ$925.9 million total sales (of which nearly 20 percent was returned to the Lottery Grants Board which oversees distribution of funds to various community causes).[39] TAB's website saw a total turnover of approximately NZ$340 million in 2009-10.[40]

Sweden

The wholly government-owned Svenska Spel holds a monopoly over all gambling in Sweden, including online gambling—a policy which has survived criticism from the European Union as well as various challenges including a high-profile legal battle between the Swedish government and British bookmaker Ladbrokes.[41] But the government is rumored to be considering breaking the monopoly nevertheless, at which point Sweden would likely become a huge area of interest for offshore operators.[42]

---

[36] *Dutch Government Seeks to Allow Online Gambling*, REUTERS, Mar. 19, 2011, http://www.reuters.com/article/2011/03/19/us-netherlands-gambling-idUSTRE72I20F20110319; *Dutch Government Paves the Way for Legalized Online Gambling*, CASINO PEOPLE, May 21, 2011, http://www.casinopeople.com/news/dutch-government-paves-the-way-for-legalized-online-gambling.html.

[37] GamingZion, Dutch Gambling Laws, http://gamingzion.com/Netherlands (last visited Mar. 6, 2012).

[38] GamingZion, Online Gambling Sites in New Zealand, http://gamingzion.com/new-zealand (last visited Mar. 6, 2012).

[39] NZ LOTTERIES, BRIEFING FOR INCOMING MINISTER 1 (Dec. 2011), http://www.nzlotteries.co.nz/wps/wcm/myconnect/lotteries2/nzlotteries/resources/ce471b804a1bd4cca29d-f7a90e10a990/Incoming+ministers+briefing+paper+2011.pdf.

[40] NEW ZEALAND RACING BOARD, ANNUAL REPORT 2010 at 15 (2011), http://static.tab.co.nz/control/data/nzrb-annual-reports/NZRB_Annual_Report_2010updated_graph.pdf.

[41] Brian K. Trembath, *Legal Update: Sweden*, CASINOAFFILIATEPROGRAMS.COM (Feb. 9, 2012), http://www.casinoaffiliateprograms.com/blog/legal-update-sweden.

[42] GamingZion, Online Gambling Sites in Sweden, http://gamingzion.com/Sweden (last visited Mar. 6, 2012).

Turkey

The state-owned IDDAA is the only Turkish entity permitted to offer online gambling services, and it only offers sports betting. As in many Middle Eastern countries, other gambling is strictly proscribed, both online and in land-based establishments.[43]

Free Market Jurisdictions

Alderney

Part of the British Channel Islands, Alderney offers several categories of licenses for remote gambling and extraterritorial Internet gambling servers.[44] Rather than taxing gaming deposits or revenue directly, it has two categories of license, with fees depending on the business type and size.

Category One licenses are for business-to-consumer operations, and the fee depends on the operator's annualized net gaming yield: for a license with no previous licensable activity in Alderney, the fee is £35,000; a renewal by a licensee whose annualized net gaming yield is less than £1 million costs £35,000; where yield falls between £1 million and £5 million, the renewal fee is £70,000; where it is between £5 million and £7.5 million, the renewal fee is £100,000; and a renewal by a licensee whose annualized net gaming yield equals or exceeds £7.5 million costs £140,000.[45]

Category Two licenses are £35,000 per year and enable business-to-business gambling transactions, such as the operational management of the gambling platform.[46] Both forms of license provide tax-exempt status for the licensee, including from VAT or other sales taxes.[47] Temporary licenses are available for £10,000 per year, and carry the same obligations and privileges as a full license, but can be used for no more than 29 days continuously or 59 total days within a six-month period.[48]

Alderney asserts that "its regulatory and supervisory approach meets the very highest of international standards"[49] but the jurisdiction—like others offering extraterritorial licenses—has not been free from controversy. In April 2011, the U.S. Department of Justice directed the Federal Bureau of Investigation to seize the domain of Full Tilt Poker, operating

---

[43] GamingZion, Online Gambling Sites in Turkey, http://gamingzion.com/turkey (last visited Mar. 6, 2012).

[44] Viaden Gaming, Alderney Online Gambling Legislation, http://www.viaden.com/products/alderney_license.html (last visited Mar. 6, 2012).

[45] Alderney Gambling Control Commission, Fees, http://www.gamblingcontrol.org/applicants9.php (last visited Mar. 6, 2012).

[46] Viaden Gaming, Alderney Online Gambling Legislation, *supra* note 44.

[47] Id.

[48] Alderney Gambling Control Commission, A Temporary eGambling License, http://www.gamblingcontrol.org/applicants5.php (last visited Mar. 6, 2012).

[49] Alderney Gambling Control Commission, Home, http://www.gamblingcontrol.org (last visited Mar. 6, 2012).

under an extraterritorial license issued in Alderney at the time, calling it "a global Ponzi scheme."[50] Alderney responded by revoking Full Tilt Poker's license the following September.[51]

Costa Rica

Over two hundred Internet gambling sites base their operations in Costa Rica, which is popular for its permissive regulatory environment, robust infrastructure, and growing economy.[52] Because Costa Rica does not have a licensing regime specifically for online gambling, the jurisdiction merely requires a $15,000 corporate license fee with $1,500 quarterly renewals.[53]

Recently elected President Laura Chinchilla attempted a Fiscal Reform plan which would have imposed a 15 percent GGR tax on Free Trade Zone businesses (including Internet gambling operators),[54] but the plan was abandoned due to resistance from the Minister of the Presidency, the Costa Rican Association of Casinos, the Association of Call Center Employees, and the political opposition party.[55]

Isle of Man

Like Alderney, the Isle of Man is a Crown Dependency of the United

---

[50] Press Release, United States Attorney Southern District of New York, Manhattan U.S. Attorney Moves to Amend Civil Complaint Alleging That Full Tilt Poker and Its Board of Directors Operated Company as a Massive Ponzi Scheme Against Its Own Players (Sept. 20, 2011), *available at* http://www.justice.gov/usao/nys/pressreleases/September11/amendedfulltiltpokercomplaintpr.pdf. The sites of PokerStars (based in Isle of Man) and Absolute Poker (licensed by the Kahnawake Gaming Commission) were also seized at that time. Jacqui Cheng, *FBI: Online Poker Sites 'Bet the House' on Money Laundering, Fraud*, ARS TECHNICA (Apr. 2011), http://arstechnica.com/tech-policy/news/2011/04/major-online-poker-sites-seized-charged-with-money-laundering.ars.

After reaching an agreement with the Department of Justice, PokerStars continues to operate and has become the world's largest poker room with licenses in Malta, Belgium, Italy, France, Denmark, Estonia, and the Isle of Man. *PokerStars.eu Launched After Acquiring Malta License*, POKERNEWSREPORT (Feb. 14, 2012), http://www.pokernewsreport.com/pokerstars-eu-launched-after-acquiring-malta-licence-7484. The site remains closed to U.S. customers except for the purpose of withdrawals from U.S.-owned accounts. *See* PokerStars Statement on the Blocking of Players from the United States, http://www.pokerstars.com (last visited Mar. 6, 2012).

[51] Nathan Vardi, *Full Tilt Poker's License Revoked*, FORBES (Sept. 29, 2011), http://www.forbes.com/sites/nathanvardi/2011/09/29/full-tilt-pokers-license-revoked.

[52] Viaden Gaming, Online Gambling Licensing in Costa Rica, http://www.viaden.com/products/costarica_license.html (last visited Mar. 6, 2012).

[53] *Id.*

[54] Mike Godfrey, *Costa Rican Tax Reform Needed, Says IMF*, TAX-NEWS.COM (Apr. 15, 2011), http://www.tax-news.com/news/Costa_Rican_Tax_Reform_Needed_Says_IMF_48819.html.

[55] Jaime Lopez, *Taxation and Fiscal Reform Legislative Plans Back in the Oven*, THE COSTA RICA STAR (Jan. 13, 2012), http://news.co.cr/business/taxation-and-fiscal-reform-legislative-plans-back-in-the-oven/13/01/2012.

Kingdom and a popular jurisdiction for locating extraterritorial Internet gambling operations, with offerings including sports books, betting exchanges, online casino games, live dealing, peer-to-peer ("P2P") games, mobile phone betting, fantasy football (and similar games), pari-mutuel and pool betting, network gaming, lotteries, certain "spot-the-ball" style games, and network services.[56]

Isle of Man's regulatory framework was established under the Online Gambling Regulation Act of 2001 ("OGRA"), which requires a license for included games, with some activities being exempt from licensure.[57] Fees include a £5,000 application fee and £35,000 for an annual license, which is granted for five-year terms.[58]

Exempted activities include the U.K. National Lottery, gambling covered by a Betting Office or Casino license, spread betting, exempted activities defined by the Insurance Act of 1986,[59] free-to-play games, and ancillary services such as marketing, administration, information technology services, customer support, and disaster recovery facilities.[60]

Kahnawà:ke

Located in Quebec, Canada, the Kahnawà:ke Mohawk Territory provides a home to online casinos and poker rooms regulated by the Kahnawà:ke Gaming Commission.[61] The Commission issues four categories of license: an Interactive Gaming License awarded to a single data center within the Territory; Client Provider Authorizations ("CPAs") allowing each operator to use the single licensed data center; Secondary Client Provider Authorizations for operations located in another jurisdiction; and Key Person Licenses for managers of the Client entities.[62]

Application fees are C$25,000 for each CPA and C$5,000 for each Key Person, with annual licenses costing C$10,000 and C$1,000-C$2,500 respectively, plus a C$5,000 renewal fee being imposed every two years for CPAs.[63] 34 licensees are

---

[56] Isle of Man Gambling Supervision Commission, Guidance for On-line Gambling 6-7 (Dec. 14, 2011), *available at* http://www.gov.im/lib/docs/gambling//external-guidancev61.doc.

[57] *See id.* at 6.

[58] *Id.* at 13-14.

[59] *Available at* http://www.gov.im/lib/docs/ipa/insurance/InsuranceAct1986.pdf.

[60] Online Gambling Regulation Act 2001 § 3, *available at* http://www.gov.im/lib/docs/info-centre/acts/ogra2001.pdf.

[61] CasinoMan.net, Kahnawake, http://www.casinoman.net/reviews/gambling-jurisdictions/kahnawake.asp (last visited Mar. 6, 2012); Viaden Gaming, Online Gambling Licensing in Kahnawake, http://www.viaden.com/products/kahnawake_license.html (last visited Mar. 6, 2012).

[62] Kahnawake Gaming Commission, Permit Holders, http://www.gamingcommission.ca/permitholders.asp (last visited Mar. 6, 2012).

[63] Kahnawake Gaming Commission, Fees—Interactive, http://www.gamingcommission.ca/docs/ApplicationRelatedCosts.pdf (last visited Mar. 6, 2012). Fees are listed in Canadian Dollars.

listed with the Gaming Commission, operating a total of 139 gaming sites.[64]

Panama

The operation of Internet gambling businesses in Panama is free of deposit or revenue taxes if the operator only accepts extraterritorial wagers—licensees may not accept business from Panamanians.[65] Furthermore, the Panama Gaming Control Board requires payment of a master license fee of $40,000, which is valid for up to seven years. Then an annual license fee of $20,000 applies, though master licensees may grant sub-licenses subject only to this annual fee.[66]

Limited Free Market Jurisdictions

Belgium provides a good illustration of the implementation of a limited free market model. Before 2012, the Belgian national lottery had an exclusive monopoly right to offer remote games. Enacted in 2011 and implemented January 1, 2012, the new Belgian Gaming Act permits very limited licensure of third-party operators.[67] Only three Internet gaming licenses have been granted so far—to PokerStars.be, Partouche.be, and Casino777. be.[68] Each operator's tax rate differs by region, but as of late 2010 the Walloon government reportedly announced a flat tax of 11 percent on all online gaming volume.[69] The Gaming Act also criminalizes any participation in, advertising for, or recruiting for unlicensed games of chance—in effect, compelling internet service providers to block Belgians from accessing unlicensed gambling sites appearing on a regularly updated blacklist.[70]

Greece and Poland also are in the process of licensing online gaming,

---

[64] Kahnawake Gaming Commission, Interactive Permit Holders List (by URL), http://www.gamingcommission.ca/interactiveURL.asp (last visited Mar. 6, 2012).

[65] CASINO CITY, GLOBAL GAMING ALMANAC 177 (2011), *available at* http://www.casinocitypress.com/common/gga_panama.pdf.

[66] *Id. See also* Viaden Gaming, Panama Internet Gaming License, http://www.viaden.com/products/panama_license.html (last visited Mar. 6, 2012).

[67] Steven De Schrijver & Pieter Paepe, *Online Gambling Law in Belgium: Some Recent Developments*, WHO'S WHO LEGAL (Oct. 2011), http://www.whoswholegal.com/news/features/article/29234/online-gambling-law-belgium-recent-development.

[68] *Controversial Belgian Gambling Law Enters Into Force*, ONLINECASINOADVICE.COM (Jan. 4, 2012), http://www.onlinecasinoadvice.com/news/controversial-belgian-gambling-law-enters-into-force.

[69] Koen Platteau, *Controversial New Gambling Legislation in Belgium*, OLSWANG (Sept. 1, 2010), http://www.olswang.com/newsarticle.asp?sid=110&aid=3115.

[70] *Id. See also* Joe Valentino, *Online Gambling News from Belgium, Greece and Georgia*, CASINO ADVISOR (Dec. 15, 2011), http://www.casinoadvisor.com/online-gambling-news-from-belgium-greece-and-georgia-news-item.html (discussing Belgium and Greece's challenges with regard to offshore operators); Maggie B., *Pokerstars is Granted Belgium License While Others Are Blacklisted*, CASINO SCAM REPORT (Feb. 10, 2012), http://www.casinoscamreport.com/2012/02/10/pokerstars-is-granted-belgium-license-while-others-are-blacklisted (describing blacklist, including operators such as Chilipoker.com, 888.com, Titanpoker.be, and Everestpoker.be).

and will likely issue only a limited number of casino licenses. Greece applies a fairly high GGR tax in addition to basic license fees,[71] and Poland has licensed a single operator subject to a variable turnover tax (depending on the game offered).[72] Spain, a hybrid model jurisdiction, has limited the licensure of cross-sports betting and horseracing mutuel betting, which are subject to a variable GGR tax depending on the game.[73]

Licensing Fee Models with Gross Gaming Revenue Tax

Antigua and Barbuda

Now home to only ten licensees,[74] the twin-island nation of Antigua and Barbuda saw a peak in online gambling revenues of nearly $2.4 billion in 2001 from 59 licensees—representing about 60 percent of the global online gambling market at the time.[75] This activity has since dramatically declined, in large part owing to the passage of UIGEA[76] in the United States and a subsequent dispute between the nations before the World Trade Organization.[77]

Antigua and Barbuda uses a GGR tax model at a rate of 3 percent of "net win" (synonymous with GGR), with operators being entitled to a maximum cap of $50,000 per month on taxes.[78] Additionally, operators can deduct software licensing and development costs up to 40 percent of their GGR, as well as charge backs on credit cards for up to 18 months after the original charge. Operators must maintain financial records and provide ready access to them to authorized government agencies. Gaming licensee fees are $75,000 annually and wagering licenses are $50,000 per year.[79]

Curaçao

Curaçao, a constituent country of the Dutch Kingdom since the dissolution of the Netherlands Antilles in October 2010, has adopted a fairly straightforward approach to online gambling regulation. Curaçao issues

---

[71] *See infra.*

[72] *See infra.*

[73] *See infra.*

[74] Antigua and Barbuda Financial Services Regulatory Authority Directorate of Offshore Gaming, Active Licensees, http://www.antiguagaming.gov.ag/licensees%20active.asp (last visited Mar. 6, 2012).

[75] Antigua WTO, Antigua Economic and Gambling Data, http://www.antiguawto.com/WTO_Economic_gambling_data.html (last visited Mar. 6, 2012) (citing GLOBAL BETTING AND GAMING CONSULTANTS, QUARTERLY eGAMING STATISTICS REPORT (May 2007)).

[76] Unlawful Internet Gambling Enforcement Act of 2006, *supra* note 32.

[77] *See* Antigua WTO, Antigua-United States WTO Internet Gambling Case, http://www.antiguawto.com/WTODispPg.html (last visited Mar. 6, 2012) (summarizing the dispute).

[78] Antigua and Barbuda, Offshore Financial Sector: Internet Gaming, http://www.antigua-barbuda.com/finance_investment/offshore_sector.asp (last visited Mar. 6, 2012).

[79] *Id.*

one type of license to cover a comprehensive assortment of gaming services, including all games of skill, chance, and sports betting. Company formation in Curaçao enables application for an "Ezone permit" to avail the operator of Curaçao's low 2 percent GGR tax and to qualify for exemption from VAT.[80]

Dominican Republic

The Dominican Republic offers Internet casino and sports betting licenses.[81] Licensure requires a one-time payment of $15,000 in addition to a $15,000 application fee (or $10,000 if it is the second or third application), and the country imposes a 5 percent GGR tax with a $50,000 annual minimum thereafter.[82] While land-based casinos in the Dominican pay the corporate tax of 25 percent -29 percent plus fees based on the number of tables in operation and a gross tax on slot machine sales, offshore licensees are exempt from these taxes and levies as long as their revenue is not Dominica-sourced.[83]

Estonia

A relative newcomer to Internet gambling despite its robust land-based gambling industry, Estonia licenses operators to provide games of chance, games of skill, and pari-mutuel betting services.[84] The jurisdiction imposes a 5 percent sales tax that excludes player winnings.[85] Operators require two licenses: an activity license and an operating license, the issuance of which is the responsibility of the Estonian Tax and Customs Board.[86]

Estonian regulations require the country's internet service providers to block offshore gambling sites that do not have an Estonian gambling

---

[80] Curacao eGaming, Guidance Notes: Operating Under a Curacao eGaming License 1 (Aug. 1, 2011), *available at* http://www.curacao-egaming.com/pdf/Curacao_eGaming_Guidance_Notes_2011.pdf.

[81] SloGold, Dominica Internet Gaming Licenses, http://www.slogold.net/dominica_gambling_license_get_gaming_sportbook_licence_in_dominica.html (last visited Mar. 6, 2012).

[82] *Id.*

[83] Viaden Gaming, Online Gambling License in the Dominican Republic, http://www.viaden.com/products/online-gambling-license-in-dominican-republic.html (last visited Mar. 6, 2012).

[84] Viaden Gaming, Online Gambling License in Estonia, http://www.viaden.com/products/estonia-gambling-license.html (last visited Mar. 6, 2012). Estonia's Gambling Tax Act, passed April 22, 2009, lays out taxes imposed on Internet gambling as the "amounts received as stakes in games of chance and games of skill . . . from which the winnings have been deducted." Gambling Tax Act § 1(1)(5), *available at* http://www.emta.ee/index.php?id=980 (last visited Mar. 6, 2012).

[85] *Estonia Regulating Online Gambling, One Step at a Time*, Gambling Results (Dec. 19, 2011), http://gamblingresults.com/internet-gambling-facts/20111219-estonia-regulating-online-gambling-one-step-at-a-time.

[86] *See* Estonian Tax and Customs Board, http://www.emta.ee/index.php?lang=en (last visited Mar. 6, 2012).

license.[87] Although this policy runs counter to European Union policy, Estonian regulators claim that the situation is temporary, and only necessary in these early stages of online gambling development.[88]

Greece

The online casino industry in Greece is reportedly worth over €2 billion, a fact which, combined with Greece's current economic hard times, has deterred the nation from banning Internet gambling as it originally considered. Instead, it is working toward a license-and-tax approach.[89] License fees have not been entirely settled upon, but legislation passed in August permits licensure of Video Lottery Terminals ("VLTs") and 10-50 online casinos, with rumors that fees will be approximately €15,000 per VLT and somewhere "in the order of €1-5 million" for five-year casino licenses.[90]

The Greek Finance Ministry originally intended to levy a 6 percent deposit tax on Internet operations, but has instead decided to implement a 30 percent GGR tax, which is toward the higher end of the scale for E.U. countries.[91] While the Remote Gaming Association was reportedly pleased with the switch, it subsequently turned its energies toward convincing the Greek government to lower the GGR tax rate "to be more into line with other countries that have licensed remote gambling."[92]

Philippines

Previously the Philippine Amusement and Gaming Corporation ("PAGCOR") held sole rights to all Internet gaming activities in the Philippines and issued an exclusive license to one company—Philweb—until the year 2032. Legislation passed in 1995 allowed the creation of the Cagayan Economic Zone Authority ("CEZA").[93] CEZA, also known as

---

[87] *Gambling News: Estonia Begins Blocking "Unlicensed" Gambling Sites*, OLSWANG (Mar. 24, 2010), http://www.olswang.be/newsarticle.asp?sid=110&aid=2926.

[88] Viaden Gaming, *supra* note 84.

[89] *Greek Online Gambling Taxation Scheme*, CASINO PEOPLE (Mar. 29, 2011), http://www.casinopeople.com/news/greek-online-gambling-taxation-scheme.html.

[90] Konstantinos Veletas, *What to Know About the New Greek Gaming Law*, CASINOAFFILI-ATEPROGRAMS.COM (Sept. 26, 2011), http://www.casinoaffiliateprograms.com/blog/what-to-know-about-the-new-greek-gaming-law.

[91] *Greek Online Gambling Taxation Scheme*, *supra* note 89.

[92] *Id.* (quoting "a spokesperson from the RGA"). *See also* John W., *EGBA Challenges Greek Online Gambling Law*, ONLINE CASINO REPORTS (Dec. 6, 2011), http://www.online-casinoreports.com/news/theheadlines/2011/12/6/egba-challenges-greek-online-gambling-law.php (describing expanded criticism and challenges by the RGA and European Gaming and Betting Association over Greece's online gambling legislation under E.U. law).

[93] Triple i Consulting, Online Gambling License Philippines, http://www.tripleiconsulting.com/main/philippines-business-guides-tips-and-news-blog/179-online-gambling-license-philippines (last visited Mar. 6, 2012).

Cagayan Freeport, is a Philippines Tax Incentive Zone created with the goal of turning the Philippine province of Cagayan into a self-sustaining economic center.[94] Online casinos and sports books domiciled in the Economic Zone pay CEZA's special 5 percent gross income tax rate,[95] an Interactive Gaming License fee of $40,000, and a low 2 percent GGR tax.[96]

United Kingdom

The United Kingdom is the largest economy regulating Internet gambling under a GGR tax model.[97] Previously taxing turnover at 6.75 percent, which reportedly led a lot of bookmakers to move their telephone and Internet operations offshore, the British regulatory model imposes a 15 percent GGR tax on top of basic licensing fees.[98] Despite an 11 percent decrease versus the prior year due to operators moving offshore, gross online gambling yield in the United Kingdom was approximately $1.027 billion for the year ended March 31, 2010.[99]

Online gambling, which is regulated by the U.K. Gambling Commission, includes remote casinos (providing games such as American roulette and blackjack, as well as P2P games like poker), remote betting, remote bingo, and remote lotteries.[100] Rather than offering a single Internet gambling permit, licenses are issued by game type and are either non-remote (that is, in-person) only, or allow remote operations from land-based premises.[101]

---

[94] Triple i Consulting, Cagayan Economic Zone Authority, http://www.tripleiconsulting. com/main/philippines-tax-incentive-programs/cagayan-economic-zone-authority (last visited Mar. 6, 2012).

[95] Triple i Consulting, Online Gambling License Philippines, *supra* note 93.

[96] Vegas 365, Philippines, http://www.vegas365.com/philippines (last visited Mar. 6, 2012).

[97] Of the surveyed countries, only France's gross domestic product ("GDP") is larger— the World Bank puts France's GDP at $2.560 trillion in 2010 vs. the United Kingdom's at $2.246 trillion; France uses a turnover tax model, as discussed *infra* Section E. World Bank, Gross Domestic Product 2010, http://siteresources.worldbank.org/DATASTATIS-TICS/Resources/GDP.pdf.

[98] Malta-Tax, British Online Gambling Laws, http://www.malta-tax.com/betting/malta-online-gaming.htm (last visited Mar. 6, 2012). *See also* HM CUSTOMS AND EXCISE, *supra* note 16, at 2.

[99] ERNST & YOUNG, MARKET OVERVIEW: THE 2011 GLOBAL GAMING BULLETIN 69 (2011), *available at* http://www.ey.com/Publication/vwLUAssets/2011_global_gaming-bulletin/$-FILE/2011%20Global%20Gaming%20Bulletin.pdf. British residents are not prohibited from gambling with offshore providers, but a bill is being considered that would require all Internet gambling sites operating in the United Kingdom to be licensed by the U.K. Gambling Commission. *UK Parliament Discusses Controversial Online Gambling Law*, ONLINECASINOADVICE.COM (Feb. 10, 2012), http://www.onlinecasinoadvice.com/news/uk-parliament-discusses-controversial-online-gambling-law.

[100] Gambling Commission, About Remote Gambling (Including Online Gambling), http://www.gamblingcommission.gov.uk/gambling_sectors/remote/about_the_remote_gambling_indu/about_remote_gambling.aspx (last visited Mar. 6, 2012).

[101] Gambling Commission, Do I Need a License, http://www.gamblingcommission.gov.

For example, operators wishing to provide general betting on virtual or real events via the Internet must pay an application fee from about £3,000 up to about £64,000 based on annual gross gambling yield (where for general betting, an annual gross yield of less than £500,000 qualifies the operator for the lowest rate, and the highest of seven tiers is represented by those operators generating an annual gross yield of over £500 million).[102] The annual remote betting license then costs from about £3,000 up to about £160,000 per year depending on annual gross gambling yield.[103] Remote casinos pay similar license application and annual fees, but remote lottery operators pay much less.[104]

Licensing Fee Models with Deposit/Turnover Tax

Belize

Belize licenses online operators to provide any type of gambling in compliance with the extraterritorial market being served.[105] The jurisdiction applies a turnover tax of 0.75 percent.[106] Extraterritorial licenses cost between $50,000 and $100,000,[107] and require being an International Business Company with incorporation in Belize, adequate capitalization, subjectivity to government audits, and appropriate identity verification.[108] Furthermore, operators may not accept wagers from residents of Belize—that is, operators are granted extraterritorial licenses only.[109]

---

uk/gambling_sectors/remote/getting_a_licence-_what_you_ne/do_i_need_a_licence.aspx (last visited Mar. 6, 2012).

[102] Gambling Commission, How Much Will My Operating License Application Cost—Betting?, http://www.gamblingcommission.gov.uk/gambling_sectors/betting/getting_a_licence_what_you_ne/applying_for_a_licence_-_betti/apply_for_an_operating_licence/how_much_-_application_fee.aspx (last visited Mar. 6, 2012).

[103] Gambling Commission, How Much Will My Operating License Annual Fees Cost—Betting?, http://www.gamblingcommission.gov.uk/gambling_sectors/betting/getting_a_licence_what_you_ne/applying_for_a_licence_-_betti/apply_for_an_operating_licence/how_much_-_annual_fees.aspx (last visited Mar. 6, 2012).

[104] *See* Gambling Commission, Apply for an Operating License—Casinos, http://www.gamblingcommission.gov.uk/gambling_sectors/casinos/getting_a_licence_what_you_ne/applying_for_a_licence_-_casin/apply_for_an_operating_licence.aspx (last visited Mar. 6, 2012) (describing casino license fees); Gambling Commission, Applying for a License—Lotteries, http://www.gamblingcommission.gov.uk/gambling_sectors/lotteries/getting_a_licence-what_you__n/applying_for_a_licence_-_lotte.aspx (last visited Mar. 6, 2012) (describing lottery license fees).

[105] LowTax Network International, Gambling License Belize, http://www.etc-lowtax.net/english/gambling_license_belize.htm (last visited Mar. 6, 2012).

[106] *Id.*

[107] Online Casino City, Belize, http://online.casinocity.com/jurisdictions/belize (last visited Mar. 6, 2012).

[108] LowTax, *supra* note 106; SloGold, Belize Gambling License, http://www.slogold.net/belize_gambling_license_get_gambling_licence_in_belize.html (last visited Mar. 6, 2012).

[109] Online Casino City, *supra* note 107.

Cyprus

Previously a haven for online casino operators paying a relatively low 10 percent GGR tax, the Cypriot government has approved a bill that proposes to ban online gambling with the exceptions of sports betting and lotteries, which will be subject to a 3 percent turnover tax.[110] As in Belize, licenses require compliance with various criteria such as adequate capitalization and customer identity and age verification.[111]

France

The largest nation by GDP with regulated online gambling,[112] France imposes a 7.5 percent turnover tax on general gambling, horse racing, and sports betting, and taxes online poker at 2 percent of the amount wagered.[113] According to critics, these tax rates are "considered some of the highest in Europe."[114] For example, KPMG argues that France's adoption of a relatively high turnover tax and limited licensure model is overly burdensome on operators—decreasing competition and market value, as well as choice for consumers and tax revenue.[115] With reference to Italy's 20 percent GGR tax, KPMG estimated two years ago that by the end of 2012, Italy's gambling turnover will be approximately four times that of France, rendering France's gambling market "immaterial" by comparison.[116]

As predicted by critics of the French system, the French online gaming market has seen a recent decline in gambling revenue, as well as loss of market share in the European Union.[117] In response, and specifically in an effort to limit French gaming through offshore providers (and thus mitigate the associated loss of French gambling tax revenue), the French government has directed Internet service providers to block sites not licensed by the French online gaming regulatory authority ("ARJEL").[118] Further-

---

[110] *Cyprus Approves Online Casino Ban*, DUROCHER (Mar. 9, 2011), http://www.durocher. org/gambling-news/cyprus-online-casino-ban.

[111] *Id. See also* N. Pirilides & Associates, Gambling Law in Cyprus, http://www.pirilides. com/en/cyprus/publications/gambling-law-in-cyprus/70 (last visited Mar. 6, 2012) (describing pending legislation as well as operator application requirements).

[112] *See supra* note 98 (comparing France's GDP with that of the United Kingdom).

[113] *France Passes Bill to End State Monopoly on Online Gambling*, THE TELEGRAPH (Apr. 6, 2010), *available at* http://www.telegraph.co.uk/news/worldnews/7561071/France-passes-bill-to-end-state-monopoly-on-online-gambling.html.

[114] *French Online Gambling Operators Lobby for Taxation Reforms*, ONLINE-CASINOS.COM (May 20, 2011), http://www.online-casinos.com/news/news2010637.asp.

[115] KPMG, TAXATION OF ONLINE GAMBLING: THE CASE FOR A TAX REGIME BASED ON GROSS PROFITS 13 (2010) (on file with author).

[116] *Id.* at 13-14.

[117] *French Online Gambling Market Slows*, CASINOS ONLINE (Feb. 8, 2012), http://www. casinos-online.co.uk/news/20120208/french-online-gambling-market-slows.

[118] Emilis Pakenas, *Online Poker Regulations Take Effect in France and Belgium*, POKER WORKS (Jan. 5, 2012), http://pokerworks.com/poker-news/2012/01/05/online-poker-regulations-take-effect-in-france-and-belgium.html. The operators licensed in France are among the most prominent: PokerStars, PartyPoker, iPoker network, 888, Everest, as well

more, ARJEL expanded the number of licensed operators to 34 as of February 7, 2012.[119] And one of the reasons France legalized online sports betting in 2010—the FIFA World Cup—may have been a significant factor in the decline of sports betting in 2011, a possibility that critics tend to avoid highlighting.

Malta

Malta was the first member of the European Union to legalize and regulate online gambling through its Lotteries and Gaming Authority ("LGA").[120] For all practical purposes, Malta is a free-market jurisdiction with its low 0.5 percent turnover tax rate (with an annual cap, described below), low-tax onshore tax regime, and broad network of double-taxation agreements.[121] It licenses a comprehensive assortment of games under a four-tiered classification system: Class 1 licenses cover casinos; Class 2 licenses apply to fixed odds, pool, and spread betting; Class 3 includes P2P games (such as poker and betting exchanges); and Class 4 licenses are for operations managers and ancillary companies such as software vendors.[122]

After the costs of incorporating in Malta and a €2,330 application fee, a license of any of the four types only costs €7,000 per year for a five-year term, with a five-year renewal fee of €1,165.[123] Furthermore, the already low annual gaming tax is capped at €460,000. But casino licenses are subject to a "differential gaming tax" of €4,660 for each of the first six months, then €7,000 per month, and P2P operators are subject to an additional 5 percent tax on real income.[124]

Poland

Despite its well-established land-based casino industry, Poland has taken a very restrictive approach to online gambling, outlawing all gambling except sports betting sites, which pay a high 12 percent turnover tax.[125] Furthermore, though Poland does not characterize its model as a

---

as two French operators, Partouche and Winamax. *Id.*

[119] CASINOS ONLINE, *supra* note 117.

[120] Viaden Gaming, Malta Online Gambling Legislation, http://www.viaden.com/products/malta_license.html (last visited Mar. 6, 2012).

[121] Malta-Tax, Malta Online Gaming Licenses, http://www.malta-tax.com/betting/malta-online-gaming.htm (last visited Mar. 6, 2012). *See also* Malta-Tax, Maltese Tax Vehicles, http://www.malta-tax.com/tax-vehicles/index.htm (last visited Mar. 6, 2012) (describing onshore tax regime).

[122] Viaden Gaming, *supra* note 120.

[123] Viaden Gaming, Malta Online Gambling Licensing Procedures, http://www.viaden.com/products/malta_procedures.html (last visited Mar. 6, 2012).

[124] *Id. See also* Malta Lotteries & Gaming Authority, Remote Gaming, http://www.lga.org.mt/lga/content.aspx?id=86949 (last visited Mar. 6, 2012) (describing online gaming sector with links to specific game and license type descriptions as well as lists of licensees in each Class).

[125] *Poland Forbids Online Gambling While Praising Sportsbooks*, GAMINGZION (Apr.

monopoly, Czech bookmaker Fortuna Entertainment Group is the only licensed operator to date.[126]

Hybrid Models

Australia

Australia's approach to Internet gambling is complex, particularly because each state and territory—like each of the United States—regulates its own gaming activities, subject to a few national restrictions. The Interactive Gambling Act ("IGA") generally restricts online gambling, making it unlawful for Australia-based operators to offer casino-style games such as roulette, poker, craps, or blackjack to anyone located in designated countries (that is, Australian jurisdiction), but excluding from the Act specific sports and race wagering, lotteries, and keno.[127] Thus, the IGA does not prohibit Australians from gambling with offshore providers, nor does it prohibit Australian operators from providing gambling services to extra-territorial customers.[128] Operators in Australian states and territories offer the activities excluded from the IGA—online sports betting, keno, and lotteries—to varying degrees, and subject to different regulatory models.

The Australian state of New South Wales adopted a monopoly model for its regulated lottery, and a license fee model with graduated GGR tax for sports betting and keno. The state granted a forty-year exclusive lottery license to New South Wales Lotteries Corporation Pty Ltd., a subsidiary of Tatts Group Ltd., which pays 66.1 percent of player loss in taxes.[129] Wagering on racing and sports is conducted by TAB Limited and licensed bookmakers, whose remote betting authorities are granted under New South Wales's Racing Administration Act.[130] Replacing the previously applied

---

11, 2011), http://gamingzion.com/gamblingnews/poland-forbids-online-gambling-while-praising-internet-sportsbooks-2000.

[126] Krystof Chamonikolas, *Fortuna Jumps to 3-Month High on Poland Expansion*, Bloomberg (Jan 25, 2012), http://www.bloomberg.com/news/2012-01-25/fortuna-jumps-to-3-month-high-on-poland-expansion-prague-mover.html. *See also* Fortuna Ent. Group, Regulatory Announcement (Jan. 24, 2012), *available at* http://www.afm.nl/registers/kgi_documents/201201240000000009_2011-01-24%20Fortuna%20-%20 20%20000%20subscribers%20for%20on-line%20bets_ENG.pdf.

[127] Interactive Gambling Act 2001 §§ 6, 8A-D, 15 (as amended Oct. 19, 2011), *available at* http://www.comlaw.gov.au/Details/C2011C00840.

[128] Australian Policy Online, Review of the Interactive Gambling Act 2001, http://apo.org.au/node/26111 (last visited Mar. 6, 2012).

[129] New South Wales Government Office of Liquor, Gaming & Racing, Public Lotteries, http://www.olgr.nsw.gov.au/public_lotteries_home.asp#top (last visited Mar. 6, 2012); New South Wales Government, The Treasury, Office of Financial Management, Interstate Comparison of Taxes 2010-11 at 37 (2011) (hereinafter Interstate Comparison of Taxes), *available at* http://www.treasury.nsw.gov.au/__data/assets/pdf_file/0018/19242/TRP10-02_dnd.pdf.

[130] Racing Administration Act 1998, *available at* http://www.legislation.nsw.gov.au/sessionalview/sessional/act/1998-114.pdf; New South Wales Government Office of Liquor,

bookmakers' turnover tax, pari-mutuel sports betting is subject to a 19.11 percent tax on player loss, and fixed odds sports betting is subject to a 10.91 percent GGR tax.[131] Keno is taxed at 8.91 percent for the first A$86.5 million in player loss, and 14.91 percent thereafter.[132]

The Northern Territory accepts applications—without a fee—for an unlimited number of extraterritorial licenses to provide online gaming to offshore customers, subject to a low 4 percent GGR tax rate.[133] Bookmakers are taxed at 10 percent of gross monthly profit (replacing a turnover tax as of January 2010), which is capped at A$250,000 per year.[134] Online keno is subject to a 20 percent tax on gross profit.[135]

Adopting a monopoly model for remote gambling across the board, Queensland has granted a sole keno license to Jupiters Gaming Pty Ltd., a sole lottery license to Golden Casket Lottery Corporation, Ltd., and a sole wagering license to Tattsbet Ltd.[136] The government taxes at 20 percent of monthly commission on totalizators and fixed odds betting, 29.4 percent of monthly gross revenue after commissions from Jupiters (in addition to a A$195,900 quarterly license fee), 45 percent of monthly gross profit from Golden Casket (in addition to its A$195,900 quarterly license fee), 55 percent from instant scratch-offs, and 59 percent from soccer pools—all collected in arrears.

As is the case in each Australian jurisdiction, the only lawful online gambling is that which the federal Interactive Gambling Act does not prohibit. However, in South Australia, if there is no State law license, permit or authorization for the gambling, both the gambler and the gambling provider will commit an offence. So, not only can there not be any lawful Australian licensed internet casinos in this State, neither can there be any lawful off-shore internet gambling. The gambler in South Australia commits an offense and (to the extent that South Australian law can apply extra-territorially) so does the internet casino.[137]

The state of South Australia takes a more free-market approach, permitting anyone to apply for inexpensive lottery and bookmaker licenses. Bookmakers' licenses are available at relatively little cost. However, the li-

---

Gaming & Racing, Sports Betting, http://www.olgr.nsw.gov.au/racing_sports_betting.asp (last visited Mar. 6, 2012).

[131] INTERSTATE COMPARISON OF TAXES, *supra* note 129, at 32.

[132] *Id.* at 39.

[133] Northern Territory Government Department of Justice, Licensing, Regulation and Alcohol Strategy: Internet Gaming—FAQ No. 1, http://www.nt.gov.au/justice/licenreg/documents/gaming/fs_ig_faq.pdf (last visited Mar. 6, 2012); Mary Swire, *Australian Online Gaming Operation Wins 50% Tax Cut*, TAX-NEWS (Nov. 21, 2001), http://www.tax-news.com/news/Australian_Online_Gaming_Operation_Wins_50_Tax_Cut_6349.html.

[134] INTERSTATE COMPARISON OF TAXES, *supra* note 129, at 32.

[135] *Id.* at 39.

[136] Queensland Government Office of Liquor and Gaming Regulation, Major Gaming License Holders, http://www.olgr.qld.gov.au/industry/gaming_licensing/major_licence_holders/index.shtml (last visited Mar. 6, 2012).

[137] INTERSTATE COMPARISON OF TAXES, *supra* note 129, at 32-40.

censes can only be granted to natural persons or to companies made up entirely of individual licensees. Commercial lotteries are a monopoly vested in a State-owned statutory corporation (the Lotteries Commission), which will begin its online sales activity mid-year 2012.

Taxes on totalizators and sports betting by South Australians will have been phased out by mid-2012.[138] Sports betting involving wagers accepted from extraterritorial customers is taxed at 0.25 percent of turnover.[139] The state lotteries, soccer pools, and keno operators pay 41 percent of net gambling revenue to South Australia's Hospitals Fund. However, each of these has to pay product fees to the racing industry of 10 percent of net wagering revenue, (NWR) except for SA TAB, which has to pay 40 percent of NWR. (It should be noted that they all pay federal goods and services tax of one-eleventh of net wagering revenue, less product fees).[140]

The Australian island state of Tasmania authorizes the operation of race and sports betting, simulated (casino) games, lotteries, betting exchanges, and pari-mutuel wagering via telecommunications devices (including the Internet).[141] License costs are based on "fee units," where one unit is valued at A$1.40.[142] The application for a Tasmanian Gaming License is 30,000 fee units (unless reasonable costs exceed 30,000 units, in which case the Tasmanian Gaming Commission can charge the applicant the excess amount).[143] License fees vary by gaming activity: for sports and race wagering, they cost 200,000 fee units; for lotteries and simulated gaming, they cost 300,000 fee units; and for betting exchanges and totalizators, they cost 350,000 fee units.[144]

Taxation of Tasmanian operators also depends on the gaming activity. There is no taxation on sports betting or race wagering operators after the initial license fee. Lotteries (the main outliers in an otherwise mostly GGR-oriented scheme) are taxed at 35.55 percent of turnover. Simulated gaming is taxed according to gross annual profit: the first A$10 million of gross profit is taxed at 20 percent; gross profit between A$10 million and A$20 million is taxed at 17.5 percent; and gross profit exceeding A$20 million is taxed at 15 percent. Additionally, gross profit relating to wagers made by residents outside of Australian territory is taxed at 4 percent. Bet-

---

[138] *Id.* at 31.

[139] *Id.* at 32.

[140] *Id.* at 37-39.

[141] Tasmania Department of Treasury and Finance, Tasmanian Gaming License Guide to Applicants 6 (May 2009), *available at* http://www.tenders.tas.gov.au/domino/dtf/dtf.nsf/LookupFiles/TasmanianGamingLicenceGuide.pdf/$file/TasmanianGamingLicenceGuide.pdf.

[142] Fee units are adjusted each year according to a formula based on consumer price index changes. *See* Department of Treasury and Finance, Fee Units, http://www.tenders.tas.gov.au/domino/dtf/dtf.nsf/v-ecopol/5D8E36BF957730DDCA2578880019C068 (last visited Mar. 6, 2012).

[143] Tasmanian Gaming License Guide to Applicants, *supra* note 141, at 8.

[144] *Id.* at 9.

ting exchanges pay 5 percent of commission received, and tote board operators pay a flat levy of 4.7 million fee units.[145]

For the fiscal year 2010-11, Tasmania collected less than A$2.5 million in Internet gaming and wagering taxes, a significant drop from previous years (about A$6.72 million in 2009-10 and nearly A$8 million for the previous year), mainly because of legislation lowering the betting exchange tax from 15 percent to 5 percent. But the state collected Internet gaming and wagering license fees of approximately A$1.5 million, a three-fold increase over previous years.[146] Lotteries (available online, but including land-based retailers) generated nearly A$84 million in tax revenue on slightly more than A$290 million in player expenditures.[147]

In Victoria, only Tabcorp has a license to conduct online wagering.[148] Tabcorp and Tatts Group Ltd. formed a joint venture to oversee Club Keno, which is operated by Tatts Group and pays 24.24 percent of player loss in taxes, subject to a minimum player return of 75 percent.[149] Separately, ten-year lottery licenses were awarded to Tatts Group and Intralot (each offering different lottery products), which both pay 79.4 percent of player loss (and are subject to a 60 percent player return requirement).[150] Sports betting is taxed at the same rates as in New South Wales.[151]

Finally, Western Australia's Lottery West operates the online lottery, which pays 40 percent of net subscriptions (sales less commission and prizes) to hospitals, 5 percent to the arts, 5 percent to sports, and 12.5 percent to eligible organizations.[152] Racing bet servicers have a choice between two methods of taxation: (1) a 1.5 percent turnover tax, or (2) the greater of a 20 percent gross profit or 0.2 percent turnover tax.[153]

Denmark

In contrast to Australia, Denmark's hybrid model is relatively simple. Denmark's state-owned operator, Danske Spil, holds a monopoly on online gambling licenses for horse racing and online bingo.[154] Other online sports

---

[145] *Id.*

[146] TASMANIAN GAMING COMMISSION, 2010-11 ANNUAL REPORT 16, *available at* http://www.treasury.tas.gov.au/domino/dtf/dtf.nsf/LookupFiles/TGCAnnualReport2010-11.PDF/$file/TGCAnnualReport2010-11.PDF.

[147] *Id.*

[148] Department of Justice, Victoria, Australia, About Wagering License, http://www.gamblinglicences.vic.gov.au/wagering-licence/about-wagering-licence.html (last visited Mar. 6, 2012).

[149] INTERSTATE COMPARISON OF TAXES, *supra* note 129, at 39.

[150] *Id.* at 37; Department of Justice, Victoria, Australia, Lotteries Licenses Review, http://www.gamblinglicences.vic.gov.au/lotteries-licences.html (last visited Mar. 6, 2012).

[151] *See* INTERSTATE COMPARISON OF TAXES, *supra* note 129, at 32.

[152] *Id.* at 37.

[153] Government of Western Australia Department of Racing, Gaming and Liquor, Western Australian Race Fields: Racing Bets Levy, http://www.rgl.wa.gov.au/Default.aspx?NodeId=74 (last visited Mar. 6, 2012).

[154] *Denmark Online Gambling Tax Approved by E.C.*, CASINO PEOPLE (Sept. 22, 2011),

betting and online casinos pay a 20 percent GGR tax, which prompted negative reactions from land-based operators, who pay between 45 percent and 71 percent GGR tax.[155] The lower tax rate for online operators was justified by the highly competitive nature of the international market in which they participate, compared to land-based operators' lower competition (being geographically restricted to Danish territory).[156]

Gibraltar

Gibraltar's regulatory model is divided between bookmakers and internet casinos. Bookmakers are subject to limited and strict licensing, and are taxed at 1 percent of turnover with an £85,000 annual minimum and £425,000 maximum. Licenses are renewable for only £2,000.[157] Internet casinos, on the other hand, are only subject to a 1 percent GGR tax (with the same minimum, maximum, renewal fee, and limited licensing as bookmakers).[158] The jurisdiction is generally not licensing new entrants, so along with strict prerequisites for licensure, online gambling licenses are very hard to come by. Extraterritorial services can only be directed at jurisdictions where such activities are not illegal.[159]

Italy

The third-largest surveyed nation by GDP, Italy had originally entered the online gambling market with a turnover tax ranging from 2.5 percent to 5 percent across the board.[160] Reacting to concerns from gambling operators and associations about competition in the European Union online gaming market, Italy introduced a GGR tax in 2010 at a rate of 20 percent for online casinos (after an initial license fee of €300,000 with lower renewals after each year of operation), and expects substantial growth as a result.[161] Despite this shift towards a GGR model, however, electronic lottery terminals, sports and horse race wagering, bingo, other lotteries, and games of skill are still taxed at a rate of 3 percent of total turnover.[162]

---

http://www.casinopeople.com/news/denmark-online-gambling-tax-approved-by-ec.html.
[155] *Id.*
[156] *Id.*
[157] SloGold, Gibraltar Remote Gambling License, Betting Gaming License, Offshore Poker Licenses, http://www.slogold.net/gibraltar_gambling_license_get_gaming_sportbook_licence_in_gibraltar.html (last visited Mar. 6, 2012).
[158] *Id.*
[159] *Id.* Furthermore, licensees must be controlled and managed from Gibraltar; must submit lists of key personnel including shareholders, directors, and executives to the regulatory authority; and may not maintain any bank accounts outside of Gibraltar. *Id.*
[160] KPMG, Taxation of Online Gambling: The Case for a Tax Regime Based on Gross Profits 14 (2010) (on file with author).
[161] *Id.* Viaden Gaming, Online Gambling Regulation in Italy, http://www.viaden.com/products/italy_license.html (last visited Mar. 6, 2012).
[162] *Id.*

Spain

New regulation in Spain applies varying tax models and rates according to the type of gaming activity. Mutuel sports betting, sports betting exchanges, horse racing counterpart betting, other mutuel or counterpart betting, raffles, contests, and random combinations are regulated by a highly competitive bidding for licenses, and subject to a turnover tax varying from 10 percent to 35 percent depending on the game category.[163] However, cross-sports betting, horse racing mutual betting, and other games are taxed at 15 percent to 20 percent of GGR (or commission, in the case of P2P games), depending on the type of game.[164]

Generally speaking, Spain's newly enacted hybrid model emphasizes turnover tax as a method for regulating Internet gambling. The authors at KPMG point out that this runs counter to most European Union members such as the United Kingdom, Italy, and Denmark, as well as some Autonomous Communities within Spain itself, such as the Community of Madrid and Basque Country.[165]

Vanuatu

Providing an illustration of a relatively straightforward free-market-oriented hybrid tax model, the small island nation of Vanuatu also divides its model by game type. For general gaming, operators are subject to a 2.5 percent GGR tax with two licensing regimes: sports books pay an application fee of $35,000 and annual payments of $30,000; and other operators pay a $75,000 application fee and $50,000 annually. Fixed odds wagering is effectively free market, subject merely to the above licensing fees and a very low 0.1 percent turnover tax.[166]

REGULATED ONLINE GAMBLING IN THE UNITED STATES

Current Regulation of Gambling in the United States

Of the fifty states and District of Columbia, only Hawaii and Utah outlaw all forms of gambling.[167] The U.S. gambling industry as a whole generated more than $92 billion in revenue in 2007 through commercial

---

[163] KPMG, *supra* note 14, at 5.

[164] *Id.*

[165] *Id.*

[166] LowTax, Vanuatu: Offshore Business Sectors (Vanuatu Electronic Gaming), http://www.lowtax.net/lowtax/html/jvaobs.html (last visited Mar. 6, 2012). *See also* GamblingLicenses.com, Interview with Geoff Sheehan of Interactive Gaming Consultants, Dec. 10, 2001, *available at* http://www.gamblinglicenses.com/PDF/Vanuatu_interview_Geoff_Sheehan.pdf (describing regulatory environment in Vanuatu).

[167] Joint Committee on Taxation, *Overview of Federal Tax Laws and Reporting Requirements Relating to Gambling in the United States* 2 (JCX-28-10), May 17, 2010, *available at* http://www.jct.gov/publications.html?func=startdown&id=3683.

casinos, Indian casinos, state lotteries, and racetrack casinos.[168] According to the American Gaming Association, commercial casinos operate in twenty-two states, generating a total gross casino gaming revenue of about $34.6 billion in 2010.[169] The twenty-two states with commercial casinos generally tax on GGR, from a low in Nevada of 6.75 percent,[170] up to 50 percent in Illinois and 55 percent on slot machines in Pennsylvania.[171] The exception is Maine, which applies a 1 percent turnover tax in addition to a 42 percent GGR tax.[172] A handful of states also apply a per-person, per-visit admission tax of $2 to $3, and South Dakota charges a $2,000 annual per-machine tax on gaming devices.[173] As a result of commercial casino revenue alone, these twenty-two states enjoyed a tax revenue in 2010 of more than $7.5 billion.[174]

Although traditional (land-based, dockside, or riverboat) gambling activities are governed by the states, Internet gambling implicates federal law. Applicable federal legislation is primarily found in the Wire Act[175] and Unlawful Internet Gambling Enforcement Act ("UIGEA"), although other federal and state statutes may also apply.[176] Specifically, the Wire Act provides:

Whoever being engaged in the business of betting or wagering knowingly uses a wire communication facility for the transmission in interstate or foreign commerce of bets or wagers or information assisting in the placing of bets or wagers on any sporting event or contest, or for the transmission of a wire communication which entitles the recipient to receive money or credit as a result of bets or wagers, or for information assisting in the placing of bets or wagers, shall be fined under this title or imprisoned not more than two years, or both.[177]

Although some have long held that this section broadly prohibits Internet gambling,[178] a recent memorandum by the U.S. Department of Justice opines that the Wire Act is only applicable to betting in relation to sporting events or contests and does not prohibit states from operating lotteries online.[179] By extension, activities such as online poker and other games of

---

[168] *Id.* at 1.

[169] Data compiled from American Gaming Association, State Information, http://www. americangaming.org/industry-resources/state-information (last visited Mar. 6, 2012).

[170] Nevada employs a graduated tax on GGR of up to 6.75% plus up to an additional 1% to local jurisdictions, and taxes in the state can actually be as low as 3.5%.

[171] *Id.*

[172] *See id.* at http://www.americangaming.org/industry-resources/state-information/maine.

[173] *See id.* (describing South Dakota's tax regime, and Illinois, Indiana, and Missouri's imposition of admission taxes).

[174] *Id.*

[175] 18 U.S.C. § 1084 (2006).

[176] 31 U.S.C. §§ 5361-5367 (2006).

[177] 18 U.S.C. § 1084(a).

[178] *See, e.g.,* Joint Committee on Taxation, *supra* note 168, at 11.

[179] Whether Proposals by Illinois and New York to Use the Internet and Out-of-State Transaction Processors to Sell Lottery Tickets to In-State Adults Violate the Wire Act, Op.

skill, as well as casino games not involving sporting events, can be viewed as similarly outside the Wire Act's prohibitions.

On the other hand, UIGEA targets operators of gambling sites (as well as financial intermediaries) by prohibiting the acceptance of any financial instrument in connection with unlawful Internet gambling, which it defines as the interstate transmission of bets or wagers contrary to state or federal law.[180] Furthermore, several bills have been introduced in Congress that would authorize and provide for the licensure and taxation of online gambling operators.[181] Of note, the taxing schemes provided for in the proposed Internet Gambling Regulation and Tax Enforcement Act of 2010,[182] Internet Poker and Games of Skill Regulation, Consumer Protection, and Enforcement Act of 2009,[183] and Bipartisan Tax Fairness and Simplification Act of 2010[184] all provided for tax schemes (at various rates) based on "deposited funds"—that is, a license fee with deposit tax model.[185] Whether or not regulated online gambling becomes widespread in the United States may ultimately be dependent on state action and not federal action.

The Trend Toward Internet Gambling

Perhaps ironically, then, the first jurisdiction in the United States that moved to legalize online gambling was not a state, but the District of Columbia. Its program "iGaming" was to offer online poker, blackjack and bingo through Greece-based Intralot, but the program was repealed before it launched, reportedly due to a lack of opportunity for public scrutiny.[186]

Of the states, Nevada appears to be leading the charge in legalizing online gambling by fast-tracking legislation to permit and regulate online

---

Off. Legal Counsel Vol. 35 (Sept. 20, 2011), *available at* http://www.justice.gov/olc/2011/state-lotteries-opinion.pdf.

[180] 31 U.S.C. §§ 5363, 5362(10).

[181] Linda J. Shorey et al., *Taxing Schemes Proposed in Connection with Federal Bills That Would License Internet Gambling Operators*, K&L GATES (May 2010), *available at* http://www.klgates.com/taxing-schemes-proposed-in-connection-with-feder-al-bills-that-would-license-internet-gambling-operators-05-24-2010.

[182] H.R. 4976, 111th Cong. (2009).

[183] S. 1597, 111th Cong. (2009).

[184] S. 3018, 111th Cong. (2009).

[185] *Id.* (All three bills were referred to committee with no further action during the 2009-10 session.)

[186] Theo Emery, *Disputes in Washington End Online Gambling Program*, N.Y. TIMES (Feb. 16, 2012), *available at* http://www.nytimes.com/2012/02/16/us/disputes-end-online-gam-bling-deal-in-washington-dc.html?pagewanted=all; Tom Howell Jr., *Online-Gambling Bill's Future Uncertain*, WASH. TIMES (Feb. 12, 1012), *available at* http://www.washingtontimes.com/news/2012/feb/12/online-gambling-bills-future-uncertain. *See also* Justin Jouvenal & Michael Laris, *'Hot Spots' Part of D.C. Officials' Plan to Allow Internet-based Gambling In City*, THE WASH. POST (Apr. 13, 2011), *available at* http://www.washingtonpost.com/local/politics/dc-officials-plan-to-allow-internet-based-gambling-at-hot-spots-in-city/2011/04/13/AFbTRHZD_story.html (describing practical implementation of the envisioned program more fully).

poker between players. Proposed Nevada Gaming Commission regulation 5A.170[187] provides that gross revenue received by an establishment from the operation of interactive gaming is subject to the same license fee provisions as the games and gaming devices of the establishment, unless federal law otherwise provides for a similar fee or tax.[188] Specifically, operators would pay a license fee and monthly taxes based on gross revenue as in current land-based operation: 3.5 percent of the first $50,000 of monthly revenue; 4.5 percent of the next $84,000 of monthly revenue; and 6.75 percent of revenue exceeding $134,000 per month.[189]

In Florida, initially fervent attempts to legalize gambling in general and create a state Gaming Control Commission (primarily for the establishment of three large land-based casinos, but also through a set of regulations that would allow online gaming from internet cafes) have slowed, and the bill will not be seen again until the 2013 session, at the earliest.[190]

New Jersey's bill to allow for the operation of online casinos—as long as their servers were located in Atlantic City—passed easily through the state legislature but was vetoed by Governor Chris Christie last year; Christie reportedly rejected the theory that server location restrictions would pass New Jersey's constitutional muster.[191] Meanwhile in Iowa, State Senator Jeff Danielson plans to introduce a bill that would legalize online poker.[192]

And in California, lawmakers are considering legalizing online gambling for its claimed significant revenue potential, estimated by supporters at $100 million to $250 million per year.[193] The recently introduced "Internet Gambling Consumer Protection and Public-Private Partnership Act of 2012" proposes legalization of intrastate gambling in California, with operators being required to make a $30 million up-front "use-it-or-lose-it" deposit against which subsequent monthly gross gaming revenue taxes would be drawn.[194]

---

[187] *Available at* http://gaming.nv.gov/documents/pdf/reg5A_proposed_v11_11dec13.pdf.

[188] *Id.*

[189] Nevada Gaming Commission and State Gaming Control Board, Gaming License Fees and Tax Rate Schedule, http://gaming.nv.gov/taxfees.htm (last visited Mar. 6, 2012).

[190] *Florida En-Route to Allow Online Gambling in the State,* GAMINGZION (Jan. 10, 2012), http://gamingzion.com/gamblingnews/florida-en-route-to-allow-online-gambling-in-the-state-2420; Lizette Alvarez, *Florida Mega-Casino Bill Is Withdrawn,* N.Y. TIMES (Feb. 3, 2012), *available at* http://www.nytimes.com/2012/02/04/us/florida-lawmaker-withdraws-casino-bill.html.

[191] Lisa Fleisher, *Christie Vetoes Online Gambling Bill,* WALL ST. J. (Mar. 3, 2011), *available at* http://blogs.wsj.com/metropolis/2011/03/03/christie-vetoes-online-gambling-bill.

[192] Lynn Campbell, *Iowa Will Attempt to Follow Lead of Nevada, D.C. in Legalizing Online Poker,* IOWAPOLITICS.COM (Feb. 1, 2012), http://www.iowapolitics.com/index.iml?Article=259831.

[193] Penelope Lemov, *The Pros and Cons of Internet Gambling,* GOVERNING (Feb. 16, 2012), *available at* http://www.governing.com/columns/public-finance/col-pros-cons-gambling-internet-online-poker.html.

[194] S.B. 1463, 2011-2012 Sess. (Cal. 2012).

Recommendations and Survey Summary

Perhaps the most obvious policy goals of legalizing and regulating online gambling are to provide consumer protection and to generate tax revenue. Furthermore, the regulation of online gambling may reduce the prevalence of unlicensed or extraterritorially licensed operators. Jurisdictions considering the legalization and regulation of online gambling must structure their licensing and taxation models in such a way as to best achieve these goals. It seems likely that, whether at the federal or local level, or across multiple jurisdictions, regulators will have to choose whether to adopt licensing fee regimes with a tax on either volume or profit—that is, a deposit tax or GGR tax. In addition, a high initial license fee, which should be credited as a deposit on taxes for a stated period of time, would help ensure the licensing jurisdiction has limited its financial risk through collections of taxes up-front. The central tax issue is therefore whether a deposit tax or GGR tax model would be more appropriate. As shown, a tension exists between the gaming industry preference for a GGR tax model and the regulatory preference for a deposit tax. While a GGR tax model seemingly tends to lower the business risk borne by operators, the timing of a deposit tax—as customers establish online accounts, as opposed to periodically calculated and collected in arrears—is preferable from a regulatory standpoint, and might make more sense in the context of online gambling.

A deposit tax also is more efficient because it is game neutral, as opposed to the calculation of GGR for operators offering a variety of game types. In the case of multi-jurisdictional regulation, a deposit tax is a tax on player funds where the place of residence or location of the player is readily identifiable, thus providing accountability and auditability advantages for the relevant locale. Calculations for operators are easy and transparent, as is verifying that they have paid the correct amount—reducing costs for both operators and regulators. Finally, a deposit model creates additional enforcement mechanisms by enabling regulators to impose the deposit tax liability (plus penalties) on players using unlicensed sites.

The "net deposit" model offers a neat compromise between pure volume-based and profit-based tax models. As discussed in Part II, operator concerns regarding a deposit tax are mitigated by giving tax credits for withdrawals from customer accounts (or customer withdrawals from accounts—for example, in the event that the customer has not played at all). This method lowers the perceived operator-side business risk and still allows regulators to collect fees as deposits are made, simplifying the regulatory system and lowering the costs involved for all parties. Alternatively, operators could charge a penalty for early customer account withdrawal or closure, but this may deter some customers from participating and could diminish the overall market to the detriment of operators and regulating jurisdictions alike.

On the other hand, a hybrid model might be developed—as illustrated by the large economies of Australia, Italy, and Spain. Certain gambling activities such as online casinos might be taxed according to a GGR model at a moderate rate, while others such as lotteries, bookmakers, and games of skill would not be inhibited by a net deposit model at a competitive rate. Despite their complexities, hybrid models could also be tailored for each specific jurisdiction. Different states have very different existing gambling markets, so each could adopt a model that suits its regulatory, economic, and social needs.

The five largest economies surveyed above in Part III have adopted different approaches to regulated Internet gambling. The largest, France, has adopted a turnover model at a rate of 7.5 percent across the board, but is arguably losing market share to other jurisdictions such as Italy and Spain. The United Kingdom has treated its online gambling market similarly to its land-based market through the application of a 15 percent GGR tax on top of a somewhat complex licensing regime. Canada (ranked fourth) prefers a monopoly model, where each Province operates its own gaming sites. Finally, Italy (ranked third) and Spain (ranked fifth) both utilize hybrid models with turnover and GGR taxes based on game category.

The following chart summarizes the survey:

Nation / State	GDP Rank*	Online Game Categories	Tax Model Summary
A. Monopoly Models			
Austria	12	Games of chance.	Government operator.
Canada	4	Provincial governments operate online lotteries, fixed odds, and casino games.	Government operator.
Hong Kong	15	Pari-mutuel betting and lottery.	Exclusive rights in Hong Kong Jockey Club.
Hungary	17	Lottery, sports betting, and prize draw ticket games.	Government operator.
Macau	21	Horse Racing.	Exclusive operator paying 35 percent GGR tax.
Netherlands	7	Online casinos, bingo, poker, and sports.	Government operator.
New Zealand	18	Totalizators and Lotteries only.	Government operator.
Sweden	11	Comprehensive.	Government operator.
Turkey	8	Sports betting.	Government operator.

B. Free Market Jurisdictions			
Alderney	N/A	Comprehensive.	License fees vary from £35,000 to £140,000 depending on revenue tier.
Costa Rica	20	Comprehensive.	$15,000 corporate and license fee with $1500 quarterly renewals; no additional taxation.
Isle of Man	27	Comprehensive.	£5,000 application, £35,000 per year (for 5-year terms).
Kahnawake	N/A	Online casinos and poker rooms.	License fees only, no taxation.
Panama	22	Comprehensive.	Seven-year master license is $40,000; additional annual fee of $20,000.
C. Limited Free Market Model			
Belgium	10	Comprehensive.	Taxation (a reported 11 percent flat tax) per individual licensing agreements, very limited on a per-game basis.
D. Licensing Fee with GGR Tax			
Antigua and Barbuda	30	Comprehensive.	3 percent GGR tax (with a cap of $50,000 per month); gaming license is $75,000 annually and wagering license is $50,000 annually.
Curacao	26	Comprehensive.	2 percent GGR tax; monthly fee of about $5,000 for 2 years.
Dominican Republic	19	Comprehensive.	5 percent GGR tax with a $50,000 minimum, plus $15,000 license fee.
Estonia	24	Chance, skill, pari-mutuel betting.	5 percent sales tax plus licenses at the rates of: €48,000 for games of chance; €32,000 for games of skill; and €3,200 for tote boards.

*GDP rank is relative to other surveyed jurisdictions using data from World Bank, Gross Domestic Product 2010, http://siteresources.worldbank.org/DATASTATISTICS/Resources/GDP.pdf."N/A" indicates data is either unavailable or not applicable.

Greece	14	Comprehensive.	30 percent GGR tax. VLT licenses are about €15,000 ea.; and limited online gaming licenses will be somewhere in the order of €1-5 million for a five-year term.
Philippines	16	Casinos, sports books, sports betting.	5 percent corporate tax and 2% GGR tax, plus a range of licensing fees.
United Kingdom	2	General betting, bingo, pools (licensed brick and mortar operators).	15 percent GGR tax.
E. Licensing Fee with Turnover Tax			
Belize	28	Comprehensive.	0.75 percent turnover tax.
Cyprus	23	Sports betting and lotteries.	3 percent turnover tax.
France	1	Comprehensive.	7.5 percent turnover tax.
Malta	25	Comprehensive.	0.5% percent turnover tax.
Poland	9	Casino games by Fortuna.	2-45 percent turnover tax, depending on the game (only one licensee so far).
F. Hybrid Models			
Australia	6	Online wagering, lotteries, and keno.	Complex hybrid model with differing models and rates by states and territories.
Denmark	13	The state-owned monopoly, Danske Spil, holds the sole online gambling licenses for horse racing and online bingo. Online sports betting and casinos licensed on limited basis.	Hybrid 20 percent GGR tax for online casinos and online sports betting, and state monopoly over horse racing and bingo.

Gibraltar	29	Bookmakers:	1 percent turnover tax capped at £425,000 annually; minimum gaming tax £85,000 annually. Licenses renewable annually for £2,000.
		Internet casinos:	1 percent GGR tax; similar caps and fees.
Italy	3	Online gambling, with exceptions below:	20 percent GGR tax.
		VLTs, sports and horse racing, bingo, lotteries, and games of skill:	3 percent turnover tax.
Spain	5	Mutual sports betting, sports betting exchange, horseracing counterpart betting, other mutual betting, other counterpart betting, raffles, contests, random combinations:	10-35 percent turnover tax depending on the game; limited licensure.
		Cross-sports betting, horseracing mutual betting, other games:	15-20 percent GGR tax depending on the game; limited licensure.
Vanuatu	31	General gaming:	2.5 percent GGR tax. $35,000 application plus $30,000 annually for sports books; other operators pay $75,000 application plus $50K annually.
		Fixed odds wagering:	0.1 percent turnover tax, plus above license fees.

4

Technical Compliance

Richard Williamson

"The success of each is dependent upon the success of each other."
John D. Rockefeller, Jr.

This quote embraces the concept of the system of controls that is the essential underpinning to the gaming industry's success. In the aftermath of an operational situation that draws the attention of casino management, regulators, reporters, and editorializers, the inevitable question arises: "How do we prevent this from happening again?" To fully answer this question, it is necessary to convey the expectations for involved parties, create the rules of engagement, and establish a level of oversight that corresponds to a particular jurisdiction's regulatory tolerance for unlawful and undesirable operations. Over the many years of regulated gaming operations, and even prior to any formal government oversight, gaming controls and procedures have evolved, typically in response to hard-learned lessons. In the absence of organized and documented controls, success is achieved only by chance and the probability of failure remains at a higher level than is necessary. Effective controls, which should use defined procedures and segregated duties, need to be designed to reveal the occurrence of fraud, embezzlement, a loss of assets, or falsified financial reports within a reasonable time. Though these controls need to be self-policing in their prescribed execution, they are not the only form of oversight intended for compliance testing. The regulator approves the controls, inspects the implementation of same, and conducts (or requires an authorized independent entity to conduct) audits testing adherence to the required controls. Statistical sampling allows for efficient, objective, and reliable analysis of data and consequently provides a scientifically derived confidence level with an expected deviation rate.

Two Case Studies On Risk Tolerance

Gaming jurisdictions establish their risk tolerance through adopted controls. This practice is not restricted to the gambling industry; it also is a central concept in many other contexts including the accounting profession, occupational and health safety practices, rules of the road, the FAA, the FDA, and now the detection of anticipated terroristic activities. All travelers routinely boarded planes for years without having to remove their shoes. The procedures implemented by the US government have demonstrated that the risk tolerance for another terrorist-related aviation disaster is very low. In contrast, two cases involving Internet gambling are extreme examples where the risk tolerance appeared to be high. In these cases the operational problems were discovered outside the regulatory structure when they could have been revealed or prevented through implementing a more effective oversight scheme. A lesson learned from these examples involves the timing of audits for financial transactions. The second example demonstrates the need for analyzing risks and creating appropriate rules to guide product analysis. New jurisdictions implementing Internet gaming should note these two examples and draft their rules to avoid history from repeating itself on their watch.

A September 20, 2011, press release from the United States Attorney regarding United States v. Full Tilt Poker stated:

> In reality, Full Tilt Poker did not maintain funds sufficient to repay all players, and in addition, the company used player funds to pay board members and other owners more than $440 million since April 2007. Between April 2007 and April 2011, Full Tilt Poker and its Board distributed approximately $443,860,529.89 to Board members and owners. By March 31, 2011, Full Tilt Poker owed approximately $390 million to players around the world, including approximately $150 million to United States players. However, the company had only approximately $60 million in its bank accounts.[1]

Full Tilt also was plagued by a U.S. payment processing network that had been disrupted, preventing the company from pulling money from customers' bank accounts to fund online gambling credits.

Instead of disclosing the problem, prosecutors said, Full Tilt maintained a false image of financial stability by crediting players' accounts with $130 million in "phantom funds." When players gambled with these funds and lost to other players, a "massive shortfall" developed, they said.[2]

The first case involved Full Tilt Poker operating with a license from the Alderney Gambling Control Commission (AGCC). Here, the fraudulent activity did not involve financial transactions from gambling activities. Rather, efforts by the U.S. government obstructed many of the deposits from U.S. patrons. Notwithstanding this, Full Tilt Poker recorded the attempted deposits as being received and created financial statements to that effect. When the scheme was ultimately revealed, the AGCC took

[1] Press Release, U.S. Attorney S. Dist. of N.Y., re *United States v. Full Tilt Poker* (Sept. 20, 2011), *available at* http://www.justice.gov/usao/nys/pressreleases/September11/amendedfulltiltpokercomplaintpr.pdf
[2] Tiffany Hsu, *Full Tilt Poker Built Ponzi Scheme, Federal Prosecutors Say*, L.A. Times, Sept. 21, 2011, http://articles.latimes.com/2011/sep/21/business/la-fi-online-poker-20110921

appropriate action regarding its licensee's failure to adhere to the regulations.

In the second case, player observations and not regulatory oversight revealed the fraudulent activity associated with the Absolute Poker site, which was licensed by the Kahnawake Gaming Commission. The vehicle for the player fraud was a software design that enabled the perpetrator to view the players' hole cards during the game. Two questions surface in this situation; What controls could or should have been in place to detect the system feature that enabled other patrons to be exploited? Have other Internet gaming regulators studied and adopted controls to detect within a reasonable time non-compliance for these particular violations as well as others? The Kahnawake rules were not part of this review and no opinion can be offered regarding whether there now exists one or more rules to guide operators, software developers and test labs to avoid a similar event. There was nothing obvious in the rules of the four jurisdictions studied herein that anticipates or thwarts this particular criminal act.

Regulators generally require professional consulting assistance to create effective rules to combat these technical problems. Certain areas of control are anticipated in the enabling legislation for Internet gambling and then controls are further defined in accompanying regulations. As these and future regulatory infractions are discovered, the rules should be modified through the adoption of appropriate controls. Indeed, this is the evolutionary nature of regulations in the gambling industry.

No regulator, operator, or jurisdiction wants to be associated with these two high-profile examples of fraudulent activities. Internet gaming, like terrestrial gaming, is dependent on the reliability of the equipment, the design of adequate controls, and the management's implementation of these controls. Without the commitment of both the operator and regulator to evaluate, test, and document the various systems associated with Internet gaming, no real assurance exists that unauthorized or undesired activities will be promptly detected.

In an atypical manner for a regulatory body, subsequent to the formal hearings on Full Tilt Poker, the AGCC engaged Peter Dean, the former Chairman of the British Gambling Commission to conduct a formal, independent inquiry "…to review and report on the actions taken by AGCC in relation to companies together trading as Full Tilt Poker, with particular reference to the appropriateness, timeliness and fairness of such actions."[3] The report generally gave the AGCC high marks and stated; "… a regulatory inspection is not designed to uncover fraud, but is an operational process review."[4] Regulators might wonder, however, if the regulatory controls are not designed to detect fraud in a timely manner, how then is fraud to

---

[3] Peter Dean, *Report by Peter Dean to the Alderney Gambling Control Comm'n*, Alderney Gambling Control Comm'n 1 (Mar. 26, 2012), *available at* http://www.gamblingcontrol.org/userfiles/file/FTP%20Report%2026%20March%202012.pdf

[4] *Id.* at 8.

be discovered and on what time schedule? Surely the prevention and detection of fraud needs to reside within the adoption and implementation of a regulatory framework. The rules examined in this chapter are viewed with respect to their effectiveness from the perspective of whether they are meaningful, enforceable and auditable.

Although the examples of the Full Tilt Poker case in Alderney and the Absolute Poker situation in the Kahnawake jurisdiction are not the subjects of this chapter, they are useful knowledge when considering what controls should be in place to avoid a similar set of circumstances and for any activity deemed worthy of being subjected to regulatory oversight.

Well-designed rules need effective implementation. Regulators do not like surprises. They want to know the status of their licensees' compliance from the results of their own oversight and not from investigations by foreign jurisdictions. This was not the case in Alderney. As Mr. Dean states in his report, the AGCC was just as surprised as its licensee; "The (United States) DoJ's operations were covert and a well-kept secret until revealed to the world by the unsealing of the indictment in the Southern District of New York on 15 April 2011."[5] The DoJ did not find anything that was not available through an audit process. The DoJ as a law enforcement agency chose not to involve the AGCC or any Alderney law enforcement entity in its investigation. One can only speculate on the reasons for DoJ's silence but the message advises regulators who want to avoid surprises to 'know your licensee'.

Regulators cannot assume that their respective adopted regulatory scheme is effective based on a compliance certification of its operation. Compliance with an ineffective rule does not make the operation secure. Close evaluation of gaming operation rules to be adopted and subsequent reviews of their effectiveness through empirical data or other reliable means will reveal whether the rules are of such caliber and implemented with sufficient frequency and thoroughness that a failure in compliance will raise timely suspicions leading to initiate an investigation and to limit the exposure of non-compliance.

JURISDICTIONAL COMPETITION

Adopting technical controls in egaming jurisdictions present unique challenges. In a terrestrial environment, casino operators must make physical and financial commitments when entering a jurisdiction. The same is not true for Internet gaming as was noted by Mr. Dean in his report to Alderney:

Smaller jurisdictions that regulate egambling, such as Malta, Gibraltar, the Isle of Man and Alderney, are to some extent in competition with each other. Potential licensees can and do shop around with a view to finding the jurisdiction that best suits their needs having regard to political stabil-

---

[5] *Id.* at 8.

ity, the business environment, technical infrastructure, tax regime, costs of licensing and so on.[6]

The "...and so on..." could be technical standards including infrastructure requirements. Because Internet gaming businesses can easily move and still have a global presence from wherever they set up shop, jurisdictions may find themselves competing to attract and keep businesses; however, this type of competition could frustrate the effectiveness of regulations.

Developing Rules

The process for coordinating the approach to create quality rules is by drawing on the best sources available. There is more to creating rules than merely copying another jurisdiction's regulations. In fact, copying rules and making changes without analysis of policy goals often results in an ineffective process since the actual intent or implementation does not accompany the regulations. Experience with external professionals helps the regulator understand and appreciate the full scope of services that are available. To begin the process of designing a system to regulate the technical elements of a gaming operation, a jurisdiction must identify all of the gaming system's components and then decide to what extent each component should be controlled. Once established, the minimum technical standards can be developed for each component if necessary and collectively as a system. Accompanying operational controls are guides for the audits that will be conducted. Technical standards guide both the testing process and the development of internal controls. It is important that a jurisdiction take ownership of its adopted rules. No changes should ever occur without adherence to an established and transparent process for adopting and modifying regulations.

Expert Advice

To various degrees, all jurisdictions rely on the expertise of independent companies and organizations in the performance of regulatory duties. Government agencies typically are not staffed with personnel equipped to certify the adequacy of the companies or organizations providing professional services. In these cases, therefore, reliance on the certifications of these external entities is essential. Consequently government agencies must have reliable metrics to establish and maintain the qualifications of these independent organizations. Examples are accounting firms performing certified financial audits that are required to be qualified to standards established by a state government agency and testing laboratories that operate in adherence with applicable requirements of the International Organization of Standardization (ISO).

When working with outside professionals, questions will undoubtedly surface regarding interpretations of advice received on gambling rules. The

---

[6] *Id.* at 6.

regulator has ultimate responsibility to interpret any particular technical standard or mandate the need for new internal controls. Indeed, the final interpretation of any expert advice may require additional controls or, due to technological advances, the relaxation of some requirements. Importantly, when a statute cites a minimum standard as a required control, the regulator needs a greater knowledge of the subject to adopt effective standards that provide better guidance for implementation of the rules. Clearly expressed standards leave little interpretation to their intent and increase the potential of operational predictability.

TESTING INTERPRETATIONS AND INSTALLATION VERIFICATION

Typically, the integrity of gaming products is evaluated using rules that are common to many jurisdictions; however, the interpretation of the rules and the prescribed minimum operating requirements vary across jurisdictions. Gaming systems, game programs, and monitoring tools are subjected to a battery of evaluations designed to verify compliance with regulations and to establish predictable results in technical laboratory environments. The testing procedures that exist today are the result of an evolution in technology, operating environments, and test lab experience. Solid testing standards form the foundation for successful processes to monitor, audit, investigate and confirm the integrity of an Internet gambling operation from an operational perspective. The installation inspection and verification is likely the most important initial step in evaluating compliance because it establishes the base line against which future examinations will be compared. Ensuring the compliance of a gaming product operation is the foundation upon which the internal controls and auditing procedures are based. Traditionally, jurisdictions require compliance verification processes be conducted prior to live action and thereafter the monitoring process is initiated. Without a requirement that the regulator establish an initial baseline compliance inspection, any subsequent monitoring for product compliance will likely yield information which does not reliably measure the integrity of the gaming systems or identify points of failure.

This chapter examines technical standards already adopted by jurisdictions and compares their effectiveness, with particular emphasis on the oversight necessary to ensure operational compliance. A close review of the selected rules will reveal the jurisdiction's intended depth of regulatory oversight and thus the risk tolerance of that jurisdiction. A study of these rules and others not included in this study can reveal that some jurisdiction's oversight consists of very effective technical standards despite a very high-risk tolerance regarding the required oversight. Staffing and funding plays a big part in ensuring operational integrity. This chapter is intended to objectively evaluate the regulatory landscape of controls and help the reader draw conclusions about a jurisdiction's intended level of risk tolerance. In short, the focus of this chapter is observing rules in jurisdictions where technical solutions are needed to achieve regulatory goals and mandates. One constant across jurisdictions is that where technical solutions are warranted, testing by qualified entities is necessary to ensure compliance.

THE TESTING PROCESS

Testing an Internet system has many similarities to testing terrestrial casino equipment. Both forms of gambling use computer systems designed to operate and monitor gaming activities. All Internet gaming activities occur on servers designed to accommodate and monitor peer to peer gambling activities, casino games, common outcome games like bingo or keno, sports betting, or other contests like chess or backgammon. In basic terms, there are two forms of testing. When a test lab verifies that a system and games work as designed, that is called a functional test. Because a functional test alone cannot verify whether the system or games are in compliance with jurisdictional rules, test labs also must look to the jurisdiction's adopted rules for criteria that can be made part of a test plan.

If a rule is not sufficiently specific about acceptable test results and measuring compliance, test labs may not have a useful or appropriate method for testing compliance. For example, a rule may state that "The system must … if utilised in any peer to peer game, ensure that over the specified periods that no one Player has any advantage over any other Player playing the same game."[7] A test lab cannot create a test plan for this rule until it reviews the licensee's submission, and the effectiveness of the design is ultimately a judgment call. The evaluation will likely be based on the implementation of accompanying internal control procedures. In this specific case, the rule calls not for internal controls but for the system to have the oversight capability. Further, the effectiveness of any technical approach that is developed to ensure compliance with this rule cannot be measured without empirical evidence. The ultimate proof of compliance, and the value of such a rule, requires the development of an audit procedure to measure the effectiveness of the system's features. Evaluating the effectiveness of any procedure developed to comply with this rule will largely depend upon the associated risk tolerance for the prohibited activity. Thus, although the rule sounds good and its intent appears to be clear, there is no guidance regarding what evaluative approach is acceptable or how its effectiveness will be measured. In all fairness, a written policy may exist to establish what is deemed to be acceptable but that information cannot be gleaned from the rule.

---

[7] Isle of Man, The Online Gambling (Systems Verification) (No. 2) Regulations, Schedule 1 (1)(d) (2007), *available at* http://www.gov.im/lib/docs/gambling/Regulations/onlinegamblingsystemverification.pdf

Rule Structure And Topics

In this study of rules from several jurisdictions, two basic regulatory approaches emerge. Some jurisdictions provide descriptions of standards as a guide: characteristics of what ought to be done within the application of the standard. The use of "should" appears throughout these descriptions with little specificity as to the actual design of a compliant product. The second approach establishes standards that provide very specific requirements to which the applicant must fulfill without deviation. This review showed that in every case rules were silent on the specific technology of system components, thereby leaving that choice to the licensee. Under the first rule structure described, the licensee documents the method of compliance and then submits that manner of compliance to the regulator for evaluation; the regulator may require testing by a third party or conduct an internal review or both. Under the second rule structure described above, the minimum acceptable criteria are specifically set forth and the licensee either develops a product or selects a pre-approved product; the licensee then submits the product for evaluation with the required documentation.

Collectively, the sampled Internet gaming rules require the licensee to provide documentation to demonstrate that the operator's procedures meet minimum guidelines for creating and implementing physical controls for the server room, authorized server room locations, compliant firewalls and external connections, encryption practices or similar security provisions, a logical security methodology, a documented personnel hierarchy for data access and responsibilities, report creation capabilities, disaster recovery procedures, domain name server requirements, software change procedures, and authentication algorithms. Not all of these subjects were addressed within each of the selected jurisdiction's rules. Knowing that all of these subjects do not receive equal treatment within the rules studied is important if someone intends to copy from these rules.

Software Authentication

The objective of controls concerning software authentication is to ensure that the software operating at an Internet site is identical to the software that was tested and approved to operate the site. The rules reviewed in the various jurisdictions mandate an inspection to verify compliance of the installed software but often with little specific description of what details of the inspection need to be recorded. Actual practices may have evolved to a policy of specific information being recorded but without that underlying information, simply copying a jurisdiction's rules could leave important aspects of the oversight operation undocumented. Verification of test lab report documentation against the actual installation can be accomplished by a technical review with the services of a test lab. The on-site review at the time of the installation or at the inaugural go-live will provide verification of the system details. Besides this verification, implementation of other control procedures such as remote access and firewall installations need to be considered. The inspection process provides assurances that the installed operating system represents what was documented or tested. A rule mandating that a "…system must be authenticated prior to execution using a means approved by the Chairman."[8] establishes that verifications of the installed software, system components and system configurations are performed. The method that will be *approved by the Chairman* is not made clear and using this rule would require research to determine what authentication and documentation methods are acceptable. Besides an initial baseline verification, there may be rules to test continued compliance. The verification process in Nevada continues pursuant to the following rule:

Interactive gaming systems must be capable of verifying that all control programs contained on the interactive gaming system are authentic copies of approved components of the interactive gaming system automatically, at least once every 24 hours, and on demand.[9]

This rule provides for a system to conduct a perpetual verification process that will enable designated personnel to verify the system within every 24 hour period. To ensure that these authentication events can be reviewed, the rules require that the results of each "…authentication must be retained and be accessible for a period of 90 days."[10] The authentication process is a very important tool for verifying that the system is operating in the same manner as when it was last inspected. This method also recognizes that the subsequent failure of a component is a potential threat to the integrity of the system: "[t]he interactive gaming system must provide a mechanism to visually notify the operator of any control program that fails an authentication."[11] Indeed, Nevada uses a belt and suspenders approach. If the system administrator does not confirm a failed authentication notice within 72 hours, the rule requires "the interactive gaming system to automatically stop any gaming related functions."[12] This rule is very straight forward in its intent and provides the developer and testing entity with explicitly detailed processes when creating and verifying the product.

The situations that can cause a failed authentication are varied. The testing lab's scientists understand the architecture of gaming systems and, as part of their testing, target areas intended to be protected by this rule. Gaming systems are very complex and failures can occur in numerous areas. Testing is best conducted by intentionally causing several failures to ensure that all the required actions do, in fact, occur as articulated in the rules. The process of testing involves documenting the results of each

---

[8] Nev. Gaming Regulation 14, Attachment 1: Technical Standards for Gaming Devices & Associated Equip., Standard 6: Interactive Gaming Systems & Associated Equip., § 6.140(2) (2012), *available at http://gaming.nv.gov/modules/showdocument. aspx?documentid=2914*
[9] *Id.* at § 6.140(3).
[10] *Id.*
[11] *Id.*
[12] *Id.*

particular testing procedure; the self authentication process, visual notice of the failed authentication, verifying that no response to the failed authentication notice does cause the system to cease operations, verifying that the system maintains a log of authentications and the results for 90 days, and testing the manner in which the system handles game activity in progress when the system is required to automatically stop.

Alderney's rule for self monitoring critical components touches on the authentication concept but does not articulate the expected component reaction once a failure occurs: "IGSs (Internet gaming systems) should implement self-monitoring of critical components."[13] The remaining two jurisdiction's rules do not have language that provides such specific instruction on software verification. There may be undocumented practices in place within these jurisdictions but without having the regulatory requirements in writing, implementation will be subjective. Of course, if a system were to operate as required by Nevada, there is no apparent reason why any of these other three jurisdictions would object to its operating methodology.

System Recovery

The objective of controls concerning system recovery is to ensure all player activity is captured to resolve any player disputes after a technical failure. In the competitive world of Internet gaming, being on-line one hundred percent of the time is a mission critical goal. Customer service is part of that critical goal particularly when technical situations may interrupt the gaming activity. A system that captures all player activity after a technical failure best supports effective customer relations by offering the ability to resolve any player disputes. The gaming site's reputation can only be maintained if the system can successfully recover and still retain play activity. As important, it protects the assets of the operation against false claims of monies due. Properly implemented, this process of monitoring the software integrity allows the operator to comply with the following rules:

Interactive gaming systems must be able to save information pertinent to any game, session, player session or interactive gaming account such that all game, session, and account information can be recovered in the event of a power loss or other critical failure of the interactive gaming system.[14]

Interactive gaming systems must be capable of performing the following administrative activities to resolve incomplete games: … Maintain a record of any game that fails to complete along with the reason why the

---

[13] Alderney, Technical Standards Extract Document v2.0, § 5.2.14 (2012), available at http://www.gamblingcontrol.org/userfiles/file/Technical%20Standards%20Document%20 v%202_0%20120330.pdf
[14] *Id.* at § 6.140(5).

game failed to complete. This record should include all information necessary to continue a partially complete game and should be retained indefinitely or until the game is resolved or voided…[15]

These rules require administrative activities to record the reason(s) games are not completed. Accompanying internal controls must direct specific personnel to create the required logs and or documents. The intent of these rules is to document the activity for proper settlement of any claims. Using the word 'should' in the last rule quoted indicates that the regulator understands that retaining all the information under certain circumstances of failures may be difficult. Using *should* does, however, seem to be inconsistent with the specific direction of rule § 6.140(5) previously cited. The testing process can identify some of those failure circumstances but the operator is given some latitude for compliance with this rule. Use of the word 'should' generally indicates regulatory flexibility.

These rules regarding information recovery are very clear in their intent yet the technical implementation is challenging due the various situations that result in incomplete games. System developers need to design to a variety of failures and develop data capturing methods for unanticipated circumstances. In a different set of rules examined from the Isle of Man the requirement was written, "The system must…integrate contingencies for loss of continuity of play;…" [16] In similar fashion to Nevada, without citing specific recovery methods regarding the nature of the contingencies, the methods which achieve the stated goal will probably vary widely. Furthermore, in a jurisdiction with many systems, the appropriate forensic examination processes will differ. Due to the technical nature of this area, the test lab is left to conduct a functional examination of the recovery methods incorporated into each system and opine on whether the system's design meets the rule as the regulatory authors intended.

From the developer and test lab's perspective, finding the regulatory intent is always a challenge. When entire segments of rules for a jurisdiction are not fully developed beyond the concept, the test lab must document the regulatory intent in its test scripts based on clarity provided by the regulator. Proper testing procedures require that the rule interpretation be documented, test scripts be revised, and then reissued through the test lab's quality system. Confirmation of regulatory intent is an important part of producing and documenting consistent test results.

This complexity of system and component failures is compounded because each system approval sets a precedent. For a jurisdiction to enforce more stringent product designs after issuing approvals is always a regulatory challenge regarding disparate treatment to licensees, grandfathering approvals, sunset provisions, and challenges to adopting rule modifications. In reality, the rules of Isle of Man, Malta or Alderney do not anticipate the licensee implementing a daily self-authentication methodology that would

---

[15] *Id.* at § 6.180(2).
[16] Isle of Man, *supra* note 7, at Schedule 1 (1)(c).

result in a system shut down. Again, if a system were to operate as required by Nevada, the three other jurisdictions mentioned earlier would have no obvious reason to object to such a system's operating methodology nor to require such a methodology for previously approved systems. Although not prescriptive in nature, the Nevada rules provide the most clear guidance for the desired system recovery goals.

GAME INTERRUPTIONS

The objective of controls designed to prevent game interruption is to protect the player when their ability to complete a game is interrupted primarily due to an Internet connectivity problem. The cause of the interruption can occur on either end of the connection or from problems with the service provider. The rules in Malta mainly pertain to circumstances where the player's computer or network connection was the cause of a game interruption.

A licensee shall take all reasonable steps to ensure that the licensee's approved computer system enables a player whose participation in a game is...interrupted by a failure of the telecommunications system or a failure of the player's computer system that prevents the player from continuing the game, to resume...[17]

The Malta rule will most likely be a combination of system design and accompanying internal controls. The method of compliance with this rule will require the internal control to ensure that the steps taken are reasonable with respect to their effectiveness.

The Isle of Man requires that "The System must... integrate contingencies for loss of continuity of play...".[18] This rule may also be applicable to system recovery but is primarily concerned with the customer play experience.

In Alderney the requirement for malfunctioning or non-responsive games consists of the following: "[t]he message 'Malfunction Voids All Pays and Play' or its equivalent should be clearly displayed on the rules for each game. Detail the procedures which describe what will be done in the event of non-responsive or problem games."[19] On its face, this rule is not a test to be conducted by a test lab. Compliance with the rule appears to be a procedure documented in internal controls. Even from the cited Malta rule one could conclude that the situation may involve some computer guided automated actions once a game failure occurs and that a computer programmed mechanism designed to comply with the intent of this rule would be tested for its functionality and effectiveness.

Nevada directs the operator to incorporate the following procedures:

---

[17] Malta, Remote Gaming Regulations, § 47(1) (amended 2011), *available at* http://www.lga.org.mt/lga/content.aspx?id=87374
[18] Isle of Man, *supra* note 7, at Schedule 1 (1)(c).
[19] Alderney, *supra* note 13, at § 4.5.1.

Interactive gaming systems must be capable of performing the following administrative activities as it relates to incomplete games or tournaments:

(a) Maintain a record of any game or tournament that fails to complete along with the reason why the game or tournament failed to complete if the reason is known. This record should include all information necessary to continue a partially complete game or tournament and should be retained indefinitely or until the game or tournament is resolved or voided;

(b) Resume an incomplete game or tournament if all information and authorized players are available and acknowledge the game is to be resumed; and

(c) Return all wagers or any awards previously agreed upon to players in the event an incomplete game or tournament cannot be finished.[20]

As a precursor to establishing gaming activities with a patron the Nevada rules require the operator to verify whether any incompatibilities exist in the patron's computer:

Authorized player software used in conjunction with the interactive gaming system must be able to detect any incompatibilities or resource limitations with the authorized player system that would prevent proper operation of the authorized player software and prevent any installation or gaming activity. Authorized players must be notified of any incompatibility and/or resource limitation preventing operation.[21]

This Nevada rule is a pure technical implementation and is a solid requirement to avoid several problems. The rule does not state that the gaming activity cannot occur when an incompatibility is detected, that judgment call appears to belong to the operator. In the Nevada rules, the regulatory requirements are not specific regarding technology; therefore, any submission from an operator or developer must be evaluated to determine whether the solution is one to be tested, whether the solution will be an internal control procedure, or both. Most controls are likely to include both technical and internal controls that are interdependent. Guidance from the Nevada rules is more specific regarding the intended outcome but, like the other jurisdictions, it does not dictate how the matters are to be resolved and in what combination of automation and internal controls.

Regulators adopting any of these rules will need to establish their own technical specifications and level of oversight which will certainly evolve with available technology and experience. In general, rules are not to be written and forgotten, continued evaluation of rule effectiveness is necessary to manage risk.

---

[20] Nev. Gaming Regulation, *supra* note 8, at § 6.180(2).
[21] Nev. Gaming Regulation, § 6.150(2).

SOFTWARE CHANGE CONTROLS

Software change controls in the terrestrial world often involve mandated oversight as a necessary step to prevent the installation of unauthorized software upgrades or modifications and to establish a known good at a specific point in time. This process may be largely an internal control procedure but system requirements can assist in conducting a review for adherence to rules for unauthorized software changes. This area of control also touches on system access controls. Best practices for rules monitoring changes to Internet gaming software are those that provide the regulator with certainty that only authorized software has been installed and those actions are accompanied with a record of all changes regardless of whether or not they were authorized.

Some necessary background on software verification methodology can be gleaned from established procedures. Testing and auditing conducted to ensure whether the approved programs have been modified requires verification of the electronic message digest of specific system components. If the electronic signatures change from the previous version of software, it is common to require a source code review to evaluate the nature of the changes. Alderney and Malta regulations specifically reference concern regarding changes to source code. Isle of Man rules are silent on the matter as is Nevada. The difference for Nevada is that it has its own test lab. That Nevada's rules are silent on the matter of source code reviews is consistent with prior practice since the same language is absent in Nevada Regulation 14 for Technical Standards for Gaming Devices and On-Line Slot Systems. State operated labs in the United States have a common practice for manufacturers to submit source code which is always subject to review. That said and in light of Nevada outsourcing testing to independent test labs, clear instruction from each jurisdiction of what needs to be submitted for testing is preferable.

A key element to ensuring gaming integrity for software is the use of cryptographic hash algorithms for creating message digests or hash values for the purpose of verifying that software has not been changed. In the thirty years prior to this publication the use of message digests have become standard practice in the gaming industry, particularly since each program is tested once and then used in hundreds of different locations. This evaluation technique enables a relatively simple but robust verification process to be available to hundreds of regulators and operators to ensure that a program has not changed since its original evaluation. The most significant and convenient factor is that the verification tools do not require access to the original program for comparison. In gaming, the risk tolerance has been set low for changes to game programs. If the message digest of a program scheduled for installation does not match what has been recorded and approved in the test lab report, the person performing the verification will have no clue as to why the message digest is different. Due to the robust nature of cryptographic algorithms, a different signature can be the result of either a one bit change or modifications of massive sections to the program. This lack of knowledge about what exactly has changed is a safety net to preclude modified software from being installed.

The message digest is universally accepted in the gaming industry as an essential control mechanism. The verification solutions available are generally open source, thus they generally do not require a solution that is subject to a patent fee. The rules of the jurisdictions evaluated for this chapter do not universally acknowledge the use of message digests but they do put restrictions on changes to the systems. In Malta, the rule reads, "No changes to the gaming system shall be made without the prior approval of the Authority and additional certification of compliance."[22] The manner in which an operator complies with this generic rule will depend on commercially available solutions like the use of message digests. While the rule does not require a specific mechanism to verify software changes, the use of message digests would be an acceptable solution and is readily available.

The Isle of Man attempts to protect software while maintaining some room for negotiation by the operator within the text of the rule: "[t]he System by means of which Gaming or a Lottery is conducted may not, without the prior approval of the Commissioners, be altered in any way which is likely to affect its compliance with the requirements of Schedule 1, subject to Regulation 3(2)."[23] Under this rule, the operator could potentially implement an unauthorized change and thereafter claim it had not violated the regulation because the software modification did not, in the operator's opinion, have an impact on the requirements of Schedule 1. The good intentions of the Isle of Man provision place the regulator in the defensive position of having to evaluate after the fact whether there really was an effect on compliance with Schedule 1.

The approach in Alderney requires the creation of a base line with this rule: "The licensee should take a snapshot / hash of the system (including database structure) after supervised installation of all software, in order to facilitate subsequent system identification and auditing."[24] This directive is a good approach to providing enough information to properly audit the operation and/or conduct a forensic evaluation. The language 'should take a snapshot' and 'supervised installation' makes that process somewhat vague regarding the actual procedures for creating the snapshot and for the necessity of a witness and who that witness must be. While the procedures for following this rule may be well understood within Alderney, a jurisdiction copying this rule could not know the nuances to its implementation without further investigation. This rule is, however, a good procedure for establishing a solid audit trail with some added clarification.

---

[22] Malta, *supra* note 17, at § 27.

[23] Isle of Man, *supra* note 7, at § 3(1).

[24] Alderney, *supra* note 13, at §5.3.1(iv).

The last rule on this subject is from Nevada, which is very explicit regarding how the software is to be verified:

Interactive gaming systems must provide, as a minimum, a two-stage mechanism for verifying all program components on demand via a communication port and protocol approved by the chairman. This mechanism must employ a hashing algorithm which produces a message digest of at least 128 bits and must be designed to accept a user selected authentication key or seed to be used as part of the mechanism (e.g. HMAC SHA-1). The first stage of this mechanism must allow for verification of control programs. The second stage must allow for verification of all program components, including graphics and data components. The interactive gaming system must also provide the same two-stage mechanism for verifying all program components on demand via an operator user interface where the results are displayed on that interface.[25]

The Nevada rule explicitly requires two methods to be available for software verification, which is in addition to the mandated system self-verification cited in Standard 6, §6.140(2). This requirement is consistent with Nevada Gaming Regulation 14 rules which apply to gaming devices used in terrestrial casinos. Manufacturers accustomed to Regulation 14 rules will be able to quickly demonstrate compliance in the Internet gaming context. If this method is new to the developer, there is a design and learning curve necessary to meet this standard. Note, however, that there is no mandated oversight for software installation. The operators are always subject to inspection by Nevada regulators and, as has been addressed, there will be several ways to verify the software including the self-verification process that occurs every twenty-four hours.

To establish a solid audit trail and depending on available resources, the optimal approach to monitoring software changes involves verification by regulatory personnel or an independent trusted resource, use of a robust software verification tool, system logging of changes, and automated and on-demand verification methodology. Accompanying these processes should be a clear segregation of duties. Any action of significance needs to be verified by an individual with a different reporting line. Risk tolerance for any activity that can impact the operation's integrity will guide the level of oversight. When drafting rules for software change controls, these factors need to be incorporated into the rules. Nevada's rules are a sound basis but could be enhanced.

Random Number Generators

The gaming operation's soul for its integrity is ensuring the randomness of its games. Electronic gaming requires use of a random number generator (RNG) to produce random outcomes like dealing cards, drawing bingo balls and selecting outcomes of casino style games. The oversight

---

[25] Nev. Gaming Regulation, *supra* note 8 ,at § 6.140(4).

of game outcomes and play activity are addressed in the rules and include the RNG. Controls concerning the RNG attempt to assure that the RNG algorithm does not create predictable results. The complex rules addressing this area include RNG security, seeding methodology, scaling, cycling, mapping, and even mechanical RNGs. Jurisdictions have to provide the guidance for developers and test labs to follow. This is a highly specialized area and statisticians that conduct this analysis will generally apply a series of industry-accepted tests to ensure randomness. Each jurisdiction in this study has criteria for random number generators. When compared, the rules were similar and, in reality, the approach that statisticians use when evaluating RNGs will be fairly consistent regardless of the jurisdiction's guidance.

Both Malta and the Isle of Man use virtually identical language and are both disciples of security technologist Bruce Schneier as is evidenced by specifically referencing that his philosophy be followed. The Isle of Man's Online Gambling Regulations devote key language in its Schedule 1 chapter titled *Randomness*. Of particular interest was that a specific set of tests were cited as an example of what would be an acceptable analysis, "…e.g. Marsaglia's Diehard" set of tests…".[26] The only improvement to this requirement would be to mandate passing all the Diehard tests unless otherwise authorized. This exception to passing all the tests would enable flexibility for those limited situations when a RNG's application does not impact gaming integrity. Additional language within the Isle of Man's *Randomness* section of the rules regarding unpredictable data, the inability to reproduce a series and the random seeding methodology are very good guidelines and are specifically directed to the implementation of the RNG. The Isle of Man provides further guidelines with this rule: "The outcome of any Game or Lottery, as the case may be, and the return to the Participant, must be independent of the CPU, memory, disk or other components used in the computer or other device used by the Participant."[27] This rule requires that RNG activity occur at the host.

Section 4.3 of Alderney's Technical Standards Extract Document devotes much quality effort towards the subject of a RNG within the subheadings of suitability, failure, seeding, metamorphic games, mapping, and scaling algorithms. With the exception of metamorphic games, these terms are described within the rules as a guide to the developer and analytical statisticians.[28] Alderney provides instructions for specific applications of the RNG, including that no adaptive behavior could occur by evaluating the RNG outcome with previous occurrences.[29] This is an important rule established by Alderney to direct that game play cannot be altered based

---

[26] Isle of Man, *supra* note 7, at Schedule 1 (3)(a).
[27] Isle of Man, *supra* note 7, at Schedule 1 (5); *see also* Malta, *supra* note 17 at Schedule 3, Regulation 25, § 4.
[28] *Id.*
[29] *Id.* at § 4.3.2(c).

on previous events. The term for this concept is adaptive behavior and the material rule is as follows:

A customer who plays a game represented as being based on a random event should have an equally likely chance of obtaining any possible combination every time a game is played. *It is improper for the return to player to be manipulated by the system or manual intervention to maintain a constant return to player.*[30]

The Alderney treatment of the RNG is thorough but a clear understanding and definition of all terms within a set of rules is necessary. The new regulator is cautioned from adopting rules in their entirety without first understanding all aspects of the rules and, in the instant case, how the metamorphic feature works.

Nevada defines an interactive gaming system as a *gaming device* and thereby draws upon its minimum standards for gaming devices as its guide for the RNG that is used in the interactive gaming system.[31] Pursuant to that definition, Nevada requires that the RNG used for the cards meet its existing rule found in Regulation 14:

Must use a random selection process to determine the game outcome of each play of a game. The random selection process must meet 95 percent confidence limits using a standard chi-squared test for goodness of fit.[32]

Nevada made this rule more robust when the Chairman issued a notice that provided "…clarification and guidance in areas not explicitly covered in the current Technical Standards or Regulations."[33] Besides new language regarding seeding, cycling, restricting each RNG selection for a single game, use of separate RNGs and seeds for applications of simultaneous games or tables, and guidance on use of RNGs, a specific rule was added for the application of shuffling cards:

Gaming devices that use a software random number generator (RNG) as part of the random selection process to produce a predetermined set of outcomes (i.e. a shuffled deck of cards) must:

1. Sufficiently encrypt or otherwise protect this information from being accessible to anyone. In addition, video poker games must not determine replacement cards prior to the player selection hold cards and initiating a draw.

2. Prevent the use of this information for the purpose of tracking deck composition and "count" that would otherwise result in a violation of NRS 465.075 (Use or possession of device to obtain advantage at playing game in licensed gaming establishment).[34]

---

[30] Alderney, *supra* note 13, at § 4.7.3.
[31] Nev. Gaming Regulation, *supra* note 8, at § 14.010(10).
[32] *Id.* at § 14.140(2).
[33] Chairman of the Nev. Gaming Control Bd., Notice to Licensees, #2012-51, at cover page (May 24, 2012), *available at http://gaming.nv.gov/modules/showdocument. aspx?documentid=3450*
[34] *Id.* at 2.

Random number generators are a key element for the integrity of a game and when implementing RNG regulations, the 'devil is in the details.' The more clarity that the rules provide in the application of RNGs, the more consistency there will be among the approved products. Regulators that prefer clear guidance on this subject can look to any of these jurisdiction rules as a basis and should seek the assistance from a gaming expert on statistical tests. These rules all speak to the development, implementation and analysis of the RNG which, in step with the calculation of payout percentages, is probably the most complex technical analysis associated with electronic gaming.

INTEROPERABILITY

Isle of Man permits players registered on an Isle of Man licensed site to place wagers on games hosted by a business partner which, though not licensed by the Isle of Man, has been pre-approved by the Isle of Man Gambling Supervision Commission.[35] Since the Isle of Man rules require the licensee to maintain detailed records of this type of gambling activity, test labs may be requested to verify the interoperability capability of the system for which approval is sought with all the authorized Gambling Supervision Commission systems. If this testing is not deemed necessary, it is a reflection on the risk tolerance regarding logging of not only the routine activity but also the capability to capture the gaming activity information necessary to resolve the anomalies that will occur. Companies working with business partners not licensed by the Isle of Man may conduct their own functional tests to ensure that all data is captured but it is not a mandated practice. Best practices to establish and maintain integrity will require interoperability testing with all systems that generate data deemed critical.

INTERNAL CONTROLS

Internal controls are policies and procedures that are designed to prevent and detect errors or irregularities that may occur in the operation of a business. They are also intended to assist a business to operate effectively and cost-efficiently. Internal controls are the integral ingredient that makes technical standards effective. Without an internal control directing, for instance, that automatically generated error logs be regularly reviewed, the ability to detect a significant error in a timely manner is lost. Internal controls reflect the implementation of regulations and are effectively the operator's employee manual and audit guide. There are two schools of thought on the creation, approval and maintenance of internal controls.

In all cases in this study, each jurisdiction requires the submission of internal controls as a prerequisite to securing a license to operate. These internal controls also serve as a template for conducting operational audits.

---

[35] *Id.* at Appendix G, "Remote game-play."

Internal controls are typically created by the operator and reflect the operating procedures necessary to comply with the regulations. It is challenging for regulators to review and evaluate internal controls. The approach taken by Nevada is to solicit professional assistance and share the burden of review and responsibility by requiring an annual independent audit of internal controls.

> ...each operator shall direct an independent accountant engaged by the operator to perform observations, document examinations and inquiries of employees to determine compliance with the operator's internal control system using procedures approved by the chairman.[36]

Nevada's Minimum Internal Control Standards for Interactive Gaming is a very thorough treatment of required duties to address the risks of non-compliance. Within that document are numerous auditing procedures to be performed for events on a daily, weekly, monthly, quarterly and annual schedule. This document is a solid base for establishing an audit program. None of the other jurisdictions provided a similar mandated audit schedule. Since all rules require report generation, it is important that reports be reviewed on a schedule reflecting jurisdictional risk tolerance because the reports are the window on gaming activity.

System Modifications

Regulations guide the internal controls that establish the methods by which systems will secure information, establish a segregation of duties, provide failsafe procedures, capture data, and create reports. Such technical operational requirements can be evaluated during the test lab's compliance analysis. An operational audit like a Statement on Accounting Standards (SAS) 70 audit could be conducted to evaluate the impact of system changes on internal controls prior to implementation or approval. SAS 70 audits do not, however, encompass source code reviews. The impact of system changes on operations are generally evaluated by a test lab when submitted for review. Both Alderney and Malta have rules very similar to the following Isle of Man rule:

The System by means of which Gaming or a Lottery is conducted may not, without the prior approval of the Commissioners, be altered in any way which is likely to affect its compliance with the requirements...[37]

Nevada's interactive gaming regulations are silent on the issue of reviewing system changes after the initial testing and approval. Heretofore, licensed Nevada manufacturers have understood that changes to their equipment necessitated a resubmission to Nevada's test lab for review and approval. There always has been and still exists the need for discussions

---

[36] Nev. Gaming Regulation 6: Accounting Regulations, § 6.105(3) (2012), available at http://gaming.nv.gov/modules/showdocument.aspx?documentid=2941
[37] Isle of Man, *supra* note 7, at § 3(1).

between the gaming equipment manufacturers and regulators as to what changes can occur on electronic gaming equipment without the necessity of being re-tested. Again, accepting gaming equipment changes without regulatory evaluation is a risk tolerance discussion and none of these jurisdictions wanted that risk. There will be many changes to systems that will not require testing and it will be an evolutionary process to identify and categorize what changes do not need to be tested and approved in order to accommodate modifications without adding risk. A virus protection software update is an example of a change that would not or should not need to be tested until proven otherwise. Most likely, common sense will prevail and jurisdictions will establish a dynamic document of permitted changes and internal control procedures to establish audit trails. This area involves an active regulatory agency to be able to facilitate reasonable commercial requests while guarding against any impact on gaming integrity.

EMERGENCY APPROVALS

Internet gaming systems are complex, designed to be robust for continuous service, and require routine support for various duties including executing backups, hardware maintenance, and installation of software updates for product enhancements and fault corrections from both third party vendors as well as in-house developers. The review and approval of routine modifications will be processed according to the policies established by the respective agencies. Emergency situations will occur and thus pose challenges for the risk assessment of the corrective actions. Procedures are needed to expedite changes, minimize risk, and provide a prescribed method that can be consistently applied regardless of when the event occurs, particularly when minimum regulatory staffing is in place and the necessary personnel with authority to approve changes are unavailable.

A review of the rules used for this study revealed that no procedures exist for an emergency situation. Emergencies, however, are inevitable and will require immediate action to prevent cheating or to correct a malfunction. An emergency situation could and most likely will occur at an inopportune moment making impractical the ability to operate under all the normal processes to implement corrections in a timely manner. The normal process for approvals on a regular basis necessitates that someone take the time to properly document the correction, have the correction independently subjected to quality assurance testing, have the results reviewed by the regulator, obtain an official approval, and then install the change with the requisite regulatory procedures.

While developing a process to expedite a fix is commercially acceptable, the process must also prevent ad hoc hot fixes from being introduced to the system without some appropriate oversight. Jurisdictions need to establish that, prior to installing any emergency fixes, the operator and developer collaborate on the analysis of the situation, document the proposed corrective action, obtain authorization from a designated operational authority and subsequently, within a specified time, submit the fix for review according to the normal provisions of the jurisdiction. In the absence of a documented procedure, the regulator risks that systems could remain operational without necessary corrections, the nature of the problem may impact the integrity of the system for either the player or operator or both, the system could be rendered unavailable thus causing an unnecessary loss of revenue and a negative impact on a site's stability, or ad hoc fixes could be introduced and cause further unanticipated problems. The risks of ad hoc fixes are always present under any circumstance but particularly when the anomaly is an intermittent problem or the time available to evaluate the correction does not allow it to be thoroughly vetted. Best practices will direct that a system of procedures be followed to facilitate and document a logical process for corrective actions.

System Maintenance

Every jurisdiction wants its licensees to operate reliable systems. Operators hire qualified personnel to oversee the gaming operation but implementation of the necessary procedures to ensure system and component reliability cannot be assumed. In fact, a conflict of interest may exist between company officials that approve departmental budgets and those seeking approval of the purchase orders related to maintaining or upgrading the systems. Artfully created regulations can eliminate much of this conflict of interest by requiring certain procedures for ensuring system reliability. Alderney's rule § 5.4.2, *Hardware Reliability,* requires the licensee to document the following:

i) Describe the licensee's scheduled hardware replacement programme.

ii) Describe the licensee's production hardware rotation programme. *It is recommended that hot standby components be rotated regularly into productions use to ensure they are up to date and in working order.*[38]

What will be deemed an acceptable program of replacement and rotation is left as subjective. A policy will most likely evolve, documentation and publication of that policy best serves the licensees. This emphasis on reliability is further supported by Alderney in the following requirement by identifying criteria that will be used to deem a system unreliable:

Operating System Reliability

i) *...Operating system reliability will be measured in terms of re-boots not due to non-redundant system faults and the time taken for restoration. System re-boots that occur due to the failure of a redundant component will be counted as Operating System Failures. A reliable operating system is one that re-boots less than once per week and requires less than 10 minutes to return to service.*

---

[38] Alderney, *supra* note 13 at § 5.4.2.

ii) Operating System Reliability will be tested during evaluation.[39]

A test lab can evaluate re-boots of the system in seven-day periods during testing and incorporate the results of that observation in its report. This rule provides clear criteria for the jurisdiction's measurement of reliability, however, the rule does not specify whether the operator is required to document these occurrences during live operation. This live operation observation may actually occur in practice, but a jurisdiction adopting these rules would want to provide more explicit guidance. Even without guidance for auditing methods, the Alderney rules provide the clearest direction of all the rules evaluated, particularly since none of the other jurisdictions in this study have a metric to measure reliability.

DATA SECURITY

Security of the data being transmitted was addressed in each of the sampled regulations. The Isle of Man and Malta have identical data security regulations, as follows: "[b]oth the Online Gambling and financial transactions software must be congruent and secure."[40] Isle of Man goes further by adding under the heading *Betting*, "Any software utilised must be capable of providing for congruent and secure betting and financial transactions."[41]

In Alderney the rule does not specifically require encryption to secure transactions: "[s]ystem applications should be able to parse all messages in accordance with design to ensure messages are communicated in a planned, approved, reliable and secure manner."[42] This regulation permits the system developer to explore different options to reach the objective of the rule. As a matter of course, the implemented method will be tested to verify its compliance to the spirit of the rule.

Nevada's approach is similar to Alderney in that '...interactive gaming systems that transmit and store information about authorized players must encrypt or otherwise protect this information using a method approved by the chairman."[43] This directive does not limit security to use of encryption as the only solution. This rule permits developers to take advantage of advances in technology without the delay of the jurisdiction needing to adopt rule changes to accommodate a different solution to data security. That said, in §6.160 of the same Nevada rules there is a tighter control on data communication, "Communications between any interactive gaming system components, authorized player systems and authorized player software must be encrypted by a means approved by the chairman."[44]

---

[39] *Id.* at § 5.4.3.
[40] Isle of Man, *supra* note 7, at Schedule 1 (2), Malta, *supra* note 17 at Schedule 3, Regulation 25, § 2.
[41] Isle of Man, *supra* note 7, at Schedule 2 (1).
[42] Alderney, *supra* note 13, at § 5.7.5.
[43] Nev. Gaming Regulation, *supra* note 8, at § 6.110.
[44] *Id.* at § 6.160(1).

Depending on the flexibility of the regulatory environment to readily adopt rule changes, the requirement to encrypt data as a minimum standard is the clearest guidance for developers to implement.

Data Storage

Data backup and storage is critical to proper regulation because this information is necessary for a variety of regulatory functions including audits and player dispute resolutions. Major corporate financial scandals prompted enacting the Sarbanes-Oxley Act (SOX) in the USA and adoption of similar rules by the European Union that address mandatory IT procedures for companies, including data storage. Besides rules adopted by gaming jurisdictions, a regulator should review and incorporate standards for data storage from SOX or the EU as part of the regulatory scheme. Each jurisdiction in this study anticipated that the information generated by systems would need to be preserved and stored. Malta requires the submission of information about the control system which includes a description of "an adequate system of data backup…"[45] Malta's rules do not provide guidance beyond this requirement. Aldereney's treatment of the backup requirement is expanded by requesting documentation for the following areas:

Adequate off-site transaction logging (IN CONJUNCTION WITH daily backups of customer accounts) to ensure all customer monies can be recovered in the event of a disaster rendering the site inoperable.

Adequate off-site transaction logging (IN ADDITION TO daily backups of customer accounts) to ensure all customer monies can be recovered in the event of a disaster rendering the site inoperable.[46]

In §5.8.1, Aldereny anticipates the use of critical information backups for data recovery in the event of system failures or other unanticipated calamities. The definition of what Alderney considers critical or vital information is:

The IGS [independent gaming system] shall treat all transactions involving monies as vital information to be recovered in the event of a failure.

The IGS shall treat records of any game that fails to complete and the reason why the game failed to complete as vital information to be recovered by the IGS in the event of a failure.[47]

Alderney rules include a comprehensive list of *Recordable Events* that the IGS should keep which includes, but is not limited to, patron identification information, session information, game and jackpot configurations, large wins, and communication failures.[48] "The licensee should retain gambling information (either archived or on-line as determined

---

[45] Malta, *supra* note 17, at § 20(2)(j).
[46] Alderney, *supra* note 13, at § 4.4.3.
[47] Id. at § 5.8.1.
[48] *Id.* at § 5.8.4.

by the licensee) for a period of six years."[49] The Isle of Man requires data backup procedures to "…occur at least daily and that the data is held for a minimum of six years."[50] No further direction on data storage is provided. Nevada's technical standards state the following, "The interactive gaming system must be equipped with a mechanism to back up any data required to be stored on the interactive gaming system."[51] In the Minimum Internal Control Standards for Interactive Games, however, there is a meticulous description of the backup procedure required to operate in Nevada. To ensure that the backup data is usable, should the occasion require, the Nevada regulation is specific:

> Daily backup and recovery procedures are in place and, if applicable, include:
>
> a.   Application data.
> b.   Application executable files (unless such files can be reinstalled).
> c.   Database contents and transaction logs.[52]

To avoid surprises regarding what is and is not being stored, whether the information is readily available, and to protect access to and modification of records, the rules for data storage need to be explicit in their direction to ensure that all necessary data is stored and available for its successful use when needed. Nevada's Minimum Internal Control Standards provide the most comprehensive treatment of data storage with requirements of maintaining original and all subsequent document versions, a unique hash signature for each version, logging of personnel who change documents, maintaining an index system, providing for limited access through logical security, and providing a complete record of administrative activity.[53]

DISASTER RECOVERY

Comprehensive disaster recovery planning is the best insurance to provide for business continuity. Not all plans will enable the enterprise to continue without some business interruption but comprehensive planning will secure the necessary customer information and financial transactions to restore operations and maintain patron confidence. Nevada provides instructions regarding mandated data recovery precautions, including semi-annual recovery testing with minimum document review requirements,[54] regulations on permitted storage locations and authorized access

---

[49] *Id.*

[50] Isle of Man Gambling Supervision Comm'n, Guidance for On-Line Gambling at § 3.5.14.

[51] Nev. Gaming Regulation, *supra* note 8 at § 6.160(4).

[52] Nev. Gaming Control Bd., Minimum Internal Control Standards, Interactive Gaming v6, §49 (2012), *available at* http://gaming.nv.gov/modules/showdocument. aspx?documentid=4553

[53] *Id.* at § 54.

[54] *Id.* at § 48.

thereto,[55] and daily back-up system log reviews and maintenance require-ments.[56] All these procedural requirements must be documented in the licensee's internal controls and submitted to the Nevada regulators. Backup procedure testing in a test lab should include verifying that the data backed up is adequate to be used in a recovery situation. In Nevada, the ability to recover files must be tested quarterly by the operator with a record of such testing.[57] Even though the recovery procedures are not specifically addressed in all of these rules, the purpose for creating backups is to ensure the continuity of services during and after emergencies, thus warranting the time and effort to perform the appropriate testing.

Establishing a backup process is integral to a disaster recovery policy. Disasters can run the gamut of total destruction of the operation due to fire or flood to major component failures. To adequately prepare for un-anticipated disasters, operators have to think of 'perfect storm' scenarios. Prophylactic procedures to thwart a disaster include appropriate physical building architectural designs which address the risks of the particular geo-location, restricting access to specific personnel, and dynamic access controls. Similar to safety drills, unless you actually test the controls you will never be sure that the process works. The server room is particularly important in an iGaming context since all gambling activity occurs in a virtual casino hosted on the servers.[58] When adopting rules for security of the IT environment, subtle differences may be critical to the operation. Regardless of the mandated rules, it behooves the operator to implement physical designs and controls that will protect "…against damage from flood, fire, earthquake or other forms of natural or manmade disasters…".[59] As noted, the Nevada minimum internal control procedures require test-ing the recovery capability of gaming systems.[60] Aldereny's procedures re-quire some form of hardware rotation practice and scheduled hardware replacement programs.[61]

Disaster prevention consists of a multi-layered set of policies and pro-cedures that collectively protect the operation. Besides the backup process-es, the operator needs to make provisions for power loss, climate control, network security, unique logins with required and regular changes, fire-walls, remote access controls, logging of a variety of activities to include all administrative access, and independent reviews of the logs because the

---

[55] *Id.* at § 50.

[56] *Id.* at § 51.

[57] *Id.* at § 53.

[58] For a more detailed analysis of the subject regarding physical and network security and remote access, the reader is encouraged to compare the highly detailed chapters from Alderney (Alderney, *supra* note 33 at Appendix N, 123-28) and Nevada (Nev. Gaming Control Bd., *supra* note 52 at §§ 1-29) which are similar but with certain enhancements in the Nevada rules.

[59] Nev. Gaming Control Bd., *supra* note 52 at § 4.

[60] *Id.* at § 53.

[61] Alderney, *supra* note 13 at § 5.4.2.

logs are useless if no one looks at them. Nevada has a very strong requirement to ensure a continuous source of power by requiring the operator
to install, as part of the IT environment, "[r]edundant power sources to
reduce the risk of data loss in case of interruption of power."[62] Monitoring
these areas speaks to the risk tolerance of the jurisdiction. Verifying that all
these controls are properly implemented and maintained requires active,
disciplined, and knowledgeable oversight. One method of reducing risk is
to require an independent third party to conduct an operational audit, similar to the requirements of having financial documents audited by accounting experts. Malta's approach to disaster recovery is to require the license
applicant to submit "...a disaster recovery plan...".[63] The required disaster
recovery plan for Malta may well include other mission critical procedures
that are also required to be documented including the following:

> ...procedures and standards for the maintenance, security, storage...of
> equipment to be used to conduct remote gaming;
> ...procedures for the setting up and maintenance of security facilities in-
> cluding general compliance and internal controls relating to critical sys-
> tems;
> ...an adequate system of data backup;...[64]

While the Maltese rules do not provide minimum standards for any
of these procedures, there is a provision for some potential oversight: "[t]
he Authority may at its sole discretion, submit or direct the applicant or
licensee to submit the proposed control system or an approved control
system, to an audit."[65] The rules are silent regarding what credentials are
required to perform the audit and whether, in fact, the function can be
performed by anyone other than a Maltese official.

Alderney's approach to security is to require the submission of a document in which the operator is to

> [d]escribe the physical premises (or cross reference to other ICS sections
> where the premises are already described), describe the security risks pre-
> sented by those particular circumstances, and describe the controls de-
> signed to mitigate those risks.[66]

Alderney rules also advise that the primary server should be restricted
to authorized personnel and that the test environment should be physically
isolated from the production system.[67]

Isle of Man provides licensing information for disaster recovery services in its Guidance for Online Gambling document.[68] The Isle of Man

---

[62] Nev. Gaming Control Bd., *supra* note 52 at § 4(a).

[63] Malta, *supra* note 17, at § 20(2)(i).

[64] *Id.* at §§ 20(2)(g-h), (j).

[65] *Id.* at § 21(1).

[66] Alderney, *supra* note 13, at § 5.2.12(i).

[67] *Id.* at §§ 5.2.12(ii-iii).

[68] GUIDANCE FOR ON-LINE GAMBLING, *supra* note 50, at §2.2, §3.2.2 and §3.2.5.

approach may provide a comprehensive disaster recovery plan through established professionals but subject details are not articulated in the regulations. There is guidance regarding what data needs to be secured, the Isle of Man requires that "All deposits, withdraws and other transactions must be maintained in a system audit log." and that "All account transactions must be backed up so as to be capable of being recovered in case of system failure."[69]

Based on reviewing the rules of these jurisdictions, it is recommended that regulators seeking to provide detailed guidance for disaster recovery should study both Alderney and Nevada rules as their base.

TIME SYNCHRONIZATION

Time synchronization among all the system components is important for reports, forensic analysis, and time stamping events. Each set of jurisdiction rules refers to recording the time of significant events, however, some variations exist in the required detail of time-related recordings. Malta and Isle of Man have no specific reference to the synchronization of time for all system components. Alderney has a rule that requires the use of the same time, but it seems to be referencing the same time zone, "All time stamping should be in a single time. If not Universal Time (UT) then the difference to UT should be apparent."[70] A licensee could easily interpret this rule that all event time logs should use the same time zone but that synchronization is not required *per se*. This premise is further supported by Alderney's specific reference to synchronizing the time between progressive jackpot controllers and slave controllers.[71] Nevada removes any speculation about its intent to synchronize time among system components: "[t]he interactive gaming system must be equipped with a mechanism to synchronize the time and date between all components that comprise the interactive gaming system."[72] Under the Nevada rules all events are required to be logged by using exactly the same time standard, regardless which component was processing the transaction. For compliance verification, the developer will submit the system to a test lab for evaluation and the synchronization mechanism will be a part of the overall evaluation. Provided a jurisdiction deems it important to log all events in real time to provide an audit trail for transactions, mandating time synchronization is important.

---

[69] Isle of Man, The Online Gambling (Registration and Accounts) Regulations, § 9(2) and § 9(5). *available at* http://www.gov.im/lib/docs/gambling/Regulations/onlinegamblingregistrationandacc.pdf.
[70] Alderney, *supra* note 13, at § 5.7.4(iii).
[71] *Id.* at § 4.29.12.
[72] Nev. Gaming Regulation, *supra* note 8 at § 6.160(3).

TERMS OF AGREEMENT

Most gaming sites require the player to agree to terms of service before being allowed to play on the site. The terms of agreement establish the contractual relationship between the operator and player on several points including use of data, dispute resolution, game rules, deposit and withdrawal requirements, eligibility to gamble on the site and many others.

Isle of Man and Malta rules do not require players to agree to terms and conditions as a prerequisite to completing the registration process. Malta does require in its rules that "The player of an authorized game shall comply with all the rules…". This rule must be made available to a player but no affirmative agreement is required by the player to adhere to these rules.[73] There is no prohibition to an operator requiring adherence to a player agreement. Alderney does require the customer registration process to "…include the prospective customer's agreement to the terms and conditions of the licensed operation."[74] Alderney provides a comprehensive treatment of the minimum requirements for the terms and conditions which includes but is not limited to dispute procedures, self-imposed limits and self-exclusion, credit terms, explanation of fees, consent to confirmation of age, identity and residence, clarity in the explanation of the rules, consequences of improper behavior, and adherence to laws of Alderney.[75] Nevada provides several items that it deems necessary for terms and conditions. Nevada requires that "[i]nteractive gaming systems must have the capability to require an individual to affirm…" consent to the prescribed terms and conditions "…before an interactive gaming account can be established remotely."[76] For Alderney and Nevada, the requirement that users must agree to the terms and conditions before an account can be activated would be part of the product evaluation. The content of the terms and conditions should be the subject of regulatory legal analysis.

PLAYER ACCOUNT REGISTRATION AND CONTROLS

Each jurisdiction studied in this chapter requires the creation of a profile for each patron. Controls limiting access to patron's files are an important security and audit function. The Isle of Man rules mandate privacy, establish penalties for violation of privacy, provide comprehensive procedures for account security, and mandate encryption of patron data. The use of encryption is required by Nevada for the transmission and storage of patron information.[77] In Nevada § 6.160, the state requires the operator to secure player information by making the following demand: "Communications between any interactive gaming system components, autho-

---

[73] Malta, *supra* note 17, at § 34.
[74] Alderney, *supra* note 13, at § 3.1.1, 3.1.2.
[75] *Id.* at § 3.1.2
[76] Nev. Gaming Regulation, *supra* note 8 at § 6.110(2).
[77] Nev. Gaming Regulation, *supra* note 8 at § 6.110(3).

rized player systems and authorized player software must be encrypted by a means approved by the Chairman."[78] Nevada registration requirements include that the "[i]nteractive gaming systems must employ a mechanism to collect the following information prior to the creation of any interactive gaming account…"[79] which includes verification of the individual's identity, age, address and that the individual is not on a list of excluded persons.[80] If a jurisdiction intends to use this rule, the *system* will need to perform all the duties to which this rule alludes. The rule requires that a gaming account not be created if the "…information is found to be unsuitable…"[81] How the system complies with this rule is the evaluation conducted in the testing process. A credible information source for this process must be approved by the Nevada chairman.

Alderney requires the operator to describe the security methods implemented to protect against unauthorized access and requires a minimum of what is acceptable which includes the use of an user ID and password, challenge questions, and "compensating controls" to mitigate the low security of email for communication.[82]

In Isle of Man rules, the operator must exclude players under eighteen years of age and record the name, age and place of residence of the player.[83] Before a player is permitted to gamble, the Isle of Man requires the player be offered one of two options for minimizing exposure:

(a) a maximum stake or bet, or maximum total stakes or bets, per session, or

(b) a maximum total stakes or bets in any period (not being less than 7 days).[84]

Isle of Man's Gambling Supervision Commission has issued its "know your customer" (KYC) requirements, in conjunction with the anti-money laundering (AML) and countering of financing of terrorism (CFT) procedures.[85] This checklist is a guide to the operator when establishing procedures it needs to perform when gathering intelligence on its customers. Malta too requires player registration prior to participation in any authorized games and lists the minimum criteria to be secured,[86] but no guidance is provided with respect to what evidence is necessary to support the validity of the registration details. Malta requires the player to be at least eighteen years of age, to secure the player's identity, obtain the player's place of residence and a valid e-mail address.[87]

---

[78] Nev. Gaming Regulation, *supra* note 8 at § 6.160(1).
[79] *Id.* at § 6.110(4).
[80] *Id.*
[81] *Id.* at § 6.110(2).
[82] Alderney, *supra* note 13, at § 3.2.6(iii, iv, v).
[83] Isle of Man, *supra* note 69, at § 5.3.
[84] *Id.* at § 5.2.
[85] *Id.* at Appendix E.
[86] Malta, *supra* note 17 at § 32.
[87] *Id.* at § 32(2)(b).

With no minimum guidance to data security, the operator is directed to maintain a *secure* online list of registered players.[88] From a testing perspective, what constitutes 'secure' for patron information would be the focus of the evaluation for compliance with this rule. Best practices will dictate a minimum standard for credible sources for patron identification and clearly establish that point at which enough information has been verified to permit a player to gamble.

Multiple Accounts

Gaming policy may dictate that players do not have more than one account to prevent cheating, circumvention of problem gambling regulations and money laundering. Multiple accounts present challenges regarding monitoring financial transactions particularly when the jurisdiction permits transfers between player accounts and when monitoring play activity. Malta[89] and Nevada[90] specifically restrict patrons to one account. Alderney permits players to have multiple accounts with guidance to establish controls to "…mitigate the various risks stemming from the practice."[91] In the Isle of Man, "The operator shall not to encourage a Player to hold more than one account."[92] This rule does not prohibit multiple accounts. For Malta and Nevada, system developers will need to prevent duplicate accounts for each authorized player which will impact on the patron identification verification process. Testing will challenge the established processes.

Fund Transfers Between Player Accounts

Like the restriction on multiple accounts, prohibiting players from transferring money between patron accounts is deemed to be an aid in preventing money laundering issues. Jurisdictions vary in their approach for the transfer of funds, which, among other things, could be indicative of a player with multiple accounts. Malta is silent on the issue of transferring funds between players. Interestingly, Alderney permits multiple accounts and transfers of funds between accounts while acknowledging that such a practice could be facilitating money laundering or problem gambling.[93] The operator is encouraged to develop controls to mitigate these risks.[94]

Isle of Man permits fund transfers between players, and the rules advise that the system must maintain a record of fund transfers that exceed an amount that "…the Commissioners may from time to time direct by notice

---

[88] *Id.* at § 32(4).

[89] *Id.* at § 32(5).

[90] Nev. Gaming Regulation, *supra* note 8 at § 6.110(13).

[91] Alderney, *supra* note 13, at § 3.2.5.

[92] Isle of Man, *supra* note 69, at Schedule – Rules as to Accounts.

[93] *Id.* at § 3.3.5(v).

[94] *Id.*

in writing to the Operator."[95] There is a fund transfer threshold that the system must maintain. A test lab will verify the system's ability to capture and record such activity.

This is a risk tolerance issue. Jurisdictions need to weigh the liabilities associated with permitting fund transfers with the desire to provide this particular customer service.

RESPONSIBLE GAMING

As noted more extensively in Chapter 8, the responsible gaming tools provided to players are intended to limit gambling, to establish a cooling off period, or to totally exclude a player from account access. As a basis for player inquiries about their online activities, Malta[96], Alderney[97] and Nevada[98] require their licensees to provide players access to their online activity. Nevada is very specific regarding the report content.[99]

Isle of Man gives details regarding betting activity that must be maintained.[100] Given the nature of the mandated betting activity that must be retained, the creation of a patron report is certainly possible. If an operator wanted to provide such a report by committing to it in their terms of agreement, the availability of the report by patrons could be verified when the system was being tested. The Isle of Man rules, however, do not require the operator provide this activity report.

Patrons that feel compelled to set boundaries on their gambling activities will have access to certain features to accommodate them. In Malta, for example, the rules provide a very comprehensive list of required mechanisms to be available to the player as well as rules for the operator. The operator must post a warning and provide for wagering limits within a set time, implement controls to establish loss limits and time limits, make available a reality check which can suspend play and provide a state-of-the-nation snapshot of the gambler's activity to that point, a real time clock always visible to the patron, and self exclusion on a temporary and permanent basis.[101] The operator is bound to ensure limitations are immediately enforced and that any changes for relief of the restrictions requires seven days to implement.[102]

Alderney directs the operator to create self-limit mechanisms in a very user-friendly and accessible manner regarding limits on deposits, wagers, losses, time gambled, and transactions.[103] For an Alderney site, "...when a

[95] Isle of Man, *supra* note 7 at Schedule 1, § 11(b).
[96] Malta, *supra* note 17, at Part II: Definitions, "player's account."
[97] Alderney, *supra* note 13, at §3.3.7.
[98] Nev. Gaming Regulation, *supra* note 8 at § 6.110(11).
[99] *Id.*
[100] Isle of Man, *supra* note 7, at Schedule 2, § 5.
[101] Malta, *supra* note 17, at §§ 42-44, 46.
[102] *Id.*
[103] Alderney, *supra* note 13, at § 3.5.4.

customer logs into a system the last time they logged in is displayed."[104] Isle of Man's Online Gambling Regulation Act is silent on responsible gaming issues.

Nevada mandates that mechanisms be established for players to set limits and the mechanism will "...require that the authorized player acknowledge how the limit works, and whether or not the limit may take effect in the middle of a game session or player session."[105] The controls to be available on Nevada licensed sites are limits on wagers, losses, time on device, and deposits.[106] The self exclusion option requires the operator to remove the player from all mailing and marketing lists.[107] Jurisdictions examining responsible gaming rules can assemble a comprehensive set of rules from studying these and probably other jurisdiction rules. The operation of these controls and their compliance to the specific language requiring how they work would be tested for compliance. Best practices for responsible gaming controls are subject to the regulatory philosophy. That said, the more options available to a player would seem to best serve those that need such controls.

ACCOUNT ACCESS CONTROLS

Another control feature to protect player's accounts is a system to monitor and detect player inactivity or to permit the player to indicate that they will be temporarily unavailable. This control is designed to prevent a legitimate player's account from being used by someone else while the legitimate player is not at their terminal. While not articulated in the Malta Remote Gaming Regulations, there exists a Lotteries and Gaming Authority (LGA) questionnaire in which operators are to respond to a series of questions. Two on-point questions are: "Do terminal logins time-out after inactivity?", and "Do online sessions time-out after inactivity?"[108] The subject of these questions is not specified within the regulations. Although these questions do not provide any detailed guidance or mandate such monitoring, they indicate the jurisdiction's intent to regulate this area of system access.

Alderney permits the operator to terminate a valid game where there is inactivity exceeding thirty minutes and the operator has made attempts to advise the customer to complete the game.[109] Nevada has a similar rule to Alderney regarding the thirty minutes of inactivity.[110] Nevada has incorporated

---

[104] *Id.* at § 3.5.5(viii).
[105] Nev. Gaming Regulation, *supra* note 8 at § 6.110(14).
[106] *Id.*
[107] *Id.* at § 6.110(15)(c).
[108] Malta: Lotteries and Gaming Authority, *LGA Compliance Audit Questionnaire,* §§ 9.5.7, 9.5.8 (2005), *available at* http://www.lga.org.mt/common/file_provider. aspx?id=633568262274998750
[109] Alderney, *supra* note 13, at § 4.8.3(v).
[110] Nev. Gaming Regulation, *supra* note 8 at § 6.120(8).

in its regulations requirements to permit players "...to indicate they are away from the authorized player system."[111] This rule provides details regarding how the operator is to handle any gambling activity that may be occurring at the time the player notices the operator of their away status and the requirement to re-authenticate the player upon the return to the game.[112] Isle of Man rules do not address the subject but also does not preclude an operator from providing these controls. The Nevada rules are the most comprehensive in this area.

PLAYER PROTECTIONS

Being restricted to only poker, Nevada has offered player protections by requiring operators to:

- Provide a mechanism to reasonably detect and prevent player collusion, artificial player software, unfair advantages, and ability to influence the outcome of a game.[113]
- Provide authorized players with the option to join a table where all authorized players have been selected at random; [114]
- Inform authorized players when they join a game or table with two or more authorized players that originally joined that table as a group or were invited to play at that table by another authorized player.[115]
- Interactive gaming systems must not employ artificial player software to act as an authorized player.[116]

These rules are unique among the field of jurisdictions examined and provide the player with intelligence and options that should protect the majority of players from unscrupulous players. These rules tend to show that Nevada operators are at least attempting to provide a more level playing field in this highly competitive and popular game that attracts a lot of novices.

ARTIFICIAL PLAYER SOFTWARE OR BOTS

The term 'bots' or artificial player software refers to computer programs that aid in the play of poker or other games such as chess. The world became aware of the most famous bot in 1996 when there was a match and a subsequent rematch between IBM's *Deep Blue* computer and the then current world chess grandmaster Barry Kasparov. The events were documented in the book *Kasparov and Deep Blue*.[117] For chess, all the options are visible to the players. In poker, however, the opponent, whether human or a bot, cannot know all the options because the game uses hidden cards.

---

[111] *Id.* at § 6.120(9).
[112] *Id.*
[113] Nev. Gaming Regulation, *supra* note 8, at § 6.190(7)(a).
[114] *Id.* at § 6.190(7)(d).
[115] Id, at § 6.190(7)(e).
[116] *Id.* at § 6.190(8).
[117] BRUCE PANDOLFINI, KASPAROV & DEEP BLUE (1997).

That said, if a player uses a bot it still puts other players in the same game at a distinct disadvantage. If an operator uses a bot to simulate another player in a game, it would be the equivalent of using a poker expert that works for the house in a game without revealing that fact to the other players. Likewise, gaming policy may dictate that the games are not fair to players unless all players can only rely on their own skill or at least are aware when another player is using a bot.

Alderney directs the operators of multi-customer games like poker to "[w]arn customers how bots can affect their play."[118] Still, Alderney has not attempted to restrict bot use. Isle of Man and Malta are both silent on the use of bots and make no mention of a player warning requirement. Nevada seeks to prevent the use of bots by directing the operator to develop a detection mechanism.[119] The method that will be developed will most likely require testing, but its effectiveness will be difficult to analyze and measure. The question is whether the effort to develop a detection mechanism will have a sufficient return on integrity to justify the total expenditure. Regulators are urged to research this area carefully before making a rule that is difficult to implement. A study of the mechanisms developed to comply with Nevada's rules would be a good start.

CASINO GAMES

Casino games differ from online poker in significant ways. They are house-banked, meaning that the player is wagering against the operator as opposed to other players. The operator earns revenue by maintaining an advantage in the game over the player, called the house advantage. Moreover, casino games can involve other features such as progressive jackpots, which increase by a small amount for every game played and are paid when a player achieves a certain random outcome on a casino game. Each of these distinctions involve different regulatory concerns.

Nevada only permits poker for Internet wagers and therefore has no rules for these casino games on the Internet.

The Alderney rules for casino games include progressive features and all the rules that are typically associated with terrestrial devices, except for the physical security elements associated with a cabinet and peripheral devices. Random number generators (RNG), displays, game rules, fairness, metering, and game recovery are important game related features. There are rules that apply to all games, for example game play must be fair, but beyond that most games have their own specific design standards, game rules and control features. Of the jurisdictions studied, Alderney has the most comprehensive approach to identifying and regulating games and game features.[120] Subjects within Alderney

---

[118] Alderney, *supra* note 13, at § 4.9.1(ii).
[119] Nev. Gaming Regulation, *supra* note 8, at § 6.190(7)(a).
[120] *See* Alderney, *supra* note 13, at § 4.

rules include fairness, transaction logging, spinning wheels, winning pay lines, symbol features, appropriate language for instructions, award symbol explanations, winning patterns, trigger symbols, free games, bonuses, keno, artwork, prize limits, game types (roulette, dice, scratch tickets, video poker, blackjack), rake and fees, meters, and progressives.[121] Also included in this section is a chapter called *Information on Percentage Return to Player*.[122] This rule requires that the website make available information regarding the lowest theoretical return to player (RTP) for each game type taking into consideration the house advantage and can also post on websites RTP data from output testing.[123] The Alderney rules are the most comprehensive of those examined but the reader should examine the thoroughness of the rules with game experts before adoption.

Isle of Man and Malta provide no guidance for the lawful RTP percentages nor mandate posting the minimum as is required in Alderney. None of the jurisdictions studied have requirements about the odds of winning combinations. Typically, since the introduction of the Telnaes[124] patent for virtual reel technology in the early eighties, jurisdictions have adopted odds requirements for awards on slot machines or video lottery devices in the name of fairness. Video reels do not need to use the virtual reel technology since there is no mapping to physical reels. Establishing odds requirements is a factor of the game's fairness since providing the RTP alone is only part of the information regarding the chances of winning.

Simulated Table Games

Simulated games are the electronic versions of terrestrial casino table games. The rules established by Alderney address many aspects of these games including the theoretical return to the player, determining game results, fairness (as the jurisdiction defines), rules of play, multiple player games, game security and displayed information.[125] Alderney's rules address certain details of the games, for instance, that simulated dice must be the same as dice used in terrestrial casinos.[126] Alderney stands alone in its treatment of simulated game rules. Nevada is silent on this topic due to the narrow scope of its authorized Internet gaming. Knowledge of table games is important to regulating them in the virtual world and soliciting game experts is recommended when creating regulations for simulated games.

---

[121] *Id.*

[122] *Id.* at § 4.3.6.

[123] *Id.*

[124] U.S. Patent No. 4,448,419 (filed Feb. 24, 1982).

[125] Alderney, *supra* note 13, at § 4.9.

[126] *Id.* at § 4.9(iv)(b).

SUMMARY

This evaluation, while not exhaustive, is intended to highlight that there are vast differences in the approach of jurisdictions to regulate and verify compliance. Definitions, terminology, and even fundamental aspects of the regulated activity are not treated the same across jurisdictions. The common thread throughout this chapter, however, has been risk tolerance. If the regulator and operator want consistent and auditable results, that fact must be made known in the form of clear and concise regulations. Writing cost effective, manageable and meaningful regulations is difficult. The hierarchy of regulation begins with the enabling legislation; all regulations are then created pursuant to the act. Internal controls are the operator's guide for its employees to perform their duties in compliance with the regulations and, quite often, there are prescribed procedures that provide specific direction about the implementation of regulations where more clarity is needed.

The results are unpredictable when one simply selects rules from a variety of jurisdictions and assembles them into one document since the terms and references therein differ and conflicts in the details will undoubtedly surface. Gaming regulations are endlessly copied and implemented. When a jurisdiction elects to adopt rules from another jurisdiction, a common observation is that subtle modifications are often made without the knowledge and experience that molded and shaped the adopted rule. With experience the rules will undergo continuous modification.

"Experience is what you get when you didn't get what you wanted. And experience is often the most valuable thing you have to offer."[127]

---

[127] RANDY PAUSCH, THE LAST LECTURE 149 (2008).

5

The Protection Of Customer Funds

Nick Nocton

Nick Nocton

INTRODUCTION

The protection of customer funds is fundamental to the integrity of remote gambling operations and the industry generally. The requirement for players to deposit funds with operators in anticipation of their use in wagering transactions is an inherent aspect of the remote gambling sector. Moreover, customer funds and data are of great value, to the player, the operator and to others, and therefore significant regulatory issues arise from their supply by players to operators for use in gambling. Issues of trust and security are critical to a well-regulated industry.

Players are increasingly aware of the risks involved in depositing funds with an online gambling operator, particularly after high-profile cases, including that of Full Tilt Poker. The Full Tilt case focused debate on regulatory measures to minimize the potential loss of customer funds in the hands of operators.

APPLICATION OF GENERAL LICENSING PRINCIPLES

The licensing principles that underpin most remote gambling regulatory regimes promote the interests and protection of the consumer, fairness and transparency in gambling, and are directed at minimizing criminal involvement. These general principles are relevant to this topic, and in particular to the protection of the consumer. However, the extent to which regulators prescribe particular mechanisms, for example by way of licence requirements on their licensees, to address these regulatory risks differ significantly. This chapter considers and compares several mechanisms to derive what might be described as best practice. It is not, however, an encyclopaedic analysis of all possible mechanisms for consumer protection and ultimately the question of what is "best practice" is a subjective one and must take into account the unique circumstances facing each jurisdiction.

BACKGROUND

Several interrelated elements to an online gambling regulatory regime exist that help to minimize the risk of loss of customer funds. These include the effective scrutiny of licence applications to verify the fitness, propriety, and financial standing of an applicant and those who own and/or work for that entity. Similarly, the effective inspection and monitoring of operators through compliance, reporting and monitoring procedures help identify and minimize risks. Such licensing and compliance functions are fundamental to an effective regulatory regime, and a coherent and robust licensing system, including a detailed and rigorous assessment of licence applicants and assiduous compliance and enforcement procedures, will enhance the protection of customer funds. Indeed, as the former Chairman of the British Gambling Commission, Peter Dean has said:

> *"Gambling regulators worldwide recognise that the best control is at the point of entry, and they take pains to ensure that no unsuitable applicant is granted a licence in the first place".*[1]

Of course, in any given jurisdiction these other indirect measures (such as the proper scrutiny of licence applicants) provide the context within which the specific mechanisms directed at customer funds protection operate, and are indirectly relevant to their effectiveness. These contextual factors vary considerably between jurisdictions, and accounting for all such factors when undertaking a comparative analysis of the particular mechanisms used to protect customer funds is not possible. Factors that are also relevant in this context include the size of the operator and the amount of funds it holds for players, the second aspect of which will be greatly influenced by the products that the operator offers.

While this chapter makes occasional reference to such related regulatory measures, it does not concentrate analysis on the indirect measures that collectively provide consumer protection. Instead, it is left to readers' broad understanding of the other factors, including from their reading of the other chapters in this text, to assist in this regard. Rather, this chapter focuses on those licence conditions and other mechanisms imposed by regulators specifically to address the manner and terms on which customer funds are held by a regulated online gambling operator, and to attempt to assess their relative suitability and effectiveness.

Traditionally, the protection of customer funds in the gambling regulatory field has tended to focus on ensuring that operators could meet their potential liability in respect of pay-outs, or winnings. For example, a bookmaker would tend to face his greatest exposure if a series of heavily backed favorites were to win. While a sensible bookmaker would price his odds accordingly, a regulator would typically require assurances that the

---

[1] Peter Dean, "Full Tilt Poker Review:" A Report by Peter Dean to the Alderney Gambling Control Commission, at 6, March 26, 2012.

bookmaker's risk management systems are robust and effective, and that he is in a financially secure position, meaning he can pay out irrespective of the outcome of those events on which he has offered betting markets.

Similarly, with bricks and mortar casinos, regulators typically require operators to hold a reserve reflecting their potential exposure to customer winnings, often on a worst case scenario basis. Having said that, in September 2011 the British Gambling Commission removed altogether the requirement for terrestrial casinos in the UK to maintain a gaming reserve, citing the disproportionate cost of maintaining a reserve when compared to the actual risk to customers. Evidence suggested only a small risk existed that any given reserve would ever be required to be called upon.[2]

In a physical environment, of course, operators tend not to retain customer funds in respect of future gambling, hence the focus on potential exposure to winnings. Similarly, in the online, or "remote" sphere, those betting on sporting or other events, and those playing bingo, casino games and slots online, typically do not deposit and leave large sums with the gambling operator for use in future gambling sessions.

The growth of community games such as online poker, however, has forced regulators to grapple with the issue of operators holding players' "stacks", often on an ongoing basis, meaning that some operators receive very significant sums of money to be held on behalf of players. Consolidation in the market, and the huge significance of liquidity in poker (and other P2P products), means that a few operators, especially in poker, hold large amounts of customer funds, as highlighted by the Full Tilt Poker case.

As a result, the issue of securing customer funds is no longer merely a question of covering potential exposure, but also of ensuring the protection of potentially very significant customer deposits, in particular against possible misappropriation and the claims of creditors in the event of insolvency.

Several high-profile examples in recent years have involved the potential or actual loss of customer funds. In the case of the betting exchange Sporting Options in 2004, the operator allegedly used customer funds instead of its own funds to support liquidity on the exchange. More recently, Worldspreads Limited, a spread betting subsidiary of Worldspreads plc, which was listed on the Alternative Investment Market in London and the Irish Stock Market ESM, ceased trading in March 2012 following the discovery by new management of "accounting irregularities". Reportedly, some £13 million was "missing" from its client accounts.[3]

---

[2] *See generally* British Gambling Commission: *Licence Conditions and Codes of Practice Supplement 9*, September 2011.
[3] Dan Townend, *World's End for WorldSpreads*, GAMBLING COMPLIANCE (19 March 2012), http://cdn03.duonox.com/node/48778

In June 2012, Purple Lounge–an online casino and poker web-site–and 5050 Poker, both licensed in Malta, reportedly ceased trading due to money owed players. In July 2012, the 5050 Poker website posted notice from the Board of its holding company to shareholders and customers saying, among other things, that the operating costs of 5050 Poker Limited had long exceeded revenues, meaning the company used players' funds for the operations. It also stated that the Board of the holding company had been unaware of this because management of 5050 Poker had presented false information to it.[4] The company has been placed into liquidation.

These examples and that of Full Tilt Poker demonstrate the increasing importance of considering the various mechanisms which are adopted by different regulators, often in combination, to seek to ensure that customer funds are protected and of seeking to draw conclusions as to those that are most effective and desirable.

The question arises, however, whether player funds can be ever fully protected. In his report to the AGCC following the regulatory proceedings that led to the suspension and revocation of the various licences held for the operation of Full Tilt Poker, Peter Dean said the following:

> *"Gambling regulators differ in their attitudes on this topic, which range from caveat emptor at one extreme to favouring a complete safety-net at the other, though total protection is not achievable in practice."*[5]

Understanding why such an esteemed former regulator considers total protection of customer funds not to be achievable in practice is important.

Let us consider the movement of funds in the first instance. When a consumer instructs his bank to transfer monies from his own account to the account of an online gambling operator, or a payment-processing intermediary, he loses control of those funds. Even while a player's money is within his own bank account, technically the player is not legally the owner of the funds; rather, the bank will have legal title to the monies and the player will be a creditor of the bank. The account represents, for the purposes of English law at least, a *chose in action*: recognition on the part of the bank that the account holder has deposited funds with it that must be repaid to him according to the terms of the contract between them.[6]

In the financial crash of 2008, customers of the Northern Rock bank in the United Kingdom queued to withdraw funds from the bank in fear that its imminent collapse would leave them out of pocket and merely creditors seeking recovery in the anticipated insolvency of a bank. Similar historic "runs" on banks have occurred and are symptomatic of the bank, which is a debtor of its customer, holding the customer deposits. The funds are the

---

[4] 5050Poker, http://www.5050poker.com ((last visited Aug. 23, 2012).
[5] Dean, *supra* note 1, para. 59
[6] ALASTAIR HUDSON, THE NATURE OF PROPERTY IN EQUITY AND TRUSTS

assets of the bank, albeit with corresponding liabilities owed to customers, and are at risk if a bank collapses.

Nevertheless, banking crises apart, once a player instructs his bank to transmit funds to an operator, those funds are generally exposed to a greater risk than they were when held by the player's own bank "on his account". In broad terms, under the terms and conditions of a gambling website, the player agrees to transfer funds to be deposited within the customer account of the operator. Once the funds are transferred, the player becomes a creditor of the operator. Applicable clearing house rules govern the funds in transit. To the extent that those funds may be held by a payment processor, the gambling operator (rather than the player) would normally be the creditor of the payment processor, because the direct contractual relationship will be between them, rather than between the processor and the customer.

While the details are not directly relevant to the present topic, the use of credit card providers and the relationship between the card provider and the player further complicate matters. In this case, the player authorizes the transfer of monies to the operator and legal title to those monies generally transfers from the player's bank (or card provider) to the operator's bank. At that point, once the funds have been received into the bank account nominated by the gambling operator, legal title will be held by the operator's bank. The gambling operator will be a creditor of the bank and the player will be a creditor of the operator. This explanation is but some evidence that securing the safety of a customer's funds is a far-from-straightforward task.

Trust Accounts

Thus, in common law jurisdictions such as the United Kingdom, where the concept of *equitable* or *beneficial* ownership exists alongside that of legal ownership, one possible solution is to take steps to create a trust (whether expressly or constructively) in respect of funds deposited. So long as the trust is properly created and exists, the level of protection of those funds increases because the depositing bank is placed on notice that, while the gambling operator may be entitled, within the terms of its customer agreement, to call upon those funds for use in gambling, it is not and never has been *beneficially* entitled to the funds held in the trust account.

Beneficial ownership in those funds would remain with the customers who deposited the monies with the operator unless and until they use the funds to gamble according to the customer agreement. In essence, the arrangement should ensure that customer funds never become the property of the operator, unless and until wagered and lost by the player, or in the case of a P2P operator, until the funds are properly designated as commission or rake.

The use of trust accounts is routine in common law jurisdictions, and not only in the gambling sector. For example, in the United Kingdom, lawyers and some other professionals deposit client funds in client accounts expressed to be trust accounts. If the professional is insolvent, there is no doubt that the funds held in the client account are not assets of the professional (and that they never have been) but remain assets of the clients. This clarity, however, is partly achieved as a result of express statutory provision in the law and supplementary regulations that provide for how such funds must be held and how such accounts must be designated and managed.

In the absence of a similar statutory provision, a company or person may nevertheless seek to establish a trust in respect of the funds held in a segregated bank account, whether expressly or constructively, and gambling operators often do. Whether the monies in such a trust account, however, are fully protected in the event of insolvency or otherwise is questionable.

When a gambling operator becomes insolvent, an administrator has a duty to identify and realize the assets of the insolvent operator. In practice, this means that he will carefully scrutinize the trust arrangements. For example, he will check that the trust arrangements are genuine and have not been imposed over funds properly belonging to the operator, for example in an attempt to defraud creditors.

An administrator would not seek to exercise his powers in respect of assets that did not properly belong to the operator, but he will be under a duty to creditors, and to the court, to ensure that assets that do belong to the operator are available for distribution. For this reason, practitioners must exercise considerable care in establishing the arrangements for trust accounts to hold customer funds, including with regard to the relevant provisions in customer agreements.

There are of course different ways in which a trust can be created and these will to some extent depend on the law of the relevant jurisdiction. This chapter will not analyse the law of any particular jurisdiction, but instead highlight the fact that a trust need not require the involvement of an independent trustee (at least under English law). Clearly, where funds are held and managed by an independent trustee this would provide additional security, including against fraud on the part of the operator or someone within the operator's business, and potentially greater protection in the event of insolvency of the operator.

However, a system involving an independent trustee can be costly and onerous for the operator and may be considered disproportionate by some, especially where it is possible (as under English law) to establish a trust without the same level of formality and oversight. Under English law, a form of trust may arise where a creditor provides funds to a debtor for a particular purpose and where those funds will be held in an account segregated from the debtor's own funds. If the funds are misused or misapplied, the creditor may be protected by a form of secondary or resulting trust in his favour[7].

---

[7] *Barclays Bank Ltd. v Quistclose Investments Ltd.* [1968] UKHL 4

In certain circumstances, a "trust" might fail. This is much less likely, however, where it has been properly established for genuine reasons (ideally *ab initio*) and demonstrably relates to funds deposited by customers on terms that create a trust either expressly or by construction. Accordingly, trust accounts may offer an effective means of protecting customer funds if an operator becomes insolvent.

In the event of fraud or other wrongdoing, however, trust monies remain vulnerable. For example, those required to give instructions to the relevant bank in respect of monies held on trust on behalf of customers could act in such a way as to betray that trust. Clearly, regulators can establish mechanisms that significantly reduce the possibility of a rogue individual defrauding players in this way, including by requiring the involvement of an independent trustee, but ultimately, somebody must give instructions to the bank or to the trustee regarding transfers in and out of the customer account to allow those funds be used in gambling. Moreover, for the funds to be afforded the protection offered by a trust account, they must be deposited there in the first place. At least in the financial sector, regulatory proceedings often address the improper deposit of customer funds in trading or working capital accounts.

By way of case example, Worldspreads was regulated by Financial Services Authority ("FSA") (rather than by the Gambling Commission) because the company operated spread betting in the UK. The terms of its licence required Worldspreads to operate segregated client trust accounts. The company nevertheless collapsed allegedly owing customers at least £13 million[8]. Following the departure of key management in early 2012, new management reportedly identified and notified the FSA of "accounting discrepancies" reflecting so significant a shortfall of customer funds as to require the company to cease trading.[9] Its shares were suspended and at the time of writing it is subject to the FSA's Special Administration Scheme. This was an entity subject to arguably stronger regulation than most gambling operators, and certainly more onerous licence requirements concerning the protection of customer funds than it would have been if regulated by the British Gambling Commission. Moreover, its licence terms required it to employ regulated individuals and to operate trust accounts, the status of which could not be revoked. Nevertheless, it appears to have failed with a shortfall in its customer accounts.

In practice, weaknesses in any regulatory mechanism may exist. In the case of trust accounts, principal vulnerability arises because individuals must instruct on behalf of the operator and/or the trust that the bank move funds in and out of the trust accounts. If they do so fraudulently or otherwise beyond the scope permitted by the customer agreement/trust

---

[8] SIMON GOODLEY, *Police to investigate collapsed financial bookmaker WorldSpreads*, THE GUARDIAN (MAR. 19, 2012), http://www.guardian.co.uk/business/2012/mar/19/police-investigate-financial-bookmaker-worldspreads

[9] *Id.*

deed, the protection is compromised. Likewise, customer funds may not be placed in the designated trust accounts in the first place. Besides careful monitoring by regulatory authorities, proper internal accounting practices, account reconciliation (in particular between the customers' interactive gaming accounts balances and the balances of funds held in segregated accounts), accurate and timely regulatory reporting and robust external audits are all important checks and balances to ensure suitable operation of a regulated entity. But, as Peter Dean noted, no system can offer complete protection.

Another vulnerability of a trust account system is the risk that it is not properly, and lawfully, established in the first place. For a trust account to work, it must meet the relevant legal requirements, the details of which are beyond the scope of this chapter, and may differ from country to country.

In the case of Full Tilt, which was not required to hold funds in trust accounts, the position may have been further complicated. Not only were players allegedly misled as to the level of protection afforded to their funds,[10] but their interactive gaming accounts were apparently credited with funds not yet received by the operator because of payment processing difficulties. If this was indeed the case, part of the problems occurred as a result of Full Tilt's internal procedures. This underlines why regulators should not only require funds to be placed in some form of segregated account, but should seek to ensure that internal procedures are sufficiently robust and rigorously policed to make sure that customers can only gamble with funds that are actually in the customers' account.

Having said that, although not obliging Full Tilt to use trust accounts, the applicable Alderney regulations provided detailed and extensive requirements regarding customer accounts. These regulations prohibited licensees from using funds standing to the credit of registered customer except for certain permitted purposes, included a requirement to repay players on demand,[11] and prohibited the giving of credit . Moreover, the regulations required licensees to report serious events affecting the operation[12] and to provide accurate regulatory returns and accounts evidencing, among other things, compliance with the required financial ratios mentioned below[13]. In practice, however, the operator allegedly failed to meet these and other licence conditions, and its licences were suspended and (with one exception) were subsequently revoked.

But the central issue remains that a trust account can be seen to offer a considerable measure of protection for customer funds, although in practice such measures cannot offer full protection, especially against fraud or other wrongdoing, including identity theft. It is worth noting, however,

---

[10] U.S. v Bitar and Burtnick, Superseding Indictment, S8 10 Cr. 336, U.S. District Court, Southern District of New York
[11] Alderney eGambling Regulations 2009, Reg. 231.
[12] *Id.* at Reg 4(g).
[13] *Id.* at Reg. 243.

that exactly the same can be said of customer funds held by non-gambling entities that hold customer funds, including banks, both online and offline.

Trust accounts cannot exist in quite the same form in countries where there is no recognition of the concept of an equitable or beneficial interest, and therefore the concept of trusts is not recognized. In such jurisdictions, generally, once the money is transferred to the operator, the legal system will recognize that only the operator is entitled to the funds. Accordingly, in the event of an insolvency of such an operator, such monies are *prima facie* likely to be assets of the operator and available to distribution to creditors as a whole.

However, the laws in such countries may afford a similar level of protection through mechanisms similar to trust accounts that provide that the operator only has a *nominal* interest and not an *economic* interest in the deposited funds.

A final and highly relevant potential weakness of the trust account in the context of online gambling arises due to the sheer volume and frequency of transactions that occur involving customer funds in a large and active online gambling operation. This may mean that in a given arrangement, the trustee may not properly be in control of the movement of the funds. If so, to the extent that the operator actually controls the accounts, then arguably the creation of the "trust" will have done little to enhance the protection already afforded by the fact that the funds are held in a segregated account and the relevant bank put on notice of the players' interests in the funds.

In view of the issues briefly discussed above, the imposition of a "trust" arguably does little more in practice to protect customer funds than a requirement to segregate player funds and to notify the bank of the players' interests (and to obtain an acknowledgement of that). Note, however, the following:

> "Under English law the mere segregation of money into separate bank accounts is not sufficient to establish a proprietary interest in those funds in anyone other than the account holder. A declaration of trust over the balances standing to the credit of the segregated accounts is needed to protect those funds in the event of the firm's insolvency. Segregation on its own is not enough to provide that protection. Nor is a declaration of trust, in a case where the client's money has been so mixed with the firm's money that it cannot be traced. So segregation is a necessary part of the system. When both elements are present they work together to give the complete protection against the firm's insolvency that the client requires."[14]

This assumes that client funds are placed in the client accounts, which in the Lehman Brothers case was not done. The decision of the UK Su-

---

[14] Per Lord Hope, *In the Matter of Lehman Brothers International (Europe) (In Administration) and In the Matter of the Insolvency Act 1986*, UK Supreme Court, (2012) UKSC 6

preme Court in that case, however, was that the availability of the statutory protections afforded by the Financial Services Authority's client money regime depends not on what the regulated entity actually did with the client money, but on what it *should have* done with the money. Whether this decision would apply equally to non-FSA matters remains to be seen and is not binding outside the UK, but it is an interesting decision in light of the topic of this chapter, and the possibility of increasing the protection of customer funds in the regulated gambling sector.

Full Reserves

Of the various mechanisms prescribed by regulators, those at the more restrictive end of the spectrum can be broadly described as a "full reserve." This requires the licensed sites to maintain reserves at a level at least equivalent to the balances from time to time held on players' interactive gaming accounts. Typically, these reserves must be posted either in real cash or secured by way of a bond or similar financial instrument.

The regulations promulgated by the Nevada Gaming Commission is an example of this type of mechanism. Regulation 5A.120 of the Nevada Online Gaming Regulations (the "Nevada Regulations") establishes a detailed series of requirements for all "Interactive Gaming Accounts" (a.k.a. player accounts), including detailed registration requirements and prescribed methods for the deposit and withdrawal or other debits of player funds.

Regulation 5A.125 of the Nevada Regulations requires the operator to maintain a reserve in the form of cash, cash equivalents, an irrevocable letter of credit, a bond, or a combination of these, equal to the sum of all player funds held in gaming accounts (excluding such amounts as may be available to players for play but that are not redeemable by them for cash – such as certain bonus entitlements).

A reserve held in cash form, cash equivalent or maintained by way of a letter of credit, must be held or maintained, as appropriate, by a US federally-insured financial institution. A bond must be written by a *bona fide* insurance carrier (although no US federal regulatory requirement is specified).

The arrangements for the reserve must be made pursuant to a written agreement entered into with the financial institution, either by the operator or on behalf of the operator by an intermediary or agent acceptable to the Nevada Commission.

The Nevada Regulations require these written agreements to "reasonably protect the reserve against claims of the operator's creditors other than the authorized players for whose benefit and protection the reserve is established and must provide that

1.   The reserve is established and held in trust for the benefit and protection of authorised players to the extent the operator holds the money in interactive gaming accounts for such authorised players;

2. The reserve must not be released in whole or in part except to the Board on the written demand of the Chairman of the Nevada Gaming Commission or to the operator on the written instruction of the Chairman. The reserve must be available within sixty days of the written demand or written notice. The operator may receive income accruing on the reserve unless the Chairman instructs otherwise;

3. The operator has no interest in or title to the reserve or income accruing on the reserve except to the extent expressly allowed;

4. Nevada law governs the agreements and the operators' interest in the reserve and income accruing on the reserve;

5. The agreements are not effective until the Chairman's approval has been obtained; and

6. The agreements may be amended only with prior written approval of the Chairman."

The Nevada Regulations require that operators submit to the Nevada Gaming Commission draft documentation relating to the proposed reserve arrangements for prior approval. The Nevada Board may require amendments to ensure compliance with the Regulations. Amendments to the documents must similarly be pre-approved. In this way, and the Commission interposes additional prescriptive requirements relating to the reserve, which involve a greater regulatory burden than merely requiring customer funds to be held on trust.

A Nevada licensee must calculate its reserve requirements daily and, where an operator determines that its reserve is insufficient to cover the calculated requirement, it must within 24 hours notify the Board in writing and indicate the steps it proposes to take to remedy the deficiency.

Moreover, the operator must engage an independent certified public accountant to audit the reserve records on a monthly basis and to examine whether the reserve amounts required by the Regulations for each day of the previous month were met. The operator must make available whatever records are necessary to the accountant and the accountant must report its findings in writing to the Board and to the operator no later than the tenth day of the month following. This report must include the operator's statement addressing those days on which it did not comply with the reserve requirements and the corrective measures taken.

The Board can authorize this report to be provided by an employee of the operator or an affiliate provided that the employee is independent of the operation of the interactive gaming,[15] although in practice this potentially could weaken this aspect of the overall mechanism.

The Board can demand that the reserve is increased to correct any deficiency or otherwise for good cause. If the reserve exceeds the requirements of the Regulations the Board must, upon the operator's written request, authorize the release of the excess.

---

[15] Nev. Gaming Comm'n Reg. 5A.125(7) (Dec. 2011)

Significantly, where an operator ceases to operate and its licence is either surrendered, revoked or lapses, the Board may demand payment to it of the reserve and any interest accruing on it after the operation has ceased and may interplead the funds in a Nevada State District Court for distribution to the players. The reserve also may be paid to such other persons as the Court may determine are entitled to it and the Board may take such other steps as are necessary to effect the proper distribution of the funds.

The Nevada Regulations further require that, in addition to the reserve, an operator must maintain cash equal to 25 percent of the total amount of player funds held in customer accounts (excluding those funds not redeemable for cash) together with the full amount of any progressive jackpots related to interactive gaming.

Failure to comply with any provision in these Nevada Regulations will be evidence of unsuitable methods of operation and grounds for disciplinary action. The Commission may impose licence conditions and other regulatory sanctions including suspension, revocation of licences and fines on the finding of any disciplinary matter.

The Nevada Regulations require interactive gaming service providers (such as B2B operators) who act for an operator to comply with the same Regulations to the extent as an operator. Nevertheless, an operator remains obliged to ensure, and remains responsible for, compliance with the Regulations regardless of the delegation of any operational responsibilities to an interactive gaming service provider.

These arrangements place a far greater burden of compliance on a licensed operator than merely to maintain a segregated trust account for player funds, and by incorporating significant reporting obligations (including monthly independent audits of the reserve) and monitoring and enforcement rights, the Nevada Regulations aim to create a robust mechanism. Not only must the operator hold the necessary funds (or their equivalent) in the relevant accounts (or be provided for) but the funds must be seen to be held or provided for, as appropriate, and very regular reconciliations and reporting will significantly reduce the risk of misappropriation. With such regulatory prescription and absent any misappropriation by the operator or a third party, endangerment of player funds is less conceivable in the event of insolvency. Moreover, the Nevada authorities are relying on the enhanced compliance monitoring requirements to make this far less likely.

MALTA

The Lotteries and Gaming Authority (LGA) in Malta requires licensees to keep player funds in segregated accounts and with a credit institution approved by the LGA. The funds held in such segregated accounts (but including the funds in transit or in the process of being cleared by the banking system or credit card processors), must be at least equal to the aggregate amount standing to the credit of players in their interactive gaming accounts. Any shortfall must be made up by the licensee from its own funds within 30 days following the end of the month in which the shortfall occurs.[16]

The credit institution must declare and affirm in writing that it will not attempt to enforce or execute any charge, write-off, set-off or any other claim against the client account, that it will not combine the client account with any other account in respect of which there is a debt owed to it by the licensee and that it will credit any interest payable in respect of the client account only to that account.[17] The licensee must provide copies of these affirmations to the LGA.

Besides these default requirements, the LGA may, for just cause, require by means of a directive that the licensee takes out a bank guarantee in favor of the LGA in such amount and for such period of time as may be determined by the LGA and if the licensee fails to comply with this requirement within three working days of the issue of the directive, the LGA may suspend the licence. However, such a bank guarantee requirement does not affect the requirement regarding the sufficiency of player funds in segregated accounts as described above.

Finally, the licensee must instruct and authorize the financial institution that holds the player funds to disclose such information as may be requested by the LGA in respect of players' accounts.

These requirements are more prescriptive than those of some other leading European remote gambling jurisdictions, and bear some similarities to the Nevada Regulations, although the Nevada regulations are more demanding, in particular by requiring a monthly audit by an independent auditor of the client accounts.

Having said that, the effectiveness of the Maltese regulations is now the subject of scrutiny following the recent cases of Purple Lounge and 5050 Poker, mentioned above.

GREAT BRITAIN

The Gambling Commission in Great Britain currently exercises a far less prescriptive approach to how customer funds are maintained. Gambling operators licensed by the British Gambling Commission pursuant to the terms of the Gambling Act 2005 are subject to a series of Licence Conditions and Codes of Practice attaching to their operating licences, many of which are specific to remote gambling operating licence holders, given the distinct nature of the provision of interactive gaming services. The Gambling Commission maintains this suite of conditions and codes of practice, in addition to its remote gambling and software technical standards, which set out a series of operational and technical specifications.

---

[16] Malta Remote Gambling Regulations, Reg. 40(2)
[17] Id. at 40(3).

The Licence Conditions and Codes of Practice include the following condition that applies to all remote operating licences (with the exception of ancillary remote licences):

Protection of Customer Funds
Licensees who hold customer funds for use in future gambling must set out clearly, in information made available to customers in writing, whether they protect customers' funds in the event of insolvency and the method by which this is achieved."[18]

While the Gambling Commission undertakes very careful scrutiny of licence applicants, their ownership, management and financial standing, and has ongoing monitoring and compliance functions (and may impose such specific additional licence conditions as it thinks fit), the licence condition set out above is the only general licence condition relating directly to protection of customer funds in the event of insolvency of a British remote gambling licensee. Many readers may find this surprising, and it perhaps represents an example of what Peter Dean refers to as a "*caveat emptor*" approach, although this likely refers to jurisdictions that do not even require such a notification[19].

There are reporting requirements with regard to key events that may have a significant impact on the nature or structure of the licensee's business and that must be notified to the Gambling Commission as soon as reasonably practicable and in any event within five working days of the licensee becoming aware of the event's occurrence. These include, in the case of licensees who are companies, the presentation of a petition for the winding-up of the company or any group company, and, in the case of individuals, the presentation of a petition for their bankruptcy or sequestration, or their entering into individual voluntary arrangements with creditors. Also, where licensees must have their accounts independently audited, any unplanned change of auditor, including a change prompted by a dispute or resulting from the auditor being unable or unwilling to sign an unqualified audit report, must be notified as a "key event", as must the departure of certain key individuals, any breach of a banking covenant or covenant with any other lender, any default in the repayment of the whole or part of any loan on its due date, the fact that a Court judgment remains unpaid 14 days after the date of the judgment and the commencement of any material litigation.[20] It might be suggested that in circumstances where customer funds are not protected in the event of insolvency the notification to the regulator of an insolvency event (even assuming that notification is actually made as it should be) may do little to enhance player protection, but the regulator may take such steps as suspending a licence to mitigate customer losses.

---

[18] Gambling Commission "Licence Conditions and Codes of Practice" (December 2011), General Condition 4.
[19] Dean, *supra* note 1, at 59.
[20] Gambling Commission, *supra* note 17, at General Condition 15.2

Other reporting requirements, and requirements regarding provision of general and regulatory returns, include the provision of detailed information with regard to operational matters. Nevertheless, British regulation remains noticeably non-prescriptive with regard to provision of specific protections for customer funds.

The British Gambling Commission's Remote Gambling and Software Technical Standards do require the provision of detailed customer account information via the interactive gaming service (online, on mobile or through interactive television), which are intended to ensure that customers can access up-to-date information with regard to their current balances, movement of funds between products and the like. However, these provisions are designed to allow customers to understand easily the status and activity of their interactive gaming account, but do not directly address the issue of protection of the funds held on behalf of the customer against creditors of the licensee's business (including other customers) or the wrongdoing of the licensee or others.

However, the Gambling Commission can impose such licence conditions as it thinks fit,[21] albeit that the imposition of conditions may be the subject of the general appeal process provided for in the legislation, and an unreasonable or disproportionate condition may possibly be set aside by the Gambling Appeals Tribunal.

Much of this, however, is theoretical. At the time of writing (July 2012), British law permits the promotion of gambling services in the United Kingdom or to UK residents by operators who are not licensed by the Gambling Commission, provided they are regulated in the European Economic Area, which for the purposes of the Gambling Act includes Gibraltar, or one of the "white listed" jurisdictions. The white list includes Alderney, the Isle of Man, Tasmania and Antigua. The effect of this has been to discourage remote gambling operators from establishing their operations in Britain and thus of having to obtain licenses and pay remote gaming and/or betting duty, plus direct taxes in Great Britain. Instead, those targeting British residents have generally established themselves in low-tax or no-tax jurisdictions on the "white list", including some British operators who have moved their interactive gambling operations offshore to take advantage of this anomaly. Accordingly, with one or two notable exceptions, the British Gambling Commission tends not to regulate significant online operations. As such, it could be said that the effectiveness of the system with regard to protection of customer funds has not particularly been tested.[22]

Moreover, considering LCCP General Condition 4 in a vacuum is unfair. In practice, when faced with particular circumstances, the Commission may impose additional licence conditions to protect customer funds.

---

[21] Gambling Act 2005, Section 77

[22] The collapse of Sporting Options predated the Gambling Act 2005 which came into force in September 2007 (and the creation of the Gambling Commission itself).

Certainly, with a change to the UK's regime for the licensing and regulation of remote gambling expected in 2014,[23] with a move to regulation at the point of consumption, the Commission and Parliament will consider what, if any, different and additional requirements might be imposed.

Indeed, in early 2013 the Commission announced a consultation on what additional or alternative measures might be appropriate to protect customer funds. Its starting point is apparently to consider whether "caveat emptor" is an appropriate approach. It is likely that even if the Commission does conclude that customers should be free to assume the risks associated with unprotected funds, customers must do so with the benefit of enhanced notice of the basis on which their funds are held. It is expected that the consultation, at a minimum, will recommend enhanced requirements for the provision of information to customers, which is clearly desirable.

The Commission will also consider the competing merits of various trust arrangements. It will likely be particularly interested in considering the merits and potential pitfalls of less formal trust measures.

The Commission is also likely to consider regulator-held reserves to be disproportionately costly, bureaucratic, and overly static; these reserves may not adequately reflect the constantly changing nature of customer deposit levels. Additionally, the Commission is likely to consider capital adequacy requirements to be insufficient without additional measures.

The Commission's consultation paper (not yet published when this chapter was completed) will also consider a number of related and important concepts which further complicate this area. For example, what should be included in any definition of "customer funds"? Should it include monies in transit to the operator, but still in the payment processing system? And would a requirement for an operator to "top up" customer funds with its own monies (e.g. to reflect such funds that are not yet received) potentially undermine the effect of a trust in respect of all customer funds?

These and other issues are extremely important when considering the suitability of any measures. The Commission's decision to consult on this topic is most welcome and the regulator will no doubt provide an important lead once it reaches its final conclusions.

Licences are likely to be subject to more prescriptive requirements with regard to customer funds protection than under the current law, but exactly what will be required remains to be seen.

GIBRALTAR

A similarly non-prescriptive approach to that currently exercised by the British Gambling Commission is adopted in Gibraltar, which has

---

[23] Department of Culture, Media and Sport, July 14, 2011, www.culture.gov.uk/news/media_releases/8299.aspx

close connections with the British system. In Gibraltar, while there may be a less-prescriptive approach than in some other leading jurisdictions, the regulator nevertheless pursues a notably "hands-on" approach with its licensees, partly as a result of the importance of the industry in the jurisdiction, and partly due to the geographic proximity of the licensees to the regulator, Gibraltar being such a physically small jurisdiction, but which does require a meaningful operator presence.

The Gibraltar regulator's approach places considerable importance on the initial licensing stage, and historically, Gibraltar licences have generally been awarded only to operators of significant size and financial substance who have demonstrable records of regulatory compliance. Furthermore, as the regulator works cheek-by-jowl with its licensees, ongoing compliance and monitoring are considered to be very proactive. In this sense, the "contextual" factors briefly discussed above are perhaps even more significant aspects of the consumer protection regime in Gibraltar than in many other jurisdictions. That is not to say that such factors are not of critical importance to other regulators, but Gibraltar is an example of a jurisdiction that relies to a large extent on such indirect means of ensuring consumer protection. In essence, the Gibraltar perspective seems to be that ultimately it is the fitness and propriety of the operator, as well as its financial standing and integrity, which are the most significant factors in ensuring that player funds are adequately protected. Gibraltar relies on these factors and, of course, robust, ongoing compliance and enforcement measures.

Having said that, the regulator does require its licensees to offer an appropriate level of protection for customer deposits, which may be a combination of measures, using a risk-based approach, taking into consideration the size of the operation, the products offered and the extent of customer deposits (which may depend, for example, in the poker context, not only on the size of the operator, but also on matters such as the value of the games and profile of the customers, who may be higher rollers on some platforms than others).

Gibraltar champions a bespoke approach based on relative risk, according to numerous factors, some of which have been touched upon briefly in this section. Such a bespoke approach is considered further in the conclusions to this chapter.

ALDERNEY

The Alderney Gambling Control Commission (AGCC) has entered into Memoranda of Understanding with numerous international gambling regulators, including the Nevada Gaming Commission and a number of regulators in Europe and has been at the forefront of the development of remote gambling regulation since its inception. Nevertheless, its online gambling regulatory regime has recently faced considerable scrutiny, including the protection of customer funds in the hands of its licensees, because it was the regulator of Full Tilt Poker.

The Alderney e-Gambling Regulations 2009 provide that e-gambling licensees may not have recourse to funds standing to the credit of a registered customer except to debit amounts payable in respect of gambling transactions at the direction of the customer, to debit inactive funds in accordance with terms and conditions of its approved internal control system (which must be accepted by the customer prior to the addition of the funds), and to facilitate player to player transfers as directed by the customer in accordance with approved terms and conditions.

Regulation 243 requires that Category 1 e-gambling licensees (that is B2C operators) must at all times satisfy the financial ratios established by the Commission and must by no later than the 20th day of each month submit to the AGCC a report detailing their financial position in the preceding calendar month by reference to the ratios. Category 2 e-gambling licensees (B2B), temporary licensees and foreign gambling associate certificate-holders (that is, certified non-Alderney associates) must provide similar reports for the purpose of satisfying the Commission with regard to their financial position.

The AGCC financial ratios require that operator current assets must exceed current liabilities at all times, that cash must exceed player balances, and that total assets must exceed total liabilities by at least 25 percent.

Monthly and quarterly regulatory reports are reviewed by external auditors and licensees are also under an ongoing obligation to provide notice of certain key events, including any non-compliance with the capital ratios.

However, like the British Gambling Commission, the AGCC did not at the time of the Full Tilt case specifically require licensees to hold player funds in segregated accounts. This has now changed, however, with the enactment of The Alderney eGambling (Amendment) Regulations 2012 ("the 2012 Regulations").

The 2012 Regulations amend the 2009 Regulations to introduce an additional requirement on licence-holders who hold funds standing to the credit of registered customers, to hold those funds in a bank account that exists solely for the purpose of holding, and only holds, funds standing to the credit of customers' accounts, and which is segregated from any bank account not fulfilling these criteria.[24]

The 2012 Regulations came into force on January 1, 2013 and require the segregation of customer funds. Although they do not specifically require that those funds are held on trust, it is understood that players' interests in the funds must be notified to the relevant bank.

The 2012 Regulations permit the AGCC to waive the requirement in Regulation 230A where a person has provided a written guarantee, in terms approved by the AGCC, to

---

[24] The Alderney eGambling (Amendment) Regulations 2102, Reg. 230A.

1. remit all funds standing to customers' credit in the event the licensee is unable to do so,
2. maintain at all times such deposits and reserves as are necessary to satisfy that undertaking, and
3. demonstrate at any time, at the request of the AGCC, that it maintains adequate deposits and reserves.[25]

The new regulation 230A further requires the licensee to provide a monthly report to the AGCC in a prescribed format detailing the total funds standing to the credit of registered customers and the balance of all bank accounts that hold customer funds.

Further, the licensee must notify each of its customers, using a "clear and robust" mechanism approved by the AGCC, of the potential risks associated with funds standing to their credit in the event of the licensee's insolvency.

Accordingly, the AGCC has significantly tightened its requirements as to customer funds protection. Although it has not gone as far as some other jurisdictions, like Nevada, have chosen to, the new regime in Alderney does require segregation of funds and the notification of the customers' interest in the funds to the relevant bank, in addition to regular reconciliations, alongside the pre-existing capital ratios, monthly and quarterly reporting requirements and a risk-based inspection regime. Whether these measures are sufficient to protect customer funds in the event of an operator's insolvency is a moot point but the AGCC may have reservations about the effectiveness of many of the measures discussed in this chapter.

In respect of the monitoring and inspection of licensees, all licensees are notified whether they represent a normal or "heightened" risk in the eyes of the regulator, with the latter category receiving more frequent inspections and scrutiny. The analysis of risk in this context is understood to include various criteria, including the nature of the activities undertaken, the locations in which business is conducted, an assessment of competence, location of bank accounts, payment processors used, and any evidence of loss-making activities.

Isle of Man

Meanwhile, in the Isle of Man, regulations adopted in December 2010[26] now permit licensees to use a trust account arrangement to protect customer funds, rather than more cumbersome bond or bank guarantee mechanisms previously required. These regulations require payment of all player funds received into a client account, which must be held by an Isle of Man-licensed bank and which account must include the words "client account" in its title.[27] Client monies must be held on trust.[28]

---

[25] *See Id.* at Reg. 230A(2).
[26] Online Gambling (Participants' Money) Regulations 2010.
[27] *See Id.* at 41 and 4.1
[28] *See Id.* at 4.2

This method of funds protection will satisfy the Isle of Man regulators' requirement for customer funds to be protected by an "approved player protection mechanism" for the purposes of Section 6(2) of the Online Gambling Regulation Act 2001, although operators are also permitted to continue to use methods such as bank guarantees.

Operators must maintain additional funds to cover any shortfall between the total money available in the approved player protection mechanisms and the total value of player funds recorded on the operator's system.[29]

The Regulations state that funds held in such client accounts are held on trust, thereby strengthening the status of such trust monies.[30]

The Isle of Man Gambling Supervision Commission has made much of these player protections in various statements in the wake of the Black Friday indictments and in particular because Pokerstars was able to refund its players while Full Tilt was not.[31]

Indeed, Isle of Man licensee PokerStars has since established a more elaborate trust mechanism, apparently to meet the requirements of the French regulator ARJEL with respect to PokerStars' French customer funds. These trusts are apparently administered entirely independently by an FSA-regulated trust company, and subject to a number of "trigger events" that will automatically trigger payouts to players. The intention behind this arrangement is apparently to ensure that the independent trustee always maintains under its control sufficient funds to meet the operator's player liabilities. Whether the volume and frequency of transactions means that this is practicable is another matter, and whether comparable arrangements are affordable for less-significant operators remains to be seen, but it is an interesting development.

IAGR eGambling Guidelines 2008

The general approaches adopted in Great Britain and Gibraltar and, prior to the implementation of its 2012 Regulations, Alderney, reflect (and are likely to have significantly influenced by) the eGambling Guidelines published in 2008 by the International Association of Gambling Regulators (IAGR),[32] which were an attempt to provide good practice guidance and to establish minimum criteria but without prescribing any particular methods to achieve the aims identified. This approach, recognizing that there are generally more ways than one to achieve (or seek to achieve) desired regulatory goals, certainly reflects the approach of the British, Gibraltar and Alderney regulators to date.

Besides recommendations regarding how customer accounts should be managed, IAGR recommended that:

---

[29] *See Id.* at 5(2)

[30] *See Id.* at 6

[31] *See, e.g.,* www.egrmagazine.com/news/player_protection_the_final_frontier.

[32] IAGR eGambling Guidelines, September 8, 2008

"Operators must provide information to customers about whether they protect customer funds and the methods which they use to do so and about how they deal with unclaimed funds from dormant accounts".[33]

The IAGR guidelines were derived from work undertaken by the IAGR eGambling Working Group in 2006, so some time has passed since the preparatory work on them, and they expressly acknowledge that the industry is dynamic and fast moving and that the working group will continue to consider developments in eGambling and where appropriate propose amendment to the guidelines. It will be very interesting to see what this esteemed group of highly-experienced regulators recommends as best practice in the future, particularly in light of the developments in various jurisdictions.

CONTINENTAL EUROPEAN APPROACHES TO PLAYER FUND PROTECTION

The development of regulated online gambling markets in certain continental European countries over the last decade has given rise to a series of different treatments for the many regulatory challenges presented by online gambling, including the protection of customer funds.

The majority (though not all) of these jurisdictions require operators to deal with their residents on a country-specific URL basis, meaning, for example, that an operator who may transact with worldwide customers on its ".com" website, must establish an entirely distinct operation using a ".it" site for Italy and a ".fr" site for France, even though there may be certain common back office functions provided to the various sites.

The desire for such jurisdictions to ensure that their residents play on "ring-fenced" sites and are not mixed with players from other jurisdictions has tended to mean that the default position regarding customer funds is that they too must be ring-fenced from the funds of customers playing on the operator's other websites. This has tended to lead to prescriptive requirements regarding the terms on which such funds are held generally.

In addition, because the licensing and regulation in such jurisdictions (and Nevada, above) are at the point of consumption as opposed to the point of origin (like with Alderney, Gibraltar, Malta and the Isle of Man), the regulations can be more demanding. Operators are, in effect, required to comply or to exit the market. This may also have encouraged the authorities to impose more demanding requirements.

Italy

Many believe that the Italian online gambling regulatory system is unusual in that the regulator enters into what is in effect a tripartite contrac-

---

[33] *Id.* at 3.2.6.4.

tual arrangement with the licensed gambling operator on the one hand and the operator's players on the other.

The standard licence agreement requires a licensed operator to open dedicated bank accounts in the name of the operator into which all deposited funds must be placed. The licence agreement provides that these deposited funds can only be used for transactions authorised by the relevant players in accordance with approved customer agreements. They are therefore held in segregated accounts and the funds cannot be co-mingled with the operator's money.

Further, if player funds that were deposited in a dedicated player account have not been used by that player for a period of three years, the operator may be required to transfer the money to the regulator. Moreover, the standard licence agreement requires the provision of customer and transaction data to the regulator's Central Control System, allowing it to monitor operational matters including the position with regard to player funds in real time. The data relating to deposits of funds into client accounts is therefore stored not only in the operator's own system, but also in the Central Control System. The intention is that the regulator will habitually monitor the segregated client accounts and check the reconciliation of the monies held in those accounts with data relating to interactive gaming accounts held in the name of players with licensed operators.

Also as part of the licensing process, licensees must accept a service chart that specifies certain requirements with regard to the transparency of gaming accounts and the safety and privacy of player data. This service chart stipulates that all funds in player accounts must be immediately recognisable by the Central Control System and in turn that the player must also be able to see his own account details and evidence of any funds he has used in interactive gambling.

This tripartite relationship between the operator's platform, the Central Control System and the player involves a real-time connection between the operator's platform and the Central Control System that is assured by compliance with certain communication protocols that in turn require that relevant data is uploaded to the Central Control System. These protocols are product- and sector-specific and there is a specific communication protocol relating to game accounts, which addresses all of the data that the regulator requires to see in real time on the Central Control System.

The gaming platform must be certified by an accredited testing laboratory and pass connectivity and communication protocol tests between the operating platform and the Central Control System before the operator can go live. The operator's platform may be located on servers anywhere within the European Union, but the Central Control System is located in Rome.

In this way, the Italian system provides for the regulator to monitor key operational data in real time, including constantly updated figures for customer account balances and bank account deposits.

France

The French regulator, L'Autorité Administrative Indépendante de Régulation des Jeux en Ligne (ARJEL), oversees a similar regime to the Italian model, although the monitoring by ARJEL might be described as more passive. Licensees must transact with French players only on ".fr" servers (the so-called "frontal operateur") located in France, although they are permitted to provide supporting transactional services from elsewhere, on the "platform operateur".

International players may be served through this ".fr" site, but the operator may not deal with French players on its ".com" or other websites. French player funds must be segregated not only from the operators' funds, but also from those held on behalf of international players. French player funds must be held in an account held with a French bank and operators must provide technology to allow the customer accounts to be monitored and transaction to be audited.

The system overseen by ARJEL contains a raft of particularly onerous regulatory requirements, a number of which relate (directly or indirectly) to customer account protections. For example, on registration, a player must send personal identity verification documents to the operator (or its agent) by post. Similarly, the operator must send an account verification code to the player at his registered address. Such measures provide heightened security, but are very costly to comply with, slow down the completion of the registration process and lead to high customer registration attrition rates. They are unpopular with international operators who do not generally have to deal with comparable measures in other jurisdictions and who argue that the costs undermine their ability to provide consumer choice and value.

The French model is typically enigmatic. On the one hand, it takes very seriously such issues as customer account protection and aims to require some measures that (even though they may be unwieldy) offer arguably greater protections against, for example, fraud than in other jurisdictions. But on the other hand, the logistical difficulties and costs of compliance imposed (taken together with an aggressive tax regime) have meant that some of the largest and leading operators are struggling to make reasonable returns on their investment in the market. Some big names have even withdrawn from the French market and anecdotal evidence suggests that players are actively seeking unlicensed operators, who offer better odds, choice and liquidity. Without wishing to generalize too greatly, some aspects of the French regime, although well-intended, seem to be self-defeating, although the requirements regarding segregation of player funds are not known to be high on the list of operator gripes.

French customers of Full Tilt Poker were left out-of-pocket (at least until the Pokerstars acquisition and refinancing of player balances). So, at least in the Full Tilt case, the regulations did not achieve their intended effect. ARJEL President Jean-François Villotte has since been quoted as wanting the French parliamentary review of gaming laws to increase the levels of protection required, saying that mere segregation of funds is inadequate and that a form of trust arrangement is desirable:

> *"More than just a segregated account, it is necessary to have the legal means to protect player funds and this is the purpose of trusts and trust companies. In the review team we will ask that the law expressly states this."*[34]

As noted above, PokerStars took steps following Black Friday (amid heightened concerns regarding security of funds) to establish the trust briefly discussed in the Isle of Man section above to administer its French customers' funds, despite this additional layer of protection not being a strict requirement.

Denmark

The Danish online gambling regulations also require an operator to establish a player funds account segregated from any other bank accounts, which must have a balance equal to all player balances, including deposits and actual winnings not yet credited to customers, but does not need to include an amount equal to potential winnings on outstanding bets.

The relevant bank must issue a declaration promising not to seek any fulfilment from funds held in the account. The account has the status of a client account and is referred to as a "set-off-free" account. It must be reconciled against customer balances at least once every 24 hours.

With regard to data security, the Danish gambling regulations take advantage of the fact that all Danish citizens are issued an identification number. The individual players must use their identification number each time they log in to gamble and the Danish Regulatory Authority issues each player with a series PIN numbers that are required to be used each time the customer logs on. Each PIN code can only be used on one occasion and the PIN codes will only work if used with the corresponding identification number of the authorized player. By this method, a greater level of data security is ensured by minimizing the possibility of identity theft with respect to the gaming.

CONCLUSIONS REGARDING PROTECTION OF CUSTOMER FUNDS

As the online gambling industry grows, and the volume of customer funds held on deposit, especially in respect of poker, grows, the number of examples of companies failing with deposits owing to customers has increased. Recent examples, especially that of Full Tilt Poker, suggest that the days of *"caveat emptor"* with regard to customer deposits should be consigned to regulatory history. The least that regulators should require of

---

[34] www.Pokerfuse.com, September 26, 2012.

licensees is establishment of segregated bank accounts into which player funds must be deposited, with the relevant banks required to acknowledge players' interests in the funds. Whether or not such accounts are described as "trust" accounts, they should, if properly established, prove of value in minimising the risk to such funds as are held in them in the event of an insolvency of an operator.

Of course, such measures do not solely prevent misappropriation, and the imposition of technological means for monitoring either in real time or on a very regular basis the reconciliation between the amount of funds held in respect of player liabilities and the balances on players' interactive accounts will reduce the risk of misappropriation, whether by the operator or by third parties.

The imposition of an independent trustee to administer trust funds might increase security, but whether such measures are practical in view of the volume and frequency of transactions is not obvious. Moreover, such measures may be prohibitively expensive to implement, and thus may not represent the best approach in all circumstances.

Perhaps the most complete measure is a requirement to have in place a bond or other financial instrument guaranteeing an amount at least equivalent to the balance of player funds from time to time, as this does not require the funds themselves to be held in a particular way, and cannot itself be "dipped into". Of course, logistical obstacles exist to the successful implementation of such a measure, including the constantly fluctuating, and potentially ever-increasing amounts of player funds deposited with the largest operators. But such a bond could form an effective anchor for a suite of measures put in place by a responsible and well-regulated operator.

All of these measures, however, carry considerable costs of compliance – especially any form of insurance or a requirement, such as in Nevada, to maintain an excess of cash over and above the amount of player funds. Certain operators will always be resistant, and a temptation may exist among regulators to afford more latitude to certain operators (or certain types of operation), especially where some regulators might be said to be in competition among themselves for licence applications.[35] And a risk-based approach may be quite reasonable provided that the assessment of risk is appropriate. Not all operations present the same type or level of risk.

It might well be argued, of course, that if a player chooses to deposit funds with an operator who does not offer specific protections he should be free to do so, provided that the player has been provided with, or had access to, sufficient information to enable him to make an informed choice.

A consequence of the Full Tilt problems, however, may be greater customer awareness of the potential risks and heightened scrutiny of the measures put in place by operators at the behest of regulators. In short, custom-

---

[35] Dean, *supra* note 1, at 34.

ers will expect, and are entitled to receive, protections commensurate with the regulatory risk.

While the Nevada approach is admirable, and may represent a gold standard for customer funds protection with regard to poker (to which the Nevada Regulations are limited), it does not necessarily lend itself as well to the regulation of all forms of gambling, nor perhaps to all jurisdictions. For example, a small online betting operator holding no large customer balances does not present a comparable regulatory risk as a large poker network holding thousands of players' chip stacks. Such prescriptive requirements may be easier to impose in a point of consumption licensing regime, as highlighted above.

So a balanced approach may continue to make sense in many circumstances. And for those regulators, such as the AGCC, the GRA and the British Gambling Commission, who regulate non-poker operators (as well as poker operators), a risk based approach may be suitable, provided always that the assessment of risk is appropriate, suitable monitoring is undertaken of operators who present the greatest risks, and the default position (i.e. minimum requirement) for all operators is that customers' funds be placed in trust, or similar, accounts. Of course, this is not currently the case with all such regulators and it remains to be seen whether and how all regulators individually, and collectively through organizations such as IAGR and GREF (Gambling Regulators European Forum), choose to develop their requirements.

6

Financial Transactions and Money Laundering

Stuart Hoegner*

A FRAMEWORK FOR INVESTIGATING FINANCIAL TRANSACTIONS AND STANDARDS

In almost any private enterprise, accepting value from customers—the "consideration" in the transaction—is a key element of the contract, and critical to the business's success. Most business owners do not give the issue much thought beyond the risk of fraud or counterfeiting. The sale takes place if the cash tendered is real, if the check is supported by the requisite funds, or if the credit card issuer allows the transaction. Seller and buyer are ad idem and each party gets what she wants.

Internet gaming and betting demand different considerations. Online interactive gaming, as with many other e-commerce channels, is a non-face-to-face business. Short of land-based marketing promotions or tournaments, operators rarely meet their customers or even speak with them by telephone. This has implications for consumer protection measures and fraud prevention. The underlying activity (gaming and betting) is problematic. Internet gaming has only been regulated for a few years. Much of the structure people take for granted in international bricks and mortar casinos, card rooms, and sports books is still emerging in online gaming and in countries with regulated Internet gaming. Perhaps because of this, many people take the view that the online sector facilitates the transfer of illicit proceeds. Accordingly, this chapter discusses best practices in regulating transactions between licensed Internet gaming operators and their customers. This can be done through anti-money laundering initiatives.

Money laundering provides a good framework to look at financial transactions for two reasons. First, money laundering is the single biggest regulatory matter Internet gaming regulators face from a transactional standpoint. Second, money laundering is emblematic of a larger transactional discussion. It draws in many issues including the best practices that affect currency and transaction requirements. It can serve as a means to focus the discussion and still generate feedback that goes beyond money laundering itself. For example, many recommendations presented here to prevent money laundering can also prevent consumer fraud. The standards adopted in this chapter provide good practices to handle general financial transactions in online gaming. For instance, reliable protocols when processing transactions require proper identification from the transacting parties and a paper trail for subsequent audit and investigation, if necessary. Therefore, the best practices to prevent money laundering also provide a viable standard into best practices for handling currency transactions.

This chapter is one small part of a larger picture and discussion. The goal here is to use proper standards to outline anti-money laundering and financial transaction principles, and to kindle further discussion among regulators, operators, professional advisors, and law enforcement. This chapter is organized as follows:

Section 2 defines the problem. It adopts a working definition of money laundering and sets out its exclusions and limitations. It also examines the various stages of money laundering and, critically, why the world places such importance on it.

Section 3 covers the constraints of this analysis and includes a discussion about the lack of understanding of the challenge of the money laundering problem in online gaming. It covers institutional and international barriers to any one regulator's effectiveness at combating it.

Section 4 gives a very brief overview of the current rules to prevent money laundering as adopted by the Financial Action Task Force (the "FATF") and five jurisdictions that have elected to regulate Internet gaming: Alderney, the Isle of Man, Kahnawake, Malta, and Nevada.

Section 5 discusses five key groups of best practices recommended for online interactive gaming to combat this problem:
1. Regulate the sector;
2. Adopt a risk-based approach;
3. Ensure the parties are transparent;
4. Make transactions fully traceable; and,
5. Foster control and security of the gaming environment.

Section 6 sets out two interesting payment systems in current use, PayPal and Bitcoin, then discusses each of them against the recommended standards.

Money Laundering and Why It Matters

What is Money Laundering?

The FATF states that money laundering is the processing of proceeds associated with criminal acts to disguise their illegal origin.[1] Several competing, but

---

[1] Financial Action Task Force: Money Laundering FAQ, *available at* http://www.fatf-gafi.org/document/29/0,3746,en_32250379_32235720_33659613_1_1_1_1,00.html.

broadly similar, definitions of money laundering are available.[2] Unsurprisingly, a law and economics approach to money laundering characterizes it as a service that satisfies a direct need governed by the laws of supply and demand.[3]

It is an offense under the Canadian Criminal Code (the "Canadian Code") to inter alia:

> Use, send, deliver, transport, transmit, dispose of, or otherwise deal with proceeds or property with intent to conceal or convert those proceeds or that property, knowing that such proceeds or property derives directly or indirectly from a "designated offense" under the Canadian Code. A designated offense is:
>
> 1. An offense that may be prosecuted as an indictable offense under federal law;
> 2. Conspiracy to commit or attempting to commit such an indictable offense; or,
> 3. Being an accessory after the fact to such an indictable offense.[4]

In the United States, one central definition of money laundering is found in title 18, section 1956 of the U.S. Code, which "criminalizes virtually any dealings with proceeds from a range of specified unlawful activities when those dealings are aimed at furthering the same specified unlawful activities, or at concealing or disguising the source, ownership, location, or nature of the proceeds."[5] The U.S. Supreme Court has addressed the issue of whether "proceeds" within the meaning of section 1956 refers to revenues ("receipts") or profits. Instead of agreeing on a single definition of "proceeds" for all specified unlawful activities, the Court ratified both approaches, depending on the nature of the underlying offense.[6]

---

[2] *See, e.g.* Anthony Cabot & Joseph Kelly, *Internet, Casinos and Money Laundering*, 2 J. Money Laundering Control 134 (1998); Andres Rueda, *The Implications of Strong Encryption Technology on Money Laundering*, 12 Alb. L.J. Sci. & Tech. 1, 7 (2001); Joseph M. Kelly & Mark Clayton, *Money Laundering and Land-Based Casinos*, 14 Gam. Law Rev. & Econ. 275 (2010); Mark D. Schopper, *Comment, Internet Gambling, Electronic Cash & Money Laundering: The Unintended Consequences of a Monetary Control Scheme*, 5 Chap. L. Rev. 303, 313 (2002); Jon Mills, *Internet Casinos: A Sure Bet for Money Laundering*, 19 Dick. J. Int'l L. 77, 78–79 (2000–2001); Alison S. Bachus, *From Drugs to Terrorism: The Focus in the International Fight Against Money Laundering After September 11, 2001*, 21 Ariz. J. Int'l & Comp. L. 835, 837 (2004); Amy Walters, Comment, *The Financial Action Task Force on Money Laundering: The World Strikes Back on Terrorist Financing*, 9 Law & Bus. Rev. Am. 167 (2003); Wendy J. Weimer, *Cyberlaundering: An International Cache for Microchip Money*, 13 DePaul Bus. L.J. 199, 203 (2000–2001); George Mangion, *Perspective from Malta: Money Laundering and Its Relation to Online Gambling*, 14 Gam. L. Rev. & Econ. 363 (2010); and, Roger C. Molander et al., *Cyberpayments and Money Laundering: Problems and Promise*, xi (1998), *available at* http://www.rand.org/content/dam/rand/pubs/monograph_reports/1998/MR965.sum.pdf.

[3] Gál István László, *Some Thoughts About Money Laundering*, 139 Studia Iuridica Auctoritate Universitatis Pecs Publicata 167, 168 (2006).

[4] Criminal Code, R.S.C. ch. C-46 § 462.31(1) (1985).

[5] Michael F. Zeldin & Richard W. Harms, *Anti-Money Laundering Compliance Programs: Principles from Traditional Financial Institutions Applied to Casinos*, 1 Gam. L. Rev 343, 344 (1997).

[6] United States v. Santos, 128 S.Ct. 2020 (2008).

While many concepts of money laundering are available from statutes, international recommendations, case law, and academic literature, the definition used in the European Union's Third Directive on the Prevention of the Use of the Financial System for the Purpose of Money Laundering and Terrorist Financing[7] (the "Third Directive") is both comprehensive enough to be meaningful and concise enough to be workable. Article 1, section 2 of the Third Directive provides as follows:

For the purposes of this Directive, the following conduct, when committed intentionally, shall be regarded as money laundering:

1. The conversion or transfer of property, knowing that such property is derived from criminal activity or from an act of participation in such activity, for the purpose of concealing or disguising the illicit origin of the property or of assisting any person who is involved in the commission of such activity to evade the legal consequences of his action;

2. The concealment or disguise of the true nature, source, location, disposition, movement, rights with respect to, or ownership of property, knowing that such property is derived from criminal activity or from an act of participation in such activity;

3. The acquisition, possession or use of property, knowing, at the time of receipt, that such property was derived from criminal activity or from an act of participation in such activity;

4. Participation in, association to commit, attempts to commit and aiding, abetting, facilitating and counselling the commission of any of the actions mentioned in the foregoing points.

Two Limitations of the Money Laundering Definition

The definition of money laundering in the Third Directive is the definition that concerns this chapter. However, this definition presents two interesting issues:

1. What to do about money laundering where the underlying gaming transaction is illegal under domestic law?

2. Should this discussion include financing of terrorism?

The first concern is the legality or illegality of Internet gaming itself in any jurisdiction other than the licensing jurisdiction (if and where the two are different). If an online interactive operator conducts an illegal business in any particular place by accepting the bet or wager, then Art. 1(2)(c) of the Third Directive may be engaged. The operator would acquire and use customer property (i.e., funds) presumably with the knowledge that those funds were derived from criminal activity. Or, as one scholar has put it:

"Where, as currently in the US and some European countries, e-gaming offered by private operators is *per se* illegal, the knowing use of such funds by e-gaming firms arguably becomes money-laundering because, under the

---

[7] Commission Directive 2005/60, art. 1, 2005 O.J. (L 309) 15, 20.

'all crimes' laundering model mandated by FATF, e-gaming is a predicate act and all concealment, disposal and assisting in the disposal of funds etc. obtained from e-gamers becomes money-laundering. Thus, in the US and in some EU countries, e-gaming offered by private operators presents a serious problem of money-laundering because (*and only because*) e-gaming is criminal and because many people like to bet, both on-line and off-line. By contrast, the identical behaviour engaged in within the UK presents very little money-laundering risk because the gambling is not a predicate crime (emphasis in original)."[8]

An Internet gaming regulator can and, as a matter of principle, perhaps should ensure that its interactive gaming licensees accept business only in jurisdictions where online bets are not a criminal act. The State of Nevada, for example, regulates intrastate online poker only; a Nevada gaming operator complying with local law should not deal with funds gained from an illegal bet or wager. No predicate gambling law violation exists because the interactive gaming that Nevada regulates is legal, provided it is undertaken by state-licensed operators.

A regulator may have difficulties assessing whether a foreign bet or wager is legal. Aside from principle, regulators must acknowledge the risk of over-regulation, as well. In the words of one regulator, "there is an impact to everything that we do."[9] If Internet gaming regulatory standards are too low, then regulators run the risk of censure by the International Monetary Fund (the "IMF") and the FATF, among others. If regulatory standards are too high compared to other credible jurisdictions, a licensing body's stakeholders may become dissatisfied;[10] operators and consumers might migrate to more lightly-regulated jurisdictions. This 'voting with their feet' effect can lower the overall international regulatory standards, thereby hurting the consumers the regulator seeks to protect in the first place.[11]

Is such a principled rule about definitively not allowing operators to accept business where the underlying bet or wager is or may be illegal raising the standard "too high?" It is difficult to say. Nevada does it, but many others do not. For example, Rational Entertainment Enterprises Ltd., the operator of www.pokerstars.com, is a licensee in the Isle of Man.[12] Rational accepts wagers from customers in Canada, which may violate the relevant gaming provisions of the Canadian Code. Is Ratio-

---

[8] Michael Levi, *Money Laundering Risks and E-Gaming: A European Overview and Assessment—Final Report*, 13 (2009), *available at* http://www.egba.eu/pdf/Levi_Final_Money_Laundering_Risks_egaming%20280909.pdf.

[9] Interview with Steve Brennan, Chief Executive, Isle of Man Gambling Supervision Commission (Feb. 3, 2012) [hereinafter Brennan Interview].

[10] *Id.*

[11] *Id.*

[12] The Isle of Man Gambling Supervision Commission, http://www.gov.im/gambling/licensees/.

nal engaged in money laundering by these actions?[13] Again, an answer is elusive. Hypothetically, if the Isle of Man were to introduce a more invasive rule about the location of its licensees' customers, that may give a regulatory advantage to its competitors. Still, as Internet gaming becomes increasingly regulated by international bodies, the issue is bound to come up more frequently. The trend among regulators will shift to increased respect for national laws and regulatory agencies, and gradually shift towards prohibiting operators from taking business in states where it may be unlawful. In the meantime, many regulators will put the burden for making these decisions on their licensees, which is easy but, on some level, unsatisfying. At the same time, operators will act unilaterally to publish and respect extensive lists of restricted territories from which they will not accept gambling transactions.[14]

The second issue is how to combat the financing of terrorism. Until recently, the FATF had nine special recommendations designed to combat terrorist financing.[15] In February 2012, these nine special recommendations were merged into 40 recommendations covering both money laundering and terrorist financing[16] (the "40 Recommendations"). Concern about terrorist financing remains central to the FATF's work.

Some safeguards used to prevent money laundering can also prevent the financing of terrorism. For example, part of "knowing one's client" should mean checking a client name against the current Specially Designated Nationals List maintained by the Office of Foreign Assets Control (the "OFAC") in the U.S. Department of the Treasury. By its very nature, this exercise inhibits terrorist financing. However, terrorist financing and money laundering issues can be distinct. Money laundering is generally more useful to criminal enterprises when larger amounts of cash or property are involved. Lower reporting or investigation thresholds restrain larger-scale money laundering. Different considerations can apply in terrorist financing, where even "very small amounts of laundering may be critical to terrorists' success."[17] For example, "an examination of the financial connec-

---

[13] The Isle of Man Gambling Supervision Commission's position is that all operators must target markets that they are legally entitled to. If licensed operators are in any doubt, they are to take their own legal advice in the matter.

[14] *See, e.g.,* RESTRICTED COUNTRIES FOR PADDYPOWER.COM, http://www.paddypower.com/bet/help?page=/al/12/2/article.aspx?aid=1566&tab=browse&bt=4&r=0.9481073

[15] FINANCIAL ACTION TASK FORCE: FATF IX SPECIAL RECOMMENDATIONS (2008), *available at* http://www.fatf-gafi.org/media/fatf/documents/reports/9%20Special%20Recommendations.pdf.

[16] FINANCIAL ACTION TASK FORCE: INTERNATIONAL STANDARDS ON COMBATING MONEY LAUNDERING AND THE FINANCING OF TERRORISM & PROLIFERATION— THE FATF RECOMMENDATIONS (2012), *available at* http://www.fatf-gafi.org/dataoecd/49/29/49684543.pdf [hereinafter 40 Recommendations].

[17] Levi, *supra* note 8, at 10. *See also* Interview with John Carlson, Principal Administrator, Financial Action Task Force (Feb. 1, 2012) [hereinafter Carlson Interview]; and, Michael Specter, *The Deadliest Virus,* THE NEW YORKER, Mar. 12, 2012, at 36. (In the Specter article, the author addresses the threat of biological terror by means of a pandemic spread

tions among September 11 hijackers showed that most individual transactions were small sums far below the reporting threshold and consisted only of wire transfers. The individuals appeared to be foreign students receiving money from their parents or grants for their studies."[18]

The FATF has not identified Internet gaming as a critical conduit for terrorist financing. Many mechanisms are used to get money to terrorists, but Internet gaming is not one of them.[19] (The hawala underground banking system in India and Pakistan is a more noteworthy vehicle for Al Qaeda funding.[20]) But, as the discussion will show, money laundering in regulated jurisdictions does not seem to be a particular problem now, either.[21] The best way to address terrorist financing in Internet gaming is to mandate rigorous know your client ("KYC") standards in all cases and restrict payment processing to a few key banks regulated in a small number of first world states. Regulators generally appear to have little appetite for adopting such tough standards.

Some bulwarks can prevent both money laundering and terrorist financing. Given the low reporting and enhanced customer due diligence thresholds in some Internet gaming jurisdictions, other sectors are at greater risk than Internet gaming. Furthermore, because both legal and criminal activities can finance terrorism, the scope of behaviours necessary to generate such small amounts may be "so vast that it is almost unmonitorable without sophisticated aggregate models and/or listing individuals and institutions believed to constitute such a threat."[22] In the context of a risk-based methodology, the risk in Internet gaming appears to be low. However, unless and until far stricter requirements are introduced, some conceptual risk remains.

---

through a flu-like virus and states: "While scientists disagree sharply about whether it would be easy to replicate such a virus in a laboratory, and whether it would be worth the effort, there is no question that we are moving toward a time when work like this, and even more complex biology, will be accessible to anyone with the will to use it, a few basic chemicals, and a relatively small amount of money.")

[18] Walters, *supra* note 2, at 178–179.

[19] Carlson Interview, *supra* note 17. Also note the comments of Frank Catania, former Director of the New Jersey Division of Gaming Enforcement, from 2001: "No one at any level in law enforcement has ever alleged, asserted, or, as far as I know, theorized, that terrorist organizations have ever used on-line gaming to launder money." Testimony of Frank Catania: Hearing on H.R. 556 and H.R. 3215 Before the H. Sub-comm. on Crime, 107th Cong. (2001).

[20] *Compare* Walters, *supra* note 2, at 171.

[21] *See generally*, Evan Osnos, *The God of Gamblers: Why Las Vegas is moving to Macau*, THE NEW YORKER, Apr. 9, 2012, at 49. (Osnos avers that land-based casinos are part of a widespread money laundering problem in Macau; one source calls Macau "a cesspool" of financial crimes.)

[22] Levi, *supra* note 8, at 10. (As with the Specially Designated Nationals List at OFAC, such a list—while perhaps not capable of distilling all international terrorist threats—can be maintained and should be checked.)

Money Laundering Stages

The various stages of money laundering—the process through which property is converted or transferred and its transactions concealed and disguised—are often referred to as the placement, layering, and integration stages.[23]

The placement stage involves the movement of proceeds—almost invariably cash[24]—from criminal undertakings into the financial system. Conceptually, this may be as straightforward as a deposit of illegal drug profits into a bank account or the purchase of chips at a casino table game using small denomination bills.[25] The placement phase "is the most vulnerable to law enforcement detection because it involves the physical disposal of cash."[26] The resistance to cash as a deposit method on Internet gaming websites (except when deposited indirectly by credit or debit card through a licensed financial institution) serves as a bulwark against the use of Internet gaming site operators to place funds at this stage of the laundering. However, a barrier like this could be threatened by payment solutions that provide, for example, anonymity for their users.[27]

After funds have been placed into the financial system, the money launderer often engages in a series of transfers and conversions of the illicit funds in the layering stage. These movements—or 'layering' of multiple transactions—are intended to distance the original proceeds from their source,[28] disguise their owner, and obscure the money trail.[29] This stage is seen as the most international and complex phase of the laundering cycle; funds are typically moved around multiple foreign accounts.[30] An example of layering is the transmission of illegal funds from one bank to a different bank in another country, followed by investing and moving the funds within a foreign market to avoid detection.[31] Understanding the justification for currency movements and adopting standards that either prohibit or mandate operators to report suspicious transactions can prevent Internet gaming operators from being used to layer transactions.

Finally, integration is the "folded clothes" of money laundering. In this stage, "funds re-enter the legitimate economy."[32] For example, after a

---

[23] *See, e.g.,* Money Laundering FAQ, *supra* note 1; Cabot & Kelly, *supra* note 2, at 134; Rueda, *supra* note 2, at 88–91; Bachus, *supra* note 2, at 842–845; and, Schopper, *supra* note 2, at 313.

[24] *See* Ping He, *A Typological Study On Money Laundering*, 13 J. MONEY LAUNDERING CONTROL 15, 16 (2010); MHA CONSULTING, *The Threat Of Money Laundering Through The Online Gambling Industry*, 5 (2009), *available at* http://www.rga.eu/data/files/final__mha_report_june_2009.pdf [hereinafter MHA Report].

[25] *See* Cabot & Kelly, *supra* note 2, at 141.

[26] Bachus, *supra* note 2, at 842.

[27] Rueda, *supra* note 2, at 88.

[28] Money Laundering FAQ, *supra* note 1.

[29] Bachus, *supra* note 2, at 844.

[30] *Id.*

[31] *Id.*

[32] Money Laundering FAQ, *supra* note 1.

money launderer enters the financial system and a creates a series of movements to obscure the source of funds and ownership, either the launderer or an accomplice might withdraw funds from a bank account or investment account and use them legitimately in the economy or for purchases to further develop illegal activity and profits.[33] Internet gaming operators' aversion to cash transactions and the propensity to send withdrawals to licensed intermediaries provides a check point on this part of the laundry cycle. However, anonymity can cut through this barrier. Proper rules governing withdrawals, peer-to-peer transactions, and anonymity can curb integration.

Why does money laundering matter? Why do we—or should we—care? There are at least three answers:

- Money laundering undermines the rule of law.
- Money laundering negatively impacts business.
- Money laundering impedes economic development.

First, money laundering undermines the rule of law. Allowing money laundering to go unchecked permits criminals to enjoy the spoils of their illicit activity and use their profits to potentially pursue new illegal activities. In a very real sense, money laundering can make crime pay. It also can allow for criminal elements to acquire large sectors of an economy and corrupt public officials through the laundry.[34] This has the potential to foster "an environment where criminal activity permeates a country's economic and political system,"[35] thereby undermining trust in and respect for the law.

Second, money laundering hurts business. Widespread money laundering can draw businesses into its web and make them complicit in criminality, albeit unwittingly.[36] By undermining the financial system, money laundering also may instigate a lack of confidence by business in a state's institutions. Because honest business people may not know which institutions to trust in a place where money laundering is abundant, they may decline investment and cut off credit. The FATF cites volatility in money demand, international capital flows, and risks to bank soundness among additional business risks.[37] This instability and uncertainty stifles production and increases transaction costs to businesses and consumers.

Finally, money laundering hinders economic development. Shrinking businesses means aggregate output declines on a macroeconomic level. Partly as a result of the effects on businesses and society, widespread money laundering harms the potential economic development of any state because honest, long-term investors are reluctant to invest in economies fuelled by illicit funds.[38]

---

[33] *See* Bachus, *supra* note 2, at 845.
[34] Money Laundering FAQ, *supra* note 1.
[35] Bachus, *supra* note 2, at 841.
[36] Money Laundering FAQ, *supra* note 1.
[37] *Id.*
[38] Bachus, *supra* note 2, at 841.

EVEN THE BEST PRACTICES HAVE CONSTRAINTS

The best practices to prevent money laundering have limitations. For example, the extent of the money laundering problem associated with Internet gaming is unknown. Moreover, money laundering is an international, multi-faceted, and multi-institutional issue. The best practices of one operator, or even one state, can only make a limited difference. The various constraints on what is known about money laundering and on what regulators are—or each regulator is—capable of doing must be explained before discussing current applicable safeguards and formulating a prescriptive approach to the issues.

The Size of the Problem is Unclear

Estimates of the size of the global money laundering problem vary. Several years ago, some estimated between US$300 billion and US$500 billion were laundered internationally each year.[39] More recently, others relying on IMF data have suggested that the problem is bigger, and that worldwide money laundering was valued at from US$590 billion to US$1.5 trillion annually, or between two and five per cent of the world's aggregate gross domestic product.[40] The FATF states "that overall it is absolutely impossible to produce a reliable estimate of the amount of money laundered and therefore the FATF does not publish any figures in this regard."[41] Key problems that make it hard to quantify size of global money laundering include the lack of recording basic statistics, estimation problems of yet-undiscovered criminality, and the emphasis on proving guilt over demonstrating the proceeds or profits from crime.[42] However, "[w]hat one can say with a reasonable degree of confidence is that the proceeds of serious crime that is generated annually globally is going to be a large number running into the hundreds of billions of dollars. While you may not be able to come up with a precise number, it's significant."[43] Respective money laundering and Internet gaming experts are not aware of any figures that quantify it.[44]

Many commentators presenting the risks and concerns about Internet gaming as a money laundering channel either cite conceptual concerns without any quantitative evidence or express their concerns with so many qualifications that no reasonable person would disagree. Examples are as follows:

One article cites "many prosecutors agree[ing] that it is easy and economical to launder criminal proceeds through offshore casinos."[45] Howev-

---

[39] Cabot & Kelly, *supra* note 2, at 134; Mills, *supra* note 2, at 78.
[40] Bachus, *supra* note 2, at 835; László, *supra* note 3, at 167. This range relies upon data put together by the IMF based on 1996 figures. Money Laundering FAQ, *supra* note 1.
[41] Money Laundering FAQ, *supra* note 1.
[42] Carlson Interview, *supra* note 17.
[43] *Id.*
[44] *Id.*; Brennan Interview, *supra* note 9.
[45] Mills, *supra* note 2, at 78.

er, the author presents this statement without any particular discussion of exactly how the proceeds are laundered, whether it includes regulated and unregulated jurisdictions, or which offshore jurisdictions cause concern.

As a second example, the (unenacted) Unlawful Internet Gambling Funding Prohibition Act[46] (the "UIGFPA") listed the following as a congressional finding: "Internet gambling conducted through offshore jurisdictions has been identified by United States law enforcement officials as a significant money laundering vulnerability."[47] But again, the bill's authors failed to discuss the amount of proceeds caught up in the alleged laundry.

Furthermore, Jonathan Gottfried states the following: "Unregulated Internet casinos may pose several money-laundering risks, particularly at the layering stage. The speed, international character, and possible anonymity of certain Internet gambling transactions, together with the potential of transferring large sums of money, may attract money launderers to online gambling operations."[48] For one thing, no commentator who supports legal Internet gambling would suggest that it should not be regulated; appropriate regulation of the industry is a *sine qua non* for preventing money laundering. For another, most serious proponents of Internet gaming oversight and control are not advocating player anonymity, especially with the transfer of "large sums of money;" unregulated or under-regulated environments that allow anonymity risk attracting criminals who engage in money laundering.

Others have arrived at more nuanced and less alarmist formulations. Fifteen years ago, Anthony Cabot and Joseph Kelly stated that "[t]he connection between money laundering and Internet gambling is one of the most complex issues facing regulators,"[49] which was true in 1998 and is still true today. Two years later, the U.S. Congress's General Accounting

---

[46] H.R. 556, 107th Cong (2001).

[47] *Id.* at § 2(4). *See also* Schopper, *supra* note 2, at 311, citing this provision of the UIGFPA. This finding was absent from the Unlawful Internet Gambling Enforcement Act of 2006 § 802, 31 U.S.C. §§ 5361–5367 (2006).

[48] Jonathan Gottfried, *The Federal Framework For Internet Gambling*, 10 Rich. J.L. & Tech. 26, 20 (2004), *available a*t http://law.richmond.edu/jolt/v10i3/article26.pdf. *Compare* Jonathan Schwartz, *Click the Mouse and Bet the House: The United States' Internet Gambling Restrictions Before the World Trade Organization*, 2005 U. Ill. J.L. Tech. & Pol'y 125, 130 (2005), citing Gottfried.

[49] Cabot & Kelly, *supra* note 2, at 144. They also cite a 1998 FATF annual report with regard to concerns about money laundering through Internet casinos in "several countries" offering "complete anonymity to potential gamblers … placing their bets by way of credit card." Financial Action Task Force, Annual Report 1997–1998, 47 (1998) *available at* http://www.oecd.org/dataoecd/13/51/34326611.pdf. As will be shown, the FATF now has specific recommendations covering Internet gaming operators. If regulators are fully implementing those recommendations and their own controls, query how applicable those concerns are today. "Several countries" should not be taken as impugning all countries. Finally, remember that neither this chapter nor any reasonable observer is advocating complete anonymity, though it is not exactly clear how complete player anonymity is ever obtained through the use of a legitimate credit card possessed by the player.

Office (now the Government Accountability Office) (the "GAO") reported to Congress on some of the issues in Internet gaming.[50] The report noted that representatives of law enforcement expressed concerns that Internet gaming could be a "powerful vehicle for laundering criminal proceeds."[51] At the same time, law enforcement officials conceded that no adjudicated cases involve money laundering through Internet gaming sites.[52] By contrast, banking representatives and gaming regulators did not view Internet gaming as particularly susceptible to or as posing any particular risks in respect to money laundering.[53] The GAO report made no recommendations to Congress. Additionally, several experts claim that money laundering is not much of a problem in regulated Internet gaming. Some offer little discussion about their assertions and conclusions;[54] many others also offer thoughtful reasoning about why money laundering is not a material issue in regulated online gaming.[55]

In a money laundering roundtable from three years ago,[56] several gaming experts discussed whether they were aware of any evidence of money laundering by means of the Internet in any global jurisdiction. Frank Catania said that he had not seen any such evidence.[57] Alan Pedley, an Internet gaming expert and former regulator, indicated that he had seen one instance in Australia, but the vulnerabilities leading to that instance had been addressed and corrected. Pedley added that he had encountered historical opportunities for money laundering that had since been "plugged," i.e., addressed.[58] Mark Clayton, a gaming attorney in Nevada and former member of the Nevada Gaming Control Board, concluded that he agreed with the previous comments in the roundtable suggesting "that Internet gaming properly regulated is already difficult to launder money through."[59] In an MHA Consulting report from 2009, the authors concluded that "there appears to be little evidence that remote gambling has, to date being [sic] particularly susceptible to money laundering and terrorist financing. The United States has published the results of official government studies concluding that online gambling is not a likely accessible avenue for money

---

[50] U.S. Gen. Accounting Office, *Internet Gambling: An Overview Of The Issues* (2002), *available at* http://www.gao.gov/new.items/d0389.pdf.
[51] *Id.* at 5.
[52] This was said to be, in part, because of a "lack of any industry regulations or oversight (emphasis added)." *Id.*
[53] *Id.*
[54] *See, e.g.* Mangion, *supra* note 2, at 363: "Interestingly, statistics prove that online gaming is less prone to money laundering than land-based gambling in venues such as casinos and on a race track." (No such statistics are cited.)
[55] *See, e.g.* Sue Schneider, *Money Laundering and Terrorist Financing in the I-Gaming World*, 14 Gam. L. Rev. & Econ. 657 (2010).
[56] Joseph M. Kelly et al., *How Vigilant Should We Be against Money Laundering?*, 13 Gam. L. Rev. & Econ. 278 (2009).
[57] *Id.* at 280.
[58] *Id.*
[59] *Id.* at 282.

laundering"[60] because the identities of gamblers are known, financial transactions are in electronic formats, and all of the wagering is recorded.[61] Put another way, money laundering risks associated with Internet gaming "are comparatively modest, due to the high traceability of e-gaming transactions and the customer identification controls in the regulated sector."[62]

All of these perspectives are important because regulation of Internet gaming—and implementing sound financial transaction rules—is a public policy issue. In any question about policy, one must understand the issues in order to understand the problem. How inconvenienced and compliance-focused must we be so that we can prevent money laundering? Doesn't the answer depend on the size of the money laundering problem in online interactive gaming? Do the costs of regulation versus the costs of the problem make financial sense? Does regulated Internet gaming account for half of the money laundering undertaken worldwide? Eighty per cent? Or does it make up a very small amount? If regulated Internet gaming is the vehicle through which a substantial amount of money is laundered, then public policy makers should allocate more resources to prevent it. If very little goes through a regulated Internet gaming laundry, then that also conveys information about: a) the current efficacy of anti-money laundering protocols; and, b) what other resources, if any, need to be devoted to the problem.

The absence of a working quantitative estimate is not a good reason to ignore the issue. Without a reliable measurement, however, policy makers are proceeding without useful—if not critical—information to decide how many resources they need to allocate to create rules, fund investigations and ensure ongoing compliance, that is, how to fund the legal and institutional machinery that prevents money laundering.

One Regulator's Effectiveness is Limited

The second set of constraints on the effectiveness of regulators deals with interconnectedness; money laundering is an international and multi-institutional problem. To prevent it, operators must rely on multiple functionalities.

First, money laundering is, as recognized by the Third Directive, "frequently carried out in an international context."[63] As noted by the FATF, criminals will seek to exploit the differences between anti-money laundering agencies. They will move their networks and operations to states with weak or ineffective countermeasures.[64] The movement of capital—facilitated by modern technology—makes this a continuous search by criminals for the global path of least resistance. Moreover, from an exclusively inves-

---

[60] MHA Report, *supra* note 24, at 31.
[61] *Id.*
[62] Levi, *supra* note 8, at 4.
[63] Commission Directive 2005/60, art. 1, 2005 O.J. (L 309) 15.
[64] Money Laundering FAQ, *supra* note 1.

tigative standpoint, tracking flows of cash through financial institutions is an international exercise. Effective money laundering investigations and prosecutions require the co-operation of different sovereign governments.[65] Accordingly, an Internet gaming regulator with the best proven methods for deterring money laundering is at the mercy of the weakest link in a global financial chain. Operators in the financial system can be shut out of transactions based upon risk, but the exposure and limitation fundamentally remains: any regulator will be constrained by the global nature of both Internet gaming and money laundering.

Second, regulatory effectiveness depends on multiple institutions; the interconnectedness of financial institutions, regulators, and intermediaries at a national level precludes any one institution from providing a complete solution to the problem. For instance, if a gaming regulator has stringent controls on financial institutions that deal with Internet gaming, but the state's banks experience a breakdown of their respective money laundering controls, then the operators could become part of an illicit laundry. For this reason, the IMF adopts a cross-institutional perspective in its various country reports.[66]

Finally, anti-money laundering controls appeal to many facets of Internet gaming. This point can seem abstract, but consider some specific ways different factors can affect the fight against laundering. Among others, cash limits on transactions, assessments of suitability, control over local operating nexus, and the act of gaming regulation itself can affect money laundering. But what about something like location verification? This can be a serious risk factor, for example, where a customer's location is a country on the FATF's list of jurisdictions that require countermeasures or is on its deficiencies list.[67] Consider an Internet gaming site's random number generator ("RNG"). A corrupted RNG can turn a gaming website into a laundering vehicle for players or members of the operator's staff.[68]

The Rules

This section examines how international jurisdictions approach legal issues and handle financial transactions while preventing operators from becoming part of an illicit scheme. It starts with the FATF's recommendations and then canvasses five jurisdictions on their approaches to money laundering controls: Alderney, The Isle of Man, Kahnawake, Malta, and Nevada.

---

[65] Mills, *supra* note 2, at 84–85; Bachus, *supra* note 2, at 773.

[66] *See, e.g.* International Monetary Fund—Country Report 09/278, *Isle of Man: Financial Sector Assessment Program Update—Detailed Assessment of Observance of AML/CFT* (2009), *available at* http://www.imf.org/external/pubs/ft/scr/2009/cr09278.pdf [hereinafter IMF Isle of Man Report].

[67] Location verification is addressed in Chapter 11.

[68] *See* Cabot & Kelly, *supra* note 2, at 144.

The FATF and the 40 Recommendations

The G7 countries established the FATF in 1989.[69] The FATF was convened in response to mounting concern about global money laundering,[70] and "was given the responsibility of examining money laundering techniques and trends, reviewing the action which had already been taken at a national or international level, and setting out the measures that still needed to be taken to combat money laundering."[71] The FATF's current mandate is to set standards and promote effective implementation of legal, regulatory, and operational measures to combat money laundering, terrorist financing, and other related threats to the integrity of the international financial system. The FATF also works with other international stakeholders to identify national-level vulnerabilities with the objective of protecting the international financial system from misuse.[72]

The FATF has 36 members: 34 jurisdictions and two international organizations (the Gulf Co-operation Council and the European Commission).[73] The FATF works closely with eight regional bodies that are FATF associate members.[74] The FATF also has many observers, including the United Nations, the IMF, the World Bank, and the Organization for Economic Co-operation and Development.

The FATF's work has been instrumental in coordinating the fight against global money laundering.[75] Perhaps because of the FATF's specialization (expressed in its mandate, for example), the depth of its membership, and the importance placed on its work by its members, the 40 Recommendations represent *the* accepted international standards for anti-money laundering principles and procedures and have been adopted or endorsed by many nations and international bodies.[76]

---

[69] FINANCIAL ACTION TASK FORCE: ABOUT THE FATF, *available at* http://www.fatf-gafi. org/pages/0,3417,en_32250379_32236836_1_1_1_1_1,00.html. *See also* Walters, *supra* note 2, at 168; Rueda, *supra* note 2, at 15–16; and, Alan E. Sorcher, *Lost In Implementation: Financial Institutions Face Challenges Complying With Anti-Money Laundering Laws*, 18 TRANSNAT'L LAW 395, 405 (2005).

[70] ABOUT THE FATF, *supra* note 69. *See also* Walters, *supra* note 2, at 168.

[71] ABOUT THE FATF, *supra* note 69.

[72] FINANCIAL ACTION TASK FORCE, MANDATE (2012-2020), *available at* http://www. fatf-gafi.org/media/fatf/documents/FINAL%20FATF%20MANDATE%202012-2020.pdf. Today, the FATF continues to develop and promote policies to combat money laundering and terrorist financing. ABOUT THE FATF, *supra* note 69. This it does through, *inter alia*, regularly revising the 40 Recommendations and their respective interpretive notes and by conducting evaluations of countries and industries to monitor and assess their compliance with the 40 Recommendations; these two broad functions are likely the two most significant areas of current activity for the FATF. Carlson Interview, *supra* note 17.

[73] FINANCIAL ACTION TASK FORCE, MANDATE (2012-2020), *Id.*, at Annex A.

[74] *Id.*

[75] Rueda, *supra* note 2, at 16.

[76] Sorcher, *supra* note 69, at 406; Walters, *supra* note 2, at 169; DEPARTMENT OF FINANCE CANADA, *Strengthening Canada's Anti-Money Laundering and Anti-Terrorist Financing Regime, Consultation Paper 1* (2011), *available at* http://www.fin.gc.ca/activty/consult/pcmltfa-lrpcfat-eng.pdf.

As one commentator noted, they "are the most comprehensive set of anti-money laundering directives yet created for governments, legislatures, law enforcement, financial institutions and businesses."[77]

The FATF issued a series of recommendations in 1990 to combat money laundering.[78] These were subsequently revised in 1996 and 2003,[79] but the process of revision and review is ongoing. In 2001, in response to an expanded mandate, the FATF issued eight special recommendations against terrorist financing; a ninth was added in 2004.[80] Until 2012, these collective recommendations were called the "40+9." As previously noted,[81] all of the FATF's recommendations have now been consolidated into the (current) 40 Recommendations.[82]

The FATF recommends a risk-based approach to money laundering. This is enshrined in the first of the 40 Recommendations.[83] The risk-based approach means identifying and assessing the risks of money laundering and terrorist financing by individual countries and, based on that assessment, ensuring "that measures to prevent or mitigate money laundering and terrorist financing are commensurate with the risks identified ... Where countries identify higher risks, they should ensure that their AML/CFT [anti-money laundering and countering the financing of terrorism] programs adequately address such risks. Where countries identify lower risks, they may decide to allow simplified measures for some of the 40 Recommendations under certain circumstances."[84] The FATF calls this approach an "essential foundation" for efficiently allocating resources and implementing the 40 Recommendations.[85] The risk-based approach is a key element of the guidance issued by the FATF for casinos.[86]

The 40 Recommendations expressly include and apply to Internet casinos. So-called designated non-financial businesses and professionals ("DNFBPs") in the 40 Recommendations include casinos and, in a footnote, the FATF clarifies that references to "casinos" include "Internet casinos."[87]

---

[77] Walters, *supra* note 2, at 169.

[78] FINANCIAL ACTION TASK FORCE: THE 40 RECOMMENDATIONS, *available at* http://www.fatf-gafi.org/document/28/0,3746,en_32250379_32236920_33658140_1_1_1_1,00.html#40recs.

[79] *Id. See also* FINANCIAL ACTION TASK FORCE: HISTORY OF THE FATF (2012), *available at* http://www.fatf-gafi.org/pages/aboutus/historyofthefatf/.

[80] *Id. See also* 40 Recommendations (2008), *supra* note 16.

[81] *See supra* text accompanying notes 15 and 16.

[82] 40 Recommendations, *supra* note 16.

[83] *Id.* at 11.

[84] *Id.*

[85] *Id.*

[86] FINANCIAL ACTION TASK FORCE: RBA GUIDANCE FOR CASINOS (2008), *available at* http://www.fatf-gafi.org/dataoecd/5/61/41584370.pdf.

[87] 40 Recommendations, *supra* note 6, at 113. The 40 Recommendations do not distinguish between Internet casinos, Internet bookmakers, Internet poker rooms, or other types of Internet betting or gaming. However, there is little reason to suppose that very similar anti-money laundering policy concerns would not apply across all of these channels. In each case, funds are being wagered on participating in various games or

Accordingly, recommendation number 22 sets out that the customer's due diligence and record-keeping requirements in recommendations 10, 11, 12, 15, and 17 apply to casinos, including Internet casinos.[88] Recommendation 23 provides that the provisions for internal controls, foreign branches and subsidiaries, higher-risk countries, suspicious transaction reporting, tipping-off, and confidentiality in recommendations 18–21, inclusive, all apply to casinos and, by extension, to Internet casinos.[89] In addition, recommendation 28 states that DNFBPs should be subject to regulation and supervision; this includes assessing the suitability of Internet casino owners.[90] Finally, recommendation 14 states that providers of money or value transfer services ("MVTS") should be licensed or regulated and compliant with relevant FATF recommendations.[91] MVTS are businesses that accept cash and other monetary instruments, then pay corresponding sums in cash or in other forms to a beneficiary.[92] The MVTS definition clearly includes a service like PayPal, for example.

Most FATF recommendations relevant to this chapter are summarized in Table 1.

Many of the Internet gaming jurisdictions canvassed here have requirements that overlap significantly with the 40 Recommendations or expressly appeal to the 40 Recommendations in establishing anti-money laundering policies and procedures.

---

external contingencies. With respect to games, this is so whether the games are house-banked (e.g., craps) or not (e.g., poker). The FATF has left it to individual countries to further define "Internet casinos" using a risk-based approach. In practice, however, the FATF believes that "Internet casinos" would likely include all above-mentioned types of Internet gaming and betting. Accordingly, all references herein to "Internet casinos" will be taken to include all of these wagering options and operations.

[88] *Id.* at 14–19.
[89] *Id.* at 18–21.
[90] *Id.* at 23–24.
[91] *Id.* at 17.
[92] *Id.* at 119.

Table 1

Selected FATF Recommendations Relevant to Internet Gaming Regulators

No.	Recommendation
10	**Customer Due Diligence**

- Financial institutions should be prohibited from keeping anonymous accounts or accounts in obviously fictitious names.

- Financial institutions should be required to undertake customer due diligence measures when, inter alia: establishing business relations; carrying out occasional transactions above the applicable designated threshold (US\$/€3,000, in the case of Internet casinos); there is a suspicion of money laundering or terrorist financing; or, the financial institution has doubts about the veracity or adequacy of previously-obtained customer identification data.

- The principle that financial institutions should conduct customer due diligence should be set out in law.

- Customer due diligence measures include the following:

  (a) identifying the customer and verifying the customer's identity using reliable, independent source documents, data or information;

  (b) identifying the beneficial owner, and taking reasonable measures to verify the identity of the beneficial owner, such that the financial institution is satisfied that it knows who the beneficial owner is;

  (c) understanding and obtaining information about the purpose and intended nature of the business relationship; and,

  (d) conducting ongoing due diligence on the business relationship and scrutiny of transactions undertaken throughout the course of that relationship.

- Financial institutions should be required to apply customer due diligence measures, but should determine the extent of such measures using a risk-based approach.

- Financial institutions should be required to verify the identity of the customer and beneficial owner before or during the course of establishing a business relationship or conducting transactions for occasional customers.

- Where the financial institution is unable to comply with the applicable customer due diligence requirements, it should be required not to open the account, commence business relations, or perform the transaction, or it should be required to terminate the business relationship; and, the operation should consider making a suspicious transactions report in relation to the customer.

11	**Record-Keeping**

- Financial institutions should be required to maintain, for at least five years, all necessary records on transactions to enable them to comply swiftly with information requests from competent authorities. Such records must be sufficient to permit reconstruction of individual transactions (including the amounts and types of currency involved, if any) so as to provide evidence for prosecution of criminal activity.

- Financial institutions should be required to keep all records obtained through customer due diligence measures, account files and business correspondence, including the results of any analysis undertaken (e.g., inquiries to establish the background and purpose of complex, unusual large transactions), for at least five years after the business relationship has ended, or after the date of the occasional transaction.

- Financial institutions should be required by law to maintain records on transactions and information obtained through customer due diligence measures.

- The customer due diligence information and the transaction records should be available to competent domestic authorities.

12	**Politically Exposed Persons**[93]

- Financial institutions should be required, in relation to foreign politically exposed persons ("PEPs") (whether as customer or beneficial owner), and in addition to performing normal customer due diligence measures, to:

  (a) have appropriate risk-management systems to determine whether the customer or the beneficial owner is a PEP;

  (b) obtain senior management approval for establishing (or continuing, for existing customers) such business relationships;

  (c) take reasonable measures to establish the source of wealth and source of funds; and,

  (d) conduct enhanced ongoing monitoring of the business relationship.

- Financial institutions should be required to take reasonable measures to determine whether a customer or beneficial owner is a domestic PEP or a person who is or has been entrusted with a prominent function by an international organization.

- The requirements for all types of PEP should also apply to family members or close associates of such PEPs.

14	**MVTS**

- Countries should take measures to ensure that natural or legal persons that provide MVTS are licensed or registered, and subject to effective systems for monitoring and ensuring compliance with the relevant measures called for in the FATF Recommendations. Countries should take action to identify natural or legal persons who carry out MVTS without a license or registration, and to apply appropriate sanctions.

| 15 | New Technologies |

- Countries and financial institutions should identify and assess the money laundering or terrorist financing risks that may arise in relation to: the development of new products and new business practices, including new delivery mechanisms; and, the use of new or developing technologies for both new and pre-existing products. In the case of financial institutions, such a risk assessment should take place prior to the launch of the new products, business practices or the use of new or developing technologies. They should take appropriate measures to manage and mitigate those risks.

| 17 | **Reliance on Third Parties** |

- Countries may permit financial institutions to rely on third parties to perform elements (a)–(c) of the customer due diligence measures set out in recommendation 10 or to introduce business, provided that the criteria set out below are met. Where such reliance is permitted, the ultimate responsibility for customer due diligence measures remains with the financial institution relying on the third party.

- The criteria that should be met are as follows:

  (a) a financial institution relying upon a third party should immediately obtain the necessary information concerning elements (a)–(c) of the customer due diligence measures set out in recommendation 10;

  (b) financial institutions should take adequate steps to satisfy themselves that copies of identification data and other relevant documentation relating to the customer due diligence requirements will be made available from the third party upon request and without delay;

  (c) the financial institution should satisfy itself that the third party is regulated, supervised or monitored for, and has measures in place for compliance with, customer due diligence and record-keeping requirements in line with recommendations 10 and 11; and,

  (d) when determining in which countries the third party that meets the conditions can be based, countries should have regard to information available on the level of country risk.

- When a financial institution relies on a third party that is part of the same financial group, and: that group applies customer due diligence and record-keeping requirements, in line with recommendations 10, 11, and 12, and programmes against money laundering and terrorist financing, in accordance with recommendation 18; and, where the effective implementation of those customer due diligence and record-keeping requirements and AML/CFT programmes are supervised at a group level by a competent authority, then relevant competent authorities may consider that the financial institution applies measures under (b) and (c), above, through its group programme, and may decide that (d) is not a necessary precondition to reliance when higher country risk is adequately mitigated by the group AML/CFT policies.

| 18 | **Internal Controls and Foreign Branches and Subsidiaries** |

- Financial institutions should be required to implement programmes against money laundering and terrorist financing. Financial groups should be required to implement groupwide programmes against money laundering and terrorist financing.

- Financial institutions should be required to ensure that their foreign branches and majority owned subsidiaries apply AML/CFT measures consistent with the home country requirements.

| 19 | **Higher-Risk Countries** |

- Financial institutions should be required to apply enhanced due diligence measures to business relationships and transactions with natural and legal persons, and financial institutions, from countries for which this is called for by the FATF. The type of enhanced due diligence measures applied should be effective and proportionate to the risks.

| 20 | **Reporting of Suspicious Transactions** |

- If a financial institution suspects or has reasonable grounds to suspect that funds are the proceeds of a criminal activity, or are related to terrorist financing, it should be required, by law, to promptly report its suspicions to the financial intelligence unit (the "FIU").

| 21 | **Tipping-Off and Confidentiality** |

- Financial institutions and their directors, officers, and employees should be:

  (a) protected by law from criminal and civil liability for breach of any restriction on disclosure of information imposed by contract or by any legislative, regulatory or administrative provision, if they report their suspicions in good faith to the FIU, even if they did not know precisely what the underlying criminal activity was, and regardless of whether illegal activity actually occurred; and,

  (b) prohibited by law from disclosing ("tipping-off") the fact that a suspicious transaction report or related information is being filed with the FIU.

| 22 | **DNFBPs: Customer Due Diligence** |

- The customer due diligence and record-keeping requirements set out in recommendations 10, 11, 12, 15, and 17 apply to casinos—including Internet casinos—when customers engage in financial transactions above the US$/€3,000 threshold.

| 23 | **DNFBPs: Other Measures** |

- The requirements set out in recommendations 18–21 apply to all DNFBPs, subject to certain qualifications that do not apply to Internet casinos.

28	Regulation and Supervision of DNFBPs

- Casinos—as DNFBPs—should be subject to a comprehensive regulatory and supervisory regime that ensures that they have effectively implemented the necessary AML/CFT measures. At a minimum:

  (a) they should be licensed;

  (b) competent authorities should take the necessary legal or regulatory measures to prevent criminals or their associates from holding, or being the beneficial owners of, a significant or controlling interest in, holding management functions in, or being operators of, a casino; and,

  (c) competent authorities should ensure that casinos are effectively supervised for compliance with AML/CFT requirements.

Alderney

Alderney is the third-largest of the Channel Islands, located off the French coast of Normandy and approximately 60 miles from England.[94] Alderney is a British Crown Dependency, is self-governing, and is independent of and not subject to the United Kingdom Parliament.[95] But, the United Kingdom handles the external defense needs and foreign affairs for the Channel Islands, as well as their relationship with the European Union.[96] Alderney does not form part of the EU, but it is inside the customs union.[97]

The key piece of legislation governing Internet gaming conducted from Alderney is the Alderney eGambling Ordinance, 2009 (the "Alderney Ordinance").[98] Among other things, the Alderney Ordinance details two

---

[93] Politically exposed persons are defined in the 40 Recommendations as follows: "Foreign PEPs are individuals who are or have been entrusted with prominent public functions by a foreign country, for example Heads of State or of government, senior politicians, senior government, judicial or military officials, senior executives of state owned corporations, important political party officials. Domestic PEPs are individuals who are or have been entrusted domestically with prominent public functions, for example Heads of State or of government, senior politicians, senior government, judicial or military officials, senior executives of state owned corporations, important political party officials. Persons who are or have been entrusted with a prominent function by an international organisation refers to members of senior management, i.e. directors, deputy directors and members of the board or equivalent functions. The definition of PEPs is not intended to cover middle ranking or more junior individuals in the foregoing categories." Id.

[94] John Clitheroe & Richard McMahon, *Alderney*, INTERNET GAMBLING REPORT 531 (10th ed., Mark Balestra, ed., 2007).

[95] *Id.*

[96] *Id.*

[97] *Id.*

[98] The Alderney eGambling Ordinance, 2009, *available at* http://www.gamblingcontrol.org/userfiles/file/Alderney%20eGambling%20Ordinance%202009%20final%20version.pdf

basic forms of Internet gaming licence that may be obtained: a Category 1 eGambling licence (for business-to-consumer operators) and a Category 2 eGambling licence (for business-to-business operators).[99] The Alderney Gambling Control Commission (the "AGCC") is the body charged with granting[100] and revoking licences,[101] creating and enforcing regulations,[102] and monitoring the industry's licensees from Alderney.[103] Only Alderney companies may hold Category 1[104] or Category 2 eGambling licences.[105]

The Alderney Ordinance mandates that the AGCC must make regulations providing for the way in which an eGambling licensee is "obliged to take steps to comply with applicable international measures in respect of money laundering and terrorist financing."[106] These components are in the Alderney eGambling Regulations 2009 (the "Alderney Regulations").The suitability requirements for licensure under licence Categories 1 and 2 are as follows:

Sections 16 and 17 of the Alderney Regulations detail the procedure for applying for a Category 1 or 2 eGambling Licence. The Alderney Regulations also set out criteria against which the applicant is to be considered.[107] While comprehensive, the application fee to cover processing and—crucially—investigation of the applicant (£10,000)[108] is low compared with other leading jurisdictions (e.g., Nevada). Whether a complete investigation of suitability of an enterprise can be done for this amount is an open question. The AGCC, however, may require further investigation and other costs from the applicant.[109] The required documents for eGambling licence applicants in Schedule 1 to the Alderney Regulations are not comprehensive. For example, an applicant in Alderney only needs to disclose "known" shareholders holding 3% of the issued and outstanding share capital of the applicant or the applicant's "parent." Audited accounts are requested, but the application does not expressly question previous liquidation, insolvency, or bankruptcy prceedings. (Note that section 21 has "the applicant's current financial position and financial background" as criteria against which the regulator assesses the applicant for licensure.[110])

---

[99] *See id.* at §4(1). *See also* Alderney eGambling Regulations 2009, §§ 3–6, *available at* http://www.gamblingcontrol.org/userfiles/file/2009_regs_consolidated_with_2010%20 %201%20%202%20and%202011%20amendments.pdf. Other forms of licensure and certifications are also available, e.g., Temporary eGambling licenses and key individual certificates.

[100] The Alderney eGambling Ordinance, *supra* note 98, at §§ 4, 5, and 7.

[101] *Id.* at § 12.

[102] *See, e.g. id.* at §§ 4(2) and 4(3).

[103] *See, e.g. id.* at §§ 14, 15, and 21.

[104] Alderney eGambling Regulations, *supra* note 99, at § 3(3).

[105] *Id.* at § 5(4).

[106] The Alderney eGambling Ordinance, *supra* note 98, at § 22(2)(e).

[107] Alderney eGambling Regulations, *supra* note 99, at § 21.

[108] *Id.* at Sched. 21.

[109] *Id.* at § 27.

[110] *Id.* at § 21.

When licensing key individuals, the initial investigatory and processing fee (£1,000)[111] is low. The criteria for assessment, however, are broad[112] and the disclosure[113] requires more information than in the case of eGambling licence applicants. Overall, how well the Alderney rules and procedures function in terms of admitting only suitable organizations and individuals is unclear.

Other key components of the anti-money laundering protocols contained in the Alderney Regulations are in Schedule 16. Section 1 of Schedule 16 gives details on the completion of a business risk assessment as a pre-condition for approval of the eGambling licensee's internal control system. The concept of risk—consistent with the FATF's required risk-based approach—runs throughout the Schedule.[114]

Category 1 (business-to-consumer) licensees must undertake customer due diligence measures:

1. Subject to section 4 of Schedule 16,[115] before registering a customer;[116]
2. Immediately after a registered customer makes a deposit equal to or greater than €3,000—the FATF threshold—or makes a deposit that brings the total deposits in any 24 hour period equal to or greater than €3,000;[117]
3. When it reasonably knows or suspects that a person is engaged in money laundering or terrorist financing;[118]
4. When it doubts the truth or sufficiency of any information previously obtained for purposes of customer identification or verification.[119]

Operators must practice enhanced customer due diligence when a Category 1 eGambling licensee does business with a customer who is a PEP[120] or a customer "established or situated" in a country that does not apply or insufficiently applies the 40 Recommendations.[121]

The Alderney Regulations require each Category 1 eGambling licensee to undertake an individual risk assessment of each customer according to that licensee's internal control systems.[122] Alderney's anti-money laundering guidance (the "Alderney Guidance") states that the Category 1 eGambling licensee must collect personal information including "unique

---

[111] *Id.* at Sched. 21.
[112] *Id.* at § 142.
[113] *Id.* at Sched. 9.
[114] *See, e.g.* "high risk" customers referred to in *id.* at Sched. 16, § 6(1)(a).
[115] Allowing identification and verification procedures after registration under certain circumstances.
[116] Alderney eGambling Regulations, *supra* note 99, at Sched. 16, § 2(a).
[117] *Id.* at Sched. 16, § 2(b).
[118] *Id.* at Sched. 16, § 2(c).
[119] *Id.* at Sched. 16, § 2(d).
[120] *Id.* at Sched. 16, § 3(1)(a).
[121] *Id.* at Sched. 16, § 3(1)(b).
[122] *Id.* at § 227(2).

identifiers contained within official documents such as driver's licences, passports or identity cards."[123] The Alderney Guidance, however, basically leaves things up to the Class 1 operator, providing that it "must determine, in accordance with the risk based approach set out in its Business Risk Assessment the extent of the identification and verification information to ask for, what to verify, and how this information is to be verified in order to be satisfied as to the identity of its customer, beneficial owner or underlying principal."[124] This more flexible approach was in effect when the author registered and deposited a small amount of funds with an Alderney Category 1 eGambling licensee. No details of official government documents were requested or provided; only name, address, country of residence, date of birth, and credit card information were given.[125]

An example from the Alderney Guidance indicates a mechanical approach to deposit-based verification. The example posits a customer making a deposit of €2,950 and then subsequently making a further deposit of €100 23 hours later.[126] In such a case, customer due diligence should be performed. By contrast, a customer depositing €2,950 and a further €100 25 hours thereafter would not automatically trigger customer due diligence, "however the licensee may consider the transactions to be linked for other reasons, which would trigger CDD [customer due diligence]."[127] If repeated, such transactions should be seen as higher risk under a risk-based approach.

If a Category 1 eGambling licensee cannot comply with the regular customer due diligence procedures, the licensee must not register the customer[128] or must terminate the customer relationship,[129] and determine if disclosure is required[130] in compliance with the Disclosure (Bailiwick of Guernsey) Law, 2007[131] (the "Disclosure Law") or the Terrorism and Crime (Bailiwick of Guernsey) Law, 2002[132] (the "Terrorism Law"). General provisions in the Alderney Regulations also require that the Category 1 licensee must perform ongoing and effective monitoring of any existing custom-

---

[123] ALDERNEY GAMBLING CONTROL COMMISSION, *The Prevention of Money Laundering and Combating the Financing of Terrorism—Guidance for the eGambling Industry Based in Alderney* 24, *available at* http://www.gamblingcontrol.org/userfiles/file/AML%20and%20 CFT%20guidance%202010.pdf%20LdeL.pdf.

[124] *Id.* at 23.

[125] This may be in accordance with, among other things, the terms of subsection 227(4) of the Alderney Regulations.

[126] Alderney Gambling Control Commission, *supra* note 123, at 28.

[127] *Id.*

[128] Alderney eGambling Regulations, *supra* note 99, at Sched. 16, § 5(a).

[129] *Id.* at Sched. 16, § 5(b).

[130] *Id.* at Sched. 16, § 5(c).

[131] The Disclosure (Bailiwick of Guernsey) Law, 2007, *available at* http://www. gamblingcontrol.org/userfiles/file/60.pdf.

[132] The Terrorism and Crime (Bailiwick of Guernsey) Law, 2002, *available at* http://www. gamblingcontrol.org/userfiles/file/Terrorism_and_Crime_(Bailiwick_of_Guernsey)_ Law,_2002_(Consolidated%202010.pdf.

er relationship,[133] including scrutinizing complex[134] or large and unusual transactions[135] or unusual patterns of transactions[136] (Category 2 licensees are addressed separately.[137])

Section 7 of Schedule 16 covers reporting suspicious activities, with reference both to Part I of the Disclosure Law, which covers financial and non-financial services, and to section 12 of the Terrorism Law. Both Category 1 and Category 2 licensees must follow the reporting requirements in Schedule 16. The Alderney Regulations require both Category 1 and Category 2 eGambling licensees to appoint a money laundering reporting officer and define that officer's responsibilities.[138] Provisions ensure that "relevant employees" receive training in, inter alia, the Alderney Ordinance and the Alderney Regulations;[139] internal procedures and controls to prevent money laundering;[140] the identity and responsibility of the money laundering reporting officer;[141] and, the detection of unusual or suspicious transactions.[142]

For purposes of record-keeping, the rules generally require five year retention periods for both Category 1 and 2 licensees, consistent with the 40 Recommendations. For example, transaction documents or copies must be kept for five years, starting from the date the transaction and/or any related transaction(s) were completed.[143] Licensees must retain customer due diligence information for five years starting from the date the person ceased to be a customer.[144] The Alderney Regulations also make provisions for retaining copies of documents in case a court order requires them.[145] The AGCC's Technical Standards and Guidelines for Internal Control Systems and Internet Gambling Systems specify that a licensee must retain all "gambling information" (inclusive of customer account and session information) for six years.[146] Guernsey imposes sanctions against certain blacklisted persons (notably terrorist organizations), and those sanctions apply to Alderney; therefore, Alderney must prohibit certain transactions (including gaming transactions) with or involving those persons.[147]

---

[133] Alderney eGambling Regulations, *supra* note 99, at Sched. 16, § 6(1).
[134] *Id.* at Sched. 16, § 6(1)(c)(i).
[135] *Id.* at Sched. 16, § 6(1)(c)(ii).
[136] *Id.* at Sched. 16, § 6(1)(c)(iii).
[137] *Id.* at Sched. 16, § 6(1A).
[138] *Id. at* Sched. 16, § 7(1).
[139] *Id.* at Sched. 16, § 8(1)(b)(i).
[140] *Id.* at Sched. 16, § 8(1)(b)(iv).
[141] *Id.* at Sched. 16, § 8(1)(b)(v).
[142] *Id.* at Sched. 16, § 8(1)(b)(vi).
[143] *Id.* at Sched. 16, § 9(1)(a).
[144] *Id.* at Sched. 16, § 9(1)(b).
[145] *Id.* at Sched. 16, § 9(2).
[146] ALDERNEY GAMBLING CONTROL COMMISSION, *Technical Standards and Guidelines for Internal Control Systems and Internet Gambling Systems* 106–107 (2010), *available at* http://www.gamblingcontrol.org/userfiles/file/ICSG%20Version%203_1%20DRAFT%20 v2_0_b.pdf.
[147] *See, e.g.* GUERNSEY FINANCIAL INVESTIGATION UNIT, *Guernsey Renews Sanction Regime Al-Qaida and Taliban, available at* http://guernseyfiu.gov.gg/article/6481/Guernsey-

For banking and payment processing methods and providers of Category 1 licensees, the Alderney Guidance is somewhat helpful in addressing risks:

> The risks of money laundering can be reduced by ensuring that deposits originate from an account with a recognised financial body in the name of the customer. In addition, the risk of money laundering can be further reduced by ensuring that withdrawals are made to the same credit/debit card or account as the original deposit came from. Those Category 1 eGambling licensees that make use of alternative deposit or withdrawal methods (such as third party payment processors) should be aware that this increases the risk of money laundering and their business risk assessments must address this factor.[148]

The IMF's most recent detailed assessment report for Guernsey from January 2011 provides an objective third party view of how the AGCC is doing at deterring money laundering. While the IMF agrees that the AGCC's supervision of interactive gaming operators is extensive,[149] it also notes some areas of concern. One worry is the lack of consistent police record checks on individuals in the licensing process, creating "a risk that the industry may be infiltrated by criminals."[150] Another concern raised is a request for reimbursement through a different payment mechanism than that used by a customer to deposit funds or through payment mechanisms that allow transactions between players. The AGCC requires controls on such payments, but they are at the AGCC's discretion; they are not prohibited under the Alderney Ordinance or the Alderney Regulations. The IMF's "assessment team did not find wide use of these mechanisms during the on-site visit but the vulnerabilities of the payment mechanism is [sic] still present in absence of legislative or regulatory prohibitions."[151] The IMF also remarked on what it called "insufficient" suspicious transaction reporting by gaming operators, given the risk level and the transaction volume conducted by the industry.[152]

Isle of Man

The Isle of Man is another Crown Dependency[153] in the Irish Sea between Britain and Ireland.[154] As with Alderney, the UK Parliament does

---

Renews-Sanction-Regime-Al-Qaida-and-Taliban.

[148] Alderney Gambling Control Commission, *supra* note 123, at 13.

[149] INTERNATIONAL MONETARY FUND, *Guernsey: Detailed Assessment Report on Anti-Money Laundering and Combating the Financing of Terrorism* 275 (2011), *available at* http://www.imf.org/external/pubs/ft/scr/2011/cr1112.pdf.

[150] *Id.* at 15.

[151] *Id.* at 231.

[152] *Id.* at 266.

[153] Claire Milne, *E-Gaming in the Isle of Man: A Primer*, 14 GAM. L. REV. & ECON. 371 (2010).

[154] Miles Benham, *The Isle of Man*, in INTERNET GAMBLING REPORT 507 (10th ed., Mark

not legislate in respect of the Isle of Man's internal affairs, but it is responsible for its defense and foreign affairs.[155] The Isle of Man is not a member of the EU, but it is inside the customs union.[156]

The Isle of Man's Internet gaming and betting regulatory jurisdiction uses the Online Gambling Regulation Act 2001 (the "Isle of Man Act").[157] This outlines the Isle of Man Gambling Supervision Commission's (the "GSC's") authority to issue licences to conduct online gambling,[158] to set the conditions of licensure,[159] and to cancel or suspend a licence.[160] The two key classes of licence are the standard licence (for business-to-consumer operators)[161] and the network services licence (for business-to-business operators).[162] Both licences require a Manx corporation to be the licensee.[163]

The Isle of Man Act establishes that the GSC cannot grant any licence unless it is satisfied that the licensee is under the control of[164]—and that its activities are under the management of—persons of integrity.[165] The application fee for a licence is £5,000,[166] which appears low for normal investigatory costs. The government may request additional funds to defray investigatory costs if necessary. There is no fee required for investigation of key officials, which seems inadequate. The required forms for licence applicants are not onerous. For example, only shareholders with more than five per cent of the issued share capital of the applicant company must disclose their names and shareholdings and complete personal declaration forms. Audited accounts are requested, but there are no express inquiries about previous insolvencies or other events. Separate disclosure is required of a parent corporation, but the same five per cent rule with respect to disclosure of shareholders of the parent also is in effect. The personal declaration forms are not robust. Disclosure only of a key individual's "main personal banking account" is required. They do not require information about other

Balestra, ed., 2007).
[155] Milne, *supra* note 153.
[156] *Id.*
[157] ONLINE GAMBLING REGULATION ACT 2001, ch. 10 (IOM), *available at* http://www.gov.im/lib/docs/gambling/Regulations/onlinegamblingregulationact2001.pdf.
[158] *Id.* at § 4(1).
[159] *Id.* at § 6.
[160] *Id.* at § 13.
[161] *See generally* ONLINE GAMBLING (LICENCE FEES) REGULATIONS 2009, S.D. 257/09 (IOM), *available at* http://www.gov.im/lib/docs/gambling/Regulations/onlinegamblinglicencefeesregul.pdf.
[162] *See generally* ONLINE GAMBLING REGULATIONS (AMENDMENT) (NETWORK SERVICES) REGULATIONS 2011, S.D. 003/11, *available at* http://www.gov.im/lib/docs/gambling//networkregulations.pdf.
[163] ONLINE GAMBLING REGULATION ACT 2001, ch. 10 (IOM), *supra* note 157, § 4(1).
[164] *Id.* at § 4(2)(a).
[165] *Id.* at § 4(2)(c).
[166] ISLE OF MAN GAMBLING SUPERVISION COMMISSION, *Guidance for Online Gambling* 13 (2011), *available at* http://www.gov.im/gambling/applications.xml (follow "Guidance Notes for making an Online Gambling application" hyperlink).

assets or any liabilities except for a yes/no check box concerning a default status on credit cards, mortgages, or other financial liabilities.

All licensees are under the term "licence holder" in the Proceeds of Crime (Money Laundering—Online Gambling) Code 2010 (the "Isle of Man Code"),[167] which details procedures and rules that all licence holders in the Isle of Man must follow.[168] The Isle of Man Code mandates that a licensee must undertake a risk assessment to determine the measures necessary when carrying out player or business participant due diligence or enhanced due diligence;[169] the risk assessment estimates the risk of money laundering using several factors.[170] Moreover, the Isle of Man anti-money laundering guidance (the "Isle of Man Guidance") advocates a risk-based approach to all aspects of the Isle of Man Code.[171] The Isle of Man Code prohibits the acceptance of cash by a licence holder from any customer or business participant—and prohibits acceptance of cash on its behalf by any third party—in relation to Internet gaming.[172] It also expressly prohibits the maintenance of accounts by anonymous licensees[173] or those who use fictitious names,[174] in line with the 40 Recommendations.

The customer due diligence requirements in the Isle of Man are less confusing than the comparable Alderney requirements. When a player establishes an account with a B2C licensee, the licensee must "require the prospective participant to provide satisfactory information as to his identity … as soon as reasonably practical after contact is first made between them."[175] This means that B2C licensees in the Isle of Man must obtain the full name, residential address, date of birth, place of birth, and nationality of each player at registration.[176] This is input by the player. The player does not have to tender copies or numbers of government documents at this stage.

In the B2C model, further identification requirements are engaged when "a qualifying payment is to be made to a participant [player] in relation to online gambling."[177] Licence holders are to establish, maintain, and operate procedures that require a customer to produce satisfactory evidence of her

[167] PROCEEDS OF CRIME (MONEY LAUNDERING—ONLINE GAMBLING) CODE 2010, S.D. 509/10 (IOM), *available at* http://www.gov.im/lib/docs/gambling//amlgamblingcode2010final.pdf.

[168] *Id.* at § 3.

[169] *Id.* at § 5(1).

[170] *Id.* at § 5(2).

[171] Isle of Man Gambling Supervision Commission, *supra* note 166, at 12.

[172] Proceeds of Crime (Money Laundering—Online Gambling) Code 2010, *supra* note 167, at § 3(2).

[173] *Id.* at § 4(1)(a).

[174] *Id.* at § 4(1)(b).

[175] *Id.* at § 6(1).

[176] Isle of Man Gambling Supervision Commission, *supra* note 166, at 30; Brennan Interview, *supra* note 9.

[177] Proceeds of Crime (Money Laundering—Online Gambling) Code 2010, *supra* note 167, at § 7(1).

identify prior to making the qualifying payment.[178] A qualifying payment is one that exceeds €3,000,[179] or a payment that, when taken with all other payments within thirty days preceding the date the payment is to be made, exceeds €3,000 in aggregate.[180] This is consistent with the €3,000 threshold set for casinos by the 40 Recommendations. The documentation required here, i.e., to be "obtained and retained"[181] by the licensee, is generally some form of government-issued identification.[182]

Evidence of identity for business participants—including suppliers and business customers in a B2B model—is addressed in section 8 of the Isle of Man Code. Enhanced due diligence for certain players, suppliers, and business customers is also covered; these measures apply to, among others, PEPs[183] and to persons located in a country that the licensee has reason to believe does not apply or insufficiently applies the 40 Recommendations.[184] Licensees also must take ongoing monitoring steps.[185]

According to the GSC's Chief Executive, these minimum thresholds are in line with the 40 Recommendations. He adds, however, that in applying a risk-based approach, many of Isle of Man's licensees elect to implement further due diligence controls and identification procedures at earlier transactional stages and where increased risk is perceived.[186] In fact, this is the case with Paddy Power, a major interactive gaming and betting operator licensed by the Isle of Man.[187] Paddy Power, consistent with section 6 in the Isle of Man Code, obtains information at the point of registration, i.e., full name, residential address, date of birth, place of birth, and nationality. At the deposit stage, Paddy Power engages most of its risk assessment protocols.[188] Paddy Power has a dedicated customer security team and runs constant reports based upon deposits reaching certain thresholds, and they check customers who fit various risk profiles.[189] For example, if a new customer makes deposits using a credit card in the ordinary course, the threshold for automatic review would be higher than if the deposit method were by means of an e-wallet or a prepaid voucher.[190] (This review applies irrespective of the €3,000 threshold detailed in paragraph 7(3)(b) of the

---

[178] *Id.* at § 7(2).

[179] *Id.* at § 7(3)(a).

[180] *Id.* at § 7(3)(b).

[181] Isle of Man Gambling Supervision Commission, *supra* note 166, at 31.

[182] *Id.*; Brennan Interview, *supra* note 9.

[183] Proceeds of Crime (Money Laundering—Online Gambling) Code 2010, *supra* note 167, at § 9(2)(a).

[184] *Id.* at § 9(2)(b).

[185] *Id.* at § 10.

[186] Brennan Interview, *supra* note 9.

[187] The licensee in the Isle of Man is Paddy Power Holdings Limited. Paddy Power plc is a publicly-traded corporation on the Irish and London stock exchanges.

[188] Interview with Robert Reddin, Compliance Manager, Paddy Power (Feb. 10, 2012) [hereinafter Reddin Interview].

[189] *Id.*

[190] *Id.*

Isle of Man Code, which only applies to withdrawals.) Reports are generated based on, inter alia, frequency and patterns of play, payment activities, and deposit and withdrawal methods.[191] The thresholds and risk profiles in these reports are dynamic and subject to constant revision and refinement.[192]

When a Paddy Power customer appears on one or more reports, the enterprise will seek to validate that customer by using a suite of tools and inquiries. This ranges from inquiries placed against external proprietary databases of information to direct questioning of the customer to determine the source of funds.[193] If Paddy Power cannot ascertain the sources of funds, it will file a suspicious transaction report with the relevant Isle of Man authority.[194]

According to Paddy Power's compliance manager, who is the enterprise's deputy money laundering reporting officer, in compliance with Isle of Man law, the vast majority of their B2C customers are electronically verified within a short period after their initial deposit to their online interactive gaming account.[195]

The Isle of Man Code requires the licensee to generate and maintain records of all transactions with players and business participants sufficient to demonstrate compliance with money laundering regulations.[196] These records must be kept for at least six years from: the date the player or business participant formally ceased to be a player or business participant;[197] or, the date of the last transaction carried out by the player or business participant.[198] The GSC takes the view that all gaming sessions on the licensee's site are required to be tracked, recorded, and available for access by appropriate authorities to comply with the minimum six-year retention rule.[199]

When reporting suspicious transactions, each licensee must appoint a money laundering reporting officer,[200] who is the lynchpin of the licensee's internal and external reporting procedures. This reporting officer must be sufficiently senior within the organization[201] (or must have sufficient experience and authority, if not within the organization)[202] and must have direct access to the directors or managing board of the licensee.[203] Among other

---

[191] *Id.*

[192] *Id.*

[193] *Id.*

[194] *Id.*

[195] *Id.*

[196] Proceeds of Crime (Money Laundering—Online Gambling) Code 2010, *supra* note 167, at § 12.

[197] *Id.* at § 13(1)(a).

[198] *Id.* at § 13(1)(b).

[199] Brennan Interview, *supra* note 9.

[200] Proceeds of Crime (Money Laundering—Online Gambling) Code 2010, *supra* note 167, at § 16(1).

[201] *Id.* at § 16(2)(a).

[202] *Id.* at § 16(2)(b).

[203] *Id.* at § 16(2)(c).

functions, the money laundering reporting officer initiates the disclosure of any applicable suspicious transaction reports to the Isle of Man Financial Crime Unit.[204] Staff screening and training by a licensee is addressed in sections 17 and 18, respectively, of the Isle of Man Code.

Interestingly, in a reflection of the FATF's recommendation 15 (new technologies), the Isle of Man's rules require a licensee to maintain appropriate procedures and controls to prevent "the misuse of technological developments for the purpose of money laundering or the financing of terrorism."[205] This is a clear call for constant vigilance about the exploitation of new technology; it demonstrates the risk-based approach adopted by the Isle of Man.

Tipping-off is covered in the Isle of Man Guidance. The offense itself is described in subsection 6.8.4(1)–(3), while the penalties associated with the offense are described in subsection 6.8.4(4). There is a current list of sanctions imposed by the Isle of Man as well as against selected territories and institutions.[206]

With respect to banking and payment processing, interviews with the GSC and with an operator regulated in the Isle of Man were insightful. The regulator acknowledged that, in an ideal world, the Isle of Man's operators would only accept credit and debit cards for payments from major providers.[207] The GSC, however, prefers a risk-based approach as advocated by the 40 Recommendations. According to the law, its licensees have a requirement in the Isle of Man to understand with whom they're doing business. This extends to banks' and payment intermediaries' internal controls and procedures for their own users and customers.[208] On the operator side, Paddy Power, for example, takes a risk-based approach but tries to deal with "cleaner" operators: the larger organizations that have a positive market reputation and are heavily regulated.[209]

The most recent detailed assessment report compiled by the IMF for the Isle of Man is from 2009. The GSC received generally positive marks in this assessment. However, the IMF noted that additional resources—particularly staffing resources and specialist skills—would need to be allocated to the GSC to keep pace with its workload and the growth of the Internet gaming sector in the Isle of Man.[210]

---

[204] *Id.* at § 16(3)(f). The money laundering reporting officer's role is expanded upon in Isle of Man Gambling Supervision Commission, *Online Gambling Guidance Notes for the Prevention of Money Laundering and Countering of Terrorist Financing, supra* note 166, at 10–12.

[205] Proceeds of Crime (Money Laundering—Online Gambling) Code 2010, *supra* note 167, at § 19.

[206] Isle of Man Treasury Department, *Sanctions and Export Control in the Isle of Man* (2012), *available at* http://www.gov.im/treasury/customs/sanctions.xml.

[207] Brennan Interview, *supra* note 9.

[208] *Id.*

[209] Reddin Interview, *supra* note 188.

[210] IMF Isle of Man Report, *supra* note 66, at 20 and 207–208.

Kahnawake

The Mohawk Territory of Kahnawake is an aboriginal community of approximately 8,000 people located 20 minutes from Montreal, Canada.[211] The entire territory occupies approximately 20 square miles.[212] The Mohawk Council of Kahnawake (the "Mohawk Council") is the governing body in and for the territory and is composed of eleven chiefs and one grand chief, all of whom are popularly elected by the community.[213] Kahnawake has consistently and historically asserted sovereignty over its affairs and territory. Kahnawake has its own police force, court, schools, hospital, fire services, and social services.[214]

The Kahnawake Gaming Commission (the "KGC") was established by the Kahnawake Gaming Law, enacted by the Mohawk Council in 1996.[215] The KGC's basic mandate is to regulate and control gaming within or from Kahnawake.[216] Assessing the suitability of interactive gaming licensees and implementing money laundering controls is done under the rubric of the Regulations Concerning Interactive Gaming (the "KGC Regulations"),[217] originally promulgated by the KGC in 1999.

The KGC Regulations set out two types of licence: the Interactive Gaming Licence (only one of which has been issued by the KGC, to Mohawk Internet Technologies, a band-empowered entity wholly owned by the Mohawk Council); and the Client Provider Authorization (the "CPA"). The CPA is the licence obtained by private Internet gaming operators seeking to be "licensed" by Kahnawake. The holder of a CPA may conduct interactive gaming from Kahnawake, "but only from the co-location facility that is owned and operated by the holder of a valid Interactive Gaming Licence."[218]

An applicant for a CPA must complete prescribed forms and provide copious information.[219] The data solicited in this process is extensive and useful to determining suitability. The cost for applying is US$25,000, which includes the estimated cost of the KGC conducting due diligence on the applicant and any individuals who have provided personal information forms in addition to that application.[220] The application cost for each proposed key person licence is US$5,000.[221]

---

[211] Murray Marshall, *Kahnawake*, INTERNET GAMBLING REPORT 321 (5th ed., Mark Balestra, ed., 2002).
[212] *Id.*
[213] *Id.* at 322.
[214] *Id.*
[215] *Id.*
[216] *Id.*
[217] REGULATIONS CONCERNING INTERACTIVE GAMING (1999) (Kahnawake), *available at* http://gamingcommission.ca/docs/RegulationsConcerningInteractiveGaming.pdf.
[218] *Id.* at § 34.
[219] *Id.* at §§ 35(a)–35(f).
[220] *Id.* at § 35(g).
[221] *Id.* at § 35(h).

What is much more interesting to an assessment of anti-money laundering controls in Kahnawake than the suitability process or its cost is the absence of many specific money laundering rules and procedures in the KGC Regulations. The bulk of the money laundering provisions are farmed out by means of section 168, which provides as follows: "Authorized Client Providers will comply with the recommendations of the Financial Action Task Force ("FATF") as they pertain to gaming establishments."[222] In other words, the 40 Recommendations—at least as they apply to Internet casinos—are imported wholesale into the KGC Regulations. A violation of any of the 40 Recommendations is therefore a violation of the KGC Regulations. Because of the breadth of the 40 Recommendations and how many other agencies seek to mimic or incorporate their terms, this may not be a bad approach.

However, difficulties exist in both principle and in practice with such an approach. While the 40 Recommendations are continually being revised and updated, the FATF devotes few resources specifically to Internet gaming and betting. The 40 Recommendations and the RBA Guidance for Casinos include Internet gaming considerations. Full-time online interactive gaming regulators, however, may be in a better position than the FATF to take the 40 Recommendations and add specific additional provisions that benefit the sector and potentially reduce money laundering.

In addition, certain provisions of the 40 Recommendations suggest an ongoing monitoring role by regulators. For example, recommendation 28 provides that competent authorities, which include gaming regulators, should ensure that casinos are effectively supervised for compliance with anti-money laundering requirements. In this context, it is odd for the KGC Regulations only to mandate CPA-holder compliance with the 40 Recommendations when the 40 Recommendations provide continuing obligations with which the KGC is supposed to comply.[223] By foregoing the creation of detailed local rules, the KGC may be relinquishing some of its responsibilities to its stakeholders, thereby making itself less responsive and, ultimately, less relevant as a regulatory body.

This approach may be easier to support in practice—if not conceptually—if the specific provisions in the KGC Regulations were complete. Section 163 states that the KGC "will establish specific rules and procedures for Authorized Client Providers for the purpose of anticipating and preventing suspicious activities whereby monies obtained by illegal means are used for the purpose of interactive gaming."[224] The KGC, however, has no such specific rules and procedures. Another provision establishes that CPA-holders must file suspicious activity reports with the KGC under cer-

---

[222] *Id.* at § 168.

[223] Perhaps not too much should be made of this point. If asked, the KGC might state that its obligation to comply with the 40 Recommendations is well understood and should be taken for granted.

[224] Regulations Concerning Interactive Gaming, *supra* note 217, § 163.

tain conditions, in a form to be provided by the KGC.[225] But the KGC has not prescribed forms for this purpose.

Other aspects of the KGC Regulations raise questions. For instance, they state that the KGC will cooperate and, "when appropriate, provide information concerning actual or potential money-laundering activities of which it becomes aware, to the Kahnawake Peacekeepers and/or such other domestic or international agency or agencies that are appropriate."[226] It is unclear whether such agencies would include Canada's FIU (referred to in recommendation 20 of the 40 Recommendations), the Financial Transactions and Reports Analysis Centre of Canada ("FinTRAC"). This point is the corollary of the FATF's concern about a lack of anti-money laundering regulations in Kahnawake, discussed below. Also, the threshold triggering a suspicious activity report (US$5,000)[227] and the prohibitions on withdrawals in excess of US$10,000 (absent identification)[228] seem to be incongruent with the US$/€3,000 threshold set out in the 40 Recommendations.

Another interesting distinction is that, unlike Alderney and the Isle of Man, the KGC Regulations do not require the CPA be issued to a locally formed entity. Requiring a corporation that is licensed and regulated by gaming authorities to be set up in the licensing jurisdiction may be preferable and the best practice to ensure effective oversight. Nevertheless, regulators may control a licensee in other ways such as through supervision of its technology, the presence of a licensee's books and records in the jurisdiction, having a local office and presence, and any number of other requirements.

Finally, this section would be incomplete without mentioning the FATF's concerns about Kahnawake detailed in its latest mutual evaluation report on Canada from February 2008.[229] In the mutual evaluation, the FATF describes the activities and organization set out by the Mohawks in regulating Internet gaming and betting and states that the KGC Regulations "were designed to ensure that all interactive gaming and gaming related activities ... satisfy three basic principles: (1) that only suitable persons and entities are permitted to operate within Kahnawake; (2) that the games offered are fair to the player; and (3) that winners are paid."[230]

The FATF, however, expressed serious concerns about Kahnawake from a money laundering perspective, as follows:

> [T]hese activities [the regulation of Internet gaming and betting] are not subject to AML/CFT regulations and Canada's federal and provincial gov-

---

[225] *Id.* at § 165.

[226] *Id.* at § 169.

[227] *Id.* at § 165.

[228] *Id.* at § 167(a).

[229] FINANCIAL ACTION TASK FORCE, *Third Mutual Evaluation on Anti-Money Laundering and Combating the Financing of Terrorism—Canada* (2008), *available at* http://www.fatf-gafi.org/dataoecd/5/3/40323928.pdf.

[230] *Id.* at 231.

ernments are faced with substantial challenges in determining the appropriate course of action to take concerning Internet gambling. The industry has grown rapidly and generates huge revenues. Canada must either enforce its prohibition effectively or introduce comprehensive AML/CFT regulation for the industry.[231]

The statement that regulation by Kahnawake is simply "not subject" to anti-money laundering regulations might be pitching the case too high. As discussed, anti-money laundering protocols are present in the KGC Regulations. The issue is whether they are complete and appropriate to the responsibilities faced by a tier one regulator. For example, the interaction between Kahnawake and FinTRAC in the context of the KGC Regulations and the 40 Recommendations has been highlighted as an area lacking clarity.

Malta

Malta is an interesting jurisdiction for its location and the interplay of its anti-money laundering rules with its Internet gaming and betting regulatory agencies. Malta is an archipelago near the centre of the Mediterranean Sea, strategically positioned between Sicily and North Africa. Malta is a full member of the EU, a member of the Schengen area, and a member of the euro zone.[232] Internet gaming in Malta and its licensure is governed primarily by the Lotteries and Other Games Act (the "LOGA").[233] Section 9 of the LOGA establishes that the Lotteries and Gaming Authority (the "LGA") is charged with inquiring into the suitability of all licensees under the LOGA,[234] ensuring that all gaming is kept free from criminal activity,[235] and advising the Maltese Minister of Finance when creating applicable regulations.[236] The main regulations regarding online gaming and betting created under the LOGA are the Remote Gaming Regulations (the "Malta Regulations").[237]

The Malta Regulations provide for the issuance,[238] suspension, and cancellation[239] of remote gaming licences for Internet gaming and betting operations. The initial grant is subject to a "fit and proper" determination of those persons involved in the applicant corporation pursuant to subsection

---

[231] *Id.*

[232] European Union, *Malta, available at* http://europa.eu/about-eu/countries/member-countries/malta/index_en.htm.

[233] Lotteries and Other Games Act (Malta), *available at* http://www.lga.org.mt/lga/content.aspx?id=87374 (follow "Lotteries and Other Games Act, 2001" hyperlink).

[234] *Id.* at § 11(c).

[235] *Id.* at § 11(e).

[236] *Id.* at § 11(k).

[237] Remote Gaming Regulations, S.L. 438.04 (2004) (Malta), *available at* http://www.lga.org.mt/lga/content.aspx?id=87374 (follow "Remote Gaming Regulations English Version" hyperlink).

[238] *Id.* at §§ 7–8.

[239] *Id.* at § 13.

8(2) of the Malta Regulations. As with Alderney and the Isle of Man, an applicant for a remote gaming licence must be incorporated under and comply with the Malta Companies Act.[240] The Malta Regulations provide for four classes of gaming licence that encompass everything from business-to-consumer gaming and betting exchanges to business-to-business network models.[241] At least one "key official" must be appointed by each gaming or betting licensee,[242] who must personally supervise the operations of the licensee of which she is a key official[243] and ensure that the licensee complies with all applicable laws and regulations, conditions of licensure, and directives issued by the LGA.[244]

An application for any of the four classes of remote gaming licence requires remittance of a €2,330 fee.[245] This covers the administration and investigation costs. This is a low fee and may not sufficiently cover thorough investigation costs. A separate fee is not required for key officials of each licensee. The Malta Regulations, however, permit the LGA to requisition actual investigative, inspection, and other costs from the licensee or proposed licensee "when objectively reasonable."[246] Interestingly, the fee schedule calls for special fees (sometimes based on an hourly rate)[247] when the LGA must review and pre-approve a contractual relationship between a licensee and a supplier.[248]

The application form itself solicits useful information. For example, it requires a listing of "all proposed/registered beneficiaries" of the corporate applicant. Presumably, this means all registered shareholders of the corporation, not merely those over a particular threshold percentage. The application also seeks disclosure of details concerning patents and proposed trademarks in connection with the licensed Internet gaming operations. The key official personal declaration form, however, may not elicit some useful pieces of information. The application seeks information about previous assignments in bankruptcy of the individual, for instance, but does not expressly solicit full financial statements from the prospective key official.

With suitability out of the way, the money laundering rules and procedures should be examined. The LOGA provides that, notwithstanding the provisions of the Prevention of Money Laundering Act (the "PMLA")[249]

---

[240] *Id.* at § 4.
[241] *Id.* at 1st Sched. Reg. 3.
[242] *Id.* at § 15(1).
[243] *Id.* at § 15(2)(a).
[244] *Id.* at § 15(2)(b).
[245] *Id.* at 2nd Sched. Reg. 6, § 1.
[246] *Id.* at § 6(3).
[247] *Id.* at 2nd Sched. Reg. 6, § 5.
[248] *Id.* at § 11(4)(e). This provision only applies when the supplier is to receive a percentage of the profits of the remote gaming operation or a commission.
[249] PREVENTION OF MONEY LAUNDERING ACT (Malta), *available at* http://justiceservices. gov.mt/DownloadDocument.aspx?app=lom&itemid=8842&l=1.

the Minister of Finance may provide guidelines for gaming licensees and their employees about transactions that may raise money laundering suspicions.[250] (No such specific guidelines for gaming licensees have been issued.) The LOGA also mandates that, where any employee of the LGA and any "officer or employee of a licensee or other person acting on behalf of a licensee or under an arrangement with him" has reason to suspect a money laundering transaction has taken place or will take place, that person has an affirmative duty to act in accordance with regulations made under both the PMLA and the LOGA.[251] The Malta Regulations also mention money laundering generally, e.g., whether the applicant has followed policies and will take affirmative steps to prevent money laundering is one of the 'fit and proper' tests.[252]

While the foregoing provisions appear to imply that Internet gaming licensees are within the scope of the PMLA, the Prevention of Money Laundering and Funding of Terrorism Regulations (the "PMLA Regulations") only define "relevant activity" as including the activities of "casino licensees."[253] ("Subject persons" include persons carrying out relevant activities.[254]) In the PMLA Regulations, "casino" has the same meaning as in Malta's Gaming Act[255]—and "casino licensee" is construed accordingly[256]—but the Gaming Act only says that "'casino' means such premises in relation to which the Minister [of Finance] has granted a concession," which does not expressly include remote gaming.[257] Accordingly, it is relevant to question whether or not Internet gaming licensees are specifically subject to the provisions of the PMLA and its regulations. Irrespective of any ambiguity, and given the application of the Third Directive to "casinos" in Malta, as Malta is a full EU member, local counsel and operators in Malta *act like* the provisions of the PMLA and the PMLA Regulations apply to Internet gaming licensees in Malta.[258] Obviously, any lack of clarity on this point is less than ideal from a best practices perspective.

With respect to specific guidance similar to what has been produced by Alderney and the Isle of Man, the Financial Intelligence Analysis Unit (the "FIAU") in Malta, has issued a series of Implementing Procedures (the

---

[250] Lotteries and Other Games Act (Malta), *supra* note 233, at § 61(1).

[251] *Id.* at § 61(2).

[252] Remote Gaming Regulations, *supra* note 237, at § 8(2)(g).

[253] PREVENTION OF MONEY LAUNDERING AND FUNDING OF TERRORISM REGULATIONS, S.L. 373.01 (2008) (Malta), § 2(1)(g) (definition of "relevant activity"), *available at* http://www.justiceservices.gov.mt/DownloadDocument.aspx?app=lom&itemid=10454&l=1.

[254] *Id.* at § 2(1) (definition of "subject person").

[255] GAMING ACT (Malta), *available at* http://www.justiceservices.gov.mt/DownloadDocument.aspx?app=lom&itemid=8867&l=1.

[256] Prevention of Money Laundering and Funding of Terrorism Regulations, *supra* note 253, at § 2(1) (definition of "casino").

[257] Gaming Act (Malta), *supra* note 255, at § 2 (definition of "casino").

[258] Interview with Olga Finkel, Managing Partner, WH Partners (Mar. 20, 2012).

"Malta Guidance").[259] The Malta Guidance is an attempt by the FIAU to outline the requirements and obligations of the PMLA and its Regulations and to assist in designing and implementing systems to detect and prevent money laundering and terrorist financing.[260] The Malta Guidance adopts a risk-based approach at one stage,[261] and requires implementation of procedures to manage the money laundering risks,[262] but then expressly states that the risk-based approach itself is optional.[263]

The Malta Guidance mandates certain customer due diligence procedures similar to those adopted in the Isle of Man. The Isle of Man requires a B2C licensee to obtain the full name, residential address, date of birth, place of birth, and nationality of each player at account setup. The more general identification requirements in the Malta Guidance require official full name; place and date of birth; permanent residential address; identity reference number, where available; and nationality.[264] The only additional requirement is the identity reference, but customers do not need to produce documents to an online gaming licensee at this stage. When a player triggers a verification of identity threshold (for example, when a player makes a deposit or withdrawal of €2,000 or more, consistent with both the Third Directive and the provisions of subsection 9(1) of the PMLA Regulations), verification procedures include submission of valid government-issued identification documents to the gaming licensee.[265] Extra due diligence is recommended with PEPs,[266] and extra caution suggested in business relationships with persons from jurisdictions that are not "reputable jurisdictions."[267] The Malta Guidance also asserts that operators should pay special attention to any money laundering threat that may arise from new or developing technologies or from products that may favor anonymity.[268]

The Malta Guidance contains various record-keeping requirements. These include items like customer due diligence documents and details on

---

[259] *Implementing Procedures Issued by the Financial Intelligence Analysis Unit in Terms of the Provisions of the Prevention of Money Laundering and Funding of Terrorism Regulations—Part I* (2011), *available at* http://www.fiumalta.org/library/PDF/23.08.2011%20-%20Implementing%20Procedures%20-%20FINAL%20%28With%20amendment%20dates%29.pdf [hereinafter Malta Guidance].

[260] *Id.* at 10.

[261] *Id.*

[262] *Id.* at 54.

[263] *Id.* at 57.

[264] *Id.* at 20.

[265] *Id.* at 20–22.

[266] *Id.* at 50.

[267] *Id.* at 38. "Reputable jurisdiction" in § 2 of the PMLA Regulations means "any country having appropriate legislative measures for the prevention of money laundering and the funding of terrorism, taking into account that country's membership of, or any declaration or accreditation by, any international organisation recognised as laying down internationally accepted standards for the prevention of money laundering and for combating the funding of terrorism, and which supervises natural and legal persons subject to such legislative measures for compliance therewith."

[268] Malta Guidance, *supra* note 259, at 50.

transactions—including withdrawals and deposits—by players.[269] Consistent with the rules set out by the FATF on records retention, the Malta Guidance establishes that a licensee must retain these records for no less than five years.[270] The Malta Regulations mandate data retention requirements for financial reports[271] and about each game played in the gaming system itself (including, inter alia, player balances, stakes played, and results).[272]

Each licensee must appoint a money laundering reporting officer.[273] Consistent with other reporting officer relationships, this officer must occupy a senior position within the organization where she can effectively influence the company's anti-money laundering policy.[274] The money laundering reporting officer must have a direct reporting line to the directors and have authority to act independently in carrying out her responsibilities.[275] Furthermore, licensees must ensure that employees are aware of the organization's anti-money laundering policies and train their employees to recognize and handle suspicious transactions.[276] External reporting of suspicious transactions to the FIAU is provided for in subsection 15(6) of the Malta Regulations and is set out in greater detail in the Malta Guidance.[277] Tipping off offenses are briefly covered in the Malta Regulations.[278]

Controls over financial intermediaries working with Internet gaming operators are not specifically addressed in the Malta Guidance. (No part of the Malta Guidance is specifically directed at online interactive gaming licensees, perhaps owing to the ambiguity in whether the PMLA applies to the LGA's remote gaming licensees in the first place.) The Malta Guidance establishes some customer due diligence measures for intermediaries that licensees can rely on in certain circumstances, but it does not permit ongoing monitoring measures by another person or third party.[279]

Finally, Malta maintains a series of international lists that identify various parties subject to sanctions or other restrictive measures.[280]

---

[269] *Id.* at 65–66.

[270] *Id.* at 67.

[271] Remote Gaming Regulations, *supra* note 237, at 3rd Sched., Reg. 25, § 7.

[272] *Id.* at § 9.

[273] Malta Guidance, *supra* note 259, at 70.

[274] *Id.*

[275] *Id.*

[276] *Id.* at 82.

[277] *Id.* at 72–75.

[278] Remote Gaming Regulations, *supra* note 237, at § 16(1).

[279] Malta Guidance, *supra* note 259, at 51. There is a limited exception to the customer due diligence requirements where the third party undertakes currency exchange or money transmission or remittance services, but the exception only applies if the subject person relying on the third party is itself a financial institution whose main business is currency exchange or money transmission or remittance services. Malta Guidance, *supra* note 259, at 52. Clearly such an exception does not apply to Internet gaming operators licensed by the LGA.

[280] MALTA FINANCIAL SERVICES AUTHORITY, *International Sanctions*, *available at* http://www.mfsa.com.mt/pages/viewcontent.aspx?id=105.

Nevada

The final jurisdiction in our survey is the U.S. state of Nevada. In many ways, Nevada exemplifies best practices. Nevada—specifically Las Vegas—is almost a metonym for international bricks and mortar gambling, or at least for land-based gambling in the United States. Thus far, Nevada has elected to actively regulate and accept applications for licensure of intra-state interactive poker only.[281] Nevada's interactive gaming regulations allow for three basic types of licence: an interactive gaming operator licence;[282] a licence to manufacture interactive gaming systems;[283] and, a service provider licence.[284]

The process for determining suitability in Nevada is impressive and expensive. The initial licence fee for an establishment to operate interactive gaming is US$500,000.[285] The inquiries and investigations made by the state Gaming Control Board (the "GCB") are extensive and the burden of proof is at all times on the applicant.[286] As far as investigations, these costs (accumulated on an hourly basis by GCB agents) are fully charged to an applicant for licensure. Estimates of investigatory costs "can be very high and range from $30,000 for a very simple investigation to over a million dollars for a complex investigation involving foreign citizens. In addition, the costs of investigating the corporation often exceed $50,000 to $100,000."[287] Investigations do not begin unless and until the estimated investigation fees are paid.[288] Historically, every shareholder of a private corporation applying for a non-restricted licence in Nevada had to be found suitable by the GCB. Recent amendments to the Nevada Gaming Control Act and attendant regulations, however, now allow persons holding five per cent or less of the issued and outstanding shares of a private licensee to merely register with the GCB and submit to its jurisdiction.[289] Persons applying for registration, however, still must complete extensive applications. That said, whether a corporation seeking a non-restricted licence is publicly traded or not, the GCB can require any person holding any beneficial interest in the licensee to undergo a full finding of suitability.[290]

---

[281] Nev. Gaming Comm'n. Reg. 5A.140(1)(a) (2011) (providing that operators shall not accept or facilitate wagers "on any game other than the game of poker and its derivatives as approved by the chairman and published on the board's website").

[282] Nev. Gaming Comm'n. Reg. 5A.030 (2011).

[283] Nev. Gaming Comm'n. Reg. 14.020 (2011).

[284] Nev. Gaming Comm'n. Reg. 5.240(2)(d) and Reg. 5.240(3).

[285] NEV. REV. STAT. § 463.765 (2001); Nev. Gaming Comm'n. Reg. 5A.040 (2011).

[286] See, e.g. Nev. Gaming Comm'n. Reg. 15.1594–4 (1973).

[287] Anthony Cabot, *Obtaining a Non-Restricted Gaming License in Nevada*, 6 *available at* http://www.lrlaw.com/files/Uploads/Documents/Obtaining%20Nonrestricted%20Gaming%20License.pdf.

[288] *Id.*

[289] *See, e.g.* NEV. REV. STAT. § 463.5735 (2011). Nevada Senate Bill 218 was signed into law on May 16, 2011.

[290] *See, e.g.* NEV. REV. STAT. §§ 463.5735(3) (2011) and 463.643(1)–(2) (2011).

The investigation is thorough. Disclosure through the Multi-Jurisdictional Personal History Disclosure Form, for example, touches on everything relevant from a suitability perspective, as befits its length (the form itself, plus relevant attachments, can easily run into the hundreds of pages). A suitability investigation will go into every aspect of an applicant's finances.[291] Anecdotes about the bizarre things arising in investigations are legion. For example, one story involves a team of gaming control agents flying to the east coast of the U.S., auditing a safe deposit box of a license applicant at a bank, and discovering US$25,000 labelled "payoff funds."[292]

An application for licensure as an operator of interactive gaming in Nevada will be made, processed, and determined in the same manner as a non-restricted gaming licence application.[293] The same high (non-restricted gaming licence) standard applies to a licence applicant for becoming a manufacturer or distributor of an interactive gaming system[294] and to any service provider who receives payments based on earnings or profits from any gambling game (including, for example, marketing affiliates paid a percentage of rake on an interactive poker network).[295]

Anti-money laundering mandates and rules in Nevada come from two primary sources: the federal Bank Secrecy Act of 1970 (the BSA)[296]—as amended by subsequent enactments, including the United and Strengthening America by Providing Appropriate Tools Required to Intercept and Obstruct Terrorism (USA PATRIOT) Act of 2001—and the provisions of the state gaming regulations and Minimum Internal Control Standards (the "MICS") (collectively, the "Nevada Regulations").[297]

With respect to the BSA, "a casino, gambling casino, or gaming establishment" is included in its provisions if it has annual gaming revenue in excess of US$1 million and: is licensed as a casino, gambling casino, or gaming establishment under the laws of any U.S. state or political subdivision thereof; or, is an Indian gaming operation conducted under the Indian Gaming Regulatory Act (other than an operation limited to class I gaming).[298] Casinos and card rooms subject to the BSA must:

1. Collect information and make reports about currency transactions—including cash in and out, the purchase of chips, safekeeping deposits, and marker purchases—in excess of US$10,000, whether the transaction is suspicious or not;[299]

---

[291] Cabot & Kelly, *supra* note 2, at 137.

[292] *Id.*

[293] Nev. Gaming Comm'n. Reg. 5A.030(2) (2011).

[294] Nev. Gaming Comm'n. Reg. 14.020(2) (2011).

[295] Nev. Gaming Comm'n. Reg. 5.240(3)(a)(ii) (2011) and Reg. 5.240(7)(a) (2011).

[296] For a useful overview of the BSA provisions, *see generally* Michael Gordon et al, *Panel Discussion: Money Laundering, Cybercrime and Currency Transactions*, 11 U.S.-Mex. L.J. 219, 219–220 (2003).

[297] Nev. Gaming Comm'n. Minimum Internal Control Standards (2012).

[298] 31 U.S.C. § 5312(a)(2)(X) (2006).

[299] 31 U.S.C. § 5313(a) (2006); 31 C.F.R. § 1021.311 (2011).

2. Report any suspicious transactions, and make sure that no person involved in the transaction is notified that the transaction has been reported (tipping-off);[300]
3. Set up "anti-money laundering programs including, at a minimum, the development of internal policies, procedures, and controls; the designation of a compliance officer; an ongoing employee training program; and an independent audit function to test programs;"[301] and,
4. Consult lists of known or suspected terrorists (e.g., the OFAC's Specially Designated Nationals List) to determine if anyone seeking to open an account appears on such a list.[302]

The Nevada Regulations require operators to implement procedures designed to detect and prevent transactions that may be associated with money laundering and other criminal activities and to ensure compliance with all federal money laundering laws.[303] In other words, Nevada law compels compliance with its own money laundering prevention system, the BSA, and other statutes. This broad mandate is given specific effect throughout the Nevada Regulations.

One example of this specificity is the customer due diligence performed during player registration. At the creation of a player's authorized interactive gaming account, the Nevada Regulations set out information that interactive gaming operators must collect. This information includes the player's name,[304] the physical address where the player resides,[305] his or her date of birth,[306] and the player's social security number (if a U.S. resident).[307] It also includes confirmation that the player has not been previously self-excluded[308] and is not on the Nevada blacklist.[309] Unlike other jurisdictions examined here, Nevada requires, within thirty days of providing registration information, that the interactive gaming operator must perform procedures to verify the information and that the operator must limit the player's gaming activity during that verification period.[310] The player, however, may not deposit more than US$5,000 into her account during the verification period, which is a high threshold.[311] All the same, the player cannot withdraw funds during the verification period, which is a good check to have in place.[312] The verification procedures must be recorded and maintained, and the MICS suggest that the licensee obtain and record credentials from the

---

[300] 31 U.S.C. § 5318(g).
[301] 31 U.S.C. § 5318(h)(1).
[302] 31 U.S.C § 5318(l)(2)(C).
[303] Nev. Gaming Comm'n. Reg. 5A.080 (2011).
[304] Nev. Gaming Comm'n. Reg. 5A.110(2)(a) (2011).
[305] Nev. Gaming Comm'n. Reg. 5A.110(2)(c) (2011).
[306] Nev. Gaming Comm'n. Reg. 5A.110(2)(b) (2011).
[307] Nev. Gaming Comm'n. Reg. 5A.110(2)(d) (2011).
[308] Nev. Gaming Comm'n. Reg. 5A.110(2)(e) (2011).
[309] Nev. Gaming Comm'n. Reg. 5A.110(2)(f) (2011).
[310] Nev. Gaming Comm'n. Reg. 5A.110(5) (2011).
[311] Nev. Gaming Comm'n. Reg. 5A.110(5)(a) (2011).
[312] Nev. Gaming Comm'n. Reg. 5A.110(5)(b) (2011).

player and record and verify the date of birth and physical address from external sources.[313] If the verification has not occurred within thirty days, the operator must immediately suspend the interactive gaming account.[314]

Some parallel identification requirements exist between the BSA and Nevada's regulations; for example, when a report on a transaction amount exceeds US$10,000, operators need to file the appropriate reports. The items to be verified and recorded include name, account number, and social security number or taxpayer identification number (if any).[315] For non-residents or aliens, verification of identity "must be made by passport, alien identification card, or other official document evidencing nationality or residence."[316]

Robust provisions exist for transfers of amounts between an interactive gaming account and the same player's land-based casino account.[317] Furthermore, when a player makes an in-person withdrawal request at a bricks and mortar gaming establishment (after transferring from her interactive gaming account), casinos must record certain particulars and the player must sign for the withdrawal.[318] The player must present identification for the withdrawal at the casino.

Authorized gaming players may hold only one interactive gaming account with an operator;[319] anonymous interactive gaming accounts or accounts in fictitious names are prohibited.[320] Funds transferred into an interactive gaming account from one financial institution may not be transferred out of the interactive gaming account to a different financial institution.[321] Transfers from one authorized player to another authorized player are not permitted (except for wins and losses at the virtual poker tables).[322]

Besides the suspicious activity reports required under federal law, the Nevada Regulations contain their own provisions for reporting "suspicious wagering" when the wager is suspected of being in violation of federal or state law[323] or where the wager "[h]as no business or apparent lawful purpose or is not the sort of wager which the particular authorized player would normally be expected to place and the licensee knows of no reasonable explanation for the wager after examining the available facts, including the background of the wager."[324]

---

[313] Nev. Gaming Comm'n. Minimum Internal Control Standards § 76 (2012).
[314] Nev. Gaming Comm'n. Reg. 5A.110(6)(a) (2011).
[315] 31 C.F.R. § 1010.312 (2011).
[316] *Id.*
[317] *See* Nev. Gaming Comm'n. Minimum Internal Control Standards §§ 71–73 (2012).
[318] Nev. Gaming Comm'n. Minimum Internal Control Standards § 89 (2012).
[319] Nev. Gaming Comm'n. Reg. 5A.120(2)(a) (2011).
[320] Nev. Gaming Comm'n. Reg. 5A.120(3) (2011).
[321] Nev. Gaming Comm'n. Reg. 5A.120(7) (2011).
[322] Nev. Gaming Comm'n. Reg. 5A.120(9) (2011).
[323] Nev. Gaming Comm'n. Reg. 5A.160(1)(a) (2011).
[324] Nev. Gaming Comm'n. Reg. 5A.160(1)(b) (2011).

On records retention, Regulation 5A.190 states that operators must maintain "complete and accurate records of all matters related to their interactive gaming activity," including player identities, player registration, and complete game histories for every game played on the interactive gaming system.[325] Consistent with the FATF standard, operators must preserve these records for at least five years after they are made.[326]

Finally, regarding payment processing intermediaries, Nevada regulators may require licensure of the processor either as a Class 1 service provider (i.e., required to submit to the same process as a non-restricted licence applicant) or as a Class 2 service provider (i.e., only required to make a restricted licence application), depending upon the nature of the relationship with the operator and the intermediary's relationship to the flow of funds between operator and customer. Irrespective of how such intermediaries are licensed, however, Nevada takes a strong interest in evaluating and monitoring the payment processors used by operators. For example, section 82 of the MICS requires that the interactive gaming operator's internal control standards delineate: procedures established for the use of each payment processor,[327] all deposit methods available to authorized players, and a complete description of the entire process for each method.[328]

Nevada has consulted widely and adopted the best practices into the Nevada Regulations, particularly on suitability and customer due diligence. When the Nevada rules are considered alongside the BSA, it forms an impressive bulwark against money laundering.

THOUGHTS ON BEST PRACTICES

Given the breadth of the FATF's recommendations—and the depth and expertise of the FATF itself—many best practices reflect the 40 Recommendations. The suggested best practices for currency and transaction handling and prevention of money laundering in online gaming are as follows:

1. Regulating the sector;
2. Adopting a dynamic, risk-based approach;
3. Transparency of all participants;
4. Traceability of all transactions; and,
5. Control of operators by regulators and security of their operations.

Almost any set of systems will generate overlap. For example, regulation strongly implies assessments of suitability, but suitability assessments

---

[325] Nev. Gaming Comm'n. Reg. 5A.190 (2011).

[326] *Id.* The GCB also takes the view that the provisions of Regulation 6.060 (producing to the GCB audit division or the tax and license division, on request, all records required to be maintained by Regulation 6) also applies to all interactive gaming records. Regulation 6.060 also requires a five-year minimum retention period.

[327] Nev. Gaming Comm'n. Minimum Internal Control Standards § 82(a) (2012).

[328] Nev. Gaming Comm'n. Minimum Internal Control Standards § 82(b) (2012).

are covered under the heading of transparency. Also, should knowing the sources of client funds be grouped with transparency or traceability? (In this list, they are put under traceability because that category tracks transactions through the financial system, from their original sources through subsequent Internet gaming operations. However, the clear role of knowing the client and how the client obtains her funds is acknowledged.) This taxonomy tries to keep the groupings as discrete as possible.

Internet Gaming Should be Regulated

The best practices for regulation assume regulation. Whether the industry should be regulated at all, however, is not universally agreed. Many continue to believe that Internet gaming should be banned outright or ignored by policy makers. For example, many states in the US and provinces in Canada with land-based casinos do not have a fully-functioning and local government-sanctioned online gaming model in place. Some large countries (e.g., India and China) do not have a regulated Internet gaming and betting industry. From an anti-money laundering standpoint only, the need for regulation of the industry is obvious. Simple prohibition increases the chances for money laundering; regulation cuts against it. Regulators, however, must have appropriate funding to properly undertake their work. Regulation of the industry requires continuing resources and commitment by policy makers.

Recommendation 28 in the 40 Recommendations establishes that Internet casinos "should be subject to a comprehensive regulatory and supervisory regime" that ensures they have effectively implemented the necessary components of the 40 Recommendations.[329] Minimum requirements include having competent authorities to license Internet casino operators.[330] The rationale for this approach ranges from the preservation of freedom to undertake (what some find to be) objectionable activities, while minimizing or "managing down" collateral harms,[331] to the futility of trying to prohibit those activities.[332]

From the perspective of preventing money laundering, the case for regulation of the Internet gaming sector is strong. According to Cabot and Kelly, most experts agree that if land-based "casinos are to be kept free of criminal domination and its association with money laundering, they must be subject to strong administrative control."[333] The same connection to strong regulation is applicable to preventing money launder-

---

[329] FINANCIAL ACTION TASK FORCE, INTERNATIONAL STANDARDS ON COMBATING MONEY LAUNDERING AND THE FINANCING OF TERRORISM & PROLIFERATION—THE FATF RECOMMENDATIONS, *supra* note 16, at 23.

[330] *Id.*

[331] *See, e.g.* Levi, *supra* note 8, at 26.

[332] *See, e.g.* K. Alexa Koenig, *Prohibition's Pending Demise: Internet Gambling & United States Policy*, 10 PITT. J. TECH. L. & POL'Y 1, 36–37 (2009–2010).

[333] Cabot & Kelly, *supra* note 2, at 136.

ing in an online context and, in fact, the authors go on to note the negative relationship between strong Internet gaming regulation and money laundering opportunities.[334] The other thing to note from Cabot and Kelly is that the role for regulators transcends suitability assessments; suitability is a necessary, but not sufficient, precondition for preventing money laundering.[335]

Regulation suggests that a blanket prohibition will not work, even if prohibition is desirable as a matter of principle. One example of the United States' attempt at prohibition is the Unlawful Internet Gambling Enforcement Act (the "UIGEA").[336] The irony of the approach adopted in the UIGEA is that it makes money laundering easier and more likely by prohibiting involvement of the regulated credit card industry in transferring funds to online gambling websites.[337] (Prohibiting instead of regulating Internet gaming discourages legitimate U.S. casino operators from entering the market while encouraging "entry by unlicensed, unregulated, and unknown 'fly-by-night' entities."[338]) Before and after its passage, many predicted that the UIGEA would lead to the creation of complicated and unregulated processes for transferring funds to US-facing Internet gaming sites.[339] For good measure, one might have added that these alternative processes might also be illegal.[340] Poor regulatory oversight, among other things, helps money laundering thrive.[341]

Proper regulation does not mean only setting up the proper structure for online gaming and betting. It means an ongoing monitoring role consistent with Cabot and Kelly's "strong administrative control." Regulators also must have stable and sufficient funding for their activities and operations. Without proper resources, a great regulatory framework may be completely ineffective.[342] In fact, the IMF saw a lack of regulatory resources sufficient to meet the growth of the Internet gaming sector as worthy of comment in the case of the GSC.[343]

---

[334] *Id.* at 144–145.

[335] *See also id.* at 139: "Admittedly, the problem of money laundering may still remain notwithstanding the suitability of gaming operators."

[336] H.R. 556, *supra* note 46.

[337] Katherine A. Valasek, Comment, *Winning the Jackpot: A Framework for Successful International Regulation of Online Gambling and the Value of the Self-Regulating Entities*, 3 Mich. St. L. Rev. 753, 765 (2007).

[338] Schwartz, *supra* note 48, at 128. *See also* Koenig, *supra* note 332, at 36–37.

[339] *See, e.g.* Valasek, *supra* note 337, at 765. *See also* Susan Ormand, Comment, *Pending U.S. Legislation to Prohibit Offshore Internet Gambling May Proliferate Money Laundering*, 10 Law & Bus. Rev. Am. 447, 451 and 453–454 (2004). (Ormand made substantially similar points about the UIGFPA in 2004.)

[340] One can view the Internet gaming indictment in the Southern District of New York in April 2011 in precisely this context. *See Superseding Indictment*, United States v. Scheinberg et al, 10 Cr. 336 (S.D.N.Y., 2011).

[341] Valasek, *supra* note 337, at 765.

[342] Cabot & Kelly, *supra* note 2, at 137–138 (discussing the effects of a lack of resources in various quarters on land-based casino gaming regulation in New Jersey).

[343] *See supra* text accompanying note 210.

Accordingly, the first best practice is that the Internet gaming and betting sector be subject to robust regulation, extending from assessments of suitability through to effective, ongoing, and random inspection and audits. Regulation of MVTS, consistent with recommendation 14 of the 40 Recommendations, is also desirable. Regulation of such bodies will be done, at least in part, by non-gaming regulators. (See the example of PayPal in section 6.) Internet gaming regulators should consider whether any particular MVTS are regulated and assess the quality of that regulation. Regulators and operators should prefer more regulated and reputable MVTS businesses rather than less regulated and less reputable solutions.

Adopt a Dynamic, Risk-Based Approach

Regulators should implement a risk-based approach dynamic and flexible enough to adapt to changing circumstances. This is imperative in an industry as subject to technology innovations as the Internet gaming sector. A risk-based approach does not mean a lack of minimum standards or a subjective view of what constitutes "risk." It means that, besides minimum thresholds subject to constant refinement, states, regulators, and operators should deploy their resources where they will have the most impact and away from areas of comparatively little concern.

Why adopt a risk-based approach? Would an accounting audit check-box type of standard work just as well while providing clearer guidance? The answer can be found in the roots of the industry requiring regulation and in the nature of electronic commerce itself. Money laundering threats change constantly and vary across customers, jurisdictions, products, delivery channels, and over time.[344] For instance, money laundering risks may be very different in peer-to-peer games than in house-banked games or certain sports bets. Increased mobile phone and technology penetration might offer more anonymous payment options already present in a mobile market and that may have been initially intended for uses other than Internet gaming; certain types of prepaid phone cards are examples of such "crossover" technology. In this environment, the regulatory response must be as dynamic as the criminal laundering element; a prescriptive, static check-box standard would likely be off-target and not deliver benefits greater than the costs of intervention and regulation.[345] As one author succinctly puts it, the online interactive gaming business is a "stunning example of technology outpacing the law."[346] The law needs to be transparent

---

[344] REMOTE GAMBLING ASSOCIATION, *Anti-Money Laundering: Good Practice Guidelines for the Online Gambling Industry* ¶ 27, *available at* http://www.rga.eu.com/data/files/rga_aml_guidance_2010.pdf.

[345] *Id.*

[346] Lawrence G. Walters, *The Law of Online Gambling in the United States—A Safe Bet, or Risky Business?* 7 GAM. L. REV 445 (2003). Another way of making the same point is as follows: "The first challenge is that there are an 'infinite' number of ways to launder money. Laundering schemes range from simple to complex … The second challenge in

and rational to address existing threats and it must be flexible enough to match the pace of technological and market change. Consistent with these comments and with the FATF's recommendation 15, regulators should approach new technologies that favor anonymity or that otherwise challenge or undercut effective anti-money laundering procedures with caution.

The risk-based approach advocated here is the same as that adopted in the 40 Recommendations (see section 4). A risk-based approach starts with a risk analysis or assessment to determine areas of particular vulnerability or concern. The approach then seeks to ensure that adopted measures intended to prevent money laundering are both rationally connected and proportional to the identified risks. In the words of the FATF, "[t]his will allow resources to be allocated in the most efficient ways. The principle is that resources should be directed in accordance with priorities so that the greatest risks receive the highest attention."[347]

Two attributes of a risk-based approach are critical. The first is that the concept of risk is not subjective or defined by one person or institution. While room for debate exists to determine whether certain industries pose higher or lower risks, the concepts of risks employed must reflect adherence to international norms and standards, including assessments by both the FATF and the IMF. For example, it is apparent that large and anonymous cash transactions are higher-risk than traceable transactions through a reputable and licensed bank.

The second attribute is that a risk-based approach does not mean the absence of minimum objective standards. Indeed, the first of the 40 Recommendations mandates a risk-based approach, but the remaining 39 recommendations require a comprehensive framework for addressing minimum standards to deter money laundering and terrorist financing. The US\$/€3,000 threshold for casinos in recommendation 22 is one example. (There is no magic in that particular figure, but it is an objectively low figure in the context of e-commerce, and the international community—through the FATF membership—did not change that threshold in the 40 Recommendations as revised and re-issued in February 2012.) Another example is the requirement that casinos be licensed pursuant to applicable law.

Consistent with the 40 Recommendations, the risk-based approach should not dissuade us from establishing more of the best possible practices. Collectively, at least some of these thresholds form a floor on anti-money laundering standards in Internet gaming. In the next section, this chapter presents a proposal that, as part of knowing with whom one is dealing at all times, the OFAC's Specially Designated Nationals List (or a comparable local list) be consulted, that transactions with any persons or organizations on that list be refused, and that such transaction attempts be

---

detecting the money laundry cycle is the vast amount of resources that traffickers can devote to innovating money laundering techniques." Bachus, *supra* note 2, at 845–846.
[347] RBA Guidance for Casinos (2008), *supra* note 86, at 6.

reported. In the section on the traceability of transactions, the chapter recommends that regulators must be wary of allowing cash to be accepted by any intermediary between the Internet gaming operator and the customer, at least without the intermediary undertaking robust due diligence, e.g., a customer depositing funds into her account at a regulated bank in the United Kingdom and then linking her account as a deposit and withdrawal method on an interactive gaming site. Neither of these recommendations is inconsistent with or detracts from a risk-based approach.

The risk-based approach, however, can present some challenges. For one thing, it requires sound and well-trained judgment in compliance decisions, which may be perceived as more than what is required under a prescriptive check-the-box approach.[348] Accordingly, a risk-based approach demands a better trained, more expert, and therefore more expensive staff. Moreover, a risk-based approach can require a fundamental shift in mindset in some organizations in terms of accepting more interpretation and analysis—some might say ambiguity—in the compliance function.

With all of its challenges, however, the risk-based approach is the best approach to prevent money laundering and is clearly the dominant one. When layered on top of minimum standards and procedures, and where a regulator is properly structured and funded, any concerns about it can be effectively addressed. Increased analysis can lead to better protocols and decisions. Increased and targeted resources in an anti-money laundering context should have beneficial effects. The FATF sets out several specific transaction risk issues raised by Internet casinos. These include multiple accounts, changes to financial institution accounts, and the use of prepaid cards and electronic wallets.[349]

A dynamic risk-based approach is a best practice for Internet gaming regulation; this does not mean minimum standards or an empty view of risk. Coupled with robust regulation and other best practices, it is a practical and effective way of getting resources to the areas of transaction handling regulation that need them the most.

All Participants Should be Transparent

In certain key respects, phrases like transparency, know your client, due diligence, identification and verification procedures, etc., are shorthand for understanding one's customers and business partners.[350] With transparency, a mix of minimum standards and a risk-based approach is at play.

Transparency into regulatory, business, and customer relationships begins with suitability assessments by regulators. In this area, of the surveyed jurisdictions, Nevada has a commendable approach. It has a com-

---

[348] *Id.* at 8–9.

[349] *Id.* at 27–28.

[350] In this section, "business partners" will be used as a proxy for any number of parties interacting with licensed gaming operators, including suppliers, marketing affiliates, and business customers on a networked gaming model.

prehensive system for assessing the suitability of operators in the state. In the application process, operators of interactive gaming are treated in the same manner as applications for unrestricted gaming licences. Accordingly, the disclosure and investigation procedures associated with the application are thorough. This extends to key people with the prospective licensee or associated with the licensee. The costs and the investigation of staff demonstrate that Nevada regulators take the process very seriously, which is appropriate from an anti-money laundering standpoint alone. As noted, being careful about who is regulated is a starting, critical bulwark against money laundering. No magic number defines how much regulators should charge to investigate applicants and their respective associates, but it must be enough to fund meaningful and relevant inquiries.

The next stage is assessment of the operator's customers and business partners. In the latter case, regulators should license some of these parties as service providers. Beyond licensure, however, regulators should mandate that Internet gaming operators implement checks and procedures to evaluate these parties. In the case of business partners, these checks include a full and robust inquiry by the operator into the nature, backers, finances, and management of the prospective business partner. Of tantamount importance are the internal and external procedures followed by the business partners who deal with their own customers or the customers of the licensee on the licensee's behalf.

The positions of MVTS or other financial intermediaries are of utmost concern because they process payments for Internet gaming licensees. Here, a risk-based approach must be taken. Banks in well regulated and respected jurisdictions should be perceived as low-risk; debit and credit cards issued by such institutions and used to fund customer accounts should be seen, accordingly, as a reduced risk. Beyond that, operators should use caution when selecting MVTS partners, although a service like PayPal is relatively low-risk. PayPal is an electronic wallet regulated as a money services business in the United States. Upon registering and funding a PayPal account, one must link to an already-issued credit card or bank account, meaning that PayPal itself interfaces with trusted institutions in the financial system.

Internet gaming operators should approach any MVTS business or intermediary who accepts cash on an anonymous basis with great caution. This warning does not include banks and other financial institutions that perform proper due diligence on depositors, as those transactions are not anonymous. Regulators should mandate such caution for their licensees. It might be possible that MVTS that accept cash could become suitable intermediaries provided that they collect and maintain satisfactory player due diligence and, crucially, that they maintain comparatively low thresholds on the amount a customer can deposit on a card or voucher (i.e., these would need to be below the US$/€3,000 withdrawal threshold in place in the 40 Recommendations).

As to customer due diligence in a B2C gaming operation, procedures in Nevada and the Isle of Man are suitable. Measures need to comply with FATF recommendation 10. Minimal information may be acceptable at the customer registration stage, and such information need not necessarily be checked against an external database. (That said, the Nevada example of requiring a verification check when registering every player is a standard to which all regulators should aspire.) However, the US$/€3,000 threshold should trigger enhanced customer due diligence procedures accompanied by attempts to verify the customer's identity with government-issued documents, and requiring direct customer contact. In addition, the risk-based procedures of a regulated company like Paddy Power demonstrate the best practices in this category. They identify potential issues based on deposit methods, number of deposits, excessive payment methods linked to a user, and many other risk factors.

Customers must be prohibited from establishing fictitious accounts, from having accounts in trust on behalf of others, or from setting up multiple accounts on any particular gaming site. Circumvention procedures should be in place to enforce this rule, as well. In particular, a "one account only" policy can minimize corruption of a peer-to-peer game like poker (where one player could otherwise control two hands at a table instead of one).[351] It also minimizes the possibility of intra-account transactions that are undertaken for no objective reason other than to move funds around and attempt to obfuscate their source.

Separate and apart from risk-based approaches for dealing with certain customers, there are some players who operators should refuse to service. It is in their—and the public's—best interest to respect the Specially Designated Nationals List maintained by OFAC[352] and to decline to engage in a business relationship of any kind with listed persons. They also need to implement measures that use private or alternate databases to prevent circumvention of this requirement by those listed.

The OFAC list is just one example. Regulators must comply with local law, so such a prohibited list could leverage the OFAC list, local prohibited lists or other sources. Regulators may augment such a database with their own investigative or monitoring findings, as appropriate. Transparency is key to the best practice for regulators; its essence is knowing with whom one is dealing. It extends from assessments of suitability by the regulator to risk-based assessments, minimum due diligence and investigation standards.

---

[351] Collusion goes well beyond having two accounts in the same name and controlled by the same person. It can take many forms and is constantly targeted by reputable Internet gaming sites. A broader discussion of collusion in peer-to-peer games is beyond the scope of this chapter.

[352] U.S. TREAS., *Office of Foreign Assets Control Specially Designated Nationals and Blocked Persons, available at* http://www.treasury.gov/ofac/downloads/t11sdn.pdf.

All Transactions Should be Traceable

The concept of traceability is the ability to follow and, where necessary, to reconstruct transactions. Traceability is a key feature in both preventing money laundering and in investigating and prosecuting money laundering offenses that have already occurred.

Regulators and operators must determine the financial choke points of criminal activity. Choke points are entryways and exits through which funds must pass as they are disseminated throughout the economy.[353] These choke points are opportunities to record transactions and customer identities, "thereby creating a 'paper trail' that law enforcement can use to trace laundered funds from which they were originally derived."[354] Placing a transaction on a credit card, depositing money to a PayPal e-wallet, and withdrawing funds from a bank are examples of instruments passing through a choke point in the system. Many money launderers seek to circumvent these choke points, which is why large cash transactions and anonymous cards that contain electronic money can cause concern. The best anti-money laundering practices must try to, as much as possible, guide consumers, business partners, and transactions through functioning and reliable choke points in the financial system. Accordingly, the Isle of Man prohibits licensees from accepting cash from customers and business participants. Where there is a parallel bricks and mortar and interactive structure, as in Nevada, rules similar to the Nevada Regulations address transfers between land-based and Internet channels.

Operators need to remain diligent and question the sources of funds of a business partner or a customer. The origin of any party's funds and establishing the identity of that party is a crucial check on their ability to launder funds through an Internet gaming business. Both bulwarks are important and related, but should be considered as separate, discrete tests. A customer may conclusively establish her identity, but that may say nothing about that customer's sources of funds. Examining the origin of funds may be required if red flags are raised in identifying the customer. If the risk profile of the customer as a whole is raised through identity verification, then the operator should be on guard about other aspects of the customer relationship, including the customer's sources of funds.

However, even with a low risk profile and definitive identification, when transactions go above larger thresholds—such thresholds to be established by reference to international risk factors—operators must make inquiries into a customer's sources of funds. Such inquiries may seek to obtain proof of a customer's income or wealth and should be designed and handled carefully, both to follow local disclosure and privacy laws and to conform to good business practice. Operators should employ similar rules when Internet gaming licensees establish business relationships with suppliers and customers.

---

[353] Rueda, *supra* note 2, at 9.
[354] *Id.*

In certain circumstances, ascertaining the origin of funds has to be mandatory. For instance, consistent with the FATF's recommendation 12, this must be done with PEPs. It seems only fair that most PEPs should not automatically be denied Internet gaming or business relationships, if desired by all parties, but particular care must be taken to ensure that the relationship does not advance corruption in the PEP's home jurisdiction, for example.[355]

Another situation that requires determination of sources of funds is when the business partner or customer of the Internet gaming licensee is from (i.e., is ordinarily resident in or has substantial connections to) a jurisdiction that is present on the FATF's counter-measures or deficiencies lists.[356] Here again, nationals or other parties hailing from those countries should not automatically be shut out of business relationships entirely, but a higher degree of scrutiny should apply. With recommendation 29, enhanced due diligence with principals from these various jurisdictions is mandatory, but requiring an investigation of the sources of funds from these countries may be perceived as going beyond the current scope of the 40 Recommendations.

The record-keeping requirement is inextricably linked to the paper trail and choke points concepts; without suitable recording of transactions at the choke points and preservation of those records, the paper trail may not be fully re-created. From a money laundering perspective only, the following information should be retained by Internet gaming operators for at least five years (i.e., the timeframe set out in the FATF's eleventh recommendation):

- Information and copies of documents obtained in any customer or business partner due diligence process;
- Information obtained through the risk assessment process and review relating to any customer or business partner;
- The results of all inquiries into and investigations of any customer or business partner;
- Full financial details, including wiring information and financial intermediary information, of every deposit and withdrawal made by each customer; and,
- The full records of each game or bet played by each customer, including the stakes brought to the table, the cards played with results of each hand, and funds won or lost.[357]

---

[355] A PEP's relationship with the Internet gaming operator should be subject to enhanced ongoing monitoring, as well.

[356] At the time of writing, the jurisdictions subject to an FATF call on its members and other jurisdictions to apply counter-measures are Iran and North Korea. The jurisdictions on the FATF's deficiencies list—and that have not made sufficient progress in addressing the deficiencies or have not committed to an action plan developed with the FATF to address the deficiencies—are Cuba, Bolivia, Ethiopia, Ghana, Indonesia, Kenya, Myanmar, Nigeria, Pakistan, Sao Tome and Principe, Sri Lanka, Syria, Tanzania, Thailand, and Turkey. *See* Financial Action Task Force, FATF Public Statement—16 February 2012, *available at* http://www.fatf-gafi.org/document/18/0,3746,en_32250379_32236992_49694738_1_1_1_1,00.html.

[357] This five-year requirement is without prejudice to any additional requirements that may

Copies of these records should be kept when produced to regulators or to law enforcement, unless it breaches applicable law. An Internet gaming operator's regulator should receive everything it requests; regulators are entitled to this information. Unless otherwise prohibited, when the local FIU or other law enforcement requests assistance, regulators should be notified and operators must comply. Regulators should mandate co-operation with international financial crime authorities and other investigators with authority, provided that such co-operation does not conflict with an operator's regulatory obligations.

Finally, operators should implement suspicious transaction reports and the money laundering reporting officer usually coordinates these reports. Based on the risk-based approach, it is possible that operators must make a report to law enforcement even if there is no financial transaction with an Internet gaming licensee, for example, when a new customer's identity cannot be sufficiently verified or when operators refuse a large transaction.

Sound traceability principles require an effort to push Internet gaming and betting transactions through legitimate and effective choke points. This implies prohibiting licensees from accepting cash. Impeccable re-cord-keeping and reporting standards are a must, and should complete any good approach when tracking the flow of funds through a regulated gaming environment.

Regulators Need to Control the Gaming Environment and Foster Security

Best practices include some form of broad control to secure multiple parts of the gaming structure. It protects access to data and encompasses security measures to ensure that any data retained is not corrupted or ac-cessed by unauthorized parties. In order to control the flow of information and reporting and to support other preferred practices, it also includes ap-pointing a suitably-empowered money laundering reporting officer. Final-ly, it is imperative to guard the confidentiality of investigations and prevent tipping-off.

Several regulators (e.g., the Isle of Man and Malta) require local corpo-rations to be established in order to apply for and obtain Internet gaming licensure. This has the benefit of providing a corporate presence in the li-censing jurisdiction with which regulators are familiar. It also, in a sense, forces the applicant to "commit" to the jurisdiction, although this com-mitment takes several forms, including completion of the application, paying the application fee, and disclosures. Moreover, the local corpora-tion requirement means that regulators have a greater level of control over

---

be imposed by regulators, applicable law, or other areas of the business itself. For example, tax auditors may want certain financial records retained for a longer period. Similarly, regulators and internal technical staff may want remote gaming and betting logs to be kept longer. The minimum five years may variously apply to the period after which a particular transaction was completed or the end of a business or customer relationship.

the licensee. Applicable corporate law may require a corporation to have its books and records or offices in the country, pay local taxes, and have technology in line with the local regulating jurisdiction. These become instruments that a regulator can reach out and influence in order to bring a recalcitrant licensee into line, if necessary. It is also administratively easier for a regulator to coordinate with other local authorities to discipline an Internet gaming licensee. For this reason, local corporation nexus is always preferable when establishing the best practices for regulators.

However, in some senses a local corporation is a proxy for control; the proxy should not be confused with actual control of a licensee. If a jurisdiction does not have the means to licence local corporations, or if it has not done so, then it may still be possible for Internet gaming regulators to have control over the licensee, at least in principle. Gaming regulators can mandate that there be a local corporate, technology, physical office, or other presence whether a corporation hails from the jurisdiction or not. Clearly, a local corporation requirement makes things easier for the regulator to control. Whether there is a requirement for a corporation from the licensing jurisdiction or not, there must be suitable integration between gaming regulations and other local laws—and gaming regulations must be robust enough in their own right—to ensure that regulators have sufficient control of Internet gaming licensees.

In an anti-money laundering context, regulators must be able to reasonably and quickly access any required records in an acceptable form. As important, Internet gaming regulators must have effective control over who has access to those records. This provides a trail for regulators to know how records have been accessed or modified and to prevent data corruption, thus supporting the data retention recommendation. It also serves as a warranty to the betting public that its licensees are operating in a well-run jurisdiction that takes data protection and privacy seriously.

The money laundering reporting officer function promoted by certain jurisdictions is also worth including in our list of recommended practices. The officer must have experience commensurate with a director-level role. She must also be senior enough in the organization and have a direct reporting relationship to the enterprise's corporate directors. Such an officer can be the point person and liaison for addressing money laundering and other compliance efforts with gaming regulators. This could be extended to certain global co-ordination efforts with regulators, law enforcement, and others (e.g., the FATF), thus potentially addressing money laundering's international character. While the money laundering reporting officer works for the licensee, sufficient independence can be written into relevant rules and procedures to ensure that she can attain a higher level of control for the regulator on the inside of the licensee. Aside from control, a money laundering reporting officer can be a salutary staff addition; she can lead and co-ordinate staff with anti-money laundering training and procedures.

Finally, as an adjunct to data protection and preserving the integrity of any investigation by either the licensee, the regulator, or law enforcement, rules that prohibit tipping-off must be implemented. Suitable penalties for breach of tipping-off rules need to be in place. These regulations should extend to anyone who has knowledge of a relevant investigative process or with anyone who has a duty to report suspected activity in the organization. Because the group of people who have a duty to report money laundering suspicions to the appropriate authorities is potentially large, those subject to tipping-off restrictions are also numerous. This recommendation should be backed up by protections for good-faith disclosures by any employees or agents.

Sufficient control of licensees and securing the Internet gaming regulation and operational structure is essential. Local corporate requirements are desirable but may not be essential in all cases. Regulators must have access to and control over availability of data logs and records. Operators need to appoint a suitably trained and higher ranking money laundering officer and provide relevant training to staff. It is also imperative that operators implement tipping-off and confidentiality measures that regulators monitor.

Selected Payment Intermediary Issues

A comparison of two e-commerce payment intermediaries within the best practices framework demonstrates the strengths and weaknesses of each. One of these intermediaries (PayPal) was brought to market more than ten years ago and is in use by highly regulated gaming operators. The other mechanism, Bitcoin, was only started in 2009, but has been in the news of late. PayPal meets the various applicable tests for being a low-risk and usable payment mechanism. Bitcoin causes more concern.

PayPal

As discussed previously, PayPal is an electronic wallet that has been variously described as "a peer-to-peer payment system"[358] and "not electronic money *per se*" but an approximation of the use of e-money.[359] PayPal was launched in 1999.[360] PayPal initially processed Internet gaming charges but agreed to cease doing so in 2002 upon its acquisition by eBay.[361]

PayPal is a system that allows its customers to deposit into e-wallets, i.e., accounts maintained on the PayPal system that shows credits (liabilities) to PayPal's customers, with cash held as the corresponding debits (assets). (A PayPal customer may transfer US$100, say, from her asset account at a financial institution into another asset account, being her PayPal e-wallet

---

[358] Ormand, *supra* note 339, at 452.
[359] Schopper, *supra* note 2, at 318.
[360] *Id.*
[361] Ormand, *supra* note 339, at 452.

Table 2

Best Practices Summary for Internet Gaming Regulators

No.	Best Practice
1	**Regulation** • Establish suitable rules, procedures, and institutions to regulate Internet gaming and ancillary activity. • Regulation must be robust and continuing. • Regulators must have sufficient resources to do their jobs.
2	**Risk-Based Approach** • Assessing risk should be in accordance with international norms and standards. • Must be dynamic and flexible in order to address new risks; reject overly mechanical approaches. • Minimum standards still apply, which are also subject to constant refinement. • Pay particular attention to new technologies, especially new technologies that favor anonymity or otherwise undercut effective anti-money laundering procedures.
3	**Transparency** • Regulators must fully inquire into prospective licensees and their associates; the cost of licensure must be commensurate with a high standard. • Regulated MVTS and financial intermediaries should be favored over unregulated parties; intermediaries accepting cash should be approached with caution. • Strong due diligence and enhanced due diligence minimums are needed. Separate from the minimum thresholds, operators must have robust internal feedback on activity that may generate risks. • Each player may have only one gaming account per operator. • Transactions and business with certain parties (e.g., on the OFAC list) should be prohibited outright.
4	**Traceability** • Customers, business partners, and transactions should be funnelled through financial choke points; Internet gaming operators should never accept cash from customers or business partners. • Sources of funds should be ascertained as part of a heightened risk profile and above higher transaction thresholds. Determining the origin of funds must be mandatory in certain cases. • Suitable record-keeping and suspicious transaction reporting standards are required for traceability.
5	**Control & Security** • Strongly prefer licensees to be locally-incorporated. In any event, ensure that regulators have sufficient levers to control and discipline its licensees. • Regulators must have timely access to relevant records and be able to control access to those records. • A suitably trained and independent money laundering reporting officer must be appointed; other staff in the organization must receive anti-money laundering training. • Tipping-off should be prohibited and good-faith disclosures about suspected money laundering should be protected within the bounds of applicable law.

account.) Once an account is established and funded, the PayPal customer can then use her funds in e-commerce and other channels to purchase goods and services. In Internet gaming enterprises where PayPal may be used, a customer may transfer funds to her online gaming account from PayPal and may withdraw to PayPal from the online gaming account. One of the attractions of using a service like PayPal is that it can be cheaper than using other forms of payment.[362]

The success of PayPal should not cause any particular concern to those seeking to suppress money laundering within Internet gaming. PayPal is currently available as an e-wallet for use on Internet gaming sites in more heavily regulated markets. More important, PayPal is itself regulated in the United States, for example, offering a good example of a well-regulated and supervised MVTS. PayPal has a money services business registration number issued by the U.S. Department of the Treasury and is licensed in a majority of U.S. states.[363]

The procedure for depositing into one's PayPal account is limited. While the registration information itself is minimal, one must deposit to or withdraw from PayPal from a credit card or an account with a regulated financial institution. Sufficient due diligence is required at the credit or debit account stage. This mixture of regulation as a MVTS provider and interaction with licensed financial institutions, together with relevant anti-money laundering procedures on the part of Internet gaming operators, makes PayPal a comparatively low-risk payment intermediary in a well-regulated online gaming environment.

Bitcoin

By contrast, Bitcoin is an electronic payment system that has received a great deal of recent attention and generated controversy. Bitcoin the payment system should not be confused with bitcoin the currency. While some aspects of Bitcoin are promising and deserve praise, the difficulties associated with identifying how its users spend Bitcoins means that this technology is not suitable for use by Internet gaming operators in a controlled and monitored marketplace.

Bitcoin was invented by Satoshi Nakamoto (a "preternaturally talented computer coder," or team of coders, and certainly an alias) in January 2009.[364] This non-fiat currency is controlled entirely by software. A total of 21 million bitcoins are scheduled for release through this software, almost all of them over the coming 20 years.[365] Every ten minutes, coins are dis-

---

[362] On the factors favouring a move away from credit cards towards electronic wallets and other payment systems (including PayPal), *see generally* Rueda, *supra* note 2, at 29–36.

[363] PAYPAL, *PayPal State Licenses, available at* https://www.paypal-media.com/licenses.

[364] Joshua Davis, *The Crypto-Currency: Bitcoin and its Mysterious Inventor*, THE NEW YORKER, Oct. 10, 2011, at 62.

[365] *Id.*

tributed through a process resembling a lottery.[366] Bitcoin "miners" play this lottery over and over; the fastest computers employed by miners win the most bitcoins released by the software.[367]

As a store of value and a medium of exchange, bitcoins have a mixed track record. Bitcoins started trading at less than a penny each. However, as more merchants began to accept bitcoins, their value appreciated. By September 2011, the exchange rate for bitcoins was US$5 (down from US$29 the previous June).[368] More recently, bitcoins have reached prices in excess of $220. There are several Internet betting and gaming websites—including sealswithclubs.eu, btcsportsbet.com, and satoshidice.com—operating exclusively using bitcoins. Other sites offer Bitcoin as a payment mechanism.

According to its inventor(s), bitcoin was developed to address "the inherent weaknesses of the trust based model" of electronic commerce.[369] Central banks must be trusted not to debase a currency; retail, commercial, and other banks must be trusted to safeguard money on behalf of customers.[370] In the estimation of Bitcoin's inventor, history is littered with evidence of breaches of that trust.[371] Accordingly, Nakamoto set out to establish an electronic payment system based on cryptographic proof and not trust, allowing any two parties to transact directly with each other without a trusted intermediary (like a bank, or PayPal).[372] With bitcoins, transactions are non-reversible and, through encryption of each transaction, does not permit the same bitcoin to be spent more than once (eliminating fraud).

The critical aspect of bitcoin is its anonymity, or its lack of transparency in discerning who is transacting what and when. It has been said of bitcoin that "[b]uyers and sellers remain anonymous, but everyone [on the network] can see that a coin has moved from A to B."[373] Nakamoto states as follows: "The public can see that someone is sending an amount to someone else, but without information linking the transaction to anyone. This is similar to the level of information released by stock exchanges, where the time and size of individual trades, the 'tape,' is made public, but without telling who the parties were."[374]

---

[366] *Id.*

[367] *Id.*

[368] *Id.*

[369] Satoshi Nakamoto, *Bitcoin: A Peer-to-Peer Electronic Cash System* 1, *available at* http://bitcoin.org/bitcoin.pdf [hereinafter Bitcoin Design Paper].

[370] Satoshi Nakamoto, *Bitcoin: Open Source Implementation of P2P Currency*, *available at* http://p2pfoundation.ning.com/forum/topics/bitcoin-open-source.

[371] *Id.*

[372] Bitcoin Design Paper, *supra* note 369, at 1.

[373] Davis, *supra* note 364, at 65.

[374] Bitcoin Design Paper, *supra* note 369, at 6. The analogy is very carefully worded, but it only works if law enforcement, the stock exchange, or other authorized parties can easily ascertain who the underlying parties are to the transaction. This is by no means clear from the use of Bitcoin.

How easily can the parties to a bitcoin transaction be identified by law enforcement? One organization that examined bitcoin calls the anonymity in the payment system "complicated"[375] and concludes that it is possible to map many bitcoin users to public keys, and that "large centralized services such as the exchanges and wallet services are capable of identifying considerable portions of user activity."[376] An apparent member of the Bitcoin development team has been quoted as follows: "Attempted major illicit transactions with bitcoin, given existing statistical analysis techniques deployed in the field by law enforcement, is pretty damned dumb."[377]

Assuming, without deciding, that the concerns about the lack of anonymity in bitcoin are true, the critical issue is whether deployment of statistical analysis techniques or other methods to obtain this information for regulators or law enforcement should be necessary in a well-regulated Internet gaming environment. It appears from the comments by the developers themselves and other analysts that the data is not easily producible to regulators within a short period of time. One Internet freedom advocate from Electronic Frontier Finland has expressed concerns about Bitcoin and said that "[w]e need to have a back door so that law enforcement can intercede,"[378] which is not comforting to the extent that it implies that law enforcement cannot presently intervene.

Whether data on the identity of transacting parties is difficult to obtain or unobtainable, bitcoin poses problems. These sorts of barriers should not be allowed to impede the work of regulators, law enforcement, and other lawful parties. Accordingly, bitcoin is not a currency or a payment system that is ready for adoption in an online interactive gaming jurisdiction striving for best practices. In fact, bitcoin is a great example of approaching new technologies with caution, as suggested in the 40 Recommendations and the practices adopted by this chapter. Attempts to reduce fraud by not allowing the same virtual money to be spent twice are commendable, and the lack of trust in banks is understandable. Making transactions effectively non-reversible is an interesting idea, although there are consumer protection issues separate and apart from these matters that should be addressed. But the challenges to parties' transparency need to be met squarely before bitcoin or equivalent substitutes can be adopted in well-regulated Internet gaming and betting.

---

[375] Fergal Reid & Martin Harrigan, *An Analysis of Anonymity in the Bitcoin System* 1, *available at* http://arxiv.org/pdf/1107.4524.pdf.

[376] *Id.* at 12.

[377] Adrian Chen, *The Underground Website Where You Can Buy Any Drug Imaginable*, GAWKER, *available at* http://gawker.com/5805928/the-underground-website-where-you-can-buy-any-drug-imaginable.

[378] Davis, *supra* note 364, at 70.

Conclusion

This chapter examined money laundering and why it matters. The constraints and limitations on this analysis have been acknowledged and explored. The FATF's 40 Recommendations and the anti-money laundering rules and procedures in Alderney, the Isle of Man, Kahnawake, Malta, and Nevada have been examined. Based on the comparatives available, we have set forth some thoughts on five best key practices that regulators may be wise to adopt. Finally, two payment systems have been looked at and some thoughts given about how they stack up against good practices in terms of preventing money laundering.

Any discussion like this is always part of a broader puzzle. It is not the definitive comment on the subject. In an industry as young, dynamic, and subject to technological change as Internet gaming, a 'last word' in a book chapter is overly ambitious. It is, however, hoped that this article may serve as a useful overview of anti-money laundering and financial transaction principles and good standards, as well as a tool to encourage more detailed discussion among regulators, operators, and law enforcement.

7

Internet Gambling Advertising Best Practices

Lawrence G. Walters*

INTRODUCTION

In the evolving realm of digital media and technology, any successful business must implement a marketing plan designed to keep pace with Web 2.0 developments. Adapt or die, as the saying goes. Online gambling is no exception; however, the unsettled legal issues associated with the underlying gambling activity itself complicate the efforts to develop an effective, compliant advertising strategy. That—combined with the paucity of existing advertising regulation and the absence of established, industry-wide best practices for online gambling advertising—begets an environment calling out for clarity and consistency.

As with most Internet-based media, online gambling advertising is inconsistently regulated and often unaddressed by most nations. Although some regulatory authorities have cobbled makeshift parameters through case law or scholarship, the lack of guiding precedent or universal standards is increasingly problematic. That said, the purpose of this chapter is to describe the existing legal environment relating to online gambling advertising, such that it is, and offer up suggested industry best practices for advertisers and media outlets. The development of recognized industry advertising practices will hopefully ward off mandatory governmental regulation, which often goes further than necessary to address any legitimate governmental interests in protecting against fraud, or excluding minors and problem gamblers. Taking into account the often negative perception associated with gambling as a "vice" activity in parts of the world, adherence to constructive, thoughtful online advertising standards is vital to effectively preserve the industry's integrity and foster its future development and legitimacy. As technology advances, so do target demographics, thus the legal parameters and ads themselves must evolve accordingly. This chapter provides a glimpse into the developing world of online gambling advertising, in the context of best practices solutions.

To explore the best practices relating to online gambling advertising, some effort must be devoted to outlining the current legal climate and the myriad of factors that may lead to the legality of such promotional materials being called into question. Accordingly, this chapter will discuss the legal standards employed by select countries, in an attempt to glean necessary principles for development of regulation or best practices. Given that so many countries have left the matter of online gambling as a whole, untouched, the author highlights three countries: the United States, Canada and the United Kingdom as providing the most detailed framework for existing and future regulatory policies. Further discussion will be devoted to evaluating the available legal remedies, i.e., injunctions, administrative proceedings, and criminal/civil penalties. Ideally, this chapter will serve to enlighten both online gaming businesses and regulators, who both must consider the wisdom of various policy options in formulating appropriate standards or restrictions on Internet gambling advertising content and methods.

CURRENT LEGAL CLIMATE IN SELECT JURISDICTIONS

United States of America

While the legality of various forms of online gaming is an unsettled question in the United States, the legal issues relating to advertising Internet gambling services are even more difficult to ascertain. The main reason for this distinction is that the power of the United States government to regulate a particular activity (like gambling) is not co-extensive with its ability to regulate or ban *advertising* for that same activity. In other words, while the government may regulate (or completely prohibit) the conduct of gambling itself, it is less free to regulate commercial speech about that conduct, under the First Amendment.[1] Therefore, affiliates, promoters and marketing agencies associated with the marketing of online gaming are less constrained, from a legal perspective, than those individuals or companies operating the gambling venture itself.

For decades, the Communications Act of 1934; 18 U.S.C. § 1304[2] (hereinafter "§1304") prohibited the radio or television broadcast of advertising for gambling activities. Although §1304 appeared only to prohibit the advertising of information concerning lotteries, various regulatory and enforcement agencies had interpreted the law to include proscribe other forms of gambling advertisements as well. Throughout the years, exemptions had been carved out, allowing advertising for Indian casinos, state

---

[1] *Greater New Orleans Broadcasting Assn. v. U.S.*, 527 US 173,(1999).
[2] 18 U.S.C. § 1304

lotteries, jai alai, and other activities. Private casinos, however, were not granted an exemption, and accordingly, U.S. casino gaming interests devoted substantial efforts to invalidating or limiting §1304. Those efforts finally succeeded in 1999, when the federal ban was struck down by a unanimous Supreme Court decision in *Greater New Orleans Broadcasting Association v. United States.*[3]

In deciding the *Greater New Orleans* case, the Supreme Court ruled that the broadcasting ban violated First Amendment free speech rights provided by the U.S. Constitution as the ban was so wrought with exceptions that it could not fulfill its stated purpose, or advance the government's interest of minimizing the alleged ills of gambling. Citing to the hypocrisy that some form of gambling was legal in nearly every state,[4] the Court specifically held that in connection with gambling advertisement, the power to prohibit or regulate particular conduct does not necessarily include the power to prohibit or regulate speech about that conduct.[5] In coming to this conclusion, the Court looked to the principles set forth in *Central Hudson Gas & Electric Corp. v. Public Service Commission of New York.*[6] Using the *Central Hudson* test, a court must first determine whether the First Amendment applies at all. In doing so, the proper inquiry is whether the advertisement concerns a lawful activity and is not misleading or fraudulent. Once it is determined that the First Amendment applies to a particular kind of commercial speech at issue, the speech may be restricted only if:

- The government's interest in doing so is substantial;
- The restrictions directly advance the government's asserted interest; and,
- The restrictions are no more extensive than necessary to serve that interest.[7]

The first element of the test can be a nuisance for the online gaming industry, and also the point where many cases are won or lost. Although the government may a substantial interest in regulating gambling in general, proving that such interest extends to online gambling is difficult, as the typical 'parade of horribles' associated with gambling and its establishments tend to not apply in the virtual world.[8]

Although U.S. advertising outlets have generally not been criminally prosecuted,[9] the last decade has demonstrated that governmental authorities still

---

[3] Greater New Orleans, *supra* note 1.

[4] 527 U.S. at 187, n.5.

[5] 527 U.S. at 193.

[6] 447 U.S. 557, 100 S.Ct. 2343, 65 L.Ed.2d 341 (1980).

[7] *Central Hudson,* 447 U.S. at 566.

[8] For example, online gambling cannot be accused of causing increased prostitution or drunkenness. Nor can the government seriously maintain that Internet gaming is controlled by organized crime. In seeking to justify any form of gambling advertising, the government typically introduces this 'parade of horribles' allegedly caused by gambling. Typically, the government will claim that land-based gambling increases local crime, fosters prostitution, causes corruption and results in the infiltration of organized crime. The same cannot logically be said about online gambling.

[9] The notable exception appears to be DME Global Marketing & Fulfillment, Inc., a Flor-

target Internet gambling advertisers and media outlets.[10] Legal concerns relating to online gambling advertising came to a head in mid-2003, when the U.S. Department of Justice ("DOJ") launched its campaign designed to combat the activity under the theory that the widespread advertising of online gambling misled the public into thinking that online gambling was lawful.[11] The DOJ took the position that such advertising rendered the any cooperating media outlets guilty of aiding and abetting Wire Act (and other statutory) violations, and conspiracy to violate the same.[12]

This campaign prompted a test case initiated against the DOJ by a gambling industry resource website. The court, however, ruled that the site did not have standing to mount the challenge, thus failing to clarify the muddied waters of online gambling advertising law.[13] Casino City, a Louisiana company that operates the Casino City Network, filed a complaint in federal court against the Department of Justice. The complaint alleged that it advertised lawful overseas companies that offer online casino and sports betting, and was threatened with prosecution based on threats and subpoenas from the Justice Department. Casino City sought a judicial declaration that the aiding and abetting statutes cannot be constitutionally applied to criminalize online gambling advertising. Unfortunately for the industry, the District Court refused to issue a ruling on the merits of the First Amendment claims, and dismissed the case on the grounds that Casino City had not been threatened directly with legal action by the DOJ. But the court went even further than it had to in order to resolve the case, and issued rulings on the constitutional claims. In doing so, it noted that the advertising involved in the case was directed to "illegal activity, namely Internet gambling."[14] The court further stated that the speech was not protected by the First Amendment because it was misleading and contained

---

ida marketing company that was included as a defendant in the Indictment returned against BetOnSports.com; Criminal Case Number 4:06CR337 CEJ, (E.D. MO). Most other legal actions against U.S. advertisers have been civil in nature, and have focused on extracting monetary penalties against the targeted media outlets. *See also,* note 19.

[10] K. Smith, "They're Baaack - Next Round of Subpoenas Targets Esquire," *Interactive Gaming News* (April 21, 2005), available at *http://www.igamingnews.com/index. cfm?page=artlisting&tid=5823&k=bodog%20poker. See also,* E. Swoboda, "State AGs Appeal to U.S. Congress for Help in Fighting Online Gambling," *Interactive Gaming News* (March 24, 2006).

[11] *See,* Correspondence from John G. Malcolm, Deputy Asst. Attorney General, Criminal Division, United States Department of Justice (06.11.03). A copy of the letter can be viewed at *http://www.igamingnews.com/articles/files/NAB_letter-030611.pdf.*

[12] In seeking to apply either the conspiracy or aiding and abetting laws to advertisers, the government would need to prove a close association between the promoter and the casino operator. Depending on the theory utilized, then, the government might not need to prove that someone actually gambled online or that the conspirators knew that the advertising scheme was illegal.

[13] Complaint at 2, *Casino City, Inc. v. U.S. Dep't of Justice,* No. 04-557-B-M3 (M.D. La. Aug. 7, 2004).

[14] Ruling at p. 14

information regarding illegal activities, namely Internet gaming.[15] The court made no effort to distinguish between the types of gambling advertised (which could have impacted the legal analysis), but instead concluded that all online gambling is simply illegal.

Shortly after the *Casino City* case ended, the DOJ began pressuring several advertising outlets, such as Google, Microsoft and Yahoo!, into cessation of their online gambling advertising activities, and seeking the imposition of monetary penalties for past infractions. Subtly, but greatly, expanding its war of intimidation against Internet gambling, the DOJ effectively forced the media powerhouses to pay over $31.5 million in fines to settle claims that the companies had promoted illegal gambling by running ads on the Internet.[16] During this influx in attention from the government came one of the first legal decisions to apply the *Greater New Orleans* case to offshore gambling advertising; the BetOnSports.com ("BoS") prosecution by the U.S. Department of Justice.[17]

Charged with various federal racketeering violations based on their involvement in online gambling activity that reached U.S. players, several BoS principles, and its marketing company, all found themselves in hot water with the U.S. government.[18] The defendants argued that the First Amendment to the U.S. Constitution protected the company's advertising statements as a form of commercial speech, which can only be banned or regulated if the government meets the *Central Hudson* test.[19] Analogizing their case with *Greater New Orleans*, the BoS defendant claimed that the gambling activity in question was legal in the jurisdictions where it was conducted.[20] Therefore, because BoS was fully licensed to provide online gambling in those jurisdictions, the advertising in question should be deemed legal within the U.S. as well. Completely ignoring the fact that the *advertising* of the gambling activity was at issue, not the gambling activity itself, the government countered with the argument that Internet gambling is illegal in the specific states where the bets are made.[21] The court

---

[15] *Id.*

[16] DOJ Fines Microsoft, Google, and Yahoo $31.5 Million for Advertising of Internet Gambling, *Tech Law Journal* (12/19/2007), found at *www.techlawjournal.com/topstories/2007/20071219.asp.*

[17] *U.S. v. David Carruthers*, et al., Case No.: 4:06CR337CEJ(MLM), (E.D. MO May 7, 2007). *See also*, Indictment, available at http://www.nytimes.com/packages/html/technology/gambling-indict.pdf.

[18] DME Global Marketing & Fulfillment, Inc., a Florida marketing company and its individual owners, were included as co-defendants in the Indictment returned against BetOnSports.com. The alleged unlawful activities, specific to the advertising outlet include: disseminating advertising in the United States and online to direct traffic to websites such as www.betonsports.com and telephone call centers, including such innocuous direct marketing activities such as mailing brochures, coupons, and flyers, and placing print, radio and television advertising. *See also*, Indictment, available at http://www.nytimes.com/packages/html/technology/gambling-indict.pdf.

[19] Carruthers, *supra* note 17.

[20] Order at p. 13.

[21] *Id.*

accepted the government's argument and issued a preliminary ruling stating, "To hold otherwise would effectively permit any activity licensed in a foreign jurisdiction to be legal in the United States without reference to local law."[22]

Also included in the twenty-two count BoS indictment was an unfair advertising claim arising from alleged violation of the Federal Trade Commission's (FTC)[23] Deceptive & Unfair Trade Practices Act, which prohibits false or misleading advertising.[24] The government alleged that BoS had made fraudulent and deceptive statements – which would not be protected by the First Amendment - in its promotional material when it claimed that its gambling-related services were "legal."[25] BoS claimed, on its website, that its betting services were, in fact, lawful, as evidenced by the company's legal licensure in Antigua, Barbuda and Costa Rica (the jurisdictions which acted as hubs for the business).[26] The DOJ disagreed and argued that advertisements directed at U.S. customers containing such language were illegal regardless of the jurisdiction of origin.[27] However, a guilty plea effectively ended the case before a decision could be rendered on the merits, so the preliminary ruling represents the first and only substantive analysis of the First Amendment advertising issue raised by the *Greater New Orleans* case, as applicable to Internet gambling.

While the government has various prosecution options available in its effort to criminalize online gambling advertising, any such effort directed against U.S. advertisers will inevitably be countered by a Free Speech defense under the First Amendment; thus creating a unique legal climate specific to the U.S. The First Amendment's protections extend to commercial speech such as advertising and, despite the defeat suffered on the BoS case; any effort to prosecute advertisers, affiliates, or media outlets may run afoul of those constitutional protections.

The government cannot do, through criminal law enforcement, that which it is prohibited from doing directly through legislation. Meaning, if an outright ban on Internet gambling advertising is unconstitutional, so would be a *de facto* advertising ban accomplished through aggressive law enforcement actions. The economy is global, and Internet gambling is a global industry. Many consider U.S. attempts to prohibit rather than regulate Internet gambling to be ill-advised, and an example of overreaching by U.S. authorities. Nevertheless, it seems that the U.S. government will continue its attempt to restrain online gambling advertisements reaching

---

[22] Order at p. 14.

[23] Notably, the FTC has not been actively involved in prosecuting gambling promotions since the BoS case.

[24] 15 U.S.C. §§ 45, 52, respectively. Accordingly, promotion of a gambling activity that can be deemed "unfair" significantly increases the potential for legal liability, and in the BoS case, this could have proved problematic regardless of the means or medium used to communicate the message.

[25] Carruthers, *supra* note 17.

[26] *Id.*

[27] *Id.*

U.S. players until some recognized legalization scheme comes into being at the state or federal level.

Canada

Although it by no means openly embraced online gaming, Canada has taken a much more careful approach in applying its gambling laws to online gambling promotion. While selected online gambling promotions reaching Canadian provinces could violate the country's anti-gambling laws, the Canadian government – both provincial and federal – has yet to pursue a prosecution for such marketing activities. Under Canadian law, an illegal "gambling" conviction requires some form of risk, reward and consideration present within the gaming activity in question.[28] Using the "consideration" element as the proverbial wildcard, Canadian Internet advertisers capitalize on the grey space within the law and have taken to marketing so-called "freeroll" websites. Commonly promoted as "instructional" in nature, the freeroll sites allow users to gamble online without the risk of losing any monetary consideration, thus bypassing the relevant Criminal Code provisions.[29] Notably, this concept of offering free play on a "Dot Net" variant of a company's "Dot Com" domain name was briefly adopted by companies advertising to the U.S beginning in about 2003, but most such advertising ceased after the adoption of the Unlawful Internet Gambling Enforcement Act of 2006[30] ("UIGEA"), coupled with the aggressive stance taken by the U.S. Department of Justice against any online gambling businesses.

Should an online gambling advertising entity find itself within the Canadian Crown's sights, three Criminal Code provisions could pose a problem for the promoter:[31]

- Advertising of sports betting services [C.C.C. s-s. 202(1)(h)][32]
- Advertising of lotteries and games of chance [C.C.C. s-s.
- 206(1)(a)]
- Importing gambling advertising [C.C.C. s-s. 202(1)(g)][33]

---

[28] Canadian Criminal Code Section VII – Disorderly Houses, Gaming & Betting.

[29] "Freeroll" sites are prohibited from providing links or generating pop-up ads directing users to "real-money" gambling websites.

[30] 31 U.S.C. §§ 5361.

[31] The Canadian Criminal Code provisions listed above have the potential to impact any online advertiser, which includes those involved in affiliate marketing. Although it appears that there has never been a prosecution involving an affiliate marketer of online gambling content, arguably the Criminal Code could be triggered if a computer located within the Canadian borders is utilized to direct online traffic to sports booking websites (s-s. 202(1) (h)) and/or websites offering casino-type games of pure chance (s-s. 206(1)(a)).

[32] Subsection 202(1)(h) of the Code makes it an offense to "advertise, print, publish, exhibit, post up or otherwise give notice of any offer, invitation or inducement to bet on, to guess or to foretell the result of a contest, or a result of or contingency relating to any contest."

[33] Subsection 202(1)(g) makes it an offense to "import or bring into Canada any information or writing that is intended or is likely to promote or be of use in gambling, book-making, pool-selling or betting on a horse race, fight, game or sport."

With the law distinguishing between "gaming" and "betting," Subsection 202(1)(h) could be interpreted as a prohibition on advertising related to betting activities, therefore, clearly encompassing sports booking services regardless of their location. Consequently, sports book websites advertising in Canada typically adopt the "freeroll" business model. Subsection 202(1)(h) may have been drafted so specifically and is construed so rigidly as a direct result of the country's government sanctioned online sports betting lotteries offered within the Canadian provinces.[34]

Addressing games of chance specifically, Subsection 206(1)(a) could proscribe any marketing promotion involving casino games that allow the player to post stakes, for example; roulette or other lottery-style games. Subsection 206(1)(a) of the Code makes it an offense to, "among other things, advertise or cause to be advertised any proposal, scheme or plan for disposing of property by any mode of pure chance." Should the advertised game require an element of skill at any point, such as (arguably) casino card games like blackjack or poker, the content will likely fall within the law's apparent loophole. Notoriously labeled as a "game of mixed chance and skill," poker websites are the most likely to capitalize on this grey area within the Canadian Criminal Code. Despite that Subsection 206(1)(a) expressly lists "cards" as a forbidden means of "disposing of property" for gaming purposes, Canadian case law states that such disposal via card play must occur while participating in a "game of pure chance" to trigger criminal violation.[35]

Although it does not expressly reference advertising like the previous two Criminal Code provisions, Subsection 202(1)(g) could be interpreted as applicable to gambling promotions. Given the law's focus on importation of material that is "intended [...] or likely to promote...gambling or betting," the scope of the law is effectively narrowed, therefore only applying to advertising content produced outside of Canada and then used within the country's borders.[36]

Similar to the United States' First Amendment, Canada provides its own potential freedom of expression defense to Internet gambling advertising violations. Found in the *Canadian Charter of Rights and Freedoms* (the "Charter"), Canadian citizens are guaranteed the "freedom of [...] expression, including freedom of the press and other media of communication."[37] Such freedoms are subject to the "reasonable limits prescribed by law as

---

[34] Most of the Canadian provinces maintain government operated lottery commissions to their citizens; some of the provinces provide online sports booking as a part of their lottery services. Thus, any private entity offering those same services online and/or promoting such services would be in direct competition with the Canadian government.

[35] *R. v. Shabaquay*, 2004 CarswellOnt 2309 (Ont. Ct. of J.)

[36] Notably, the Criminal Code does not include exporting "gambling" material to Canada in violating s-s. 202(1)(g). Accordingly, only the Canadian-based recipient of the advertising materials in question runs the risk of being charged under this provision.

[37] s-s. 2(b)

can be demonstrably justified in a free and democratic society."[38] Arguably, the online gambling advertising prohibitions listed in the Canadian Criminal Code could infringe on the speech-related freedoms set forth in the Charter, however, the infringement may be upheld based on the Charter's "reasonable limits" savings clause.[39] Laws criminalizing speech have generally been upheld as lawful where the Court found that the government's objective in enacting the provisions was to "avoid harm to society."[40] Debatably, the legislative intent behind the above referenced "anti-gambling" statutes is not to ban gambling promotion, but rather to restrict it to circumstances where the gambling activity in question is licensed by the province (e.g. province- operated lotteries and/or online sports booking).[41]

United Kingdom

In 2007, with the enactment of its Gambling Act of 2005, the United Kingdom liberalized the European gaming sector by reforming almost all previous restrictions on gaming advertising within the country.[42] The Act obligates enforcement of advertising guidelines[43] through the UK's Advertising Standards Authority ("ASA"), which develops advertising code through its two entities: the Committee of Advertising Practice ("CAP") and the Broadcast Committee of Advertising Practice ("BCAP").[44] The guidelines, directed at the entities which are statutorily permitted to advertise in the UK,[45] state that any gambling promotions are prohibited

---

[38] § 1; *See also, R. v. Oaks* [1986] 1 S.C.R. 103.

[39] In determining if the Canadian government is justified in infringing on the free speech rights of online gambling promoters, the court would look to the following test: 1) Is the law designed to achieve an objective that is of sufficient importance to warrant overriding freedom of expression? 2) If so, is there a rational connection between the criminal sanction and that objective? 3) Is the impairment on expression minimal in light of the standard imposed? 4) Is the criminal prohibition proportionate, when one weighs the importance of the objective sought against the degree of the infringement? *Id.*

[40] *Id.*

[41] *R. v. Andriopoulos*, [1993] O.J. No. 3427 (Gen. Div.); aff'd 1994 CarswellOnt 3947 (C.A.). In a decision from the Ontario Court of Appeal, *Andriopoulos* holds that gambling is permitted when there is sufficient control of the activity by the province so as to ensure that the public interest is protected. Accordingly, when a province regulates a particular form of gambling within its jurisdiction, the courts may safely assume that there is sufficient protection for the public and the gambling activity is compliant with the Canadian Criminal Code.

[42] *See* Gambling Act of 2005, available at: http://www.legislation.gov.uk.

[43] *See* Gambling Industry Code for Socially Responsible Gaming (2007). The Code affords local authorities the ability to impose sanctions on Internet gaming operators whose advertising does not comply with the relevant guidelines.

[44] *See generally* Advertising Standards Authority website, available at: www.asa.org.uk.

[45] Entities permitted to advertise in the United Kingdom include all European Economic Area countries, as well as those countries specifically chosen to be on the UK's "white list." The UK Dept. of Culture, Media and Sport maintains a list of jurisdictions that license Internet gaming operators (e.g. – Alderney, Antigua, Barbuda, Isle of Man, and Tasmania). Inclusion on the White List allows licensees based in those particular jurisdictions to

from misleading or offending the viewing public, and further, must not be geared towards children or problem gamblers.[46]

Arguably even more importantly, the Gambling Act was one of the first regulations in the world to address potential issues related to Internet-based gambling.[47] The Act states that entities outside of the European Economic Area ("EEA") members are not permitted to advertise any form of "foreign gambling" in the UK other than a lottery.[48] Despite this restriction, Internet gambling entities that are licensed within any of those EEA states fall within a loophole of the Act, and can advertise their services within the UK.[49] This lack of regulation for foreign advertising entities, coupled with disturbing statistics,[50] has several members of Parliament concerned. As a result, in early 2011, the UK's Secretary of State for Culture, Olympics, Media & Sport, Jeremy Hunt, announced his intent to make extensive amendments to the country's gaming laws in an attempt to launch new consumer protection efforts in the gaming industry.[51] Wanting to tighten regulations on foreign gambling entities advertising in the UK,[52] Hunt is hoping his efforts will ultimately "protect the public from gambling entities that don't meet UK standards, but have been allowed to profit from [the country's] lax approach to Internet gambling."[53]

---

advertise in the United Kingdom.

[46] Although advertisers are no longer banned from offering incentives and/or inducements in gambling-related advertising, the promotions must still abide by the advertising code and be deemed socially responsible. "The Codes make it clear that gambling advertisements should not portray, condone or encourage gambling behaviour that is socially irresponsible or could lead to financial, social or emotional harm, nor should they exploit the susceptibilities, aspirations, credulity or lack of knowledge of children, young persons and other vulnerable persons. The provisions apply to advertisements for 'play for money' gambling products and advertisements for 'play for free' gambling products that offer the chance to win a prize or explicitly or implicitly direct the consumer to a 'play for money' gambling product.

[47] Section 89 of the Gambling Act details the licensing process for remote gambling operations, which have been noted as applying to Internet-based gambling.

[48] Section 331 of the Gambling Act states that when associated with remote gambling specifically, "foreign gambling" is defined as "remote gambling none of the arrangements for which are subject to the law about gambling of an European Economic Area state (whether by being regulated, exempted, prohibited, or otherwise)."

[49] *Id.*

[50] "Crackdown on foreign internet gambling operators amid addiction fears," *Daily Mail* (Jan. 14, 2011), available at www.dailymail.co.uk/news/article-1347027/Crackdown-for-eign-internet-gambling-operators-amid-addiction-fears.html.

[51] D. Katz, "UK Culture Secretary Aims to Curb Online Gambling Ads," *Poker News Daily* (Jan. 18, 2011), available at http://www.pokernewsdaily.com/uk-culture-secretary-aims-to-curb-online-gambling-ads-17696.

[52] Secretary of State Hunt proposes to "reign in all remote gambling" in the United Kingdom by requiring that any company offering gaming-related services in the UK be licensed in the country and, more importantly, subject to UK law.

[53] Katz, *supra* note 51.

Other Jurisdictions

Mexico

In Mexico, governmental permission must be sought before advertising online casino games and sports betting.[54] Several criteria are included in the statute, including confirmation that the gaming enterprise has secured a proper permit, that the advertisement is accurate (and not deceptive), and that all ads include a statement that minors are prohibited from participating. Although the requirement of a permit before airing an advertisement offends traditional North American Free Speech principles, as a "prior restraint" on expression, the Mexico statute contains other laudable elements, such as exclusion of minors and problem gamblers, which are consistent with industry best practices.

Israel

Until fairly recently, advertising of online gambling activities was prevalent in Israel. However, in the wake of several police raids on Internet gambling advertising portals, such advertising is now scarce. Israel, like many countries, has not enacted specific legislation dealing with the advertising of online gambling activities. Law enforcement simply relies on the country's existing "terrestrial" legislation to battle the alleged unlawful marketing. Notably, however, Israel has taken a general position against online gambling. With its seminal case law criminalizing involvement in online gambling websites, ranging from ownership to mere technical maintenance, most online gaming advertising outlets have good reason to err on the side of caution when dealing with potential Israeli customers.[55]

Singapore

Singapore, like many other countries, lacks any laws regulating online gambling. Given that the country regulates gambling activities under archaic statutes enacted to monitor gambling dens during the country's colonial period, conflicting opinions exist as to how, or if, the laws could be interpreted in conjunction with cyberspace.[56] The Singapore government, however, has chosen to take a firm stance against gambling by enacting stringent guidelines for the advertising of land-based casino operations.[57]

---

[54] *Art. 10, Regulation for the Implementation of the Federal Gaming & Drawings Act of 1947* (Reglamento de la Ley Federal de Juegos y Sorteos, 2004). The *Regulation* went into effect on October 15, 2004.
[55] *Shimon Dabush vs. Connective Group Ltd. et. al.; State of Israel vs. Shauli et. al.*
[56] Private Lotteries Act (Cap. 250); Betting Act (Cap. 21); Common Gaming House Act (Cap. 49); Betting & Sweepstake Duties Act (Cap. 22).
[57] *Id.* Casino operators are required to seek approval from Singapore's Ministry of Community Development for all casino advertising and promotions (e.g. - membership drives, rewards and loyalty programs, drawings and contests). Casino operators risk a fine of up to $100,000 if found in breach of the guidelines. Policymakers have reasserted that the

Arguably, the same regulations would apply to online gambling activities. But such speculation is doubly inconclusive, as the issue has yet to reach the Singapore courts and country's online gambling industry appears in no hurry to launch such promotional content.

Ireland

Ireland has not passed specific laws related to online gambling advertising. Gaming in Ireland is governed by the Gaming & Lotteries Act 1956 which, due to its age, does not make any reference to online gambling, let alone the advertising of such.[58] Ireland's Gaming & Lotteries Act contains provisions restricting the promotion of "unlawful gaming"[59] and the advertising of lotteries,[60] both of which *could* encompass the marketing of Internet gambling activities. Recognizing the need to stay relevant in the cyber economy, however, Ireland is undertaking a review of its gambling laws and is expected to announce the details of the draft legislation within the year.[61] With the proposals rumoured to mirror the United Kingdom's gambling regulations, the new legislation will more than likely address online gambling advertising.[62]

Costa Rica

Some Central American countries have openly encouraged the development of the online gaming industry, thus choosing not to implement laws against advertising within the industry.[63] For example, the nation of Costa Rica – despite the strong presence of online gambling entities in that jurisdiction – has adopted no regulations relating to online gambling advertising, or online gaming in general. The adoption of regulations is highly unlikely due to the country's desire to capitalize on its label as an international hub for sports betting operations, and thereby encourage foreign gambling companies to relocate to Costa Rica.

---

casinos are meant for tourists and the new measures are designed to prevent the casinos from targeting Singaporeans.

[58] *See generally*, Gaming & Lotteries Act 1956.

[59] Section 4(1) of the Gaming and Lotteries Act 1956 states that "no person shall promote or assist in promoting or provide facilities for any kind of [unlawful] gaming ..."

[60] Section 21(1) of the 1956 Act has a similar provision specifically in relation to lotteries and that section provides that "no person shall promote or assist in promoting a lottery" that is not deemed to be lawful. In addition, Section 22 of the 1956 Act prohibits all print and radio advertisements of lotteries (including bingo).

[61] The new legislation is not expected to be made law until late 2013.

[62] *Written evidence submitted by the United Kingdom Advertising Association*, Parliament Session 2010-2012, available at: http://www.publications.parliament.uk/pa/cm201012/cm-select/cmcumeds/writev/gambling/m74.htm.

[63] E.g. Panama; Costa Rica.

Sweden

Officially authorized to do so in 2003, Sweden permits limited online gambling through a government-controlled operator, Svenska Spel.[64] Using a state monopoly model, Svenska Spel is the only authorized Internet gambling operator licensed through the Swedish government.[65] Similar to the United Kingdom, Sweden is especially concerned with the effect of advertising on problem gamblers.[66] Unlike the UK, however, Swedish gambling advertising law has been tested in court. Although addressing terrestrial gambling advertising, in 2010, the Stockholm District Court upheld the legislation that prohibits advertising unlawful gambling within state borders. With the court finding that Swedish criminal code warranted greater penalties for advertising originating from another state or country, as compared to similar material originating within state borders, online advertising entities should be cautious of Sweden's clear distinction between foreign and domestic advertising outlets.[67]

CRITIQUE OF CURRENT APPROACHES TO ONLINE GAMBLING ADVERTISING

Advertising related to online gambling activities is often not regulated, or occasionally treated identically to the gambling activity itself. But distinct considerations exist when developing regulatory policies and best practices relating solely to promotional activities like marketing and advertising. Whether due to the content's association with traditionally iniquitous activities or simply the boundless nature of the Internet, most current regulatory practices are disconnected, conflicting and often problematic. Although several jurisdictions throughout the world have implemented laws regulating gambling advertising in its print or terrestrial broadcasting form, the difficulty in translating those laws into the online world is noteworthy.[68] Although commercial in nature, online gambling promotions are expressive activity, and deserve unique consideration as a form of speech. Governmental bodies should be more cautious, and the resulting regulation more narrowly tailored, given the expressive nature of the activity involved. Online gambling advertising is by no means entitled to be

---

[64] *See* Lotterilagen (Lotteries Act of 1994) amendments (August 1, 2002).

[65] *Id.*

[66] Problem gamblers compile approximately .5-.6 percent of Sweden's population. See generally, *British Gambling Prevalence Survey of 2007*.

[67] Joined Cases C-447 & 448/08, *Sjöberg v. Åklagaren*, [2011] 1 C.M.L.R. 11.

[68] *See e.g.*, 16 C.F.R. Part 255: Guides Concerning the Use of Endorsements and Testimonials in Advertising (the FTC Endorsement Rule). In an effort to adapt regulations targeted at Web 2.0 environment, the FTC updated its Guides Concerning the Use of Endorsements & Testimonials in Advertising. The revised Guide basically updates the earlier Guide with particular attention to the use of endorsements, and testimonials on blogs, in word-of-mouth advertising campaigns and on new media platforms, and became effective December 1, 2009.

a marketing free-for-all, but any regulation should be limited to achieving a specified, legitimate governmental interest. Greater regulation of online gambling advertising, merely because it involves gambling, is illogical and unwarranted.

Jurisdictional disparities pose a serious issue for online gambling promotions. As a result, lawmakers in various countries have proposed legislation requiring gambling advertising outlets to employ geo-targeting[69] efforts to limit the reach of advertisements to an audience legally entitled to engage in the gaming activity. Although these proposals have yet to pass in their respective jurisdictions, it may only be a matter of time before legislators succeed in their efforts to force online gaming sites to use current technology to limit the reach of their advertisements. Geo-targeting is an Internet-based marketing tool that allows an advertising outlet the ability to target a promotional campaign at a limited set of recipients based on geographic location. Most marketing initiatives that support geo-targeting allow the advertiser to control where the promotional materials are displayed based on individualized restrictions like country, state, city, or proximity within a given physical address. Lawmakers often sing the praises of this marketing technique without taking into account the feasibility of its use for the average online gambling entity. It is true that with the help of geo-targeting advertising, online gambling promoters could direct their campaigns solely to jurisdictions where the underlying gambling activity is completely lawful. Some in the industry have even used the technique already.[70] However, with effective geo-blocking solutions still fairly pricey, and so many countries still in limbo on whether online gambling ads are even a problem, industry advertisers–particularly small affiliates–are forced to evaluate whether efforts are worthwhile. Geo-targeting is just one example of several solutions du jour bombarding online gambling advertisers that may be effective, but will no doubt take a considerable amount of time to resonate as an industry standard. While voluntary geo-blocking may be an effective tool to be considered by advertisers in developing best practices, mandating its use under the pain of civil or criminal penalties may be too much for many promoters to bear.

As referenced above, current legislative struggles with online gambling marketing seem to ignore the distinction between a gambling violation and a violation of advertising laws. To bypass such a clear distinction not only subjects today's online advertisers to potentially excessive penalties, but sets an extremely dangerous precedent for all future Internet-based marketers. Most jurisdictions have well-settled gambling laws that denote specific aspects of gambling as criminal acts, often punishable by incarceration or asset seizure.[71] On the other hand, most jurisdictions have yet

---

[69] Noted promotional technique is also known as "geo-blocking."

[70] For example, the technique was required by court order in *141 Domain Names* case to avoid forfeiture of online gambling domain names.

[71] *See, e.g.,* Unlawful Internet Gambling Enforcement Act of 2006 (UIGEA); U.S. Wire Act

to address the legality of online gambling advertising, let alone penalties associated with such activities. Because an unmistakable division exists between an advertisement and the underlying conduct being advertised, logically, penalties arising from online gambling marketing should not rise to the same severity as a violation of gambling laws. Moreover, penalties associated with Internet-based gaming ads should be limited to civil sanctions such as injunctions, fines or consent decrees restricting future conduct.[72] While criminal penalties like incarceration may be more effective in inducing compliance, expressive activity like advertising must be afforded due deference. An evolved approach to online gambling advertising regulation would limit penalties to those that are civil in nature.

Under the U.S. model, advertising regulations are generally enforced, at the federal level, by the Federal Trade Commission ("FTC"). This administrative agency typically encourages compliance through civil, as opposed to criminal, remedies.[73] The FTC further issues policy statements or warning notices to companies alleged to be engaged in deceptive advertising, in an effort to alter the content of future promotions, without actually taking enforcement action. Occasionally, administrative complaints will be initiated, resulting in consent decrees whereby the alleged violator agrees to take some remedial action and perhaps pay some fines or costs of investigation. In more serious cases, the FTC will seek court injunctions, to halt the offending marketing practices. Only in the most egregious of advertising cases, however, should the harsh penalties of criminal prosecution be invoked.[74] The underlying reasons for this approach relate to the expressive nature of the advertising activity, and the sensitivity to potential censorship concerns. Concerns over potential self-censorship are even more probable if incarceration is threatened as a penalty. Only where specific intent to violate the law exists, coupled with a compelling governmental concern (such as willful marketing to minors) should criminal penalties be an available remedy.[75] Model advertising regulations should include defenses based on good faith efforts, or substantial compliance, to further protect the expressive activity at issue. Much like print or terrestrial commercial speech, if the advertiser knows it cannot be held strictly liable for rogue advertisements reaching improper jurisdictions so long as it has made reasonable efforts to avoid such occurrences, self-censorship becomes less likely. Any restriction on advertising practices necessarily impacts speech, which should enjoy a favored position as part of the marketplace of ideas. Any advertising reg-

---

of 1961; Travel Act; Wagering Paraphernalia Act; Illegal Gambling Business Act; Professional & Amateur Sports Protection Act of 1992; Racketeer Influenced & Corrupt Organizations Act (RICO).

[72] See supra, note 9.

[73] See generally, 16 C.F.R. 1.61.

[74] For example, intentional misrepresentation, deceptive, etc, which will be covered by other existing laws such as fraud.

[75] See U.S. v. X-Citement Video, 513 U.S. 64 (1994).

ulations should be cognizant of these concerns, and use the least restrictive means of accomplishing any legitimate governmental objective.

Suggested "Best Practices" in Regulating Online Gambling Advertising

In developing best practices for marketing ventures, regardless of the industry, looking to existing laws and regulations is helpful as a guide and evidence of the current regulatory viewpoint. Such laws may impact the method used to convey the commercial message, or the content of the message itself. Given existing efforts to capitalize on technological advancements in communication, such laws may include restrictions on the use of unsolicited commercial e-mail communications (i.e. "spam"), instant messages ("spim"), message board posts, and even unsolicited calls and text messages to mobile devices. Laws restricting these activities are generally developed with consumer protection in mind, and adhering to them (or standards modeled from them), even if an entity is not jurisdictionally required to do so, may provide the ancillary benefit of evidencing a public commitment to consumer protection. Demonstrating such commitment, at the current stage of development in the online gambling industry, will help foster a cooperative environment in which the industry will ultimately flourish through effective self-regulation. Adapting "best practice" approaches premised on voluntary industry regulation of the *type* of media used to distribute online gambling advertisements as well as the *content* contained within those ads, would appear to yield the best results when implemented on a global scale. Such approach was effective for the Hollywood motion picture and the music recording industries in avoiding potentially oppressive content regulations.

Self-Regulation Based on the Advertising Medium or Method

In the United States, the Controlling the Assault of Non-Solicited Pornography and Marketing Act of 2003[76] ("CAN-SPAM") governs the transmission of what is commonly referred to as "spam." CAN-SPAM generally requires[77]:

- Accurate header information. For example, the "From" field and underlying IP address of the sender must be accurate.[78]
- The physical address of the sender.

---

[76] 15 U.S.C. § 7701.

[77] This particular list focuses solely on electronic mail messages that do not contain "sexually oriented material." E-mail containing sexually oriented material must conform to additional requirements as set forth at 15 U.S.C. § 7704(d).

[78] While the majority of CAN-SPAM factors are only applicable to "commercial" messages which advertise or promote a commercial product, this requirement is also applicable to "transactional" and "relationship" messages, which are messages that a business sends existing customers and which concern a transaction or the specific, already-established relationship between the sender and recipient.

- An accurate subject heading.
- Opt-out capability, either via a return e-mail address or some other clear and conspicuous mechanism that allows the recipient to opt-out of future commercial messages.
- A disclaimer that clearly and conspicuously indicates that the message is an advertisement.

Arguably, avoiding any form of deception is a best practice. Accurate header information and subject fields are obvious positive attributes for marketing material. Similarly, a functioning opt-out mechanism is reasonable, especially when limiting the ability to opt-out to commercial messages unrelated to any existing business/customer relationship. Even if a customer opts-out of "commercial"[79] messages, as that term is defined by CAN-SPAM, such opting-out does not prohibit a business from sending unsolicited messages about a customer's account or about new features that may be added to a service to which the customer already subscribes.

Numerous misconceptions exist relating to CAN-SPAM; the most dangerous of which is that CAN-SPAM has no effect if a recipient has given some prior consent to receiving the message. While consent does affect *some* of the above requirements, consent does not completely negate the requirements. For example, even if a user of a poker site has consented to receiving commercial messages, an opt-out mechanism is still required. In fact, under CAN-SPAM – assuming the substantive elements of the law are met - a business does not need prior affirmative consent before sending an unsolicited commercial message. It truly is an opt-*out* mechanism. There is, in effect, an implied consent prior to the recipient exercising the opt-out right.

Canada's anti-spam law, sometimes referred to as the Fighting Internet and Wireless Spam Act[80] ("FISA") was passed in December 2010 and is set to take effect in the near future. Presuming that the law is unchanged between now and when it is becomes effective, FISA employs an opt-*in* approach to e-mail marketing. Therefore, consent must be obtained either impliedly or expressly prior to sending the message.

Of these two countries' mechanisms, a hybrid approach may be worthy of consideration. CAN-SPAM's allowance of an initial unsolicited commercial message is obviously valuable from a business perspective, however, obtaining prior consent before sending additional commercial messages may offer the site operator or advertiser an additional layer of good faith if its promotional activities were questioned. Whether through regulation or best practices, the concerns of consumers over being bombarded with

---

[79] The term "commercial electronic mail message" means any electronic mail message the primary purpose of which is the commercial advertisement or promotion of a commercial product or service (including content on an Internet website operated for a commercial purpose). The term "commercial electronic mail message" does not include a transactional or relationship message. 15 U.S.C. §§ 7702(2)(A), (2)(B).

[80] *Canadian House Government Bill C-28* – Fighting Internet and Wireless Spam Act (FISA).

irrelevant and often annoying commercial messages on every conceivable electronic device should be considered. Importantly, prior consent should not, and arguably, *cannot*, be legally obtained through dubious promotional techniques or suspect contractual drafting; i.e. burying the consent in the middle of a lengthy Terms of Service document, or combining consent with other necessary consumer responses during a sign-up process. Just as consent to a website's Terms of Service should be obtained by clear and conspicuous means, the same standard should apply to consent to receive non-relationship-based commercial solicitations directed to online gaming customers. For example, a separate check box allowing the site operator to send the customer promotional material from partner or third party sites may be an effective way to obtain prior consent.[81] The decision to create such an obvious opt-in procedure will depend on factors such as the jurisdiction(s) in which the site intends to operate, the jurisdiction(s) in which the site intends to target its marketing, and the jurisdiction(s) which may potentially assert legal authority over the site. Irrespective of the legal requirements, some form of conspicuous consent or opt-out procedure is consistent with recommended industry best practices.

With gambling addiction being one of the foremost social concerns in regulating online gambling advertising, operators and promoters would be well served to take this issue into account when developing industry best practices.[82] As stated above, offering a self-exclusion option is an important industry best practice. Accordingly, developing an industry-wide database comprised of problem gamblers that have chosen to opt-out of certain online gambling advertisements would serve both purposes of social responsibility and suggested advertising guidelines. Accessible to participating online gambling advertising outlets across the globe, the database would house the e-mail addresses and other electronic contact points for consumers that have indicated their desire to no longer receive online gambling solicitations. Similar to the FTC's National Do Not Call Registry, any entity accessing the database would be required to certify that it is doing so for the purpose of preventing distribution of solicitations to parties who have chosen to opt-out from contact.[83]

Using CAN-SPAM as a model for potential best practices has some advantages. The statute imposes requirements relating to identification of the party

---

[81] The author recognizes that many customers will simply ignore such a box and, consequently, providing that option may not be desirable.

[82] *See generally,* British Gambling Prevalence Survey 2010, available at: www.gamblingcommission.gov.uk/PDF/British%20Gambling%20Prevalence%20Survey%202010.pdf. The National Centre conducted this survey for Social Research on behalf of the United Kingdom's Gambling Commission.

[83] Any advertising entity that accesses the database would be required to certify, under penalty of law, that it is accessing the database solely in an effort to comply with industry-regulated, voluntary best practices attempting to foster socially responsible online gambling marketing activities. Use of the database for any other purposes could subject the advertising entity to industry sanctions.

sending the commercial message, and the promotional nature of the message itself.[84] CAN-SPAM's physical address and advertising disclaimer requirements, however, can be burdensome for some businesses for two reasons:

- Not all businesses want to publish their physical location;[85]
- A clear and conspicuous disclaimer that a message is an advertisement or solicitation is almost guaranteed to result in the message being filtered by the inevitable multiple spam filters that exist between the sender and recipient.

In these areas, voluntary best practices may diverge from legal compliance methods. Certainly, any online gaming e-mail advertisements targeting U.S. consumers should comply with the applicable legal requirements. Given the burdensome nature of these requirements, however, they are unlikely to be voluntarily adopted as best practices. Only through legislative reform will the compliance obligations change, although the difficulties associated with applying U.S. law extraterritorially often results in foreign promoters disregarding these obligations.

Irrespective of whether promoters decide to comply with the disclosure and disclaimer requirements of CAN-SPAM, inclusion of an opt-out requirement is recommended. Adopting this minimally disruptive opt-out and/or database exclusion standards will be beneficial to the industry's image and demonstrate commitment to effective self-regulation.

Online gambling advertising best practices do not end with simply establishing e-mail marketing guidelines. As discussed earlier, various countries have expressed intent, or at the very least, willingness to apply dated "terrestrial" gambling promotion laws to Internet marketing activities. Any legal success in doing so could easily foster motivation to employ those same obsolete regulations to mobile device-based promotions and other yet to be developed technologies. Mobile devices and social media applications are quickly becoming the predominant way in which businesses identify and communicate with their customers.[86] In the U.S., old laws are being repurposed to address changing technologies. For example, the Telephone Consumer Protection Act of 1991[87] ("TCPA"), which predates short message service ("SMS") text messaging, has recently been interpreted to include promotional SMS text messages as "calls." The TCPA

---

[84] 15 U.S.C. § 7704(a)(5).

[85] This is especially true for business entities in so-called "vice" industries like gambling and adult entertainment, where anonymity is not only preferred among industry participants, but can also be a key component in success.

[86] *See generally*, Justin Smith & Charles Hudson, "Inside Virtual Goods," *The US Virtual Goods Market 2009-10 Report*. The rise of social networking and the influx of gaming integrated with these social networking sites is clearly indicative of the other technological mediums of which online gambling advertisers must be aware. In 2010, Facebook had more than 500 million users worldwide, with over 100 million of those users in the U.S. alone, and along with several other social networking websites offering "social and casual games," were projected to generate more than $1 billion in virtual goods and advertising revenue.

[87] 47 U.S.C. § 227.

has its own triggering events and requirements concerning consent, some of which differ from CAN-SPAM. In fact, the TCPA is more of an opt-*in* model, requiring "prior express consent" before sending an unsolicited commercial advertisement. Should an online gambling advertiser choose mobile marketing as part of its gambling promotion strategy, at a minimum, prior express consent must be obtained by a clear and conspicuous process under the TCPA. Accordingly, when collecting a user's cell phone number, regardless of the communication medium used in the collection, a recommended best practice would be to encourage the marketing entity to capture and log the users' consent to receiving the gambling promotion messages on their mobile devices.

Under CAN-SPAM and the TCPA, the company that is responsible for initiating or procuring the e-mail or text advertisement is ultimately legally responsible for the message. This means that any commercial messages that an affiliate might be sending for an online gambling advertising outlet will be attributed to that advertising outlet.[88] This puts a substantial risk on initiating party, especially when dealing with content like online gambling advertisements that may be unlawful in certain jurisdictions. This risk is also the reason that many affiliate programs flatly prohibit their participants from using e-mail as a marketing medium. Care should be taken when using e-mail marketing methods, to ensure compliance with the relevant jurisdiction's spam laws. Moreover, standardized best practices should be used to provide recipients with accurate, truthful information, avoid targeting minors, exclude compulsive gamblers, and allow anyone to halt future undesired communications. With this responsibility falling on the shoulders of the program operator, it would serve gambling advertising outlets well to implement proper policing procedures to ensure that their affiliate marketers are not overstepping various legal and ethical boundaries.

Some websites also employ a "Refer-a-Friend" model wherein an existing customer is given some benefit[89] for filling out a form that initiates a marketing e-mail to the user's friend. The generated e-mail would likely identify the referring friend and suggest that the recipient visit a given website and play any of the several casino games offered to users. When the recipient registers as a user of the site, the referring friend could receive something as minimal as temporary access to a high stakes online poker game. Despite that the promoted site did not trigger the chain of events that lead to the recipient receiving that e-mail, under the FTC's interpretation of CAN-SPAM that e-mail was, in effect, sent by the promoted site, not by the referring friend. Arguably the referring friend was induced to

---

[88] Affiliate marketing is a highly efficient and inexpensive way to market online gaming and betting sites. Affiliates use their computer servers to direct traffic to websites, and are paid commission for the customers they acquire.
[89] Such a "benefit" does not have to be monetary in nature. The FTC restrictions encompass any sort of advantage given to the referring user, for example, virtual tokens, game credits, future discounts, etc.

send, and then rewarded for sending, the message. As such, in keeping with the attempt to develop advertising best practices within the gambling industry, it would be wise to maintain the e-mail marketing requirements set forth above even for e-mails purportedly sent at the volition of third parties who receive some benefit for initiating the communication.

Similarly, under the TCPA, if the required "prior express consent" does not include consent for someone other than the company obtaining such consent to actually send certain promotional text messages, then the company who obtained the consent, but did not actually send the messages, is subjected to potential liability. For example; Company A obtains its users' prior express consent to receive promotional text messages from its "affiliates and brands," but Company A's users actually receive promotional text messages from Company B. Regardless whether Company B had some type of a marketing relationship with Company A, if it was not a legal "affiliate or brand," Company A has opened itself up to a myriad of legal consequences.[90] Clearly, this indicates that the specific language used in obtaining consent from advertising recipients is critically important.

These examples, under U.S. law, demonstrate how a website's affiliates and/or marketing partners can expose the website's operators to liability. While some requirements may appear unfair or heavy-handed, they provide an opportunity to inform best practices protocol that might satisfy regulators and politicians in other countries, and ultimately result in some level of legislative reform in the U.S. Only if a website operator or affiliate program operator can be sure that its affiliates and/or marketers are sending messages that comply with the website's established best practices should e-mail be allowed as a method to market the website. This can be accomplished by providing the affiliate or marketer with specific text or e-mail templates that must be used, along with insistence on clear, written affiliate agreements outlining any prohibited marketing practices.[91] Also, any time that prior express consent is sought, the website operator must consider the scope of consent sought to be obtained. An "affiliate" marketer might not be a legal "affiliate" of the website as defined by the jurisdiction's relevant case law or statutes. Finally, if using a "refer-a-friend" model, any resulting messages or transmissions should conform to the site's best practices for sending e-mail and should not be considered an independent message sent by the user, such that it is immune from the site's policies.

Another danger area for online gambling advertising is with the increasingly popular practice of using published "reviews" to generate business. Many consumers have become accustomed to immediately scrolling down to the consumer reviews of any product or service offered online, before making the decision to purchase. Online gambling

---

[90] Satterfield v. Simon & Schuster, Inc., 569 F.3d 946 (9th Cir. 2009).

[91] Many operators that manage affiliate programs disclose to their marketers upon registration, that deviation from the relevant e-mail template or text language is grounds for termination from the affiliate program.

services are no different. The value (and danger) of truthful, reliable consumer reviews cannot be understated in the ecommerce environment. Many websites employ a "reviewer affiliate" model wherein an affiliate with some tie to the business purports to "review" the services found on a website. The review will often contain links back to the site or service being reviewed, and those links often have affiliate tracking codes embedded in them to ensure payment or other compensation is sent to the affiliate for any resulting sign-ups or clicks. In the U.S., the FTC has crafted guidelines for such "endorsements" that require that the review or endorsement disclose any "material connection" between the reviewer and the company providing the product or service being reviewed.[92] As with CAN-SPAM and the TCPA, the company responsible for causing the review to be published will be legally responsible for it. As mentioned at the beginning of this section, the purpose of such regulations is consumer protection, and this is especially true with promoting controversial entertainment activity such as gambling.[93] While a review with embedded affiliate codes in the links back to the reviewed site may be recognized as an obvious "paid review" by some, others may genuinely think that the particular website provides the "best" casino game on the Net, or that it has the "highest payouts," and that it is completely "lawful" in every aspect – if such claims are made in the reviews. Under current FTC policy if the reviewer received any sort of credit or incentive for writing that endorsement, the website operator is responsible for making sure that the material connection between the reviewer and the reviewed content is conspicuously identified. This fair disclosure of any tie between purported "reviewers" and the service being reviewed should be an integral part of any best practices list.[94]

Careful monitoring of affiliate activity is an essential component of any best practices regime. Affiliate promotions should be monitored and occasionally audited through independent verification tools, to ensure compliance with the gaming company's policies, and applicable law. Spot-checking promotions and other activity will provide valuable feedback. Requiring the affiliate to provide advance or contemporaneously published advertising copy to the promoted site also qualifies as a responsible best practice. Finally, affiliates should agree to comply with any existing or future advertising rules established by the promoted gaming site, to ensure sufficient flexibility as the legal environment evolves. By implementing policies designed to ensure affiliate compliance with best practices, gaming sites will

---

[92] FTC, *supra* note 70.

[93] The author makes no "value judgment" regarding gambling or gaming activity, but simply observes that gambling – despite its ancient roots – has in modern history often been viewed as a "vice" activity, or social ill, as opposed to a mainstream product or service, in many countries.

[94] While not directly addressing "fake reviews" and online affiliate marketers, Canada's Competition Act is similar to the U.S.'s FTC Act in that it prohibits false and misleading representations in marketing.

not only protect their affiliates, but also their own companies from claims based on vicarious liability theories.

Self-Regulating Based on the Advertising Content

Prevention of misleading advertising is a serious concern for most lawmakers in regulating online gambling promotions. Regulating content in any form requires a delicate balance of recognizing individual rights in conjunction with societal obligations. This is especially true in dealing with a so-called "vice" industry like online gambling. For example, in the U.S., any law affecting commercial speech must be clear, narrowly tailored and supported by identified, legitimate governmental goals.[95] Because of this rigorous standard imposed on advertising-related regulations, legislative bodies must be cognizant of infringing on what could be legally protected commercial speech. As this standard arises from the U.S.-specific First Amendment, notably not all countries place such rigid restrictions on their advertising. In addressing best practices in a worldwide industry, however, online gambling marketers might consider the benefits of such advertising standards when applied via self-regulatory guidelines instead of government-imposed laws.

Although many online gambling promotions may not rise to the level of "deception," advertisements in such an under-regulated industry often ride the line of "misleading" when attempting to capitalize on a global market. Given the anonymity that comes along with advertising in the virtual world, advertised services must be accurately portrayed in any promotional materials. Online gaming marketing is particularly vulnerable, where a simple opinion from a player could be seen as a fraudulent promise to future users. For example, online gambling promotions should not guarantee a specific rate of return on wagers, provide false or exaggerated probabilities of success, or even draw success rate comparisons between it and competitors without specific, factual bases. Although statements of opinion used in marketing materials should certainly remain within the realm of protected speech, implementing self-governed guidelines to avoid deceiving consumers–whether intentional or not–would aid in leveling this global playing field, and legitimizing the industry as a whole. For example, using promotional materials laden with statements declaring a particular website provides *"The best chance of winning on the Internet!"* could qualify as a misleading opinion statement. So although, this statement is (and should be) completely *legal*, it may warrant caution from a best practices perspective.

In examining this concept of misleading online gambling, advertising outlets must consider that their services are *not* legal in all jurisdictions, despite the ability to reach all such jurisdictions. Accounting for this, a beneficial best practice would not only be to prohibit false claims of legality, but to

---

[95] Intermediate scrutiny: i.e., not vague / restricting access by minors, ensuring truth in advertising, addressing compulsive gambling.

take the concept a step further and warn the consumer of potential illegality. The beauty and the curse of the World Wide Web is just that; it is worldwide. Online gambling promotional materials will inevitably reach consumers located in jurisdictions that have outlawed Internet gambling. If the industry adopts standards proscribing blanket statements of legality in its advertising, this ostensibly lessens the potential for claims that consumers were being misled into believing their online gambling activities were perfectly legal.[96] Because e-commerce business models cultivate legal inconsistencies by their very nature, judicious use of disclaimers and disclosures should be adopted. Encouraging advertising outlets to include a warning of sorts, thus notifies consumers that they have a duty in determining if participation in the advertised gaming conduct is illegal in their particular jurisdiction. Although some of the above-referenced proposals may be resisted initially, introducing self-regulated, heightened standards in online gambling advertising will foster a cooperative environment with legal and legislative bodies, as the online gambling industry continues its struggle for worldwide legitimacy.

CONCLUSION

Although some of the world's most politically visible countries have introduced varying forms of regulation for modern online gambling advertisements, the Internet-based gaming community has an obligation as a whole to cooperate in enacting self-regulatory principles, and demand a higher level of professionalism and truth in advertising from each other. The information contained herein is intended to instill an understanding of the ongoing evolution of the Internet gambling industry and its multifaceted marketing concerns. Because legal scrutiny of online gambling advertising is still in its infancy, the best practices and procedures identified in this chapter will ideally play a part in the development of more definitive, industry-wide standards. Many countries are just now evaluating their stance on Internet gambling and related activities. Voluntary development of best practices, at this crucial time in the industry's overall development, will help ward off overreaching mandatory regulation, and fulfill laudable goals including exclusion of minors and compulsive gamblers, and inclusion of truthful, accurate information regarding the increasingly popular pastime of online gambling.

---

[96] *See generally,* BetOnSports.com prosecution. *See also,* http://www.usatoday.com/tech/news/2009-11-03-betonsports-founder-prison_N.htm. Prosecutors said the company falsely advertised that its gambling operations were legal, and misled gamblers into believing that money transferred to BetOnSports.com was safe and available to withdraw at any time. Instead, investigators said, the money was used to expand operations, including purchase of a rival betting firm.

8

Responsible Gaming

Frank Catania, Sr., Esq., Gary Ehrlich, Esq.,
and Antonia Cowan, Esq.

Introduction

Responsible governments, regulators, and operators across the globe accept that when a new form of gaming is legalized and made available to the public, those who profit from such gaming must formulate and implement policies to minimize any harm resulting from that activity, especially to the most vulnerable members of society.[1] The Financial Services Regulatory Commission of Antigua and Barbuda provides an example of a jurisdiction's express commitment to social gambling responsibility:

> The Financial Services Regulatory Commission ("the Commission") recognises that for a small group of people, gaming may be a problem adversely affecting their personal lives and the lives of those closest to them. What is for the vast majority of participants an enjoyable leisure, social activity can for a small percentage of the population become a problematic behaviour. Similarly, shopping, the consumption of alcohol, eating, and physical exercise are a few examples of otherwise normal activities [which] if unmanaged, abused or used as a mechanism to escape everyday problems and inner conflicts can become a problematic activity. We at the Commission believe that we have a responsibility to consumers of gaming services provided by our licencees and to the global industry by being key participants in the promotion of responsible gaming to ensure the delivery of gaming services in a socially responsible environment.

> We are very cognizant that we licence and regulate a service which is not always viewed favourably. With this in mind our social responsibility commitment is underpinned by four main objectives:

---

[1] *See* Garry Smith & Dan Rubenstein, *Socially Responsible and Accountable Gambling in the Public Interest*, 25 J. Gambling Issues 54, 54-60 (2011), *available at* http://jgi.camh. net/doi/pdf/10.4309/jgi.2011.25.5.

1. **To Strengthen** the industry's commitment to responsible gaming and social responsibility;
2. **To Enhance** the capacity for operators to conduct business in a manner which promotes responsible gaming and the jurisdiction's social responsibility commitment objectives;
3. **To Protect** consumers gaming with a site licensed in our jurisdiction that they are gaming with an operator who adheres to our regulatory and licensing objectives; and
4. **Accountability**, operators will be held accountable to incorporate industry best practices with respect to responsible gaming and the delivery of gaming services in socially responsible environment.

The Commission and the Antigua Online Gaming Association (AOGA) are committed, and will collectively embark on a national, industry-wide initiative to address social responsibility issues confronting the industry and to ensure that the Commission's key objectives are adopted to achieve full observance of our polices; to ensure the delivery of gaming services in a socially responsible environment.

In support of this, there will be the establishment of a "Gaming Addiction Research and Education Fund." The Antiguan remote gaming industry and the Commission will assist in educating the public on the risks associated with online gaming, increasing social awareness, particularly with minors, as well as providing resources for the treatment of problem gambling. The Commission is united with the AOGA on the importance of these measures. We will not only continue to meet, and in most cases exceed international standards of best practice, but more importantly work collaboratively with e-gaming jurisdictions globally towards preserving and safeguarding the health and welfare of on-line players worldwide.[2]

"Responsible gaming"[3] policies are designed to ensure that legalized gambling takes place in a socially responsible manner.[4] Some jurisdictions stress the importance of responsible gaming provisions. For example, the United Kingdom Gambling Commission requires its gaming licensees to put into effect policies and procedures intended to promote socially re-

---

[2] Ant. & Barb. Fin. Services Regulatory Comm'n, Social Responsibility Commitment, http://www.antiguagaming.gov.ag/gamingresponsibily.asp (last visited Aug. 18, 2012).

[3] Although the terms "gaming" and "gambling" have distinct origins, they have come to be used interchangeably. Solely in the interest of uniformity, the term "responsible gaming" will be used throughout this Chapter, with the understanding that "responsible gambling" is used in many jurisdictions around the world as well.

[4] *See, e.g.,* Conditions and Codes of Practice Applicable to Remote Gen. Betting Licences, Remote Pool Betting Licences, Remote Betting Intermediary Licences, Remote General Betting Ancillary Licences, at 13, [United Kingdom] Gambling Comm'n., *available at* http://www.gamblingcommission.gov.uk/pdf/Licence%20conditions%20and%20codes%20of%20practice%20-%20remote%20betting%20-%20October%202010.pdf.

sponsible gaming.[5] The Standards of the European Gaming and Betting Association (EGBA) also provide another illustration of a typical "responsible gaming" policy statement:

PRINCIPLE 1 – PROMOTE RESPONSIBLE GAMBLING AND BETTING

The EGBA Members are committed to promoting socially responsible gambling and betting, and working with customers, employees and relevant industry stakeholders to help manage and control problem gambling. EGBA Members will ensure that proper controls are established, implemented, and enforced, and that gambling and betting takes place in a responsible gaming and betting environment.[6]

Similarly, e-Commerce and Online Gaming Regulation and Assurance (eCOGRA) requires operators seeking its imprimatur or seal of approval to "commi[t] to promoting socially responsible gambling, and working with players, employees and relevant industry stakeholders to help combat problem gambling."[7] Additionally, seal holders must "ensure that proper controls are established, implemented and enforced, and that gambling takes place in a responsible environment."[8]

Responsible gaming policies such as these are usually embodied in specific responsible gaming provisions, which vary among regulatory jurisdictions. The best responsible gaming provisions, however, contain three core elements. First, responsible gaming provisions provide sufficient information to players so they can understand the nature of the gaming activity and make informed decisions regarding their participation.[9] Second, responsible gaming provisions ensure a fair, well-regulated, and controlled gaming experience for all players.[10] Finally, responsible gaming provisions minimize the potential social, health-related, and economic harm to vulnerable players.[11]

These elements are broad enough to encompass most, if not all, of the issues addressed in other Chapters of this book. This Chapter, however, focuses on what, in human terms, is the most compelling aspect of responsible gaming: protecting at-risk customers from the consequences

---

[5] *Id.*

[6] EUROPEAN GAMING AND BETTING ASS'N STANDARDS (FEBRUARY 2011), *available at* http://www.egba.eu/pdf/EGBA-Standards-October-2011.pdf (last visited Sept.4, 2012).

[7] eCOGRA GENERALLY ACCEPTED PRACTICES, at 4 (2012), *available at* http://www.ecogra.org/Documents/eGAP_-_Approved_26_April_2012.pdf.

[8] *Id.*

[9] *See* TASMANIAN GAMING COMM'N, PREAMBLE TO RESPONSIBLE GAMBLING MANDATORY CODE OF PRACTICE FOR TASMANIA(2012), *available at* http://www.treasury.tas.gov.au/domino/dtf/dtf.nsf/LookupFiles/MandatoryCodeofPracticeFinal.pdf/$file/MandatoryCodeofPracticeFinal.pdf; EGBA Standards, Principle 1, http://www.egba.eu/en/consumers/standards.

[10] *Id.*

[11] *Id.*

of gambling disorders.[12] Section2 of this Chapter explains the nature and prevalence of gambling disorders. Section 3 identifies the various types of current gaming jurisdictions and shows how some of the provisions in these jurisdictions can serve as models. Section 4 explains a mechanism used to ameliorate problem gambling, "player limits," notes examples of current player limits provisions in several jurisdictions, and provides a list of suggested best practices for "player limits" provisions. Section 5 discusses "self-exclusion" and "time-out," mechanisms that are frequently used to prevent problem gambling. Finally, Section 6 suggests miscellaneous responsible gaming provisions that should be part of responsible gaming provisions.

NATURE AND PREVALENCE OF GAMBLING DISORDERS

Like many other human behaviors, gambling can be harmful to some participants.[13] Indeed, excessive gambling can affect not only the gambler but also those around the gambler.[14] The "potential for gambling-related personal suffering and social disruption has accountability implications for governments in terms of duty of care, informed consent, and articulating priorities vis-à-vis revenue generation and protection of citizen welfare."[15]

The primary responsibility for addressing the social consequences of gaming rests with governments and regulators. At the same time, responsible private gaming businesses also have a role to play. As stated by the American Gaming Association in the context of casino gaming:

> Gaming is, first and foremost, an entertainment industry, and members of the gaming industry want everyone who visits a casino to be there for the right reasons—to simply have fun. The industry doesn't want people who don't gamble responsibly to play at its casinos, period.[16]

Thus, policy makers have an important responsibility to enact laws and promulgate regulations that promote responsible gaming. However, to formulate policies that ensure socially responsible online gaming, policy makers must first assess the scope of the problem. This involves analyzing the answers to several questions. First, what constitutes a gambling disorder or problem? Second, how significant is the problem, that is, what percentage of the online gaming public suffers from a gambling disorder or problem? Finally, what dangers does online gambling pose to those suffering from a gambling disorder or problem?

A "gambling disorder" has no universally accepted definition. In the revised version of its widely used encyclopedia of mental illnesses, the

---

[12] *See, e.g.,* CONDITIONS AND CODES *supra* note 4, at 13.
[13] Smith and Rubenstein, *supra* note 1, at 56.
[14] *Id.*
[15] *Id.*
[16] AM. GAMING ASS'N, RESPONSIBLE GAMING, http://www.americangaming.org/social-responsibility/responsible-gaming (last visited Aug. 18, 2012).

American Psychiatric Society proposes to re-label its previous diagnosis of "pathological gambling" as "gambling disorder," to reclassify it from an impulse control to an addiction disorder, and to re-define it as follows:

A. Persistent and recurrent problematic gambling behavior as indicated by four (or more) of the following in a 12-month period:

1. needs to gamble with increasing amounts of money in order to achieve the desired excitement;
2. is restless or irritable when attempting to cut down or stop gambling;
3. has repeated unsuccessful efforts to control, cut back, or stop gambling;
4. is often preoccupied with gambling (e.g., persistent thoughts of reliving past gambling experiences, handicapping or planning the next venture, or thinking of ways to get money with which to gamble);
5. gambles often when feeling distressed (e.g., helpless, guilty, anxious, depressed);
6. after losing money gambling, often returns another day to get even ("chasing" one's losses);
7. lies to conceal the extent of involvement with gambling;
8. has jeopardized or lost a significant relationship, job, or educational or career opportunity because of gambling;
9. relies on others to provide money to relieve desperate financial situations caused by gambling.

B. The gambling behavior is not better accounted for by a Manic Episode.[17]

The National Council on Problem Gambling (NCPG), an American non-profit organization whose mission is to increase public awareness, has formulated a useful working definition of problem gambling which includes, but is not limited to, pathological or compulsive gambling:

Problem gambling is gambling behavior which causes disruptions in any major area of life: psychological, physical, social or vocational. The term "Problem Gambling" includes, but is not limited to, the condition known as "Pathological", or "Compulsive" Gambling, a progressive addiction characterized by increasing preoccupation with gambling, a need to bet more money more frequently, restlessness or irritability when attempting to stop, "chasing" losses, and loss of control manifested by continuation of the gambling behavior in spite of mounting, serious, negative consequences.[18]

Those who suffer from "problem gambling" can be seriously affected. Some of the typical adverse consequences have been identified by the government of Tasmania, a highly regarded online gaming regulatory jurisdiction:

---

[17] PROPOSED DRAFT REVISIONS TO DSM DISORDER AND CRITERIA, AM. PSYCHIATRIC ASS'N, DSM-5 DEV., R 37 Gambling Disorder, http://www.dsm5.org/ProposedRevisions/Pages/proposedrevision.aspx?rid=210(last visited Aug. 25, 2012).
[18] THE AM. COUNCIL ON PROBLEM GAMING, www.ncpgambling.org/i4a/pages/index.cfm?pageid=1 (last visited Aug. 25, 2012).

[F]inancial difficulties such as being unable to find enough money to pay bills and living expenses (e.g. rent, food, providing for others including children);
psychological and emotional problems such as stress, anxiety, depression, anger, loss of self esteem and being unable to control one's own behaviour;
loss of time for work or study due to gambling;
family and relationship difficulties, missing out on family commitments due to gambling activities and causing problems with relationships with others;
physical health problems through loss of sleep, self neglect, poor diet, smoking and alcohol use/overuse; and
legal issues and police involvement.[19]

Studies of casino gaming suggest that approximately 1 percent of adults meet the existing criteria for gambling disorder, while an additional 2-3 percent can be considered problem gamblers.[20] Studies conflict on whether problem gambling rates are higher among online gamblers.[21]

Little evidence supports a conclusion that online play *causes* problem gambling.[22] Nevertheless, certain specific features of online gambling may facilitate problem gambling. These features include its 24/7 availability, its faster speed of play, the variety of games offered, the smaller permissible bet size, players' anonymity and isolation, the possibility that players may gamble while impaired or under the influence, and players' decreased perception of the value of money.[23] On the positive side, the nature of online

---

[19] RESPONSIBLE CONDUCT OF GAMBLING (2012) at 23, [TASMANIA] DEP'T OF TREASURY & FIN.(2012), *available at*http://www.treasury.tas.gov.au/domino/dtf/dtf.nsf/LookupFiles/WorkbookV3.PDF/$file/WorkbookV3.PDF.

[20] Malcom K. Sparrow, *Can Internet Gambling Be Effectively Regulated? Managing the Risks*, at 61 (Dec. 2, 2009), *available at* http://www.hks.harvard.edu/fs/msparrow/documents--in%20use/Can%20Internet%20Gambling%20Be%20Effectively%20Regulated--Managing%20the%20Risks--12-02-2009.pdf; *See* THE AM. COUNCIL ON PROBLEM GAMING, www.ncpgambling.org/i4a/pages/index.cfm?pageid=1 (last visited Aug. 25, 2012).

[21] *Compare* CENTRE FOR THE ADVANCEMENT OF BEST PRACTICES, RESPONSIBLE GAMBLING STANDARDS FOR REMOTE GAMBLING PREPARED FOR NOVA SCOTIA GAMING CORP. at 8 (2009)("Prevalence study research suggests that online gamblers are significantly more likely to have gambling problems compared to other gamblers."),*with* Sparrow, *supra* note 20, at 62("[S]tudies specific to online gambling . . . have indicated that online gambling does not inherently encourage excessive gambling."), *and* Laura M. Fontanills, *Smaller Risk of Addiction in Web Gambling*, HARVARD CRIMSON, April 19, 2009 ("A recent study conducted by the Harvard Medical School Division on Addictions suggests that the widespread availability of Internet gambling has not led to an increase in the number of people addicted to gambling. The study actually found that gamblers who visit gaming Web sites are more likely to self-regulate their betting behavior based on their pattern of wins and losses.").

[22] RESPONSIBLE GAMBLING STANDARDS, *supra* note 21, at 9.

[23] RESPONSIBLE GAMBLING STANDARDS, *supra* note 21, at 7-8; Sparrow, *supra* note 20, at 62-63. *See* [Australian] RESPONSIBLE GAMBLING ADVOCACY CTR., REVIEW OF THE INTERACTIVE GAMBLING ACT 2001, at 6 (Oct. 2011), *available at*http://www.dbcde.gov.au/__data/assets/pdf_file/0020/142580/RGAC_Submission_to_Review_of_the_Interactive_

gambling provides operators with the technological ability to offer effective and innovative measures to reduce potential "problem gambling" risks.[24]

One commentator has identified two approaches to minimizing harm to those with gambling issues.[25] One approach is to regulate all gamblers equally by building protections into the games, venues, and conditions of play.[26] The other approach is to isolate and treat problem gamblers differently.[27] Under the latter approach, players can choose to identify themselves as having a gambling problem and enroll in self-banning and other programs to prevent them from gambling.[28] These strategies are not mutually exclusive and, as indicated below, most jurisdictions employ both.

RESPONSIBLE GAMING PROVISIONS AMONG VARIOUS JURISDICTIONS

As online gaming has exploded globally, gaming regulation also has expanded and developed. Online gaming regulatory jurisdictions presently fall into three unofficial groups or "tiers." In Tier 1 jurisdictions, governments closely regulate gaming and emphasize player protection and compliance.[29] Governments in Tier 2 jurisdictions impose some regulation, but focus more on attracting operators.[30] Finally, governments in Tier 3 jurisdictions allow companies to conduct online gaming with little or no external regulation.[31]

Tier 1 jurisdictions include, but are not limited to, the United Kingdom (UK) and those on the UK's "white list." The "white list" is a list of countries whose licensed operators are permitted to advertise within the UK.[32] To be included on the UK white list, the licensing jurisdiction must be approved by the UK.[33] Additionally, a jurisdiction must have a connection to the European Union (Alderney, Isle of Man, Gibraltar, Cyprus, and Malta) or demonstrate that it has a licensing and regulatory system sufficient to ensure the suitability, solvency, and social responsibility of its gaming op-

---

Gambling_Act_2001.pdf.

[24] RESPONSIBLE GAMBLING STANDARDS, *supra* note 21, at 9.

[25] William R. Eadington, *Trends in Gambling and Responsible Gaming in the United States and Elsewhere*, Dec. 1, 2003, *available at* http://www.888betsoff.com/links/04_presentations/Eadington.pdf.

[26] *Id.* at 24.

[27] *Id.*

[28] *Id.*

[29] Jamie Wiebe & Michael D. Lipton, *Overview of Internet Gambling Regulations*, at 13-20 (2008), *available at* http://www.gamblingresearch.org/content/research.php?cid=3563&appid=3073.

[30] *Id.*

[31] *Id.*

[32] ONLINE CASINO WHITE LIST, http://www.onlinecasinowhitelist.com/ (last visited Aug. 19, 2012).

[33] *Id.*

erators (Tasmania and Antigua and Barbuda).[34] Individual states in the United States and certain private organizations including eCOGRA and EGBA also have gaming requirements in place similar to those of Tier 1 jurisdictions.[35]

The features shared by Tier 1 jurisdictions and the leading industry groups suggest certain global "best practices" in the area of responsible online gaming. These best practices are the baseline standards necessary for socially responsible online gaming regulations.[36]

What follows is a sampling of the responsible gambling approaches of various Tier 1 jurisdictions. These approaches can serve as a model for other gaming jurisdictions seeking to establish or strengthen their responsible gaming laws or regulations. Like many Internet and land-based gaming regulations, however, responsible gaming provisions are frequently expressed in general terms or provide only minimum standards. This leaves operators to formulate the specific means of compliance, subject to the approval of the regulators.[37]

Gibraltar

Gibraltar has several gaming regulations that focus on minimizing problem gaming. First, gaming operators in Gibraltar must have on their websites a direct and conspicuous link to a problem gambling treatment organization.[38] Second, operators must have a "problem gambling" warning on the entry page of their websites.[39] Third, operators must have a self-exclusion policy and designate an employee to formulate responsible gambling polices and train staff.[40] Finally, Gibraltar operators must have systems in place to warn gamblers not to gamble beyond their means, to allow gamblers to participate in the self-exclusion program, and to allow gamblers to set their own limits (e.g., by deposits, time or gambling amounts).[41]

---

[34] *Id.*

[35] *See* eCOGRA GEN. ACCEPTED PRACTICES *supra* note 7; EGBA STANDARDS, *supra* note 6.

[36] *See generally* INTERNET RESPONSIBLE GAMBLING STANDARDS, NATIONAL COUNCIL ON PROBLEM GAMBLING, (suggesting standards and identifying other leading sources of responsible gaming practices), *available at* http://www.ncpgambling.org/i4a/ pages/index.cfm?pageid=4492; RESPONSIBLE GAMBLING STANDARDS, *supra* note 21; EGBBA, BENCHMARKING STUDY (2008), *available at* http://www.egba.eu/pdf/EGBA_ Benchmarking_Study_final_version.pdf.

[37] *See, e.g.*, NEV. GAMING COMM'N REG. § 5A.0.70 (stating that operators of interactive gaming shall establish, maintain, implement and comply with the standards adopted and published by the Gaming Commission Chair. The statute also states that such minimum standards shall include internal controls.).

[38] CODE OF PRACTICE FOR THE GAMBLING INDUS., GIB. REGULATORY AUTH., § 5.5 (2008).

[39] *Id.*

[40] *Id.* at § 5.7.

[41] *Id.* at § 5.8.

Alderney

Alderney has established regulations to address problem gambling. Alderney requires licensees to establish procedures to identify potential problem gamblers.[42]If a licensee has reasonable notice that a customer is a problem gambler, the licensee must terminate the customer's account and cease marketing activities to that customer.[43] Other gambling regulations in Alderney mandate that the licensee provide self-limitations on customer game play and require a 24-hour "cooling off period."[44] Additionally, Alderney operators must provide a player protection page that contains problem gambling information and problem gambling services.[45] Alderney operators are also required to spend a designated amount or percentage of gross gambling revenue on problem gambling treatment.[46]

Isle of Man

The Isle of Man mandates several responsible gaming safeguards. First, online gambling advertisements must have hyperlinks to Gamblers Anonymous or other problem gambling websites that have been approved by the Gambling Supervision Commission.[47] Second, gaming operators must provide players with options to establish a maximum bet per session and players must wait seven days to increase a bet limit.[48] Third, operators must include provisions for self-exclusion.[49] Finally, operators must contribute to the government's "Problem Gambling Fund.[50]

United Kingdom

The UK's own regulations similarly set forth minimum requirements for the protection of problem gamblers. For example, online operators must, at regular intervals, provide players with information on "the licensee's policies in relation to, and experiences of, problem gambling."[51] Also, operators must establish policies on how they will contribute to problem gambling research

---

[42] ALDERNEY EGAMBLING REG. §236.

[43] Id.

[44] ALDERNEY EGAMBLING REG. §237.

[45] Id.

[46] ALDERNEY GAMBLING CONTROL COMM'N, TECHNICAL STANDARDS AND GUIDELINES FOR INTERNAL CONTROL SYS. AND INTERNET GAMBLING SYS. § 3.5.2-6.

[47] ISLE OF MAN ONLINE GAMBLING (ADVERTISING) REG. (2007).

[48] Id.

[49] Id.

[50] ISLE OF MAN ONLINE GAMBLING (REG. AND ACCOUNTS) REG. § 5 (2008).

[51] See, e.g., CONDITIONS AND CODES supra note 4, at 13, [UNITED KINGDOM] GAMBLING COMMI'N., available at http://www.gamblingcommission.gov.uk/pdf/Licence%20 conditions%20and%20codes%20of%20practice%20-%20remote%20betting%20-%20 October%202010.pdf.

and public education on the risks of gambling, and "how they will contribute to the identification and treatment of problem gamblers."[52] UK licensees also must develop self-exclusion procedures to ban players from their websites for at least six months.[53] Finally, operators must ensure that self-excluded customers are barred from all accounts with the operators.[54]

As is apparent from the examples noted, quality responsible gaming provisions contain some common threads, including player limits and self-exclusions. The following sections discuss these and other miscellaneous responsible gaming provisions that should form part of the law and regulations governing legal online gaming.

Player Limits and Global Best Practices

Player Limits

A common feature of gambling regulations in Tier 1 jurisdictions are provisions mandating player limits. "Player limits" are mechanisms that establish or allow players to specify their own gambling limits. Research suggests that online gamblers welcome the availability of such limits.[55] The very act of establishing limits may induce problem gamblers to reassess their behavior.[56]

Operators sometimes establish limits that apply to all players to prevent money laundering or other criminal activities. When it comes to setting limits, however, most are imposed by players themselves, using whatever procedures gaming operators have established for that purpose.[57] This section focuses on limits that help players with a gambling problem.

Jurisdictions need to consider three issues when considering provisions that address player limits. First, what kind of limits should be available to players? Second, how should such limits be established and modified? Third, what policies or procedures should operators follow once a player has established limits? A review of several regulatory schemes suggests certain best practices regarding these issues.

Alderney

Alderney provides an example of how a jurisdiction can establish player limit provisions. Under the relevant Alderney statute, players may estab-

---

[52] *Id.* at 10,12, and 16-20.
[53] *Id.*
[54] *Id.*
[55] *See, e.g.*, Sparrow, *supra* note 20, at 70-71; Responsible Gambling Standards, *supra* note 21, at 14-16; Griffiths, Wood, Parke, *Social Responsibility Tools in Online Gambling: A Survey of Attitudes and Behavior Among Internet Gamblers*, (abstract), *available at* http://www.ncbi.nlm.nih.gov/pubmed/19594379.
[56] Responsible Gambling Standards, *supra* note 21, at 17.
[57] *Id.* at 14-18.

lish limits on deposits, losses, or wagers.[58] The statute also prohibits operators from sending marketing materials to customers who have established
gambling limits.[59]

Delaware

Delaware provides another example of how a jurisdiction can establish
provisions dealing with player limits. Although no regulations have yet
been promulgated, a recently enacted Delaware statute authorizing online
lottery gaming expressly requires procedures by which players "may place
limits on the amount of money being wagered per game or during any
specified time period, or the amount of losses incurred during any specified time period." [60]

eGAP

The eCOGRA Generally Accepted Practices ("eGAP"), which set forth
the policies and procedures required for operators to obtain the eCOGRA
seal of approval, suggest three features of an effective player deposit limit
procedure with regard to money-based gambling limits.[61] First, operators
must inform players of their ability to set limits and such limit-setting must
be easy to initiate.[62] Second, the options to set limits must be flexible.[63]
Finally, operators must honor a player's request for a deposit limit immediately.[64] Operators, however, must require a "cooling off period" before
increasing a player's previously established limit.[65]

Antigua and Barbuda

Finally, Antigua and Barbuda provides a simple example of how a
player can set limits. A regulation of Antigua and Barbuda provides that
"[a] player may, by notice to the license holder, set a limit on the amount
the player may wager."[66]

---

[58] ALDERNEY EGAMBLING REG. § 237 (2009).

[59] Id.

[60] H.B. 333 § 14 (§ 4826 (c)(5)).

[61] See eGAP 1.09-1.11 ("The operator shall provide players with the option to set their own
deposit limits per day, week and month. Operators shall deal with requests to decrease
deposit limits immediately. Player requests to increase previously set deposit limits shall
only be effective after a minimum waiting period of 24 hours.

There shall be a clear link from the deposit page to the facility to set deposit limits and/or
to the Responsible Gambling page.").

[62] Id.

[63] Id.

[64] Id.

[65] Id.

[66] ANT.& BARB. INTERACTIVE GAMING AND INTERACTIVE WAGERING REG. § 139(a).

Global Best Practices Regarding Player Limits

The provisions noted above as well as similar provisions not mentioned in this Chapter, along with the relevant literature and empirical data,[67] suggest the following global best practices regarding player limits:

- **Deposit Limits**
  - Gambling sites should establish and post reasonable default limits on the amount players may deposit per day, week, and month.
  - A player's request to decrease the default limits should be effective immediately, while a player's request to increase the default limits should require a waiting period of at least 24 hours.

- **Wagering and Loss Limits**
  - Operators should provide players clear notice of, and easy access to, a mechanism to establish and pre-set wagering or loss limits.
  - Players must be able to set a wagering or loss limit by time, gambling transaction, or any other reasonable criteria.
  - Decreases to pre-set wagering or loss limits requested by a player should be given effect immediately, while increases should require a waiting period of at least 24 hours.

- **Marketing During Period Limits in Effect**
  - Gambling sites should refrain from advertising or posting any other marketing to a player during any period in which that player has established any deposit, wagering, or loss limits.

Self-Exclusions and Time-Outs, and Global Best Practices

Self-Exclusions and Time-Outs

Another characteristic of Tier 1 jurisdictions and standards promulgated by leading trade groups are "self-exclusion" programs. Self-exclusion[68] programs allow players to bar themselves from play at a specific gambling site or with a specific operator.[69] Included within self-exclusion programs

---

[67] *See, e.g.,* Sparrow, *supra* note 20, at 59-72.

[68] As pointed out in Responsible Gambling Standards, *supra* note 21, at 13n.1, "self bans should not be confused with *self-exclusions*, which apply to land-based gaming operations. The difference in terminology reflects the distinct implementation challenges that apply to land based gambling versus Internet gambling." Although this observation is technically accurate, responsible gaming provisions regarding Internet gambling are virtually unanimous in utilizing the term "self-exclusion" as opposed to "self ban," and that convention is followed in this Chapter.

[69] *See, e.g.,* Responsible Gambling Standards, *supra* note 21, at 29; Internet Responsible Gambling Standards, *supra* note 36; Benchmarking Study, *supra* note 36;

is the "time-out" or "cooling off period," a mechanism that allows players to bar themselves from play for a specific period. This "time-out" period can serve as a measure for players who want an immediate break from gambling. This period also can help players to manage their gambling during particularly tempting or risky periods (*e.g.*, days following the receipt of paychecks or around major sporting events like March Madness, Super Bowl, World Cup, etc.).[70]

Online gamblers generally view self-exclusion and time-out programs favorably and use the programs frequently.[71] Thus, not surprisingly, research concerning such bans suggests their overall effectiveness.[72] However, specific issues that jurisdictions must consider with regard to self-exclusion and time-out programs are numerous and include the following:

- How should the availability and details of the programs be communicated to players?
- How should a player register for the programs?
- What options should be offered regarding the length of the self-exclusion or time-out?
- How should the self-exclusion or time-out be enforced?
- Should a player be permitted to modify a previously selected self-exclusion or time-out and, if so, how?
- Should the regulatory authority be involved in the process and, if so, how?
- Should third parties, *i.e.*, parties other than the player, be permitted to initiate exclusion or time-out programs and, if so, how?
- What if a player who has self-excluded or requested a time-out successfully circumvents the process and gambles anyway?

Below are examples of the manner in which some jurisdictions currently address these issues.

Jurisdictions with Self-Exclusion Provisions

Antigua and Barbuda

Antigua and Barbuda's regulation governing self-exclusion is typical. First, the regulation addresses how a player can register to be excluded from the operator's website. The regulation explicitly states that the self-exclusion process should be easy to initiate and require no formal writing. E-mail or phone calls should suffice.

Second, Antigua and Barbuda's regulation sets a six-month period of self-exclusion. A six-month period for self-exclusion is a common choice

---

eGAP § 1.14; EGBA STANDARDS 1.15-1.20.

[70] RESPONSIBLE GAMBLING STANDARDS, *supra* note 21, at 13-14; INTERNET RESPONSIBLE GAMBLING STANDARDS, *supra* note 36 (suggesting time-outs of between one hour and 30 days, with longer periods available as a self-exclusion).

[71] RESPONSIBLE GAMBLING STANDARDS, *supra* note 21, at 13-14; Sparrow, *supra* note 20, at 70-71.

[72] RESPONSIBLE GAMBLING STANDARDS, *supra* note 21, at 13-14.

among other jurisdictions. Establishing the minimum period of self-exclusion, however, involves a balance. Too short a period will render the self-exclusion ineffective and too long a period may deter problem gamblers from self-excluding. This problem can be mitigated, if not completely eliminated, by making available a procedure for a shorter time-out of flexible duration.

Finally, Antigua and Barbuda's existing regulation sets forth how a player can revoke his enrollment in the self-exclusion program.[73] A player simply needs to wait at least six months and then send a written request to the Commission.

This final point of Antigua and Barbuda's regulation raises the issue whether regulators should be involved in the self-exclusion process and, if so, to what extent? Whether a player has a gambling disorder or has recovered from one involves a subjective determination that is complex even for a health care professional with full information about that player.[74] Gaming regulators who do not have any information on the player's condition would face an impossible task. It could also raise the specter of potential liability if the gaming regulators make an incorrect or unfounded determination. For these reasons, leaving regulators out of the self-exclusion process is a best practice.

Nevada

Although more states may follow, Nevada is, as of this writing, the only United States jurisdiction that has adopted a full set of online gaming regulations.[75] Nevada's online regulations include a provision that governs self-exclusion.[76] It explicitly regulates the obligations of gaming operators. First, Nevada online gaming operators must refuse play from gamblers during any period of self-exclusion.[77] One efficient method of enforcing self-exclusion is to close the gaming account of the person who has self-excluded.[78] Second, Nevada gambling operators must train their employees to ensure that they implement their self-exclusion policies.[79] Third, Nevada establishes a minimum self-exclusion period of 30 days.[80] Finally, online

---

[73] ANT. AND BARB. REG. §138 provides:

> A player may request to be self excluded from a licenced interactive gaming or interactive wagering site by means of a telecommunication device. Players that are self-excluded may not be reinstated for a period of six (6) months from the date of self-exclusion. Revocation of a self-exclusion must be requested in writing to the Commission after the six (6) month self-exclusion period has expired.

[74] *See* Section 2 *supra*.
[75] Nevada refers to "Online Gaming" as "Interactive Gaming." For simplicity's sake, this article uses "Online Gaming."
[76] NEV. GAMING COMM'N REG.§ 5A.130.
[77] *Id.*
[78] *Id.*
[79] *Id.*
[80] *Id.*

gaming operators in Nevada cannot send marketing materials to self-excluded players.[81]

eGAP Standards

The eGAP Standards governing self-exclusion allow for a time-out (cooling off) period of at least 24 hours without marketing, mandate advertisement of the self-exclusion program on a page with other responsible gambling information, and set a minimum self-exclusion period of six months.[82] They also establish a procedure by which a third party may initiate the self-exclusion process. However, an operator's employee, who must first contact the player, is the only party who may complete this procedure.[83]

Given the undeniable effects of problem gambling on those close to the problem gambler, allowing a third party such as a family member or other concerned third party to initiate an exclusion procedure has an appeal in theory. In reality, such a procedure raises many legal and practical issues, which make it difficult to administer. For example, no clear guidelines exist regarding which third party or parties can initiate an exclusion procedure, and how an operator can properly identify and evaluate the initiator. Even if the third party initiation merely results in an employee of the operator contacting the player, it seems unrealistic to expect even a highly trained employee to be able to ascertain from limited contact with a player whether that player is a problem gambler.[84] Finally, a third party-initiated procedure brought to conclusion would result in something more akin to an *involuntary* exclusion than a self-exclusion. But such a procedure is unlikely to be helpful or effective, since a problem gambler who has not affirmatively chosen to seek help can simply gamble at another site.

Gibraltar

The responsible gaming regulations of Gibraltar address the self-exclusion process in an unusually specific and detailed manner. For example, Gibraltar specifies that "self exclusion systems modeled on mainstream industry bodies' advice . . . will be regarded as effective systems."[85] This benefits operators, who do not need to "re-invent the wheel" regarding self-exclusion processes.

Likewise, if a gambler has self-excluded and that gambler successfully circumvents the self-exclusion agreement, any winnings by the gambler may be retained by the license holder.[86] In effect, this regulation precludes a self-excluded person from receiving any winnings obtained as a result of circumventing the self-exclusion. This process is an effective way to deter players

---

[81] *Id.*

[82] eGAP § 1.12-1.14.

[83] *Id.*

[84] *See* Section 2 *supra.*

[85] Gib. Reg. Auth. Code of Practice for the Gambling Industry, § v1.0.2009 (2008).

[86] *Id.*

from circumventing the program because it removes the economic incentive to do so. Allowing winnings to be retained by the operator, however, seems counter-productive. At best, this is an undue windfall to an operator who has failed to bar the self-excluded person. At worst, it gives the operator an incentive to *allow* self-excluded persons to gamble, in the hope of retaining forfeited winnings. A better approach would be to mandate that any forfeited self-excluded person's winnings go to the regulatory authority, preferably to fund programs addressing responsible or problem gambling.

Gibraltar's regulation also reflects the obvious truism that, to be effective, responsible gaming information must be offered in the language of the player.[87] Additionally, the regulation mandates accountability by requiring that a designated employee of the operator be responsible for formulation, review, and enforcement of the operator's responsible gaming policies.[88] Finally, the provisions mandate a level of proactivity by requiring operators to identify and assist problem gamblers.[89] This is difficult to accomplish in practice, however, as objective and precise criteria that indicate that a "customer may be gambling beyond their means" are lacking.

Global Best Practices Regarding Self-Exclusions and Time-Outs

The provisions mentioned above and similar provisions not included in this Chapter regarding self-exclusions and time-outs,[90] along with the relevant literature and empirical data,[91] suggest the following global best practices regarding self-exclusions and time-outs:

- Gambling sites should have comprehensive, staff-supported programs in place that cover time-outs and self-exclusions, subject to periodic review and revision.
- Self-exclusion and time-out programs should be well promoted in the appropriate language(s), be posted preferably on the registration or login pages, be easily accessible by players, and be administered by trained and knowledgeable staff.
- Operators should devise a strong enforcement process to prevent play by self-excluded players. This process should apply to all sites owned by the operator and subject to the jurisdiction of the regulator.
- Players should be informed of the self-exclusion and time-out programs' enforcement process.

---

[87] *Id.*

[88] *Id.*

[89] *Id.*

[90] *See, e.g.,* Internet Responsible Gambling Standards, *supra* note 36; Responsible Gambling Standards, *supra* note 21, at 29.

[91] *See, e.g.,* Sparrow, *supra* note 20, at 59-72. *See generally,*[Canadian] Responsible Gambling Council, *From Enforcement to Assistance: Evolving Best Practices in Self-Exclusion,* Mar.,2008,*available at*http://www.responsiblegambling.org/articles/RGC_SE%20Review_FINAL.pdf.

- The self-exclusion and time-out enforcement process should provide for the forfeiture of winnings to remove any incentive for self-excluded players to attempt to circumvent the ban.
- Any winnings forfeited by self-excluded players should not be retained by the operator, but instead should go to the regulatory authority, preferably to fund programs addressing problem gambling research, education, and treatment.
- Available time-out periods should be flexible, but no longer than the minimum self-exclusion period.[92]
- Players should be allowed to self-exclude for a period between one to six months or, if the player requests, a longer period including permanently.
- Time-outs or self-exclusions requested by a player should be effective immediately, and should be irrevocable during the period selected.
- The gambling site should refrain from advertising or posting other marketing to a player during any time-out or self-exclusion period requested by that player.
- Reinstatement at the conclusion of the selected time-out or self-exclusion period (other than a permanent ban) should require an affirmative request by the player.
- Neither regulators nor operators should be required to engage in any assessment or render any independent judgment on whether a player who has requested reinstatement at the conclusion of a selected time-out or self-exclusion period (other than a permanent ban) should be reinstated.
- Requests by players for renewals of time-outs or self-exclusions should be treated in the same manner as initial requests.
- Exclusions initiated by third parties should not be mandated because they are difficult to administer, raise complex legal issues, and are unlikely to be effective inasmuch as they run counter to the theory that problem gamblers must personally recognize their problem and choose to seek help.
- If a third party does request an exclusion, the operator should contact the player just to reiterate all relevant responsible gaming information, including the availability of player limits, time-outs, and self-exclusions.

MISCELLANEOUS RESPONSIBLE GAMING PROVISIONS AND SUGGESTED GLOBAL BEST PRACTICES

Player limits and self-exclusions form an indispensible part of any regulatory system concerned with minimizing the harm to problem gamblers.

---

[92] *See* RESPONSIBLE GAMBLING STANDARDS, *supra* note 21, at 40 (defining time-outs as "stops in play that are less than 20 continuous days").

Additionally, progressive regulators have also designed and imposed other responsible gaming provisions. These miscellaneous provisions not only protect at-risk customers from the consequences of problem gambling, but also may prevent others from developing a gambling problem or disorder.

Suggested Global Best Practices Regarding Miscellaneous Responsible Gaming Provisions

Providing Players with Gaming Information

One policy goal lawmakers and regulators should have when establishing responsible gaming provisions is to provide sufficient information to individuals so that they can understand the nature of the gaming activity. This will allow players to make informed decisions regarding their participation. Some factors that facilitate informed decision-making have been identified as follows:

- **Tips on how to gamble safely:** Where is the information located and what kind of information is provided?
- **Chances of winning and losing:** Where is the information located and what kind of information is provided?
- **Risks of gambling:** Where is the information located and what kind of information is provided?
- **Information about randomness and house edge:** Where is the information located and what kind of information is provided?
- **Signs of a gambling problem:** Where is the information located and what kind of information is provided?
- **Common myths:** Where is the information located and what kind of information is provided?
- **Interactive Tools:** Does the site offer interactive tools such as quizzes, money and time managers? If so, what are they and where are they located?
- **Self-assessment Tool:** Does the site offer a list of questions where a player may self-test for indications that they are developing problems with their gambling? If so, where is it located?
- **Limit Setting:** Can players set their own deposit or money and time limits? If so, what are they (e.g., amount or length of time)? Does the site impose limits on players?
- **Play History:** Do players have access to a history of their play, such as the amount of money or time they have spent? What kind of information is provided? How is this obtained? Do they get live messages during play to remind them, or do they have to go to a certain place in the site to get the information?
- **Help services:** Does the site provide links to resources that will help players experiencing gambling problems (e.g., helpline, counselors,

links to discussion forums or customer service representatives who can help)?[93]

The above points suggest global best practices with regard to providing players with gaming and problem gambling information. Essentially, operators should provide players with information in a prominent location and in appropriate language. That information should include:

- the rules, odds, and nature of the gaming activity, the need to maintain responsible gambling behaviors, and the risks associated with gambling;
- problem gambling, including self-diagnostic tools; and
- the availability of resources to assist problem gamblers.[94]

Reality Checks

Features particular to online gambling that may facilitate problem gambling include the following. First, gambling is available around the clock. Second, players may develop a decreased perception of the value of money.

Some jurisdictions have implemented responsible gaming provisions to counter these issues. These provisions serve as a model for global best practices on how to provide players with reality checks:

- Operators should provide players time reminders or other reality checks. Some examples are:
  - a visible clock in real-time;
  - pop-up messages notifying players when they have been playing for an extended period of time and asking whether they would like a break;
  - running displays of bets, wins, losses, and account balances, etc.[95]
- Operators should provide players easy access to their past and current account information and gambling history.[96]

Tracking Play To Detect Problem Gambling

While operators of brick-and-mortar casinos can observe players and try to detect possible problem gamblers, operators of online gambling sites are not able to make such physical observations. This raises the question of whether an online gambling operator can establish objective play-related criteria to detect problem gambling and intervene.

As one source has observed:

For the most part, experts felt that there is not yet enough information at the present time to know what the tracking criteria and ensuing interaction should be. As one expert stated, "the biggest hurdle is, what are the warning

---

[93] Responsible Gambling Standards, *supra* note 21, at 58.
[94] *See, e.g.,* Internet Responsible Gambling Standards, *supra* note 36.
[95] *Id.,* EGBA Standard 1.22.
[96] *See, e.g.,* Internet Responsible Gambling Standards, *supra* note 36; eGAP 1.06.

signs and then how to interact in a way that is not threatening." That being said, there was a fair amount of support for monitoring player behaviour, watching for potential warning signs and touching base with concerns. One expert mentioned that all players could be informed at the point of registration that the site will make contact if they notice risky gambling behaviours. A number of the experts identified what they considered red flags or warning signs, including:

- a progressive increase in time and money spent;
- numerous calls to the Customer Service requesting bonuses, complaining that the site is unfair, or complaining about losses;
- repeated requests for increases to deposit limits or increases to self-limits; [and]
- frequent changes to funding sources.[97]

Based on the empirical data, tracking play to detect problem gambling is not recommended at this time, as there is insufficient information to know either what the tracking criteria should be or what ensuing interaction with the player would be appropriate and effective. Nevertheless, if any objective outside criteria raise a suspicion of problem gambling, an operator should at least contact the player, if only to reiterate all relevant responsible gaming information, including the availability of player limits, time-outs, and self-exclusions.[98]

Funding of Problem Gambling Programs

One commentator has opined that "[t]he general public still does not recognize [problem gambling] as a public health issue," and compares the problem gambler to "the homeless derelict that many of us try to ignore as we walk through the city streets. Throw him a dollar from time to time, but easier to just walk by, shake one's head, and go to work."[99] Still, as indicated at the outset, responsible governments, regulators, and operators have come to accept that those who profit from gaming do have an obligation to minimize any resulting harm.

That obligation is frequently effected by policies or regulations that mandate funding for various programs: research on how to prevent, identify, and treat problem gambling, and public education on the risks of gambling and how to gamble safely.[100] Such funding may come from governments, operators, or even fines and penalties imposed by the regulators.

Existing responsible gaming provisions suggest that parties that directly benefit from online gambling, governments, and operators should all be

---

[97] RESPONSIBLE GAMBLING STANDARDS, *supra* note 21, at 29.
[98] *Id.*
[99] Eadington, *supra* note 25.
[100] *See, e.g.,* CONDITIONS AND CODES, *supra* note 4, at 17; ALDERNEY STANDARDS AND GUIDELINES at 47; INTERNET RESPONSIBLE GAMBLING STANDARDS, *supra* note 36; EGBA STANDARD 1.26.

encouraged or required to contribute funds to organizations dedicated to problem gambling research, education, and treatment.

Implementation of Responsible Gaming Policies

Relevant studies have identified two additional aspects of socially responsible behavior applicable to operators. One is that to solidify the operator's commitment to its responsible gaming policy, an executive should be accountable for the policy's implementation.[101] The other is that to the extent operators engage third parties in the gaming process, those third parties must be equally obligated to follow the operator's responsible gaming policies.[102]

Existing responsible gaming provisions suggest the following global best practices regarding the implementation of responsible gaming policies:

An operator should appoint a designated senior management staff member to assume responsibility for the implementation and monitoring of responsible gaming practices.[103]

Relevant third party and business partner contractual terms and conditions should provide the operator the right to terminate the contract where any third party or business partner's conduct conflicts with the operator's responsible gaming program.[104]

Playing on Credit

Gaming jurisdictions do not have a consensus with regard to the public policies of playing on credit.[105] Most sites allow customer deposits via credit cards, but operators are divided on whether to extend credit themselves.[106] For that reason, existing responsible gaming provisions suggest only the following limited global best practices regarding the issue of credit play:

Operators should not provide credit to players unless the regulatory authority permits such practice.[107]

All money and money services should be provided to players in a responsible manner that does not encourage excessive spending.[108]

---

[101] RESPONSIBLE GAMBLING STANDARDS, *supra* note 21, at 34-35.

[102] *See, e.g.,* CONDITIONS AND CODES, *supra* note 4, at 23.

[103] *See, e.g.,* INTERNET RESPONSIBLE GAMBLING STANDARDS, *supra* note 36; EGBA STANDARD 1.28.

[104] *See, e.g.,* EGBA STANDARD1.29.

[105] RESPONSIBLE GAMBLING STANDARDS, *supra* note 21, at 33, 50.

[106] *Id.*

[107] *See, e.g.,* EGBA STANDARD1.21; eGAP 1.16.

[108] RESPONSIBLE GAMBLING STANDARDS, *supra* note 21, at 51.

Conclusion

Online gaming undoubtedly brings entertainment to the people who enjoy it. Jurisdictions that allow and operators that provide it also have a number of economic benefits. At the same time, online gaming brings negative consequences to a small percentage of the population that suffers from a gambling problem or disorder. Thus, lawmakers, regulators, and operators have the responsibility to establish laws, regulations, and policies to ensure that the negative effects on these members of the population are minimized.

This Chapter has provided a basic overview of gambling disorders and problems, and suggested best practices for responsible gaming provisions that a jurisdiction can use as a starting point to establish or strengthen responsible gaming provisions. Because online gaming regulation is always evolving along with the gaming technology, however, it is always advisable to consult sources including global experts in this field concerning the latest developments.

9

Ensuring Internet Gaming that is Free from Fraud and Cheating
Better Practices and Predominantly Regulatory Challenges

Alan Littler*

REGULATORY CHALLENGES CAUSED BY THE INTERNET AND MULTI-JURISDICTIONAL NATURE OF INTERNET GAMING

Internet-borne challenges to the regulation of gaming

Following the dawn of the Internet era, legal commentators discussed whether the Internet should be seen as an area free from legal constraints as determined by national legal systems.[1] Prevailing approaches to exert jurisdiction in the land-based sphere were questioned, and opinions expressed that such approaches would fit uncomfortably within an Internet based environment. Notably, for example, David Post opined that questions generated in cyberspace "are indeed different, and more difficult than

---

* A draft version of this paper was presented at the *Internet Gaming Regulation Symposium* hosted at the UNLV William S. Boyd School of Law Las Vegas in cooperation with Lewis & Roca LLP on 18 May 2012. The author wishes to thank the organisers of this event, and participants, for a fruitful and interesting day. All intellectual property rights associated with the manuscript are reserved. Nothing in this manuscript constitutes legal advice or may be used or relied upon as legal advice. Use of or reliance upon this manuscript does not create an attorney-client relationship between the author or UNLV or any other party. All views expressed in this article are those of the author and are not necessarily held by VMW Taxand.

[1] Rather aptly referred to as *'Visions of a Post-Territorial Order'*, by Jack Goldsmith & Tim Wu, in their book WHO CONTROLS THE INTERNET? ILLUSIONS OF A BORDERLESS WORLD (2006). *See also* Michael Geist, *Cyberlaw* 2.0, 44 B. C. L. REV. 323 (2003).

the questions realised in its real space counterpart".[2] Concurrently, Jack Goldsmith viewed the issue in terms of functionality and considered that:

> "Internet activities are functionally identical to these non-Internet activities. People in one jurisdiction do something - upload pornography, facilitate gambling, offer a fraudulent security, send spam, etc. - that is costly to stop at another jurisdiction's border and that produces effects within that jurisdiction deemed illegal there."[3]

How do these concerns relate to detection and prevention of fraud and cheating in gaming services via the Internet? Negative consequences can arise if a player sits either face to face with an operator or if they sit on the other side of the globe. In either of these situations, Jack Goldsmith maintains his claim that "there is no general normative argument that supports the immunization of cyberspace activities from territorial regulation".[4] Immunization has not, or at least has not yet, consigned de facto land based territoriality to the history books but, rather, illegal extraterritorial activities challenge the capacity of territorially bound law enforcement and legal systems, as Kim-Kwang Raymond Choo reflects:

> "Extraterritoriality, the notion that the Internet has no geographic boundaries, has driven the e-commerce revolution. Unfortunately, the criminal fraternity operates online under the same free market principles while legislative and law enforcement endeavours launched against them suffer from geographical and cultural restrictions."[5]

Although such comments relating to organized crime groups abound, attempts to tackle fraud and cheating surrounding the supply of Internet gaming services are equally subject to similar challenges posed by the "criminal fraternity".

Gaming regulation and regulatory structures suffer from a lack of coherency and integration within the European and international context. Regulatory fragmentation occurs at both international and intra-national levels. When gaming regulations are both affected by and affect the regulation of other activities that relate to gaming such as sports and sports governance, then regulation often becomes disconnected.

Gaming services are readily available on the Internet,[6] with both na-

---

[2] David G. Post, *Against "Against Cyberanarchy"*, 17:1 BERKELEY TECH. L. J., 1365, 1387 (2002).
[3] Jack L. Goldsmith, *The Internet and the Abiding Significance of Territorial Sovereignty*, 5 IND. J. GLOBAL LEGAL STUD., 475, 479 (1998).
[4] Jack Goldsmith, *Against Cyberanarchy*, 65 U. CHI. L. REV., 1199, 1250 (1998).
[5] Kim-Kwang Raymond Choo & Russell G. Smith, *Criminal Exploitation of Online Systems by Organised Crime Groups*, 3 ASIAN J. OF CRIMINOLOGY, 37, 55 (2008).
[6] Monsieur Jean-François VILOTTE, 'PRESERVER L'INTEGRITE ET LA SINCERITE DES COMPETITIONS SPORTIVES FACE AU DEVELOPPEMENT DES PARIS SPORTIFS EN LIGNE. Prévention et lutte contre l'atteinte à l'intégrité et à la sincérité des compétitions sportives en relation avec le développement des paris sportifs'. Rapport à Madam Chanal JOUANNO, Ministre des Sports, le 17 mars 2011 (hereinafter 'Report of

tional and sub-national jurisdictions seeking to exert control.[7] While certain jurisdictions seek to uphold a prohibition of Internet gaming or to protect the monopoly-based supply of both land-based and Internet gaming, other jurisdictions have established open-regulated markets. Within the internal market of the European Union, some jurisdictions believe that the principle of mutual recognition for free movement of services permits their licensees to offer gaming services throughout the internal market. The evolution of the case law of the Court of Justice of the European Union ("CJEU"), however, highlighted that the principle of mutual recognition does not apply in an absolute fashion to gaming services.[8] Member States have a margin of discretion in which to design their national gambling market that can restrict the cross-border movement of gaming services into their jurisdiction. In light of the CJEU's case law, and to attempt to capture Internet gaming, an increasing number of Member States have established national licensing bodies to regulate the supply of Internet gaming services. Through doing so, they seek to achieve national standards through a regulatory system that does not (in terms of EU law) unjustifiably restrict the cross-border movement of gaming services and operators.

This has resulted in a two-layered patchwork. First, jurisdictions must decide whether the market is reserved for the incumbent offline monopolist,[9] or whether the Internet market is characterised by a limited number of operators[10] or an unlimited number of operators, all of which are subject to strict rules that determine eligibility to enter the market.[11]

Vilotte'). Point 8 notes "Le développement de l'activité de paris sportifs à travers Internet est aujourd'hui une réalité économique et sociale dont les consequences sur l'order public et sur le sport doivent être prises en compte et maîtrisées."

[7] Rousso v. State of Washington, 239 P.3d 1084 (Wash. 2010).

[8] Case C-42/07, *Liga Portuguesa de futebol Profissional, Bwin International Ltd v. Departamento de Jogos da Santa Casa da Misericórdia de Lisboa*, [2009] ECR I 7633 (hereinafter referred to as "*Santa Casa*").

[9] The Santa Casa da Misericórdia de Lisboa in Portugal enjoys such a position.

[10] This is the case in Belgium where primary legislation caps the number of online licenses in line with the numerous causus prevailing in the existing offline sector for casinos, amusement arcades and in a slightly different manner for sports-betting. Conditioning the online provision of gaming to an offline establishment is extremely contentious and highly likely to be an unjustifiable restriction on the free movement of services as enshrined in Article 56 of the Treaty on the Functioning of the European Union. *See* Alan Littler, MEMBER STATES VERSUS THE EUROPEAN UNION: THE REGULATION OF GAMBLING (2011) and more specifically Alan Littler, *Een Europese kijk op de voorgestelde wijziging van de Kansspelwet/Un point de vue européensur la propositiond'amendement de la loisur les jeux de hasard*, in Nele Hoekx & Alain-Laurent Verbeke (eds.), KANSSPELEN IN BELGIË / LES JEUX DE HAZARD EN BELGIQUE, 3-19, 21-38 (2009).

[11] A number of jurisdictions follow this approach such as Denmark, France and Italy. It also appears to be the direction which the Netherlands may very well take, following a letter of the current, albeit caretaker, State Secretary for Security and Justice to the parliament. TK 32264, nr. 25 *Wijziging van de Wet op de kansspelen in verband met de instelling van de kansspelautoriteit: Brief regering; Uitvoering van ingediende moties bij het wetsvoorstel inzake de instelling van de kansspelautoriteit*, 4 mei 2012.

Second, among jurisdictions that permit Internet operations, several differences prevail as to which forms of Internet gaming are allowed. Some Member States seek to regulate as wide of a range as possible while others are more restrictive and limit the Internet market to a few forms such as sports betting, horserace betting, and skill-based casino games (i.e. poker) as in France. In contrast, Denmark allows online casino games, online poker and online sports betting, but excludes horserace betting. Differences exist between jurisdictions in terms of what Internet based casino gaming encompasses (pure chance based, live gaming), but some jurisdictions permit a narrower range of sports betting opportunities. Differences also arise between jurisdictions regarding which events within sporting competitions to allow. Some jurisdictions restrict their licensees to only accept bets on the final outcome of a game or the score at half time, while other jurisdictions permit operators to take bets on a wider range of in-play events such as which team will score the first goal or which player will receive a red card.

Underlying these differences is a deeper layer of regulatory divergence including regulations to prevent fraud and cheating. For example:

- Jurisdictions must decide how the licensing body determines if a license applicant is eligible for a license, relating to (not to the exclusion of other considerations):
  - Their credit worthiness.
  - Their integrity through background checks on those in managerial positions.
- Jurisdictions must decide which modalities operators must employ when creating customer accounts and how operators verify an individual's identity (both when creating a player account and subsequent log-ins):
- Jurisdictions must establish national standards of consumer protection and responsible gambling measures such as:
  - Deposit limits.
  - (Self-) exclusion.
- Jurisdictions may establish infrastructural requirements that allow their national regulatory authority to supervise its licensees, which may include:
  - Requiring operators to locate the server within their jurisdiction or requiring remote access to a server located in another jurisdiction.
  - The (quasi) real-time remote collection of data, which is time and date stamped, en route to a 'safe' where it is stored.
  - Jurisdictions must maintain technical requirements such as:
  - Random number generators ("RNGs").

Absent any cross-border harmonisation or coordination, such market fragmentation along jurisdictional lines is unlikely to receive the blessing of cross-border operators attempting to satisfy the divergent requirements of numerous regulatory bodies while, at the same time, ensuring that their operations remain economically viable. Although a danger exists that some operators may tire of jurisdictions that seek to reinvent the regulatory wheel in an effort to achieve optimal regulation, such a regulatory quagmire should not be viewed with disdain. Through time and experience, EU Member States and other jurisdictions will become wiser as to which practices are best in terms of enabling them to secure their regulatory objectives while avoiding a regulatory and technical burden so cumbersome and costly that operations become devoid of economic viability. As Member States become increasingly experienced in regulating the sector, hopefully better practices will begin to emerge.

The regulation of gaming serves to uphold the interests of various elements that exist within a society. As is common with other activities, the regulation of gaming "is designed to secure benefits for some at the expense of others."[12] Regulatory approaches will balance and affect, explicitly or perhaps through unintended consequences, the interests of:

- Gamblers.
- Vulnerable persons who may become excessive gamblers.
- Gaming providers (business-to-consumer);
  - Providers of services to gaming providers (business-to-business);
- General public;
  - Consumers;
  - Non-consumers, such as children;
  - Local communities, for example: surrounding a (proposed) casino or other venue; and
  - Taxpayers.
- Beneficiaries of gaming derived revenues (such as "benevolent or public interest activities such as social works, charitable works, sport or culture."[13]).
- Regulators.
- Criminals.[14]

The definition of a best regulatory practice will depend upon the interest in question. The best practice from the perspective of a criminal is far different from the best practice that has the interest of a consumer in mind. Other instances, however, will be comparatively less distant. What the best regulatory practices are in the eyes of an Internet gaming operator that takes its corporate and social responsibilities seriously differs from those of an operator who wants to make the maximum profit possible in the shortest period of time. Best practices can be seen from a more global perspective. This chapter, however, will speak of 'better' practices to allow

---

[12] Peter Collins, GAMBLING AND THE PUBLIC INTEREST, 56 (2003).

[13] Case C-275/92, *Her Majesty's Customs and Excise v. Gerhart Schindler and Jörg Schindler*, [1994] ECR-1039 (hereinafter referred to as "*Schindler*") para. 60.

[14] Adapted from Collins' "principal categories of people whose interests need to be taken account of in examining the impact of regulating the gambling industry", *id.* at 57.

for areas where the definition of 'best' is difficult to determine, or where the objective in question may not be pursued in every regulatory jurisdiction in an absolute sense. In reality, practices have to be balanced and what may constitute a best practice with regards to one regulatory objective may interfere with upholding a best practice for another objective. For example, the supporting document for the European Commission publication *Towards a Comprehensive Framework for Online Gambling* notes that the requirements for data protection can hinder the sharing of information when tackling match fixing in the context of regulated sports betting.[15]

Peter Collins also notes that within the context of the regulation of gaming, a place exists for moral and cultural relativism[16] and, while true, some aspects of gaming regulation are relatively immune from relativism along the lines of national (gaming) cultures. One could imagine that the objective to ensure that gaming is free from fraud and cheating is one that all regulatory regimes should strive to uphold in an absolute manner. This contrasts to the attainment of other objectives, such as consumer protection where, even amongst a collection of relatively homogenous jurisdictions such as those within the EU, differences prevail in the standard to which the objective is upheld.

Cheating and Fraud: Adequate and Balanced Attention?

Overwhelmingly, the prevailing European discourse on the regulation of Internet gaming is predicated upon consumers' interests being placed at the detriment of unscrupulous or untrustworthy operators. Consequently, across the prevailing jurisdictional quagmire that private licensed operators[17] must navigate, jurisdictions dedicate considerable attention to protecting the consumer and preventing crime.[18]

---

[15] "Data protection issues are often mentioned as a barrier for sharing information, in particular with regard to match-fixing alerts involving player's sensitive information". EUROPEAN COMMISSION, *Staff Working Document, Online Gambling in the Internal Market*, SWD (2012) 345 final (hereinafter referred to as "*Staff Working Document*"), section '9.1 Existing anti-match-fixing measures'. The Staff Working Document accompanies the European Commission's *Communication Towards a Comprehensive Framework for Online Gambling*, Strasbourg, 23 October 2012, COM (2012) 596 final. These documents can be found at http://ec.europa.eu/internal_market/services/gambling_en.htm.

[16] GAMBLING AND THE PUBLIC INTEREST, supra note 12, at 7.

[17] Reference is purposefully made to 'private licensed operators' because in contrast to the provision of gaming services through a public monopolist licensing conditions and applicable measures are likely to be transparently stated. Regulation of public monopolists can be akin to a 'black hole' in which detailed regulatory conditions and provisions are less likely to be in the public domain; in the absence of private operators regulatory transparency is likely to suffer. Alan Littler, *The State may want to keep its poker face but Brussels and Luxembourg will require more than a peek at its hand: Competence and Transparency in the Gambling Sector*, presented at the 12ᵀᴴ BIENNIAL CONFERENCE OF THE EUROPEAN UNION STUDIES ASSOCIATION, Boston, Massachusetts, 3-5 March 2011.

[18] On the distinction between protecting the consumer in general and responsible

In practice, however, the prevention of cheating and fraud is unlikely to be solely a one-perspective problem. Gaming operators can be used as conduits for cheating or fraudulent activities by third parties, or become the actual victims themselves. Therefore, and in contrast to the perception that only consumers of gaming services get cheated and defrauded, this chapter addresses better practices, which cover both sides.

Section 2 discusses the definition of fraud and cheating before discussing how fraud has been perceived in EU regulatory discourse concerning gaming. Given that gaming operators can become vehicles for the fraudulent activities of other parties, this chapter also discusses sports betting and match fixing.

Section 3 addresses regulatory responses to fraud and cheating by discussing the following practices: opening customer accounts, pay out procedures, prevention of in-play fraud, the threat of criminal penalties, reporting duties that include those applicable to providers of sports betting services and determining events on which operators can accept bets.

Section 4 explores the measures that operators can take as part of their internal procedures to counter fraud and cheating and identify collusion.

Definition of Fraud and Cheating and their Relationship with Sports

Rather than attempting to provide conclusive and all encompassing definitions of cheating and fraud in all possible circumstances, this section discusses the meanings and understandings of these terms and how they manifest themselves in the regulation of gaming and in the challenge to maintain the integrity of sporting competitions.

Definitions of cheating and fraud

Cheating can be defined as acting "dishonestly or unfairly in order to gain an advantage." The United Kingdom's Gaming Act 1845, which has since been repealed by the Gambling Act 2005, was quite specific in its definition of cheating. Notably:

> ".... every person who shall, by any fraud or unlawful device or ill practice in playing at or with cards, dice, tables, or other game, or in bearing a part in the stakes, wages, or adventures, or in betting on the sides of hands of them that do play, or in wagering on the event of any game, sport, pastime, or exercise, win from any other person to himself, or any other or others, any sum of money or valuable thing...".[19]

gambling measures more specifically see Alan Littler, *Protecting consumers of gambling services; some preliminary thoughts on the relationship with European consumer protection law*, in James Devenney & Mel Kenny, European Consumer Protection: Theory and Practice (2012).
[19] §17 Gaming Act 1845, as amended by the Theft Act 1968.

Interestingly, the equivalent provision of the current Gambling Act does not define cheating. The Explanatory Notes, however, state the term "has its normal, everyday meaning." Today computer software and random number generators could replace dice and tables to achieve a dishonest win through the use of deception or fraud. This question remains: "What is fraud?" For the purposes of the current chapter, we refer to James Stephen who has defined the elements of fraud in the following manner:

> ... there is little danger in saying that whenever the words 'fraud' or 'intent to defraud' or 'fraudulently' occurs in the definition of a crime two elements at least are essential to the commission of the crime: namely, firstly, deceit or an intention to deceive or in some cases mere secrecy; and, secondly, "either actual injury or possible injury or an intent to expose some person either to actual injury or to a risk of possible injury of that deceit or secrecy."[20]

This suggests that fraud relates to gaining or attempting to gain something through deceitful and dishonest practices, which may or may not result in injury but nevertheless, addresses the possibility of injury to another party. Thus, cheating and fraud evolve around dishonesty, deception and otherwise getting something to which one is not entitled while not actually constituting theft.[21]

Fraudulent activities relating to Internet gaming are not unique to either the Internet environment or to the gaming environment. John Rothchild identifies a range of fraudulent online conduct that the Internet facilitates, such as pyramid schemes, chain letters, items paid for but not delivered, impersonation of another person or entity, and gambling itself with reference to actions by the states of Missouri and Minnesota against Delaware and Nevada corporations that provided Internet gaming sites in the mid-1990s.[22] While dishonest players can conduct the core activities of these actions without the Internet, the Internet triggers greater concern because it facilitates the commission of these activities on a wider scale. Robust 'better' regulatory practices are required to ensure the effective prohibition of such activities and to avoid the occurrence of harmful and illegal acts, including cheating and fraud in Internet gaming services.

---

[20] James Fitzjames Stephen, A HISTORY OF THE CRIMINAL LAW OF ENGLAND, vols. I-III 1883 (reprinted by William S. Hein & Co., Buffalo, NY).

[21] For the sake of completeness the Theft Act of 1968 provides a basic definition of 'theft' as:

"(1) A person is guilty of theft if he dishonestly appropriates property belonging to another with the intention of permanently depriving the other of it; and "thief" and "steal" shall be construed accordingly.

(2) It is immaterial whether the appropriation is made with a view to gain, or is made for the thief's own benefit."

[22] John Rothchild, *Protecting the Digital Consumer: The Limits of Cyberspace Utopianism*, 74 IND. L. J. 893, 904-908 (1999).

Operators must clearly separate issues of fraud and cheating from money laundering.[23] In a study by Michael Levi, he draws the line between "the making of a dishonest profit" and "hiding and transforming the proceeds of crimes that have been committed in the community." Therefore, Levi considers that fixing sporting competitions and other events on which operators accept bets amounts to fraud rather than money laundering.[24] This resonates with the notion that fraud can be dissected into two types: that "with direct financial benefits" and "fraud with further interests to influence society and economy (…laundering criminal proceeds, etc.)".[25] Money laundering processes form a machine through which criminals seek to dispose of their unjust gains and, as such, their fraudulent activities constitute 'predicate crimes' in the terminology of anti-money laundering provisions.[26]

Perception of Fraudulent Activity in EU Regulatory Discourse

During the CJEU's career in dealing with gaming issues, its appreciation of 'crime' and 'fraud' has been influenced by the cases it has received. As such, this section illustrates some findings of the CJEU's case law that considered the nature of crime and fraud in relation to gaming.

A prime illustration is the case of *Sjöberg & Gerdin* concerning Swedish legislation that prohibited the advertisement of unlawful gaming. Sweden enforced it pursuant to criminal law that permitted higher penalties to be awarded for the advertising of unlawful gaming originating outside of Sweden compared to unlawful gaming having a domestic origin. In his Opinion to the Court Advocate General Bot stated:

> … internet gaming organised by a company established in another Member State does not necessarily or in general pose greater risks of fraud and crime to the detriment of consumers than gaming organised clandestinely by a company established within the national territory.[27]

This is a potentially dangerous assumption to make. Undoubtedly, clandestine and unregulated operations exist; some operate within the borders

---

[23] Anti-money laundering measures are dealt with in Chapter 6.

[24] Michael Levi, MONEY LAUNDERING RISKS AND E-GAMING: A EUROPEAN OVERVIEW AND ASSESSMENT (September 2009). This report considers the threat that money laundering presents to the Internet gaming industry and is available via the website of the European Gaming & Betting Association (EGBA) at http://www.egba.eu/pdf/Levi_Final_ Money_Laundering_Risks_egaming%20280909.pdf.

[25] OCTA-EUROPOL, EU Organised Crime Threat Assessment 2008, p. 25. Available at http://s3.amazonaws.com/rcpp/assets/attachments/628_650_EN_original.pdf.

[26] A ready conceptualization of such processes can be garnered from the definition of money laundering as provided for in Directive 2005/60/EC of 26 October 2005 on the prevention of the use of the financial system for the purpose of money laundering and terrorist financing [2005] OJ L309/15.

[27] Joined Cases C-447/08 and C-448/08, *Criminal proceedings against Otto Sjöberg and Anders Gerdin*, [2010] ECR I-6921 (hereinafter *"Sjöberg and Gerdin"*).

of a particular jurisdiction, such as Sweden, and others in a transnational cross-border context. Yet, other regulated operators exist that supply their services to residents in other jurisdictions where they lack a license to do so. In this case, it is illegal to offer their services if they do so in breach of a local law that either requires a local license or upholds a complete prohibition of the said activity.[28] The license conditions applicable in the licensing jurisdiction, however, carry through their operations to all players accessing the licensed website. Reputable regulated operators are highly unlikely to use one set of servers that complies with the license requirements of the jurisdiction within which it is regulated, and a wholly separate IT infrastructure that supplies other markets, where it is not licensed locally. Provisions that uphold measures to counter criminal and fraudulent activity encompass all players accessing the licensed site. Therefore it would be inaccurate to suggest that players in a jurisdiction have an equal risk of crime and fraud with domestically unregulated, clandestine operators as they have with operators regulated elsewhere, but who offer their Internet gaming services locally (actively or passively) without a local license. This does not necessarily mean that operators should be able to supply numerous markets on the basis of an 'export license'.[29] A fundamental question would otherwise present itself: Why should a select number of jurisdictions be able to establish standards that other jurisdictions are expected to accept? Blindly equating regulated operators licensed in other jurisdictions with wholly unregulated operators overstates the case and has the potential to prevent or disrupt desirable cooperation and coordination at the transnational level through placing reputable regulated operators in the same camp as those that are unregulated.[30]

Against the backdrop of cross-border supply into a jurisdiction with a monopoly in place, the CJEU in *Santa Casa* illustrates their approach taken to fraud. Ostensibly, Portugal's monopoly was in place to protect consumers against fraud conducted by operators, which was found to constitute an overriding reason in the public interest and thereby justify a measure (namely the monopoly) that restricted the cross-border movement of ser-

---

[28] Although within European discourse questions will arise as to whether they were unlawfully excluded from the market and therefore cannot be sanctioned in relation to the market from which they were unlawfully excluded.

[29] Such as that of Gibraltar which is discussed in the context of EU free movement law in Case C-46/08, *Carmen MediaLtd v Land Schleswig-Holstein and Innenminister des Landes Schleswig-Holstein*, [2010] ECR I-8149 (hereinafter "*Carmen Media*").

[30] Against the backdrop of the European debate the following offers a working definition of illegal supply which is conditional upon the national licensing regime in place not being incompatible with EU law:

"illegal gambling may be defined as gambling in which operators do not comply with the national laws of the country where they offer services provided those national laws are in compliance with EU Treaty principles."

Legal framework for gambling and betting in the Member States of the European Union, Presidency Progress Report, COUNCIL OF THE EUROPEAN UNION, 11th May 2010.

vices into Portugal from elsewhere within the EU. The CJEU attributed a "high risk of crime or fraud" to the "scale of the earnings and the potential winnings offered to gamblers."[31] The Internet based environment supposedly held more risks than the offline world with the CJEU proceeding to conclude:

> "The lack of direct contact between the consumer and the on-line gambling operator gives rise to different and more substantial risks of fraud by operators against consumers compared to the traditional gambling market."[32]

For those familiar with European case law on gaming, this is nothing new; the CJEU held in the 1990s that lotteries have a 'peculiar nature' due to the associated risk of crime or fraud "given the size of the amounts which can be staked and of the winnings which they can hold out to the players," the incitement to spend which lotteries generate, and the accompanying possibility of damaging consequences to the individual and society.[33]

Having found this monopoly to be a suitable means to achieve the objectives behind the Portuguese legislation, and thus the monopoly itself, the CJEU went on to find that regulation of private operators in their Member State of establishment:

> "cannot be regarded as amounting to a sufficient assurance that national consumers will be protected against the risks of crime and fraud, in the light of the difficulties liable to be encountered in such a context by the authorities of the Member State of establishment in assessing the professional qualities and integrity of operators."[34]

Although the Portuguese authorities had cited difficulties in assessing the integrity of operators established in other Member States, the CJEU touched upon a different element The CJEU considered that national authorities find it difficult to assess the integrity of license applicants for their own national licensing regime whereas the Portuguese authorities were concerned with the difficulties they would face in establishing the integrity of operators established in other Member States. The perspective taken by the CJEU is remarkable given that Portugal made no argument to this effect nor presented evidence to suggest such difficulties prevailed.[35] Nevertheless, it furthers the notion, without an evidential base, that private operations are liable to become sources of crime and fraud.

The vast majority of jurisdictions in the European context have resisted pressure to mutually recognise export-only gaming regulatory regimes.

---

[31] *Santa Casa, supra* note 8, at para. 76.

[32] *Id.* at para. 70.

[33] *Schindler, supra* note 13, at para. 59.

[34] *Santa Casa, supra* note 8, at para. 69.

[35] For a critique of this decision see Alan Littler, *Gambling Regulation in the European Union: Recent Developments*, in Alan Littler, Nele Hoekx, Cyrille Fijnaut & Alain-Laurent Verbeke (eds.), In the Shadow of Luxembourg: EU and National Developments in the Regulation of Gambling (2011).

Their concerns may very well be reflected in the thoughts of Advocate General Mengozzi, who asked in *Carmen Media* "[w]hy should Member States be obliged to accept a licence that is not valid for those who granted it?"[36] Nevertheless, an approach whereby a locally unlicensed status is equated with untrustworthiness or fraudulent activities has two limitations. First, when operators who are regulated in some jurisdictions operate without a local license in other jurisdictions, they are often deemed to operate illegally in those jurisdictions where they lack a local license. They are viewed as unlicensed operators and this can have consequences in terms of combating fraud and cheating. Second, the assumption is that only consumers are the victims of crime and fraud rather than recognising the vulnerability of reputable operators to cheating and fraud or becoming the conduit for such activities.

The Relationship with Sports and Sports Integrity

Over recent years there have been numerous allegations that Internet sports betting activities pose a serious threat to sport while linking operators of such services to match fixing. These allegations pay little attention to the distinction between regulated and unregulated operators. Consequently, it is necessary to consider sports betting in detail given the attention that this form of gaming receives as a threat to the integrity of sport. In relation to activities that undermine the integrity of sporting competitions, the definition of corruption provides a clear indication of the issues at stake and their closeness with cheating and fraud:

"Corruption in sport involves any illegal, immoral or unethical activity that attempts to deliberately distort the result of a sporting contest for the personal material gain of one or more parties involved in that activity."[37]

The Council of Europe describes its understanding of this issue as follows:

> "the arrangement of an irregular alteration of the course or the result of a sporting competition or any of its particular events (such as matches, races) in order to obtain an advantage for oneself or for others and to remove all or part of the uncertainty normally associated with the results of a competition."[38]

Such an alteration can take shape in a variety of ways to manipulate the outcome of the game or competition so that it is not determined by merit.

---

[36] *Carmen Media*, Opinion of Advocate General Mengozzi delivered on 4 March 2010, para. 43.
[37] Samantha Gorse & Simon Chadwick, *Conceptualising Corruption in Sport: Implications for Sponsorship Programmes*, THE EUROPEAN BUSINESS REVIEW, July/August 2010: 40-45.
[38] Recommendation CM/Rec (2011) 10 of the COMMITTEE OF MINISTERS *to member states on promotion of the integrity of sport to fight against manipulation of results, notably match-fixing*, as adopted on 28 September 2011.

It is necessary to appreciate that threats to the integrity of sports do not arise solely, or even primarily, from sports betting. A report prepared for the French Ministry of Sport notes that "online betting does not create corruption in sport".[39] According to *The Prevalence of Corruption in International Sport,* the largest danger to the integrity of sports arises from doping, accounting for 95.64% of the instances of corruption, from the cases studied; 2.73% of the cases arose due to betting and non-betting match fixing. The misuse of inside information for betting purposes accounted for the remaining 1.63%.[40] The report found that match fixing is not necessarily due to sports betting; betting operators can be defrauded by such activities.

The aforementioned report from the French Ministry of Sport notes that "online gambling has increased the number of people with a personal economic interest in manipulating the outcome of sporting competitions"[41] thereby suggesting that online sports betting expands the number of people with an economic interest in manipulating sporting competitions. While the size of the Internet gaming market has expanded in recent years, Internet gaming is not only carried out by those licensed in reputable jurisdictions, but also via unregulated or under-regulated operators and syndicates in Asia. Many of the match fixing scandals over the past decade have been traced back to such syndicates, which even went as far as purchasing Belgian football clubs. While not condoning any under-estimation of the scale of the problem, nor the seriousness of the issue in terms of potential damage to sport, it is worthy to note that Forrest, McHale and McAuley write that such scandals "provoke speculation that they are the tip of a much bigger iceberg and that many other cases of 'fixing' remain undetected".[42]

Research has been conducted that seeks to establish the conditions under which sports betting is likely to constitute a threat to the integrity of sport. Forrest, McHale and McAuley identify relevant factors as:

- Liquidity—the greater the volume of betting, the greater the incentive to fix an outcome. The authors consider that "[p]otentially the greatest absolute rewards to a successful fix will be found in the most liquid markets and here the risks of detection will also be lower since high bets will be commonplace."[43]

---

[39] *Report of Vilotte* Unofficial translation of "[l]es paris en ligne n'ont pas créé la corruption dans la sport", para. 1. The Report is available at www.arjel.fr/IMG/20110323/rapport.pdf (last accessed 22 August 2012).

[40] Samantha Gorse & Simon Chadwick, *The Prevalence of Corruption in Sport: A Statistical Analysis*, CENTRE FOR THE INTERNATIONAL BUSINESS OF SPORT, COVENTRY UNIVERSITY BUSINESS SCHOOL, p. 10.

[41] *Report of Vilotte*, unofficial translation of "[l]es paris en ligne ont multiplié le nombre de personnes ayant un intérêt économique personnel direct à la manipulation des résultats des compétitions sportives", para. 2.

[42] David Forrest, Ian McHale & Kevin McAuley, *Risks to the Integrity of Sport from Betting Corruption*, A REPORT FOR THE CENTRAL COUNCIL FOR PHYSICAL RECREATION BY THE CENTRE FOR THE STUDY OF GAMBLING, University of Salford, February 2008, p. 2.

[43] *Id.* at p. 3.

- Increased competition—to remain competitive, operators must offer bets that are more vulnerable to fixing, such as single bets in football.
- Modes of betting—the development of exchange betting whereby bettors can back a proposition (i.e. that team X will win) as well as lay (i.e. bet that team Y will lose). Therefore, individuals perform the function traditionally exercised by the bookmaker.
- In-play betting where players can place bets during a particular event—the concerns raised focus on parts of a match being fixed rather than the final outcome. A player, especially in a one-on-one game such as tennis, could underperform, lose a set as agreed prior to the game, and still win the match. It is important to note that underperformance is not caused by in-play betting, as this practice has prevailed longer than in-play betting has existed, but that the availability of such bets may raise suspicions of fixing where they would not have arisen previously.

These considerations have to be balanced against the need for regulated operators to offer an attractive product range. If sports betting license holders are unable to satisfy consumer demand due to regulatory constraints on the types of bets jurisdictions allow them to offer, then the likelihood of a larger number of consumers choosing unregulated operators will be greater than when the regulated supply more accurately reflects consumer demand. In instances where the regulated supply is sub-optimal from the consumer's perspective, demands from those (operators) within the regulatory regime will create pressure upon the regulatory authorities for measures such as blocking financial transactions and blocking via ISPs to be used in an effort to hinder the ability of customers to access the offerings of wholly unregulated operators.[44] Unregulated operators are unlikely to engage in cooperative measures with sport governing bodies and, thereby, continue to pose a threat to the integrity of sporting competitions and the regulated sports betting industry.

Regulatory Responses to Cheating and Fraud

This section discusses the industry's advanced 'best practices;' reviews the regulations of several European jurisdictions, including Belgium, Denmark, France, Isle of Man, Italy and the United Kingdom; and considers provisions within the following two initiatives: a) the *RGA Technical Issues* document[45] and b) the *CEN Workshop Agreement on Responsible Remote*

---

[44] However such measures have not proven to be watertight. See for example Norwegian Gaming Board, *Evaluation of the regulation prohibiting payment transfers for gaming purposes without a Norwegian license* (FOR 2010-02-19 no. 184), 25 January 2012 and Daniel Macadam, *Norway's Payment Ban Fails To Halt Offshore Gambling in 2011*, Gambling Compliance, 30 January 2012.

[45] Remote Gambling Association, *Technical Issues: Good practice guidelines for the remote gambling industry*, published on 31 August 2012, available at www.rga.eu.com/

Gaming Measures.[46] The objectives behind the *RGA Technical Issues* document include the following highlights:

> 8 a. Support regulators in designing efficient and effective technical standards within a wider regulatory framework that takes full account of information society services, consumer experience and inherent market dynamics;
>
> d. underline the integrity and fairness of remote gambling products;
>
> e. assist with the creation of standards that will ensure that online gambling products are fair, secure, auditable and can be regulated efficiently;
>
> h. cover not just the standards themselves, but also the principles of good testing of those standards by both regulators and third party testing organisations. Wherever possible they should focus on identifying what objectives they are seeking to be achieved, and not be unnecessarily prescriptive about what means should be used to achieve them.
>
> 9. It must be remembered that these guidelines are designed to represent best practice, but national and, where relevant, international laws and regulations must be taken into account and will always have precedence.

The outcome of a CEN Workshop is a "mechanism whereby stakeholders can submit their standardisation and specification requirements and develop a result by consensus, validated in an open process." A CEN Workshop Agreement is characterised as "a voluntary standard applicable internationally and does not have the force of regulation."[47] This particular CEN Workshop Agreement on Responsible Remote Gaming Measures seeks to "develop Control Measures that are:

- Capable of adequately protecting customers and ensuring that the remote gambling operators, software suppliers and associated service providers behave responsibly; and
- Provide policy makers with easy access to a set of measures that are readily and consistently understood and can be used to address the challenges of creating a safe and secure remote gambling environment."[48]

The following issues will be considered in terms of regulatory practices to combat fraud and cheating: i) account origination and pay out procedures, ii) in-play fraud, iii) threat of criminal penalties, iv) reporting duties and v) types of bets.

Before doing so it is worthwhile to note that in practice there may be some synergies when measures are introduced to implement different regulatory objectives; the prevention of cheating and fraud may also be achieved by way of measures implemented with a view to securing a dif-

---

news.php/en/69/rga-publishes-model-technical-guidelines (hereinafter '*RGA Technical Issues*').

[46] CEN WORKSHOP AGREEMENT, *Responsible Remote Gaming Measures*, January 2011 CWA 16259 (hereinafter '*CEN Workshop Agreement*').

[47] *Id.* at 3.

[48] *Id.* at 6.

ferent objective. For example, the requirement that an operator only opens one account per player may have been introduced for the purpose of upholding responsible gaming measures in an effort to limit an individual's expenditure or loss during a certain period of time. Permitting players to hold multiple and unconnected accounts with a single operator would defeat such measures. Many jurisdictions such as Denmark, France, and Isle of Man[49] require operators to give customers the opportunity to set maximum stakes or bets per period of time. Equally, however, *IAGR Guidelines* from 2008 explained that a single account per player also reduces the scope for fraudulent activity to occur,[50] preventing players from playing against themselves in an online tournament. A rule of one account per player can help secure these two policy objectives; regulators should be aware of such synergies when formulating regulatory practices.

Account Origination and Pay Out Procedures

Procedures for opening a player account, logging into that account, and subsequently cashing out from such account help guard against fraudulent activities. Whereas many European jurisdictions seek to implement rigorous identity verification procedures at the point of account origination with the goal of achieving regulatory objectives such as preventing minors from accessing Internet gaming services, these requirements also play a role in reducing opportunities for fraudulent behaviour and cheating.

According to the *RGA Technical Issues,* a customer "should only be permitted to gamble where they hold a valid account with the operator" and that the operator "must take reasonable steps to establish the age and identity of a person before allowing them to gamble. Confirmation and verification of that information must be undertaken before funds can be withdrawn."[51] Thereafter, customers should only be able to enter their account upon supplying "minimum information such as a personal user ID and password."[52] Furthermore, the RGA standards suggest that each customer should only have "one active account per company at a time" or the operator should be able to link multiple accounts to a single individual.[53]

Within the system established in Denmark pursuant to the Act on Gaming and secondary legislation,[54] only those who are registered players of an operator can gamble or place bets. During the account opening

---

[49] Isle of Man Online Gambling (Registration and Accounts) Regulations 2008 at §5(2)(b).
[50] IAGR*eGambling Gudelines,* September 2008. Available from the International Association of Gaming Regulators.
[51] *RGA Technical Issues, supra* note 45, at 20 and 22 (Customer Identification).
[52] *Id.* at 23.
[53] *Id.* at 37 (Customer accounts).
[54] Executive order no. 66 of 25 January 2012 about the provision of online betting (Bekendtgørelse nr. 65 af 25. januar 2012 om landbaserede væddemål) and Executive order no. 67 of 25 January 2012 about online casino (Bekendtgørelse nr. 66 af 25. januar 2012 om udbud af online væddemål), both available in Danish at http://www.skat.dk/SKAT.aspx?oID=1880733&lang=us

procedure, the operator must obtain information pertaining to the identity of the consumer using a variety of information including his or her ID number. Verification of the customer's identity must occur either when the account is opened or when the first payment is made. A customer can only have one account per operator. What is particularly interesting about the Danish system is that operators are able to verify the identity of new customers via a database of national ID numbers. With the government enabling operators to verify that the national ID number provided is accurate, it would appear that this robust system would ensure that operators know to whom they have granted access to their gaming systems.

The Danish system excludes cash as a means of payment for Internet gaming, thereby preventing the possibility of anonymous play. When a player transfers funds from their bank account to the operator, the funds must be immediately credited to the customer's player account. Such transfers can only be made via payment service providers who offer their services according to Danish financial services legislation. When the player cashes out winnings, the payment can only be made to the nominated account, called a NemKonto. This account is not merely the nominated account for the relationship with the operator, but is used for a variety of purposes such as social welfare payments and tax refunds. Operators are prohibited from allowing customers to transfer payments between each other's player accounts.

Operators licensed in the Isle of Man are subject to the conditions of the *Online Gambling (Registration and Accounts) Regulations 2008* that restrict operators to offering services only to those who have an account with the operator in question. Opening an account is conditional based upon the deposit of money by credit or debit card.[55] Applicant customers must provide details of their age, identity and place of residence. An operator is required to "use his best endeavours to exclude from registration, and to cancel the registration of problem gamblers."[56] It is unclear what the standard of 'best endeavours' entails, but given that it only appears to apply to the exclusion of problem gamblers, it does not apply to other parameters when registering and verifying player identities. However, further details of applicable verification standards arise in the *Prevention of Terrorist Financing (Online Gambling) Code 2011*.[57] This code:

- Prohibits operators from maintaining anonymous accounts and accounts held in a fictitious name;[58]
- Requires operators to establish, maintain and operate procedures that require the prospective consumer to provide satisfactory in-

---

[55] Isle of Man (Registration and Accounts), *supra* note 49, at Article 1 of Schedule ´Rules as to Accounts.´

[56] Isle of Man (Registration and Accounts), *supra* note 49, at §3(4).

[57] Isle of Man, Prevention of Terrorist Financing (Online Gambling) Code 2011, Statutory Document No, 492/11.

[58] *Id.* at Article 4.

formation as to his/her identity "(either online or in writing) as soon as reasonably practicable after contact is first made" and in the absence of which there can be no Internet gaming.[59]

Prior to a payment of more than €3,000 or aggregate payments within a 30 day period amounting to €3,000, the identity of the customer must be verified under the *Proceeds of Crime (Money Laundering - Online Gambling) Code 2010*. In the absence of such verification, no payment can be made and no further gaming undertaken.[60]

In contrast to the Danish system, this approach is more descriptive and relies more upon the accuracy of the information provided by the player. The *Guidance for On-line Gambling* for Isle of Man licensees states that the requirement for identity at the stage of identifying prospective customers is "a requirement for identity, not proof of identity."[61] Therefore, an operator does not have a duty to actually verify the accuracy of the information provided, subject to the €3,000 payment threshold.

The Isle of Man places emphasis at the point when the customer cashes out. They only allow withdrawals "to the card account or other financial facility from which the initial deposit was made" or "if the operator of the card account or other facility will not accept it, by cheque sent to the Player's place of residence as stated in his registration."[62] However, such withdrawals are conditional upon positive verification of the customer's identity that consists of "a personal identification number (PIN) sent to his place of residence as stated in this registration" or other means as the Isle of Man regulator may approve.[63] This approach requires continuity in the accuracy of the information provided upon initial registration and throughout the customer-operator relationship, but does not require the degree of certainty the Danish system provides in terms of identification verification. While offering some protection against money laundering because of the procedures in place at the point of cash-out, should a consumer not cash-out, an operator would then have a lower degree of certainty in correctly identifying such a customer. Whether this is a weak point in terms of preventing cheating and fraud depends upon whether customers can commit such activities without the need for a cash-out.

The opening of an account and identity verification procedure adopted under French law contrasts with the approach of the Isle of Man.[64] Again,

---

[59] *Id.* at Article 6.
[60] *Id.* at Article 7.
[61] Isle of Man Gambling Supervision Commission, *Guidance for On-line Gambling in "Appendix E: An AML/CFT checklist"* Version (vi): 141211, effective as of 14th December 2011. Available at http://www.gov.im/gambling/licensing/.
[62] Isle of Man (Registration and Accounts), *supra* note 49, at Article 7 in Schedule "Rules as to Accounts."
[63] Isle of Man (Registration and Accounts), *supra* note 49, at Articles 5 & 6 in Schedule "Rules as to Accounts."
[64] La loi no. 2010-476 du 12 mai 2010 relative à l'ouverture à la concurrence et à la regulation du secteur des jeux d'argent et de hasard en ligne ainsi que les principes

they also have a rule of one account per player per operator, during the opening of which the operator must request details such as the individual's name, date and place of birth, and the postal address of the individual's residence. Within a period of one month after making the request to open an account, the potential customer must provide hard copies of their identification and proof that the bank account is actually in their name. Upon receipt of such documentation, the operator, after verifying the accuracy of the information provided, shall send a code to the potential customer's postal address. The customer can then open their account with this code. In the interim period before the player uses the code, he can play on the basis of a provisional account. Customers can make deposits into this provisional account, but no monies can be cashed-out until the account is upgraded from its provisional status using the code. An operator can only cash-out to the bank account registered and properly verified. Assuming that all of the mandatory documentation is reliable and proves that a person is who he claims to be, then this is a robust method of identity verification. To assume, however, that no degree of vulnerability exists for a player to falsify the information and documentation is dangerous. Considering the speed of e-commerce, this hard copy French identity verification technique is cumbersome and challenging; it is widely understood that many individuals fail to supply the necessary documentation to the operator(s) of their choice.[65]

These measures indicate different approaches when establishing the identities of players on an operator's gaming platform. The Isle of Man's approach places greater emphasis upon the point at which the player cashes-out. Denmark and France focus more attention at the stage when a player establishes their initial relationship with an operator. A better practice would require a higher burden of proof when establishing a potential customer's identity as they initially create their relationship with an operator. While reaffirming a customer's identity for cash-out purposes serves to add an additional degree of thoroughness, the need for such verification is less when more rigid controls occur at the point when individuals initially become customers.

In-play Fraud

Practices are found in a number of European jurisdictions that seek to enable the regulator to supervise the activities of their licensees and, with the threat of penalties, attain regulatory objectives.

Regardless of whether the rules relating to the fairness and randomness of games are extremely detailed and instruct licensees on the exact

---

régissant leur règles techniques (Law of 12 May 2010 regarding the opening to competition and the regulation of the online gambling sector).
[65] David Altaner, *Betting And Poker Firms Finding French Growth Elusive*, GAMBLING COMPLIANCE, 27 March 2012.

functions their software should perform, they are of limited value if the regulator is unable to verify what an operator does in practice. With data orientated scrutiny, the scope for operator-perpetrated fraud is reduced.

Belgium, Denmark, France and Italy have all established regulatory regimes that seek to enable the national authority to access data generated by Internet gaming operators as a means to verify compliance with regulatory standards and, ultimately, regulatory objectives. Regrettably, it is not always apparent how the respective national regulatory bodies analyze the data. Sub-optimal data analysis will undermine the achievement of each system in attaining its full potential.

Different jurisdictions approach securing access to accurate data and verifying the accuracy of such data in different ways. Belgium requires the operator to locate their server in its jurisdiction. Denmark and France require the passage of information from the operating systems of the licensee, commonly referred to as an 'e-vault' or 'e-safe' while Italy seeks to approve all transactions in real-time.

Unfortunately and even though the Belgian authorities have recently issued licenses for the provision of Internet gaming,[66] secondary legislation that implements technical standards has not yet been passed. Primary legislation requires that servers on which data and the gaming website are maintained must be located within a permanent establishment in Belgium.[67] It is, therefore, unclear what this measure contributes that ensures a gaming environment is free from cheating and fraudulent activities. If the Belgian authorities do not analyze the data in a coherent manner on a regular basis, then the value of such a method of data collection is questionable.

Italy has a long established system which requires real time interaction between the infrastructure of the operator and that of the regulator. This system has recently been described in the Decree of 10 January 2011 concerning the provision of tournament poker, cash poker and casino games.[68] In terms of communication between the gaming platform of the operator and the central system of the regulator, the following capabilities must be possible:

1. Request by the player to participate in a gaming session authorised by the central system.

2. Request by the licensee to the central system for validation of the right of participation.

---

[66] Daniel Macadam, *888 And Playtech Among Those Targeted On First Belgian Blacklist*, Gambling Compliance, 10 February 2012.

[67] Article 43(8)(2), Wet van 7 mei 1999 op de kansspelen, de weddenschappen, de kansspelinrichtingen en de bescherming van de spelers as amendedby Wet tot wijziging van de wet van 7 mei 1999 op de kansspelen, de kansspelinrichtingen en de bescherming van de spelers, wat de Kansspelcommissie betreft van 10 januari 2010.

[68] http://www.aams.gov.it/sites/aams2008/files/DOCUMENTI-NEW/COMUNICATI/CONCESSIONARI/decreto-simulati-bruxelles-en.pdf

3. Validation and assignment of a unique game code for the right of participation by the central system and the transfer of the unique game code to the licensee.

4. Communication to the player of validation of the participation right and the relative unique game code and charge of the relevant account.

5. Allocation of any winnings and the communication to the player with the respective credit to the player's account.[69]

In brief, this system entails that every gaming transaction with every customer of an operator's services, subject to an Italian license, must be pre-approved by the regulatory authorities and identifiable by their unique game code. Such real-time approval ensures that every transaction is traceable by its identification number; this reduces the room for an operator to engage in deviant practices. However, it is unclear how readily a regulator would discover if a particular random number generator was no longer truly random and, therefore, this illustrates the need for software testing as part of a multi-faceted approach to maintaining regulatory objectives.

France and Denmark have not undertaken technologically burdensome systems as Italy has developed, but both require licensees to permit the regulatory authorities access to their data.

Danish regulations require a gaming control system to be established that consists of the data store ('SAFE'), a security system ('Tamper Token') and a centralised register of problem gamblers that contains details of deposit limits and self-excluded players ('ROFUS'). The SAFE is an operator's data storage facility to which the Danish Gambling Authority must have online access. Operators must store a broad array of data within the SAFE. The Gambling Authority must be able to access all of the necessary information to reconstruct the interaction between customers and an operator's system. This is to secure regulatory objectives like ensuring player safety and preventing money-laundering. The Tamper Token ensures that the data recorded in the SAFE is accurate and not altered after being recorded.

While operators consider the Danish system to be a pragmatic approach, they regard the requirements of French licensees as more burdensome.[70] Each operator must have a 'Front End' or 'Frontal Opérateur,' in place, which directs all French players to their platform and records all interactions between players and the system. They must store all data from this 'Front End' in a data storage device, which is capable of:

---

[69] Luis Gil, *Regulatory Report: Italy*, GAMBLING COMPLIANCE, 24 August 2012 which provides this English description of the requirements found in the Italian legislation.
[70] Décret no. 2010-509 du 18 mai relatif aux obligations imposes aux opérateurs agrees de jeux our de paris en ligne en vue du contôle des données de jeux par l'Autorité de regulation des jeux en ligne (Decree no. 2010-509 of 18 May related to obligations imposed on licensed gaming operators regarding the game control data by ARJEL).

316 | *Regulating Internet Gaming*

- Collecting and formatting data from the Front End (referred to as a 'traced data');
- Storing such traced data; and
- Allowing the consultation and extraction of traced data.

Traced data refers to the player's identification, the IP address used by players, every game or betting event undertaken, plus all activity regarding the player's account balance. In essence, the system must record customer actions as well as functions performed by the operator's system in an effort to detect questionable game incidents and potentially fraudulent activity. Furthermore, the device must ensure that:

- Only the regulator can decrypt the stored data;
- The regulator must be able to identify whether data has been deleted or damaged;
- Only the regulator can manage the access rights to the data;
- Data contained within the device must be available to the regulator at all.times.

This monitoring system, upon which the French regulator ARJEL relies, has been described as passive in contrast to the more active approach used by its Italian counterpart in which the data actually passes through the regulator's servers.[71]

While continued scrutiny should reduce the potential for fraud, whether it does so depends upon how frequently and effectively regulators analyse the data trail; little transparency currently exists about the practices of regulators in this regard. If regulatory systems place operators under a burden to collect, store and provide access to such data, then regulatory practices should mandate that the regulator analyse this data using robust and reliable parameters. Simply collecting data for the sake of collecting it has limited value, if any at all.

The Threat of Criminal Penalties

The ability to deter fraudulent practices through the threat of penalties has a place in shaping regulatory practices. For example, Great Britain has established an explicit offense of "cheating at gambling" in the Gambling Act 2005.[72] An offense is committed when an individual cheats 'directly,' assists, or enables another person to cheat. *Mens rea* (criminal intent) is required. In contrast, should Player A do something without intent that enables Player B to cheat, then Player A will not have committed an offense.

In accordance with section 42(2) of the Act, it is not necessary for a player to have gained as a result of cheating or for the action to have actually increased the cheater's chances of winning. Therefore, disrupting the gaming process, but ultimately failing to gain in the manner intended, or in any other manner, will not serve as a defense. Again, *Mens rea* (crim-

---

[71] Pat Rodriguez, *Regulatory Report: France*, GAMBLING COMPLIANCE, 18 May 2012.
[72] Gambling Act, 2005 Section 42.

inal intent) is applied in this case. Furthermore section 42(3), without providing for an exhaustive definition of cheating, establishes that actual or attempted deception or interference with the process by which gaming is conducted or any other real or virtual game, race, event or process to which the gaming relates, is covered by the prohibition on cheating. By making reference to 'real', 'race' and 'event', this includes cheating at sports betting.

An important factor that deters cheaters is the possibility of criminal charges. The potential for such proceedings is increased in Great Britain given the mandates of the Gambling Commission.[73] This national regulatory body has the power to prosecute criminal offenses under the Gambling Act,[74] as explained in its *Licensing, compliance and enforcement statement*.[75] In describing the relationship between the Commission's regulatory powers and criminal investigative powers, it states that in "most cases" under investigation they will deal with the offenses through the exercise of regulatory powers.[76] However, the document notes that there may be situations that merit criminal investigations such as "if a licensee is suspected of cheating under section 42 of the Act" or if a licensee knowingly provided false information to the Gambling Commission.[77] If the Commission uncovers that a "serious criminal offence may have been committed," then the case may be passed onto the police or other body.[78] In common with all public institutions, the Gambling Commission functions on the basis of limited resources, but the ability to investigate suspected criminal offenses means that it does not have to rely upon the police. Furthermore, the Gambling Commission has the power to issue cautions as an alternative to prosecution.

The potential for such an offense against a licensee and threats of potential denials of future license renewals could act as a deterrent. However, for those acting wholly outside of the regulatory regime, the deterrent effect will likely be entirely diminished.

Reporting Duties

All licensees of the Gambling Commission are bound to *Licence Conditions and Codes of Practice* as a condition of their license[79] and, in this

---

[73] www.gamblingcommission.gov.uk

[74] Gambling Act 2005 Section 346.

[75] GAMBLING COMMISSION, *Licensing, compliance and enforcement policy statement*, September 2009.

[76] *Id.* at para. 6.6.

[77] *Id.* at para. 6.6.

[78] *Id.* at para. 6.7.

[79] GAMBLING COMMISSION, *Licence Conditions and Codes of Practice* (consolidated version), December 2011 (hereinafter '*Licence Conditions and Codes of Practice*'). For more information on this regulatory approach see Alan Littler, MEMBER STATES VERSUS THE EUROPEAN UNION: THE REGULATION OF GAMBLING (2011) and Alan Littler, *Sports Betting in the United Kingdom*, in Tilman Becker, (ed.) ZWISCHENBILANZZUM GLÜCKSPIELSTAATSVERTRAG FÜR LOTTERIENUND SPORTWETTEN. BEITRÄGEZUM

manner, Great Britain will be used as an example of the duty to report information to the Gambling Commission as one prong in ensuring effective enforcement. In this regard, all licenses, apart from those of betting related services, require the licensees to provide the Gambling Commission with:

> "any information that they know relates to or suspect may relate to the commission of an offence under the Act, including an offence resulting from a breach of a condition or a code provision having the effect of a licence condition."[80]

Many of these conditions do not relate to the prevention of cheating and fraud but, rather, to other matters pertinent to regulating gaming. Given that cheating is "an offence under the Act," a licensed operator is duty-bound to inform the Gambling Commission if they have reason to suspect this offense is being committed. Cheating, as defined by section 42, not only covers license holders, but also participants and other parties, suggesting that a licensed operator is obliged to inform the Gambling Commission about the activities of a cheating customer.

In light of concerns relating to match fixing and potential harm to the integrity of sports, the Gambling Act 2005 places more stringent reporting duties on holders of sports betting licenses. While they are subject to the generic duty to report their suspicion of an offense in terms of the Gambling Act and attached conditions, they are also bound to do so where they suspect this "may lead the Commission to consider making an order to void a bet."[81] Furthermore, those who accept bets or facilitate the making or acceptance of bets between others, on horse races or other sporting events governed by a sport governing body listed in a schedule to the Act, also have the responsibility to provide information to the relevant sport governing body. This duty arises when the licensee suspects that information in their possession may lead the Gambling Commission to make an order to void a bet or when they suspect a rule on betting of the relevant sport governing body has been breached. Consequently, Gambling Commission licensees are duty-bound to be aware of the rules of a variety of UK and international sports governing bodies that may or may not have different rules pertaining to sports betting.[82] Rules of governing bodies may differ between the various bodies, or at least when a horizontal comparison is made, i.e., between different sports rather than vertically - different leagues within the same sport.

Symposium 2010 der Forschungsstelle Glücksspiel, (2011).

[80] *Licence Conditions and Codes of Practice*, clause 15.1.

[81] *Id.*

[82] Gambling Act of 2005 Part 3 of Schedule 6, as amended by Statutory Instrument 2012/1633, The Gambling Act (Amendment of Schedule 6) Order 2012, refers to a broad range of UK and international sports governing bodies. Not only are highly popular sports included such as football through reference to the Union of European Football Associations, amongst others, but also competitions governed by, Bowls England, the Greyhound Board of Great Britain Limited, the London Marathon Limited and the World Darts Federation.

British licensees are required to report suspected breaches of rules on competitions organized by such bodies, which indicates a point of weakness. If an operator takes bets on a competition organised in another jurisdiction and that competition is not covered by the rules of one of the international bodies to which the reporting duty applies, then a gap emerges in the duty to report. To counter such gaps, two separate transnational initiatives have been developed; namely ESSA, [83] supported by private operators and, SportAccord,[84] supported by public monopolists, thereby representing the two sides of the private operator-public monopolist divide. The respective members of these associations commit to report suspected fraudulent activities to the sports governing bodies they have signed agreements with, and to supply information to the relevant local law enforcement agencies.

To the extent that licensees under the Gambling Act 2005 give information to international sport governing bodies, the related national counterparts in jurisdictions outside the United Kingdom will be reached by this duty to report. Therefore, because of the duty UK licensees have to report

---

[83] EUROPEAN SPORTS SECURITY ASSOCIATION, *Code of Conduct on Sports Betting for Athletes*, April 2010. According to the 'About ESSA' section of the organisation's website the European Sports Security Association was "established in 2005 by a group of leading European online sports-betting operators as a way of protecting sport from a growing tide of sporting corruption". ESSA was founded out of "[t]he realisation that match fixing could be defeated through superior technical standards" which "led the founding members to adopt high minimum standards of risk management and undertake to share intelligence on suspicious betting in order to create an early warning system through which any illegal activity could be detected, shared among the group and if necessary passed on to police." Consequently, "ESSA represents all of Europe's leading online and offline licensed, regulated bookmakers. As an early warning system, it has access to the largest database of proprietary betting data in the world. A non-profit organisation funded by its members, its intelligence on suspicious betting is passed on to relevant sporting authorities completely free of charge and its efforts in pushing the boundary in terms of security and anti-fraud best practice have contributed to the licensed, regulated sector's continued success in deterring betting-related match fixing in Europe."

"About ESSA" available at http://www.eu-ssa.org/index.php?option=com_content&view=article&id=2&Itemid=3 (last accessed 21 August 2012).
[84] SPORTACCORD, *Model Rules on Sports Integrity in Relation to Sports Betting for all International Sports Federations and Organisations*, August 2011.

According to Article 1.1 of the SportAccord Statutes (April 2011 edition), SportAccord is a "non-profit association, composed of autonomous and independent international sports federations and other international organisations contributing to sport in various fields". Article 2.1 of the Statutes lists twelve objectives of SportAccord, which include:

"1. to promote sport at all levels, as a means to contribute to the positive development of society;

6. to be a modern, flexible, transparent and accountable organisation;

10. to coordinate and protect the common interests of its Members;

11. to collaborate with organisations having as their objective the promotion of sport on a world-wide basis; …".

The Statutes are available at www.sportaccord.com/multimedia/docs/2011/05/2011_-_SPORTACCORD_STATUTES_-_ENG_.pdf (last accessed 21 August 2012).

information to international sports governing bodies, the Gambling Act 2005 has the potential to prevent fraudulent activities within and around sporting competitions in other jurisdictions.

Not all international sports governing bodies may be covered by the Gambling Act. Under the auspices of ESSA and SportAccord, operators who are signed up to one of these two initiatives are obliged to report information to the governing bodies which have entered into understandings with one or both of these organisations. To the extent that there is an agreement for information to be exchanged between ESSA or Sport-Accord and sport governing bodies not referred to by the Gambling Act, then these two initiatives will help overcome the gap in the reporting duty installed by the Gambling Act. Further research is needed, however, to precisely define such gaps in the duty to report.

What could be of more value is the duty of operators to report any suspected activity that may cause the Gambling Commission to void a bet and this is not conditional upon the rules and regulations of individual sporting bodies. The list of governing bodies does not cover all the sporting competitions on which bets may be taken and, consequently, a provision with greater scope is welcome. Therefore, sports for which the relevant governing body is not listed under the Gambling Act also benefit from the Gambling Commission's ability to void bets, dependent upon the scope of the Gambling Commission's authority.

The Gambling Commission's *Licensing, compliance and enforcement policy statement*[85] details the Commission's ability to void bets. The result of a voided bet means that any contract relating to the bet will be void and any money paid in relation to it must be paid back to the person who paid it, with such repayments enforceable as a debt. Yet, the power to void a bet will only relate to the bet in question and not bets placed by other parties on the same event. The Gambling Commission will only void bets when they are "satisfied" that they were "substantially unfair," which is defined in relation to four factors:

- One or both parties to the bet supplied information that was insufficient, false or misleading;
- One or both parties believed, or ought to have believed, that the race or event on which it was placed would contravene industry rules applicable to the event (although the Gambling Commission does not refer to whether these rules must specifically relate to betting);
- One or both of the parties believed, or ought to have believed, that cheating "had been, or was likely to be, committed in relation to the bet"; or
- One or both parties to the bet have been convicted of cheating.[86]

---

[85] GAMBLING COMMISSION, *Licensing, compliance and enforcement policy statement*, September 2009, section 5.41 et. seq.
[86] *Id.* at clause 5.34.

However, the Gambling Commission need not rely on information supplied by the market itself, but also that arising through the "information and intelligence" collected by the Sports Betting Intelligence Unit that is active for:

- Sporting events occurring in Great Britain, and/or
- Betting that involves parties based within Great Britain, and/or
- Gambling Commission licensees.[87]

Seemingly, this suggests that the Gambling Commission will receive information about situations where the licensee is not based within the United Kingdom, the event took place outside of the United Kingdom, or the person who placed the bet could also have been based outside the United Kingdom. While, in the absence of cross-border cooperation with other national regulators, presuming that they similarly have equivalent powers to void bets, the Gambling Commission has the ability to exert its influence over bets that involve parties outside the United Kingdom. For example, bets taken by a British licensee could be void when taken on a football match involving a league of another country or involving a bettor who resides outside the United Kingdom. However, it is hard to envision how the Gambling Commission could exercise jurisdiction to void a bet between a licensed operator from another jurisdiction on an event that occurred in the United Kingdom.

Therefore, this measure could be challenged by the jurisdictional reach of the Gambling Commission and may not cover all bets that have a connection to the United Kingdom. Nevertheless, the ability to void bets on the basis of cheating and the duty of operators to report suspect activity should bring the Gambling Commission into close contact with the sector it regulates, thereby, extending its authority to parties it does not regulate, but whom its licensees have contact with.

Ultimately, however, this approach attempts to rectify a situation through voiding a bet that has already happened along with any possible detriment to the integrity of the sport in question. 'Possible' seems appropriate given that the Gambling Commission does not appear to need absolute proof to void a bet. In contrast to this approach, France has taken a different route. They direct their regulatory focus towards the nature of the bets which licensees can accept.

Types of Bets

Regulation of the gaming market in France is entrusted to "ARJEL", the Aurorité de regulation des jeux en ligne.[88] Pursuant to the 'regulated opening' of the market, the land-based monopolists for horserace and sports betting relinquished their online monopolies with the establishment of a more open regulated market that allows private operators to obtain licenses

---

[87] GAMBLING COMMISSION, *Sports Betting Intelligence Unit terms of reference*, June 2010.
[88] www.arjel.fr

for Internet gaming. An unlimited number of licenses for Internet betting are available in France pursuant to legislation introduced in May 2010.[89]

The regulatory body attempts to uphold the integrity of sport, or at least attempts to ensure that its licensees do not undermine such integrity. Article 13 of the law of May 2010 and Decree no. 2010-483[90] bind license holders to the events and forms of bets they can accept.

Although competitions can be domestic or outside of France, whether sports betting licensees can offer bets on an event depends upon whether it falls into the permitted category as determined by ARJEL. This depends, in accordance with Decree no. 2010-483, on:

- The quality of the organising body, national or international;
- Rules applicable to the sporting event including publication of results;
- The age of participants in the sporting competition; and
- Whether the reputation of the event ensures that there is sufficient betting.[91]

Therefore, for football, the website of ARJEL lists many domestic, foreign and European competitions licensees can offer bets on, including those in the premier and secondary leagues. However, ARJEL needs opinions from national sporting federations so they can understand the specifics of each sport and the risks of manipulation with some types of results.[92] By doing so, they prevent licensees from accepting bets on particular results that are vulnerable to manipulation.[93] Decree 2010-438 permits operators to accept bets on the final results of a competition and results from phases within a competition. However, the results must be definable in an objective, quantifiable manner. Operators can accept bets on certain events within football matches including the final result of the match, the score at halftime, the next player to score, and headed goals.[94] If this approach is to be effective, then presumably the types of bets most susceptible to manipulation and posing the greatest threat to the integrity of sport are excluded. The decision making-process needs to be based upon an evidence-based risk analysis and not merely conjecture.

French law also seeks to prevent conflicts of interest between betting operators and competition organizers (Article 32 of the Law of May 2010) by granting ARJEL the authority to review contracts between operators

---

[89] Loi no. 2010-476 du 12 mai 2010, which also provides for the regulation of Internet poker.

[90] Décret no. 2010-483 du 12 mai 2010 relatif aux compétitions sportives et aux types de résultats sportifs définis par l'Autorité de régulation des jeux en ligne.

[91] Décret no. 2010-483, Article 2. II.

[92] Report of Vilotte, para. 60.

[93] *Id.* at para. 61 "Il s'agit de limiter des risques de fraude sportive, en refusant notamment l'organisation de paris sur des categories de compétitions ou des types de résultats présentant un risque important de manipulation."

[94] Available at http://www.arjel.fr/-Football-.html.

and organizers of sporting competitions. This measure is designed to ensure that operators do not take bets on a competition if they have direct or indirect control over the organizer or if they have a financial interest in the competition. Additionally, participants within a competition are prohibited from disclosing inside information, which, to comply with the Code on Sport, the competition organizer must ensure.

The Law of May 2010 has led to an amendment of the Code on Sport, which notes that the contract specifies operators have the obligation to detect and prevent fraud and exchange information with the sports federation or competition organizer. It then establishes a basis for the federation or organizer to charge a fee for the costs incurred in detecting and preventing fraud.[95]

Vilotte considers that this approach allows sports and competition organizers to place contractual obligations upon operators to remain transparent with their betting activities conducted pursuant to that contract. This relates to information about the liquidity bet upon events covered by the contract and any occurrences which are not present in the normal course of betting operations.[96] Accordingly, this places a legal framework for the relationship between sports and operators, and thereby enables the regulatory authority to combat threats to the integrity of sporting competitions. However, Vilotte notes that the objective of ARJEL is to protect the domestic market "that is to say French bettors".[97] Therefore, he considers that ARJEL is only concerned with the protection of sporting events in France. Thus the competence of ARJEL is limited to bets offered by its own licensees and is seemingly unable to counter threats to the integrity of sports from operators based in other jurisdictions.

This illustrates the limitation of nationally focused measures when responding to the threat of cheating, fraud, collusion and match fixing. How effective the French regulatory regime is compared to the British one remains to be seen. Ultimately, the French regulator lacks the ability to void bets in a manner comparable to its British counterpart. While British license holders are duty bound to report suspicious behaviour to the Gambling Commission, they are permitted greater economic freedom in terms of not having any limitation of the type of bets they can accept. In contrast, the freedom of French licensees to choose which events and the type of bets they can accept is restricted by the regulator.

Although this is quite a specific analysis on the issue of fraud, it illustrates that when developing practices to deal with issues that do not touch gaming alone, regulatory approaches should have a broad scope. Integration, in this context between gaming and sports, needs to be fostered.

---

[95] Article L. 333-1-2- du code du sport.
[96] Report of Vilotte, para. 75.
[97] *Id.* at para. 78

OPERATOR BASED MEASURES

Internet gaming creates a considerable volume of data, which is of interest to both regulators and operators. It ensures that regulatory standards are met and that an operator is not vulnerable to fraudulent activities. Operational practices such as opening an account, identity verification, payment transfers (with the accompanying anti-money laundering measures) contribute to the reduction of fraudulent activity. However, operators need to remain diligent in their combat of fraud; it threatens revenues and damages their reputations. The considerable data trail Internet gaming generates offers a wealth of information at operators' disposal to assist them in establishing thresholds and creating software that continuously monitors the website's activities.

Regulatory agencies pay little, if any, attention to measures or the need to implement measures to combat fraud against an operator with the only exception being the generic provisions against it. Submissions to the consultation process for the *Green Paper on on-line gambling in the Internal Market,*[98] published by the European Commission, provide samples of the types of fraudulent activity perpetrated against operators. For example, one operator notes that customers charge back on their credit cards in an attempt to recoup losses they incurred while gambling with chip dumping, which creates another danger. Chip dumping means that online poker players agree to intentionally lose chips to other players, then split the winning funds between them.[99] A report by TÜV Rheinland Secure iT details collusion that arises in tournament and player-to-player games, particularly poker, where players meet at a table and "pretend to be opponents like all of the other players, but illicitly come to an arrangement and share the winnings."[100] Such an illicit arrangement is likely to include a degree of deception and, therefore, constitutes cheating.

In terms of collusion between players in a tournament, operators can review player behaviours to detect fraudulent activity. Suspicious behavioural patters include those when:

- two or more customers always sit down at the same virtual poker table,
- two or more customers have the same account or credit card data,
- two or more customers have similar user names, similar passwords, similar addresses.[101]

---

[98] EUROPEAN COMMISSION, *Green Paper on on-line gambling in the Internal Market,* 24 March 2011, COM(2011) 128 final (hereinafter '*Green Paper on on-line gambling*').
[99] See BETFAIR, *Responses to the Green Paper On on-line gambling in the Internal Market* available at https://circabc.europa.eu/faces/jsp/extension/wai/navigation/container. jsp?FormPrincipal:_idcl=navigationLibrary&FormPrincipal_SUBMIT=1&id=c974a5bc-234e-4614-90c6-02e73c1512c8 which contains all the responses to the Green Paper consultation which have been authorised for publication (hereinafter '*Responses to the Green Paper.*'
[100] TÜV RHEINLAND SECURE IT GMBH, *Opinion: What can the Internet do?*, Cologne, June 2009 (hereinafter '*What can the Internet do?*'), prepared on behalf of bwin, p. 22.
[101] *Id.*

Furthermore, customers with multiple accounts or collaboration between customers may be identified by similar details, user names and passwords, e-mail addresses along with identical bank accounts and the same log-in times and gaming interests.[102] Betfair[103] notes how it has a fraud management system with "neural learning capabilities" to profile customer behaviour by analyzing variables that include "customer information, login data, player activity and deposit patterns in order to identify anomalous behaviour".[104] This particular system uses a continuous analysis of trends and patterns in fraudulent behaviour to modify the thresholds used in the profile models.[105]

Permitting only a single account per customer provides one way of averting fraudulent activity and, therefore, requirements to open an account and identity verification procedures prove significant. Regardless of how robust account opening requirements and identity verification procedures are, if two or more account holders decide to collude, then operators must rely on data analysis. Regulatory requirements in some jurisdictions require that a single bank account must be connected to the player account. Then, when a player cashes out, the operator will only transfer the funds to the account from which the stake or deposit was originally paid.[106] However, if two spouses open separate player accounts and use their joint bank account, then this would be one situation when an operator would have the same bank account connected to more than one player account.

Should an individual with fraudulent intent manage to pass the account opening and verification checks, or should players who open accounts in good faith and subsequently engage in fraud, then an operator's best line of defense is to analyse their gaming behaviour. It requires further research to obtain information from a broad range of operators about their practices and techniques to combat fraud if they are even willing to publically reveal them; only limited information about such techniques has reached the public domain.

Regulatory measures on how to combat collusion are shallow. The Isle of Man provides that, in the case of peer-to-peer games, the licensee must

---

[102] *Id.*

[103] To gain an impression about the services which Betfair provides, the "About Us" section of the Betfair Group's website states:

"Betfair is one of the world's largest international online sports betting providers and pioneered the first successful Betting Exchange in 2000. The Betting Exchange, where customers come together in order to bet at odds sought by themselves or offered by other customers, has eliminated the need for a traditional bookmaker. Driven by world-leading technology the company now processes over five million transactions a day from its three million registered customers around the world. In addition to sports betting, Betfair offers a portfolio of innovative products including casino, exchange games, arcade and poker." *See* http://corporate.betfair.com/about-us/betfair-group.aspx (last accessed on 22 August 2012).

[104] BETFAIR, *Responses to the Green Paper*, answer to Question 29.

[105] *Id.*

[106] This requirement is important for anti-money laundering policies.

ensure that, over a specified period of time, no player has any advantage over another player of the same game. This suggests that one person's play cannot, over a prolonged period, become detrimental to another player of the same game. However, this example does not offer any practical guidance or insight into how to reach such an objective.[107]

The *CEN Workshop Agreement* and *RGA Technical Issues* provide some guidance. However, they do not precisely replicate one another. Under the heading "Anti-collusion and anti-deception measures" the CEN document reads:

> "Preventative and detective controls or technology should be in place to ensure that the prospect of cheating through collusion (external exchange of information between different customers) is prevented.

> Under their terms and conditions, poker rooms should not permit the use of robots by customers with a view to providing them with an advantage over other customers, and should have procedures in place to monitor the rooms for robots, and upon detection stopping their use."[108]

Equivalent provisions from the RGA, found under the headings "Multi-customer games"[109] and "Peer-to-peer gaming and the use of robots"[110] are:

> "129. Multi-customer games (e.g. peer to peer poker) with outcomes that can be affected through collusion between customers must not be permitted unless clear rules, compensating controls or technology is put in place to minimise the risk of cheating.

> 130. Multi-customer games with outcomes that can be affected through the use of automated electronic devices or ancillary computer systems must have warnings in the game rules so that customers can make an informed decision whether or not to participate.

> 131. Where local licensing allows for their use, when operators use programs to participate in gambling on their behalf in peer-to-peer gambling (e.g. "robots"), information must be displayed, which clearly informs customers that the operator uses this kind of software.

> 132. W here peer-to-peer(s) customers may be gambling against programs deployed by other customers to play on their behalf, information must be made easily available that describes that this is possible.

> 133. The information must warn customer of the risks of gambling against robots and of using robots themselves, that is, that the predictability of robots may be exploited by other customers."

---

[107] Statutory Document No. 731/07, Online Gambling (Systems Verification) (No. 2) Regulations 2007, Schedule 1 'Requirements with which systems much comply for gaming and lotteries', Article 1(d).
[108] *CEN Workshop Agreement, supra* note 46, at 6.19 and 6.20.
[109] *RGA Technical Issues, supra* note 45 at 129-130.
[110] *Id.* at 131-135.

A distinct difference exists between the two sets of standards in this context. While the CEN standards preclude the use of robots through detection and subsequent disablement, the RGA standards suggest that they can be used as long as operators use measures to minimise the risk of cheating. Unfortunately, the RGA's *Technical Issues* do not describe the potential preventative measures that operators could use in this context; rather, they place greater emphasis on providing information to consumers. Operators adhering to the RGA's standards must inform their customers of the risks of gaming with robots, namely customers who could find themselves playing against robots and customers seeking to rely on robots themselves.[111]

It is arguable whether merely informing consumers of such risks offers an adequate degree of protection against the risk of what some consumers could perceive as fraudulent play. Whether an individual is aware of the associated risks depends upon how operators present the information and the customer's awareness of the risks. Although operators are also susceptible to incur damage through collusive behaviour, they have immediate access to more information than a single consumer. Operators are also in a better position to take appropriate action, while consumers' only realistic course of action is to quit playing on a particular site. Michael Levi notes that the interest of operators in such circumstances is not purely financial, but rather, reputational or regulatory damage. Operators must take measures to prevent such losses - a valuable practice in the longer term.[112]

Operations that offer sports betting rely upon monitoring player behaviour as a means to remain alert to possible manipulation of competitions or customers' use of insider knowledge. However, any reporting agreements or obligations are only effective if operators have specific information. In the same vein, as indicators of collusive behaviour, certain elements in sports betting can be indicative of betting behaviour that could reflect a threat to the integrity of sports. These include:

- Customers placing bets on sports that they do not normally bet on;
- Customers placing unusually high bets relating to past play;
- Customers attempting to carry out transactions from a different country than that of their registration; and
- Customers using a different deposit method than normal.[113]

Both the *CEN Workshop Agreement* and *RGA Technical Issues* provide guidance in this regard but do not indicate either the type of information that could indicate suspicious betting activities or the technical requirements to expose such anomalies. The *CEN Workshop Agreement* states:

"6.21 For sports betting there should be procedures for identifying suspicious betting transactions and patterns which might identify a threat to

---

[111] Information on how to report suspected robot use, when it contravenes an operator's terms and conditions, should be made easily available. *Id. at* 134.

[112] MONEY LAUNDERING RISKS AND E-GAMING: A EUROPEAN OVERVIEW AND ASSESSMENT, *supra* note 24 at 15.

[113] *What can the Internet do?*, *supra* note 106 at 23.

the sport's integrity or an offence of cheating. Where a threat is identified there should be a procedure for notifying the relevant sporting body or Regulatory Authority in line with applicable data protection requirements.

6.22 Effective risk control mechanisms should be in place for managing events offered, bet sizes and prices, taking into consideration available cash and cash equivalents."

Similarly the comparable provision within the *RGA Technical Issues* reads:

"144. Operators should have in place mechanisms to identify unusual and suspicious betting patterns. These are necessary to protect the operator and the consumer against fraud and to assist sports in combating any threat to their integrity."

As noted above, experience shows that operators also need to draw upon the overall betting patterns of both pre-match and live betting and note if the volume of bets placed is exceptionally high. Over time operators will build up knowledge of what is a normal degree of liquidity for betting on sports and the different levels within that particular sport, with lower levels of liquidity anticipated for lower league sports. If levels are out of the normal range, then this should trigger a response. Secondly, monitoring activities can identify changes in odds. Indeed, the history of Internet sports betting is punctuated with moments where operators have highlighted movements in betting patterns that have indicated fraudulent activity was under way and therefore all bets have been pulled.[114]

Technical or more detailed information on how operators configure their systems is not widely available; further research is needed to elaborate on how they set parameters and how they review player behaviour. A distinct need exists for operator-initiated measures that combat fraud and cheating within their platforms and to prevent the use of sports betting for match fixing purposes; whether or not regulators should require such measures has not yet been considered. Best practices do not have to originate only by regulation; with experience, operators can develop their own internal practices for responding to risks associated with fraud and cheating.

CONCLUSION

The focus of regulation reflects that cheating and fraud within gaming services is widely perceived as operators acting against consumers. The risk of such activities intentionally perpetrated by highly reputed operators is slim. Nevertheless, there is a need for regulatory and licensing agencies to be explicit, although not disproportionate, in the conditions they mandate

---

[114] *See, e.g.,* instances provided for in *The Prevalence of Corruption in International Sport.*

for licensees. However, this does not secure the degree of protection afforded by local regulatory and licensing regimes where an operator is not licensed in that particular jurisdiction.

The protection of operators, and those who use their operations, against cheating and fraud receives far less attention with regulatory authorities. Not only does the potential arise for individuals to cheat or defraud an operator, customers may attempt to cheat or defraud each other. In such circumstances, not only can customers suffer but operators, too, because the integrity and value of their services diminish. With this in mind, the regulatory practices of several European jurisdictions have been reviewed regarding the opening of customer accounts and the pay out stages of Internet gaming operations licensed by their authorities. In terms of protecting players against the fraudulent practices of operators, several European jurisdictions have adopted technology-based solutions that enable them to supervise the actual gaming services provided.

Regulated operators have no interest in supporting fraudulent practices that surround sports. Match fixing scandals may exist with sports betting, but this does not mean that properly regulated sports betting operators are to blame. Rather, due to the systems in place and duties to report information, they are often well intended and obliged to report suspicious activities to the proper authorities. Regulated operators have nothing to gain from being the cause of nor the conduit of illicit gambling activities. From a regulatory perspective, to achieve the best practices in gaming regulation, integration with other policy areas, such as sports and sports governance, is necessary; neither can successfully stand alone.

The best practices for operators should correspond with effective regulatory practices of governing bodies, whether sports federations or public regulatory authorities. Accordingly, the Staff Working Document to the European Commission's Communication *Towards a comprehensive framework for online gambling* notes that "it seems that the various bet monitoring systems currently in place should be better coordinated and complement each other, in order to increase the overall efficiency of detection of match-fixing threats. To that end, a higher level of cooperation" seems necessary both at national and international level."[115] This is reflected in the Communication itself that details the "clear need for more cooperation between betting operators, sport bodies and competent authorities including gambling regulators, both at national and international level."[116]

Regulatory approaches and regulatory authority are divided along jurisdictional lines. Such fragmentation weakens the response and the use of information gathered where cheating and fraud occur in a

---

[115] *Staff Working Document*, '9.1 Existing anti-match fixing measures'.
[116] *Towards a comprehensive European framework for online gambling*, '2.5 Safeguarding the integrity of sports and preventing match-fixing'.

cross-border context. These conflicts present challenges not only for relationships between regulators and operators, but also between regulators and their peers.

Given the diversity of the issues present, all better regulatory practices need to be implemented and executed at an international level where appropriate and not merely between authorities within a single jurisdiction. With time and experience, such cross-border and cross-discipline activity generates its own best regulatory practices.

10

Age Verification

J. Blair Richardson

On September 20, 2011, the United States Department of Justice issued an opinion ("DOJ Opinion") allowing states to permit forms of online betting not involving sports.[1] The opinion was issued in response to requests by the states of Illinois and New York for clarification of the applicability of the Wire Act of 1961 ("Wire Act") to intrastate lottery tickets sold online. The Wire Act generally bans wagering over any telecommunications system or systems that cross state lines or national borders. Although the opinion dealt specifically with lottery tickets, several states interpret it to allow other forms of intrastate online gambling. These states have already legalized other forms of online gambling or propose to do so in the near future.[2]

With rapid growth in the online gambling market anticipated following the DOJ Opinion, more minors will seek to gamble. Whether gambling debts of minors are legally unenforceable (and therefore uncollectible) or whether law expressly prohibits gambling by underage individuals, the

---

[1] *Whether Proposals by Ill. & N.Y. to Use the Internet and Out-of-State Transactions Processors to Sell Lottery Tickets to In-State Adults Violate the Wire Act*, 34 Op. Att'y Gen. (2011) [hereinafter *DOJ Opinion*]. The opinion concludes:

> Given that the Wire Act does not reach interstate transmissions of wire communications that do not relate to a "sporting event or contest," and that the state-run lotteries proposed by New York and Illinois do not involve sporting events or contests, we conclude that the Wire Act does not prohibit the lotteries described in these proposals. In light of that conclusion, we need not consider how to reconcile the Wire Act with UIGEA, because the Wire Act does not apply in this situation. Accordingly, we express no view about the proper interpretation or scope of UIGEA.

DOJ Opinion at 13. Although it is not the purpose of this review to analyze the legal ramifications of the DOJ Opinion, there is a strong legal basis for interpreting the DOJ Opinion as allowing other forms of intrastate non-sporting event wagering.

[2] *See infra* Part III.

business and legal risks of allowing minors access to online gambling sites are dramatic. As a result, robust age verification has become a growing business and legal necessity for any responsible online gambling provider. Numerous options for *bona fide* online age verification exist, and a number of commercial providers offer such services.

First, this chapter outlines the general risks to businesses from allowing minors to gamble and summarizes various age verification alternatives that are available to minimize and manage such risks affordably.[3] Next,

---

[3] This overview does not attempt to undertake an assessment of the societal costs of allowing minors to gamble, but such costs are nonetheless significant. The UK Gambling Commission has published a thorough review of this and other issues related to underage gambling. *See* Gill Valentine, *Literature review of children and young people's gambling* (September 2008), http://www.gamblingcommission.gov.uk/pdf/literature%20review%20 of%20children%20and%20young%20peoples%20gambling%20-%20sept%202008.pdf. Reports by the Ipsos MORI Social Research Institute also provide further relevant information on the subject of children's gambling behaviors. *See British Survey of Children, the National Lottery and Gambling 2008-09* (July 2011), http://www.natlotcomm.gov.uk/assets-uploaded/documents/Children%20and%20gambling%20-FINAL%20VERSION%20 140709.pdf. Specifically, the survey aimed to:

- Measure current levels of gambling among 12 to 15 year olds, including levels of addictive gambling;
- Compare levels of gambling on the National Lottery with underage participation in other forms of gambling such as slot machines;
- Profile young gamblers, and those who show a predisposition towards problem gambling behaviors;
- Investigate levels of exposure to free trial gambling games on the Internet and rates of play of online gambling games;
- Look at the awareness of gambling advertising, the appeal of gambling and barriers that do, or would, prevent children gambling; and
- Assess children's awareness of age restrictions affecting young people's participation in gambling and other activities.

Id. In addition, Ipsos MORI Social Research Institute conducted a survey of 11-16 year-olds on behalf of UK National Lottery Commission in June 2011. *See Underage Gambling in England and Wales,* http://www.natlotcomm.gov.uk/assets-uploaded/documents/ipsos-mori-report-on-behalf-of-the-commission_1316537803.pdf. The overall aim of this study was to explore children's gambling behaviors, especially amongst those ages 11-15 who are not legally entitled to buy National Lottery tickets. Specifically, the survey set out to cover the following key issues:

- Children's rates of gambling on different types of game
- Gambling patterns and behaviors of underage players of the National Lottery
- Use of the National Lottery website
- Awareness of legal ages restrictions for the National Lottery and other age-limited activities.

Id; see also UK National Lottery Commission's Response to the findings of the 2011 Ipsos MORI Young People Omnibus, http://www.natlotcomm.gov.uk/assets-uploaded/docu-

this chapter provides examples of the relevant age verification provisions in current and proposed legislation that reveal a trend toward the use of databases of government issued identification for online age verification.

Overview Of Business And Legal Risks

Contracts with minors concerning debts are unenforceable in most jurisdictions.[4] It is self-evident that no gaming operator would want to allow an individual to engage in gaming when the operator will be unable to collect payment from a person who is not of age. The cost of unenforceable, uncollectible gaming debts is a business risk that gaming operators can greatly limit by pre-qualifying players as adults through age verification. Taking reasonable steps to minimize the risk in this manner is imperative as a matter of good business judgment.

Beyond financial risk mitigation, existing laws and regulations now expressly mandate the implementation of a meaningful program to limit minors' use of gambling websites. For example, Nevada, one of only three states with legislation currently permitting online gambling, requires "robust and redundant" age verification.[5] Age verification in Nevada is thus not optional; it is a legal necessity. Likewise, in the United Kingdom, the Gambling Act of 2005 expressly extends its reach to Internet (or "remote") gambling facilities, and makes it an "offense if [any person] invites, causes or permits a child or young person to gamble." However, the Gambling Act creates a safe harbor if appropriate age verification steps are taken.[6] Thus, even if a minor obtains access to a UK remote gambling facility, the age verification safe harbor insulates the facility from liability. In the United States, legislative proposals at the federal and state levels contain similar age verification mandates for Internet gaming.[7] Together these developments signal that *bona fide* age verification is, and will continue to be, an essential component of lawful and responsible online gaming.

---

ments/summary-of-findings-and-the-commissions-response_1316536694.pdf.

[4] *See, e.g.,* N.Y. Gen. Oblig. Law § 3-101, et seq. (McKinney) (A minor may disaffirm most contracts if disaffirmed within reasonable time after reaching majority. Exceptions are (1) certain loans; (2) married infant buying home; (3) providing medical care for self/child; (4) for performing athletic or arts services if court-approved; (5) life insurance if 15 or over; or (6) if veteran or veteran's spouse). *See also* D.C. Code § 28-3505 (1964) (An action may not be maintained to charge a minor upon an acknowledgment of, or promise to pay, a debt unless promise made in writing after age of majority).

[5] Nevada Operation of Interactive Gaming Regulations, Nev. Gaming Reg. 5A.070(4); http://gaming.nv.gov/modules/showdocument.aspx?documentid=2942. *See infra* Part III. B.

[6] *See* Gambling Act 2005, § 63. Section 42 of the Act defines a "child" as an individual who is less than 16 years old, and a "young person" as an individual who is not a child but who is less than 18 years old. *See infra* Part III.C.

[7] Existing and proposed laws and regulations governing online gambling in the United States and the UK are discussed in Part III.B and C.

Forms Of Age Verification

The Standard: Use of Government-Issued ID Database for Age Verification

In recent years, there has been a significant change in the business and legal requirements for online identity and age verification. Websites' use of government-issued ID databases for age verification addresses consumer privacy concerns and provides an effective and widely accepted solution.

Government-issued ID databases search governmental records to find evidence that individuals are registered at the address they claim to be and are legally adults. These systems are already used successfully by a number of sites in the online gambling industry. For example, investigative reporters from CBS's *60 Minutes* television news show tested various UK gambling sites and found that the sites using government-issued ID databases as age verification were able to bar a 16-year old from access. Sites that did not utilize a government-issued ID database failed the test.[8]

A government-issued ID can be in the form of an electoral roll registration, a driver's license, passport, state or national identity card, or any other government-issued legal documentation. One common hallmark of a government-issued ID is that it contains a date of birth provided under an oath or affirmation of veracity made to the government. Such IDs are typically issued after the individual presents other official documents to the issuing agency. Often these records are the only valid sources for date of birth and other personal information obtained under oath. Furthermore, government ID databases are maintained as public records, so they are accessible for verifying information or documents presented to the operator of a gaming site. Conversely, other sources of age verification are self-reported, informal and do not have the same high reliability.

Many laws, such as US tobacco and alcohol purchase restrictions, already require government-issued ID for access to age-restricted products in the offline world. Using this standard online does not require the consumer to purchase any special technology or hardware. Almost all adults, regardless of income or nationality, hold some form of government-issued ID. Major institutions, public and private, rely on government-issued ID for age verification as opposed to credit card possession, credit reports or consumer databases that might otherwise be available as unverified evidence of an individual's age.

Moreover, government-issued ID databases are more reliable than other types of private data. Additionally, government-issued ID databases create fewer privacy issues because the information is based on public

---

[8] *See 60 Minutes: Online Gambling-Age Verification Demo* (November 2005), http://video.google.com/videoplay?docid=-6867789129477811430 .The sites that successfully prevented youth access were using Aristotle's Integrity system, based on a database of government-issued ID.

records, not commercially collected private behavior. A gaming site operator's use of regulated government record databases in insuring compliance with and enforcement of age verification laws online comports with offline behavior and norms. From a privacy perspective, using these government databases is far more appropriate than alternatives, such as privately compiled consumer profiles, dossiers, or credit data, which may not have been collected with the consumer's consent. Thus, real-time ID checks against a government-issued ID and other public records are currently available, affordable, and continuously expanding.

Discredited Methods of Age Verification

Pseudo-Verification Based on Presentation of a Credit or Debit Card

Some Internet gambling operators have allowed remote access by minors under the fiction that self-reporting of age plus possession of credit cards and debit cards verify age. An earlier study demonstrated the fallacy of this approach.[9] Sometimes referred to pejoratively as the "porn" standard, this is the method of choice for pseudo-age verification by purveyors of online pornography. This method is not only fraught with legal pitfalls, but it falls far short of meeting reasonable risk mitigation standards.

Credit or debit cards are merely payment mechanisms marketers and card companies encourage consumers under the age of eighteen to use. They are routinely marketed to minors and issued without independent age verification, thus making possession of a credit card an unreasonable tool for verifying age in transactions that are not face-to-face. Accordingly, credit card companies have stressed the inadequacy of their cards for age verification. For example, Visa, the largest card company in the world, testified before the US Congress that access to a credit or debit card proves nothing about a person's age:

Access to a credit card or a debit card is not a good proxy for age. The mere fact that a person uses a credit card or a debit card in connection with a transaction does not mean that this person is an adult. Many individuals under the age of 17 have legitimate access to, and regular use of, credit cards and debit card…. Moreover, using access to a credit card or debit card as a proxy for age actually could result in an inadvertent commission of criminal acts . . . .[10]

---

[9] *See, e.g.,* David Batty, *Call to Block Child Gambling Online,* GUARDIAN (July 26, 2004), http://www.guardian.co.uk/uk_news/story/0,3604,1269498,00.html. Batty states in the article, "Internet gambling websites should introduce age-verification checks to prevent children from betting online, a children's charity urged today. The call by the charity NCH came after it found that a 16 year-old girl was able to register with 30 gambling websites after lying about her age. Only seven sites requested verification of her age when she claimed to be 21…."

[10] Mark McCarthy, Visa VP for Public Policy, Testimony Before the Congressional Commission on Online Protection (June 9, 2000), *available at* www.copacommission.org/meet-

This testimony remains as true today as when it was first presented to Congress. Visa's Buxx card is targeted to teens,[11] and the Solo card is expressly targeted to children as young as eleven. The Solo website, in fact, states the following:

> *How old do you have to be to get Solo?*
>
> You can open accounts that include Solo with NatWest from age 11 onwards and with HSBC from age 13 onwards. If you are interested in getting Solo, you should go to your nearest branch of either of these banks or visit their Web sites for more information.[12]

Minors may not legally gamble under any circumstances, even with parental permission. It is, therefore, both indefensible and irrelevant to suggest that a minor's possession of a card proves legal qualification to gamble. A brick-and-mortar casino may not allow a minor to gamble simply because the minor presents a debit or credit card, and there is no reason for remote gambling providers to be allowed to claim "reasonable" reliance on such cards as proof of age. Consequently, a number of the card companies have expressly prohibited use of their cards for age verification.[13]

---

ings/hearing1/maccarthy.test.pdf

[11] *See* HTTP://USA.VISA.COM/PERSONAL/CARDS/PREPAID/BUXX_BENEFITS.HTML#HOW (last visited Feb. 28, 2013). The Visa Buxx Card is marketed as Visa's "Prepaid Debit Card for Kids":

> How It Works
>
> Visa Buxx is a reloadable prepaid card designed especially for teens. They get the freedom to make purchases—online, in stores, and anywhere Visa debit cards are accepted—while you get the reassurance that comes from setting boundaries around how much they are allowed to spend.
>
> Convenience meets control
>
> - Your teen only spends what's on the card. The purchase amount is deducted from the balance. If they spend over the balance, the transaction will be declined.
> - You can add funds anytime — online, over the phone, or with convenient automatic transfers from your checking or credit card account. That means fewer trips to the ATM and a quick way to get money to your teen in an emergency.
>   (Fees may apply. Learn more ›)
> - Visa Buxx can be used everywhere Visa debit cards are accepted, online and in stores, worldwide.

[12] SOLO, *http://www.solocard.co.uk/faqs.html* (last visited Feb. 28, 2013).

[13] *See, e.g.*, American Express Merchant Reference Guide § 3.3 (October 2012), *available at* https://www260.americanexpress.com/merchant/singlevoice/singlevoiceflash/USEng/pdffiles/MerchantPolicyPDFs/US_%20RefGuide.pdf ("Merchants must not use the Card to verify a customer's age."); *see also* Card Acceptance Guidelines for Visa Merchants § 3 (2011) ("The merchant must not use the account number for age verification or any purpose other than payment").

Furthermore, the ineffectiveness of using cards for age verification increases as card companies and online merchants seek to place more cards in the hands of the coveted teenage consumer. This fact, coupled with major card companies' ban on age verification uses, makes it dangerous for any online gambling site to rely on a practice that is so ineffective for risk-mitigation.

Comparing a Website Visitor's Personal Information with Consumer Database or Credit Report

Some sites have chosen to "verify" age by comparing the personal information provided by a website visitor with consumer transaction data or credit reports. This type of age verification is generally less reliable and unnecessarily creates consumer privacy concerns.

Everyday activities by minors create an improper illusion of age verification. Consumer transaction databases contain records of credit card transactions, magazine subscriptions, self-reported age information and similar information. Accordingly, minors routinely become part of consumer databases by registering a cell phone, opening a bank account, joining a book club, or using an ATM card. That is, minors engaging in commerce will create a record or trail that places them in commingled databases of consumer transactions. These commingled databases also contain implied and inferred information, including age estimates. Thus, consumer transaction databases are particularly inappropriate for the purposes of age verification risk mitigation and legal compliance.

Credit report searches create a unique problem because searches may be entered in the consumer's credit record and recorded as a "soft hit." This may prompt two undesirable consequences: (1) it may lower the customer's credit score, and/or (2) it may impact an employer's, bank's or other lending institution's evaluation of an individual. For example, even if a person's actual credit score is not affected, banks and other institutions may have access to "soft hit" information as part of a due diligence process. If a potential employer or bank is able to see that an individual has opened, for instance, ten gaming accounts in the past six months, it might deny him everything from a job, to a credit card to housing simply because he places some casual wagers. Therefore, gambling sites that are selecting the form of age verification to best reduce risk should factor in negative consequences for their customers. Certainly, states with licensing standards for age verification service providers should require disclosure of any impact on credit scores resulting from use of credit reports in these circumstances.

Selecting an Age Verification Service Provider

The wide disparity in available age-verification services and service providers makes the selection of an appropriate provider paramount to effective risk mitigation.[14] Factors to consider include:

---

[14] Some providers in various age-restricted markets in the United States and/or Europe

Reputation and References – Numerous data privacy scandals have dominated news coverage in recent years, and gambling websites should weigh all available information before entrusting proprietary customer data to anyone.

Privacy Protections – Gambling websites should consider whether the service provider is releasing personal information or match codes.

Legal Requirements/Source of Data - If gambling websites want to insure that their age verification meets the legal standards to qualify for safe harbor treatment, a critical question is whether the age-verification provider uses consumer data, credit reports, or government-issued ID databases.

Licenses – Does the service provider have the necessary licenses required by the jurisdictions in which the gambling website will be operating?

Extent of coverage – For example, how many nations and how many citizens are in the database?

Service Guarantees – A gambling website should determine whether the service provider provides a guarantee or indemnification agreement to stand behind the accuracy and efficacy of its work.

Speed - A gambling website should consider the time it takes to complete the age verification process from the moment the information is submitted by a website visitor.

Compatibility – A gambling website should determine whether the age verification system requires new hardware and whether it works across standard computer operating systems.

Insurance – A gambling website should consider whether the provider insures transactions against fines imposed for underage access.

Additional Fulfillment Services – A gambling website should determine what services are offered to verify consumers who are not approved through the database comparison process.

Additional Customer Screening Services – A gambling website should consider whether the service provider can determine if the financial transactions involve any Politically Exposed Persons and others with whom such commerce is prohibited.

---

include Aristotle International, Veratad, IDology, Equifax, Experian/192.com, GB Group, Lexis/Nexis, Acxiom, NetIDme, and GreenID/GDC. The Integrity Global Checklist for Compliance Officers is available at http://integrity.aristotle.com/files/2012/07/Integrity-Global-Compliance-Checklist-2012.pdf.

Legal Trends In Online Age Verification: Codification Of The Government-Issued Id Database Standard For Internet Commerce

The Significance of the PACT Act

The federal Prevent All Cigarette Trafficking (PACT) Act, 15 U.S.C. § 375, et seq., became effective June 30, 2010. The law addresses the requirements for sales of cigarettes ordered online, and represents a significant development in the field of online age verification in commerce. For the first time, the US government recognized and codified the use of commercially-used databases of government records as the standard for verifying age to prevent minors' access to cigarettes ordered over the Internet.

Specifically, the law provides that a seller who mails or ships cigarettes cannot accept an order online without verifying age "through the use of a commercially available database or aggregate of databases, consisting primarily of data from government sources, that are regularly used by government and businesses for the purpose of age and identity verification and authentication."[15] Moreover, the law makes clear that the database used is

---

[15] 15 U.S.C. § 376A(b)(4) (2010):

Age verification

(A) In general

A delivery seller who mails or ships tobacco products—

(i) shall not sell, deliver, or cause to be delivered any tobacco products to a person under the minimum age required for the legal sale or purchase of tobacco products, as determined by the applicable law at the place of delivery;

(ii) shall use a method of mailing or shipping that requires—

(I) the purchaser placing the delivery sale order, or an adult who is at least the minimum age required for the legal sale or purchase of tobacco products, as determined by the applicable law at the place of delivery, to sign to accept delivery of the shipping container at the delivery address; and

(II) the person who signs to accept delivery of the shipping container to provide proof, in the form of a valid, government-issued identification bearing a photograph of the individual, that the person is at least the minimum age required for the legal sale or purchase of tobacco products, as determined by the applicable law at the place of delivery; and

(iii) shall not accept a delivery sale order from a person without—

(I) obtaining the full name, birth date, and residential address of that person; and

(II) verifying the information provided in subclause (I), through the use of a commercially available database or aggregate of databases, consisting primarily of data from gov-

not to be in the possession or control of, or subject to manipulation by, the seller.

The PACT Act reflects the trend in the US toward the use of government-issued identification for Internet, mail-order, or telephone order age verification because such identification indicates a degree of reliability that is commensurate with the seriousness of preventing access to age-restricted products and services by minors. Likewise, California's Stop Tobacco Access to Kids Enforcement (STAKE) Act, the state's tobacco control statute, requires age verification for online orders "by reference to an appropriate database of government records."[16] Similarly, the Virginia law regulating Internet tobacco orders requires an effort to verify age using a "commercially available database of valid, government-issued identification that contains the date of birth or age of the individual placing the order."[17] However, the PACT Act creates stricter standards than these state

---

> ernment sources, that are regularly used by government and businesses for the purpose of age and identity verification and authentication, to ensure that the purchaser is at least the minimum age required for the legal sale or purchase of tobacco products, as determined by the applicable law at the place of delivery.
>
> (B) Limitation
>
> No database being used for age and identity verification under subparagraph (A)(iii) shall be in the possession or under the control of the delivery seller, or be subject to any changes or supplementation by the delivery seller.

Id.

[16] The Stop Tobacco Access to Kids Enforcement (STAKE) Act, CAL. BUS. & PROF. CODE § 22963 (providing an example of workable statutory language and structure). § 22963(b)(1)(A) states that before enrolling a person as a customer or distributing tobacco to be shipped pursuant to Internet, mail, and telephone order:

> The distributor or seller shall attempt to match the name, address, and date of birth provided by the customer to information contained in records in a database of individuals whose age has been verified to be 18 years or older by reference to an appropriate database of government records kept by the distributor, a direct marketing firm, or any other entity.

Id. If the merchant is unable to verify age through this procedure, §22963(b)(1)(B) requires the merchant to obtain an "age verification kit" from the customer – specifically, an attestation from the customer that he or she is at least 18 years old, and a copy of a valid form of the customer's government-issued identification.

[17] *See* VA CODE ANN. § 18.2-246.8. Age verification requirements:

> A. No person shall mail, ship, or otherwise deliver cigarettes in connection with a delivery sale unless prior to the first delivery sale to a consumer such person...2. Makes a good faith effort to verify the information contained in the certification provided by the prospective consumer pursuant to subsection A against a commercially available database of valid, government-issued identification that contains the date of birth or age of the individual placing the order, or obtains

statutes by making clear that the government records database cannot be in the possession or control of, or subject to manipulation by, the seller.[18] As discussed in more detail below, some recently proposed online gambling legislation reflects the legal trend toward codifying the government-issued ID database check for age verification. While no system is or can be expected to be perfect, this type of verification is evolving into the preferred and legally mandated standard.

United States

At the time of this writing three states, Nevada, Delaware, and New Jersey, have current laws legalizing intrastate online gambling.[19] The federal government and a growing number of other states have put forth legislative proposals to allow online gambling. Examples of the relevant age verification provisions in current and proposed legislation are set forth below. Several provisions reflect the trend toward requiring the government-issued ID database check to verify age.

Laws Permitting Intrastate Online Gambling

Nevada

Nevada has passed a law permitting intrastate online gambling websites.[20] Nevada regulations will allow state casinos to operate online gambling sites by the end of 2012 for players within Nevada state borders. All online bets must be placed within Nevada until either federal law or the Justice Department states that bets may be accepted from outside the state.[21]

---

a photocopy or other image of the valid, government-issued identification stating the date of birth or age of the individual placing the order....

Id.

[18] *See* 15 U.S.C. § 376A(b)(4)(B).

[19] In addition, at least two states, Illinois and Minnesota, have each authorized an Internet intrastate lottery following issuance of the DOJ Opinion. *See* 20 ILL. COMP. STAT. 1605 (2009). The Illinois lottery law states "[t]he Department [of the Lottery] must establish a procedure to verify that an individual is 18 years of age or older." *Id.* at 7.15. IL Admin. Code Section 1770.145(d)(1), Internet Pilot Program, states that establishing that a player is at least 18 years old may be accomplished by utilizing "any combination of commercially available or custom identity verification software, geolocation software, geofiltering software, public databases, Department databases and financial entity 'know your customer' (KYC) processes...." *See* http://www.ilga.gov/commission/jcar/admin-code/011/011017700001450R.html (last visited Feb. 28, 2013).

Minnesota uses the last four digits of an individual's Social Security Number for age verification. *See* MINNESOTA STATE LOTTERY, HTTPS://WWW.MNLOTTERYSUBSCRIPTION.COM/HELP.ASPX (last visited Feb. 28, 2013) ("How do I open an account? Open an account with these four easy steps: Enter name, date of birth, address, email, and *last 4 digits of players SSN (to be used as a PIN and for age verification....*)(emphasis added)).

[20] *See* NEV. REV. STAT. 463.745 (2011) et *seq.*

[21] NEV. GAMING REG. 5A.240 ("A license granted by the commission to be an operator

The Nevada statute's legislative findings and declarations provide that the state leads the nation in gaming regulation and enforcement, and is uniquely positioned to develop an effective and comprehensive regulatory structure for interactive gaming. It further provides that to prepare for possible federal legislation, the state must develop the necessary structure for licensure, regulation and enforcement.22

Specifically, the statute provides that a "comprehensive regulatory structure, coupled with strict licensing standards, will ensure the protection of consumers, prevent fraud, guard against underage and problem gambling and aid in law enforcement efforts."23 During hearings on the bill before the Nevada Assembly Committee on Judiciary, legislators addressed age verification based on government-issued ID database checks and expressed concerns regarding harms suffered by families if children were able to access online gaming sites.24

Moreover, the regulations promulgated under the enabling statute require the establishment of minimum standards including controls for "[r]egistering authorized players to engage in interactive gaming," as well as controls for "[i]dentification and verification of authorized players to prevent those who are not authorized. . . from engaging in interactive gaming."25 The regulation expressly requires that the procedures and controls "incorporate *robust and redundant* identification methods and measures in order to manage and mitigate the risks of non face-to-face transactions inherent in interactive gaming."26

Nevada law sets twenty-one as the minimum age to gamble online.27 Neither the statute nor the regulations define what "robust and redundant" methods would be for age verification of those claiming to be at least twenty-one. However, use of a credit card would be particularly ineffective for verifying ages. Eighteen is the well-known minimum age at which one can

---

shall not allow a licensee to offer interactive gaming from Nevada to individuals located in jurisdictions outside the state of Nevada unless the commission determines: a) That a federal law authorizing the specific type of interactive gaming for which the license was granted is enacted; or b) That the board or commission is notified by the United States Department of Justice that it is permissible under federal law to operate the specific type of interactive gaming for which the license was granted.").

[22] Nev. Rev. Stat. § 463.745(1) and (3).

[23] Nev. Rev. Stat. § 463.745(2) (emphasis added).

[24] *See* Nev. Minutes of the Meeting of the Assemb. Comm. on Judiciary, 76th Sess. (March 24, 2011) *available at* http://leg.state.nv.us/Session/76th2011/Minutes/Assembly/JUD/Final/534.pdf (provides legislative history for AB 258).

[25] Nev. Gaming Reg. 5A.070(3).

[26] Nev. Gaming Reg. 5A.070(4) (emphasis added).

[27] *See* Nev. Gaming Reg. 5A.110(2)(b) ("An operator may register an individual as an authorized player only if the individual provides the operator with the following information: ... (b) The individual's date of birth showing that the individual is 21 years of age or older"); Nev. Gaming Reg. 14, Attachment 1, Technical Standard 6.010(4)(b) ("Interactive gaming systems must employ a mechanism to collect the following information prior to the creation of any interactive gaming account: ... (b) The individual's date of birth showing that the individual is 21 years of age or older").

obtain a credit card in most circumstances without the need for a co-signer if ability to repay is shown. Although the Nevada regulation's "robust and redundant" standard has not been clarified, the requirement of a government-issued ID database is the most likely methodology to satisfy Nevada's age verification requirements.

Delaware

Delaware joined Nevada as one of the first states to legalize online gaming since the issuance of the DOJ Opinion. The Delaware Gaming Competitiveness Act of 2012,[28] signed into law June 28, 2012, permits Internet gambling within the state's borders "under the supervision of a Director who shall be appointed by the Secretary of Finance with the written approval of the Governor and hold broad authority to administer the system in a manner which will produce the greatest income for the State."[29]

The law states that in authorizing Internet gambling, it is the further purpose of the General Assembly to "[e]xpand access to certain lottery games by offering them on the Internet in a well-regulated and secure system designed to create a positive customer experience that limits access to minors, those with gambling problems, and others who should not be gaming."[30]

That statute was amended to provide that anyone under the age of eighteen who participates in an "Internet ticket game," and anyone under the age of twenty-one who wagers on "Internet table games" or "Internet video lottery" is guilty of a misdemeanor.[31] In addition, the law now provides

---

[28] *See* DEL. CODE ANN. tit. 29, § 4801 et seq.

[29] § 4801(a).

[30] § 4801(c)(1).

[31] § 4810(a). Title 29, § 4803(i)-(1) of the Delaware Code defines the restricted games as follows:

> (i) "Internet Lottery" shall mean all lottery games in which the player's interaction with the game operated by the Office occurs over the Internet (which, for purposes of this chapter, shall include any public or private computer or terminal network, whether linked electronically, wirelessly, through optical networking technology or other means), including Internet ticket games, the Internet video lottery and Internet table games.

> (j) "Internet table games" shall mean a lottery game in which the player's interaction with the game operated by the Office occurs over the Internet through a website or network of a video lottery agent, rather than at a table game in a video lottery facility, and in which the game is an Internet variation or compilation of a table game or table games, provided that the game is expressly authorized by rule of the Director.

> (k) "Internet ticket games" shall mean a lottery game in which the player's interaction with the game operated by the Office occurs over the Internet through a website or network of the Office, and in which the winner is decided by chance

that "[n]o licensed video lottery agent, sports lottery agent, or employee of such agents shall allow a person under the age of 21 to wager on … Internet table games, or Internet video lottery."[32] Violation of this age restriction results in a misdemeanor.

However, the following facts constitute a defense to prosecution: (1) the underage person presented proof of age or photographic identification that would lead a reasonable person to believe that the underage person was over the minimum age required in this section or (2) the appearance of the underage person was such that an ordinary prudent person would believe that the person was over the minimum age required in this section.[33] Although, regulations have yet to be promulgated defining standards for age verification, the statute requires the Director to accomplish this at the "earliest feasible time."[34]

New Jersey

On February 26, 2013, New Jersey became the third state to legalize online gaming. New Jersey Assembly Bill No. 2578 bill permits only Atlantic City casinos to host online gambling for those located in the state.[35] The bill does not contain any age or identity verification stan-

---

through mechanical or electronic means, and which shall include keno but which shall not include the video lottery, table games, and other forms of the Internet lottery.

(l) "Internet video lottery" shall mean a lottery game in which the player's interaction with the game operated by the Office occurs over the Internet through a website or network of a video lottery agent, rather than at a video lottery machine in a video lottery facility, and in which the game is an Internet variation of a video lottery game, and which shall not include keno, table games, and other forms of the Internet lottery.

Id.

[32] § 4810(c).

[33] § 4810(d).

[34] Title 29, § 4826(c)(6) of the Delaware Code provides:

(c) The Director [authorized to operate an Internet Lottery] shall have the duty to promulgate such rules and regulations governing the Internet Lottery as the Director deems necessary and desirable in order that the Internet lottery be initiated at the earliest feasible time in a manner that provides for the security and effective administration of such games, including but not limited to: …(6) mechanisms to exclude from the Internet lottery persons not eligible to play by reason of age, inclusion on a list of self-excluded persons in §4834 of this title, or inclusion by the Director on a list for exclusion pursuant to § 4835 of this title…

Id.

[35] New Jersey Assembly Bill No. 2578 ("An Act authorizing Internet gaming at Atlantic City casinos under certain circumstances and amending and supplementing the 'Casino Control Act', P.L.1977, c.110 (C.5:12-1 et seq.), amending P.L.1981, c.142, and repealing section 11 of P.L.2011, c.18".)

dards, instead leaving such decisions to the New Jersey Division of Gaming Enforcement.[36]

Proposed Legislation

Numerous bills have been proposed at the federal and state level in the past two years to legalize Internet gambling. Several of these have contained provisions reflecting the trend toward online age verification by government-issued ID databases. The adoption of bills such as these with similar provisions included would signal a further national coalescence around this standard.

U.S. Congress

H.R. 1174, proposed in the 112th U.S. Congress, sought to establish federal licensing requirements for Internet gambling operators.[37] The proposed Congressional findings contained in the bill state:

Internet gambling in the United States should be controlled by *a strict Federal, State, and tribal licensing and regulatory framework to protect underage and otherwise vulnerable individuals,* to ensure the games are fair, to address the concerns of law enforcement, and to enforce any limitations on the activity established by the States and Indian tribes.[38]

Proposed changes to 31 U.S.C. § 5383 stated that any application for a federal license shall contain documentation containing "detailed evidence of the applicant's plan for complying with all applicable regulations should a license be issued, *with particular emphasis on the applicant's ability to... protect underage and problem gamblers.*"[39]

The bill proposed a legal age of twenty-one. The bill sought to require, at minimum, applicants include in the license application a description of a "comprehensive program" intended "*to verify the identity and age of each customer through the use of commercially available data sources or any approved government database that is available for access in real-time through*

---

[36] *See, e.g.,* New Jersey Code § 5:12-76(y), as amended:

> 76.   General Duties and Powers.
>
> The Division of Gaming Enforcement shall have the general responsibility for the implementation of P.L.1977, c.110 (C.5:12-1 et seq.), and to issue any approvals necessary as hereinafter provided, including without limitation, the responsibility to:
>
> ....
>
> > y. License, regulate, investigate and take any other action regarding all aspects of authorized games conducted through the Internet.

[37] Internet Gambling Regulation, Consumer Protection, and Enforcement Act, H.R. 1174, 112th Cong. (2011).

[38] H.R. 1174, § 2 (modifying Chapter 53 of Title 31 U.S. Code § 5381) (emphasis added).

[39] H.R. 1174, § 2.

an automated process."[40] It is unknown at this time whether a similar bill will be submitted in the 113th U.S. Congress.

California

Two bills have been proposed in California to legalize online poker. California Senate Bill 678, the Authorization and Regulation of Internet Poker and Consumer Protection Act of 2013, introduced February 22, 2013, would authorize intrastate online wagering on poker. The two-page bill proposed delegating to California's Gambling Control Commission the establishment of all regulations for licensing and operation of Internet poker sites.[41]

California Senate Bill 51 ("S.B. 51"), the Internet Gambling Consumer Protection and Public-Private Partnership Act of 2013, was introduced December 19, 2012. [42] Among the provisions in the 51-page bill is a requirement that a license applicant's proposal state how it will facilitate compliance with:

(1) Age and location verification requirements reasonably designed to block access to minors and persons located out of state; and

(2) Appropriate data security standards to prevent unauthorized access by any persons whose age and current location have not been verified in accordance with this chapter and applicable regulations.[43]

S.B. 51 sets the minimum legal age for online wagering at twenty-one,

---

[40] H.R. 1174, § 2.

[41] California S.B. 678, the Authorization and Regulation of Internet Poker and Consumer Protection Act of 2013. The bill's provisions read as follows:

> THE PEOPLE OF THE STATE OF CALIFORNIA DO ENACT AS FOLLOWS
>
> SECTION 1. Chapter 5.2 (commencing with Section 19990) is added to Division 8 of the Business and Professions Code, to read:
>
>> CHAPTER 5.2. Authorization and Regulation of Internet Poker and Consumer Protection Act of 2013
>>
>> 19990. Internet poker Web sites may be operated within the borders of this state in accordance with this chapter and all other applicable laws and regulations.
>>
>> 19991. The California Gambling Control Commission shall establish a regulatory framework for both of the following:
>>
>> (a) The licensure of eligible entities to operate Internet poker Web sites.
>>
>> (b) The operation of Internet poker Web sites within the borders of the state.
>>
>> 19992. Eligible entities may apply to the commission for licensure pursuant to this chapter.

[42] *See* the Internet Gambling Consumer Protection and Public-Private Partnership Act of 2013, S.B. 51, *available at* http://www.leginfo.ca.gov/pub/13-14/bill/sen/sb_0051-0100/sb_51_bill_20121219_introduced.html

[43] S.B. 51 (amending CAL. BUS. & PROF. CODE § 19990.24 (i)(1) and (2)).

and includes age verification requirements virtually identical to the standards previously codified by the California STAKE ACT, the core of which is "reference to an appropriate database of government records."[44]

Because California's minimum age would be twenty-one, the use of a credit card for age verification purposes would not only be ineffective due to the prevalence of credit cards in the hands of those under twenty-one, but also a violation of credit card company rules. In addition, the use of a credit card for age verification is not included in the required age verification methodology.[45]

Hawaii

In Hawaii, Senate Bill 768, introduced January 18, 2013, sets eighteen as the minimum legal age to gamble and requires documentation verifying age. Section 13(a) states:

---

[44] *See* S.B. 51's age verification provision, amending CAL. BUS. & PROF. CODE § 19990.35(c):

(c) A registered player shall not be less than 21 years of age.

(1) Online games shall not be provided, directly or indirectly, to any person under 21 years of age.

(2) Each licensee shall do all of the following:

(A) Prior to registering a person as a registered player or permitting a person to play an authorized game, the licensee shall verify that the person is 21 years of age or older. The licensee or seller shall attempt to match the name, address, and date of birth provided by the person to information contained in records in a database of individuals who have been verified to be 21 years of age or older by reference to an appropriate database of government records. The licensee also shall verify that the billing address on the check or credit card offered for payment by the person matches the address listed in the database.

(B) If the licensee is unable to verify that the person is 21 years of age or older pursuant to subparagraph (A), the licensee shall require the person to submit an age-verification kit consisting of an attestation signed by the person that he or she is 21 years of age or older and a copy of a valid form of government identification. For the purposes of this section, a valid form of government identification includes a driver's license, state identification card, passport, official naturalization or immigration document, such as an alien registration receipt card or an immigrant visa, or United States military identification. The licensee also shall verify that the billing address on the check or credit card provided by the person matches the address listed in the government identification.

[45] For a good discussion on the policy background of California's Internet gambling legislation *see* Bradley Valerius, *The Foundations of Internet Gambling Policy: California*, FOR THE BETTER GOOD (1st ed. April 16, 2012) *available at* http://www.forthebettorgood.com/wp-content/uploads/2012/05/Cali-IGamingPolicy-4TBG.pdf.

A person desiring to wager money on the corporation's web-site shall register for an account by providing documentation verifying the identity of the individual and that the person is at least eighteen years of age.[46]

Furthermore, Section 17 provides that the corporation operating the gambling site shall establish the age verification requirements.[47] However, the Hawaii bill does not set the standards for age verification other than to say that they must be "reasonably designed to block access to minors."[48] It is likely that reference to other state or federal statutes will determine what documentation and standards would meet this requirement.

UK Age Verification Legislation Concerning Online Gambling

The minimum legal age for most types of gambling in the UK is eighteen.[49] In 2009, the UK Gambling Commission wrote to licensed bookmakers to remind them they must have effective policies and procedures in place to prevent anyone underage from gambling or entering a betting shop. The notice followed a "mystery shopping exercise" undertaken by the Commission throughout England revealing that in 98 of the 100 shops visited, a seventeen year old was allowed to place a bet illegally. The Commission stated that it would continue with its mystery shopping exercises and threatened regulatory action if necessary.[50]

---

[46] *See* S.B. No. 768, 27th Leg. § 13(a) (Haw. 2013), *available at* http://www.capitol.hawaii. gov/session2013/Bills/SB768_.HTM.

[47] *See* S.B. No. 768 § 17.

[48] *Id.*

[49] The 18 or over minimum age limit applies to adult gaming centers ("amusement arcades"), betting shops, bingo halls, casinos and online gambling. Exceptions are: a) National Lottery tickets and scratch-cards for which the minimum legal age is 16 years, and b) Category D electronic gaming machines (in Family Entertainment Centers for which there is no minimum legal age. *See Consumer Protections Measures Provided by Gambling Operators*, GAMBLE AWARE (last visited Aug. 15, 2012), http://www.gambleaware.co.uk/consumer-protection/.

[50] *See* UK Underage Gambling Press Release, UK GAMBLING COMMISSION (May 11, 2009), http://www.gamblingcommission.gov.uk/gh-media/latest_news/2009/under_age_gambling.aspx:

> The Gambling Commission (the Commission) has written to licensed bookmakers to remind them that they must have effective policies and procedures in place to prevent young people under the age of 18 from gambling or entering a betting shop.
>
> This follows a recent mystery shopping exercise undertaken by the Commission throughout England that revealed a disturbing failure rate. The exercise covered all the major betting operators in Great Britain, accounting for around 80% of betting shops, and the initial results show that in 98 of the 100 shops visited a 17 year old was allowed to place a bet at the counter.
>
> The Director of Regulation at the Commission, Nick To-

Bona fide and effective age verification by UK gaming operators is therefore a financial and legal necessity. In addition to the goal of risk mitigation, age verification serves the critical purpose of establishing defenses in the event of prosecution for allowing a minor to gamble. For example, Part 4 of the Gambling Act in the United Kingdom, "Protection of Children and Young Persons," expressly makes it an "offense if [any person] invites, causes or permits a child or young person to gamble."[51] A person found guilty of an offense under this bill is subject to imprisonment, a fine or both.[52]

The law does not impose strict liability for allowing a minor to gamble. It may be that in passing the Act the UK Parliament recognized that no screening system will be flawless. Thus, the Act creates a safe harbor for those who have a "reasonable belief" that their customer is not a minor. The crux of this defense is that the person charged, "took all reasonable steps" to determine the individual's age.[53] The Gambling Commission amendments set forth Social Responsibility Code Provisions that identify what will constitute reasonable steps for "remote" (online) gambling sites

---

filuk, has already met with senior executives at the companies involved to discuss these results and the action the operators plan to take to speedily address the situation.

Nick Tofiluk said "It is illegal for young people under the age of 18 to gamble or to enter a betting shop. We are extremely concerned at these results - further mystery shopping exercises will be conducted to ensure that controls are adequate and effective." The Commission will continue with its mystery shopping exercises and will not hesitate to take regulatory action where necessary.

Id.
[51] Gambling Act, 2005, c. 19, § 46(1)
[52] *Id.* at § 62.
[53] § 63 in Part 4 of the Gambling Act states:

Reasonable belief about person's age

(1) Where a person is charged with an offence under this Part of doing anything in relation to an individual who is a child it is a defense for the person charged to prove that

(a) he took all reasonable steps to determine the individual's age; and

(b) he reasonably believed that the individual was not a child.

(2) Where a person is charged with an offence under this Part of doing anything in relation to an individual who is a young person it is a defense for the person charged to prove that

(a) he took all reasonable steps to determine the individual's age, and

(b) he reasonably believed that the individual was not a young person.

Id.

to verify a customer's age.[54] If followed, these steps should create a safe harbor from prosecution for allowing a minor to gamble.

For UK residents using any payment method other than a credit card, the Gambling Commission's proposals state that "unless the licensee has established that a third party has satisfactorily carried out age verification," age verification procedures must include, *inter alia*, credit checks and database searches which list names and addresses of individuals over the age of eighteen.[55] Therefore using government-issued ID database checks would

---

[54] *See* GAMBLING COMMISSION, LICENCE CONDITIONS AND CODES OF PRACTICE , 22 (December 2011), *available at* http://www.gamblingcommission.gov.uk/pdf/LCCP%20consolidated%20version%20%20December%202011.pdf:

All remote licences (including ancillary remote betting licences), except gaming machine technical, gambling software, ancillary remote casino, ancillary remote bingo and remote betting intermediary (trading rooms only) licences

Social responsibility code provision

Licensees must have and put into effect policies and procedures designed to prevent underage gambling, and monitor the effectiveness of these.

Such procedures must include:

a) warning potential customers that underage gambling is an offence;

b) requiring customers to affirm that they are of legal age;

c) regularly reviewing their age verification systems and implementing all reasonable improvements that may be made as technology advances and as information improves;

d) ensuring that relevant staff are properly trained in the use of their age verification procedures;

 in particular customer services staff must be appropriately trained in the use of secondary forms

 of identification when initial verification procedures fail to prove that an individual is of legal age;

e) enabling their gambling websites to permit filtering software to be used by adults (such as

 parents or within schools) in order to restrict access to relevant pages of those sites.

Id.

[55] *Id.* Subsection (f) provides:

in the case of any UK resident customer who deposits money using any type of payment method other than a credit card, and unless the licensee has established that a third party has satisfactorily carried out age verification, the following age verification procedures:

i) verifying additional information about the customer, such as carrying out searches of credit reference and other databases that list names and addresses of individuals over the age of 18;

ii) carrying out secondary age verification checks in any circumstances which give the operator reason to suspect that the person may be underage;

be more reliable and the quickest way to satisfy this requirement while assuring a requisite level of financial risk mitigation.

For non-UK residents using any payment method other than a credit card, the proposed regulations state "unless the licensee has established that a third party has satisfactorily carried out age verification," then age verification procedures must include taking all reasonable steps to make use of information publicly available for age verification purposes from whichever country the potential customer is a resident, in addition to following procedures similar to those used for UK resident customers.[56] Therefore, using government-issued ID database checks would also be

---

iii) not permitting the customer to withdraw any winnings from their account until age

verification has been satisfactorily completed; and

iv) in any event, a requirement that if age verification has not been satisfactorily completed within 72 hours of the customer applying to register to gamble and depositing money:

- the account will be frozen

- no further gambling will be permitted until age verification has been successfully completed

- if on completion of age verification the customer is shown to be underage, the

operator must return to the customer any money paid in respect of the use of the gambling facilities, but no winnings shall be paid.

Id.

[56] *Id.* Subsection (g) provides:

in the case of any non-UK resident customer who deposits money using any type of payment method other than a credit card, and unless the licensee has established that a third party has satisfactorily carried out age verification, the following age verification procedures:

i) taking all reasonable steps to make use of information available for age verification purposes from whichever country the potential customer is resident in; and

23 LCCP 11/04

ii) each of the following steps, unless they can not reasonably be implemented or, in the case of the fourth bullet point, a period of more than 72 hours was reasonably required:

- verifying additional information about the customer, such as carrying out searches of credit reference and other databases that list names and addresses of individuals over the age of 18

- carrying out secondary age verification checks in any circumstances which give the operator reason to suspect that the person may be underage

- not permitting the customer to withdraw any winnings from their account until age verification has been satisfactorily completed

- a requirement that if age verification has not been satisfactorily completed within 72 hours of the customer applying to register to gamble and depositing money:

- the account will be frozen;

more reliable and the quickest way to satisfy this requirement for non-UK resident customers, while assuring greater risk mitigation. That is, while reliance on credit cards may temporarily allow a gambling website to avail itself of a safe harbor from prosecution in the UK, the site's financial risk mitigation procedures will remain unnecessarily deficient because the card companies' merchant rules themselves prohibit the use of cards for age verification [57]

Conclusion

It is expected that more minors will attempt to gamble following the DOJ Opinion and the likely increase in Internet gaming. Similarly, the corresponding financial and legal risks relating to underage gambling will likely increase. As a result, more jurisdictions will pass online gambling legislation including age verification requirements. Thus, service providers utilizing government-issued ID databases are becoming a business and legal necessity for any responsible online gambling service operator.

    - no further gambling will be permitted until age verification has been successfully completed; and

    - if on completion of age verification the customer is shown to be underageall deposits held by the operator are returned to the customer and nowinnings paid.

Id.

[57] *See e.g.* American Express Merchant Reference Guide, *supra* note 13.

11

Proposal for an International Convention on Online Gambling

Marketa Trimble[*]

Marketa Trimble[*]

INTRODUCTION

The regulation of online gambling[1] has generated much discussion in countries around the world, but the option to enhance national regulations by an international convention, although sometimes mentioned, has remained at the margins of the discussions.[2] It is surprising that this option

---

[*] The author would like to thank Jennifer Anderson of the Wiener-Rogers Law Library at the University of Nevada, Las Vegas, and Gary A. Trimble for their research and editing support. The author also thanks David Briggs, Rao Coca, Professor Eric Goldman, Professor Thomas Main, Sanford Millar, Phillip Ryan, David G. Schwartz, and the participants of the 2012 Internet Law Works-in-Progress Symposium for their comments and suggestions. This chapter was preceded by the author's blog post at the UNLV Law Blog: Marketa Trimble, *Is It Time for an International Convention on Online Gambling?*, October 3, 2011, *available at* http://unlvlawblog.blogspot.com/2011/10/is-it-time-for-international-convention.html (last visited June 19, 2012).

[1] This article uses the term "gambling" instead of "gaming" because it proposes international cooperation in the area that might be more accurately described as "gambling." *See infra.*

[2] Marketa Trimble, *Is It Time for an International Convention on Online Gambling?*, October 3, 2011, *available at* http://unlvlawblog.blogspot.com/2011/10/is-it-time-for-international-convention.html (last visited Oct. 9, 2011).

Recent proposals for cooperation appear to be either limited territorially or focused on the creation of a single new international regulation rather than cooperation among countries with various regulatory approaches. *See, e.g.*, European Parliament Resolution of 15 November 2011 on online gambling in the Internal Market, 2011/2084(INI) ("[I]n some areas there would be clear added value from a coordinated European approach, …given the cross-border nature of online gambling services."); Margaret Devaney, *Online Gambling and International Regulation: An Outside Bet*, 18(3) Information & Communications Technology Law 273 (2009) (suggesting cooperation among EU member states); Katherine A. Valasek, *Winning the Jackpot: A Framework for Successful International Regulation of Online Gambling and the Value of the Self-Regulating Entities*, MICH. ST. L. REV. 735 (2007)

has been neglected because an international convention on online gambling could facilitate the effective enforcement of national online gambling regulations and respect individual national approaches to online gambling that have been or will be adopted. Regardless of a jurisdiction's approach to online gambling—whether it wants to allow and regulate online gambling or prohibit it partially or entirely—all jurisdictions would benefit from cooperation with other jurisdictions.

The problem with existing proposals for international cooperation regulating online gambling is that these proposals have focused on achieving uniformity in national approaches—whether to legalize and regulate the activity, or to prohibit it altogether. However, the regulation of online gambling is unlikely to emerge as a uniform international law, at least not in the near future, because countries' views about online gambling vary greatly. In federal countries such as the United States and Germany, even the individual states have very different opinions about online gambling.[3] Past proposals have lacked sufficient support precisely because they have required countries to accept a uniform international standard. Although the adoption of a uniform international standard would be helpful from some perspectives,[4] it appears unachievable now or anytime soon.

Because countries lack consensus about a proper approach to online gambling, online gambling regulation is and will continue to be based on territorially defined gambling laws. These laws apply only within the

---

(suggesting the creation of an international regulatory scheme); Eric Pfanner & Heather Timmons, *U.K. Seeks Global Rules for Online Gambling*, The New York Times, November 2, 2006; John D. Andrle, *A Winning Hand: A Proposal for an International Regulatory Schema with Respect to the Growing Online Gambling Dilemma in the United States*, 37 Vand. J. Transnat'l L. 1389 (2004) (suggesting an international regulatory scheme); John Warren Kindt & Stephen W. Joy, *Internet Gambling and the Destabilization of National and International Economies: Time for a Comprehensive Ban on Gambling Over the World Wide Web*, 80 Denver U. L. Rev. 111, 152 (2002). For proposals focused on criminal enforcement *see* Anthony Cabot, *Internet Gambling in the Information Age*, Nevada Lawyer, March 1999, 20-22, at p. 22; Anthony Cabot, The Internet Gambling Report IV 395-403 (2001).

[3] *See, e.g.*, Devaney, *supra* note 2, p. 276 (identifying "four categories" of "approaches towards Internet gaming:" "maximum protection/compliance, prohibition, laissez-faire and tolerance"). *See also* GREF Position Statement on Gambling on the Internet, Gaming Regulators European Forum, adopted May 15, 1998, *available at* http://www.gref.net/statements.html (last visited Mar. 30, 2012), par. 2 ("[I]t is a matter for individual Governments, either at national or at autonomous regional level, whether or not they wish to permit any forms of gambling to be offered on the Internet in their territories and, if they do, under what circumstances or conditions particular forms of gambling are to be allowed.").

[4] Proponents of legalization or prohibition of online gambling see the potential for a uniform standard to maximize their goals internationally (*e.g.*, prevention of fraud, money-laundering and other criminal activities, protection of minors). One common benefit heralded by the proponents of a uniform standard for online gambling is the ease of enforcement of a uniform standard on the Internet. *See also* Kevin F. King, *Geolocation and Federalism on the Internet: Cutting Internet Gambling's Gordian Knot*, 11 Colum. Sci. & Tech. L. Rev. 41, 66-74 (2010) (presenting the arguments for and against "jurisdictional differentiation" in Internet gambling laws).

borders of a particular jurisdiction and do not extend beyond national borders unless they target conduct that has effects within a jurisdiction. Enforcing territorially limited laws on the Internet has been challenging, and online gambling laws suffer from the same enforcement problems that other territorially limited laws do.

Countries have a limited ability to enforce their laws against persons and entities outside their territories. Regardless of the manner in which a country defines the territorial scope of its jurisdiction—whether prescriptive or adjudicatory—the territorial extent of its enforcement power, and therefore the true extent of its jurisdiction, is limited by its physical access to persons, accounts, or facilities, and by the willingness of other countries to enforce decisions rendered in the country. Countries can effectively enforce their regulators' or courts' decisions only by sanctioning an entity (by freezing the entity's accounts or seizing its property) or by persuading other countries to recognize and enforce its decisions against the entity abroad.

Because the Internet enables website operators to strategically locate their assets to avoid having a physical presence in countries of potential enforcement, it is often difficult, if not impossible, for countries to enforce territorially defined laws on the Internet directly against the operators. As a result, countries have sought to employ their enforcement power over entities other than website operators, such as Internet service providers or payment processors, whom the operators need in order to conduct business. While practically feasible, enforcement against these entities is not without controversy or practical limitations.[5] As discussed further below, content filtering by Internet service providers raises serious concerns about the protection of free speech and the freedom to conduct business, and enforcement against other third parties, such as payment processors, may not serve well the needs of the particular regulation.

These regulatory and enforcement limitations illustrate the need to seek international solutions to enforcement problems. The borderlessness of the Internet[6] and the global business environment require international cooperation in enforcement. The strong public policies that shape the current or future national regulation of gambling in general and online gambling in particular should be the significant driving forces that will propel the negotiations of an international convention.

Solving the enforcement problems of online gambling regulation is certainly important from a public policy perspective, as countries strive to

---

[5] On the problems with "derivative liability" in online gambling regulation generally *see, e.g.,* Testimony of Eric Goldman before the National Gambling Impact Study Commission's Regulatory, Enforcement and Internet Subcommittee, December 1, 1998, *available at* http://eric_goldman.tripod.com/articles/gamblingarticle.htm (last visited June 16, 2012).

[6] The use of geolocation by website operators and filtering by Internet service providers challenges the original concept of the "borderless" Internet. *See, e.g.,* Marketa Trimble, *The Future of Cybertravel: Legal Implications of the Evasion of Geolocation,* 22 FORDHAM INTELL. PROP. MEDIA & ENT. L.J. 567 (2012).

implement their policies. At the same time, gambling operators should be presented with a clear legal framework. Although the popular perception has been that gambling operations are insufficiently regulated or not regulated at all, the gambling industry is highly regulated in many jurisdictions where gambling is legalized, and the global players in the industry are accustomed to complying with multiple national regulatory schemes. These industry players should have the opportunity to shape their operations on the Internet while respecting multiple national territorially defined laws. Academics and practitioners have expressed a similar desire for clarity in the legal framework governing general global online operations for Internet intermediaries with respect to secondary liability concerning online content posted by third parties;[7] a similar pro-business approach should be pursued in the area of online gambling.[8]

This chapter outlines a proposal for an international convention on online gambling (hereinafter referred to as the "Convention") and analyzes some of the challenges that the drafters of such a convention will likely encounter. The intent is not to list all the provisions of the Convention but to provide outline material for critical review and discussion to propel further development of this proposal or inspire alternate proposals. Drafting the Convention would require extensive negotiations among countries with substantial input from gaming law experts, regulators, online gambling operators, and other stakeholders, including public health officials and representatives of civil society.

The analysis in this chapter demonstrates that the Convention would be feasible, although it would not be without challenges. Critics will question the solutions offered and argue that rather than supporting an international convention, the analysis below proves that an online gambling convention is not feasible and/or not helpful. There are indeed significant challenges to be overcome. Some challenges are law-related and raise significant issues

---

[7] Many countries provide safe harbors that protect Internet service providers from liability for third-party content; however, no international agreement clarifies the transnational application of the rules. For proposals to solve the Internet service provider secondary liability issues *see, e.g.*, Graeme B. Dinwoodie et al., *The Law Applicable to Secondary Liability in Intellectual Property Cases*, 42 N.Y.U. J. INT'L L. & POL. 201, 209-229 (2009); Principles on Conflict of Laws in Intellectual Property, European Max Planck Group on Conflict of Laws in Intellectual Property, Final Text, December 1, 2011, Article 3:604(2) and (3), *available at* http://www.cl-ip.eu/files/pdf2/Final_Text_1_December_2011.pdf (last visited Aug. 20, 2012) (proposing a special provision on secondary liability for intermediaries). For the relevant national legislation *see, e.g.*, 17 U.S.C. §512 (Digital Millennium Copyright Act); 47 U.S.C. §230 (Communications Decency Act); Mark A. Lemley, *Rationalizing Internet Safe Harbors*, 6 J. TELECOMM. & HIGH TECH L. 101 (2007); Directive 2000/31/EC of the European Parliament and of the Council of 8 June 2000 on certain legal aspects of information society services, in particular electronic commerce, in the Internal Market, Articles 12-15.

[8] Some critics may point out the differences between the public's perceptions of the public benefit provided by Internet intermediaries (whose activities are generally perceived as beneficial to society) and online gambling providers (whose contributions to the larger societal good are debated).

including freedom of speech and national sovereignty. Further challenges are practical and technological, such as the possibility that users will evade geolocation tools installed by website operators. Still other challenges are political, such as overcoming public opposition to a strengthening of enforcement on the Internet. This chapter identifies and analyzes these various difficulties and suggests that they could all be successfully addressed.

Before outlining the individual provisions of the proposed Convention, this chapter offers some general thoughts about the motivations for an online gambling convention. Part I explains the suitability of online gambling for international action; both the Internet and gambling itself pose transnational challenges that imply an international solution. Part II discusses the question of the proper timing for the proposal and addresses the argument that the proposal may be premature, given the current variability of national and sub-national gambling regulations. It is precisely because countries are currently searching for viable solutions to online gambling regulation that this Convention would be timely. Part III presents the individual provisions of the proposed Convention, article by article. Each provision is justified, explained and discussed in view of its implementation. The Conclusions address potential arguments that critics may raise in opposition to the proposed Convention, including the lack of incentives for some countries to sign and adhere to the Convention, and contemplate the possible advantages of concluding the Convention within the World Trade Organization ("WTO") framework.

THE SUITABILITY OF ONLINE GAMBLING FOR AN INTERNATIONAL CONVENTION

With few exceptions, online gambling has been debated at national levels rather than at the international level. The Antigua and Barbuda complaint filed with the WTO against the United States and the arbitration proceedings that followed are an example of online gambling being debated at the international level.[9] In the European Union ("EU"), online gambling is not regulated at the EU level *per se*,[10] but it has been subject to decisions by the Court of Justice of the European Union,[11] and online gambling has

---

[9] WTO Dispute DS285; Request for Consultations by Antigua and Barbuda filed on March 27, 2003, WT/DS285/1. *See also* Isaac Wohl, *The Antigua-United States Online Gambling Dispute*, Journal of International Commerce and Economics, July 2009, *available at* http://www.usitc.gov/publications/332/journals/online_gambling_dispute.pdf (last visited Mar. 30, 2012); I. NELSON ROSE, MARTIN D. OWENS, JR., INTERNET GAMING LAW, 252-265 (2d ed. 2009). *See also* Statement of Jay Cohen, President, Antiguan Online Gaming Association, Hearing before the Committee on Financial Services, U.S. House of Representatives, 111th Cong., No. 111-92, December 3, 2009, Appendix, pp. 235-236.

[10] For EU legislation affecting online gambling *see* Green Paper on On-line Gambling in the Internal Market, COM(2011) 128 final, March 24, 2011, section 1.2, pp. 10-13 [hereinafter "Green Paper"].

[11] E.g., Dickinger and Ömer, Case C-347/09, September 15, 2011; Sjöberg and Gerdin, Joined Cases C-447/08 and C-448/08, July 8, 2010; Markus Stoβ and others, Joined Cases

also been addressed by the European Commission and the European Parliament.[12] As the WTO and EU examples show, there are international and transnational legal frameworks that apply to online gambling.[13] For now, however, online gambling regulations are primarily a matter of national or state law. Nevertheless, online gambling is suitable for an international convention, as explained in this section.

The problem of any national regulation on the Internet, including the regulation of online gambling, lies in the inability of a country to enforce its regulations against persons or entities outside the country when those persons or entities commit acts outside the country that cause effects inside the country. For a country to be able to regulate effectively, its regulators must be able to prohibit operations by those who do not comply with its regulations. However, regulators can only enforce regulations on the Internet if they have enforcement power over a party (either directly against a website operator or indirectly against an intermediary)—meaning that the party's officers, and/or its assets, including its servers, must be located within the regulating jurisdiction for enforcement actions to be effective.[14] In fact, under such conditions, the regulation of an activity on the Internet can *de facto* expand with no territorial limits; a regulator may require a party to act in a certain manner on the Internet regardless of where any particular content is accessible.[15]

Concerns about the limitations of enforcement on the Internet have led jurisdictions to require that online gambling operators locate their servers within the countries' territories if they want to obtain an online gambling license in these countries. For example, Nevada and the Isle of Man both require that online gambling operators licensed by their jurisdictions locate their servers in the jurisdictions' territories.[16] The Gaming

---

C-316/07, C-358/07 to C-360/07, C-409/07 and C-410/07, September 8, 2010. *See also* Martin Lycka, *Online Gambling: Towards A Transnational Regulation?*, 15(4) Gaming Law Review and Economics 179, 186-187 (2011) (discussing relevant case law of the Court of Justice of the European Union).

[12] Green Paper, *supra* note 10. For other activities of the European Commission in the area of online gambling *see* Gambling, The EU Single Market, European Commission, *available at* http://ec.europa.eu/internal_market/services/gambling_en.htm (last visited March 29, 2012); Lycka, *supra* note 11, pp. 187-189 (on the activities of the European Commission in the area of gambling). *See also* European Parliament Resolution of 15 November 2011 on online gambling in the Internal Market, 2011/2084(INI).

[13] Of course, given the maturation of the European Union it is arguable that any EU-level actions should be viewed at this point as more akin to actions taken by a federal country than a regional organization.

[14] Naturally, parties may comply with regulation voluntarily and there are a variety of reasons for them to do so. On voluntary compliance in general *see, e.g.*, MARKETA TRIMBLE, GLOBAL PATENTS: LIMITS OF TRANSNATIONAL ENFORCEMENT 132 (2012).

[15] This is the phenomenon that Michael Geist described as the rule of cyberlaw 2.0. Michael Geist, *Cyberlaw 2.0*, 44 BCLR 323, 357 (2003).

[16] *See, e.g.*, Regulations of the Nevada Gaming Commission and State Gaming Control Board, section 14.010.10, as of March 12, 2012 ("The core components of an interactive gaming system, including servers and databases running the games on the interactive

Regulators European Forum has recommended that "those ... licensed [to operate online gambling] ... be required to establish their operation in the territory of the jurisdiction concerned so that the operation can be properly controlled an[d] policed."[17] Naturally, these types of requirements place significant limitations on global enterprises that intend to utilize cloud computing for their services or have other legitimate reasons why they might wish to locate their servers or other assets outside a particular licensing jurisdiction.

More importantly, even if a regulator imposes an obligation on online gambling operators to place their servers or other assets in the particular country to qualify for a license, some operators choose not to apply for the license. Instead, these operators have assets located outside of the regulator's jurisdiction but still provide online gambling to users connecting to the Internet from the regulator's jurisdiction. In this familiar scenario, the regulator has very limited options on how to exclude such operators from operating in the regulator's territory; the regulator cannot enforce any regulations against the operator *directly* if the regulator has no actual enforcement power over the operator.[18]

Countries have attempted to work around their inabilities to enforce their regulations on the Internet over parties outside their enforcement power through various means, and not only in the online gambling area. China uses its "Great Firewall" to prevent users in China from accessing prohibited websites outside China,[19] and other countries have mandated content filtering by Internet service providers, such as cable companies that connect users to the Internet, to make content unavailable to users who connect to the Internet through their services.[20] In the United States

---

gaming system and storing game and interactive gaming account information, must be located in the State of Nevada except as otherwise permitted by the chairman or his designee."). *See also* Statement by Mary Williams, Chief Secretary, Isle of Man Government, Hearing before the Committee on Financial Services, U.S. House of Representatives, 111th Cong., No. 111-92, December 3, 2009, Appendix, p. 253 ("A competent regulator of internet gambling must be able to impose effective sanctions against unregulated or non-conforming operators. The key officers and employees of the licensee must be located in the Isle of Man... The licensee's data servers also must be located in the jurisdiction..."). *See also* Lycka, *supra* note 11, pp. 189 (listing Estonia, France, Bulgaria, Poland, and Romania as examples of countries that require online gambling servers to be located in their territories, and suggesting that the requirement might be incompatible with EU law).

[17] GREF Position Statement on Gambling on the Internet, *supra* note 3, par. 3.

[18] *See, e.g.,* Report by Mr. Oxley to Accompany H.R. 4411, 109th Cong., Rept. 109-412, 2006, p. 9 ("According to the [American Gaming Association], its major concern is that offshore Internet gambling sites 'frustrate important state policies, including restrictions on the availability of gaming within each State.'").

[19] For a description of the firewall *see, e.g.,* Jyh-An Lee, Ching-Yi Liu, *Forbidden City Enclosed by the Great Firewall: The Law and Power of Internet Filtering in China*, 13 Minnesota J. L. Sci. & Tech. 125, 130-135 (2012). On other examples of nationwide filtering of the Internet by governments *see also id.*, 142-143.

[20] Jonathan Zittrain, Benjamin Edelman, *Documentation of Internet Filtering Worldwide*, Berkman Center for Internet & Society, Harvard Law School, *available at* http://cyber.law.

authorities have taken action against online gambling operators by seizing their domain names[21] and by targeting financial institutions used by the gambling operators.

Each of these means of enforcement on the Internet presents difficulties. Seizures of domain names are not very effective against operators who have no interest in conducting legal business in the jurisdiction that seized their domain name; the operator can merely continue to do business under a different domain name. Financial institutions, such as payment processors, have struggled to comply with laws that enforce anti-gambling regulations through the institutions.[22] Firewalls and filtering by service providers raise serious human and constitutional rights issues;[23] the Court of Justice of the European Union recently held that an obligation to implement time--unlimited general filtering violates the rights of both Internet users and Internet service providers.[24] The Stop Online Piracy Act proposed in the United States has been attacked on similar grounds.[25]

With firewalls and filtering condemned for potentially violating fundamental rights, and enforcement through financial institutions criticized for the difficulties that the enforcement causes in practice, the least controversial and most straightforward method for achieving website oper-

---

harvard.edu/filtering/ (last visited July 27, 2011).

[21] E.g., Commonwealth of Kentucky v. 141 Internet Domain Names, Franklin Circuit Court, 08-CI-1409, Order of Forfeiture of Domain Defendants, March 8, 2012. For a review of laws applicable to seizures *see* Jack Mellyn, *"Reach Out and Touch Someone": The Growing Use of Domain Name Seizure as A Vehicle for the Extraterritorial Enforcement of U.S. Law*, 42 Geo. J. Int'l L. 1241 (2011). To the consternation of those who oppose seizures of domain names, the Internet Corporation for Assigned Names and Numbers (ICANN), which administers the domain name system, published a Guidance for Preparing Domain Name Orders, Seizures & Takedowns, *available at* http://www.icann.org/en/about/staff/security/guidance-domain-seizures-07mar12-en.pdf (last visited Mar. 30, 2012).

[22] *See, e.g.,* Hearing before the Committee on Financial Services, U.S. House of Representatives, 111th Cong., No. 111-146, July 21, 2010, comments by Edwin Williams, President and CEO of Discovery Federal Credit Union, p. 23; Testimony by Edwin Williams, *id.*, Appendix, pp. 58-61; Testimony of Wayne Abernathy on behalf of the American Bankers Association, Hearing before the Subcommittee on Domestic and International Monetary Policy, Trade, and Technology of the Committee on Financial Services, U.S. House of Representatives, April 2, 2008, No. 110-102, Appendix, pp. 46-58.

[23] *See, e.g.,* Opinion by Advocate General Pedro Cruz Villalon in Scarlet Extended SA v. Société belge des auteurs, compositeurs et éditeurs SCRL (Sabam), Court of Justice of the European Union, C-70/10, April 14, 2011; Wendy Seltzer, *Free Speech Unmoored in Copyright's Safe Harbor: Chilling Effects of the DMCA on the First Amendment*, 24 Harv. J.L. & Tech. 171 (2010); Christoph B. Graber, *Internet Creativity, Communicative Freedom and a Constitutional Rights Theory Response to "Code is Law,"* i-call Working Paper, November 2010, p. 5, *available at* http://ssrn.com/abstract=1737630 (last visited February 6, 2011).

[24] Scarlet Extended SA v. Société Belge des Auteurs, Compositeurs et Éditeurs SCRL (SABAM), Case C-70/10, November 24, 2011; Belgische Vereiniging van Auteurs, Componisten en Uitgevers CVBA (SABAM) v. Netlog NV, Case C-360/10, February 16, 2012.

[25] Stop Online Piracy Act, H.R. 3261, 112th Cong. (SOPA); Laurence H. Tribe, *The "Stop Online Piracy Act" (SOPA) Violates the First Amendment, available at* http://www.scribd.com/doc/75153093/Tribe-Legis-Memo-on-SOPA-12-6-11-1 (last visited May 9, 2012).

ators' compliance with territorially defined laws is through geolocation. Geolocation tools installed by website operators determine the location of a user and allow the operators to tailor content accessible to a user based on the user's location.[26] Geolocation can use data that a user self-reports and/or Internet protocol information;[27] however, additional data, such as the duration of ping requests, or GPS or Wi-Fi information, may also assist in identifying a user's location. A number of vendors offer to website operators geolocation tools with varying degrees of sophistication and accuracy.[28] Website operators use geolocation for targeted advertising, price differentiation, and prevention of fraud, for example.

With increasing frequency, website operators employ geolocation tools not only voluntarily—for example, to enhance user experience or improve transaction security—but also mandatorily, to comply with territorially defined legal obligations, whether the obligations arise under contract or from legislation. Legislators, regulators, and law enforcement agencies have begun to consider and accept geolocation tools as the standard means for achieving compliance with territorially defined regulation on the Internet. The Italian government, for example, requires website operators to use geolocation tools to prevent users located in Italy from accessing certain online gambling content that is prohibited in Italy.[29] In Germany, several courts have

---

[26] Today, geolocation tools rely on IP addresses; however, in the future, other data may assist operators in determining users' locations. On geolocation in general *see, e.g.,* Trimble, *supra* note 6; Dan Jerker B. Svantesson, *"Imagine There's No Countries": Geo-Identification, the Law, and the Not-So-Borderless Internet,* 10 No. 9 J. INTERNET L. 1 (2007); Kevin F. King, *Geolocation and Federalism on the Internet: Cutting Internet Gambling's Gordian Knot,* 11 COLUM. SCI. & TECH. L. REV. 41 (2010). This chapter leaves aside the discussion of problems with verifying other user characteristics, such as age. Some technological solutions combine geolocation with verification of other information about the user; for example, SafetyNet combines geolocation with a fingerprinting device in its verification that both the user and the device (a USB key) are present in the same location. Responsible Gaming Networks Pty Ltd., Safety Net, http://www.responsible.com.au/page/internet_solution.html (last visited June 14, 2012).

[27] For an explanation of Internet protocol addresses *see, e.g.,* Trimble, *supra* note 6, 594-597.

[28] *E.g.,* Neustar (former Quova), http://www.quova.com/ (last visited May 22, 2012); GeoComply, http://geocomply.com/ (last visited May 22, 2012); Responsible Gaming Networks Pty Ltd., Safety Net, http://www.responsible.com.au/page/internet_solution.html (last visited June 14, 2012).

[29] According to Quova, one geolocation tools provider, "[g]eolocation technology is a requirement in online licensing applications in Italy. [...] An operator wishing to obtain an online gaming licence in Italy is required to note during its license application the technology that will be used for geolocation. [...] The use of geolocation technology is required in order to enable an operator to identify the geographical origin of the player who attempts to access the gaming website. This is needed in order to prevent Italians having [sic] access to non-authorised sites managed by the same operator. [...] France has studied Italy's model and has developed a similar system which is expected to come into force some time during the year." *Geolocation; Ensuring Compliance with Online Gaming Regulations,* Quova, 2010, p. 6.

accepted geolocation as "a viable and technically feasible method of determining website visitors' locations,"[30] and have ordered website operators to use geolocation tools to limit access to certain content from particular German states.[31] In an agreement between the U.S. Attorney's Office for the Southern District of New York and Poker-Stars, an online gambling company operating out of the Isle of Man,[32] the U.S. Attorney's Office required that PokerStars "utilize geographic blocking technology relating to I.P. addresses."[33]

Although geolocation and the filtering of content by website operators based on user location defeats the borderlessness of the Internet,[34] enforcement problems remain. Utilizing geolocation for the purposes of compliance with territorially defined laws requires that a website operator install sufficiently effective geolocation tools to filter content based on a user's location. If operators from outside a jurisdiction do not install tools and do not filter content voluntarily (or do not do so properly)—and thereby allow users from the jurisdiction to access content that is illegal in that jurisdiction—then regulators will often be powerless to stop them. Regulators in the jurisdiction have no power to enforce the requirement to geolocate and filter if the regulators have no enforcement power over the operator (meaning that the regulators have no access to the operator's officers, assets, or servers).

In such a situation—and absent enforcement against a third party such as an Internet service provider or a payment processor—the jurisdiction will need to obtain assistance from other jurisdictions that do have the requisite enforcement power over the operator. Facilitating this assistance is the primary goal of the Convention proposed in this chapter. While the regulation of the online gambling industry can also benefit from other aspects of international cooperation,[35] cooperation among countries in enforcement is the most significant reason to consider this international Convention.

---

[30] Oberverwaltungsgericht Nordrhein-Westfalen, 13 B 646/10, July 2, 2010. The decision refers to other German cases in which the German courts agreed that geolocation may be used to comply with their territorially limited decisions. *See also* Oberverwaltungsgericht Nordrhein-Westfalen, 13 B 676/10, July 13, 2010.

[31] But *cf.* earlier opinions by German courts concerning geolocation, *e.g.* Oberverwaltungsgericht Lüneburg, 11 ME 399/08, April 3, 2009. "[I]t is not without a question whether at this time enough technically matured possibilities exist to exclude the internet access only from Lower Saxony." *Id.*

[32] PokerStars, http://www.pokerstars.net/about/ (last visited Apr. 27, 2011).

[33] A letter by the U.S. Attorney for the Southern District of New York re United States v. Pokerstars, et. al., 11 Civ. 2564 (LBS), April 19, 2011, *available at* http://www.rakeback. com/images/doj-pokerstars-domain-name-reinstatement.pdf (last visited Apr. 25, 2011), p. 1. In this case, the U.S. government's leverage over the company was the company's U.S.-registered domain name.

[34] *See infra* for a discussion of the evasion of geolocation.

[35] *See, e.g.*, European Parliament Resolution of 15 November 2011 on online gambling in the Internal Market, 2011/2084(INI) (suggesting cooperation in setting common standards for operators or a framework directive at the EU level; id., par. 15).

Online gambling is only one of the types of Internet conduct for which international cooperation could facilitate effective enforcement—any other conduct on the Internet faces the same enforcement problems that online gambling does. Online gambling, however, is particularly suited to pave the way for a model international convention on enforcement of national laws because countries have a strong and shared desire to enforce their online gambling laws. Notwithstanding the significant differences among jurisdictions in their views on gambling, there seems to be a common understanding that any regulation or prohibition of gambling activities must function effectively.[36] This understanding emanates from the strong public policies that underlie countries' approaches to gambling: moral perceptions,[37] concerns for the protection of consumers (players)[38] and public health,[39] the desire for tax revenue,[40] the need to prevent crime,[41] and other policies. An equilibrium among the various public policies shapes each country's legislative and regulatory solutions for gambling; national equilibria vary according to each country's historical, social, cultural and political makeup, and may be influenced by a country's current fiscal situation.

The differences among national solutions to online gambling do not prevent countries from negotiating an international convention to facilitate the effective enforcement of laws and regulations on online gambling.

---

[36] *See, e.g.*, Statement of Tom Malkasian, Vice-Chairman of the Board, Commerce Casino, Hearing before the Committee on Financial Services, U.S. House of Representatives, No. 111-146, 111th Cong., July 21, 2010, Appendix; Green Paper, *supra* note 10 ("In view of recent trends, restrictions imposed to online gambling by each Member State can be expected to continue to vary considerably, with the effect that what is, or will become, considered a legal offer in one Member State will continue to be deemed 'unlawful' (in that it has not been implicitly or explicitly authorised) in the territory of another Member State. It follows that, subject to the legal conditions set out above, effective enforcement will be essential to ensure the achievement of the objectives of a Member State's gambling policy." *Id.*, 7.)

[37] *See, e.g.*, Dickinger and Ömer, Court of Justice of the European Union, C-347/09, September 15, 2011, par. 45; Devaney, *supra* note 2, p. 274.

[38] *See, e.g.*, Dickinger and Ömer, *supra* note 37, par. 100.

[39] *See, e.g.*, Green Paper, *supra* note 10, pp. 19-23; Julia Hörnle, *Social Policy and Regulatory Models*, in JULIA HÖRNLE & BRIGITTE ZAMMIT, CROSS-BORDER ONLINE GAMBLING LAW AND POLICY (2010), 10-77, at 11-17; Executive Summary of the First Written Submission of the United States, WT/DS285 (Nov. 14, 2003), *available at* http://www.antiguawto.com/wto/11_US_Exec%20sum_1st_Written_Submissn_14Nov03.pdf (last visited Oct. 9, 2011); Kindt & Joy, *supra* note 2, pp. 114-116; Valasek, *supra* note 2, pp. 762-765.

[40] *See, e.g.*, the Hearing before the Committee on Financial Services, U.S. House of Representatives, No. 111-146, 111th Cong., July 21, 2010.

[41] *See, e.g.*, Green Paper, *supra* note 10, pp. 26-29; Hörnle, *Social Policy and Regulatory Models*, *supra* note 39, pp. 17-22; Executive Summary of the Second Written Submission of the United States, United States—Measures Affecting the Cross-Border Supply of Gambling and Betting Services, WT/DS285 (Jan. 16, 2004), *available at* http://www.ustr.gov/webfm_send/794 (last visited Oct. 9, 2011); *Liga Portuguesa de Futebol Profissional v. Departamento de Jogos da Santa Casa da Misericórdia de Lisboa*, Court of Justice of the European Communities, C-42/07, September 8, 2009, par. 62-72; Kindt & Joy, *supra* note 2, pp. 118-121; Valasek, *supra* note 2, pp. 765-767.

As opposed to the many international conventions that exist specifically to harmonize national laws, this Convention would be conducted to respect and maintain the differences in national approaches to online gambling and permit countries to enforce their individual solutions. All approaches would enjoy equal standing, regardless of whether online gambling would be permitted and regulated, or prohibited altogether.

It is possible that countries that wish to permit and regulate online gambling have much common ground, and that there is room for negotiating an agreement that would transcend the "agree to disagree" framework of the limited convention that is proposed in this chapter. In fact, the increasing internationalization of the gambling industry suggests that online gambling regulation would benefit from cooperation among the regulators of countries that permit online gambling, particularly in the areas of licensing and technological standardization. For example, the recent developments concerning Full Tilt Poker revealed that regulators should cooperate if they wish to be successful in regulating businesses that operate in multiple countries.[42] From an operator perspective, cooperation among regulators could bring large savings in resources. A global operator such as WMS Industries, one of the leading manufacturers in the gambling industry and one that holds licenses in more than 380 jurisdictions,[43] would benefit from an agreement among national regulators on the unification of licensing standards, or at least the introduction of a uniform licensing application format. Technological standardization is another clear candidate for international cooperation among gambling regulators. The proposed Convention would not foreclose any possibilities for further conventions or agreements that would complement this proposed Convention or align any aspects of online gambling regulation not addressed in this Convention.

The Timing of a Convention

An international convention that would respect the differences in national approaches to online gambling should be desirable to all countries, regardless of their positions on online gambling. The Convention is timely regardless of the fact that some countries wish to permit online gambling, some wish to prohibit it, and some are undecided; it is timely even though disagreements persist within individual countries about whether online gambling should be permitted.[44] Despite the ongoing uncertainty about

---

[42] Full Tilt Poker Review, Report by Peter Dean to the Alderney Gambling Control Commission, March 26, 2012, *available at* http://www.gamblingcontrol.org/userfiles/file/FTP%20Report%2026%20March%202012.pdf (last visited Apr. 1, 2012); *Full Tilt Poker Licence Revoked by Alderney Authority*, BBC News, September 29, 2011, *available at* http://www.bbc.co.uk/news/business-15115224 (last visited Apr. 1, 2012).

[43] Scott Schweinfurth, Executive Vice President, WMS Industries, at the 2011 IAGA International Gaming Conference, Las Vegas, September 30, 2011.

[44] The dynamics of the developments in the regulation of online gambling are evidenced

the current status and future development of online gambling regulation in some countries, this is the best moment to propose and negotiate an international convention on online gambling precisely because online gambling, at least from the global perspective, is in its formative stages.

National online gambling regulations differ, as do levels of national expertise in regulating gambling. Although some commentators have observed a general trend toward a liberalization of online gambling,[45] some anti-gambling stronghold jurisdictions maintain their positions against online gambling,[46] and even the countries that regulate online gambling differ in their approaches to regulation. The jurisdictions that regulate online gambling often have pioneering regulations that have made their jurisdictions popular for the registration of online gambling operators. For instance, the Mohawk Territory-Kahnawake Gaming Commission in Canada has regulated Internet gambling since 1999.[47] Alderney,[48] Gibraltar,[49] the Isle of Man,[50] and Malta[51] also are among the well-known jurisdictions that regulate online gambling. Jurisdictions that make certain gambling illegal differ in whom and in what conduct they penalize. For example, U.S. legislation permits intrastate online gambling[52] but makes gambling across state lines unlawful by prohibiting the "acceptance of any financial instrument for unlawful Internet gambling."[53] South Africa regulates online gambling and penalizes not only companies that provide illegal online gambling in South Africa, but it also imposes liability on Internet service providers who allow users in South Africa to access illegal online gambling websites and makes users who gamble on such websites liable.[54] Within individual countries, state or provincial legis-

---

by the fact that a helpful November 2008 overview of various approaches to online gambling regulation is significantly outdated in March 2012. Hörnle, *Social Policy and Regulatory Models, supra* note 39, p. 29.

[45] *See, e.g.,* Lycka, *supra* note 11, p. 180 (suggesting that "the regulatory trend leans towards liberalization, rather than towards restriction of online gambling markets").

[46] *See also supra* note 3.

[47] Kahnawake Gaming Commission, http://www.gamingcommission.ca/faq.htm / (last visited May 22, 2012).

[48] Alderney Gambling Control Commission, http://www.gamblingcontrol.org/ (last visited March 30, 2012).

[49] Remote Gambling, http://www.gibraltar.gov.gi/remotegambling (last visited March 30, 2012).

[50] The Isle of Man Gambling Supervision Commission, http://www.gov.im/gambling/ (last visited March 30, 2012).

[51] Malta's Lotteries & Gaming Authority, http://www.lga.org.mt/lga/ (last visited March 30, 2012).

[52] Unlawful Internet Gambling Enforcement Act of 2006, 31 U.S.C. § 5362(10)(B) and (C).

[53] Unlawful Internet Gambling Enforcement Act of 2006, 31 U.S.C. § 5363; *see also* Report by Mr. Oxley to Accompany H.R. 4411, 109th Cong., Rept. 109-412, 2006, p. 8 ("The … Act … prohibits the acceptance of any bank instrument for unlawful Internet gambling."). For other related legislation in the United States *see* the Report by Mr. Sensenbrenner to Accompany H.R. 4411, 109th Cong., Rept. 109-412, 2006, pp. 8-9.

[54] In South Africa all three actors—the gambling website operator, the Internet service

lation on online gambling may differ. The United States and Germany are examples of federal countries in which individual states disagree on online gambling policies; this makes a consensus on any gambling regulation at the federal level difficult, if not impossible. In Germany, during the negotiations of the 2007 treaty among the individual Länder, some of the Länder were in favor of legalizing online gambling, while others resisted.[55] The final wording of the 2007 treaty stipulated that the Länder would not legalize online gambling.[56] A new treaty signed by fifteen of the sixteen Länder in December 2011 liberalizes online gambling to some extent.[57] The sixteenth Land, Schleswig-Holstein, had adopted its own law regulating online gambling in September 2011.[58]

In the United States, bills have been introduced at the federal level to both legalize and regulate some or all forms of Internet gambling;[59] however, individual states hold opposing views on online gambling. For example, Nevada undertook steps toward legalizing online gambling as early as 2001,[60] but Utah has consistently voiced strong opposition to any form of gambling. In March 2012, Utah adopted an act making a person "guilty of gambling" and making gambling and "intentionally provid[ing] or offer[ing] to provide any form of Internet or online gambling" punishable as a misdemeanor.[61] Additionally, the Utah act states that "[w]hether or not any federal law is enacted that authorizes Internet gambling in the

---

provider, and the end user—are liable for illegal online gambling. *See On-line Gambling Transactions Are Outlawed in South Africa*, GAUTENG GAMBLING BOARD, *available at* http://www.ggb.org.za/index.php?option=com_content&view=article&id=3: news-flash-2&catid=3:newsflash (last visited Nov. 19, 2011). Compare this with the situation in the United States, where the Unlawful Internet Gambling Enforcement Act of 2006 does not apply to players who place bets. Gerd Alexander, *The U.S. on Tilt: Why the Unlawful Internet Gambling Enforcement Act Is A Bad Bet*, 2008 DUKE L. & TECH. REV. 6, 29 (2008). *See also* Federal Wire Act, 18 U.S.C. § 1084 (2006); S. Rep. No. 588, 87th Cong., 1st Sess. (1961) (and its associated legislative history). *Cf.* also Strafgesetzbuch [StGB] [Penal Code], May 15, 1871, Reichsgesetzblatt [RGBl] 127, as amended, § 284-85 (on unlawful operating of gambling and participating in unlawful gambling).

[55] Julia Hörnle, *Social Policy and Regulatory Models, supra* note 39, pp. 36-37.

[56] *Id.*, p. 37.

[57] Caroline Freisfeld, *Glücksspielstaatsvertrag ist unterzeichnet*, Frankfurter Allgemeine, December 15, 2011, *available at* http://www.faz.net/aktuell/wirtschaft/lotto-und-wetten-gluecksspielstaatsvertrag-ist-unterzeichnet-11564729.html (last visited March 30, 2012).

[58] In January 2013 Schleswig-Holstein repealed the law and decided to join the treaty. *Schleswig-Holstein schließt sich Glücksspielvertrag an*, Reuters Deutschland, January 24, 2013, *available at* http://de.reuters.com/article/domesticNews/idDEBEE90N03V20130124 (last visited January 26, 2013).

[59] Internet Gambling Regulation, Consumer Protection, and Enforcement Act, H.R. 1174, 112th Cong.; Internet Gambling Prohibition, Poker Consumer Protection, and Strengthening UIGEA Act, H.R. 2366, 112th Cong.

[60] *See, e.g., Nevada's Online Gaming Regulations, Changes Adopted December 22, 2011, available at* http://gaming.unlv.edu/reports/NV_online_reg_changes.pdf (last visited May 29, 2012).

[61] Internet Gambling, H.B. 108, Section 2(3)(a).

states, this section acts as this state's prohibition of any gambling, including Internet gambling, in this state."[62]

Although online gambling regulation enforcement problems are not at the root of all disagreements about regulation, online enforcement problems are certainly among the major concerns that critics of online gambling raise,[63] and the concerns contribute to confusion about the feasibility of effective regulation of online gambling. If enforcement concerns could be removed from national discussions on online gambling regulation, an agreement on national regulation might be easier to achieve, meaning that the current unsettled state of affairs would be assisted by an international convention of the kind proposed here.

Gambling operators who want to comply with national laws are ready for online gambling to be permitted and regulated in more countries, particularly in the United States. Manufacturers are creating applications for online gambling and many have tested their applications in either jurisdictions that permit online gambling or other jurisdictions as games not for stakes. For example, IGT provides online gambling applications outside the United States in countries that permit online gambling,[64] WMS sells online gaming applications in the United States where they are available on iTunes for users to play as non-gambling entertainment, and Aristocrat supplies online gaming applications to U.S. land-based casinos that want to prepare for any future legalization of online gambling in the United States. Additionally, some operators outside of the traditional gambling industry are engaged in activities that appear to be in preparation for legalized gambling; they offer non-gambling games on their websites or on social media websites.[65]

Given the diversity of national opinions, it would be pointless to promote any uniform international approach to online gambling. However, a proposal that would make it possible to enforce differing national regulations on the Internet could facilitate the development of national laws on online gambling by removing the existing cross-border enforcement obstacles that discourage national legislatures from adopting national solutions.

The Convention proposed here would benefit even those jurisdictions with sophisticated regulatory frameworks for online gambling already in place. These jurisdictions could continue to offer advantageous conditions to online gambling operators while they also offered their turnkey regulatory solutions and other incentives to new operators to induce the new

---

[62] Internet Gambling, H.B. 108, Section 2(5).

[63] See, e.g., Kindt & Joy, supra note 2, p. 149; see also supra note 18.

[64] IGT, Online and Mobile Gaming Partners, available at http://www.igt.com/gb-en/games/online-and-mobile-gaming-partners.aspx (last visited Oct. 8, 2011).

[65] Zynga serves as an example here. Paul Tassi, Zynga Wants to Get Into the Online Gambling Game, Forbes, January 23, 2012, available at at http://www.forbes.com/sites/insertcoin/2012/01/23/zynga-wants-to-get-into-the-online-gambling-game/ (last visited Mar. 29, 2012).

operators to base their operations in these jurisdictions. Operators would want to be based in sophisticated jurisdictions to benefit from those jurisdictions' favorable online gambling regulation and enjoy the convenience of dealing with experienced gambling regulators. To the extent that other countries tolerate the sophisticated jurisdictions' regulations, the sophisticated jurisdictions could regulate worldwide the conduct of the online gambling operators licensed by their jurisdictions.[66]

The Convention will constrain the worldwide reach of a particular country's regulation because the Convention creates an obligation for countries to assist each other in the enforcement of their respective national online gambling regulations. However, the Convention itself does not foreclose the possibility that operators may benefit from one country's regulation worldwide. As long as other countries do not request assistance from the regulating jurisdiction, operators in the regulating jurisdiction will be governed globally by the law of the regulating jurisdiction. Some countries already permit online gambling operators to operate in their territories without a national license as long as they hold a valid license in some specified country,[67] and this would continue to be possible even under the proposed Convention. For the jurisdictions in which gambling regulations require that licensees comply with the laws of foreign countries, the proposed Convention would not change the playing field but, as explained below,[68] only enhance the ability of local regulators to enforce their own regulatory framework.

Proposal for the Convention

This section suggests the content of individual Convention provisions and identifies and analyzes difficulties and concerns that the proposed solutions generate.

Article 1 – The Scope of the Convention

The Convention establishes rules for cooperation among countries—parties to the Convention—in enforcing national rules concerning online gambling. Countries remain free to regulate gambling in any manner they deem proper; this freedom applies also to states and other smaller jurisdictions within a federation or confederation. The freedom to maintain its own national gambling laws does not mean that a country will be able to comply with the Convention without implementing the Convention into its national laws. Instead, it is likely that the implementation will require existing national laws and regulations to be adapted or new laws to be adopted to comply with and assist in the functioning of

---

[66] Note that the proposed Convention does not address retrospective remedies; it provides only for the enforcement of prospective remedies—injunctions.

[67] Green Paper, *supra* note 10, p. 15.

[68] *See infra* Article 4.

the Convention. However, the implementation will not require countries to change their positions on the legality or illegality of online gambling. The countries that wish to permit and regulate online gambling and the countries that wish to prohibit online gambling may both continue to maintain their positions.

The Convention requires that countries respect various positions on online gambling as legitimate choices to be made by nations, and that the Convention operate equally without regard to which position a country takes on online gambling. The principle of non-discrimination among countries based on their stance on online gambling is important; countries should not give preference to assistance requests[69] from countries that share their position on online gambling or delay requests from countries that take a different position.

The Convention concerns only online gambling; it is not intended to apply to land-based gambling. This restriction on the scope of the Convention is meant to prevent its provisions from being applied to land-based gambling issues; any attempts to extend the application of the provisions to land-based gambling might create unnecessary controversies that would impede the adoption of the Convention. However, if the negotiators to the Convention decide that some of the provisions of the Convention, such as the provision on cooperation in the exchange of information, would advance the international regulation of land-based gambling as well, parts of the Convention could also apply to land-based gambling.

Article 2 – Definitions

One of the most challenging tasks for the proposed Convention—as it is for any international convention—is the drafting of definitions, because definitions specify the scope of the Convention. The definitions should aim at the highest common denominator, the most comprehensive scope on which countries can agree, and would therefore not necessarily originate from national laws or other documents, although these are certainly places where negotiators could seek guidance.

"Online"

Whether the term "online" is used or is replaced by some other term, the Convention will apply only to activities that occur on the ubiquitous network that is known as the Internet. Because the term "Internet" describes only one of the protocols that are used on the network, a more precise definition must be formulated.

International treaty and national law provisions that concern the Internet use general descriptions. For example, the Convention on Cybercrime applies to "computer systems," which are defined as "any device

---

[69] *See infra* Article 4 for a discussion of enforcement requests.

or a group of interconnected or related devices, one or more of which, pursuant to a program, performs automatic processing of data[.]"[70] This definition is too broad for the purposes of this Convention because the definition would include intranet gambling—for example, gambling offered on hand-held devices within the internal network of a land-based gambling operation. This type of gambling should remain outside the scope of this limited Convention. The definition that the European Commission proposed in its 2011 Green Paper on On-line Gambling in the Internal Market is similarly broad: "On-line gambling services are any services ... that are provided at a distance, by electronic means and at the individual request of a recipient of services."[71] The definition of the Internet in the Unlawful Internet Gambling Enforcement Act may be closer to the definition appropriate for this Convention: "The term 'Internet' means the international computer network of interoperable packet-switched data networks."[72]

"Gambling"

One of the potentially contentious provisions of the Convention is the provision that will specify what types of gambling will be covered by the Convention. Listing specific games is clearly problematic since new games are being developed constantly; rather, a general definition should be formulated.

In the European Union, the definition in the 2000 E-Commerce Directive excludes from its scope "gambling activities which involve wagering a stake with monetary value in games of chance, including lotteries and betting transactions."[73] The 2006 Unlawful Internet Gambling Act defines gambling as "plac[ing], receiv[ing], or otherwise knowingly transmit[ing] a bet or wager," and specifies the term "bet or wager" in detail.[74] In Nevada, "gambling" (or "gaming") "means to deal, operate, carry on, conduct, maintain or expose for play any game ... defined [by the statute], or to operate an inter-casino linked system."[75] The Nevada statute defines a "game" as "any game played with cards, dice, equipment or any mechanical, electromechanical or electronic device or machine for money, property, checks, credit or any representative of value," and provides a non-exhaustive list of examples of such games.[76] The definition in the Convention should be built on a

---

[70] Convention on Cybercrime, Budapest, November 23, 2011, Article 1(a).

[71] Green Paper, *supra* note 10, p. 14.

[72] Unlawful Internet Gambling Enforcement Act, 31 U.S.C. §5362(5).

[73] Directive 2000/31/EC of the European Parliament and of the Council of June 8, 2000, on certain legal aspects of information society services, in particular electronic commerce, in the Internal Market, Article 1(5)(d).

[74] Unlawful Internet Gambling Enforcement Act, 31 U.S.C. §5362(1) and (10)(A).

[75] N.R.S. §463.0153.

[76] N.R.S. §463.0152.

compromise from among the various national, transnational, and state definitions.[77]

It is important to keep in mind that each definition will be subject to a separate interpretation by each signatory country which may, in the process of implementation, adjust its interpretation to its particular goals. This built-in flexibility for separate interpretations of the definition of the term "gambling" could likely facilitate an agreement on the general formulation of the term.

"Requesting national authority"

According to the enforcement mechanism outlined in the Convention, a country's national authority—the requesting national authority—will send a request for enforcement assistance to another country's national authority—the requested national authority.[78] Ideally, there should be one or a limited number of requesting national authorities per country. The definition should be formulated generally and include an obligation for countries to communicate to a central repository—administered either by the country-depository of the Convention or by the Secretariat[79]—the name and contact details of their national authorities.[80] This mechanism of communications allows countries to efficiently change the designations of their authorities and quickly update contact details whenever necessary.

"Requested national authority"

On the receiving end of the request for enforcement assistance is the requested national authority—the authority that receives requests from other countries' requesting national authorities. While many countries might choose to designate one authority as both their requesting and requested national authority, other countries might decide to designate two different authorities to handle the separate functions. As with the definition of requesting national authority, the definition of requested national authority should be formulated generally and include a requirement that the names and contact details of requested national authorities be communicated to the central authority.[81]

"National regulating authority"

While the enforcement provision employs the terms "requesting national authority" and "requested national authority," other provisions of

---

[77] For examples of other national definitions of the term "gambling" see Lycka, *supra* note 11, p. 180.
[78] See *infra* Article 4 for a discussion of the enforcement assistance.
[79] See *infra* Article 8.
[80] See *infra* Article 7.
[81] See *infra* Article 7.

the Convention will use the term "national regulating authority." In countries with legalized gambling, national authorities will exist to serve as the "national regulating authority." In some countries these authorities may perform all three of the functions of "national regulating," "requesting national," and "requested national" authorities; in other countries these functions may be distributed between two or among three different authorities. Federal countries may designate multiple national regulating authorities—"national" in this case indicating that they are equivalent authorities of a single country, not that they are federal-level authorities. As with the requesting and requested national authorities, the names and contact details of national regulating authorities should be communicated to the central authority.[82]

A problem may arise for countries with no legalized gambling and no existing "national regulating authority" for gambling. To remedy the lack of an existing appropriate authority, the countries would have to appoint *some* national authority, even if it were not gambling related, to perform the functions of the "national regulating authority." In countries that enforce anti-gambling laws, appropriate authorities may emerge within the general law enforcement agencies (such as the justice department, justice ministry, or attorney general's office). In countries with no gambling laws, or countries that have never enforced their anti-gambling laws, new authorities would have to be created or an existing authority would have to be tasked as the national authority within the meaning of the Convention.

Article 3 – Exchange of Relevant Information

To facilitate effective enforcement, countries should cooperate by exchanging relevant information via their national regulating authorities. This exchange of information must be without prejudice to national rules on data protection, whether they be rules on personal data protection (privacy rules) or other rules protecting certain types of data or data in certain situations. Countries should be permitted to deny requests for information if the requests concern protected data, or to postpone delivery of the data, for example if immediate delivery could jeopardize an ongoing criminal investigation.[83]

It is important to maintain the discretion of the country that receives a request for information to deny or postpone the exchange of information. In addition to any legal barriers that may prevent the sharing of information with other jurisdictions, a country's reason for denying an exchange of information may stem from the country's doubt as to whether the request for information is, in fact, motivated by the goals of regulating online gambling and therefore within the scope of this Convention. The Convention

---

[82] *See infra* Article 7.
[83] For a similar provision *see, e.g.*, the Council of Europe's Convention on Cybercrime, Article 27(5).

could provide for a dispute settlement mechanism, as described below,[84] to allow for the resolution of disputes concerning requests for information if the proffered ground for the denial or postponement of information exchange were contested by the requesting country.

Article 4 – Enforcement Assistance

The core of the Convention is the provision on enforcement assistance. Because a country cannot enforce its online gambling regulations against an operator with no assets or other presence in the country, the country must seek assistance from other countries where the operator does have assets or a presence. To effectuate enforcement, the requesting national authority of the country sends a request for assistance to the requested national authority of a country in which the operator has assets or some other presence. Countries that address the online enforcement problem by imposing indirect liability on and effectuating enforcement against third parties, such as payment processors (a solution adopted by the United States), can maintain such liability and enforcement mechanisms. However, the Convention certainly does not require that such indirect liability be imposed, and in fact is designed to facilitate an environment in which the indirect liability of and enforcement against third parties are not necessary.

The functioning of the enforcement assistance can be illustrated as follows: Authorities in country A, which prohibits online poker, discover that operator O offers online poker to users accessing O's website from country A. The authorities in A cannot enforce its regulations against O because O has no assets in A; O operates from country B, where all of its assets and officers are located. Therefore, based on the proposed Convention, A's national requesting authority sends a request to B's national requested authority. In response to A's request, B takes measures to make O use appropriate filters in country B to prevent users in A from connecting to O's online poker site. O would have to use geolocation tools to determine the location of its users and, for any users connecting from A, O would have to adjust the content accessible to these users to meet A's regulations against online poker.

This scenario is only an illustration of the functioning of the mechanism; the enforcement assistance would certainly not be limited to online poker or to a complete denial of access to gambling. For example, other countries may seek an operator's compliance with technological requirements for online slot machines and request that the operator exclude users connecting from such countries from accessing particular slot machines.

The law of the requesting country will determine what decisions by which agency in the requesting country shall trigger the filing of an enforcement assistance request with a requested national authority, and the requesting country's law shall also provide for any appeals or remedies that

---

[84] *See infra* Article 9.

the operator may pursue in the requesting country with regard to the effects of the enforcement assistance request. In the above example, A's law will specify the procedural and substantive requirements necessary for an agency in A to render a decision that causes A's requesting national authority to submit an enforcement assistance request to B's requested national authority. Once B's requested national authority receives the request, B's authority will not scrutinize whether A's request is based on a decision in A that complies with A's procedural and substantive requirements. If operator O wants to object to the submission of the request, O must seek redress in A under A's law. A's requesting national authority would have to notify B's requested national authority if A's decision were to change, in which case B should cease enforcement against O.

The success of the mechanism is predicated on the use of geolocation tools and a limitation of access to content that is based on a user's location. Geolocation and filtering are not new to the gambling industry; for example, some existing online gambling operators already prevent users that connect to the Internet from the United States from connecting to their gambling pages. Online gambling operators also use geolocation tools to prevent fraud. However, the imposition of (as opposed to the voluntary compliance with) an obligation to geolocate in the requested country in order to filter out users from the requesting country presents legal difficulties and could raise concerns over free speech protections and the freedom to conduct business in the requested country. In addition to the legal issues it raises, geolocation-based enforcement is not free from technological problems.

Enforcement of Public Laws Applied by Administrative Agencies

One problem—perhaps the most significant problem—of the proposed enforcement assistance mechanism is that it concerns enforcement of 1) public laws and 2) decisions by administrative agencies. Countries are not obligated to assist each other in enforcing the decisions of their counterpart administrative agencies. Court decisions may often be recognized and enforced because of the principle of comity. Although countries have failed to agree on an international convention to facilitate the recognition and enforcement of foreign judgments,[85] the principle of international comity suggests that, save for exceptional circumstances, countries should recognize and enforce the decisions of courts of other countries.[86] Arbitration

---

[85] The proposal to draft a convention on jurisdiction, recognition and enforcement of foreign judgments in civil and commercial matters encountered great disagreement among the negotiating countries, and resulted in the adoption of a very limited Convention on Choice of Court Agreements. The negotiations of the general convention were reopened in 2012. *See* Ongoing Work on International Litigation and Possible Continuation of the Judgments Project, Preliminary Document No 5 of 5 March 2012, *available at* http://www.hcch.net/upload/wop/gap12pd05e.pdf (last visited Mar. 29, 2012).

[86] For the grounds for the non-recognition of a foreign-country judgment, *see, e.g.,* Uni-

decisions enjoy a greater certainty of enforcement abroad thanks to a wide-ly-adopted and respected international convention on arbitration awards.[87] However, neither the principle of comity nor the international convention on arbitration awards extends to the recognition and enforcement of decisions that arise out of public laws (or laws that are penal in nature)—such as tax laws, for example—or decisions by administrative agencies. Decisions concerning the regulation of online gambling would be both based on public laws and likely rendered by administrative agencies. Although in many countries parties can file appeals with courts against decisions by administrative agencies, the Convention should not require appellate decisions. Because of the instantaneous nature of conduct on the Internet and the weight of public policy concerns that are involved, the Convention should permit a decision by an administrative agency to trigger the enforcement assistance of Article 4 with the understanding that the requested national authority will cease enforcement if the decision in the requesting country is overturned.

As for the decisions of a country's national authorities concerning public laws, other countries may choose to provide assistance to support such decisions; however, it is ultimately a matter for the requested country's authorities to decide as to whether the requested country will cooperate. This discretion ensures that the assistance will not violate the requested country's national legal requirements. For example, a Red Notice issued by the International Criminal Police Organization (Interpol) notifies countries of a person of interest and of the request for a provisional arrest. Although the requested country may arrest the person, the Red Notice does not mandate that the person remain in custody nor that the person automatically be handed over to the requesting country; the national law of the requested country will determine whether the person will remain in custody, and an extradition proceeding will determine whether the person will be extradited to the requesting country.[88] The different result in the case of the proposed Convention is that the decision by a requesting national authority should translate directly into a corresponding action by the requested national authority, with only a minimal basic scrutiny in the requested country; the basic scrutiny should ensure that no significant public policies of the requested country would be offended by the enforcement.

One solution to the problem of the enforcement of decisions concerning the gambling laws of foreign countries is to incorporate into a national law an obligation for gambling operators to comply with the foreign gam-

---

form Foreign-Country Money Judgments Recognition Act, 2005, Section 4.

[87] *See* Convention on the recognition and enforcement of foreign arbitral awards, 1958.

[88] Similarly, when a judicial authority requests the cooperation of a foreign judicial authority through a letter of request or a letter rogatory, the foreign judicial authority should cooperate, but only within the limits of its own country's laws. The decision whether to provide the requested assistance (evidence) lies with the requested national judicial authority. Convention on the Taking of Evidence Abroad in Civil or Commercial Matters, 1970, Articles 9 and 10.

bling laws of all countries in which the operators operate; only if an operator so complies will a country grant an online gambling license to the operator. This solution is known to the industry; for example, under Nevada law, "[a] licensee shall not, in a foreign gaming operation, knowingly ... [v]iolate a foreign, federal, tribal, state, county, city or township law, regulation, ordinance or rule, or any equivalent thereof, concerning the conduct of gaming."[89] In assessing applications for licenses, the Alderney Gambling Commission considers *inter alia* an applicant's character and "the manner in which the applicant currently conducts any form of [online gambling] in any jurisdiction."[90] The Commission "may have regard to any other licence ... allowing the applicant ... to conduct any form of gambling lawfully in ... another jurisdiction,"[91] loss of such a license,[92] and "any penalties or sanctions ... imposed ...by gambling or other regulators outside Alderney."[93] The licensee must notify the Gambling Commission of any changes in the status of the licensee's license in any foreign jurisdiction.[94] Additionally, Alderney imposes obligations on its licensees to comply with foreign online gambling advertising requirements,[95] and to "keep abreast of international developments as they affect the lawfulness" of online gambling to make sure that its licensees do not provide online gambling "where to do so would constitute criminal activity by its customers."[96]

While the incorporation of the obligation to comply with foreign gambling laws solves the problem of enforcement of foreign public laws, the foreign compliance requirement creates a new problem. The incorporation implies that a national regulating authority must assess the legality of the operator's actions in a foreign jurisdiction under that jurisdiction's laws. As the "Black Friday" situation has shown, the assessment of legality under foreign laws may be difficult,[97] and only the national regulating author-

---

[89] N.R.S. 463.720. "A foreign gaming operation" means a gaming operation outside the State of Nevada. N.R.S. 463.680. Originally, the statute required Nevada gaming licensees to obtain approval prior to operating gaming outside of Nevada, with the Gaming Control Board assessing the foreign gaming regulations before approving the licensee's operations in the foreign jurisdiction. Since 1987 the assessment of foreign gaming regulations has not been required, and since 1993 no prior approval for foreign gaming operations has been required for Nevada licensees.

[90] Alderney eGambling Regulations 2009, as amended in 2010 and 2011, *e.g.*, sections 21(1)(a) and (h), 22(1)(b)(i), 41(1)(a), 42(1)(b)(i), 65(1)(a), 66(1)(a) and (h), 67(b)(i), 85(1)(a), 102(1)(a), 122(a).

[91] *Id., e.g.*, sections 21(2) and 41(2)(a), 42(2); for certificates section 58(1)(b)(i), 65(2), 66(2), 85(2).

[92] *Id., e.g.*, section 41(2), 42(2).

[93] *Id., e.g.*, section 41(2)(b).

[94] *Id., e.g.*, sections 4(h)(i), 6(h)(i), 8(1)(e)(i), 60(g)(i).

[95] *Id.*, sections 4(c)(ix), 6(c)(ix), 8(1)(c)(ix), 60(b)(ix).

[96] *Id.*, sections 4(f), 6(f), 8(d), 60(e).

[97] See, e.g., Report by Peter Dean to the Alderney Gambling Control Commission, *26 March 2012, available at* http://www.gamblingcontrol.org/userfiles/file/FTP%20Report%2026%20March%202012.pdf (last visited May 14, 2012) (The Alderney Gambling Control Commission "takes the view, as do other reputable gambling regulators, that it

ity of the foreign country can definitely assess the legality of actions in its jurisdiction. The enforcement assistance proposed in this Convention would enhance laws like the laws of Nevada and Alderney because it would provide a mechanism under which national regulating authorities would be notified of any illegal foreign conduct by their licensees, and it would set a standard for the licensees to follow to comply in a territorially limited manner with foreign regulatory requirements. Once notified of illegal conduct, national regulating authorities could act within the scope of their national laws; they would not enforce foreign public laws or decisions by foreign administrative agencies, but they would enforce their own national laws based on their own decisions.

In a country with a foreign compliance obligation, the national regulating authority may act against an operator as soon as it receives the relevant information under Article 3 of the Convention. While actions by a national regulating authority in response to information obtained under Article 3 would be only a matter of that authority's national law, an action by the requested national authority under Article 4 would be required as an international obligation under the Convention. As noted earlier, the Convention should provide for assistance in enforcing the decisions of administrative agencies with the understanding that any assistance would cease if the requesting national authority notified the requested national authority that the decision of the requesting country's administrative agency had been overturned by an appellate body. In such a case, an operator who had been damaged by the decisions of the requesting country's authorities could pursue a remedy in a proceeding in the requesting country (not in the requested country) based on the requesting country's law.

The Convention must permit the requested national authority to scrutinize the content of a request against its own national public policy and allow for a public policy exception to enforcement of the request; however, the requested national authority cannot deny an enforcement assistance request solely because the request has as its objective the imposition of geolocation and filtering on the operator, because this form of enforcement is accepted by all countries who sign the Convention.[98] The means of achieving compliance with an order to geolocate and filter (*e.g.*, contempt orders) in the requested country will be governed by the law of the requested country. While an operator would not be able to object in the requested country to the requesting national authority's request (only a proceeding in the requesting country would be permitted for that purpose), the operator would be able to raise a public policy objection in the requested country against the enforcement of the request and would be a party to contempt proceedings in the requested country.

---

cannot be responsible for interpreting or enforcing the laws of other jurisdictions." *Id.*, par. 36.). On "Black Friday" in general *see also* I. Nelson Rose, *Poker's Black Friday*, 15 Gaming Law Review and Economics 327 (2011).

[98] *See infra* for a discussion of standards setting for geolocation.

The Convention provides for a possibility for a requested national authority to deny enforcement assistance if the requesting country appears to have a viable means of enforcement against the operator (*e.g.*, against the operator's assets in the requesting country) but uses (or rather misuses) an enforcement assistance request under the Convention. Such a situation could conceivably occur if a requesting country were trying to save resources that it would have to expend to enforce a decision against the operator domestically. The requested national authority may decide *sua sponte* to deny enforcement assistance in this situation or decide to deny enforcement after an objection by the operator (who might have its own reasons for preferring enforcement in the requesting country instead of the requested country). Disputes between countries concerning this type of misuse of enforcement assistance requests could certainly arise and could be subject to the dispute resolution mechanism discussed below.[99]

A Territorially Limited Remedy and Free Speech Concerns

The remedy that the Convention seeks to provide consists of the installation of geolocation tools and the filtering of content by an online gambling operator. The problem with the enforcement of such remedies on the Internet has been the effect that the enforcement can have in the country where the tools are installed. Even if the remedies are defined in a territorially limited manner (in the example above the remedy should prevent users connecting from A from accessing O's online poker), the remedies can have implications outside the specified territory (A), and in particular in the country where such measures must be installed and operated (B).

In the United States, the *Yahoo!*[100] and *Viewfinder*[101] cases demonstrate the problem. In *Yahoo!*, a U.S. court refused to enforce a French judgment that ordered Yahoo! to prevent users connecting to the Internet from France from accessing Nazi memorabilia offered on its pages. In *Viewfinder*, a U.S. court refused to enforce a French judgment that ordered a U.S. company to remove certain content that was found to infringe intellectual property rights in France. In both cases the U.S. courts found the foreign judgments to be contrary to U.S. public policy because the judgments did not comply with the robust free speech protections of the First Amendment to the U.S. Constitution.

The effects of the two French judgments were limited—or should have been interpreted as being limited—to the territory of France, meaning that they should have been satisfied by a territorially limited enforcement measure that would have affected only users connecting to the Internet from France. Arguably, geolocation and filtering based on user location would

---

[99] *See* Article 9 *infra*.
[100] Yahoo!, Inc. v. La Ligue Contre Le Racisme et L'Antisemitisme, 169 F.Supp.2d 1181 (N.D. Cal. 2001), *rev'd en banc*, 433 F.3d 1199 (9th Cir. 2006).
[101] Sarl Louis Feraud Intl. v. Viewfinder, Inc., 489 F.3d 474 (2d Cir. 2007).

have allowed for such a targeted enforcement. However, the U.S. courts concluded that requiring U.S. companies to adjust their activities in the United States in the manner required by the French courts, even if only with effects outside the United States,[102] would be incompatible with the First Amendment free speech protections under U.S. law. Similarly, consistent with a line of court decisions concerning foreign libel judgments, the 2010 SPEECH Act allows only foreign libel judgments that are compatible with the level of protection of free speech safeguarded by the First Amendment to be recognized and enforced in the United States, suggesting that also in these cases, enforcement will be impossible even if a remedy targets acts outside of the United States.[103]

The question thus becomes whether the enforcement by a national gambling authority of its own decision based on a request by a foreign requesting authority (B's decision prompted by A's request) could cause the same free speech protection concerns that recognition and enforcement of foreign judgments concerning libel, intellectual property, or speech in general may pose. Undeniably, a limitation on speech occurs not only in the requesting country (A) but also in the requested country (B); although only users connecting to the Internet from the requesting country (A) should feel the effects of the limitation, it is in the requested country (B) where the online gambling operator has to expend the resources to obtain and maintain geolocation tools and a content filtering system. However, this type of limitation on speech seems sufficiently tailored to the particular needs of the online gambling regulation.[104] The operator would have to prevent access only to users accessing the Internet from the requesting country (A) and only to the extent that the content accessible from the requesting country violates the requesting country's online gambling regulation. In countries that incorporate a foreign compliance requirement, the geolocation and filtering will achieve compliance not only with the foreign online gambling regulation but also with the national law of the requested country that mandates compliance with foreign gambling laws.

It is possible that a requesting country may attempt to use an enforcement assistance request under the Convention to curtail free speech; for example, a country may send a request claiming that an operator is violat-

---

[102] Note that—at least at the time of the *Yahoo!* Decision—the issue of whether geolocation tools were sufficiently reliable was contested. *See* Declaration of Bennet Laurie in Lieu of Direct Testimony at 12, Nitke v. Ashcroft, 253 F. Supp. 2d 587 (S.D.N.Y. 2005) (No. 01 Civ. 11476).

[103] Securing and Protecting our Enduring and Established Constitutional Heritage (SPEECH) Act, 28 U.S.C. §§ 4101–05 (2010).

[104] "Electronic communications related to gambling should be able to be regulated under the First Amendment, but only if such regulations are narrowly and precisely drawn in order to avoid chilling permissible electronic communications." Testimony of Eric Goldman before the National Gambling Impact Study Commission's Regulatory, Enforcement and Internet Subcommittee, December 1, 1998, *available at* http://eric_goldman.tripod.com/articles/gamblingarticle.htm (last visited June 16, 2012).

ing the country's laws while in fact the country is really seeking to censor the operator's speech. This might occur if a country attempted to prevent the operator from endorsing on its website a candidate for a political position. For such situations, the Convention must preserve the discretion of the requested country to deny any enforcement assistance if the requested country suspects that the requesting country's request is prompted by motives that are not related to online gambling regulation.[105] The dispute resolution mechanism proposed below could be employed to solve countries' disagreements on free speech.

Disputes about the scope of a remedy should be resolved within the requesting country. The requesting national authority should be specific in describing the material that should be made inaccessible to users connecting from the requesting country and in describing who should make the material inaccessible. Only with sufficiently specific information can the requested country enforce the specific decision of the requesting country. If an operator considers the requesting country's decision to be contrary to the requesting country's law, either in terms of subject matter or territorial scope, the operator should seek redress in the requesting country, not in the requested country.

Enforcement through Geolocation

A problem of geolocation enforcement is the establishment of basic minimum standards that countries will use to judge whether geolocation is deemed sufficiently effective and therefore compliant. Standards are very important because, as Malcolm Sparrow has pointed out in his study on online gambling, "licensed sites may have an incentive to be lax with geolocation controls: excluding users from certain states lowers their overall customer base. Therefore, a regulator must ensure that geolocation controls are updated frequently and meet desired standards of quality."[106] In fact, the regulating authority of a requested country may not have sufficient incentive to impose on operators located in its territory a requirement to effectively geolocate and filter out users connecting from other jurisdictions. Therefore, it is necessary for countries to agree on minimum standards for acceptable geolocation.

Some critics will argue that no geolocation standard is sufficient for the purposes of compliance because they deem geolocation ineffective *per se*. Indeed, the effectiveness of geolocation can be diminished by users evading geolocation; tools exist that allow users to change the information on

---

[105] For example, as the Council of Europe's Convention on Cybercrime does, this Convention could formulate the exception to apply whenever the requested country "considers that execution of the request is likely to prejudice its sovereignty, security, *ordre public* or other essential interests." Council of Europe's Convention on Cybercrime, Article 27(4)(b).
[106] Malcolm K. Sparrow, *Can Internet Gambling Be Effectively Regulated? Managing Risks*, Hearing before the Committee on Financial Services, U.S. House of Representatives, 111th Cong., No. 111-92, December 3, 2009, Appendix, pp. 108-109.

their Internet-connected devices that identifies their location, and cause the users to appear as if they are located in a jurisdiction other than the one in which they are physically located.[107] Although the reliability of geolocation tools continues to improve, so do the capabilities of tools designed to allow users to evade geolocation. At present the number of users evading geolocation based on Internet protocol addresses appears to be rising for three primary reasons: geolocation and content filtering based on user location are becoming more pervasive, evasion tools are becoming increasingly user-friendly, and users are becoming more aware of location-based filtering.[108]

The fact that geolocation may be evaded and that the legal status of acts of evasion of geolocation is unsettled may suggest that geolocation is an unsuitable compliance method.[109] However, geolocation methods are being improved constantly; they do not rely only on Internet protocol addresses but utilize other data, such as mobile telephone networks,[110] GPS data,[111] and Wi-Fi signals.[112] When geolocation is augmented with additional information—including data that the user must provide that is difficult to alter—the ability to evade is diminished. To gamble online, users must provide a credit card number and a billing address, and usually additional information that allows the operator to verify their identity and age. Although the input of the additional data may be manipulated, the data can confirm or call into question the results of geolocation and decrease the chance that a user can successfully misrepresent his location.[113] Additionally, it is possi-

---

[107] For an extensive analysis of the evasion of geolocation and its legal implications *see* Trimble, *supra* note 6.

[108] Contributing to the rising numbers of users evading geolocation is also the increasing awareness by users that website operators are tracking their activities on the Internet and the resulting use, by many users, of anonymization tools. The use of such tools may in some instances lead to the evasion of geolocation. *See* Trimble, *supra* note 6, 602-604. *See also* Liana B. Baker and Yinka Adegoke, *Olympics Fans Find Ways to Circumvent NBC's Online Control*, Reuters, July 31, 2012, *available at* http://www.reuters.com/article/2012/07/31/us-olympics-tech-workaround-idUSBRE86U02R20120731 (last visited Aug. 20, 2012).

[109] *See* Trimble, *supra* note 6; SOPA, *supra* note 25.

[110] Testimony of Keith Marsden, Managing Director 192business.com, Hearing before the Committee on Financial Services, U.S. House of Representatives, 111th Cong., No. 111-92, December 3, 2009, Appendix, p. 272.

[111] *E.g.*, Responsible Gaming Networks Pty Ltd.'s Safety Net system with its USB Player Protection Key, *supra* note 28.

[112] *E.g.*, GeoComply, *supra* note 28.

[113] Advice on where to obtain offshore accounts is readily available on the internet. *See, e.g.,* Radar O'Reilley, *Complete Guide to Offshore Accounts for Funding Online Casino and Poker Play*, 2007, *available at* http://www.blackjackforumonline.com/Complete_Guide_to_Offshore_Bank_Accounts.htm (last visited Oct. 17, 2011). For the response of a geolocation provider to the cybertravel problem *see, e.g., What Is Screen Sharing Software and How Is It Used?*, *available at* http://geocomply.com/blog/what-is-screen-sharing-software-and-how-is-it-used/ (last visited June 14, 2012).

ble that future legislative efforts will settle the legal status of the evasion of geolocation.[114]

Recent legislative proposals have formulated geolocation standards in general terms, leaving it upon regulatory agencies to determine the detailed requirements for geolocation tools. For example, according to the Unlawful Internet Gambling Enforcement Act of 2006, one requirement for a gambling operation to be excluded from the definition of "unlawful gambling" is that "the bet or wager and the method by which the bet or wager is initiated and received or otherwise made [be] expressly authorized by and placed in accordance with the laws of such State, and the State law or regulations include … location verification requirements *reasonably designed to block access* to … persons located out of such State[.]"[115] One bill that has been proposed to amend the 2006 Act, the Internet Gambling Prohibition, Poker Consumer Protection, and Strengthening UIGEA Act of 2011, would require that an Internet poker facility "demonstrate to the qualified State agency that such facility maintains appropriate safeguards and mechanisms, in accordance with standards established by the qualified State agency, … to … ensure, *to a reasonable degree of certainty*, that the individual placing a bet or wager is physically located in a jurisdiction that has not prohibited such bets or wagers at the time the bet or wager is placed…"[116]

Similarly, the Convention envisions that countries establish minimum standards for geolocation tools in order to be considered effective measures under the Convention. The standards cannot be set in the Convention; they must be established separately in a manner that allows for necessary updating as the relevant technology develops. The standards should be set at the highest level possible and encourage competition in the geolocation tool market; countries should avoid imposing unreasonably detailed standards that would discourage competition among geolocation tool suppliers.

Article 5 – Cooperation in Licensing and Standardization of Technological Requirements

As mentioned earlier, cooperation among national regulating authorities in standardizing their licensing and technological requirements would be extremely beneficial. Harmonized licensing in multiple jurisdictions would not only decrease the regulatory burden on gambling operators, but it would also facilitate increased cooperation among national regulating authorities. Uniform technological requirements could bring savings in testing and regulatory approval processes.

It is possible that only some countries will be amenable to common licensing and technological standards, and therefore closer cooperation might need to be

---

[114] *See* Trimble, *supra* note 6.
[115] Unlawful Internet Gambling Enforcement Act of 2006, §5362 (10)(B)(ii)(I) (emphasis added).
[116] Internet Gambling Prohibition, Poker Consumer Protection, and Strengthening UIGEA Act of 2011, H.R. 2366, 112th Cong., section 104(d)(2) (emphasis added).

left to a separate bilateral or multilateral convention or agreement to be concluded outside this Convention. In such circumstances, the Convention could include a provision stating that the signatory countries wish to continue to pursue further cooperation in the areas of licensing and technological standards.

Article 6 – Cooperation in the Area of Responsible Gambling

The parties to the Convention should cooperate in the area of responsible or problem gambling, particularly by supporting and exchanging research on problem gambling, developing and sharing publications on problem gambling, and collecting data on problem gambling.

No responsible regulation of the gambling industry can overlook the issues of problem gambling, and countries have been active in collecting data on problem gambling. For example, according to the European Commission, fifteen of the twenty-seven EU member countries have conducted some studies on problem gambling.[117] In addition to government-sponsored studies,[118] not-for-profit organizations supported by the industry, such as the National Center for Responsible Gaming,[119] and research institutions[120] have collected information and supported research on problem gambling. It is both a matter of public interest and the responsibility of the gambling industry to pool industry resources at the international level and facilitate further research and development on strategies to address problem gambling.

Cooperation in the area of responsible gambling could include enforcement assistance concerning individual players' self-exclusion requests. If national gambling regulations provide an option for a player to self-exclude from games—either completely by preventing access to games, or partially by setting limits on wagers or losses[121]—then online gambling operators should also comply with player self-exclusion requests—even if the online operators operate from other jurisdictions. Particular attention should be paid to protecting privacy in enforcement assistance requests that concern individual players; privacy should be protected in assistance requests relating to a player's specific requests for self-exclusion that apply to all online gambling sites accessible from the player's jurisdiction, even when the sites are operated from a different country. The player should receive information explaining that a self-exclusion request may require enforcement measures that necessitate the player's data being forwarded to a foreign requested national authority.

---

[117] Green Paper, *supra* note 10, p. 20.

[118] E.g., the National Gambling Impact Study Commission in the United States established by the National Gambling Impact Study Commission Act of 1996, Pub.L. 104-169, August 3, 1996.

[119] National Center for Responsible Gaming, http://www.ncrg.org/ (last visited Oct. 7, 2011).

[120] E.g., Große Studie zum Glücksspielverhalten, April 13, 2010, http://www.schleswig-holstein.de/MWV/DE/Service/Presse/PI/2010/100413UkshStudieGluecksspiel.html (last visited March 30, 2012).

[121] *See, e.g.*, Regulations of the Nevada Gaming Commission and State Gaming Control Board, sections 5A.070.9 and 5A.130, as of March 12, 2012.

384 | *Regulating Internet Gaming*

Article 7 – Appointment of National Authorities

The Convention should include a provision that sets a time and place for parties to the Convention to deposit a document designating their national authorities under the Convention. As suggested above in the proposal for Article 2, these authorities will include the requesting national authority, the requested national authority, and the national regulating authority. Nothing in the Convention will prevent a country from designating a single agency to assume all three of the authority functions under the Convention. A country will also be free to designate multiple agencies to assume the functions of a single authority; for example, federal countries like Germany may wish to designate agencies in the individual Länder. The Secretariat (see below in proposed Article 8) could be the depository where countries would have convenient access to the information.

Article 8 – Secretariat

Although the creation of a permanent Secretariat to administer the Convention is not indispensible for the functioning of the Convention, it appears that a Secretariat would enhance the enforcement mechanism in the Convention if it were to function as a central "clearinghouse" to centralize Convention administration and maintain an expertise from which all countries could benefit. The Secretariat could serve as the depository of designations of national authorities under Article 7, the repository of problem gambling research studies (see Article 6), and the organizer of meetings on standards setting and enhanced cooperation (see Article 5).

Article 9 – Dispute Resolution

Situations may arise in which parties to the Convention will disagree on the interpretation of the Convention or its application. A requested country may disagree with a requesting country on the true purpose for which information is requested under Article 3. A requesting country may object to a requested country's postponement of the delivery of information under Article 3, or a requesting country may contest a requested country's decision to deny assistance in enforcement under Article 4 because of the requested country's suspicion that the requesting country's request is unrelated to online gambling regulation and is politically motivated (or otherwise unrelated to online gambling).

For situations in which countries disagree on either an interpretation or an application of the Convention, the Convention should provide for a dispute resolution mechanism. First, countries should be encouraged to negotiate and resolve disputes amicably between themselves. Second, the Convention may provide for arbitration of disputes before an arbitration tribunal. Third, the Convention can establish its own dispute resolution mechanism. Fourth, disputes concerning the Convention could be filed with the International Court of Justice, and fifth, if the Convention were to be concluded within the WTO framework, disputes concerning the Convention could be resolved under the WTO Dispute Settlement Understanding.[122]

CONCLUSIONS

In the regulation of online gambling it is time for countries to agree to disagree. Since the need for the effective enforcement of national gambling regulations might be the only point on which countries can agree at a time when a consensus on gambling in general, and on online gambling in particular, appears unachievable—not only at the global level but even at the level of individual countries—the Convention proposed in this chapter is designed to facilitate the effective enforcement of national online gambling regulations without requiring that countries change their current or future positions on online gambling.

Interest in the conclusion of the Convention should be shared by governments and gambling regulators in all countries. While countries that prohibit online gambling obviously have strong incentives to conclude the Convention and gain increased enforcement of their laws, what will be the incentives for regulators in jurisdictions that license online gambling operators to operate worldwide? After all, these jurisdictions have benefited from their global approach to online gambling and are unlikely to have an interest in reducing their licensing territorially. If they regulate online gambling responsibly, however, these jurisdictions already require their licensees to comply with the laws of other jurisdictions, and therefore the proposed convention does not change the *status quo* for the regulators and licensees in these jurisdictions. Gambling authorities in these jurisdictions, if they are serious about having their licensees comply with other jurisdictions' regulations, should welcome the Convention, which would assist them in detecting licensee non-compliance and promote licensee compliance with other countries' laws.

Legal and law-abiding online gambling operators also have incentives to support the conclusion of the Convention. It is important for the health of the industry to have an effective enforcement of gambling regulations. The integrity of games, personal data, and financial information must be protected to enhance players' and the general public's confidence, participation, and trust in the games offered on the Internet, and effective regulation is indispensable to achieving this goal. Gambling industry support of the Convention will emphasize the industry's commitment to its support of responsible gambling, which needs to be more than a public relations matter if the indus-

---

[122] Understanding on rules and procedures governing the settlement of disputes, Annex 2 of the WTO Agreement.

try is to address problem gambling effectively. Additionally, the Convention will level the playing field for legal online gambling operators by reducing competition from illegal gambling sites.

Some critics may be of the opinion that the Convention—and the effective enforcement of national online gambling regulations—is unnecessary because market forces will weed out illegal operators. This opinion assumes that players will ultimately opt to play only on sites that are licensed by responsible (and freely competing) regulators because the players will value the licensing and oversight that are associated with high quality online gambling regulation. While the idea of unrestrained free competition among regulators is appealing, it seems unrealistic to expect players to have sufficient information to make rational and informed choices concerning gambling sites and regulators. Implementation of strong public policies that are associated with gambling and that call for, for example, the prevention of money laundering and the assurance of responsible gambling, cannot rely solely on free competition among regulators.

The approach that calls for reliance on unrestrained free competition among regulators also ignores the fact that jurisdictions have legitimate reasons for wanting to prohibit gambling in their territories, or regulate gambling in their territories differently from other jurisdictions. Religious, moral, health, and other considerations play important roles in shaping countries' approaches to gambling, including online gambling. When countries adhere to a democratic ideal that says that populations ought to be free to choose solutions for themselves (within acceptable limits defined by fundamental human rights), countries should assist each other in enforcing these solutions within the territorial limits of individual countries.

Enforcement of laws on the Internet is complicated, and there is strong public resistance to proposals that are aimed at enhancing the enforcement of laws on the Internet (and that may include solutions that might not always comply with fundamental rights and freedoms). The negotiations of the Anti-Counterfeiting Trade Agreement showed the public's displeasure with enforcement measures targeting the Internet. Under public pressure, the Agreement negotiators were forced to eliminate a proposed three-strike enforcement measure. The Stop Online Piracy Act proposed in the United States also generated overwhelming opposition from the public, industry, and academia. Indications that the International Telecommunication Union might be interested in assisting enforcement on the Internet were also met with criticism. Undoubtedly, careful public relations work will be necessary for the success of any international convention affecting the enforcement of laws on the Internet. In the case of this proposed online gambling Convention, the public must be assured of the limited scope of the Convention and the substantial public benefits that the Convention will provide. Most importantly, however, the Convention must be carefully crafted to safeguard free speech, due process, and other rights, including the protection of privacy.

The proposed Convention is not a cure-all. Certainly, there will be countries that will opt not to negotiate and not to sign the Convention. Some countries may not participate because they intend to become safe havens for those online gambling operators who plan to offer online gambling to users accessing the Internet from anywhere, including from countries that prohibit online gambling or from countries that have different requirements for online gambling. Undoubtedly, the functioning of the Convention will improve as the number of parties to the Convention increases. As with other international treaties, it will be up to the countries with strong diplomatic and economic positions to persuade other countries to join and abide by the Convention. The status of the Convention would be enhanced if it were concluded within the WTO framework, which would not only facilitate its wide adoption by WTO member states but also strengthen its functioning by providing an established dispute resolution mechanism with sanctions that could be used to force countries to comply with the Convention, if necessary.

The executive branch of the U.S. government received a mandate from Congress in 2006 to seek cooperation with other countries in the area of Internet gambling. In adopting the Unlawful Internet Gambling Enforcement Act of 2006, Congress instructed the U.S. government to "encourage cooperation by foreign governments and relevant international fora." The government's international initiatives should focus on detecting money laundering, corruption, and other crimes, and "advance policies that promote the cooperation of foreign governments, through information sharing or other measures, in the enforcement of [the] Act."[123] The proposal for the online gambling Convention suggested in this chapter would promote cooperation among governments in the enforcement of any current or future online gambling regulation, whether it be U.S. regulation, Nevada regulation, Utah regulation, or any other regulation by any other jurisdiction in the world.

---

[123] Unlawful Internet Gambling Enforcement Act, H.R. 4954, 109th Cong., 2006, Title VIII, section 803.

About the Contributors

Anthony Cabot

Anthony Cabot is the chair of the gaming law practice at Lewis and Roca LLP with offices in Las Vegas, Reno, Phoenix, Tucson, Albuquerque, and Silicon Valley. He has practiced in the field of gaming law for over 25 years. He is a past president of the International Masters of Gaming Law, past president of the Nevada Gaming Attorneys Association and past general counsel to the International Association of Gaming Attorneys. He also serves as an adjunct professor at the Boyd School of Law.

Cabot is a prolific author on gambling law. He is the founding editor of *The Internet Gambling Report Xl* (2009). He has co-authored *Casino Credit And Collections* (2003), *Practical Casino Math* (2d ed. 2005), *International Casino Law* (3d ed January 1999) and *Federal Gambling Law* (1999).

Frank Catania

Frank Catania is a senior partner in Catania Gaming Consultants and the law firm of Catania Ehrlich & Suarez of New Jersey, and has extensive experience in gaming-related matters. His expertise stems from his years of service as Director of New Jersey Division of Gaming Enforcement, Vice President of Players International, and Deputy Speaker of the New Jersey General Assembly. Catania serves as an independent director of eCOGRA, Nevada Gold Casinos and Continent 8.

Catania is a member and served as the first president of the International Masters of Gaming Law, a non-profit association dedicated to the education and advancement of gaming law. Mr. Catania has been published on a wide variety of casino gaming and government-related topics in several national publications, regional newspapers, and trade publications. He has been instrumental in drafting gaming regulations for several gaming jurisdictions.

Toni Cowan

Toni Cowan is an attorney, licensed in New Jersey, Nevada and Pennsylvania, with expertise in state gaming compliance, Internet gaming, and federal Indian gaming compliance. Her gaming experience stems from her many years of public service as a Senior Attorney at the New Jersey Casino

Control Commission and in the Division of Gaming at the Nevada Attorney General's Office, and as a Staff Attorney at the National Indian Gaming Commission.

Cowan has published several articles on gaming-related topics. Her 2003 article on cross-border gaming, *The Global Gaming Village*, has been frequently cited, most notably by the World Trade Organization in its 2005 panel decision concerning the dispute between the United States and Antigua and Barbuda on the cross-border supply of gambling and betting services. She has a B.A. degree from the Pennsylvania State University, an M.A. from New York University, and a J.D. from Villanova University School of Law.

Gary Ehrlich

Gary Ehrlich is a Principal and Vice President of Catania Gaming Consultants. He provides legal analysis and advice to those involved in international gaming consultancy as to all aspects of land-based and Internet gaming. Ehrlich is also a partner of Catania & Ehrlich, which he co-founded with Frank Catania in 2009.

For over 25 years, Ehrlich was with the New Jersey Division of Gaming Enforcement. He ended his tenure there as Deputy Director.

Ehrlich holds a Masters of Laws from New York University School of Law, and a J.D. from Seton Hall University School of Law. He is admitted to the bar in the states of New York and New Jersey as well as the Unites States Supreme Court.

Stuart Hoegner

Stuart Hoegner is a gaming attorney and serves as a principal of Gaming Counsel Professional Corporation in Toronto, Canada. He advises his clients on games of skill and chance, contests, mergers and acquisitions, tax matters, online interactive gambling and land-based gaming issues. Hoegner's clients include the owners of top Internet poker and casino brands, sports books, First Nations operators and developers, skill games operators, gaming equipment manufacturers, poker professionals, financial institutions, and social media entrepreneurs.

He writes a regular blog on gaming law and has been widely published in tax and gaming journals in Canada and internationally.

Hoegner graduated from the University of Toronto Faculty of Law, began practicing in Ontario in 1999, and subsequently received his professional accounting designation.

Peter Kulick

Peter Kulick is a tax and gaming attorney with Dickinson Wright, PLLC, which has an international gaming law practice with offices in Michigan, Nashville, Washington, D.C., Toronto and an affiliated office in Macau.

He is a prolific author on gaming law with articles published in leading publications such as *Casino Lawyer, Casino Enterprise Management, ABA Gaming Law Gazette, Gaming Law Review* and various other gaming industry publications and frequent panelist at national gaming law and tax law conferences.

Alan Littler

Alan Littler is a member of the Gaming Team at VMW Taxand, where he is involved with Dutch and European developments in the industry. In December 2009, Dr. Littler successfully defended his Ph.D. *Member States versus the European Union: The Regulation of Gambling* at Tilburg University in the Netherlands. He then continued as a post-doctoral researcher at Tilburg University and spent autumn 2010 as a visiting research scholar at the Fletcher School of Law & Diplomacy at Tufts University, Medford, Massachusetts. His post-doctoral research focused on the regulation of gambling in relation to transparency, the GATS, and consumer protection in transnational contexts.

Sanford I. Millar

Sanford I. Millar is a Certified Specialist in Taxation Law and is admitted to practice before all courts in California. He has a sub-specialty in taxation of eCommerce, including Internet gaming. Based in Los Angeles where he has practiced since 1974, Millar is frequently consulted as an expert on business and taxation law matters in the gaming and non-gaming sectors. He has experience advising and structuring international internet game companies and has represented clients in diverse businesses in domestic and complex cross-border transactions.

Mr. Millar obtained his A.B degree in International Relations from the University of Southern California and his J.D. from Southwestern University School of Law in 1974, and a Masters in Business Taxation from the University of Southern California's Graduate School of Business. He also attended post-graduate classes at the RAND Graduate School.

Nick Nocton

Nick Nocton is a Partner in the Gaming and Betting Group at Jeffrey Green Russell, one of the United Kingdom's leading specialist teams advising on all aspects of gambling law and regulation in the UK and other leading gambling jurisdictions. Drawing from the full range of legal services provided by JGR, he provides advice on all commercial issues for clients, including technology, white labeling and affiliate arrangements.

Nocton has over 12 years' experience advising on UK and international gambling issues, specializing in licensing and regulation as well as general commercial matters. He is the Editor of IMGL's *European Gaming Lawyer* magazine, a contributor to various legal and trade journals, and a regular speaker at international gaming conferences.

Ngai Pindell

Ngai Pindell is a professor and Associate Dean at the University of Nevada Las Vegas, William S. Boyd School of Law. Professor Pindell practiced community development law in a nonprofit law firm in Baltimore, Maryland and taught the Community Development Clinic at the University of Baltimore School of Law. Professor Pindell came to the Boyd School of Law in 2000. His research interests include economic development, cities, housing, and gaming law, and he teaches Property, Local Government Law, and Wills, Trusts & Estates. He also directs the law school's Gaming Program.

J. Blair Richardson

J. Blair Richardson has served as the chief privacy officer and counsel for Integrity, the age verification division of Aristotle International, Inc., since 1999. He specializes in regulatory compliance, public record data acquisition, child protection, and privacy issues relating to the use of databases for preventing minors' access to age-restricted products and services. He is a 1979 graduate of Princeton University, and received his *juris doctor* from Fordham University School of Law in 1982. Prior to working with Aristotle, Mr. Richardson was an attorney with Winston and Strawn, Washington, D.C., specializing in litigation.

Marketa Trimble

Marketa Trimble is a professor at the University of Nevada Las Vegas' William S. Boyd School of Law. In her research, she focuses on intellectual property and issues at the intersection of intellectual property and private international law/conflict of laws. Using her extensive research experience from law schools in the U.S. and Europe, her expertise from the European Union and European governments, and her foreign language abilities, Professor Trimble conducts comparative and empirical work in her areas of interest.

She joined UNLV from Stanford Law School, where she received her second doctoral degree.

Lawrence G. Walters

Lawrence G. Walters is a partner with Walters Law Group, a 50-year-old firm whose attorneys have handled cases in virtually every United States' jurisdiction, including seven cases before the U.S. Supreme Court. His practice focuses on gaming, advertising, and Internet law, representing clients involved with all aspects of the online gambling industry. Walters has developed an international reputation on Internet law issues, and has served as a regular commentator in the national media, including appearances on *CNBC, Fox News Channel, CNN, MSNBC, 48 Hours, 20/20, Good Morning America, The Today Show* and the *O'Reilly Factor*. He has written extensively on the issue of online gambling advertising, including a yearly chapter in the widely-read *Internet Gambling Report*, several law review articles, and many legal columns.

Walters is a frequent presenter at gaming industry conferences and publishes a regular legal update column on www.GamblingLawUpdate. com. A list of his speeches and seminars is available at www.gameattorneys.com/seminars.php3.

Walters is admitted in all the state and federal courts in Florida, the Federal Circuit and U.S. Claims Court in Washington DC, the Eleventh Circuit Court of Appeal, and the United States Supreme Court. In addition, he has appeared pro hac vice in courts throughout the country. He is a member of the IMGL and President of the First Amendment Lawyers Association.

Richard H. Williamson

Richard Williamson, Senior Vice President, Regulatory - Americas for BMM Compliance is a thirty-year veteran of the gaming industry. Mr. Williamson has extensive experience in developing and implementing technical standards, internal controls, regulations and rulemaking as well as writing and interpreting gaming product testing standards.

Previously, Williamson was appointed in 2005 by the Pennsylvania Gaming Control Board as the first Director of its Gaming Laboratory Operations where he created technical standards, lab procedures and was instrumental in opening the first three slots-only Pennsylvania casinos. Before joining the PGCB, Williamson was the director of the New Jersey Division of Gaming Enforcement's slot testing laboratory for more than twenty years. During this period, the DGE lab routinely received submissions of technologically advanced products and concepts that challenged the language of existing regulations and necessitated many rule changes. Under his leadership the New Jersey lab was routinely consulted as a preeminent government operated testing laboratory.

Index

Table of Cases

D

David Carruthers, et al., *U.S. v.*, Case No.: 4:06CR337CEJ(MLM), (E.D. MO May 7, 2007), ...253n17

Departamento de Jogos da Santa Casa da Misericórdia de Lisboa, Liga Portuguesa de futebol Profissional, Bwin International Ltd v.,[2009] ECR I 7633, ...297n8

Departamento de Jogos da Santa Casa da Misericórdia de Lisboa, Liga Portuguesa de futebol Profissional, Bwin International Ltd v., [2009] ECR I 7633, ...306n31

Departamento de Jogos da Santa Casa da Misericórdia de Lisboa, Liga Portuguesa de futebol Profissional, Bwin International Ltd v., [2009] ECR I 7633, ...306n34

Departamento de Jogos da Santa Casa da Misericórdia de Lisboa, Liga Portuguesa de Futebol Profissional v., Court of Justice of the European Communities, C-42/07, September 8, 2009, ...363n41

Dickinger and Ömer, Court of Justice of the European Union, C-347/09, September 15, 2011, ...363n37, 363n38

G

Gerhart Schindler and Jörg Schindler, Her Majesty's Customs and Excise v., [1994] ECR-1039, ...299n13

Greater New Orleans Broadcasting Assn. v. U.S., 527 US 173, 119 S.Ct 1923, 144 L.Ed.2d 161 (1999), ...250n1, 251n3, 251n4, 251n5

H

Her Majesty's Customs and Excise v. Gerhart Schindler and Jörg Schindler, [1994] ECR-1039, ...299n13

I

In re Application of Cason, 294 S.E.2d 520, 523 (Ga. 1982) (*citing* Penobscot Bar v. Kimball, 64 Me. 140, 146 (Me. 1875), ...2n1

In re Bauquier's Estate, 88 Cal. 302, 307, 26 P. 178 aff 'd, 88 Cal. 302, 26 P. 532 (Cal. 1891), ...43n73

In re Farmer, 191 N.C. 235, 131 S.E. 661, 663 (N.C. 1926), ...40n54

In re Florida Bd. of Bar Examiners, 373 So. 2d 890 (Fla. 1979), ...41n61

In re Monaghan, 126 Vt. 53, 60, 222 A.2d 665, 671 (Vt. 1966), ...41n55

In the Matter of Lehman Brothers International (Europe) (In Administration) and In the Matter of the Insolvency Act 1986, UK Supreme Court, (2012) UKSC 6, ...169n14

K

Klahr, 433 P.2d 979, ...41n55

Konigsberg v. State Bar of Cal., 353 U.S. 252, 77 S. Ct. 722, 1 L. Ed. 2d 810 (1957), ...40n50, 41n60

L

M

N

O

P

Q

Quistclose Investments Ltd., Barclays Bank Ltd. v., [1968] UKHL 4, …167n7

R

R. v. Andriopoulos, [1993] O.J. No. 3427 (Gen. Div.); aff'd 1994 CarswellOnt 3947 (C.A.), …257n41

R. v. Oaks [1986] 1 S.C.R. 103, …257n38

R. v. Shabaquay, 2004 CarswellOnt 2309 (Ont. Ct. of J.), …256n35

Reese v. Bd. of Com'rs of Alabama State Bar, 379 So. 2d 564 (Ala. 1980), …41n61

Rousso v. State of Washington, 239 P.3d 1084 (Wash. 2010), …297n7

S

Sarl Louis Feraud Intl. v. Viewfinder, Inc., 489 F.3d 474 (2d Cir. 2007), …378n101

Satterfield v. Simon & Schuster, Inc., 569 F.3d 946 (9th Cir. 2009, …269n90

Scarlet Extended SA v. Société belge des auteurs, compositeurs et éditeurs SCRL (Sabam), Court of Justice of the European Union, C-70/10, April 14, 2011, …360n23, 360n24

Schware v. Bd. of Bar Exam. of State of N.M., 353 U.S. 232, 77 S. Ct. 752, 1 L. Ed. 2d 796 (1957), …41n56

Shabaquay, R. v., 2004 CarswellOnt 2309 (Ont. Ct. of J.), …256n35

Shimon Dabush vs. Connective Group Ltd. et. al.; State of Israel vs. Shauli et. al., …259n55

Simon & Schuster, Inc., Satterfield v., 569 F.3d 946 (9th Cir. 2009, …269n90

Sjöberg v. Åklagaren, [2011] 1 C.M.L.R. 11, …262n67

Société belge des auteurs, compositeurs et éditeurs SCRL (Sabam), Scarlet Extended SA v., Court of Justice of the European Union, C-70/10, April 14, 2011, …360n23

Sponick v. City of Detroit Police Dept., 49 Mich. App. 162, 211 N.W.2d 674 (1973), …51n89

State Bar of Cal., Konigsberg v., 353 U.S. 252, 77 S. Ct. 722, 1 L. Ed. 2d 810 (1957), …40n50, 41n60

State of Washington, Rousso v., 239 P.3d 1084 (Wash. 2010), …297n7

State v. Morales, 137 Ariz. 67, 668 P.2d 910 (Ariz. Ct. App. 1983), …51n89

T

Texas, Wiggins v., 778 S.W.2d 877, 889 (Tex. App. 1989), …43n72

U

United States v. Arthur Young & Co., 465 U.S. 805, 818 (1984), …71n57

United States v. Pokerstars, et. al., 11 Civ. 2564 (LBS), April 19, 2011, …362n33

9040222R00241

Made in the USA
San Bernardino, CA
04 March 2014